THE REAL NATIONAL INCOME OF SOVIET RUSSIA SINCE 1928

THE REAL NATIONAL INCOME OF SOVIET RUSSIA SINCE 1928

Abram Bergson

HARVARD UNIVERSITY PRESS
Cambridge
1961

Distributed in Great Britain by Oxford University Press, London

Library of Congress Catalog Card Number 61–15281

Printed in the United States of America

TO
S.B.; R.M.B.;
J.M.B.; E.A.B.; L.A.B.

PREFACE

This study brings to a conclusion a program of research that has been long, I fear inordinately long, in progress. It has also had many participants. I may be able to indicate in some degree my debt to others if I explain how the present volume evolved from previous work.

The story begins with an attempt, which was initiated toward the end of World War II but which only subsequently began to be pursued with some seriousness, to measure the national income of Soviet Russia for a single year, 1937. My aim, more particularly, was to compile income and outlay data for the USSR for 1937 in accord with the methodology of "national income accounting" that has by now become a familiar feature in Western countries. I also proposed to grapple somehow with the vexatious problem posed by the special nature of ruble prices, especially the many significant divergencies from "scarcity relations." Pursuit of these aims almost inevitably was impeded by other commitments, but in a manner which was to prove prophetic the task also turned out to be more formidable than was anticipated. In any event, the results of the inquiry could not be published until 1950 (in the May and August issues of the *Quarterly Journal of Economics*). Subsequently, this study was also published in a somewhat revised and extended version (*Soviet National Income and Product in 1937,* New York, 1953).

Meantime, under the sponsorship of The RAND Corporation, an effort had also been initiated to make similar calculations for other years under the five year plans. Thus, in association with Mr. Hans Heymann, Jr., I undertook to compile measurements for three interesting years: 1940, 1944, and 1948. At the same time, it was my good fortune to be able to persuade Dr. Oleg Hoeffding to assume responsibility for the difficult task of deriving corresponding data for 1928, the year when the First

Five Year Plan was launched. The results of both inquiries were published (New York, 1954) under the titles *Soviet National Income and Product in 1940–48,* by Heymann and me, and *Soviet National Income and Product in 1928,* by Hoeffding. Later still, Dr. Hoeffding and Miss Nancy Nimitz undertook to compile other measurements for all years during the period 1949–55, and the results of this inquiry have now appeared as a RAND Research Memorandum (RM-2101, April 6, 1959).

In all the foregoing studies, Soviet national income is calculated in current ruble values. Data are compiled at first in terms of prevailing ruble prices and subsequently, in order to adjust for outstanding divergencies from "scarcity relations," in terms of adjusted rubles. But for each year the values considered in either case are those pertaining to the time in question. Nevertheless, after these calculations had been under way for some time, a decision was made to extend the scope of our work still further. More specifically under continuing RAND sponsorship, inquiries were to be made into trends in Soviet prices and related aspects. Where possible, these studies were to be of a sort that might have an interest of their own, but the further researches it was hoped would also enable us to proceed from the data on the national income of the USSR in current ruble values to corresponding data in "constant" ruble values. In other words, the final aim became that of compiling measurements of Soviet "real" national income.

With this the task became large indeed, but the work was much facilitated, since at an early stage I was able to enlist the aid of Dr. Lynn Turgeon and Mr. Roman Bernaut. In association, the three of us were able in the course of time to compile and publish systematic data on price trends for most important basic industrial products (see RAND Research Memorandum RM-1522, August 1, 1955; further reports of the same sort listed therein; and *Journal of Political Economy,* August 1956). Fortunately, it was also possible for me to arrange for additional major responsibilities to be assumed by others, and in this way these further inquiries were in time also completed: into the cost of living and "real" wages, by Dr. Janet Chapman (for her preliminary results, see *Review of Economics and Statistics,* May 1954; a revised and expanded version of this study is now forthcoming); into civilian machinery prices and production, by Dr. Richard Moorsteen (his study is now in press); into the physical volume of construction, by Professor Raymond P. Powell (RAND Research Memoranda RM-1872 and 1873, February 14, 1957; RAND Research Memorandum RM-2454, September 28, 1959; *Review of Economics and Statistics,* May 1959); and into farm prices by Dr. Jerzy F. Karcz (RAND Research Memorandum RM-1930, July 2, 1957). Also, valuable research into Soviet transportation rates was carried out by Professor James Blackman, although this is as yet unpublished.

In preparing the present volume, I have drawn on all the foregoing studies, but I am pleased to acknowledge also that here, as so often in the past, consultations with Professor Paul A. Samuelson on methodological questions have always been rewarding. My indebtedness to Dr. Richard Moorsteen on an interesting aspect of index number methodology will become apparent, but after many discussions with him I find I am no longer able easily to distinguish my thoughts from his on the treatment accorded here to other facets of this matter as well.

To the profit of this study, the sterling aid of Miss Nancy Nimitz was available not only in the compilation of data on national income in prevailing values, but at many other points, not least in the computation of "real" farm income in kind and of farm employment. On "real" farm income in kind, Dr. Leon Smolinski also provided valuable assistance. As will become clear, this study has often been facilitated by the opportunity to draw on the results of independent RAND research into Soviet fixed capital, carried on by Mr. Norman Kaplan, who was also kind enough to comment on this study generally, and at different stages.

I describe in the text two intricate computations that were undertaken, one on the incidence of the Soviet turnover tax by category of retail sales and the other on the value of Soviet national income at ruble factor cost after adjustment according to the cost structure of the USA. If a high degree of accuracy was achieved in both inquiries, this is due chiefly to the understanding and careful work of Mr. Herbert Levine. In the revaluation of Soviet national income according to the U.S. cost structure, I also benefited from advice of Professor Wassily Leontief, Dr. Elizabeth Gilboy, and their associates at the Harvard Economic Research Project. My debt to Professor Alexander Gerschenkron for advice on expositional and other matters, which was already great, has here only been compounded. Dr. Oleg Hoeffding, who had advised on the work at earlier stages, was also good enough to read through and comment on a draft of the final product. A thorough and searching check of the computations, under the supervision of Mr. Russell Nichols, was not only helpful in assuring accuracy but often led to useful clarifications.

While enjoying the support of The RAND Corporation, not only the present study, but the entire program of research from which it evolved, profited much indeed from the opportunity that was thus made available for continuing consultation with Dr. Joseph A. Kershaw of the Economics Division of that organization. Dr. Kershaw was also unfailingly helpful in arranging participation in the work by permanent staff members of the Division. Mr. Charles J. Hitch, Chief of the Economics Division, was instrumental at the outset in initiating RAND sponsorship, and the fact that the work proceeded thereafter in behalf of a research department that was under his direction was a source of benefit throughout.

The project was sponsored by The RAND Corporation as part of the continuing program of research which it conducts for the United States Air Force.

Finally, the work was much aided by the fact that I had access in earlier stages to the facilities of the Russian Institute of Columbia University and in later stages to those of the Russian Research Center of Harvard University.

In the text some topics are elaborated in small print. Such passages need not be read in order to grasp the main thread of the argument. The system of transliteration from the Russian employed here is essentially that of the Library of Congress. For simplicity I have omitted the tie marks which, in the Library of Congress system, connect two Latin letters used to represent a single Cyrillic letter.

Abram Bergson

Cambridge, August 1960

CONTENTS

TABLES

APPENDIX TABLES

1

INTRODUCTION

Purpose and Limitations of the Study

This volume represents the result of an attempt to calculate for the period 1928–55 the "real" national income of the Soviet Union. The possible value of data of this sort hardly needs elaboration. Compiled as they are here in terms of "final" uses — that is, consumption, investment, et cetera — national income statistics measure summarily the growth of an economy and its evolving structure. Such data have come to be considered as practically indispensable for the appraisal of the extent and causes of a country's economic progress. Regarding Soviet Russia, these are momentous matters indeed; in the fifth decade since November 1917, they are for good reason of concern almost everywhere.

While there is no lack of applications for national income statistics, such figures are apt to be inexact even in favorable circumstances. The circumstances in Russia under the five year plans are scarcely favorable. One need not be conversant with all the technicalities to be aware that marked changes in economic structure can pose difficulties for the summary measurement of growth. Among other things, as with all "index numbers" of physical volume, "real" national income measures may vary with the prices in terms of which they are computed. Moreover, the difficulties are only compounded if prevailing prices reflect only imperfectly the "scarcity values" of different products. In the Russia of the period studied, structural changes were marked indeed. The radical shifts that occurred have probably had no precedent in modern history. The limitations of ruble prices under the five year plans perhaps are sometimes overrated, but no doubt their relation to "scarcity values" has in fact often been tenuous.

The circumstances of the Soviet five year plans would complicate the task of measurement even if reliable and abundant basic statistical data were available. It remains to say that a Western scholar has at his disposal little more than the notoriously imperfect and incomplete Soviet official statistics. The Russian government has lately been releasing a sharply increasing volume of economic statistics, to the profit of this study, but seemingly it still prefers us not to know many things or not to know them accurately.[1]

The measurement of national income, it has been said, is an art rather than a science. If this is so (and few practitioners would disagree), for Russian national income it may be felt the art must even assume an occult character. Is it really worth while to attempt such measurements in this case? The question is inevitable, and the answer must be of a familiar kind. Great as the difficulties are, they do not appear to be overwhelming. With sufficient care and industry, it should be possible to limit the range of conjecture, and even uncertain knowledge may be highly valuable on a vital theme. It is hoped that these important propositions will be validated in this volume.

No inquiry into Soviet national income can fail to profit from the pioneer work that was done in this field by a number of intrepid Western scholars, particularly Colin Clark,[2] the late Dr. Julius Wyler[3] and Dr. Naum Jasny.[4] It was felt, however, that a substantially independent calculation might make more effective use of the available statistical materials than had been done previously. The present study also differs from earlier ones in regard to methodology. Most importantly, in view of the limitations of ruble prices, Clark and Wyler abandon these altogether and value Soviet national income instead in United States dollars. Jasny

[1] On the volume and quality of Soviet economic statistics, see Abram Bergson, "Reliability and Usability of Soviet Statistics," *American Statistician,* June-July 1953.

[2] Colin Clark, *A Critique of Russian Statistics: The Conditions of Economic Progress,* London, 1939.

[3] Julius Wyler, "The National Income of Soviet Russia," *Social Research,* December 1946; "Die Schätzungen des sowjetrussischen Volkseinkommens," *Schweizerische Zeitschrift für Volkwirtschaft und Statistik,* 1951, nos. 5 and 6.

[4] Naum Jasny, *The Soviet Economy During the Plan Era,* Stanford, 1951.

retains the ruble standard but limits himself to a calculation in terms of the ruble prices of 1926–27, a year preceding the five year plans. I compute Soviet national income in terms of ruble prices, but attempt to correct the results for outstanding distortions. This approach need not necessarily be held to be superior to that of Clark and Wyler in order to be felt worth exploring. Ruble prices probably were more meaningful on the eve of the five year plans than they often were to be in later years, and Jasny's use of 1926–27 prices without adjustment has much to commend it. In view of the possible importance of index number relativity, however, I compile data in terms of the prices of different years. One of these will be 1928, or about the same date that Jasny considers.

Reference has been made to non-Soviet calculations of Soviet national income. There are, of course, also Soviet data but Western scholars have found many reasons to think that the measurement of Russian national income is too important a task to leave to Russian statisticians.[5] Ever since the early thirties, the Soviet government has limited its national income releases primarily to global figures, often in terms of percentage increases. Data on the structure of national income of the sort that have been found so valuable in the West have been largely suppressed. Whether and to what extent the figures that actually are published are unreliable, as many Western writers charge, is a matter on which it is hoped the present inquiry will shed further light, but in view of the evidence assembled to date the question is in order, to say the least. Furthermore, for years up to 1950, the calculations of "real" national income are exclusively in terms of 1926–27 ruble prices, and even if the data were

[5] On the Soviet official national income data, there is now a considerable body of literature. See in addition to the studies of Clark, Wyler, and Jasny, already cited: Paul Studenski, "Methods of Estimating National Income in Soviet Russia," in National Bureau of Economic Research, Conference on Research in Income and Wealth. *Studies in Income and Wealth,* vol. VIII, New York, 1946; Paul Studenski and Julius Wyler, "National Income Estimates of Soviet Russia," and Abram Bergson, "Comments" in *American Economic Review,* May 1947, no. 2; Naum Jasny, "Intricacies of Russian National Income Indices," *Journal of Political Economy,* August 1947; A. Gerschenkron, "The Soviet Indices of Industrial Production," *Review of Economic Statistics,* November 1947; Paul A. Baran, "National Income and Product of the USSR in 1940," *Review of Economic Statistics,* November 1947; Maurice Dobb, "Further Appraisals of Russian Economic Statistics," *Review of Economic Statistics,* February 1948; Maurice Dobb, "Comment on Soviet Economic Statistics," *Soviet Studies,* June 1949; Alexander Gerschenkron, *A Dollar Index of Soviet Machinery Output, 1927–28 to 1937,* The RAND Corporation, Report R-197, April 6, 1951; Francis Seton, "Pre-war Soviet Prices in the Light of the 1941 Plan," *Soviet Studies,* April 1952; Stuart Rice et al., "Reliability and Usability of Soviet Statistics: A Symposium," *American Statistician,* April-July 1953; Abram Bergson, *National Income of the Soviet Union,* CEIR A-5, November 1954; Donald Hodgman, *Soviet Industrial Production 1928–1951,* Cambridge, 1954; A. Nove, "Soviet National Income Statistics," *Soviet Studies,* January 1955; F. Seton, "The Tempo of Soviet Industrial Expansion" (read before Manchester Statistical Society), January 1957; A. Nove, "'1926/7' and All That," *Soviet Studies,* October 1957; R. Moorsteen, *Prices and Production of Machinery in the Soviet Union, 1928–1958.* (In press)

reliable, alternative measures in terms of a more recent base year would still be needed.

Finally, under the influence of what they consider a Marxian distinction between productive and unproductive activity, the Soviet statisticians confine their measure of national income more or less to the value of material goods produced. Services generally are excluded from national income. Not only personal services but even government services are omitted. In terms of Western concepts, therefore, the Soviet data are at best only partial measures and cannot readily be used for many purposes for which Western data customarily are employed.

As a contribution to national income literature generally, the present inquiry may be of value as an attempt to apply a familiar methodology to an economy of a radically novel sort. Also, special attention is devoted to the problems posed by index number relativity and distortions in ruble prices. Anyone who works on the former topic today must be in debt to the trail-blazing studies of Professor Gerschenkron, Dr. Gilbert, and Dr. Kravis, but this inquiry may gain in interest so far as it deals with a still little explored aspect: the effects on historical national income trends of a change in the prices in terms of which the data are compiled.[6] Similarly, although in kind if not in degree, distortions in prices such as are encountered here must prevail in other countries, the problem this poses for national income computations appears until now to have received little systematic study. The attempt to explore this topic, therefore, may also be of general interest.

In previous publications,[7] the writer, Oleg Hoeffding, Hans Heymann, Jr., and Nancy Nimitz calculated Soviet national income in terms of current ruble prices. For purposes of measuring structural relations, an attempt was also made to recompute the results in terms of more meaningful "adjusted rubles." The present attempt to calculate Soviet "real"

[6] Professor Gerschenkron focuses on the measurement of the physical volume of Soviet machinery production. See his *Dollar Index of Soviet Machinery Output, 1927–28 to 1937,* The RAND Corporation, Report R-197, April 6, 1951. Gilbert and Kravis deal with "real" national income, but with comparisons between countries rather than over time. See Milton Gilbert and Irving B. Kravis, *An International Comparison of National Products and the Purchasing Power of Currencies,* Paris, n.d.

[7] Abram Bergson, *Soviet National Income and Product in 1937,* New York, 1953 (hereafter, *SNIP-37*); Abram Bergson and Hans Heymann, Jr., *Soviet National Income and Product, 1940–48,* New York, 1954 (hereafter, *SNIP-40–48*); Oleg Hoeffding, *Soviet National Income and Product in 1928,* New York, 1954 (hereafter, *SNIP-28*); Oleg Hoeffding and Nancy Nimitz, "Soviet National Income and Product, 1949–55," The RAND Corporation, Research Memorandum RM-2101, April 6, 1959 (hereafter *SNIP-49–55*); Abram Bergson, Hans Heymann, Jr., and Oleg Hoeffding, "Soviet National Income and Product, 1928–48: Revised Calculations," The RAND Corporation, Research Memorandum RM-2544, November 15, 1960 (hereafter, *SNIP-28–48*). The foregoing will be referred to collectively as the SNIP studies.

national income is intended as a sequel to, and draws heavily on, these earlier works. On the other hand, unexpectedly to the writer, the treatment accorded the problem of national income valuation in these studies quickly became a controversial theme. While it may as well be said at once that many of the essentials of the earlier approach are to be retained, it has seemed best to consider this central question more or less afresh here, and with special reference to the present problem of measuring "real" national income. I shall also explain other aspects of the methodology used, although this too involves retracing some previous steps.

My calculations are often complex. Research methods and procedures are matters on which opinions may differ, but perhaps I should explain that my goal throughout was not an unattainable certitude but a reasonably effective use of the available data. Although guesswork was unavoidable, systematic computations seemed necessary in order to assure that full account was taken of the scattered and incomplete Soviet statistics. The volume of statistical work was also considerably magnified as a result of the decision to consider valuations given by the prices of different years and to try to adjust ruble values for major distortions. Despite all the limitations of the basic data, the problems in question seemed much too important to ignore. If an inquiry into Soviet national income were to be undertaken at all, it was felt it would have to be along the lines marked out here.

What is the margin of error in the results? Even in the best of circumstances, it would hardly be possible to give a simple answer for complex measurements such as national income calculations. Furthermore, such data are used in countless diverse ways, and figures that are not especially reliable in one use may often be sufficiently accurate in another; for example, the data may be of varying reliability depending on whether the concern is with absolute or relative magnitudes, with year-to-year or long-term changes, et cetera. In the present study, an attempt is made throughout to explain sources and methods briefly in the text and in detail in appendices. On this basis it is hoped that the reader will be able to appraise the quality and limitations of the findings. Where possible, supplementary calculations are made in order to facilitate this appraisal.

It is hoped that, in presenting the details of the calculations, a foundation will be provided for further research. The calculation of national income for a strange and secretive country is a large task. Despite a substantial effort, no doubt there are many shortcomings which might have yielded to a still greater one. If the Soviet government continues, as it has recently done, to expand its statistical releases, there will be still more opportunities for fruitful research, and it should be possible to improve on the present computations at many points. The systematic nature of the calculations may have the incidental virtue that further work is facilitated.

If there can be no simple formula for the margin of error in our calculations, there can be no very satisfactory treatment either of the vexatious problem of rounding. As a practical expedient, I generally show the results in the text as they were computed, that is, for the most part to the nearest 100 million rubles (in the case of figures in terms of 1928 ruble prices, to the nearest 10 million rubles). Some especially crude figures are rounded beyond this, but some data are shown in similarly rounded form for other reasons (for example, they may have been in this form in the source), and in any case it will readily be seen that while accuracy to the number of significant digits shown may have been achieved in some cases the truth probably is more often the reverse. Accordingly, accuracy is to be judged not so much from the number of significant figures shown but (to repeat) from the nature of the underlying calculations.[8]

Although only rather summary results are presented in the text, the temptation was great to summarize even more. Almost inevitably, the figures compiled for broad use categories (for example, consumption) tend to be more reliable and interesting than those compiled for their components (as retail sales, housing, services). If only for purposes of understanding and appraising the more aggregative data, however, the more detailed results must often be considered. If the reader is to know what is being served in the dining room, he must have some acquaintance with the ingredients used in the kitchen.

Historical and Institutional Framework

My calculations begin with 1928, the year when the First Five Year Plan was inaugurated. The trends that are to be portrayed may usefully be seen in relation to previous economic levels in Russia, particularly those prevailing under Tsarism before the first World War, and also in

[8] By appropriate use of zeros, data rounded beyond the nearest 100 million rubles generally are shown with the same number of digits as data rounded only to this point; for example, in Table 2 household retail purchases in collective government and cooperative shops in 1937, which have been calculated to the nearest billion rubles, are nevertheless shown as totaling 110.0 billion rubles. I refer here to figures in prices of years other than 1928; where reference is to data in terms of 1928 prices, by appropriate use of zeros data are shown to the nearest 10 million rubles. Since zeros usually have been inserted in this way in the case of a series of figures on the same item, the reader, I believe, can generally see whether or not this device has been used in any particular case. In any event, the manner in which the data are presented seemingly tends to limit errors in computation and transcription, and it was felt that this gain outweighed the possible confusion which might result regarding the precise number of figures that is significant in any particular instance.

relation to those of the United States. While no systematic inquiry can be attempted, a few outstanding facts may suffice to provide the necessary perspective.

Russia in 1928 produced a 19 percent larger national income than in 1913.[9] This is according to official claims in terms of 1926–27 rubles, which for the early years have yet to be subjected to close scrutiny. From more reliable data in physical units (see Table 1), it may be con-

TABLE 1

Selected Economic Indicators — Russia, 1913, and USSR, 1928

	1913	1928
Pig iron (mil. m.t.)	4.2	3.3
Steel (mil. m.t.)	4.2	4.3
Coal (mil. m.t.)	29.1	35.5
Petroleum (mil. m.t.)	9.2	11.6
Electric power (bil. kw. hr.)	1.9	5.0
Grain (mil. m.t.)	81.6	73.3
Cotton, unginned (thous. m.t.)	744	821
Meat, commercial (thous. m.t.)	1,042	678
Fish catch (thous. m.t.)	1,018	840
Cotton cloth (mil. m.)	2,582	2,678
Woolen cloth (mil. m.)	103	86.8
Paper (thous. m.t.)	197	284
Freight turnover, all carriers (1913 = 100)	100	104

Note: All data except for those on grain and cotton production are from *Narkhoz-1956*, pp. 60 ff, pp. 128, 187. Grain and cotton production figures are from N. Jasny, *The Socialized Agriculture of the USSR*, Stanford, 1949, pp. 776, 793, and 795. Except as indicated, the figures refer to production. The abbreviations used are: mil. m. t., millions of metric tons; thous. m. t., thousands of metric tons; bil. kw. hr., billions of kilowatt hours; and mil. m., millions of meters.

cluded that by 1928 the country had largely if not entirely recovered from the devastating losses suffered under the successive blows of world war, revolution, and civil war, and probably was producing a total output similar to that of Tsarist times.

As Soviet leaders of the time did not fail to point out, the swift economic recovery of the twenties was a considerable achievement, but on the eve of the five year plans, production levels still were low by Western standards. Even in the favored industrial sector, Russia remained a backward country, although perhaps not quite as much so as is sometimes assumed. The United States already had reached in 1890 the 1928 level of Soviet steel production. We surpassed Russia's 1928 coal output in

[9] TSU, *Narodnoe khoziaistvo SSSR v 1956 godu*. Moscow, 1957, p. 42 (to be abbreviated as *Narkhoz-1956*).

1871 and her electric power output in 1902. In 1928 we produced 12.2 times as much steel as Russia did, 14.7 times as much coal, and 21.6 times as much electric power.

The late S. N. Prokopovich computed that "real" wages in Russia in 1928 were 11 percent above the 1913 level.[10] In the light of physical data of the sort cited above, one wonders whether at least in the cities, the Tsarist consumption standards could actually have been surpassed, but if the ordinary Russian was not as poverty stricken under Tsarism as often is depicted he scarcely prospered, and necessarily this too was his lot on the eve of the five year plans. Among the favored workers of large-scale industry, cereal products and potatoes supplied 68 percent of the calorific value of the diet.[11] In the years 1934–38, the corresponding figure for the American population generally was 32 percent. The industrial worker during 1927–28 purchased per capita 20 meters of cotton and 1.4 meters of woolen cloth (including the cloth equivalent of ready-made articles), and 1.4 pairs of leather shoes.[12] The average city dweller occupied 5.9 square meters of floor space.[13]

With the limited data available, the comparative levels of urban and rural consumption are difficult to judge with any precision. A careful recent study[14] reaches this conclusion:

> "It is clear that the urban worker had on the average more goods at his command than did the peasant. The urban worker had more proteins in his diet and more clothes and things other than food than did the peasant, and certainly a larger share of whatever government goods and services were available."

The early trends in the division of the national product between different final uses are also difficult to gauge. From information of the sort already presented, the presumption must be that in comparison with pre-World War I, the government on the eve of the plans already was allocating an increased share of the national product to investment and a correspondingly reduced share to consumption.

In considering the calculations that are to follow, it is useful to recall also a few broadly familiar facts concerning Soviet economic organization in the period studied. As the First Five Year Plan was initiated, Soviet agriculture still was predominantly a peasant agriculture, with 97 percent of the sown area in the hands of 22 million peasant households. But soon thereafter this situation was abruptly changed, and in 1937 (as will appear, this is the second of a series of benchmark years on which attention will be focused in this study) "collective farms" and

[10] S. N. Prokopovich, *Biulleten'*, Nov.-Dec. 1937.

[11] Nancy Baster, *A Study of Economic Growth and Working Memorandum on Russian Budget Studies,* New York, 1955, p. 16.

[12] *Ibid.,* p. 19.

[13] T. Sosnovy, *The Housing Problem in the Soviet Union,* New York, 1954.

[14] Baster, *op. cit.,* p. 48.

their members controlled 89 percent of the sown area. The balance of the agricultural land was largely in the hands of "state farms," while independent peasants tilled less than one percent of the country's sown area.

More recently, the collective farms have continued to be the mainstay of Soviet agriculture, but the government allowed peasant farming to continue for a time in the new territories that it took over in 1939–40. The government has made extensive use of state farms in the new lands that it has been bringing under cultivation in the East since 1954, and the role of these organizations in agriculture generally has expanded correspondingly.

Outside of agriculture, the Soviet economy in 1928 already was largely in the hands of state enterprises, and soon thereafter this form of organization became even more universal. In 1928, state enterprises were responsible for 69 percent of the industrial output, various sorts of state-regulated cooperatives for another 13 percent, and private enterprise for the remaining 18 percent. In official reports, private enterprise accounts for but 0.2 percent of the industrial output in 1937. State enterprise had gained also at the expense of the cooperatives. Private enterprise (exclusive of farmers) still conducted 24 percent of the country's retail trade in 1928, but in the official reports the figure had dropped to null by 1931. In this sphere, the state-controlled cooperative was predominant in 1928, but its role has been greatly restricted since, although it has continued to conduct the bulk of the trade in rural localities. While private trade vanished early in the thirties, the Soviet consumer has been able to obtain supplies ever since, not only in the state and cooperative retail shops but in the so-called "collective-farm" market, where the collective farms and their member households are allowed to sell any surpluses remaining at their disposal after they have met their legal obligations to the government and their own requirements. The collective farm market is now the one completely free market in the USSR, there being no regulation of either sales or prices.

Years Studied; Boundaries

Given the lack of data and the need to limit the task to feasible dimensions, this study considers only selected "benchmark" years. These are for the pre-war period and World War II: 1928, marking the inauguration of the First Five Year Plan and the beginning of the period studied; 1937, the final year of the Second Five Year Plan; 1940, the last full calendar year before the German attack; and 1944, probably the year of peak war effort. For the postwar period, we study 1950, the final year of the Fourth Five Year Plan, and 1955, marking the end of the Fifth Five Year Plan. Annual data have also been compiled for all years during the interval 1948–55. Partly because of the greater difficulty in measuring year-to-year changes reliably, and partly because of the need to limit the expositional burden, I focus primarily on the benchmark years 1950 and 1955 during most of the study, but the annual data are referred to at various points. They are also set forth fully in the Addendum.

Regrettably it did not seem possible to extend the calculations to a year in the early thirties, and so disentangle the complex events of the first two five year plans. This period saw among other things an initial sharp decline and a subsequent recovery of consumption standards. It would have been especially interesting to separate out these contrary developments. Except for the initial decade, however, the calculations generally seem to bracket the more interesting intervals in the period studied, and so to allow an appraisal of shorter-term as well as longer-term trends. Among other things, we are able to observe the impact of accelerated industrialization in its crucial first decade, the repercussions of the purges and heightened war preparations in the late thirties, and then the shift to an all-out war economy after the German attack. Reconstruction of the devastated western areas was largely although probably not entirely completed by 1950, so use of this year as a benchmark permits us to appraise separately reconstruction and postreconstruction growth. With the aid of our annual data, we may also consider the impact of the Korean War and the aftermath of Stalin's death (March 5, 1953).

The period studied witnessed a number of changes in the boundaries of the Soviet Union. During 1939 and 1940, the Soviet government incorporated in the USSR territories (that is, the Eastern provinces of Poland, Bessarabia, and N. Bukovina, certain Finnish provinces, and the Baltic States) which formerly had a population of about 20.5 millions, or nearly 12 percent of the Soviet population within the pre-1939 boundaries. Prior to these acquisitions, the Soviet population numbered nearly 175 millions. Further territorial changes occurred in 1944 and 1945, but these were of a very minor sort as measured in terms of population.[15]

In addition to these territorial changes which were due to boundary revisions, the Russians experienced further changes in the area under their control, albeit only temporary ones, as a result of the Germans' wartime conquests. At one time or another during the war, the Germans occupied some 700,000 square miles of Soviet territory (within the post-1940 boundaries). At the beginning of 1944, however, the Red Army had regained about two-thirds of this area, and the Soviet government at that time controlled a territory with probably more than four-fifths

[15] Use is made here mainly of unpublished data supplied by Dr. John F. Kantner of the U. S. Bureau of the Census.

of the total population. By the end of the year, the Russians again controlled their entire prewar territory except for a small corner of the Latvian and Lithuanian republics.

My calculations for 1928 and 1937 refer to the USSR within its pre-1939 boundaries. Those for 1948 and later years refer to the present territory of the USSR. Soviet sources are rarely explicit regarding the territorial coverage of the statistical data underlying the measurements for 1940. For reasons set forth elsewhere,[16] I believe the calculations are more or less comprehensive for territories added in 1939 and 1940. Possibly the underlying Soviet data, taken largely from postwar sources, also reflect the territorial changes that occurred subsequently, but these changes were statistically inconsequential in any case. Although the precise scope of the measurements for 1940 is still uncertain, therefore, I believe they can be treated as essentially referring to the post-1945 boundaries.

Soviet sources are not clear either regarding the territorial coverage of their data for 1944, but I believe my calculations are properly viewed as referring more or less to the area under Soviet control on the average in the course of the year. Furthermore, economic activity in the remainder of the present Soviet territory was at an extremely low level, so that the calculations for 1944 for all practical purposes refer to the entire USSR within the present boundaries.

The calculations for all years considered during the period 1940–55, therefore, may be taken as referring essentially to the present boundaries, but they still differ significantly in territorial coverage from the calculations for 1928 and 1937. This will have to be borne in mind in interpreting the trends we show.

Part I (chapters 2 and 3) elaborates further the methodology of the study. As was implied, my measures of "real" national income were derived in two stages: national income was first computed in terms of the ruble prices prevailing in different years, and then an attempt was made to adjust the results of these computations for ruble value distortions. The computations in prevailing rubles are presented in Part II (chapters 4 to 7), while the subsequent adjustments are the subject of Part III (chapters 8 to 10). In a final section (IV, comprising chapters 11 to 15), I compare my results with those obtained in previous inquiries, summarize findings, and discuss some of the more interesting economic implications. Implications should have an interest of their own, but inquiry into this aspect will also facilitate appraisal of the reliability of the data.

[16] *SNIP-40–48,* pp. 29–30, 230 ff.

PART I

METHODOLOGY

2

CONCEPTS AND CATEGORIES

National Income Concepts

This study focuses on the measurement of gross national product. Considering the differences in the economic systems involved, this concept is understood in essentially the same way as in the national income calculations of the U. S. Department of Commerce.[1] As with the Commerce Department concept, gross national product represents the sum of the values at prevailing prices of currently produced goods and services. The sum is calculated without any deduction for depreciation on durable capital, but is net of "intermediate products" that are used up currently in the production of "final" goods.

The Department of Commerce also uses two additional concepts of national income: net national product, which differs from gross national product in that it is net of depreciation on durable capital (as so understood, it is of course the same thing as the concept national income at

[1] See *National Income, 1954 Edition* (supplement to the U. S. Department of Commerce *Survey of Current Business*), Washington, 1954; and *U. S. Income and Output* (supplement to the U. S. Department of Commerce *Survey of Current Business*), Washington, 1958.

market price which is used by many statisticians), and national income, so called, which corresponds to the concept national income at factor cost as used by statisticians generally. The latter represents the net national product or national income at market price, less indirect business taxes and certain other charges included in the value product that are not considered to be a part of the income of business enterprises and households. Regrettably, any attempt at a systematic calculation of the "real" net national product for the USSR must await the compilation of more satisfactory data than are now available on the Soviet stock of fixed capital and its current depreciation.

As it turns out, after their adjustment for distortions in ruble values, my measures of "real" gross national product come to much the same thing as measures of "real" national income, so called. Of course, the former are still gross while the latter are net of depreciation, but otherwise (to repeat) the two categories tend to converge. But in Soviet conditions it seems best nevertheless to approach the problem of national income valuation independently in the light of the nature of the prevailing prices and without any prior commitment (such as the use of the Commerce Department concept of national income, so called, would entail) as to the kind of adjustments in these prices that are in order. My calculations, therefore, are best viewed as referring to "real" gross national product. If the results also tend to represent "real" national income, so called, this is more or less incidental rather than intended.

A familiar preliminary to national income accounting is the delimitation of "final" from "intermediate" products. The former contribute directly to "welfare"; the latter only indirectly. The former alone constitute national income. What kinds of goods are to be considered as "final" for the USSR? In Table 2, the list set forth for 1937 (this is to be one of our base years) applies to my calculations generally (for 1928, household purchases in retail markets include private rather than collective farm market trade). The list is also of a familiar sort, but in national income accounting, welfare ordinarily is seen in terms of "consumers' utilities." For the USSR, presumably we must consider not only this standard but also the alternative given by "planners' preferences." Viewed in this light, I fear my list will be subject to novel as well as familiar objections.

At least to "consumers," is not government administration partly intermediate? To Soviet "planners" no doubt defense is final, but may it not be intermediate to "consumers," as Professor Kuznets contends?[2] What of the possibility sometimes suggested that Soviet "planners" consider some individual commodities, for example, steel, as wholly final

[2] Simon Kuznets, "Government Product and National Income," in International Association for Research in Income and Wealth, *Income and Wealth,* series I, Cambridge, 1951.

TABLE 2

Gross National Product of the USSR by Use in Current Prices, 1937

Outlay category	Billions of rubles
Household purchases in retail markets	
In government and cooperative shops and restaurants	110.0
In collective farm markets	16.0
Total	126.0
Housing; services	17.4
Consumption of farm income in kind	25.0
Military subsistence	2.5
Household consumption outlays[a]	170.9
Communal services	
Health care	7.9
Education	17.0
Other	0.7
Total	25.6
Government administration, including NKVD (OGPU; MVD and MGB)	7.4
Defense (as recorded in budget[b])	17.4
Gross investment	
In fixed capital	35.2
Other	24.2
Total	59.4
Gross national product	280.7

[a] Here and elsewhere the sum of "household purchases in retail markets"; "housing; services"; "consumption of farm income in kind"; and "military subsistence."

[b] Exclusive of pensions to officers, et cetera, that are included in published defense figures.

rather than (as is usually supposed) partly intermediate? Or of the further possibility also suggested that to the "planners" consumption in reality is more nearly intermediate than final? The questions are in order but for the USSR no more than elsewhere is it feasible to separate intermediate from final activities of government; and as to other aspects in question, no doubt alternative standpoints are open, but mine at least has the merit that it enables me to fall in with convention. Moreover, from the data to be presented, some recomputations may readily be made in the light of other views.

But to classify goods as either intermediate or final presupposes that, although in different ways, all alike contribute to welfare. From the standpoint of "consumers" at least, is not this too a dubious proposition for the USSR? What in particular of the NKVD, which is classified here with government administration? To "consumers," is this not more properly viewed simply as economic waste? For a country where political power is notably concentrated, familiar doubts as to the value of defense to "consumers" inevitably gain in force. In terms of consumers' utilities, therefore, should not the military outlays also be written off? These questions, too, are in order, and as will appear, although I retain the list of use categories given above, no way is found in any case to value all of them (as usually is attempted) in terms pertinent to the appraisal of welfare, as given by consumers' utilities. On the other hand, we are also interested here in welfare, as given by planners' preferences, and in this light the classification of the NKVD and military outlays as economic waste presumably would be inappropriate. Moreover, national income data are used to appraise not only welfare but "production potential." From the latter standpoint, I believe I am right that sometimes even dubious uses of scarce resources are appropriately included.

I shall have more to say later on these two familiar applications of national income data and on the relation of my calculations to them.

For a socialist economy, "government administration" needs definition. In the economic sphere, where does this category end and economic activities of a nongovernmental sort begin? For the USSR, we may reasonably be guided at this point, I think, by the Russians' own financial practice. For the purposes of this study, at any rate, government administration embraces in the economic sphere only agencies which are attached to the government budget. Broadly speaking, this means that government administration includes economic ministries (prior to 1946, commissariats) and superior organs but not agencies subordinate to the economic ministries, such as combines, trusts, and individual enterprises. Under long-standing administrative arrangements, the latter so-called *khozraschet* agencies are divorced from the government budget and financially speaking are more or less independent entities. Among other things, they generally are expected to cover current expenses out of sales revenues.[3]

Although the government limits in this way its financial responsibilities for subordinate economic enterprises, the *khozraschet* system is complex,

[3] The point in the administrative hierarchy at which an agency is detached from the budget and becomes a so-called *khozraschet* organization has varied to some extent in the course of time. Accordingly, the scope of government administration as understood here has varied correspondingly. For the period studied, probably the most important change in arrangements of this sort occurred in 1936 when the supply and procurement departments of industrial ministries were divorced from the government budget and reconstituted as *khozraschet* agencies.

At the beginning of the period studied, enterprises subordinate to trusts or similar organizations did not yet have the full status of a *khozraschet* agency, and this they acquired only subsequently, but this shift in arrangements does not seem to affect our calculations.

On the nature and scope of the *khozraschet* system, see Institut Ekonomiki, Akademiia Nauk SSSR, *Ekonomika promyshlennosti SSSR,* Moscow, 1956, chap. 16, and *SNIP-37,* pp. 13 ff, 23 ff. On special aspects of the system on which I comment further below in the text, see these same citations and also *SNIP-37,* pp. 113–119; *SNIP-28-48,* pp. 16–17 ff; *SNIP-49-55,* pp. 125 ff, 141 ff.

and not surprisingly the government at one time or another has attached agencies to its budget that are essentially of an operating character. Most importantly, the state "machine-tractor" station (MTS) servicing the collective farm, which previously had operated partially on a *khozraschet* basis, was attached fully to the government budget in 1938 and retained this status thereafter. In view of the operational character of the MTS and similar organizations, we clearly must treat it here essentially as a *khozraschet* organization rather than as a part of government administration. Actually, the government itself has long observed a distinction between superior agencies of the sort referred to above and the MTS. The former have been financed out of a budgetary appropriation to government administration, the latter out of an appropriation to "financing the national economy." Out of the latter appropriation, the government has also financed a large part of the requirements for investment in fixed and working capital of the *khozraschet* organizations and certain special measures, such as industrial resettlement, geological surveys, some limited outlays for industrial research and training that are delegated to *khozraschet* agencies (as distinct from educational agencies that are financed out of the budgetary appropriations to "education"), et cetera. The investments in fixed capital and inventories of course constitute final goods here, and with some misgivings I consider the special measures as final also. In violation of *khozraschet* fundamentals, for protracted periods the government has also granted substantial subsidies to the *khozraschet* organizations in order to permit their prices to be fixed below costs. Since the expenses covered in this fashion are in no way distinct from other expenses of the subsidized agency, it goes without saying that such activities are to be treated as intermediate rather than final.

As the foregoing implies, the *khozraschet* system provides us with a basis for distinguishing not only between government administration and operating enterprises in the economic sphere but also between intermediate and final products of the latter. Outlays recorded as expenses in the books of the *khozraschet* organization generally are considered here as intermediate; other outlays for goods and services, as final. To this rule, we make a few exceptions, including most importantly the public health measures financed out of enterprise social insurance contributions (the latter are charged as expenses), but otherwise it is observed throughout. Although this was a necessary expedient, the relevant Soviet accounting practices appear to be of a broadly conventional sort, and I believe we shall not be diverging markedly from familiar national income accounting at this point. On the other hand, we apparently are committed to include in national income some curious items, for example, "outlays for experiments not yielding results" (Soviet accountants treat this as a charge to profits rather than as an expense; as a result in our calculations, it probably finds its way into investment). Moreover, one inevitably wonders to what extent theoretically sound principles, such as the distinction made between asset debits for "capital repairs" and expense charges for "current repairs," are properly observed in practice.

Following the Commerce Department, I include in household consumption an allowance for the subsistence of the armed forces. This is in addition to the corresponding entry under defense. The latter entry, of course, is supposed to represent the value of the services of military personnel, over and above money pay. By recording military subsistence also under consumption, in effect one allows for the final disposition of such income in kind.

An awkward problem in national income accounting is posed by household processing for own consumption. While this category is difficult to measure, it may be of some consequence. Of particular concern is the overstatement of the increase in national income which, in economies undergoing industrialization, results from the transfer of processing from home to factory. Following the Commerce Department, I omit household processing for own consumption from Soviet national income, but attempt to appraise some aspects of such activities in 1928 and 1937. During the five year plans, the shift of processing from home to factory presumably was important primarily in this early period.

During the war, the Russians had at their disposal not only their own domestic output but imports obtained on Lend-Lease account. Similarly, after the war they were able to supplement their own production with reparations from ex-enemy countries. With the data avaliable, Soviet national income is best computed in terms of final outlays that include these imports. In other words, during the years when such aid is received, I calculate national income disposed of rather than national income produced. The possible extent of the divergence between these two aspects, however, will also be discussed.

Final Use Categories

The captions of our final use categories (Table 2) are broadly indicative of their scope. In explaining them, I refer primarily to the year 1937. Some questions that arise regarding the comparability of the figures compiled for different years will be considered later when data are presented for all years in terms of constant prices.[4]

Household purchases in retail markets. This is intended to represent household purchases of consumers' goods as distinct from farm producers' goods (such as tools and fertilizers, which must be classified here as either investment or production expense) and building materials used in

[4] For further details and documentation see also Appendices A-G.

private housing construction (which also become investment in our calculations). Reflecting the nature of the underlying data used, I include household purchases in rural localities in the case of government and cooperative shops but for the most part not in the case of collective farm markets. On purchases in rural collective farm markets, however, see below the comment on farm income in kind.

Housing; services. Reference is to household rental payments, including imputed rentals on privately owned housing; expenditures on utilities, transportation, entertainment, and diverse other services such as repairs and domestics; and dues paid to trade union and other organizations.

Consumption of farm income in kind. This refers, of course, to the consumption by farmers of their own produce and should correspond to their current output, less marketings, production expense, and investment in kind. As considered here, marketings probably omit and therefore farm income in kind includes most if not all rural collective farm market sales. Since such sales are omitted from retail sales, their inclusion in farm income in kind involves no double counting. Consumption of farm income in kind also includes limited amounts of investment in kind in the form of changes in farm inventories of produce available for human consumption (for example, grain inventories). Investment in kind in livestock herds, however, is allowed for in gross investment.

Military subsistence. The value of food, clothing, and other subsistence supplied to members of the armed forces.

Communal services. Military medicine financed out of the government budget appropriation to "defense" is recorded in the corresponding use category rather than under "communal services." Similarly, some very limited household outlays for private medical services and tuition charges are classified under "housing; services," rather than here.[5] But with these main exceptions, the data cited on communal services are meant to be comprehensive of outlays in the USSR on the activities included, and accordingly embrace not only expenditures recorded under the headings of "health care" and "education" in the government budget, but additional sums allotted to these activities from other sources, including the budget appropriation to "social insurance," and funds (sometimes supplemented by budgetary grants) of state enterprises, collective farms and

[5] On a very limited scale, the private practice of medicine has continued in the USSR up to the present day. Education generally was probably supplied free of charge in 1937, but the government charged some tuition for secondary and higher education prior to the adoption of its new constitution in December 1936 and (despite the constitutional provision to the contrary) tuition charges were reinstituted in 1940 and continued to be levied until 1956. Throughout the period of the five year plans, however, scholarships have been granted on an extensive scale. On the tuition charges, see Abram Bergson, *The Structure of Soviet Wages,* Cambridge, 1944, pp. 26 ff, 234 ff.

the like. In delimiting "health care" and "education," therefore, I generally fall in with Soviet budgetary practice. In the former case, this means that reference usually is to activities of a conventional kind (that is, doctors' services; upkeep of clinics, hospitals and sanitoria; public health measures, et cetera).[6] For "education," however, the cited figures include expenditures not only on schools but on libraries, museums, scientific research, and diverse other cultural activities. Capital construction is recorded under investment rather than in this category; stipends and scholarships are treated as transfer payments. "Other" communal services consist chiefly of social insurance administration.

Government administration, including NKVD (OGPU; MVD and MGB). Exclusive of the NKVD, this corresponds in 1937 to the government budget category "maintenance of government administrative organs and judicial institutions,"[7] and embraces expenditures for the upkeep of all higher and local organs of government except those concerned with internal security and defense. The superior organs administering the economy are included.

For the NKVD,[8] I also refer to a corresponding budgetary category, but one about which the Russians understandably have been especially secretive. In addition to internal security, the NKVD performs a variety of other civil control activities, such as the operation of penal institutions, fire protection, civil registration, and forest guards. For the most part, these activities must be financed out of the general budget appropriation to the NKVD and accordingly are classified under the same heading in my accounts. As part of its internal security activities, the NKVD maintains military formations of various kinds, including frontier guards, military police, troops to combat "counterrevolution," et cetera. Insofar as these activities are financed out of the NKVD, they must be considered as supplementing the defense expenditures referred to below. Under the notorious "correctional labor" system, I believe much of the upkeep

[6] Some minor sums appropriated in the government budget to "physical culture" are classified in my calculations with "health care."

[7] This is the category that appears in published summary versions of the budget. According to the official classification of the time, the pertinent activities were distributed among several budget headings.

[8] The NKVD (People's Commissariat of Internal Affairs) was organized in 1935 as the successor to the OGPU (Unified State Political Administration). In 1928, some of its functions had also been performed by a predecessor of the same name. During 1941, the NKVD in turn was dissolved, reconstituted, and then dissolved again, its functions finally being transferred partly to a successor of the same name and partly to the NKGB (People's Commissariat of State Security). Renamed ministries in 1946, these two departments continued in existence until 1953 when they were again merged into a single agency. In 1954, the new agency was once more supplanted by two agencies, the MVD and the KGB (Committee on State Security). The latter has continued in existence to date, but the former has now been supplanted by republican agencies.

of penal workers is financed out of the receipts from the sales of their products but when this is not the case they would have to be supported instead out of the budget appropriation to the NKVD. The corresponding funds likewise must be included under this heading. In the latter case, the Soviet practice might tend to rectify a shortfall in my calculations due to the omission elsewhere of any allowance for penal labor subsistence, but national income is still understated to the extent that the subsistence is financed out of sales receipts. Furthermore, household consumption is understated by the full amount of the subsistence. In the chapters following, my calculations will have to be interpreted in this light. Preferably the data should have been corrected initially for the indicated deficiencies, but in view of the uncertainties regarding the pertinent Soviet financial arrangements and the magnitudes involved, this was not feasible.[9]

Defense (as recorded in the budget). With an exception to be noted, this corresponds to the Soviet budget category "defense." The latter in turn refers to the appropriations to the departments administering the Soviet armed forces (in 1937, the Commissariat of Defense, so-called, and the Commissariat of the Naval Fleet, created in July 1937) for military pay and subsistence, munitions procurement, and diverse other types of defense procurement and expense of a familiar sort, petroleum and transport, for example. In the USSR, munitions production generally is the responsibility not of the military establishment but of departments specialized to this end. Accordingly, the budget defense appropriation for the most part (as is the case also in the United States) includes munitions costs only at the procurement stage. It follows too that while some outlays for the construction of military facilities, such as camps and fortifications, are included in the defense appropriation, investments in defense plant construction generally are not. In my calculations, however, the latter outlays should find their way into "gross investment." The budget appropriations also fail to cover premilitary training, which to some extent is given in ordinary schools, or paramilitary training provided by various voluntary societies auxiliary to the armed forces. Military pensions in the USSR are generally paid out of a budget appropriation to "social assistance," and accordingly are also omitted from that to defense. For present purposes, this is to the good, since such pensions are properly considered as transfer incomes. On the other hand, pensions are paid to officers and certain other personnel and their dependents out

[9] Actually, we are not only in the dark as to the extent that penal labor is supported out of the budget appropriation to the NKVD. Contrary to the view implied in the text, we cannot be sure either that it is omitted from household consumption. Although the eventuality seems remote, we cannot rule out that penal labor subsistence finds its way into our data on retail trade.

of the appropriation to defense. In my calculations, the budgetary defense figures have been adjusted to exclude these pensions as well.[10]

Gross investment. Investment in "fixed capital" is identified here essentially with the corresponding category in Soviet official statistics, and for the most part refers to activities of a kind usually classified in this way, including erection of permanent structures, such as factories, houses, and other buildings; construction of roads, irrigation works, and the like; purchases of new machinery and equipment; and assembly and installation work. Some additional expenditures for such items as design and research work and labor training, that are associated with a particular investment project, are also included and so also are certain other outlays, for example, on prospecting. In Soviet accounting practice, a distinction is made between "capital repairs," involving substantial renovations that are intended to restore an asset to full working life, and "current repairs," representing maintenance that is intended to keep an asset in normal working condition. Fixed capital investment is supposed to include capital but not current repairs. "Other" investment in my computations is a catchall, and supposedly includes investments in inventories, stock piles, gold production, and net exports.[11] I include here investments in livestock herds (no attempt is made, however, either here or elsewhere to allow for investments in agricultural work in process). Some outlays on prospecting and on certain other special measures (for example, industrial resettlement) probably find their way into this residual category also.

Although I have sought to explain some aspects more fully than was done previously, the concepts of national income and the final use categories employed in this volume have essentially the same meaning as those considered in the SNIP studies which serve as a point of departure. The current ruble figures for 1937 in Table 2, however, are intended to correspond with the constant ruble figures that are derived in this study, and this is true also of similar current ruble figures for other years that will be presented later. As will be explained, these current ruble data represent a slightly revised version of the current ruble data compiled in the SNIP studies.

This chapter has explained the national income concepts and final use categories considered. For purposes of further elaboration of the methodology employed, I turn now to various methods and procedures employed.

[10] The special arrangements now in force for the payment of pensions to officers, et al., date from 1941, and just what arrangements were in effect for them previously is not known, but the sums involved must have been quite small and the precise scope of the budgetary appropriation to defense in this respect was of little consequence.

[11] Net exports on commercial account. In my calculations, imports on Lend-Lease and reparations account, instead of being an offset to exports, contribute positively to the gross national product. (See page 20.)

3

METHODS AND PROCEDURES

The purpose of this study is to measure Soviet "real" national income. Understood as representing the volume of a country's final output at "constant" prices, such data summarize a country's productive activities, but economic theory teaches that different computations may also be more or less illuminating regarding more ultimate categories, particularly production potential and welfare. The analysis is abstract, and seems especially so in relation to Soviet circumstances, but an attempt to compile meaningful figures for the USSR may usefully take it as a point of departure.

The task of this chapter is to explain methods and procedures employed. As a preliminary, it may be advisable to review the pertinent theoretic principles. Space permits me to do little more than underline aspects of particular interest here. The reader may wish to refer, therefore, to relevant writings.[1] On the other hand, only a general impression

[1] See particularly W. Leontief, "Composite Commodities and the Problem of Index Numbers," *Econometrica,* January 1936; J. R. Hicks, "The Valuation of Social Income," *Economica,* May 1940; Simon Kuznets, "On the Valuation of Social Income," *Economica,* February-May 1948; J. R. Hicks, "On the Valuation of Social Income," *Economica,* August 1948; P. A. Samuelson, "Evaluation of Real National Income," *Oxford Economic*

of the theoretic rationale of the calculations may be desired. If so, one should turn at once to the explanation of methods and procedures on pages 34 ff. Although the precise meaning of some theoretic allusions may not be evident, the discussion will provide a basis to proceed.

Here are the principles in mind:

(i) For purposes of appraisal of production potential and welfare, national income must be appropriately valued. The nature of the valuation depends on which of the two applications is in question. Production potential at any time is understood in terms of the corresponding "schedule of production possibilities," that is, the schedule representing the limiting amounts of "composite commodities" of different mixes that the community might produce with available factor supplies and "technical knowledge." Supposedly, the diverse mixes are obtainable through appropriate allocations of productive factors between industries. Where the concern is with production potential, prices conform ideally to the "efficiency standard": The prices of any two products are inversely proportional to the corresponding "marginal rate of transformation." For the products concerned, the latter represents the rate at which on the margin one product may be transformed into another through reallocations of factors between industries.

If reference is to welfare, prices are supposed to conform to the "welfare standard": Prices generally correspond to consumers' "marginal utilities." In the case of investment goods, future returns are discounted at the prevailing "rate of time preference." Or rather, this is the standard applied where reference is to a community in which consumers' utilities are a prevailing end, and where welfare is understood accordingly. If resources are allocated in accordance not simply with consumers' utilities but in some measure with planners' preferences, the possibility arises that national income data may also be illuminating regarding welfare understood in terms of planners' preferences. Valuation is then in terms of the planners' "marginal rates of substitution."

(ii) In the comparison of any two periods, two computations are of interest. In one case, outputs in both periods are valued in period 1 prices; that is, use is made of the formula:

Papers, January 1950; J. L. Nicholson, "National Income at Factor Cost or Market Price?" *Economic Journal,* June 1955; I. M. D. Little, *A Critique of Welfare Economics,* 2nd ed., Oxford, 1957, chap. xii; J. de V. Graaf, *Theoretical Welfare Economics,* Cambridge, 1957, chap. xi; W. Nutter, "On Measuring Economic Growth," *Journal of Political Economy,* February 1957, and the comments by Herbert Levine and Warren Nutter, *Journal of Political Economy,* August 1958. Reference may also be made to *SNIP-37,* chap. 3. As will appear, an interesting aspect was clarified by Dr. Richard Moorsteen in a talk given at The RAND Corporation in the summer of 1958. Moorsteen is elaborating his analysis for publication in a journal article, "The Measurement of Productive Potential and Efficiency."

$$\frac{\Sigma P_1 Q_2}{\Sigma P_1 Q_1} \tag{1}$$

In the other, outputs in both periods are valued in period 2 prices; that is, one applies the familiar analogue of Formula (1):

$$\frac{\Sigma P_2 Q_2}{\Sigma P_2 Q_1} \tag{2}$$

Final outputs observed at different times ordinarily will differ in their commodity structure. Each computation, however, serves in effect to translate the final outputs of the two periods considered into equivalent amounts of some one "composite commodity" that is taken as a standard. The translation occurs simply through the hypothetical "exchange" of one commodity for another at the prices applied; thus, for the final outputs of each period, the equivalent amount of the standard composite commodity is that amount of the latter having at the given prices the same total "dollar" value as the observed final outputs. In this way, each computation may be seen as translating the observed change in final outputs into a change of equivalent "dollar" value in the standard composite. Moreover, such a translation occurs no matter what composite commodity is taken as a standard. By the same token, it also occurs in respect of the composite actually experienced in either period. In other words, Formula (1) tells us how much of a change in the volume of either of the two composites experienced would be equivalent in "dollar" value at period 1 prices to the observed change in final outputs. Similarly, Formula (2) shows what change in the volume of either composite would be equivalent in "dollar" value at period 2 prices to the observed change in final outputs.

This is true whatever the nature of the prices applied. Where the prices conform to one or the other of the two valuation standards prescribed by theory, the "dollar" equivalents of the outputs experienced tend also in some degree to be equivalent in terms of the corresponding theoretic category. In this way, the alternative computations serve as observations on the variation in the different composites experienced which in terms of the pertinent theoretic category is equivalent to the actual change in final outputs. The category itself is appraised in this light. Thus, where valuation is in terms of the efficiency standard, each computation serves as an observation on the change in the community's capacity to produce each of the two composites experienced. The change in production potential is gauged accordingly. Where the welfare standard is applied, there are observations on the hypothetical change in the volume of each composite experienced that is equivalent in terms of welfare to the observed change in outputs. The change in welfare is judged on this basis. Production potential in respect of any composite, however, varies proportionately with the volume of that composite. Because of "diminishing marginal utility," this is not true of welfare. Moreover, since household "tastes" change from period to period, the appraisal of welfare must consider this aspect as well. Finally, welfare depends not only on the volume of output but on its distribution among households.

(iii) Whether reference is to welfare or to production potential, the magnitude of the "equivalent variation" in one or another composite very likely will depend on the nature of the composite. For a nation of "meat-eaters," the proportional increases in bread and meat required to yield the same increase in welfare will be greater the smaller the share of meat in the total output. The same change in production potential generally may also mean different changes in the capacity to produce different product mixes. It follows that index number relativity has an analytic as well as statistical aspect. Not only are there alternative computations in terms of the prices of different years. The alternative computations in turn are observations on alternative "true" measures of welfare or production potential, as the case may be. Moreover, each computation bears on both "true" measures.

The two sets of prevailing prices, however, ordinarily will not be equally valid measures of the rate at which one mix may be translated into another in each period. By the same token, the two computations are probably not equally reliable observations on the equivalent variation in each composite. Schedules of production possibilities may be of diverse shapes. Conceivably they might be "linear"; that is, in any period the marginal rate of transformation is constant as successive transformations take place. In this case, prices in period 1 correctly indicate the rate at which during period 1 the mix of period 1 might be transformed into the mix of period 2, but not necessarily the rate at which during period 2 the mix of period 2 might be transformed into the mix of period 1. It follows that Formula (1) measures accurately the change in capacity to produce the period 2 composite and yet may be inaccurate regarding the change in capacity to produce the period 1 composite. The situation regarding Formula (2) is seen to be the converse of that regarding Formula (1).

More likely, schedules will be in some degree "curvilinear"; that is, in any period the marginal rate of transformation varies as successive transformations take place. In this case, prices of period 1 will no longer measure accurately the rate at which during period 1 the period 1 mix might be transformed into that of period 2. By the same token, Formula (1) no longer provides a correct observation on the change in capacity regarding the period 2 composite. Moreover, depending on the extent of the change in production structure, the error might be marked in both cases. Nevertheless, period 1 prices very possibly will still be more indicative than period 2 prices of the rate at which the stated transformation might be made. If so, Formula (1) will continue to be more reliable than Formula (2) as to the change in capacity regarding the period 2 composite. On similar reasoning, we also see that Formula (2) might well be more reliable than Formula (1) as to the change in capacity regarding the period 1 composite.

The situation in respect to the appraisal of welfare is similar, but what is in question here is the households' (planners') "indifference schedule" rather than the schedule of production possibilities, and considering this aspect there are reasons to think that, for purposes of gauging the "equivalent variation" in the period 2 mix, the case for Formula (1) is less impelling than where the concern is with production potential. The same situation obtains regarding the use of Formula (2) to gauge the "equivalent variation" in the period 1 mix.

(iv) Reference so far has been to comparisons of two periods, but the foregoing considerations are also illuminating where the concern is to compile serial data for many years. Among other things, use may be made of one or the other of two approaches: On the one hand, national income is computed for all years in terms of the prices prevailing in some one year taken as "base," that is, according to Formula (1). On the other hand, each comparison with the "base" year is made in "given" year prices, through successive application of Formula (2). If period 1 is taken as "base" year and there are three periods, these are the alternative serial measures in question (with the period 1 index taken as 100):

Period	With valuation at "base" year prices	With valuation at "given" year prices
1	100	100
2	$\frac{\Sigma P_1Q_2}{\Sigma P_1Q_1} \cdot 100$	$\frac{\Sigma P_2Q_2}{\Sigma P_2Q_1} \cdot 100$
3	$\frac{\Sigma P_1Q_3}{\Sigma P_1Q_1} \cdot 100$	$\frac{\Sigma P_3Q_3}{\Sigma P_3Q_1} \cdot 100$

In sum, by use of the first method, one obtains a series of a conventional sort where national income is valued over a protracted period in terms of the prices of a single year. Under the second method, oddly, the prices in terms of which output is valued vary over time, but this method nevertheless is also of interest so far as it may yield, for the entire period considered, alternative and often more reliable serial observations on the change in capacity to produce one and the same composite, namely that of the base year. The observations are more reliable wherever for any two years a calculation in given year prices is more indicative than one in base year prices of the change in capacity to produce the base year composite. If the concern is with welfare, the second method is seen to provide alternative observations on the variations in the base year composite that are equivalent from this standpoint, but the method nevertheless seems less meritorious here than where the concern is with production potential.

Serial data may also be computed through the chaining of successive links. Each link in turn is computed in terms of the prices prevailing at some time during the interval to which the link pertains. Where reference is made to a lengthy period during which there have been marked changes in the production structure, neither calculations in terms of the prices of a single base year nor calculations where all comparisons with the base year are in terms of given year prices may provide the basis for accurate appraisal of trends in terms of a single composite. By chaining successive links, however, one may still obtain relatively reliable observations on the "equivalent variations" in the composites actually experienced in successive intervals. If it is taken into consideration that the changing product mixes ordinarily will represent in some degree adaptations to changing factor structures, including natural resource depletion, such observations seemingly have an interest of their own. Each link indicates the performance of the economy in terms of a product mix reflecting the contemporary supplies of factors, including natural resources.

(v) Because of differences in the degree to which different factors are allocable between industries, the schedule of production possibilities depends on the period allowed. Among other things, that for the "short run," where allocations are largely limited to labor and materials, will ordinarily differ from one referring to the "long run," where in some measure capital too is allocable. There are also different variants depending on the extent to which workers may shift between occupations as well as industries. Very likely, schedules pertaining to the "long-run" are more nearly "linear" than those pertaining to the "short-run." "Linearity" is also more nearly approximated if in different industries there are no "economies" or "diseconomies" of scale to factors generally, but a "linear" schedule still may not prevail because of differences in factor proportions in different industries. Corresponding to the different schedules, there are also different concepts of production potential and different variants of the efficiency standard.

Correspondence of prices to marginal rates of transformation comes to the same thing as their correspondence to "marginal costs." Costs are computed in terms of factor prices that generally are uniform between industries and within any industry are proportional to "marginal productivities." Wage differentials also correspond to workers' "transfer prices." This is the appropriate formulation where the concern is with "long-run" production possibilities and where among other things there may be occupational shifts of workers. For other variants, the formulation in terms of costs varies correspondingly. Where reference is to the stated "long-run" variant, and there are no "economies" or "diseconomies" of scale, prices also correspond to "average cost."

The appraisal of production potential presupposes ideally the achievement of a partial economic optimum: The community is realizing its production possibilities. On this basis, the outputs experienced are taken as observations on the corresponding schedules. Also, relative factor productivities are the same in all industries. In this way, it is possible to have uniform factor prices which correspond to factor productivities in each and every industry. Similarly, appraisal of welfare presupposes ideally that households are on their "contract curves." In this way, the awkward possibility is avoided that prices conforming to relative marginal utilities for one household will not do so for another. Where welfare is understood in terms not of consumers' utilities but of planners' preferences the requirement is analogous.

The efficiency and welfare standards are independent. Either may be realized without the other. However, the community ideally may produce a "bill of goods" which is "optimal" from the standpoint of welfare. If so, prices will correspond at the same time to both standards. By the same token, calculations in terms of either standard provide a basis for the appraisal of both production potential and welfare.

Some aspects of the theory that has been outlined were only recently clarified by Dr. Richard Moorsteen and at some other points as well the analysis may still not be generally understood. It may be of value, therefore, if I elaborate somewhat on the foregoing discussion. I refer particularly to the appraisal of production potential. Of the two applications, this is the more novel. It is also more important here. The following will demand the reader's close attention, for I must still be rather concise.

Consider the simple community illustrated in Figure 1. The community produces bread and machinery in amounts designated as N_1 and N_2 in periods 1 and 2 respectively. With the change from period 1 to period 2, production potential is assumed to have increased. With its period 2 schedule of "production possibilities" (P_2P_2), therefore, the community can produce more of the two products in any given proportions than it could with the corresponding period 1 schedule (P_1P_1). Among other things, while it was able to produce in period 1 only ON_1 of bread and machinery in the proportions then obtaining, in period 2 it could produce OM_2 of the same composite. Similarly, the community's capacity to produce a composite of the period 2 sort increases from OM_1 to ON_2.

Also shown are the community's schedules of "constant dollar outputs" (D_1D_1 and D_2D_2). For any period, alternative amounts of bread and machinery given by such a schedule have the same "dollar" value in prevailing prices as the outputs actually produced. By the same token, they also represent the same "dollar" national income as that produced. Schedules of constant dollar outputs are necessarily related to schedules of production possibilities in the manner depicted; that is, at each observed position the pertinent schedule of constant dollar outputs touches and has the same gradient as the corresponding schedule of production possibilities. The gradient of the former schedule is given by the price ratio and of the latter by the marginal rate of transformation. The two gradients coincide, therefore, where prices conform to the efficiency standard. The dashed line N_2M_2'' is drawn through the point N_2 parallel to D_1D_1, and the dashed line $M_1''N_1$ is drawn through the point N_1 parallel to D_2D_2.

As the reader may verify, Formulas (1) and (2) yield these observations on the change in production capacity occurring:

	Actual change in production capacity	Formula (1) measurement	Formula (2) measurement
In respect of period 1 composite (OV_1)	$\frac{OM_2}{ON_1}$	$\frac{OM_2''}{ON_1}$	$\frac{OM_2'}{ON_1}$
In respect of period 2 composite (OV_2)	$\frac{ON_2}{OM_1}$	$\frac{ON_2}{OM_1'}$	$\frac{ON_2}{OM_1''}$

In the case illustrated, the rule explained in the text is also seen to hold; that is, Formula (1) is more reliable than Formula (2) in respect of the period 2 composite and less reliable than Formula (2) in respect of the period 1 composite. In the assumed case, schedules of production possibilities are "concave." If instead they were "convex," Formula (1) is still superior in respect of the period 2 composite and Formula (2) in respect of the Formula (1) composite unless the curvature of the schedules is pronounced.

I assume in Figure 1 that, in association with a disproportionate increase in machinery, the marginal rate of transformation changes against machinery; that is, increasing amounts of machinery must be sacrificed in order to produce a marginal increment of bread. As is readily seen, if alternatively the marginal rate of transformation changes against bread, Formula (1) is again superior to Formula (2) in respect of the period 2 composite and inferior to Formula (2) in respect of the period 1 composite whenever schedules are "convex." This is still true where schedules are "concave" unless the curvature is marked.

If the schedules are linear, Formula (1) is always fully accurate in respect of the period 2 composite and Formula (2) in respect of the period 1 composite. The reliability of Formula (1) in respect of the period 1 composite and of Formula (2) in respect of the period 2 composite depends on the extent of the change over time in the marginal rate of transformation.

Among the different cases considered, which are the more likely? In theoretic analysis, the schedule of production possibilities is usually taken to be "concave." One nevertheless hesitates to assume that this is generally so in the "real" world. At least, the "convex" case hardly can be barred where the concern is with the long-run. On the other hand, so far as the schedule is "convex," without positive evidence to the contrary one perhaps is entitled to suppose that the convexity would not be very marked.

As to the change in the marginal rate of transformation as output changes, on the most general plane seemingly anything is possible, but evidently the question posed is in effect the familiar one regarding the relative magnitude of the measurements given by the two formulas. If the marginal rate of transformation shifts against products which increase disproportionately, Formula (1) necessarily yields a

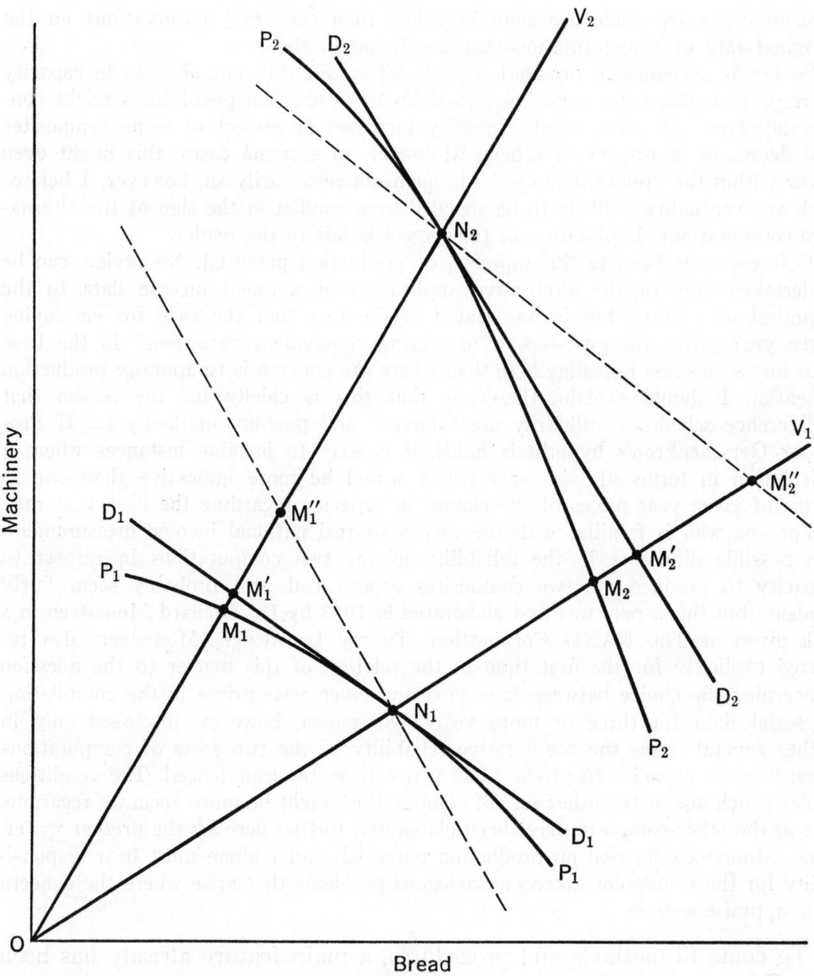

Figure 1.

higher index than Formula (2), and conversely. By the same token, we also see that the marginal rate of transformation must in fact shift against products which increase disproportionately whenever Professor Gerschenkron's well known hypothesis holds. According to this hypothesis, under industrialization the Formula (1) index ordinarily will be the greater.

In sum, to return to the main question, there is still no assurance that a calculation in terms of given year prices is more indicative than one in terms of base year prices of the change in capacity to produce the base year mix, but it is difficult to avoid the conclusion that there is generally some presumption that this is so. As is readily seen, other things equal, the presumption is greater the less pronounced is the change in production structure and the more pronounced the change in price structure. Finally, for the USSR, the presumption is heightened since, as will appear in Chapter 12, Professor Gerschenkron's hypothesis does indeed seem to hold in this case, although I fear the prices in terms of which my measurements are made are something less than the exact observations on the marginal rate of transformation that are found in theory.

So far as a change in production potential entails different changes in capacity in respect of different composites, schedules of production possibilities might conceivably cross. In other words, capacity increases in respect of some composites and decreases in respect of others. Moreover, in extreme cases, this might even occur within the "relevant range." Although not necessarily so, however, I believe such an eventuality is likely to be signaled by a conflict in the sign of the alternative computations. Exploration of this aspect is left to the reader.

Reference has been to the appraisal of production potential. No review can be undertaken here of the alternative application of national income data to the appraisal of welfare, but it was stated in the text that the case for employing given year prices for purposes of measuring "equivalent variations" in the base year mix seems less impelling here than where the concern is to appraise production potential. I should explain, therefore, that this is chiefly for the reason that indifference schedules ordinarily are "convex" and possibly markedly so. If Professor Gerschenkron's hypothesis holds, it is easy to imagine instances where a calculation in terms of base year prices would be more indicative than one in terms of given year prices of the change in capacity regarding the base year mix.

For one who is familiar with the theory of real national income measurement, the possible difference in the reliability of the two computations in respect to capacity to produce the two composites experienced, will probably seem fairly evident: but this aspect was first elaborated in 1958 by Dr. Richard Moorsteen in a talk given at The RAND Corporation. To my knowledge, Moorsteen also referred explicitly for the first time to the relation of this matter to the question concerning the choice between base year and given year prices in the compilation of serial data for three or more years. Moorsteen, however, discussed only in rather general terms the comparative reliability of the two sorts of computations regarding the capacity to produce the two composites experienced. The conditions under which one or the other sort of computation might be more accurate regarding one or the other composite have been elaborated further here by the present writer. Also, Moorsteen focused on production potential, and I alone must bear responsibility for the standpoint taken on analogous problems that arise where the concern is to appraise welfare.

To come to methods and procedures, a main feature already has been mentioned. With varying exactitude and for differing intervals, an attempt is made to compile national income data for the USSR in terms of prices of several different years. So far as different computations diverge, theory only informs common sense in holding that in principle there is much to say for an attempt actually to make the alternative measurements. In this way, we may appraise the extent of the divergence, and hence the practical import of index number relativity in any particular case. Moreover, as we have seen, national income data may be viewed as observations on the hypothetical change in the volume of output of a standard product mix that is equivalent in terms of production potential and welfare to the change in outputs actually occurring. Alternative computations of national income in terms of the prices of different years have the additional interest that they may in some measure indicate the variety of such "equivalent variations" corresponding to the range of product mixes experienced.

Index number relativity becomes possible, of course, wherever there are changes in economic structure. Alternative calculations, therefore, might be of value in practically any circumstances. They are the more in order for the USSR in the period studied in view of the radical shifts occurring in economic structure.

In the compilation of national income data, logically prior to the choice of base year is the decision as to the method to be employed in compiling serial data. A choice must be made particularly between calculations where national income in all years is valued in terms of the prices prevailing in one year taken as a base (that is, use is made throughout of Formula (1)) and calculations where all comparisons with the base year are made in given year prices (that is, through successive applications of Formula (2)). As was explained, by use of the first method, one obtains serial data of the conventional sort where national income is valued over a protracted period in terms of the prices of a single year. The second method nevertheless may well yield more reliable observations for a series of years on "equivalent variations" in the base year composite. On the other hand, this outcome is uncertain even on a theoretic plane and must be the more so in Soviet circumstances. Moreover, application of the first method facilitates illustration of the effects of alternative valuations. Last but not least, while calculations employing given year prices are not as complex as might be imagined (see note 2), the need to be concerned here about ruble price distortions makes it necessary to limit severely the number of different years for which prices are used as weights.

In this study I rely almost exclusively on the first method, using base year prices. Since computations are made for several different base years, however, it is also possible to gauge the broad trends that would result from use of the alternative method, involving valuation in given year prices. This I will attempt to do when I come to summarize my findings.

So far as we are able to apply the method where valuation is in given year prices, I believe the results in the present case will also be more or less indicative of those that might be obtained through use of the third method of compiling serial data that was referred to, that involving the chaining of successive links, each computed in terms of "contemporary" prices. For this reason, no further computations of the latter sort are undertaken.

Serial measures of national income in base year prices may be compiled by use of one or another of two familiar procedures. Data on different final uses compiled initially in terms of current prices are "deflated," that is, adjusted for changes in the price level from some base year.

Alternatively, measures of the physical volume of different commodities and services devoted to different final uses are aggregated directly in terms of the prices of the base year. In this study, I rely primarily although not exclusively on the method of deflation. At the same time, an attempt is made as far as feasible to use as deflators "variable weight" price index numbers, that is, indices given by the formula

$$\frac{\Sigma P_i Q_i}{\Sigma \dfrac{P_o}{P_i} \cdot P_i Q_i} \qquad (3)$$

where o is the base and i the given year. In national income calculations, use is very often made of the alternative "fixed weight" index numbers, that is, index numbers given by the formula

$$\frac{\Sigma \dfrac{P_i}{P_o} \cdot P_o Q_o}{\Sigma P_o Q_o} \qquad (4)$$

But while the former indices are more laborious to compile, they alone are appropriate for the purposes of reducing national income to the prices of a single base year. In ordinary circumstances, use of Formula (4) indices may still be in order insofar as they approximate those given by Formula (3), but if index number relativity may be important in the case of "real" national income measures, it may be important also in the case of price indices. Given the concern to clarify the former aspect, there was no alternative but to attempt where possible to deflate by Formula (3) indices, at least for the more important categories.[2]

The foregoing are the methods and procedures used in compiling national income data in "constant" prices. Ordinarily the task of measuring "real" national income is considered as completed when such calculations have been made. In the present study, however, the calculations initially are in ruble prices. In view of the special nature of such values, an attempt is also made to adjust for outstanding distortions that result. This, of course, requires reference to some valuation standard as a norm. It should be explained, therefore, that two standards are so referred to here. The chief is one that was considered previously in *SNIP-37*, "adjusted factor cost": Prices correspond to average cost, where factor prices generally are uniform between industries and tend on the average for the economy generally to be proportional to factor

[2] Paradoxically, deflation of current value data by variable weight price indices of the sort given by Formula (3) yields measures of physical volume in terms of constant prices of a single base year, but deflation by fixed weight price indices of the sort given by Formula (4) yields measures of physical volume in terms of variable given year prices.

productivities. For labor, factor prices also correspond to workers' transfer prices. What is the rationale of adjusted factor cost?

The formula is evidently an adaptation of the theoretic efficiency standard that is applied where the concern is to appraise production potential. For the efficiency standard valuation, factor prices supposedly are proportional to factor productivities not only on the average for the economy generally but in each and every industry. This condition is met only when the community realizes its production possibilities. Adjusted factor cost is applicable equally whether production possibilities are realized or not. In the former case, it comes to the same thing as the efficiency standard. In the latter case, it is still the same as the latter except that relative factor prices correspond to relative factor productivities not in each and every industry but on the average for the economy generally. In sum, I allow here for the possibility of a material shortfall from production potential. If resource allocation is inefficient in this way, does valuation in terms of adjusted factor cost still provide a basis for the appraisal of production potential? As we have seen, even where the efficiency standard is employed, measurements are inexact. If calculations are in terms of adjusted factor cost, no doubt they will often be more so. In any event, production potential now must be understood as referring not to the schedule of production possibilities but to the community's "feasibility locus." Reflecting the prevailing state of inefficiency, the feasibility locus falls short of but probably is broadly parallel to the schedule of production possibilities.

Since different factors vary in their allocability between industries, production potential means somewhat different things depending on the time period considered. There are corresponding variants of the efficiency standard. As is readily seen, adjusted factor cost is most easily construed as an adaptation of the variant of the efficiency standard pertaining to the "long-run." By the same token, national income data in terms of adjusted factor cost should bear especially on "long-run" production potential. Nevertheless, they presumably are illuminating also regarding "short-run" potential. Indeed, the adjusted factor cost standard itself can only be realized imperfectly in this study, and while my crude calculations clearly will not be especially indicative of "short-run" production potential, in some circumstances, particularly where structure changes markedly, one may wonder whether they are not often more pertinent to this than to "long-run" production potential. But I cannot pursue this complex theme. So far as adjusted factor cost is taken as a standard, my task will be only to appraise and adjust for divergencies of ruble prices from this formula. The comparative degree to which the adjusted data are indicative of production potential in different senses must be left to separate inquiry.

Production potential also varies depending on the extent to which workers are able to shift between occupations as well as industries (page 30). Evidently, adjusted factor cost is especially pertinent to situations where in some degree there are occupational shifts. As is rarely considered, production potential also depends on the supposition as to technology. In the real world, a community usually employs at the same time diverse technologies. Ordinarily, still other technologies are in some sense known but not applied. So far as capital is reallocated, evidently the effects on output will depend on the particular technology employed. No doubt my calculations will be more pertinent to production potential given by technologies of sorts actually applied than to that given by technologies in some sense known but not yet employed. On this aspect, I have benefited from discussion with Professor Paul Samuelson.

I said that when production potential is realized, adjusted factor cost corresponds to the efficiency standard. When it is considered that reference is to the "long-run" variants of production potential and the efficiency standard, adjusted factor cost comes to the same thing as the latter only if there are "constant returns" to scale. If there are "varying returns" in the "long-run," there is a further difference between adjusted factor cost and the efficiency standard, for the former corresponds to average rather than marginal costs. Average cost, of course, is inclusive of "rent" to permanently fixed factors.

For purposes of computing national income in terms of "final" use categories, it is necessary to prescribe valuation standards only for "final" goods, but so far as there are changes in inventories, national income as so computed will include some materials which are at the same time a factor and a product. As for "final" products generally, so for such "intermediate" products, valuation at adjusted factor cost is to be in terms of average cost, but prices so fixed may not correspond on the average to the productivities of the "intermediate" products, as seems logically required if adjusted factor cost is to parallel the efficiency standard in this regard. As is well known, however, there are generally rather limited possibilities of substitution if not among materials at least between materials and other factors. For this reason, any of a wide range of prices might correspond equally well to relative factor productivities in the case of materials. On the other hand, so far as this is not the case, there is a further difference between adjusted factor cost and the efficiency standard. I believe I am right in thinking that in the case of capital goods where there is an additional degree of freedom to determine the value of the asset, there is no comparable problem.

Where production potential is not realized, it was said that adjusted factor cost bears primarily on the community's feasibility locus which falls short of but tends to be broadly parallel to the schedule of production possibilities. Actually, the feasibility locus is usually thought of as reflecting some given institutional constraints and as such it surely is not easy to generalize about its possible shape. Indeed, one wonders whether within the limits of such constraints the locus is not apt to be somewhat indeterminate, so that reference is more properly made to a penumbra of loci than to a single locus. On the other hand, still another possibility which I for one find appealing is simply as a matter of convention to consider the feasibility locus as parallel to the schedule of production possibilities. As must also be understood, even without any serious institutional change, a resource reallocation may be associated with a change in the "efficiency locus," and admittedly this is awkward. But I venture to think that where production potential is not realized, national income data ordinarily are most readily construed as bearing on the efficiency locus as so understood. In any event, this appears so for the data compiled in this study.

As we have seen, prices conforming to the efficiency standard may also conform to the theoretic welfare standard, pertinent to the appraisal of welfare. This occurs only under ideal conditions which as may be shown already are violated if production potential is not realized. But very possibly calculations in terms of adjusted factor cost will still be broadly illuminating regarding welfare as well as production potential. Welfare, however, must be understood in terms of the prevailing ends. For the USSR, presumably these are not the conventional consumers' utilities but planners' preferences.

Although the treatment of the valuation problem in *SNIP-37* has become a controversial subject, criticism, I believe, has been directed not so much against adjusted factor cost as a yardstick for national income valuation as against its practical application to the Soviet case. Questions raised concerning the latter aspect will be considered in due course.

Adjusted factor cost is the chief standard to be considered in this study, but in adjusting the ruble national income data I try also to explore the implications of another formula not previously applied. This is the conventional variant of the welfare standard already explained: Different commodities entering into national income are valued in accord with consumers' marginal utilities. The consumers' utility standard, however, is to be applied only to household consumption. So far as consumers' utilities must often be gauged from "political" as distinct from "market" choices, extension of this standard to use categories other than consumption (that is, such items as investment and defense) encounters difficulties even in respect to a Western country. Under Soviet conditions, where consumers seemingly have only limited sway over resource allocation even politically, the proper valuation of such goods in terms of the consumers' utility standard must be a matter of opinion. Hence, while the formula perhaps can be broadly approximated for household consumption, its application to national income as a whole is precluded.[3]

I have discussed thus far the methods and procedures used to derive data in constant rubles and the valuation standards taken as norms in

[3] While no data are to be compiled expressly in such terms, our calculations provide a basis to appraise national income in relation to still another standard of a mixed sort, "consumers' utility—factor cost": Valuation generally is in accord with adjusted factor cost, but within the household consumption sector different commodities are valued relatively in accord with the consumers' utility standard. This standard may possibly be of analytic interest. If adjusted factor cost reflects at all planners' preferences, the mixed standard might be viewed as an extension to Soviet Russia of the kind of valuation that in effect is already applied to some extent in the West. Relatively to each other, consumers' goods are valued in accord with the consumers' utility standard. Supposedly the same standard is applicable to investment goods so far as these are "market determined." For the rest, however, valuation is in accord with "collective preferences" given by the prevailing political process. Needless to say, the Soviet political process is not the same as that of the West, but the formal analogy is evident.

adjusting the latter. For purposes of completing the outline of methodology, it remains to comment on the choice of base years. The calculation of "real" national income in terms of the prices of even a single base year is an exacting assignment. In order to limit my task, I focus especially on a calculation for the USSR in terms of the ruble prices of 1937, but an attempt is made also to compute Soviet national income for two years, 1928 and 1937, in terms of the ruble prices of 1928. For all years studied, the series compiled initially in 1937 prices is also partially recomputed in terms of the ruble prices of 1950. The year 1937, marking the end of the Second Five Year Plan, represents a more or less intermediate phase in the development of the Soviet economy over the period studied, while 1928 is our initial date and a year in which Soviet industrialization was still at a very early stage. (The First Five Year Plan was just beginning in this year.) By 1950, near the close of our period and the last year of the Fourth Five Year Plan, the Russians had largely made good their war damages and were entering into another phase of development which essentially still continues. My alternative national income calculations in terms of the prices of these three years should indicate fairly well the variety of measurements that must be reckoned with for the period studied.

In 1937, the base year on which I focus especially, ruble prices appear to have had more economic content than in many other years under the five year plans. This probably was true also of 1928 and 1950, and these years commend themselves as alternate base years partly on this account. In favor of 1937 as a year on which to concentrate is the further fact that information of the sort needed is relatively plentiful for this date.

The foregoing refers to my computations in established rubles. When I come to adjust for ruble distortions, I focus even more on the computations in terms of 1937 prices, but tentative recomputations are made for other base years as well.

To appraise production potential and welfare is not a simple task. As we have seen, consideration must be given not only to national income but to various other aspects, particularly "curvilinear" (as distinct from "linear") schedules and changes in "tastes" and income distribution. These matters have to be reckoned with even on an abstract plane. One need not probe very deeply to become aware that in any more realistic case the complexities only multiply. What, for example, if due to "learning curves" the production possibilities are in some measure inherently "dynamic" rather than purely "static" as theory assumes? In any event, at least in Soviet circumstances, the list of complexities already is lengthened so far as the theoretic validity of adjusted factor cost depends on the efficiency of Soviet planning. The reader will understand if I follow most students of national income in leaving the practical import of all features such as the foregoing to separate inquiry. So far as concerns the efficiency of Soviet planning, from what is said later about ruble price formation and from generally known facts, he will have some impression on this score, but I can hardly pursue this theme any more than I can the others. In sum, theory provides the basis not for the precise measurement of abstract ultimates but for the organization of broadly meaningful statistical inquiries. If this moral holds generally, it certainly applies also to the USSR. If we are to proceed, it must be on this basis.

I have followed theoretic writings in focusing on applications of global data on "real" national income, but "real" national income is computed here by type of final use, and where global measures are meaningful it goes without saying that corresponding data on outlays on different final uses are also of interest. If this is true generally, it is also true where as here the global measures are in terms pertinent to the appraisal of production potential and welfare as given by planners' preferences, and where accordingly the corresponding figures on structural trends must bear similarly on capacities committed to different uses and values realized from the planners' standpoint. When in the latter part of the study I come to summarize findings, therefore, attention properly will be directed to the results regarding not only national income but its disposition.

PART II

NATIONAL INCOME IN PREVAILING RUBLES

4

NATIONAL INCOME IN 1937 RUBLES: HOUSEHOLD CONSUMPTION

Introduction

The task of Part II is to present and explain the calculations in prevailing rubles. In this chapter and in chapter 5 I discuss the figures compiled in terms of 1937 prices. The calculations using 1928 and 1950 prices are considered more briefly in chapter 6. Chapter 7 is devoted to a summary appraisal of the calculations generally.

Turning to the computations in 1937 rubles, I take as a point of departure the current ruble figures in Table 3. Except in certain particulars, these data are drawn from the SNIP studies.[1]

[1] More specifically, the figures are taken from *SNIP-28-48* and *SNIP-49-55*. In Table 3, I have revised somewhat the SNIP estimates of outlays on housing rents (actual and imputed) in order to allow for the sharp differences in quality between public and private urban housing and between both of these and rural housing. While public housing continues to be valued at the average public housing rates, private urban and rural housing are valued at arbitrarily reduced rates. The public housing rates are in any case too low from any economic standpoint, but in compiling data on housing in constant prices it clearly is necessary to value differently the various types of housing, and it seemed just as well to incorporate the different values in our current ruble

TABLE 3

Gross National Product of the USSR by Use in Current Prices, 1928–55 (billions of rubles)

Outlay category	1928	1937	1940	1944	1950	1955
Household purchases in retail markets						
In government and cooperative shops and restaurants	—	110.0	160.0	111.0	328.0	442.0
In collective farm markets	—	16.0	26.0	30.0	47.0	51.0
Total	12.10	126.0	186.0	141.0	375.0	493.0
Housing; services	2.79	17.4	26.2	20.1	50.4	65.7
Consumption of farm income in kind	6.70[a]	25.0	42.0	25.0	61.0	85.0
Military subsistence	0.25	2.5	6.6	25.7	14.1	17.2
Household consumption outlays	21.84	170.9	260.8	211.8	500.5	660.9
Communal services						
Health care	0.54	7.9	11.6	12.6	25.0	34.0
Education	0.87	17.0	23.8	20.9	59.0	69.3
Other	0.14	0.7	1.0	0.7	1.5	1.7
Total	1.55	25.6	36.4	34.2	85.5	105.0
Government administration, including NKVD (OGPU; MVD and MGB)	0.82	7.4	13.9	14.0	36.9	27.6
Defense (as recorded in budget[b])	0.76	17.4	56.5	135.7	80.8	105.4
Gross investment						
In fixed capital	6.00	35.2	53.9	38.9	156.5	239.6
Other	1.32	24.2	13.7	14.7	51.5	45.4
Total	7.32	59.4	67.6	53.6	208.0	285.0
Gross national product	32.29	280.7	435.2	449.3	911.7	1,183.9

[a] Includes 0.30 billion rubles of farm wages in kind.

[b] Exclusive of pensions to officers, et cetera, that are included in published budgetary defense figures.

Note: Here and in succeeding tables the dash (—) means not applicable or not available.

In Table 4 are set forth the corresponding figures that have been calculated here in terms of 1937 prices.

As was explained, in deriving measures of national income in terms

data. Moreover, the question of the average value of housing generally is to be considered separately when we discuss the effects of distortions in ruble prices.

For 1949–55, I also cite revised figures on farm income in kind. The revision, prepared by Miss Nancy Nimitz, takes into account information on the scope of Soviet official farm marketings data and new Soviet official farm production and marketings statistics that were not available when *SNIP-49–55* was compiled. In the interests of consistency, I also compute farm livestock investments in kind (in Table 3, this is included in "Gross investment, other") somewhat differently than was done by Hoeffding and Nimitz. While in *SNIP-49–55* an allowance is made only for livestock investments in kind by farm households, I have sought to take into account also similar investments elsewhere. I do no more here than extend to 1949–55 methods used in *SNIP-28–48*. For purposes of the present study it also seemed in order to recalculate military pay and subsistence so that we could take into account data on the size of the armed forces released by Khrushchev in his speech before the Supreme Soviet on January 14, 1960. In

of constant prices,[2] I rely chiefly although not exclusively on the method of deflation as distinct from that involving the aggregation at base year prices of data on the physical volume of different commodities. At the same time, an attempt is made, as far as feasible, to use as deflators the logically appropriate "variable weight" price index numbers as distinct from the alternative "fixed weight" measures. In the present case, indices of the former sort are given by the formula:

$$\frac{\Sigma P_i Q_i}{\Sigma \frac{P_{37}}{P_i} \cdot P_i Q_i} \tag{5}$$

The alternative "fixed weight" index numbers are given here by the formula:

$$\frac{\Sigma \frac{P_i}{P_{37}} \cdot P_{37} Q_{37}}{\Sigma P_{37} Q_{37}} \tag{6}$$

In the balance of this chapter and all of the next I discuss the computation of the data in Table 4. Each of the final use categories listed is considered in turn. The discussion in each case is intended to outline the essentials of the computation and to provide the reader with a basis to appraise the reliability of the results. Reliability is considered in the light of diverse kinds of evidence, but discussion of questions that arise regarding economic implications (there certainly are many such, for the results are often striking) is deferred to Part IV. Details on the sources and methods are presented in Appendices A to G.

---

revising the SNIP calculations on defense, it seemed just as well to take into account too some late official figures on total budgetary outlays that presumably superseded preliminary figures on this aspect used in *SNIP-49-55*. In Table 3, I have also abandoned an arbitrary allowance for penal labor subsistence in *SNIP-49-55*.

In the SNIP studies no systematic data are compiled on the breakdown of gross investment between investments in "fixed capital" and "other." In Table 3, the figures cited on this aspect were derived in the present study. The relationship between the current ruble data compiled in the SNIP studies and those taken as a point of departure in the present work is discussed further in the chapters following and in the appendices.

[2] Perhaps I should be more explicit here regarding several terms that are to be used often in this study. By "prevailing ruble prices" I mean the actual ruble prices prevailing at any time. Such prices, therefore, are to be distinguished from "adjusted ruble prices," which correspond to the actual ruble prices after various adjustments for distortions that will be explained subsequently. On the other hand, serial data compiled in terms of either sort of ruble prices may refer to the values prevailing in a single base year, in which case they represent "constant ruble prices" (either prevailing or adjusted, as the case may be). Alternatively, the serial data may be such that the figures for any year are in terms of the values prevailing in that year. In this case the data are said to be in terms of "current ruble prices" (which again may be either prevailing or adjusted).

TABLE 4

Gross National Product of the USSR by Use in 1937 Prices, 1928–55
(billions of rubles)

Outlay category	1928	1937	1940	1944	1950	1955
Household purchases in retail markets						
In government and cooperative shops and restaurants	—	110.0	127.0	68.0	148.0	260.0
In collective farm markets	—	16.0	13.0	1.6	23.0	23.0
Total	105.0	126.0	140.0	70.0	171.0	283.0
Housing; services	10.3	17.4	19.1	13.3	21.6	32.1
Consumption of farm income in kind	35.6[a]	25.0	30.0	18.0	28.0	32.0
Military subsistence	0.8	2.5	5.0	17.2	6.0	9.6
Household consumption outlays	151.7	170.9	194.1	118.5	226.6	356.7
Communal services						
Health care	2.1	7.9	9.5	8.8	11.0	15.8
Education	3.9	17.0	19.9	14.1	24.6	28.1
Other	0.6	0.7	0.8	0.5	0.7	0.7
Total	6.6	25.6	30.2	23.4	36.3	44.6
Government administration, including NKVD (OGPU; MVD and MGB)	3.0	7.4	10.8	8.5	14.8	10.5
Defense (as recorded in budget[b])	1.9	17.4	45.8	118.0	42.4	62.0
Gross investment						
In fixed capital	10.9	35.2	39.4	24.2	66.5	112.2
Other	7.8	24.2	11.5	11.7	24.2	23.8
Total	18.7	59.4	50.9	35.9	90.7	136.0
Gross national product	181.9	280.7	331.8	304.3	410.8	609.8

[a] Includes 1.6 billion rubles of farm wages in kind.
[b] Exclusive of pensions to officers, et cetera.

Household Purchases in Retail Markets

In government and cooperative shops and restaurants. The SNIP data in terms of current rubles (Table 3) are derived for all years from Soviet official figures on the volume of retail sales of the government and cooperative trade network. As officially reported, retail sales include some institutional (as distinct from household) purchases and also some household purchases of small tools, fertilizer, and other farm producers' goods, and of building materials used in private housing construction. In order to obtain a series representing only household purchases of consumers' goods, the official figures had to be adjusted for the foregoing items on the basis of incomplete information. Among other things, according to admittedly inexact Soviet calculations, institutional purchases have declined from 11 to 12 percent of retail sales in 1937 to 7 to 8 percent recently. The adjustment for institutional purchases for all years is based on these findings. For 1955, the official figure on government and cooperative retail sales is also arbitrarily reduced by 2 percent in order to allow for an expansion in their scope in 1951, principally the inclusion for the first time of certain repair services and custom work. In the SNIP calculations, such activities are recorded under "Housing; services."

In order to deflate the current ruble figures, I rely primarily on index numbers of retail prices compiled by Dr. Janet Chapman partly for use in the present inquiry.[3] Among other things, Dr. Chapman calculates by use of Formula (5) index numbers of the prices prevailing in the state and cooperative retail network. The calculations are made for the years 1937, 1940, 1948, 1952, and 1954. In Table 4, the constant ruble figures on household purchases in state and cooperative shops and restaurants for the years 1937–55 are derived on the basis of these indices. For purposes of the deflation, Dr. Chapman's Formula (5) series is extended in a manner to be described to years which she does not cover but which I do.

In her computations for government and cooperative retail trade, Dr. Chapman uses price data obtained chiefly from Soviet price decrees, price handbooks issued for the purposes of Soviet trade administration, and reports of foreign travelers in the USSR. The index numbers are compiled from price quotations for 98 to 138 commodities and generally can be taken as representative of more than 90 percent of household purchases in the government and cooperative trade network. In terms of both the quality and quantity of price data used, however, the calculations for 1940 are less reliable than those for other years. No account is taken of products put on sale for the first time after 1937, but while Soviet information releases might often suggest the contrary, such new goods have been quantitatively of very limited importance in the Soviet retail market. Nevertheless, the omission of some products, particularly radios and certain other consumers' durables, may tend to distort the index numbers of prices somewhat in recent years.[4] According to a separate inquiry, price data for Moscow alone that are used for the period 1937–54 are closely representative of the price movements in the USSR as a whole.

[3] The indices were first published in her article, "Real Wages in the Soviet Union, 1928–1952," *Review of Economics and Statistics,* May 1954. I refer here to the revised data presented in *Real Wages in Soviet Russia Since 1928,* which is in preparation. The latter work is cited henceforth as Chapman, *Real Wages.* Dr. Chapman compiles both index numbers of retail prices paid by urban workers and index numbers of retail prices paid by the population generally. In this study, use is made of the latter measures. Reference is to a preliminary version of Dr. Chapman's monograph. In a final version, Dr. Chapman has revised a few of her figures, particularly her index numbers of prices prevailing in "commercial shops" and collective farm markets in 1944. Because of the limited importance of these two markets at the time, the effect on my measures of the physical volume of all household retail purchases in 1944 is inconsequential.

[4] Chapman, *Real Wages,* chap. 3.

Price relatives for individual commodities are aggregated by Dr. Chapman in terms of value weights derived from recently published Soviet official data on the retail sales structure. In the aggregation of relatives for individual products within commodities groups, some use is made throughout of 1937 weights and the weights generally are often estimated, but in each comparison with 1937 the weights refer primarily to the given year. Such weights, of course, are called for by Formula (5). Dr. Chapman also compiles indices in terms of Formula (6). For years since 1937, as it turns out, the indices move fairly closely together, for example, according to Formula (5), prices in 1952 were 198 percent of 1937; according to Formula (6), 216 percent.[5] This result may be due partly to the illegitimate inclusion in the Formula (5) indices of some 1937 weights but so far as the change in formula has only a limited impact a comforting implication is that possible errors in weighting may not be very consequential either.

Reflecting the wartime circumstances, the government distributed consumers' goods to households in 1944 largely through a rationing system in closed shops and to a very limited extent in unrestricted form through the so-called "commercial shops." Prices in closed shops were very low and in commercial shops astronomically high. Meager supplies were also distributed to rural households partly at about the same prices as prevailed in the closed shops and partly at increased prices. I deflate the different types of sales separately on the basis of corresponding crude indices which Dr. Chapman has compiled.

For the years 1948–55, the Soviet government has recently published its own index numbers of the prices prevailing in state and cooperative retail shops. For purposes of deflating household purchases in the state and cooperative trade network, I extend Dr. Chapman's Formula (5) series to 1950 and 1955 by reference to the Soviet official indices. Although the latter indices probably are derived according to a different formula,[6] they correspond closely to Dr. Chapman's measures since 1948, and there can be little margin for error if we interpolate to 1950 and extrapolate to 1955 on this basis. The two sets of price indices, for years that are common to both (1948 = 100 in both cases), are as follows: For 1952, the Chapman index is 66.0 and the Soviet official index 61.1; for 1954, the Chapman index is 56.7 and the Soviet official index 52.4.

Apparently Dr. Chapman's calculations agree broadly with the Soviet official data. Although the methods used to derive the latter are not entirely clear, the agreement perhaps may properly be considered as

[5] The results of Dr. Chapman's computations in terms of both formulas for all years covered are given in Appendix A.

[6] For years since 1948, I cite annual indices calculated from official indices of the prices prevailing after spring price cuts. The annual indices so derived differ slightly from official annual indices that also have been published.

reassuring regarding the reliability of both Dr. Chapman's and the official indices.[7]

In collective farm markets. The SNIP figures on sales to households in urban collective farm markets, which are deflated here, are adapted from corresponding data inclusive of sales to institutions. For all years except 1944, the latter data are given or implied in Soviet sources and were compiled by Soviet statisticians from sample surveys. They presumably are subject to error. Data on the volume of collective farm market sales are lacking for 1944; in the SNIP calculations it was possible to do little more than guess at this magnitude. In addition to the statistics it releases on the volume of collective farm market sales, the Soviet government has recently published index numbers of collective farm market prices for 1950–55, with 1940 as a base year. Although these index numbers probably were calculated from a formula other than (5), Dr. Chapman feels there is hardly any possibility of improving on them with available information. Accordingly, I use them in the deflation. The official series is extended by Dr. Chapman to other years of concern here on the basis of rule-of-thumb measures compiled from scattered information in Soviet sources on prices and quantities and in price reports by foreign observers.

Total. For all years other than 1928, this is the sum of the magnitudes already obtained for household purchases in government and cooperative shops and restaurants and in collective farm markets. For 1928, I deflate a SNIP estimate of retail sales to households in all markets. At the time, this includes sales to households by government and cooperative shops and restaurants and by private merchants. The SNIP estimate was derived by Dr. Oleg Hoeffding from detailed official data on retail trade of a sort that the Soviet government once published as a usual matter, and like the SNIP figures for 1937–55 it excludes institutional purchases in the retail market and household purchases of farm producers' goods and building materials. In deriving his estimate of household retail purchases in 1928, Dr. Hoeffding omits intravillage barter but includes intravillage cash sales. The latter are taken to amount to 1.0

[7] The official indices for 1950–55 were expressed originally in terms of 1940 as 100 percent. Dr. Chapman's calculations still are broadly in accord with the official series when the comparison is extended in this way to include 1940. As might be expected, my measures of "real" household purchases in government and cooperative trade outlets also tend to parallel corresponding official data on the "real" volume of retail sales by such outlets. See chapter 11.

The value of the agreement between the official and Dr. Chapman's data as an indication of their reliability admittedly is diminished when we consider that in compiling her measures, Dr. Chapman must ultimately rely on raw data on commodity prices and quantities that she herself obtains from official sources, but at least in the case of the price data the official figures could often be checked by reference to voluminous travelers' reports.

billion rubles, or 8.5 percent of all household retail purchases. As a rule intravillage trade, whether of a barter or of a cash sort, is omitted from total retail sales for 1937–55 as these are measured in this study, but some such trade nevertheless is represented in my data on collective farm market sales for recent years. Moreover, sales by government and cooperative shops as calculated for 1937–55 include sales made by these outlets in rural areas. In the course of time, the government and cooperative shops undoubtedly took over some of the intravillage trade that formerly was conducted privately. Under the circumstances, I believe the SNIP figure on total household retail purchases for 1928 is more or less comparable in scope to the corresponding figures for 1937–55. In any event, if there is any incomparability at this point, for reasons to appear, my data on total household consumption probably are little affected.

In deflating household retail purchases in 1928, I use an index number of all retail prices calculated by Dr. Chapman. Reference is made again to a calculation applying Formula (5), which is the appropriate one for present purposes. Using much the same kinds of sources as she employed for the period 1937–55, Dr. Chapman compiles price data for 85 kinds of consumers' goods which can be taken to represent more than 90 percent of all retail sales of such products to households. For the period 1928–37, as for later years, new products probably were of relatively limited importance in the Soviet consumers' goods market; in any case, since the concern is to compile a price index number in terms of 1928 weights, products introduced after 1928 are properly omitted at this point. In aggregating price relatives, Dr. Chapman uses weights derived largely from Soviet data on urban industrial family budgets in 1927–28. For the most part, therefore, the weights reflect the pattern of expenditures of urban workers rather than the structure of retail trade generally, but the comparative weights of foods and manufactured goods are determined from data on total retail sales, and according to trial calculations the price index numbers probably would be little affected by further adaptations of the weights to make them conform to the retail trade structure. On the other hand, Dr. Chapman finds that her measures of the change in retail prices are far more sensitive to a change in base year for the period 1928–37 than for intervals after 1937. When Formula (5) is applied, retail prices in 1928 are 11.5 percent of 1937. In terms of Formula (6), the corresponding figure is 16.8 percent. We must conclude that errors in weighting for any reason would be more consequential for the period now considered than for later years.

Dr. Chapman compiles three main index numbers of retail prices for 1928 in terms of Formula (5): Official Moscow prices are 12.4 percent of 1937 prices; and official urban USSR prices, and average prices for all USSR markets, are each 11.5 percent of 1937 prices.

The index of official prices, Moscow, is derived in the manner already described from data on the retail prices prevailing in the Moscow shops of the government and cooperative trade network. The index number of official prices, urban USSR, is derived from that for official prices, Moscow, on the basis of a calculation of the comparative trends in prices in Moscow and in Soviet urban localities generally for a limited number of commodities for which data on average urban prices are available. In 1928, the Soviet household bought consumers' goods not only in the urban shops of the government and cooperative network but also from private traders in urban localities and from both public and private traders in rural localities. There were corresponding differences in prices. On the basis of Soviet data on these comparative price levels, Dr. Chapman finds that the average level of prices in all retail markets taken together is approximately the same as that of urban official prices alone, the low prices in rural markets tending to offset the high prices in urban private trade. I deflate retail sales in 1928 by Dr. Chapman's index of prices in all retail markets, which comes to the same thing as her index of urban official prices.[8]

Housing; Services

I calculate this as the sum of several components (Table 5):

TABLE 5

Housing and Services in 1937 Prices — USSR, 1928–55
(billions of rubles)

Year	All	Actual and imputed rent	Utilities (et cetera)	Trade union and other dues
1928	10.3	2.4	7.3	0.6
1937	17.4	2.8	13.5	1.1
1940	19.1	3.4	14.4	1.3
1944	13.3	2.8	9.2	1.3
1950	21.6	3.9	15.3	2.4
1955	32.1	4.5	24.6	3.0

[8] Although there was no private trade, so-called, at the time, the Soviet consumer purchased goods in 1937 in the collective farm markets as well as in the government and cooperative retail shops. In that year, however, prices in the collective farm market appear to have approximated those charged for similar goods in the government and cooperative retail shops. Hence the urban official prices are also representative of prices generally in 1937.

Housing. The SNIP data on actual and imputed rent on housing[9] are intended to represent the value at the average rental rate charged for government owned apartments of all Soviet housing, including privately owned homes as well as government housing.[10] In order to compute this magnitude for any year, the available stocks of different kinds of housing are estimated first in terms of actual floor space and then in terms of government housing equivalent. The actual and imputed rent is obtained as the product of the total housing stock in terms of government housing equivalent and the corresponding average rental charged per square meter for government housing.

The SNIP rental figures are in terms of current rubles. For purposes of compiling corresponding data in terms of 1937 rubles, I simply repeat the SNIP computations, but apply to the housing stock for all years (expressed in terms of government housing equivalent) the average rental rate charged for government housing in 1937. In the SNIP calculations, data on stocks of urban housing (both public and private) generally could be taken or inferred from information in Soviet sources, and no doubt the rural housing stock has been more or less stable over the period studied, as is assumed, but the precise magnitude of the latter is conjectural. Furthermore, different kinds of housing had to be translated into government housing equivalent in the light of meager information on comparative depreciated values and costs, so that necessarily the exact factors applied are arbitrary. Under the circumstances, an alternative calculation (Table 6) may be of interest. One square meter of private urban housing is now taken to be equivalent to 0.4 square meter of public housing (instead of the 0.6 square meter originally allowed). Similarly, the government housing equivalent of one square meter of private rural housing is reduced from 0.4 to 0.2 square meter. The "real" computed rent varies as shown in Table 6.

My calculations make no allowance for changes in quality of different kinds of housing. The import of this limitation is difficult to judge, but I wonder whether it is correct to assume, as is often done, that the average quality of Soviet housing deteriorated markedly under the five year plans. While it is true that housing since 1928 has suffered increasingly from undermaintenance, the share of new structures in the total stock has expanded continually, and this should have been something of an offset to the undermaintenance so far as average quality is concerned. Of course, the new housing itself has left something to be desired, but recurring reports regarding the inferior quality of construction under the five year plans must be read together with the fact

[9] As revised here. See Appendix B.

[10] The data also embrace the so-called "cooperative" housing up to 1937, when the housing cooperatives were liquidated.

TABLE 6

Actual and Imputed Rent in 1937 Prices, Alternative Computations, USSR, 1928–55 (1937 = 100)

Year	As initially computed (Table 5)	With alternative valuation of private urban and rural housing
1928	86	76
1937	100	100
1950	139	146
1955	161	175

that there have been continuing although often modest gains in respect of the provision of plumbing facilities and utilities.[11]

The Soviet government charges notoriously low rentals for its housing. The problem that this practice poses for this study is considered later when we review the valuation of national income generally.

Utilities, et cetera. Soviet households spent some 13.5 billion rubles on services classified as "Utilities, et cetera" in 1937. Of this total, about 3.0 billion rubles went for railway passenger service, while the balance perhaps was divided more or less equally between urban electric power and water consumption, urban transport, and entertainment, on the one hand, and all other services, including such items as repairs, custom work, custom processing of farm goods, and domestics, on the other hand. For purposes of deriving measures of outlays on "Utilities, et cetera" in 1937 rubles, I assume that the trends in household outlays on railway passenger service in constant prices may be gauged from serial data compiled in Janet Chapman, *Real Wages,* on total passenger kilometers of service provided by Soviet railways. From information in Soviet sources, Dr. Chapman has also compiled serial figures on urban electric power and water consumption, urban transport (in terms of the number of passengers carried), and entertainment (as indicated by motion picture attendance). The trends in household outlays on these services in terms of constant prices are taken as given by these figures while expenditures on each in the base year (1937) may be judged from further data assembled by Dr. Chapman on urban workers' budgets. I arbitrarily assume that in constant prices household outlays on other services (such as repairs, custom work, custom processing of farm goods, and domestics) were constant throughout the period studied except in 1944, when they decrease with consumption generally. Very possibly such outlays tended

[11] See T. Sosnovy, *The Housing Problem in the Soviet Union,* New York, 1954, pp. 81 ff, 96 ff.

to decline in the course of time, especially in the early years. I find that farm income in kind declined somewhat in the period studied, and custom processing of farm goods may also have fallen. Repairs and custom work generally are performed by the so-called "cooperative" and "independent" artisans. The numbers of such persons similarly have tended downward in the period studied. The latter data are difficult to interpret, however, since the artisans are engaged in many other tasks as well.

Evidently I have applied here the method of aggregating data on physical volume. In addition to figures of this sort, Dr. Chapman has also compiled index numbers of the prices of services included in "Utilities, et cetera." Although based on very incomplete information, the index numbers are intended to represent the trends in the prices of "Utilities, et cetera" generally. Using these indices, the "real" outlays of households on this category may be computed by deflation. The results of the computation are shown in Table 7 together with the corresponding

TABLE 7

Household Outlays on Utilities (et cetera), 1937 Rubles, Alternative Computations, USSR, 1928–54 (1937 = 100)

Year	By aggregation of physical volume series[a]	By deflation
1928	54	39
1937	100	100
1940	107	103
1944	68	56
1948	103	117
1952	134	133
1954	168	167

[a] The figures for 1948, 1952, and 1954 are derived by application of the same methods as those for other years, on which attention is focused in this chapter. See the Addendum: Annual Data, 1948–55.

figures on "real" outlays derived by aggregation of physical volume data. The SNIP figures on outlays on "Utilities, et cetera" in current rubles that are here deflated for the most part were derived through rather arbitrary projections. For this reason, I have hesitated to rely on the method of deflation at this point. On the other hand, the SNIP current ruble figures for 1937 and 1954 are relatively reliable, and interestingly the indices obtained by deflation for these years agree closely (more closely than could have been anticipated) with those derived by aggregation of data on physical volume.

Trade union and other dues. The SNIP data are deflated by indices of average money wages in the USSR.

Consumption of Farm Income in Kind[12]

I apply here the method of aggregating physical series; that is, data that are compiled on the physical quantities of different products constituting farm income in kind are aggregated in terms of 1937 prices. The SNIP current ruble data are derived partly from calculations made in the present study, and more generally the current value of farm income in kind must be determined directly or indirectly by essentially the same procedure as is applied in determining the value of this category in constant prices. Deflation therefore could not be an especially meaningful alternative in this case.[13]

Income in kind is valued here at average prices realized on the farm in 1937. Under the collective farm market system, Soviet agricultural marketing arrangements are notably complex. Valuation at average realized farm prices means that each farm product is valued at the average of a variety of prices, including the very low fixed prices that the government pays for obligatory deliveries, the higher prices that the government pays for quasi-voluntary deliveries in excess of the obligatory amounts, and the generally still much higher prices that the farmers obtain for any surpluses they can sell on the free collective farm market. I shall discuss later the conceptual problem that is posed by valuation in terms of an average of these diverse prices; for the time being, the standard at least has the merit that it corresponds formally to the one usually used in national income calculations.

Needless to say, under the complex Soviet marketing arrangements, valuation at average realized farm prices also encounters practical difficulties, but partly for purposes of this inquiry Dr. Jerzy Karcz has compiled systematic price data of the sort needed here.[14] It is often assumed that the Soviet government has released hardly any information on the prices it pays for farm produce. This is by no means the case. Although there are many gaps, Karcz could compile his estimates of average realized farm prices for 1937 from a substantial volume of price information, including official handbooks of procurement prices, price

[12] In calculating farm income in kind, I have been greatly aided by Miss Nancy Nimitz and Leon Smolinski.

[13] Prior to their revision in *SNIP-28-48,* the SNIP current ruble data on farm income in kind for 1928–48 were computed independently and by a procedure differing from the one referred to in the text, but the figures are especially crude and an attempt to deflate them would be fruitless. As will appear, the figure for 1928 is an exception.

[14] Jerzy F. Karcz, "Soviet Agricultural Marketings and Prices, 1928–1954," The RAND Corporation, Research Memorandum RM-1930, July 2, 1957.

decrees, and sample data on average procurement prices. Collective farm market price quotations are compiled from press reports and other sources. The prices prevailing in different markets are averaged on the basis of the quantities of marketing involved. On the latter, I comment below. Karcz's data are more reliable than might have been thought possible, but chiefly because of the uncertainties regarding the precise level of the very high collective farm market prices he feels that his estimates of average prices for individual products may err by as much as 15 percent.

The present study was much facilitated also by the recent publication by the Soviet government of relatively detailed and methodologically much improved data on the volume and disposition of the output of different farm products in the USSR. Moreover, it was possible to draw here on the results of extensive researches by Western scholars, especially Naum Jasny, Nancy Nimitz, Jerzy Karcz, Gale Johnson, and Arcadius Kahan, on the meaning of such Soviet agricultural statistics. These scholars have also often made useful independent estimates.

While recently published official data are superior in quality to those that had been released previously for many years, many Western scholars have come to feel that perhaps because of sampling errors those on milk output probably are appreciably inflated. In the present calculation of farm income in kind, therefore, these Soviet data have been adjusted downward. If alternatively the official figures had been used without adjustment, income in kind in 1950 would have been 7.0 percent greater than has been computed. For 1955, the corresponding figure would have been 6.3 percent. More generally, reliable statistics on the physical quantities of different products available for farm consumption are, after marketings and production expense, difficult to come by for any country and the USSR is certainly no exception. Although involving a considerable effort, the calculations of farm income in kind chiefly on this account must be among the less reliable made in this study. The computations are subject to error generally, but because of the sparsity of the needed information on output and its disposition those for 1944 are less reliable than those for other years.

The Party Central Committee held its plenary session of January 1961 after this volume went to press, and it is still too soon to gauge fully the import for Soviet agricultural statistics of disclosures that were made in the proceedings of this session and in press reports on subsequent meetings of local party organizations. But, even after all due allowance is made for the usual excesses of Party "self-criticism," obviously "simulation" (*ochkovtiratel'stvo*), including even patent falsification (for example, forgery of procurement receipts), is now rife in the statistical reporting work of local agricultural authorities. By the same token, the conclusion is unavoidable that the official agricultural data for recent years are materially distorted.

On the other hand, the concern here is with the period up to 1955. In the light of the current disclosures, a further review of the official data used here for 1955 and earlier years must be in order. But, while "simulation" is hardly a new phenomenon in either the Soviet economy in general or in Soviet agriculture in particular, as the Party disclosures themselves suggest, the wholesale "simulation" now reported seemingly is a relatively recent development, reflecting chiefly the combined pressures of ambitious goals and in 1959–60 relatively limited harvests. The weakening of local discipline in regard to statistical reporting has to be read also in the light of the general relaxation of authoritarian police controls, although in view of their tardy response (some of the malpractices currently disclosed reportedly occurred as early as 1958) the central authorities can only be regarded as having been rather permissive in any event. By implication, the official data used here for 1955 and earlier years have their limitations but should be on a quite different plane of reliability from those published for the last several years.

Under Stalin, so far as there was local "simulation" in agriculture, it only compounded gross distortions already initiated or sanctioned by the central authorities themselves, most notably the notorious practice of reckoning harvests "on the root" rather than as actually collected. But, whether for the Stalin era or for more recent years, the official data used here are those published recently under Khrushchev's sponsorship, and it seems clear that in revising old and releasing new figures Khrushchev has generally avoided the kinds of distortions familiar under Stalin. Nevertheless, as was explained, for whatever reason, the new official data used for milk appear to be materially off the mark and hence could only be used here after adjustment. Moreover, as was not considered sufficiently before, the grain crop currently reported still represents not a true barn harvest but a somewhat elastic "bunker crop" that is sensitive to changes in moisture content. Here again it is chiefly the official data for years after 1955 that are in question, for only during these years have the recent increases in the volume of moisture-laden grain from the East become relatively sizable, but the Eastern grain was already a factor of some consequence in 1954 and 1955, and it seems necessary to reckon with some bias at this point, although the effect on my calculations of farm income in kind must be quite limited. No doubt, as the recently released official data are scrutinized further they will be found subject in some degree to still other deficiencies.

While here and in this study in general, I focus on the period up to 1955, in a concluding chapter I try to extrapolate national income to 1958. The extrapolation is crude in any event, but it rests on a calculation of national income by industry of origin, and it should be observed that for agriculture the Johnson-Kahan computation of net output employed must be affected by distortions in official data such as have been described. Hence, although growth seems to continue during 1955–58 at about the same rate as prevailed during 1950–55, possibly it slows somewhat instead.

The foregoing applies primarily to years other than 1928. For the latter year, two alternative calculations are made. On the one hand, by the method of aggregation, farm income in kind is found to be 40 billion rubles in terms of 1937 prices. On the other hand, the SNIP figure for farm income in kind in terms of 1928 prices is computed from global official data in monetary terms on farm output and its disposition. This figure may be inflated to the 1937 price level by use of the price index implied by the initial calculation of income in kind and an alternative one in terms of 1928 prices. The necessary 1928 price data have been compiled by Karcz. By the method of inflation, farm income in kind amounts to 34 billion rubles. The difference in results I believe is largely due to differences in their scope. Among other things, the first calculation includes and the second omits intrarural cash sales of farm produce. Both calculations include intrarural barter sales.

In Table 4, I cite the figure obtained by the method of inflation, that is the one that excludes intrarural cash sales. Soviet sources are not entirely explicit about the scope of the marketings data used in our calculations for 1937–55. I believe these figures largely omit, and hence our income in kind data include, much intrarural collective farm market sales. The intrarural cash sales that we omit from farm income in kind in 1928, however, may be considered as a counterpart to appreciable sales that are classified as marketings and hence are omitted from income in kind for 1937–55. I refer especially to "return sales" to rural deficit areas.

As these remarks make clear, our figures on farm income in kind for different years are not fully comparable in scope. There may be some divergencies within the period 1937–55 as well as between 1928 and these later years. The data appear, however, to be more or less complementary to those compiled earlier on retail trade. For this reason, there need be no corresponding divergencies in our figures for household consumption generally.[15]

In calculating farm income in kind for 1937–55, no deductions are made for investment in kind. The calculations are confined, however, to products used for human consumption. The amounts of investments that are included (for example, variations in farm grain stocks) must be very limited, therefore, and the resulting series can be taken to represent consumption of farm income in kind, which is of concern here. For 1928, the current ruble figure that is inflated is net of livestock investments. For all years, I include in gross investments a separately computed allowance for the latter investments.

Military Subsistence

As in the SNIP calculations, military subsistence per man is arbitrarily assumed to have amounted to about 1500 rubles a year during 1937. This is in terms of the prices paid by the defense establishment in 1937.[16]

[15] Actually, Hoeffding's breakdown of Soviet data on intrarural trade between cash and barter sales on which I rely here is arbitrary, so the precise amount of cash sales is conjectural. On the other hand, Hoeffding's estimate is perhaps of broadly the right magnitude for purposes of obtaining an income in kind figure that fits in with our data for 1937–55. In any event, our data of farm income in kind and retail sales are fully complementary for 1928. Whatever of intrarural trade is not classified as income in kind is classified as retail trade. Hence, total consumption for 1928 is unaffected by the treatment of intrarural trade.

[16] The average working class family spent 741 rubles per capita on food and clothing in 1935. See *SNIP-37*, p. 109.

Military subsistence in the aggregate is computed here for 1928 as well as 1937–48 on this assumption. For 1949–55, I also follow the SNIP studies in allowing for an annual increase of a few percent in "real" subsistence per man. Throughout, I rely on these figures on the numerical strength of the armed forces. For 1928, 562,000; 1937, 1,750,000; 1940, 3,500,000; 1944, 12,000,000; 1950, 4,000,000; and 1955, 5,500,000. These data represent a revision of corresponding figures in the SNIP studies. The revision takes account of information on the size of the armed forces released by Khrushchev in his speech before the Supreme Soviet on January 14, 1960.

5

NATIONAL INCOME IN 1937 RUBLES: OTHER OUTLAYS

Communal Services

Health care. In the SNIP studies, outlays on this category in terms of current rubles are derived mainly from Soviet budgetary statistics. From incomplete information, expenditures not included in the budgetary appropriation to "health care" (chiefly those financed out of the social insurance budget) are estimated generally to have constituted about 20 to 25 percent of the total outlays from all sources. In 1937, some 3.2 billion rubles, or 40 percent of the total outlays, budgetary and nonbudgetary, represent wage payments. In terms of 1937 rubles, the corresponding expenditures in other years are taken here to vary simply with the volume of employment of medical and other workers engaged in health care. The necessary employment figures are given in or may be estimated from statistics released in a recently published Soviet statistical abstract.[1] Nonwage outlays in current rubles are computed for all years as

[1] TSU, *Narodnoe khoziaistvo SSSR,* Moscow, 1956 (which will be cited henceforth as *Narkhoz*).

residuals on the basis of the foregoing employment data and corresponding figures on average annual wages for health care workers. The trends in the latter often had to be inferred from the trends in the average wages of Soviet employees generally. Measures of nonwage outlays in terms of constant rubles are derived by deflation. The deflator is compiled here from price data for the more important inputs, including chiefly index numbers of retail food prices, computed by Dr. Janet Chapman as part of her study of retail prices generally; corresponding index numbers of the wholesale prices of such items as fuel and power computed by Lynn Turgeon, Roman Bernaut, and me from price quotations in Soviet price handbooks;[2] and diverse other wholesale and retail price data compiled by Dr. Chapman and the latter writers. Although Dr. Chapman's indices for food and other products refer to Moscow prices and moreover to retail rather than wholesale prices, I believe they represent reasonably well the trends in the wholesale prices paid by health institutions in the USSR generally during the period since 1937.[3] For 1928, I have reduced my input price index by some 10 percent in order to allow for differences between Moscow and USSR average prices and for the probably wider trade margins of the time, compared with 1937. Although retail prices may be used on this basis to derive index numbers of input prices, as compiled here the latter leave something to be desired so far as they involve the use of base year weights and almost inevitably a number of "substitutions" in the case of less important inputs (for example, trends in the prices of short-lived equipment have to be gauged from the prices of machinery and housewares).

For purposes of appraising their reliability, my measures of total "real" outlays on health care may be compared with two alternative indicators of health care in the USSR: employment in medical institutions and the number of civilian hospital beds. While my calculations of health care outlays are based partly on employment trends, wage payments constituted but two-fifths of total expenditures on such activities in 1937. Moreover, hospital care was planned to absorb only 30 percent of the government budget appropriation for health care in the same year. Under the circumstances, the broad similarity in the different series that is observed (Table 8) could not have been predicted with any certainty, but seems to the good nonetheless. Then too, "real" out-

[2] See page 71.

[3] While health care institutions presumably often purchased foodstuffs and other consumers' goods at wholesale prices, such prices are gross of practically all "turnover taxes." Although the contrary is often suggested, institutional consumers as well as retail trade outlets pay wholesale prices gross of the tax. Only on this basis can index numbers of retail prices be at all indicative of wholesale price trends. On the turnover tax, see page 105. On the inclusion of the tax in wholesale prices paid by institutions, see the discussion of taxation of military procurements on pages 112–113.

TABLE 8

Health Care in the USSR, Alternative Indicators[a]

(1937 = 100)

Year	"Real" outlays, 1937 rubles	Wage earners and salaried workers engaged	Hospital beds, civilian
1928	26.6	35.4	40.0
1937	100	100	100
1940	120	134	128
1944	111	113	—
1950	139	182	164
1955	200	233	209

[a] For data on employment, see Appendix D. On hospital beds, see TSUNKHU, *Sotsialis-tichesKoe stroitel'stvo Soiuza SSR, 1933–38, gg*, Moscow, 1939, p. 133 (hereafter cited as SS, 1933-38), and *Narkhoz*, p. 244.

lays are found here to be quite low in 1928 and 1950 in relation to both employment and hospital beds, but one wonders whether nonlabor inputs might not in fact have been comparatively limited in both these years (the one coming at the beginning of the five year plans and the other toward the end of the reconstruction period); and for some minor categories of health care for which data are available (for example, sanitariums, rest homes, nurseries) levels of activity in 1950 seemingly were generally distinctly below that in hospitals.[4] My calculations are subject to error, however, and very possibly I do to some extent understate the volume of "real" outlays in the two years in question.

According to both the calculations of health care outlays and the employment data, the scale of Soviet health care measures declined very little during the war. The reason, I believe, is that civilian medical institutions were rendering substantial services to the armed forces. On the other hand, military medicine as such, at least so far as it was administered by the armed forces, is financed out of the defense budget and is not covered by the figures on health care expenditures or by the employment series, which refers to civilian employment alone.

The figures in constant prices that have been derived for health care strictly speaking measure "real" inputs rather than outputs. Although measures of the latter ideally would be preferable, an attempt to allow for changes in the quality of health services provided by given inputs would hardly be practical. In the case of labor inputs, it did not seem worthwhile either to try to allow for changes in working hours.

Education. Like the SNIP current ruble figures on health care, those on education are compiled from budgetary data. In the light of prewar

[4] See *Narkhoz*, pp. 247, 248.

information, expenditures over and above those financed out of the budget appropriation to "education" for years since 1940 are taken to amount to about one-sixth of total outlays from all sources. Current ruble figures are here translated into constant rubles by use of essentially the same procedures and sorts of data as are used in the corresponding calculation for health care. Although the deflator for nonlabor outlays (an unweighted average of index numbers of the prices of fuel and power, reading matter, and other inputs or surrogates thereof) is crude, such expenditures constitute but two-fifths of the total outlays in 1937 and less than this in many other years. Errors at this point, therefore, are less consequential than they might seem. If the deflator for 1928 or 1950–55 erred by as much as 25 percent, for example, "real" outlays on education would in no case err by as much as 10 percent.

As for health care, so for education some interest may attach to the relation between my results and the corresponding data on employment (Table 9). Also shown in the table are indices of school enrollment. In compiling the latter indices, I assigned to the numbers enrolled in three different branches (general schools, technicums and other secondary vocational schools, and universities and other higher educational institutions) weights corresponding to the average expenditure per student in 1937. The resulting series, therefore, shows what the trends in "real" outlays on all branches together would have been if "real" outlays per student in the three branches had remained constant at the 1937 level. In 1937, expenditures on all three branches together constituted some 60 percent of all budgetary expenditures on education. The balance went for such items as special educational programs, research, libraries, and "red corners."

In Table 9, the three series show broadly similar trends, but they diverge especially in 1928 and 1955. From 1928 to 1937 "real" nonlabor outlays may well have increased markedly in relation to both employment and enrollment as my calculations imply, but my index for 1928 is among the less reliable computed, and possibly I am in error at this point. For 1955 my index might also be in error, but in this case it falls squarely between the indices for employment and enrollment, and this is a plausible result. It only seems the more so when it is considered that, in the general schools, the postwar period has seen (as the data in the table would suggest) a marked decline in the size of classes, that is, from 29 pupils per teacher in 1940/41 to 17 per teacher in 1955/56.[5]

As for health care, so for education, my data on "real" outlays measure "real" inputs. As measures of "real" outputs, therefore, they do not reflect changes in the quality of services rendered by inputs.

Other communal services. In relation to the outlays on health care

[5] See *Narkhoz,* p. 222.

TABLE 9

Education in the USSR, Alternative Indicators[a]
(1937 = 100)

Year	"Real" outlays, 1937 rubles	Wage earners and salaried workers engaged	Students enrolled
1928	22.9	34.0	38.4
1937	100	100	100
1940	117	126	121
1944	83	88	—
1950	145	162	130
1955	165	197	138

[a] On "real" outlays and employment, see Appendix D. Data on enrollment in each of three main branches (general schools, technicums and other secondary vocational schools, and universities and other higher educational institutions) are from *Narkhoz,* pp. 221–223, and TSUNKHU, *Kul'turnoe stroitel'stvo SSSR* (reference is to the edition published in 1940, which is hereafter cited as *Kul'tstroi,* 1940 ed.), p. 9. In aggregating these data, I assign to the different branches weights corresponding to per student expenditures in 1937 (exclusive of capital outlays and stipends). These are estimated at 200 rubles in the general schools, 800 rubles in the technicums and other secondary vocational schools, and 1900 rubles in the universities. Data on total outlays in different branches are given in *Kul'tstroi,* 1940 ed., p. 31. Capital outlays and stipends are estimated roughly from data in TSUNKHU, *Kul'turnoe stroitel'stvo SSSR 1935* (I refer to the edition published in 1936, which is cited hereafter as *Kul'tstroi,* 1936 ed.), pp. 250 ff., and Narkomfin SSSR, *Raskhody na sotsial'no-kul'turnye meropriiatiia* . . . Moscow, 1939, p. 51.

and education, the expenditures for other communal services in constant prices are taken to be more or less proportional to the corresponding current ruble figure.

Government Administration, Including NKVD (OGPU; MVD and MGB)

Government administration, other than NKVD (See Table 10). In terms of current rubles, expenditures on government administration, exclusive of the NKVD, are reported in Soviet budgetary sources. I deflate these figures by index numbers of the prices of all inputs to government administration. The latter index numbers are obtained by averaging the following: (i) Index numbers of the average annual wages of government workers. For 1928–37 the earnings of government workers are given in official sources. For 1937–55, they are taken to vary with the average wages of Soviet employees generally. They did so within a percentage point from 1928 to 1937. (ii) Index numbers of the prices of nonlabor inputs to government administration. The latter inputs should be similar to those for education; in any case, for lack of an alternative, the index numbers compiled for the latter are applied again here. The two series

TABLE 10

Expenditures on Government Administration, Including NKVD, in 1937 Prices, USSR, 1928–55
(billions of rubles)

Year	Government administration, other than NKVD	NKVD
1928	2.7	0.33
1937	4.4	3.0
1940	5.3	5.5
1944	4.5	4.0
1950	5.6	9.2
1955	4.8	5.7

on wages and prices are averaged with weights of 7 to 3, respectively, which correspond to the prewar division of government expenditures between labor and nonlabor inputs.

Data are lacking on employment in government administration, but the Soviet government has recently published figures on the labor force in the "apparatus of organs of government and economic administration and social organizations." The "apparatus" includes "government administration" as understood here, but apparently it also includes employees of trade unions, and other social organizations (among them, possibly the Communist Party). The *Narkhoz* data, I believe, also cover employees in intermediate organs of economic organization (for example, trusts and combines) which operate on a *khozraschet* basis and hence are not supported out of the government budget. Before the war, employees in social and intermediate economic organizations may have totaled two-fifths of the total personnel in the "apparatus."

While the *Narkhoz* employment figures are considerably broader in scope than my measures of "real" outlays on government administration, the fact that the two series generally move closely together (Table 11) is to the good. "Real" outlays, nevertheless, decline markedly less than employment in the "apparatus" from 1950 to 1955. This may be because employment in governmental sectors of the "apparatus" declined less than in nongovernmental sectors. Very possibly, too, nonlabor inputs to governmental administration declined less than labor inputs, if indeed the former declined at all.[6] On the other hand, my computations may

[6] That nonlabor inputs declined less than labor inputs becomes all the more likely if the *Narkhoz* figures indicate the trends in employment in government administration alone. Granting this, and assuming the same indices of wages and nonlabor input prices as before, I find that "real" outlays on nonlabor inputs increased from 1.8 billion rubles in 1950 to 2.1 billion rubles in 1955. On the same assumptions, I have also calculated total "real" outlays on government administration by the same procedures as were

understate the reduction in "real" outlays on government administration that occurred, but granting this the employment figures at least tend to confirm a feature that might otherwise be questioned: that an appreciable reduction in "real" outlays did in fact take place.

NKVD. For the years 1928–44, the SNIP figures on the expenditures of the NKVD could be taken or inferred from information in Soviet budgetary reports. Since 1950, however, the government has ceased to publish data on the NKVD outlays. In the SNIP calculations, NKVD expenditures in 1950 are assumed to be the same as in 1949. Although broadly consistent with incomplete budgetary data, the figure for 1955 is something of a guess. In order to measure "real" outlays of the NKVD, the prices of inputs to this category are assumed to vary in the same way as the prices of inputs to government administration. In view of the possible importance of outlays on the subsistence of NKVD personnel and penal workers, an alternative calculation giving more weight to retail prices was also made, but the results differ little from those derived initially.

The agencies concerned with "internal affairs" in the USSR have been reorganized on a number of occasions. The current ruble figures that are deflated represent the budget appropriations made in 1937 to the People's Commissariat of Internal Affairs (NKVD), and in other years to its various predecessors and successors. Although reference is throughout, therefore, to agencies in charge of "internal affairs," the functions performed must have varied in the course of time. Among other things, the NKVD (or rather its wartime and postwar successors) apparently assumed considerable responsibilities for the care of P/W's during and after the war.

Defense (as recorded in budget)

To reduce to a common "real" dimension defense outlays made by a major power over the last several decades could never be an easy task. For Soviet Russia, difficulties are posed not only by successive revolutions in military technology but by the government's notable secrecy. The figures that have been compiled may serve nevertheless to round out my calculations of "real" national incomes. The reader will wish to use them carefully in other applications.

Military pay and subsistence. A principal component of Soviet defense expenditures is military pay and subsistence. Data on this aspect in

used for health care and education. In other words, I take "real" outlays on labor to vary with employment in the "apparatus." After computing nonlabor outlays in current rubles as a residual, I deflate them separately. On this basis, "real" outlays on government administration for all years are within 2.5 percentage points (with 1937 as 100) of the magnitudes originally computed.

TABLE 11

Expenditures on Government Administration, 1937 Rubles, Alternative Indicators, USSR, 1928–55[a]
(1937 = 100)

Year	All outlays, in 1937 prices	Employment in "Apparatus . . . ," *Narkhoz* series
1928	61.4	67.9
1937	100	100
1940	120	123
1944	102	95
1950	127	123
1955	109	91

[a] On the data in terms of 1937 rubles, see Appendix D. On the employment data, see *Narkhoz*, p. 190. According to *Narkhoz*, p. 190, employment in the "Apparatus . . ." in 1945 was 111 percent of 1937. I assume the corresponding figure for 1944 was 95 percent. This is in view of the budget outlays for "government administration" in the two years: They were, for 1944, 7.4 billion rubles, and for 1945, 9.2 billion rubles. See K. N. Plotnikov, *Biudzhet sotsialisticheskogo gosudarstva*, Gosfinizdat, 1948, p. 340.

The *Narkhoz* figures refer to employment in the "Apparatus of organs of government and economic administration and social organizations." As this caption indicates, reference is made not only to workers in government administration in the sense considered in the text but also to workers in other branches, including I believe: intermediate organs of economic administration, such as trusts and combines, which operate on a *khozraschet* basis and hence are not supported out of the government budget, and social organizations, including the trade unions and possibly the Communist Party.

According to *Narkhoz*, employment in the "Apparatus . . ." totaled 1.488 millions in 1937. The comparative importance of different branches in this total, I believe, may be judged from more detailed employment data in TSUNKHU, *Chislennost' i zarabotnaia plata rabochikh i sluzhashchikh v SSSR*, p. 120. The number of workers, as of April 1, 1936, in government institutions was 650,900; in courts and other legal agencies, 39,900; in projecting organizations, et cetera, 96,200; in agencies administering national economy, 434,000; and in social organizations, 165,500. The total number of workers in all specified branches was 1,386,500.

The *Narkhoz* employment series probably embraces all five of the foregoing branches, while "government administration," as this is understood in our national income accounts, probably comprehends only the first three branches, employing 57 percent of the total. The *Narkhoz* series, it should also be noted, differs from data for similar categories for 1928–1937 that are given in TSUNKHU, *Trud v SSSR*, 1936 ed., pp. 10-11, and Gosplan, *Tretii piatiletnii plan razvitiia narodnogo khoziaistva Soiuza SSR, 1938–42*, Moscow, 1939 (hereafter *TPP*), pp. 228–229. The reasons for the differences are not known. All three series, I believe, omit "forced labor" employed by the NKVD, but the *Narkhoz* series must omit and the other series may possibly include regular employees of this agency. Reason to think the *Narkhoz* series omits the regular employees of the NKVD is chiefly that after the war the indicated employment levels are incongruous with the greatly expanded NKVD outlays. See Table 4.

current rubles, which are compiled in the SNIP studies, have been revised here chiefly in order to take into account information on the size of the armed forces released by Khrushchev in his speech before the Supreme Soviet on January 14, 1960. For each year the corresponding figure in terms of 1937 rubles (Table 12) is obtained as the product of the size of the armed forces in that year and the outlays on military pay and subsistence per member of the armed forces in 1937. Since the concern at this point is with the changing volume of military services, it will readily be seen that this is the correct calculation to make. The alternative procedure that might suggest itself, involving the deflation of outlays on military pay and subsistence by (say) an index of consumers' goods prices, would be logically inappropriate.

TABLE 12

Defense Expenditures (as recorded in budget),[a] USSR, 1928–55, in 1937 Rubles (billions)

Year	All expenditures	Military services	Munitions	Other
1928	1.9	1.3	—	—
1937	17.4	4.0	—	—
1940	45.8	8.0	26.8	11.0
1944	118.0	27.4	70.6	20.0
1950	42.4	9.1	25.3	8.0
1955	62.0	12.6	39.4	10.0

[a] Excluding pensions to officers, et cetera.

Munitions and other procurement: reference data on prices. Exclusive of military pay and subsistence, the budgetary defense expenditures comprise outlays on munitions and other procurements.[7] Other procurements include petroleum and other industrial goods needed for current operations, materials and services needed for military construction, transportation, civilian employees of the military departments. For purposes of measuring outlays on these goods in terms of 1937 rubles (Table 12), I rely primarily, although not exclusively, on the method of deflation. As a preliminary, it may be well to describe certain serial data on prices that were referred to in the computations (Table 13). For domestically produced civilian machinery, I cite serial figures compiled partly for this study by Dr. Richard Moorsteen. Moorsteen makes diverse calculations of machinery prices. As is appropriate, reference is made here to those

[7] Certain pension payments to officers and other special military personnel and their families are included in the published budgetary defense appropriation. In Table 3, p. 46, the published figures have been adjusted to exclude these pensions, which are treated as transfers. Pension payments to military personnel generally are financed not out of the budgetary defense appropriation but out of a separate appropriation to "social assistance."

where he employs "variable weights" in accord with formula (5).[8] Although Moorsteen's index numbers are used in the computation of "real" outlays on munitions and other procurement, in this study they serve primarily as a basis for the measurement of "real" investments in machinery. Further comment on his calculations, therefore, is postponed until we come to the latter aspect.

In Table 13, the index numbers of the prices of basic industrial goods are also to be employed at several points, but may as well be explained here. They were computed by Roman Bernaut, Lynn Turgeon, and me,[9] chiefly from wholesale price quotations given in price handbooks published by sales, procurement, statistical, financial, and other administrative agencies in the USSR. The quotations represent the transfer prices obtaining in transactions between economic enterprises. The quotations are gross of turnover taxes, which, however, have been nominal or null for most industrial goods except petroleum products (see chapter 8), and probably also of the limited sales taxes that were levied prior to the introduction of the turnover tax in 1930. Most commonly they are f.o.b. shipper and fail to reflect varying freight charges. The quotations usually are all-Union and, where they are not, the trends in average all-Union prices may be approximated from such regional quotations as are given. Index numbers were compiled initially for 26 industrial branches in 6 sectors (iron and steel, nonferrous metals, fuel and power, lumber and wood products, chemicals and related products, and nonmetallic minerals) representing about 70 percent of Russia's output of producers' goods other than machinery in the mid-thirties.[10] In Table 13, the indices for all branches together correspond to Formula (6), but a partial recomputation according to Formula (5) leaves the result unchanged for

[8] Moorsteen's Formula (6) index for 1928 is 140 percent! While his Formula (5) index must be given priority here, as will become clear, the wide divergence between the two results for 1928 is one of several reasons why a reliable calculation of "real" outlays is difficult to make for this early year. The two formulas yield closely corresponding results for years since 1937, so the use of machinery prices as indicators of munitions prices does not seem to be complicated by any "base year relativity" to speak of for the more recent period.

[9] Abram Bergson, Roman Bernaut, and Lynn Turgeon, "Prices of Basic Industrial Products in the USSR, 1928–50," *Journal of Political Economy,* August 1956; Lynn Turgeon and Abram Bergson, "Prices of Basic Industrial Goods in the USSR, 1950 to 1956: A preliminary report," The RAND Corporation, Research Memorandum RM-1919, June 12, 1957. See also the underlying RAND publications cited in the former article, p. 304, note 6.

[10] For all branches, price relatives were compiled for 175 distinct articles. For a roughly comparable sector, the U.S. Bureau of Labor Statistics now prices about 95 more items than this for its wholesale price index. The BLS apparently had to deal, however, with a much more varied commodity structure and more finely differentiated prices than were encountered in the calculations for the USSR, especially in lumber where much of the difference arises.

TABLE 13

Index Numbers of Prices, Selected Branches, USSR, 1928–55
(percent)

Period	Munitions, procurement prices (assumed)	Domestic civilian machinery, wholesale prices (Moorsteen)	Basic industrial goods, wholesale prices (Bergson, Bernaut, Turgeon)	Munitions, material inputs, wholesale prices	Average annual wages, adjusted, industrial workers
1928 ÷ 1937	60[a]	70	45	60	27
1940 ÷ 1937	120	106	121	126	128
1944 ÷ 1940	80	104	106	114	120
1950 ÷ 1944	132	174	200	143	150
1955 ÷ 1950	80	80	89	87	117

[a] Including other procurement.

1928. For basic industrial goods, the choice of base year probably is not very consequential for more recent years either. In applying Formula (6), price relatives are aggregated in terms of the value of their "marketed output" or some variant thereof.

For munitions material inputs, I refer to averages of index numbers compiled by Bernaut, Turgeon, and me for three branches: quality steel, nonferrous rolled products, and inorganic chemicals. The index numbers for different branches often diverge widely, but it seemed in order to attach most weight to those for quality steel.[11] In Table 13, the indices of the average annual wages of industrial workers were calculated or estimated from incomplete Soviet official data. Average wages have been adjusted for changes in working hours.[12]

Munitions and other procurement: "real" outlays. Given the SNIP figures on military pay and subsistence in current rubles, corresponding figures on munitions and other procurement may be obtained as a residual. The Soviet government has published little information on the prices its military establishment pays for munitions. Accordingly, as is already implied, in order to measure outlays on munitions and other procurement in constant prices (Table 12), it was often necessary in the case of the former to resort to the familiar but still risky expedient of gauging price trends from the trends in prices of related goods.

I take the prices of munitions and other procurement together in

[11] Considering the U.S. wartime procurement experience, J. C. DeHaven and R. Grosse of The RAND Corporation advised me to weight the branch index numbers in the proportions 4 to 1 to 1, the weight of 4 being assigned to quality steel.

[12] See Appendix H.

1928 to have averaged 60 percent of the 1937 level. In view of the limited importance of such outlays in 1928, an error at this point could not be consequential. The stated figure nevertheless seems to be of the right order, in the light of the price trends for cognate sectors (Table 13). For 1940–55 "real" outlays on munitions and other procurement are calculated by aggregating measures of "real" outlays derived for each of these two components separately. Little can be said for my figures on other procurement for 1940–55 (Table 12). By computing this minor component separately, however, even though often by use of guesswork, I probably obtain more reliable measures of "real" defense outlays as a whole than could be derived otherwise. Since serial data on other procurement may be compiled in current as well as constant rubles, we may determine at once as a residual the outlays on munitions alone in current rubles. In deriving corresponding constant ruble data for the latter for the years 1937–40, we must consider that this period witnessed a sharp expansion of munitions production from an initially low level. Since productivity gains in this early phase of expansion most likely were minimal, I judge munitions price trends (Table 13) chiefly from the trends in munitions input prices. This means that munitions prices rose more than the prices of civilian machinery, but this seems explicable if not in terms of differential gains in productivity then in terms of differential increases in input prices.[13] It appears to be the burden of diverse official releases that the USSR produced in 1940 about 3.3 times as much munitions as it did in 1937. As computed here, munitions procurements in 1940 may have been on the order of 2.8 times those of 1937. Although Soviet official production data in terms of 1926/27 rubles may not be as fallible as is generally supposed (see chapter 11), the true increase could not have been much greater than has been calculated.

By 1944, the Russians were engaged in the mass production of munitions on a vast scale. The undocumented and unexplained official claim that the wholesale prices of munitions in 1942 were but 72 percent of the "prewar level" cannot be taken at face value, but it is not to be dismissed either, even though munitions input prices rose.[14] By the same token, I believe we must also consider seriously a variety of parallel Soviet claims regarding the wartime reduction in labor expenditures (for example, from 1941 to 1943, for airplanes, by 37.5 to 48 percent; for tanks by 50.7 to 53.8 percent); and in munitions costs (reportedly by 30 to 50 percent during the war). Claimed economies in defense expendi-

[13] The increase in the prices of munitions material inputs from 1937 to 1940 is due primarily to the 82 percent increase in the prices of nonferrous metal rolled products. These presumably were more important to munitions than to machinery.

[14] In Table 13, in computing the change in adjusted average wages from 1940 to 1944, I "discount" somewhat the wartime overtime hours in order to allow for their inferior quality. Without such a discount, the 1940–1944 index is reduced to 108 percent.

tures resulting from the cuts in munitions prices are also pertinent, although difficult to interpret.

If no price cuts were realized concomitantly for civilian machinery or basic industrial goods, and if indeed costs rose in these sectors and a price inflation could be avoided only through the use of subsidies — if these eventualities materialized (as indeed they did) — they are fully explicable in terms of the wartime circumstances. (Among other things, while output in these branches was expanded in the unoccupied areas to offset losses in the West, there was no shift to mass production methods such as occurred in the case of munitions.) They are not at all inconsistent, therefore, with a wartime cut in munitions prices.[15]

The wartime experience of the USA may also be illuminating. Despite a 20 percent increase in hourly earnings in manufacturing, the "contract prices" negotiated with individual companies in U.S. procurements in August 1945 averaged 64.0 to 80.3 percent of October 1942 for war agencies engaged in major munitions procurement.[16]

Under the circumstances, the 20 percent cut in munitions prices that is allowed (Table 13) may actually be too conservative, but the Russian claims on munition price and cost cuts and on the resultant economies in defense outlays refer primarily to 1942 and 1943. In view of their secrecy regarding 1944, the pre-1944 price trends may not have continued into the latter year. Possibly they were finally reversed. More important, "real" munitions procurements in 1944 are found here to be 2.6 times those of 1940. If Lend-Lease is excluded (see chapter 7), the corresponding figure might be 2.3. This does not seem implausible in relation to a further Soviet claim that "war production in the eastern and central regions of the USSR" during the war reached 2.5 times the "prewar" level in the whole of the USSR. N. Voznesenskii (the source also of the report cited above on munitions prices) is referring here to munitions production, and presumably in terms of 1926/27 ruble prices.

[15] The government's decision in the face of rising costs to limit wartime price increases by the use of subsidies was not unprecedented. A similar policy was followed in relation to the prices of producers' goods in the early thirties. On the other hand, the policy was initiated after 1928 and was more or less abandoned in 1936, when industrial prices generally were raised so as to cover costs. For this reason, the prices of machinery and industrial goods generally were more or less in accord with costs in 1928 and 1937. It will readily be seen that this is a matter of some importance here insofar as the price trends for these products are taken to indicate the trends in munitions prices. To complete the story, the government continued to subsidize industrial goods after the war, but again raised prices sharply in 1949 in order to re-establish the principle of profitability. If anything, the government overshot the mark in 1949, but as a result of a price cut of 1950, I believe the prices of machinery and other industrial goods generally tended once more to approximate costs. This relation appears to have been maintained in more recent years.

[16] J. P. Miller, *Pricing of Military Procurement,* New Haven, 1949, pp. 283–284.

The "eastern and central regions" probably produced about all of the wartime Soviet output.

For 1944–50, I am again guided primarily by input prices. Munitions prices rise less than might appear likely (Table 13) because postwar wage increases probably went primarily to sectors that had lagged in wartime. Although munitions production was sharply curtailed after the war, losses in productivity may have been avoided as a result of the concentration of output in the more efficient factories. Possibly there were gains. After the war, the government continued to subsidize civilian machinery and basic industrial goods as costs continued to rise, but in 1949 it sharply increased prices in order to re-establish profitable operations in these sectors. Since the 1949 increases overshot the mark, prices were cut in 1950, but in the latter year they were still far above the pre-1949 levels. The sharp increases for these products for 1944–50 (Table 13) have to be read in this light. Evidently they can shed little light on munitions price trends during this period.

On the other hand, the government has continued since 1950 to fix the prices of machinery and most other industrial goods more or less in accord with costs. For the period 1950–55, therefore, munitions prices are supposed to move with machinery prices (Table 13).

The military establishment procures many kinds of goods (for example, military subsistence, petroleum, construction materials) that are also purchased by civilian agencies. My calculations assume that the armed forces pay for these goods the same prices as other buyers.[17] Evidence is presented on pages 112 and 113 that this is substantially so and that contrary to a common belief the armed forces are not favored by any special tax exemptions, subsidies, and the like. If under the *khozraschet* system, the armed forces were not favored in the pricing of civilian goods, it seems reasonable to suppose (as by implication I have done) that normally they would also be expected to pay for munitions prices that covered their costs.

As computed here, "real" defense outlays omit investments in defense plant construction, the upkeep of the NKVD military formations and of premilitary and paramilitary units, and military pensions. These omissions, which result from reliance on Soviet budgetary data but which need not be inappropriate for present purposes, were explained in chapter 2 with special reference to 1937. It must now be observed that they affect my data throughout. Moreover, it is not known how the Russians accounted in their budget for requisitions and occupation charges levied after the war in Eastern Europe and Germany. No doubt many of these charges did not become apparent in the budget at all. Accordingly, they

[17] The SNIP current ruble data on military subsistence are compiled on this assumption. My computations for other procurement also require it.

too are not reflected in the budget defense appropriations. Very likely some research and development work on nuclear weapons is conducted outside the Soviet military establishment; the corresponding outlays are not included in the defense appropriation. There is no indication that munitions are stock-piled in any quantity outside the military establishment. One wonders, however, whether this may not be done in the case of atomic weapons. If so, additions to such stock piles also would be omitted from the defense appropriation.[18]

Gross Investment: In Fixed Capital

This is calculated as the sum of (Table 14): investments in new machinery; capital repairs to machinery; construction; and diverse other outlays classified in Soviet statistics as fixed capital investment, including land improvement and prospecting not connected with specific projects. Serial data on fixed capital investments in the socialist sector (government and cooperative enterprises; collective farms) in terms of current

[18] In my calculations, as was explained earlier, defense plant construction falls under gross investment and the upkeep of NKVD military formations under NKVD outlays. Military pensions are treated as transfers. Outlays on premilitary and paramilitary organizations might appear partly under education but otherwise their classification is conjectural. If requisition and occupation charges are not cleared through the government budget, they probably do not show up in my calculations at all. Civilian research and development expenditures are included under education. Any additions to munitions stock piles not held by the military establishment might be included in my data on gross investment.

Some information on the magnitudes of these different omissions from defense outlays may be of interest:

For the year 1940, a total of 8.2 billion rubles or about one-seventh of the budget defense outlays was appropriated to the commissariats of Ammunition, Armaments, Shipbuilding, and the Aircraft Industry and to the Chief Administration for War Construction. The appropriations were made under the budget heading of "Financing the National Economy," and probably represent mainly grants for plant construction. See *Shestaia sessiia Verkhovnogo Soveta SSSR . . . , 1940 gg,* Moscow, 1940, pp. 433–434.

The Russians in 1948 were quartering outside their borders probably substantially less than a million of their troops. At the values at which military subsistence is recorded in our accounts, the total cost of feeding these soldiers may have amounted to several billion rubles. This may be compared with the 64.3 billion rubles of defense department outlays recorded in the 1948 budget.

In the budget for 1950, expenditures on "scientific research organizations and measures" total 5.6 billion rubles. See *SNIP-49–55.* Expenditures by industrial enterprises for the same purpose were to amount to another 2.5 billion rubles. Both these sums probably include some outlays for military research and development. In the 1950 budget, recorded defense outlays amount to 80.8 billion rubles.

In 1955, the United States government spent $1.7 billions on "atomic energy development." If, as may possibly have been so, a dollar spent in this area in 1955 was worth on the order of 4 rubles, the U.S. outlays would have amounted to about 7 billion rubles. Assuming too that the U.S. expenditures may serve as a benchmark for judging the Soviet outlays for the same purposes, we may judge in this light the possible importance of their omission from the published defense figure. For 1955, the latter was 105.4 billion rubles.

TABLE 14

Gross Investment in Fixed Capital, in 1937 Prices, USSR, 1928–55
(billions of rubles)

Year	All gross investment in fixed capital	Investment in new machinery	Capital repairs to machinery	Construction	Other investments in fixed capital
1928	10.9	2.02	0.51	7.89	0.45
1937	35.2	11.0	1.4	21.5	1.3
1940	39.4	11.1	2.2	21.7	4.4
1944	24.2	8.6	1.2	12.5	1.9
1950	66.5	24.2	4.7	33.3	4.3
1955	112.2	41.4	7.9	56.8	6.1

rubles have been compiled by Norman Kaplan in an exhaustive study based on official statistics.[19] Kaplan's data are adjusted here to omit livestock investments, which I treat separately, and to include an allowance for private investment in housing and (for 1928 only) in other fixed capital, chiefly agricultural structures. Corresponding figures in current rubles on investments in new machinery and in capital repairs to machinery have been assembled by Moorsteen.[20] Because of the need to rely on incomplete and ambiguous official information, Moorsteen feels that his figures for investments in new machinery may err by a number of percent either way. I compile current ruble measures of construction, including capital repairs and assembly and installation, from similar official statistics. Outlays on other investments in fixed capital may be computed as a residual.

Machinery investment. Dr. Moorsteen assumed the responsibility for compiling index numbers of machinery prices that might be used to deflate the data on investments in new machinery. He calculates among other things variable weight, that is, Formula (5), index numbers of the sort required to translate the current ruble figures into the prices of 1937.[21] As in the computations described above for basic industrial goods, the needed price quotations are found in Soviet price handbooks. The quotations for machinery are invariably all-Union in scope. They are also inclusive of sales taxes before 1930 and of turnover taxes after that

[19] Norman Kaplan, "Capital Investments in the Soviet Union, 1924–1951," The RAND Corporation, Research Memorandum RM-735, November 28, 1951. Since the appearance of this study, Kaplan has revised and extended his calculations. I rely here on the revised and extended data which he supplied me chiefly in an unpublished memorandum of July 13, 1955, and in a letter of April 11, 1957. Kaplan's RAND report as so elaborated is cited henceforth as Kaplan, *Fixed Capital.*

[20] Moorsteen, *Machinery.*

[21] For purposes of his *Machinery,* Moorsteen goes further and deflates the investment data. I am simply retracing his steps here.

year, and while they are f.o.b. shipper, transport and distribution charges paid by the investor probably accounted for only about 10 percent of machinery costs to investors before the war.

In applying Formula (5) Dr. Moorsteen uses value of output weights. Because of the rapidly changing structure of machinery production, it was felt that as far as possible the variable weighting system called for should be strictly adhered to. Value of output weights were compiled, therefore, for all years that are compared with 1937.[22] Use is made of Soviet official production statistics, including the voluminous data recently published in Soviet statistical abstracts.

Contrary to a common belief, the Russians already were producing a respectable assortment of machinery on the eve of the five year plans, including not only such characteristic types as railway rolling stock and agricultural and textile machinery but also (although often in limited quantities) many others usually associated with more advanced stages, including tractors, automobiles, water turbines, and diesel engines. For this reason, and because of the Soviet policy of producing standardized models over protracted periods, the problem of making reliable intertemporal price comparisons in this sphere was not as difficult as might be supposed. Nevertheless, the period of the five year plans witnessed the introduction of "new" products in many branches but especially in the machinery sector, and, as Moorsteen explains, partly for this reason inaccuracies were unavoidable. In all, about two-thirds of the price comparisons could be made between prices of models known to be identical. Furthermore, of the balance, many differed in only minor respects. But some items compared may differ materially, and because of such incongruities Moorsteen considers that his index numbers for 1928 may be understated somewhat in relation to 1937. Similarly, those for later years may be overstated. Moreover, in order to complete comparisons over extended periods, it was often necessary to link relatives for different items. This is a standard procedure in index number calculations, but according to familiar reasoning is theoretically inexact. As Moorsteen explains, this theoretic limitation is quite apart from any incomparabilities involved in computing individual links. Although the resultant distortion is difficult to appraise quantitatively, it may be of some consequence in the case of Moorsteen's index numbers.

In all, price data are compiled for 19 categories of machinery comprising in most years 55 to 70 percent of all machinery produced in the USSR for investment purposes. Although some significant categories are omitted, for example, chemical equipment and ships, Moorsteen feels that these omissions do not tend generally to impart a systematic bias. The calculations refer initially to domestically produced machinery. From

[22] The "given year" weights for 1944 are compiled from output data for 1945.

sample price data, the resulting index numbers are adjusted to allow for differences between domestic prices of imported and similar domestic machinery at the beginning of the period studied. In this way, the calculations reflect more accurately the average prices paid by investors. On the basis of global Soviet data on the ruble value of Lend-Lease imports, a similar adjustment is conjectured for 1944. Machinery imports were relatively unimportant in 1937 and 1940. After the war, they occurred on some scale on reparations account and otherwise, but by 1950 they again constituted only a small fraction of total investment in machinery.

Capital repairs to machinery. In addition to his index numbers of the prices of new machinery, Moorsteen also compiles index numbers that may be used to deflate capital repairs. These are obtained by averaging with weights of 2 to 1 his index numbers of new machinery prices and corresponding index numbers of the earnings of workers in metalworking industries.

Construction. Outputs in this category are extraordinarily diverse and vary strikingly over time. The literal application to this sphere of conventional methods of measuring the physical volume of output, therefore, is a forbidding task, which students of national income understandably hesitate to undertake. Such a computation, in any event, has not been undertaken here. Instead, I have resorted to a familiar expedient: The physical volume of construction is measured by the physical volume of materials utilized.

In Table 14, the figures on construction are obtained more specifically as the product of the outlays on construction in 1937 in current rubles, and index numbers of the volume of material inputs to construction.

Professor Raymond Powell compiled the latter measures for this study.[23] As Professor Powell carefully explains, chiefly because of gaps in the underlying Soviet official data, his index numbers are imprecise even as measures of material inputs, but it was possible generally to include all major construction materials. While omitted minor materials are still consequential in the aggregate, care was taken not to allow the results to be affected by changes in coverage over time. Lacunae in the official statistics on the exact amounts of construction materials allotted to sectors other than construction are less troublesome than they might have been because of the preponderant shares generally going to con-

[23] Raymond P. Powell, "A Materials Input Index of Soviet Construction, 1927/28 to 1955," Part I, The RAND Corporation, Research Memorandum RM-1872, February 14, 1957; Part II, Research Memorandum RM-1873, February 14, 1957; Raymond P. Powell, "A Materials Input Index of Soviet Construction, Revised and Extended," The RAND Corporation, Research Memorandum RM-2454, September 28, 1959. For a summary version, see Raymond Powell, "An Index of Soviet Construction, 1927/28 to 1955," *Review of Economics and Statistics,* May 1959.

struction. The ultimate aim is to measure outputs in terms of their 1937 prices. The material inputs, thus, are aggregated in terms of their 1937 prices. Although delivered prices would have been more appropriate, the calculation is made in terms of f.o.b. shipper prices.[24]

How reliable is the material input index as a measure of Soviet construction output? As Professor Powell makes clear, the facts are complex and difficult to judge *a priori*. The relation of materials inputs to the volume of output in construction nevertheless should not be highly volatile. At least, after all due allowance is made for inflation in Soviet claims regarding mechanization and gains in labor productivity in construction, the input "coefficients" for materials should be more nearly stable than those for labor. For this reason, the materials inputs series for present purposes seemed decidedly more suitable as a "surrogate" for construction outputs than an alternative series that Powell compiles on changes in employment in construction (Table 15). The latter series is also statistically dubious, but as might be expected shows less of an increase over the period studied than the materials input series. The materials input indices also seemed preferable to another of Powell's series representing the volume of inputs of materials and labor together, although here the

TABLE 15

The Physical Volume of Construction in the USSR, Selected Indicators, 1928–55 (1937 = 100)

Year	Materials inputs, 1937 prices	Employment	Material and labor inputs, 1937 prices	Construction outlays deflated by prices of material and labor inputs
1928	36.7	59.5	47.8	45.0
1937	100	100	100	100
1940	101	97.5	99.3	102
1945	42.9	96.9	69.1	69.2
1950	155	168	161	143
1955	264	212	239	233

[24] A further calculation that Powell makes is also illuminating regarding the reliability of index numbers as measures of material inputs to construction. Inflated by appropriate index numbers of construction materials prices, the index numbers of material inputs become measures of such inputs in current rubles. By aggregating the latter data with corresponding figures on the construction wage bill, Powell obtains measures of construction inputs generally in terms of current rubles. These may be compared with independent estimates on the current ruble volume of construction outlays. Among the benchmark years considered here, in only one case, 1950, do the two series diverge by more than 10 percent.

contrary opinion is also tenable. By deflating estimated current ruble outlays on construction by index numbers of the prices of labor and material inputs, Professor Powell computes still another series of measures of the physical volume of construction (Table 15). Statistical errors apart, this series should diverge from that for material and labor inputs only insofar as the varying total outlays on construction diverge from material and labor costs.

One might wish to be able to refer here to the experience of some other country. If true measures of the physical volume of construction were available for the United States, for example, the validity of a material input series as a surrogate might be tested empirically. Such true measures, however, appear to be lacking. The measures of the physical volume of construction employed by the U.S. Department of Commerce, for example, are calculated by deflation. The deflators essentially are index numbers of input rather than output prices.[25]

Diverse related series are available, however, for the United States. Although inconclusive, analyses of these data seem to support the supposition that the material "input coefficients" in construction tend to be stable, at least in the long run.[26]

Miscellaneous investments in fixed capital. In view of their probably large labor component, these investments are deflated by index numbers of average wages in industry.

Gross Investment: Other

In current rubles, this is computed as a residual; that is, it represents the difference between, on the one hand, the gross national product determined as a sum of incomes and charges and, on the other, the sum of outlays other than those now in question. Such calculations are necessarily dubious, although in the light of incomplete information on the components of the residual, resultant errors of more than 5 percent in the totals of investment as a whole (that is, in fixed capital and in other forms taken together) are probably exceptional. Other gross investments are very heterogeneous. As far as possible, in reducing them to constant prices the more important elements are dealt with individually.

[25] The deflation is carried out separately, however, for 26 types of construction, and in some instances reference is made to the costs of standardized units of output, that is, costs of building an element of the structure, although here too reference still is often made to input rather than output prices. In the series used in its national income calculations, the Commerce Department also makes an adjustment for varying profit margins. See Powell, "A Materials Input Index of Soviet Construction, 1927/28 to 1955." Part I, The RAND Corporation, Research Memorandum RM-1872, February 14, 1957, p. 40; Norman Kaplan, "Some Methodological Notes on the Deflation of Construction," *Journal of American Statistical Association,* September 1959.

[26] See Powell, "A Materials Input Index of Soviet Construction, 1927/28 to 1955," Part I, pp. 37 ff.

Investments in livestock herds are understood here as corresponding to the value of the net increment in livestock herd numbers. Conceived in these illogical but statistically expedient terms, such investments constituted perhaps one-sixth of other gross investments in 1937. Yearly increments of different sorts of herds (cows, other cattle, hogs, sheep and goats, and, in 1928 and 1937, horses), as computed chiefly from Soviet official data on herd numbers, are valued at the estimated average prices prevailing in marketings of the different animals in question in 1937. This procedure was applied to 1937–55. In order to measure livestock investments in 1928 in terms of 1937 rubles, a Soviet current ruble figure on such investment is inflated.

As it turns out, because of the high turnover taxes, investments in inventories of consumers' goods in retail and wholesale trade are often a major constituent of other gross investments. (In 1937, they constituted but one-sixth of the total, but in a peak year, 1949, they rose to nearly one-third.) Such investments are also highly volatile. The Soviet government's decision to release in a recently published handbook of trade statistics (*Sovtorg*) extensive serial data on trade inventories, therefore, was most welcome here. Using these statistics, together with Dr. Chapman's and Soviet official index numbers of retail prices, it is possible to compile for the period studied serial data on annual investments in trade inventories. The investments are computed initially as is appropriate in terms of average prices for the year. Corresponding data in terms of average prices for 1937 may then be obtained by reference again to the Chapman and Soviet official index numbers of retail prices. In *Sovtorg*, wholesale as well as retail inventories are believed to be valued at retail prices. Since net investments as computed here in current rubles must be valued correspondingly, the use of index numbers of retail prices as deflators poses no problem at this point.[27]

Although not without guesswork, current ruble figures on the inventory investments of government and cooperative enterprises in sectors other than trade could be compiled from Soviet financial and other statistics. Such investments account for about one-third of other gross investments

[27] Nevertheless, for purposes of national income accounting, trade inventories are properly valued at acquisition prices. While an allowance might be made for distribution costs incurred in acquiring and holding the inventories, valuation at retail prices tends to inflate our data on investments in trade inventories both in terms of current and constant rubles. The inflation corresponds to unearned trade margins and turnover taxes paid by trade organizations. Moreover, since substantial turnover taxes are paid by wholesale trade organizations, the inflation probably reaches some dimensions in the case of inventories held by wholesale trade. On the other hand, when we come to revalue national income, the valuation of inventory investments in trade will be corrected for such turnover taxes after all. While the inflation nevertheless leads to an understatement in the current ruble magnitudes assigned to certain residual elements in other gross investment that are still to be considered, it did not seem in order to try to correct accordingly the calculations on the latter aspects.

in 1937. Some corresponding figures are assembled also on the structure of the inventory investments. With the aid of the latter, I deflate the totals by reference to diverse price data, including the Moorsteen index numbers of machinery prices, the Bergson-Bernaut-Turgeon index numbers of the prices of basic industrial goods, and the Chapman and Soviet official index numbers of retail prices. I also use index numbers of realized farm prices, compiled by Dr. Jerzy Karcz.[28]

For the rest, other gross investments represent a variety of activities, including money inventory investments by the MTS and collective farms (these are partly omitted from the data compiled for government and cooperative enterprises generally[29]); commodity stock-piling; gold production; the net foreign balance on commercial account; and other outlays of an investment type not classified elsewhere. Current ruble outlays on these activities are computed as a residual. In order to obtain corresponding constant ruble data, I use as a deflator a composite of index numbers of machinery prices, basic industrial goods prices, realized farm prices, and average wages.

[28] Jerzy F. Karcz, "Soviet Agricultural Marketings and Prices, 1928–1954," The RAND Corporation, Research Memorandum RM-1930, July 2, 1957. The calculations on inventory investments were facilitated by the kindness of Professor Raymond Powell and Professor Robert Campbell in putting at my disposal results of unpublished researches.

[29] Except for livestock investments, however, farm investments in kind are partly included in household consumption and partly omitted from national income altogether.

6

NATIONAL INCOME IN 1950 AND 1928 RUBLES

The recomputations in rubles of 1950 and 1928 need only brief explanation here. Details in any case are again presented in the appendices. As before, discussion of economic implications is postponed.

National Income in 1950 Rubles

I again take as a point of departure the SNIP current ruble data on the gross national product by major final use (Table 3). Dr. Janet Chapman compiles Formula (5) index numbers of retail prices not only for government and cooperative retail sales generally but for each of 22 categories of such sales, for example, grain products and legumes, meat and poultry, and textiles. She also compiles corresponding data on the structure of government and cooperative retail sales in terms of current rubles. By deflation, index numbers of the physical volume of retail sales in terms of 1937 prices may be obtained for each category. I aggregate the index numbers for the 22 categories using as category weights the relative volume of retail sales in current rubles in 1952. In relation to 1950, government and cooperative retail sales for 1937–55 in 1950 prices (Table 16) vary essentially with the resultant aggregative index numbers. In effect, then, I employ here mixed weights: 1937 weights within and

TABLE 16

Gross National Product of the USSR by Use in 1950 Prices, 1928–55 (billions of rubles)

Outlay category	1928	1937	1940	1944	1950	1955
Household purchases in retail markets						
In government and cooperative shops and restaurants	—	248.0	275.0	147.0	328.0	585.0
In collective farm markets	—	33.0	27.0	3.3	47.0	47.0
Total	235.0	281.0	302.0	150.3	375.0	632.0
Housing; services	23.9	41.2	44.9	30.8	50.4	76.2
Consumption of farm income in kind	79.6[a]	58.0	66.0	39.0	61.0	69.0
Military subsistence	1.9	5.9	11.7	40.5	14.1	22.6
Household consumption outlays	340.4	386.1	424.6	260.6	500.5	799.8
Communal services						
Health care	4.7	17.9	21.5	19.9	25.0	35.9
Education	9.1	41.1	47.9	34.0	59.0	66.9
Other	1.3	1.5	1.7	1.1	1.5	1.5
Total	15.1	60.5	71.1	55.0	85.5	104.3
Government administration, including NKVD (OGPU; MVD and MGB)	7.5	18.4	26.9	21.2	36.9	25.9
Defense (as recorded in budget)	5.4	34.3	86.6	226.2	80.8	114.6
Gross investment						
In fixed capital	30.7	88.1	95.3	55.4	156.5	261.1
Other	16.6	49.9	23.6	24.2	51.5	49.2
Total	47.3	138.0	118.9	79.6	208.0	310.3
Gross national product	415.7	637.3	728.1	642.6	911.7	1,354.9

[a] Includes 3.6 billion rubles of farm wages in kind.

1952 weights as between categories. There are reasons to think, however, that the results may approximate the desired measures in terms of 1950 prices.

For one thing, in terms of government and cooperative retail sales as computed, 1950 is more or less intermediate between 1937 and 1952 (in Table 16, 1937 is 76 and 1952 is 119 percent of 1950). Very possibly, the price structure of 1950 is similarly related to those of the other two years.[1]

[1] Evidently some such relation of price structures is presupposed if Professor Gerschenkron's hypothesis regarding the effect of base year shifts is to apply. Or rather, this is so if the hypothesis is taken to hold (as is usually done) for the measurement of changes in physical volume in terms not only of the prices of any two years com-

For another, if 1952 prices are applied within as well as between categories, "real" retail trade in 1952 is affected only to a limited extent: It is 161 percent of 1937 trade in 1937 prices and 147 percent in 1952 prices. On the index of retail trade in 1937 prices, see Table 4. The corresponding index in 1952 prices is obtained by using Dr. Chapman's Formula (6) index of retail prices as an inflator.[2] In mixed 1937–52 prices retail sales in 1952 are 157 percent of 1937. Considering the limited effect of a shift from 1937 to 1952 prices, measurement in 1950 prices should not yield a very different result.

In 1950 rubles, household purchases in collective farm markets are assumed to vary in relation to 1950 as such purchases did in 1937 rubles. The measurements for this category, therefore, continue to reflect the 1937 price structure, although the total outlays in 1950 correspond to the volume of purchases in that year in terms of 1950 prices. For 1928, household purchases in all retail markets are computed in 1950 prices by the same procedure as was used in the calculations for government and cooperative trade for 1937–55. Consequently, as with the measures for the latter category, that for 1928 reflects a mixture of 1937 and 1952 price weights.

In 1950 rubles, "real" outlays on each of the three components of "Housing; services" (that is, such items as housing, utilities, and trade union and other dues) vary in the same way as they do in 1937 rubles. In summing the components, however, I assign each a weight corresponding to the current ruble outlays of 1950 as given in the SNIP studies.

In *SNIP-49–55,* Nancy Nimitz estimates the average prices of different agricultural products realized on the farm in 1950. In order to compute consumption of farm income in kind in 1950 prices, I reaggregate in terms of Miss Nimitz' price data the farm consumption of different products as previously computed. "Real" outlays on military subsistence vary as they did in 1937 prices.

"Real" outlays on labor and nonlabor inputs to health care and education vary as before. For each use category, the two components are now summed with weights corresponding to the current ruble expenditures

---

pared but of the prices of any third year; for example, in terms of 1937 prices, the increase in physical volume between 1928 and 1955 is held to be less than that in terms of 1928 prices and more than that in terms of 1955 prices. I comment below on the applicability of the Gerschenkron hypothesis to the USSR.

[2] For 1952, the Formula (6) index has the specific form:

$$\frac{\Sigma \frac{P_{52}}{P_{37}} \cdot P_{37}Q_{37}}{\Sigma P_{37}Q_{37}} \qquad (7)$$

Applying this to retail sales in 1937 in current rubles, the result is retail sales in 1937 in 1952 rubles.

of 1950. Data on the latter aspect were derived previously. In 1950 prices, outlays on other communal services and government administration, including the NKVD, vary as before in relation to 1950.

This is true also of "real" outlays on military services, munitions and other procurement, although in the case of munitions this must be especially dubious. The three components of defense expenditures are reaggregated, however, with weights corresponding to the current ruble outlays in 1950 as calculated previously.

As before, "real" outlays on investments in fixed capital are calculated by aggregating measurements of investments in new machinery, capital repairs to machinery, construction, and other investments in fixed capital. Use is also made of the computation made earlier of the distribution among these different components of the total investments in fixed capital in current rubles. So far as "real" outlays in 1950 prices are computed by deflation, the appropriate index numbers of prices to apply are given ideally by this formula:

$$\frac{\Sigma P_i Q_i}{\Sigma \frac{P_{50}}{P_i} \cdot P_i Q_i} \tag{8}$$

From Moorsteen's calculations, it is possible to compile index numbers of the prices of machinery that tend to correspond to this formula. Investment in new machinery in 1950 prices is calculated by use of these index numbers. An appropriate deflator may be compiled similarly for capital repairs to machinery. Powell aggregates materials inputs to construction in terms not only of 1937 but of July-December 1950 prices. Although this hardly comes to the same thing as the valuation of construction outputs in 1950 prices, it is the appropriate analogue of the computation in 1937 prices to use here. Other investments in fixed capital vary as in 1937 rubles but for purposes of computing "real" outlays on fixed capital as a whole, the resultant indices are given a weight corresponding to the volume of outlays on other investments in fixed capital in 1950 in 1950 prices.

Livestock investments, inventory investments in different branches, and miscellaneous investments as previously computed are here reaggregated in terms of weights corresponding to current ruble outlays of 1950.

National Income in 1928 Rubles

As before, I begin with the SNIP figures on the gross national product by major final use in current rubles. In order to reduce current ruble data to 1928 prices (Table 17), one must apply index numbers given by this formula:

$$\frac{\Sigma P_i Q_i}{\Sigma \frac{P_{28}}{P_i} \cdot P_i Q_i} \tag{9}$$

For retail prices in 1937 this is simply the reciprocal of Dr. Chapman's Formula (6) index. Accordingly, retail sales in 1937 are deflated to 1928 rubles on this basis. Dr. Chapman's Formula (6) index for 1928 applies to all retail markets. I employ it here, therefore, to deflate all retail sales,

TABLE 17

Gross National Product of the USSR by Use in 1928 Prices, 1928–37
(billions of rubles)

	1928	1937
Household purchases in retail markets	12.10	21.20
Housing; services	2.79	4.58
Consumption of farm income in kind	6.70[a]	4.90
Military subsistence	0.25	0.42
Household consumption outlays	21.84	31.10
Communal services		
Health care	0.54	1.99
Education	0.87	4.46
Other	0.14	0.16
Total	1.55	6.61
Government administration, including NKVD (OGPU)	0.82	2.01
Defense (as recorded in budget)	0.76	10.61
Gross investment		
In fixed capital	6.00	27.45
Other	1.32	7.90
Total	7.32	35.35
Gross national product	32.29	85.68

[a] Including 0.30 billion rubles of farm wages in kind.

including collective farm market as well as government and cooperative.

"Real" outlays on housing, utilities and other services, and trade union and other dues as calculated previously in 1937 rubles are now reaggregated with weights corresponding to the current ruble expenditures of 1928. On the basis of data on farm prices in the late twenties compiled by Karcz and Smolinski, consumption of farm income in kind may be recomputed in terms of the average prices realized by farmers in 1928. Outlays on military subsistence in 1937 are deflated by the reciprocal of Dr. Chapman's Formula (6) index of retail prices.

"Real" outlays on labor and nonlabor inputs to health care and education as computed initially in 1937 prices are now summed with weights corresponding to the current ruble expenditures of 1928 as calculated earlier. In relation to 1928, other communal services and government administration vary as they did in 1937 prices.

For purposes of measuring "real" defense outlays, use is made of the SNIP data on the division of total expenditures in current rubles between military pay and subsistence on the one hand and munitions and other procurement on the other. In relation to 1928, military services vary as before. In redeflating outlays on munitions and other procurement I try to allow for the possible effect of the change in weights on the measure of price change. To this end, account is taken of available data on the impact of a shift in base year on index numbers of prices of related goods. In calculating "real" outlays on fixed capital, reference is again made to the current ruble data on outlays on different components that were compiled previously. For machinery prices, Moorsteen computes a Formula (9) index for 1937. Investments in new machinery are now deflated by use of this index. A corresponding computation is possible for capital repairs to machinery. For construction, I rely on still another computation by Powell: materials inputs to construction are valued in 1928 prices. In relation to 1928, other investments in fixed capital vary as previously. This is true also of livestock investments and miscellaneous investments. In redeflating inventory investments, use generally is made of Formula (9) index numbers. The different components of other investments are aggregated with weights given by the expenditures made on them in 1928 in 1928 rubles. The amounts of such expenditures were calculated earlier.

7

THE CONSTANT RUBLE DATA: A SUMMARY APPRAISAL

For purposes of appraising the computations in constant rubles, I first comment summarily on their reliability and then refer to some questions raised previously regarding scope.

Reliability

Although my computations all leave something to be desired, they vary in quality. The range perhaps is broadly typified by the data compiled for, on the one hand, household purchases in government and cooperative retail shops for the years 1937–55 and, on the other hand, gross investment in other than fixed capital. For the former, current ruble figures could be derived from official statistics with a minimum of adjustment, while in compiling the index numbers used as deflators Dr. Janet Chapman systematically exploits a wealth of information on prices and quantities. All things considered, the resultant constant ruble series is probably as reliable as any computed. The calculations for other gross investment are uneven, but outlays on this category in current rubles are obtained as a residual, and important components had to be deflated on the basis of very incomplete information. Taking the category as a whole, the figures for other gross investment are among the least reliable computed.

Among other categories, many clearly fall between these extremes. Specifically, I should so classify:

Household purchases in collective farm markets: Although the current ruble outlays could usually be determined from official data, price trends must be judged for some years from limited evidence and for others from official indices computed from an unknown formula.

Household purchases in all markets in 1928: Almost inevitably there are some divergences in scope between 1928 and later years, while the measurement of price trends is inherently difficult for this early period.

Housing; services: Uncertainties as to the quantity and quality of rural housing perhaps constitute the chief limitation in the case of the former. For services, little information is available on some significant components, for example, repairs and custom work, but alternative computations are reassuring.

Communal services: While trends in labor inputs may be judged from official employment data, "real" nonlabor inputs must be computed from residual current ruble figures and incomplete information on price changes. Here too, however, alternative computations are generally reassuring.

As to the remaining categories, the volume and structure of fixed capital investment in current rubles generally could be estimated from official statistics, and in deflating the machinery component we have been able to employ index numbers of prices which Moorsteen has compiled with notable care and judgment from voluminous data on prices and quantities. On the other hand, accurate measurement of machinery price trends is not entirely feasible in view of the multitude of new commodities. Then, too, in his extraordinarily thorough inquiry, Powell must have succeeded in portraying the trends in materials inputs to construction, but a question remains as to the accuracy with which the results measure construction outputs. In sum, the data on fixed capital investments are difficult to classify, although no doubt they are superior to those for a number of other categories. This may also be true of the calculations for farm income in kind, although if so, I fear this speaks not so much for their accuracy as for the limitations of some other computations.

Defense outlays in current rubles may be derived from official statistics, but the lack of information on munitions prices and on the detailed structure of expenditures puts formidable obstacles in the way of their accurate deflation. Fortunately, on this aspect it was possible to refer nevertheless to a substantial volume of data on the prices of munitions inputs and related industrial goods, but even waiving uncertainties regarding the scope of the budgetary defense appropriations, my constant ruble data on this important category must be among the less reliable compiled. The calculations for military subsistence reflect available information on the size of the Soviet armed forces. Because of doubts as to scope and structure of the NKVD outlays in current rubles, the corresponding constant ruble figures cannot be entirely meaningful or exact. These limitations necessarily affect the data on government administration including the NKVD, although for government administration alone the constant ruble figures could be computed from budgetary statistics and a broadly appropriate deflator.

I have sought to characterize the calculations for different use categories generally and without regard to possible differences as between periods. Regarding the latter, it may suffice to observe that the basic information for 1944 often is inferior in quality and quantity to that available for other years. The Soviet government has published voluminous statistics for the late twenties, but at the time data collection was still at an early stage, and comparisons of 1928 with later years encounter special difficulties because of changes in statistical concepts and more importantly in economic structure.

In appraising the possible effect of errors in any category on the measures compiled for larger aggregates, one must consider the importance of the outlays involved. At their relatively high 1950 level, for example, NKVD outlays constituted but 2.2 percent of the "real" national product. An error of even one-fourth in the price index used to deflate this category, accordingly, would alter the national product by but 0.6 percent. Again, if (as is very doubtful) "real" outlays on health care in 1950 were proportional to employment (Table 8), they would total 14.3 instead of 11.0 billion rubles, but national income would rise by less than one percent. On the other hand, defense constituted 38.8 percent of the national product in 1944. If, as Russian claims suggest, munitions prices in 1944 were 75 percent of the 1937 level (instead of the 96 percent I assume), national income rises by 20 billion rubles or nearly 7 percent. This is one of many reasons to feel that my national income calculations for 1944 are less reliable than those for other years.[1]

The computations for different use categories are substantially independent. Where larger aggregates are in question, therefore, it is reasonable to suppose that errors will often cancel out. Barring the remote contingency that inaccuracies are overwhelmingly in one direction, for example, the error in national income should be markedly less than is typical among components.

[1] The cited percentages refer to the computations in terms of 1937 rubles. In terms of 1937 "adjusted rubles," defense outlays are still more important in 1944. See chapter 9.

In commenting on reliability thus far, I have been thinking primarily of the calculations in 1937 prices. In the examples just given, reference accordingly has been made to these data. But what has been said generally applies also to the calculations in terms of 1950 and 1928 prices. Nevertheless, in appraising these alternative computations, it must be considered that the volume and variety of "new" products to be dealt with is especially great where 1928 is the base year. Where valuation is in terms of 1937 and 1950 prices, this feature is still a problem but necessarily less of one than where use is made of the earlier base year.

TABLE 18

Gross National Product by Use, USSR, 1928–55, Alternative Price Weights (1937 = 100)

Outlay category	1928	1937	1940	1944	1950	1955
Household consumption outlays						
1937 prices	88.8	100	114	69.3	133	209
1950 prices	88.2	100	110	67.5	130	207
1928 prices	70.2	100	—	—	—	—
Communal services						
1937 prices	25.8	100	118	91.4	142	174
1950 prices	25.0	100	118	90.9	141	172
1928 prices	23.4	100	—	—	—	—
Government administration, including NKVD[a]						
1937 prices	40.5	100	146	115	200	142
1950 prices	40.8	100	146	115	201	141
1928 prices	40.8	100	—	—	—	—
Defense						
1937 prices	10.9	100	263	678	244	356
1950 prices	15.7	100	252	659	236	334
1928 prices	7.2	100	—	—	—	—
Gross investment						
1937 prices	31.5	100	85.7	60.4	153	229
1950 prices	34.3	100	86.2	57.7	151	225
1928 prices	20.7	100	—	—	—	—
Gross national product						
1937 prices	64.8	100	118	108	146	217
1950 prices	65.2	100	114	101	143	213
1928 prices	37.7	100	—	—	—	—

[a] Divergences between 1937, 1950, and 1928 ruble data due to rounding rather than revaluation.

As was explained, the recomputations are in some degree only partial. The possible import of this aspect too has yet to be considered. As calculated in 1937 rubles, the gross national product in 1928 is 65 percent of 1937. In 1928 rubles, the corresponding figure is 38 percent (Table 18). Of the total difference between these two results, I find that about 18 percentage points or two-thirds is accounted for by the change in weights as between 25 use categories and subcategories. The balance of nine percentage points or one-third is due to reweighting within these categories.[2] At the same time, the latter recomputations were made systematically for use categories accounting for nearly one-half the national income in 1937. They were also made although often rather arbitrarily for still other use categories accounting for an additional 30 percent of the national income. Taking the observed results as a benchmark, I believe a more complete recomputation might possibly increase the divergence between my two indices of "real" national income in 1928 by (say) five percentage points. To what extent this would mean an increase in the index in 1937 rubles and to what extent a reduction in that in 1928 rubles is conjectural.

Except for the war year, 1944, calculation of national income in 1950 instead of 1937 prices scarcely affects the final results. In making this recomputation I reaggregate some 27 use categories and subcategories with 1950 ruble weights. Within use categories, the recomputation is less complete than that in terms of 1928 rubles, but in two important sectors where the effects of changes in price structure can be measured relatively reliably, a shift in the base from 1937 to a year in the fifties appears to have only a limited impact. (See Tables 19 and 20.)[3]

If a more complete recomputation is assumed, national income in 1950 prices probably would diverge more than is shown from national income in 1937 prices, but the discrepancy would still be relatively limited. The gap in results is greatest, however, in 1944, when it amounts to seven percentage points. Moreover, our calculations involve no revaluation within the munitions sector. If (as is conceivable) the index number effect within this category from 1937 to 1944 had been at all comparable to that in (say) machinery from 1928 to 1937, the gap between the alternative measurements of the gross national product for 1944 might have been seven percentage points larger.

[2] This follows from this further recomputation: in each of 25 use categories (for example, retail sales, government, NKVD, and new machinery investment), "real" outlays vary as computed in 1937 rubles. In further aggregations, each use category is assigned a weight corresponding to the current ruble outlays of 1928. The resulting index of "real" national income for 1928, 46.9 percent of 1937, is in mixed price weights: 1937 ruble weights within and 1928 ruble weights as between use categories. Reweighting in this fashion, I account for two-thirds of the difference between my two indices of national income in 1928 and 1937 rubles, that is, (64.8 — 46.9) ÷ (64.8 — 37.7).

[3] In Table 19, the indices in 1937 prices and 1950 prices for 1928–40 are from Table 4 and Table 16, and those for 1952 and 1954 from the Addendum. The indices in "given year" prices are obtained by use of Dr. Chapman's Formula (6) index numbers as deflators. Each comparison with 1937, therefore, is made in terms of the prices of the "given year." See Appendix A. The years considered in Table 19 are those for which Dr. Chapman's data permit us to record most faithfully the effects of base year shifts. In Table 20, the indices in prices for 1937 and 1950 are from Table 4 and Table 16. Indices in "given year" prices are obtained by use of Moorsteen's Formula (6) index numbers as deflators. See his *Machinery*.

TABLE 19

Government and Cooperative Retail Sales,
USSR, 1928–54, Alternative Weights
(1937 = 100)

Year	In 1937 prices	In 1950 prices	In prices of "given year"
1928	83.3[a]	83.6[a]	57.1[a]
1937	100	100	100
1940	115	111	110
1952	161	157	147
1954	228	229	215

[a] Including private sales.

TABLE 20

Investments in New Machinery, USSR, 1928–55, Alternative Weights
(1937 = 100)

Year	In 1937 prices	In 1950 prices	In prices of "given year"
1928	18.4	27.1	9.1
1937	100	100	100
1940	101	95.8	101
1944	78.2	65.7	70.0
1950	220	214	214
1955	376	356	353

The difference between our measurements in terms of 1928 and 1937 rubles is marked indeed. Besides, growth is more rapid in the former than in the latter case. On the other hand, a change in base year from 1937 to 1950 is seen here generally to have only a very limited effect, although the tendency as before is for growth to be reduced when a later base year is employed. According to familiar reasoning, index number relativity depends on the extent of the change in the structure of prices and production and on the correlation between them. By implication, the change in structure was nothing less than radical from 1928 to 1937. Seemingly, price changes were also distinctly correlated with production changes. More particularly, price increases tended to be restricted where production increases were great, and conversely. In contrast, the indicated change in structure after 1937 was relatively limited, although prices and production may also have varied with less dependence on each other than previously. Are such results plausible? Although the stated implications had to be underlined as a preliminary to the discussion to follow of the problem of valuation, to pursue the question posed would involve us with aspects (most importantly Professor Gerschenkron's well known hypothesis about index number relativity) which are more properly considered at a later stage. Accordingly I shall say no more about this matter at this point.

I have been considering national income as a whole. In respect of individual use categories, the recomputations are very uneven in quality. The results accordingly vary widely in the degree to which they reflect alternative price structures. The recalculations are relatively complete for household consumption outlays, for example, but could be carried out to only a very limited extent for communal services and government administration. The various series obtained have to be read in this light. As for national income as a whole, of course, the observed differences between series and time periods regarding index number relativity imply corresponding differences regarding the change in the structure of prices and production and their correlation. As we proceed, this aspect too should be kept in mind.

Some Questions of Scope

I turn to some questions of scope posed earlier, particularly uncertainties regarding penal labor subsistence, the omission of household processing for own consumption, and the inclusion of Lend-Lease and reparations.

Penal labor subsistence. As was explained, penal labor subsistence very possibly is omitted from my data on household consumption. Some of such outlays are included under NKVD expenditures, but for the rest they may also be omitted from national income.[4] As to the magnitudes involved, the size of the Soviet penal labor force is conjectural. Assuming (as may not be wide of the mark) that in the late thirties the government employed some 3.5 million prison workers,[5] and spent on each as much as (say) 750 1937 rubles a year (or one-fourth the average civilian wage and one-half the allowance for military subsistence per man in 1937), penal labor subsistence would come to 2.6 billion rubles. This is 1.3 percent of Soviet household consumption and less than one percent of the national income of 1940.

On the eve of the five year plans, the Soviet penal labor force still

[4] Such outlays are often held to be included in the Soviet "comprehensive" (as distinct from TSUNKHU) wage bill. If so, they would find their way into the SNIP estimates of national income as a sum of charges. By the same token, so far as the outlays for penal subsistence are not covered in the NKVD outlays they would also find their way into the SNIP estimates of gross investment computed as a residual. On the other hand, for years since 1940, the SNIP figures on the "comprehensive" wage bill are largely extrapolations, so the import of all this for the SNIP (and our own) data is conjectural. On the treatment of penal labor subsistence in the SNIP data, see *SNIP-28-48*.

[5] See Appendix K.

was measured only in the thousands, but under the impact of collectivization and the purges, it expanded sharply thereafter. The government also recruited many penal workers from newly annexed Western areas during and after 1939, and from Eastern Europe after the war. The extent to which new recruits exceeded releases during these years is conjectural. Reportedly the government since Stalin's death has released many workers with the result that the number of persons still confined has declined markedly. The possible trends in penal labor subsistence over the period studied have to be judged in the light of these considerations.

Household processing for own consumption. The processing of goods by households for their own consumption generally is omitted from national income computations for the very good reason that such activities are especially difficult to measure. Although the difficulties are no less for the USSR than elsewhere, the following figures may possibly serve as benchmarks for some of the pertinent magnitudes: In 1928, farm household processing of selected farm products for own consumption, at assumed 1937 factory costs, amounted to 5.8 to 6.4 billion rubles, which is 3.8 to 4.2 percent of all household consumption outlays and 3.2 to 3.5 percent of gross national product. In 1937, farm household processing amounted to 2.5 to 3.0 billion rubles, which is 1.5 to 1.8 percent of consumption outlays and 0.9 to 1.1 percent of gross national product. These rule-of-thumb data refer to farm household processing of grains, meat, wool, hides, flax, and oil seed by farm households for their own consumption. Of the two figures cited under each heading, the lower one assumes that all bread produced from the farmers' own grain is home-baked. The higher one assumes additionally that all farm flour is farm-milled. In both calculations, other products produced and consumed on the farm supposedly are processed as in Soviet industrial practice. Actually, in the years studied, Russian peasants probably had much of their grain custom ground by commercial or collective farm millers, and other products too were often processed commercially for farm consumption. Payment for such services tended to be in kind, however, and the extent to which they are included in national income is conjectural.[6]

The cited figures refer only to home processing on the farm. The relative decline in home processing from 1928 to 1937 presumably would be somewhat greater than is shown if allowance were made for the concomitant decline in corresponding activities, especially bread baking, in urban localities.

[6] Of the indicated totals for farm processing, grain processing amounted in 1928 to 1.5 to 2.1 and in 1937 to 1.2 to 1.7 billion rubles. Meat processing in 1928 was 2.2 and in 1937 0.7 billion rubles. The processing of other products therefore comes to 2.1 billion rubles in 1928 and 0.6 billion rubles in 1937. For grain, farm consumption in kind is estimated at 32.5 million tons in 1928 and 25.0 million tons in 1937. See Appendix C. On advice from Karcz, I reduce the 1928 figure to 29 million tons in order

Besides the foregoing products, Soviet households have engaged in diverse other processing activities for their own use. Although the contrary is sometimes suggested, the magnitudes involved in the case of distilling must have been relatively limited, but the scale of home processing no doubt rises appreciably if we also extend the accounting to include other aspects, particularly food preparation other than baking.

Home processing is the outstanding but hardly the only case where because of incomplete coverage of household productive activity "real" national income measurements may tend to be biased when a country undergoes industrialization. Almost inevitably such measurements usually also fail to cover in some degree diverse other productive activities of the household (for example, rural woodcutting and farm investment in kind), and as these dwindle in relative importance, "real" national income data necessarily are affected. Because of the long-standing interest of Soviet planners in relatively complete statistical reports, this feature probably is less important for the USSR than might have been supposed, but certainly here as elsewhere it is a factor, although, as always, it is a factor that is difficult to appraise quantitatively.

This still says nothing of the relative curtailment occurring under industrialization of still other household activities of a less tangible sort (for example, the housewife who goes to work has less time to devote to her children), but here particularly the student of national income is right to shrink from attempting a quantitative assessment. In any event, none will be attempted here.

Farm household processing for own consumption is related above to total household consumption and national income as calculated in this study in terms of ruble prices of 1937. The relative volume of farm household processing would rise if allowance were made for ruble price distortions. See chapters 9 and 10.

Lend-Lease; reparations. As calculated for 1944, gross national product

---

to exclude "return sales" to grain deficit areas that are omitted in 1937. Before the war, factory baking costs may have been on the order of 50 rubles and milling costs 20 rubles per ton of grain processed. See the data in A. K. Suchkov, *Dokhody gosudarstvennogo biudzheta SSSR,* Moscow, 1945, p. 41. Suchkov's figures refer to rye bread in the "third region" at an unspecified date, but probably are indicative of the magnitudes of interest here. For meat, farm consumption in kind amounted to 2.8 million tons of slaughter weight in 1928. The corresponding figure for 1937 was about 0.8 to 0.9 million tons. See Appendix C. Taking account of the illustrative cost data in G. C. Lazarovich, *Uchet i kal'kulatsiia na predpriatiiakh miasnoi promyshlennosti,* Moscow, 1952, pp. 79–84, and the trends in average money wages after 1937, processing costs may have been on the order of 800 rubles per ton of meat, slaughter weight.

Farm processing of wool, hides, flax, and oil seed is computed from the values of these products consumed in kind (Appendix C) and arbitrary coefficients on the average relation of fabricating to raw material costs in Soviet industry. On the latter, see M. V. Dmitriev, *Voprosy formirovaniia i snizheniia sebestoimosti produktsii v legkoi promyshlennosti,* Moscow, 1957, pp. 92, 178, 186, 198.

represents "disposable income" so far as it includes Western Lend-Lease aid to the USSR. My measures for postwar years also refer to "disposable income" since they include Soviet reparations receipts from ex-enemy countries. The concern at this point is to appraise the corresponding magnitude of national income domestically produced.

The United States exported to the USSR in 1944 3.5 billion dollars of goods on Lend-Lease account. Other Western countries supplied an additional half-billion of Lend-Lease aid to the USSR in the same year. In terms of Soviet prices of 1937, the total aid from all sources may have come to (say) 30 to 35 billion rubles. This is 10 to 12 percent of the gross national product of 1944 as computed. Income domestically produced, therefore, is correspondingly less. The translation of Lend-Lease from 1944 dollars to 1937 rubles necessarily is inexact.[7]

[7] To refer first to United States shipments, the totals for different commodities in 1944 (in billions of dollars) were: military exports, 1.060; machinery, scientific instruments, merchant ships, and freight cars, 0.714; automobiles et cetera, petroleum products, and other basic industrial goods, 0.837; foodstuffs and manufactured consumers' goods, 0.713; and other, including inedible vegetable oils, 0.134; the total is 3.457. See U.S. Department of Commerce, "United States Trade with Russia (USSR) During the War Years," *International Reference Service,* December 1945, p. 3.

Military exports are taken to amount to 6.5 billion 1937 rubles. In the Soviet budget for 1944, customs receipts totaled 24 to 26.5 billion rubles. Essentially, this seems to represent the value at which Lend-Lease imports totaling $4 billion was transferred to Soviet processors, distributors, and institutional consumers. See *SNIP-40–48,* pp. 43, 63, and Moorsteen, *Machinery.* The implied exchange rate of 6 rubles to one dollar is used arbitrarily to value "military exports" in terms of 1944 rubles. Munitions prices in 1944 were slightly below 1937. See Appendix E. Shipments of machinery, et cetera, are valued at 3.9 billion rubles in 1937 prices. The implied exchange rate of 5.4 rubles of 1937 to one dollar of 1944 is from Moorsteen, *Machinery.*

Shipments of autos et cetera, petroleum products, and other basic industrial goods, are first translated into United States dollars of 1950 on the basis of Bureau of Labor Statistics wholesale price indices. I compute the corresponding values in terms of 1950 rubles by reference to the ruble-dollar price ratios in N. Kaplan and W. L. White, "A Comparison of 1950 Wholesale Prices in Soviet and American Industry," The RAND Corporation, Research Memorandum RM-1443, May 1, 1955. The final total in 1937 rubles (7.5 billion) is obtained by reference to the index numbers of industrial wholesale prices in Abram Bergson, Roman Bernaut, and Lynn Turgeon, "Prices of Basic Industrial Products in the USSR, 1928–50," *Journal of Political Economy,* August 1956, and in Moorsteen, *Machinery.* The procedure used here to translate basic industrial goods into 1937 rubles is essentially the same as that used by Moorsteen to derive the implied exchange rate given above for machinery.

Bureau of Labor Statistics price indices indicate that shipments of foodstuffs and manufactured consumers' goods amounted to $1.124 billion in 1950 prices. This figure, which presumably represents wholesale values and to some extent partially processed goods, is felt to be equivalent to (say) $1.5 billion in terms of retail prices of processed goods. The corresponding magnitude in terms of 1950 rubles is 28 billion, the implied exchange rate of 19 to 1 being computed from data in N. Kaplan and E. S. Wainstein, "A Note on Ruble-Dollar Comparisons," *Journal of Political Economy,* December 1957. The total reduces to 12.6 billion rubles in terms of 1937 prices (see Appendix A), or to about 10.0 billion rubles in the same terms if trade margins and extra processing costs are omitted.

Miscellaneous United States shipments, including inedible vegetable oils, totaled

After the war, the Russians obtained reparations from Eastern Germany, Finland, Rumania, and Hungary. As far as very imperfect data permit judgment, the amounts shown in Table 21 were received during years studied here.

TABLE 21

Reparation Receipts, USSR, 1948–53

Year	U.S. 1938 dollars,[a] (millions)	Soviet 1937 rubles, at 10 rubles per 1938 dollar (billions)
1948	470	4.7
1949	440	4.4
1950	270	2.7
1951	280	2.8
1952	270	2.7
1953	210	2.1

[a] Totals for Rumania and Hungary are given in N. Spulber, *The Economics of Communist Eastern Europe*, New York, 1957, pp. 172, 182. For Eastern Germany and Finland, I rely on unpublished estimates compiled by Leon Smolinski chiefly from West German and Finnish sources.

Dollar prices of 1938 are translated into 1937 rubles at a rate of 10 to 1. This is suggested by the computations made on page 99 for Lend-Lease aid. As calculated, reparations account for two-thirds of one percent of the Soviet gross national product in 1950.

The cited figures omit various Soviet exactions, most importantly profits from the so-called joint stock companies in ex-enemy countries. Allowing for the profits from such companies in East Germany, Soviet revenues might rise by as much as 40 percent.

$0.134 billion. These shipments, together with non-United States Lend-Lease aid to Russia amounting to perhaps $0.600 billion, are taken to be worth 6.0 billion 1937 rubles. The implied exchange rate of eight 1937 rubles to one 1944 dollar obtains on the average for all other shipments.

Lend-Lease aid in 1944, thus, totals 34 billion 1937 rubles. To repeat, the Soviet government apparently transferred the aid to domestic organizations for 24 to 26.5 billion rubles. The discrepancy would be larger if allowance were made for price increases in the USSR from 1937 to 1944. What is the explanation? Probably there are several. The government transferred Lend-Lease goods to domestic organizations net of turnover taxes. My 1937 ruble data are gross of turnover taxes. Possibly the government's transfer prices were below the domestic prices of similar goods. Lend-Lease shipments to the USSR were still rising toward the end of the war. Because of the lag of Soviet imports behind Allied shipments, the former in 1944 presumably still fell short of the latter in the same year. Finally, my computations are in error.

PART III

NATIONAL INCOME IN ADJUSTED RUBLES

8

RUBLE PRICES VERSUS ADJUSTED FACTOR COST

Introduction

This part deals with the attempt to adjust for distortions in ruble prices the national income data set forth in previous pages. As was explained, two different approaches are employed. On the one hand, I take as a norm the adjusted factor cost standard of valuation pertinent to the appraisal of production potential (and perhaps also to welfare in terms of planners' preferences), and endeavor to adjust the national income data for major divergencies between ruble prices and this standard. On the other, for household consumption alone, I consider the effects of possible divergencies from the consumers' utility standard pertinent to the appraisal of welfare in terms of consumers' utilities. This chapter and chapter 9 deal with the former inquiry while the latter is the subject of chapter 10.

The task of this chapter in particular is to survey the relation of ruble prices to the adjusted factor cost standard. By appraising ruble prices from this standpoint, the discussion will provide the basis in chapter 9 for consideration of pertinent adjustments. The relation of ruble prices to adjusted factor cost was discussed in the SNIP studies, but a review will help make the present study relatively self-contained. The treatment accorded national income valuation in the SNIP studies has become the subject of a sizable literature, sometimes of a critical sort. The SNIP approach nevertheless still seems substantially valid to me, but in retracing previous steps on ruble price formation I shall also have an opportunity to express a somewhat changed standpoint. Comment on criticisms of the SNIP approach is also facilitated.[1]

The discussion of the relation of ruble prices to adjusted factor cost is involved, and may appear needlessly so when it is seen that the chief adjustments that are made in my national income data are after all of a familiar sort. Without reference to ruble price formation, however, the meaning of the adjusted figures might not be evident in Soviet circumstances. Moreover, so far as my previous treatment of the valuation problem has become controversial, what is in question, I believe, is not so much the nature of the adjustments as the interpretation of results.

The ruble price system has evolved to some extent in the course of time. We are especially interested here in the circumstances prevailing during our three base years, 1937, 1950, and 1928. In chapter 9 I shall focus primarily although not exclusively on the adjustment of national income figures that were compiled in terms of the prices of 1937. Hence, priority is properly accorded this year here as well.

Adjusted factor cost was formulated in chapter 3 in abstract terms. A more concrete definition of essentials will facilitate the survey of ruble prices from this standpoint:

[1] The most extensive critique to date of the *SNIP-37* approach to the Soviet national income valuation problem is that of Peter Wiles, "Are Adjusted Rubles Rational?" *Soviet Studies*, October 1955; "A Rejoinder to All and Sundry," *Soviet Studies*, October 1956.

Wiles's contributions in turn have already provoked numerous and diverse responses, including Joan Robinson, "Mr. Wiles' Rationality: A Comment," *Soviet Studies*, January 1956; Donald Hodgman, "Measuring Soviet Industrial Production: A Reply," *Soviet Studies*, July 1956; David Granick, "Are Adjusted Rubles Rational? A Comment," *Soviet Studies*, July 1956; John Montias, "Rational Prices and Marginal Costs in Soviet-Type Economies," *Soviet Studies*, April 1957; F. D. Holzman, "The Adjusted Factor Cost Standard of Measuring National Income: Comment," *Soviet Studies*, July 1957 .

The valuation procedures used in the SNIP studies have also been discussed in other writings. See Naum Jasny, "On the Wrong Track," *Soviet Studies*, July 1956; Michael Kaser, "Estimating Soviet National Income," *Economic Journal*, March 1957; and the reviews by F. Seton (*Review of Economics and Statistics*, November 1954); A. Nove (*Review of Economics and Statistics*, May 1955); and G. Grossman (*Journal of Political Economy*, October 1953; *American Economic Review*, June 1955).

Although the literature bearing on the "adjusted ruble" approach to Soviet national income valuation is voluminous, I believe interest centers on a relatively few analytic issues. It seems best for me to comment on the different views expressed at points in the present discussion where these issues are in question.

All commodity prices correspond to average cost. Costs are computed in terms of factor prices of a prescribed sort.

For capital, there is a net charge, "interest," corresponding to the average internal return on capital in the economy generally. The internal return is given by economies in costs realized through capital investments in different branches. There is, of course, no bar to a net charge for capital in the form of a residual income, "profits," but in this case "profits" are included in average cost. In addition to "interest" (or "profits"), there is a charge for "depreciation" determined in accord with conventional accounting principles.

The charge for land, "rent," corresponds on the average to the differential return to superior land. Similar charges are made for superior deposits in extractive industries.

As between occupations, the "wages" charged for labor tend on the average to correspond at one and the same time to differences in marginal productivities and to workers' transfer prices. For any given occupation "wages" may also vary as between industries to reflect workers' transfer prices between industries.

Similar principles apply to the relation of wages and farm incomes so far as the latter represent the rewards of labor rather than of capital or land.

Commodity prices are uniform within any market area.

In the section immediately following this, I shall consider in turn outstanding aspects of ruble price formation and ask in each case how the relation of ruble prices to adjusted factor cost is affected. I refer to features other than wages and farm incomes. In the two subsequent sections, the same sort of inquiry is made first in regard to wages and then in regard to farm incomes. Although much that is said applies generally, the discussion through these sections refers primarily to the period around 1937. In a final section, I discuss very briefly the relation of ruble prices to adjusted factor cost in 1950 and 1928.

Ruble Prices in General in 1937

Turnover taxes; subsidies. As in *SNIP-37,* so here, the notorious "turnover tax" (*nalog s oborota*) is classified as an outstanding cause of divergence between the ruble prices of 1937 and adjusted factor cost. In fact, it is by far the most important cause with which we must deal. If prices are to correspond to adjusted factor cost, necessarily there is no place for a "sales tax," understood as a budgetary charge against sales revenue based on the volume of sales rather than on the volume of employment of any particular factor. Although it has been levied in a variety of ways, the turnover tax clearly has been a sales tax in all variants. Thus, the tax has been charged variously as a flat percentage of selling price, a fixed absolute charge per unit of output, the difference between wholesale and retail prices after allowance for a standard trading margin, and so on.[2]

For purposes of national income valuation, only relative prices matter and not their general level. Hence, a sales tax need not cause any material divergence between market prices and adjusted factor cost if the tax is at a uniform rate on different commodities. The turnover tax rates of 1937, however, were by no means uniform. The variation was greatest between heavy industrial and consumers' goods, but the tax was also differentiated markedly within the latter category. The tax on coal and steel, for example, was 0.5 percent; and on most types of industrial machinery, 1.0 percent. At the same time, the tax on men's leather shoes, depending on the make, varied from 17 to 35 percent. For many types of cotton textiles, the tax at least during part of the year was 44 percent and often higher.

At the time studied, the turnover tax was levied in part on goods at a final stage of fabrication, but to a considerable extent it was also collected on raw materials and other "intermediate products." Taxes on coal and steel and (so far as they were used in further processing) textiles are examples, but there are also others, particularly petroleum and grain and other agricultural products. While sales taxes on final goods must cause a divergence between market prices and any factor cost valuation appropriate to the measurement of production potential, a question recently has been raised by J. L. Nicholson as to whether this is so in the case of taxes on "intermediate products." The issue posed is complex. Essentially, as seen here, some distinction is in order between "intermediate" and final products, but I believe I am right in thinking that for practical purposes the tax on intermediate products like one on final products is a source of divergence between market prices and an appropriate factor cost valuation. If this is so, we must also view a sales tax on intermediate products as causing a deviation of prices from adjusted factor cost. It follows too that we must treat in the same way the Soviet turnover tax, although to an important degree it is levied on intermediate products.[3]

[2] F. D. Holzman, *Soviet Taxation,* Cambridge, 1955, chap. iv and vi; A. K. Suchkov, *Dokhody gosudarstvennogo biudzheta SSSR,* Moscow, 1945, chap. ii, and the corresponding sections in the 1949, 1952, and 1955 editions of the same work.

[3] As seen by J. L. Nicholson ("National Income at Factor Cost or Market Price?" *Economic Journal,* June 1955, pp. 218 ff.), whether uniform or not, the sales tax on intermediate products is included in gross prices paid by producers who use the intermediate products. Under the circumstances, it is held, gross prices continue to correspond to the productivities of intermediate goods and hence to theoretic requirements. Nicholson is clearly right in reminding us to distinguish between final and intermediate goods

Granting that even when levied on intermediate products the turnover tax is not the same thing as a factor charge, it sometimes is suggested that in practice it may take the place of such a charge. At least, the tax serves partly to offset distortions in ruble prices due to limitations in Soviet practices in accounting for factor charges. In this way, it is held the turnover tax does not represent to its full extent a divergence from adjusted factor cost. This may be so, but it is just as well to proceed provisionally here without regard to this aspect. In practice, one distortion may always offset another, but this is a problem that is properly considered when we come to the adjustment of the national income data. I refer below, however, to one or two outstanding cases where the government may have consciously used the turnover tax as something of a surrogate for a factor charge.[4]

---

in this connection, but in the light of theoretic considerations set forth in chapter 3 I believe the matter is more complex than he assumes. For one thing, if taxes are levied on intermediate products the community tends to fall short of its production possibilities to begin with, that is, there may be an undue tendency to avoid many-stage processes in a given industry. If so, strictly speaking, neither gross nor net prices correspond to theoretic factor cost. For another, even if there is no significant inefficiency, the gross prices could not represent the underlying theoretic desideratum, the marginal rates of transformation between different products. This is seen at once if one considers that the gross prices could not indicate the rates at which the intermediate products themselves may be transformed into each other through transfers of labor and other factors.

At the same time, here, as on page 38, we must consider that there may only be limited possibilities of substitution between materials and other factors, whether by the short-cutting of stages or otherwise. One may be justified in assuming, therefore, that the shortfall from production possibilities is limited. If so, sales taxes on intermediate products seemingly may be viewed after all in the same way as sales taxes on final goods. Prices net rather than gross of such taxes tend to conform to the efficiency standard valuation.

In the foregoing I have tacitly followed Nicholson in directing my remarks primarily to a Western market economy. Evidently, however, what has been said applies equally to the "competitive solution" of socialist planning. (See A. Bergson, "Socialist Economics," in H. Ellis (ed.), *A Survey of Contemporary Economics.*) Moreover, the conclusion that sales taxes on intermediate products are, practically speaking, of a piece with those on final goods only seems to gain in force if reference is made to a socialist economy applying the Centralist Scheme, where among other things the prices of intermediate products are allowed to have only a limited influence on their allocation. Without probing very far into Soviet planning procedures, therefore, the conclusion also obtains for an economy such as the Soviet one.

In view of the foregoing, I am unable to agree with M. Kaser ("Estimating Soviet National Income," *Economic Journal,* March 1957) that the Soviet turnover tax is properly viewed as an element in a standard such as adjusted factor cost. Kaser follows Nicholson at this point.

If a sales tax on intermediate products is considered as a cause of divergence between prices and an appropriate factor cost valuation, even a uniform tax on such products can cause difficulties. This follows from differences in the extent to which different final goods are produced with marketed "intermediate" goods.

[4] In addition to the turnover tax, so-called, certain other levies were collected at the time studied which might be classified as sales taxes (for example, the tax on the "noncommodity operations" of organizations engaged in such things as custom repair work), but these are statistically of too little importance to be of concern here.

If adjusted factor cost bars sales taxes, it also bars a subsidy which permits operation at a price less than that corresponding to the charges for productive services. This too was a feature in the USSR at the time studied. Although no longer nearly as important in industry as they had been before the price reform of April 1936, subsidies still were paid in some basic industries in 1937. Furthermore, the government also granted subsidies to sectors other than industry. Among other things, under the complex accounting arrangements that obtained in the case of the government-owned machine-tractor stations, the income in kind that these agencies received for their services to collective farms was valued at nominal prices, but the government compensated the MTS for the resulting undervaluation. Since the MTS income finds its way into our accounts at the same nominal valuation as is used in Soviet accounts (actually, valuation is in terms of the very low prices the government paid the collective farms for obligatory deliveries), the corresponding compensation must be considered here as a form of subsidy. As for the turnover tax, so for subsidies, the possibility arises that a given payment might offset some other distortion in rubles prices, but again I pass by this complexity. Subsidies like turnover taxes are considered provisionally as representing to their full extent a divergence between ruble prices and adjusted factor cost.[5]

Profits; interest and depreciation; rent. Although the government has often subsidized industrial and other enterprises, under long-standing *khozraschet* rules already operative in 1937, prices supposedly are fixed ordinarily so as to cover all accounting charges for factors and at the same time to allow Soviet producers a "planned profit." What is the nature of this feature? The government's policy on the relation of prices to costs for nonsubsidized enterprises is yet to be studied systematically by Western scholars. Seemingly, at the time in question the government ultimately took part of any profits earned into the budget, but it allowed industry to retain part chiefly for purposes of meeting investment needs. Taking account of these requirements and also of the danger that "excessive" profits might weaken the *khozraschet* system, the government fixed prices so as to assure generally limited though varying "planned profits."

As will appear in chapter 10, retail prices around 1937 probably were fixed so as more or less to clear the market and limit demand to the available supply. The manner in which Soviet planners dealt financially with the resulting gaps between prices and costs is not entirely clear. Very likely, surplus revenues generally were absorbed into the budget

[5] On the accounting arrangements for the MTS and on subsidies generally, see chapter 2 and *SNIP-37,* pp. 13 ff., 57 ff., 114 ff., and 128 ff. See also the discussion of these topics in the other SNIP studies.

through varying turnover taxes, but to some extent these also accrued to the enterprise in the form of planned profits, and this category must be interpreted in this light. For basic industrial goods at the time studied, both "supply" and "demand" were determined directly in the plan, but under the *khozraschet* system enterprises have been expected to economize costs.

Given this, the government has often found it expedient to manipulate the prices of such goods to a limited extent in order to grapple with special "market situations," for example, at one time to encourage the use of ferrous metals in place of scarce nonferrous metals; at another to restrict the use of quality steel, and so on. Presumably, planned profits have been determined accordingly.

In sum, contrary to the view expressed in *SNIP-37*, at the time considered this category is by no means wholly arbitrary even from a theoretic standpoint. Nevertheless, we find no counterpart here to the factor charges called for by adjusted factor cost. Planned profits, therefore, represent another cause of divergence between ruble prices of 1937 and this standard.[6]

Under the *khozraschet* system, necessarily, there are also unplanned profits and losses due to deviations from the plan. So far as unplanned profits reflect superior administrative ability, they are in effect wages of management. Possibly, however, the unplanned profits are to be viewed partly as the counterpart of windfall gains under capitalism; if so, there is no place for them in adjusted factor cost.

Under *khozraschet,* the enterprise obtains most of its capital without payment of interest. Interest is paid on short-term loans supplied by the State Bank for seasonal and other special working capital needs, but for the rest the enterprise usually obtains investment funds either from the budget in the form of interest free grants or by reinvestment of earnings, in which case there is again no interest charge. Since profits evidently are not a surrogate, the lack of an interest charge means that prices here too have deviated from adjusted factor cost.[7]

Under *khozraschet,* the enterprise's costs include a charge for "depreciation." Ruble prices, therefore, reflect this charge. Professor Campbell confirms, however, what was suspected previously: Under conditions

[6] On planned profits and on Soviet price formation generally, see L. Maizenberg, *Tsenoobrazovanie v narodnom khoziaistve SSSR,* Moscow, 1953, and D. D. Kondrashev, *Tsenoobrazovanie v promyshlennosti SSSR,* Moscow, 1956. Both volumes were published only recently but much is said or implied regarding prewar arrangements.

[7] Although interest is charged on short-term loans, such charges are properly omitted from adjusted factor cost, since the services of the State Bank are essentially intermediate. The payments of the State Bank to primary factors, that is, essentially labor, are therefore included instead. This procedure seems the more in order since the State Bank apparently operates on the same *khozraschet* principles as economic enterprises generally.

of the five year plans the rates charged at the time studied tended to overestimate the service life of Soviet fixed assets.[8] The charges are understated the more since they are calculated in terms of original cost. Because of the price inflation under the five year plans, the corresponding allowances in terms of replacement cost would have been materially higher. Beyond this, asset values have also been understated somewhat because of the subsidization of certain construction work.

As I failed to consider in *SNIP-37,* the variation in costs among different enterprises in the same industry necessarily has posed an awkward problem for Soviet price fixing agencies, but I believe the solution for long has generally been the obvious one. Except where subsidies are resorted to, prices have been fixed to cover the average cost of and allow a profit to the entire industry. If (as sometimes has been the case) there are zonal prices, prices have been fixed in relation to the average cost of all enterprises in a given zone. At the same time, where the cost variation has been marked, by one device or another profits have often been redistributed within the industry so as to assure that different enterprises do not gain or lose unduly from circumstances beyond their control. This manner of dealing with cost variations, while perhaps objectionable from a more ultimate theoretic standpoint, evidently poses no problem here so far as it is applied to industry generally, but I believe the government has also applied it to extractive industries. Since in doing so, it has made no charge for the use of superior deposits, we must conclude that for extractive industries ruble prices have failed to reflect the rental charges that adjusted factor cost calls for.

This rather has been the procedure where operations were profitable at all. It remains to say that under its subsidy policy the government appears often to have favored extractive industries. Moreover, while after the price reform of April 1936 the government paid only limited subsidies to industry generally, it continued to make sizable grants of this sort to some extractive industries, particularly coal and lumber. The further implications as to the relation of prices and adjusted factor cost in 1937 are evident.

Among extractive industries, petroleum is a special case. Here, as elsewhere in 1937, prices appear to have been fixed in relation to average costs for enterprises generally (or in this case, for enterprises in a given region), but as an outstanding exception to the rule for basic industry, petroleum products were subject to sizable turnover taxes (for example, on the average in 1937, 71.8 percent for naphtha, 75.4 percent for kerosene, and 13.3 percent for lube oil). Possibly (as is sometimes suggested) such taxes in this case are something of a substitute for a factor charge, but

[8] Robert Campbell, "Depreciation in the Soviet Economy," *Quarterly Journal of Economics,* November 1956.

without further inquiry the degree to which the magnitudes involved are explicable in this light must be conjectural.[9]

Although land is public property in the USSR the government has made no systematic charge for its use in agriculture. As a result, some of the fruits of superior soil very likely have accrued to those who have tilled it, but under the complex agricultural procurement system prevailing under collectivization the government has tended to impose heavier burdens on more fertile and more favorably located areas.[10] In this way it has also extracted agricultural rent for its own use. Then too, the lack of any charge for land as such does not signify at all that the prices at which farm products are sold to consumers are correspondingly reduced. For agricultural raw materials, processors have paid to procurement agencies prices covering not only the latter's costs, including the prices paid farmers, but especially in the case of grain sizable turnover taxes.[11] The government has also levied at later stages additional turnover taxes on processed food stuffs and other turnover taxes on consumers' goods produced from agricultural raw materials. May we not consider the turnover tax, therefore, at least that levied on procurement agencies, as in effect agricultural rent? Here perhaps more than elsewhere the turnover tax seems akin to a factor charge, but it still is not such in the pertinent sense. Furthermore, as for petroleum one hesitates to assume that the tax on procurements corresponds in magnitude to the appropriate charges for rent.

Multiple prices. In order for prices to correspond to adjusted factor cost, they must be uniform within any given market area. A notable instance where this principle has been violated in the USSR already has been mentioned. Under the collective farm system, the government has paid diverse prices for its agricultural procurements including chiefly very low prices for obligatory deliveries and generally higher prices for additional deliveries made on a more or less voluntary basis.[12] But the concern in this study is not so much with procurements as with the ultimate disposition of raw materials, and from this standpoint the deviation

[9] Generalizations about any aspect of Soviet price formation are apt to be treacherous. Although what has been said about the government's method of dealing with cost variation I believe is broadly true of the times studied, very likely there were analytically interesting variants in addition to that for oil. At all events, this has been so in recent years.

On the policies followed in respect of cost variations among enterprises, see Maizenberg, *op. cit.*, pp. 122 ff.; Kondrashev, *op. cit.*, chap. iii. On recent Soviet practice see the last section of this chapter.

[10] *SNIP-37*, pp. 59 ff.; and Jerzy F. Karcz, "Soviet Agricultural Marketings and Prices, 1928–1954," The RAND Corporation, Research Memorandum RM-1930, July 2, 1957, Appendix A.

[11] On the relation between procurement prices and charges to processors, see also below.

[12] The Soviet agricultural procurement system under the five year plans is described in J. Karcz, *op. cit.*, Appendix A.

from adjusted factor cost seemingly has been of only limited consequence. In order to make *khozraschet* more meaningful, the government has sought to put different processors on a more or less equal footing in respect of raw materials costs, regardless of the manner of procurement. Thus, at the time studied a procurement agency that paid different prices for its purchases might nevertheless pass the produce on to processors at a single more or less average price. As was explained, the government has levied turnover taxes partly at the procurement stage. Where necessary, uniformity in price to processors might also have been achieved through differential taxes, or tax refunds. To a limited extent, before the war the government also absorbed the extra costs of high priced procurements through special appropriations under the budget item "Financing the National Economy." These appropriations are classified in this study as "Subsidies." [13]

Although the prices of agricultural raw materials generally were equalized, apparently there were exceptions; for example, in the case of leather, prices varied depending on whether supplies were obtained from procurement agencies or the meat industry. Furthermore, for purposes of stockpiling and export, grain and possibly other unprocessed agricultural goods before the war were sold to the agencies concerned at the same low prices the government paid farmers for obligatory deliveries.[14] To this extent, therefore, the ruble prices of 1937 still diverge from adjusted factor cost.

After meeting their obligations to the government and their own requirements, Soviet collective farmers have been free to dispose of their produce by selling it on the retail collective farm market. In this, since the early thirties the one free market in the USSR, prices necessarily have fluctuated, and depending on the availability of supplies in the government and cooperative retail shops they have often risen far above the official prices prevailing in the latter outlets. In 1937, however, the government and cooperative shops appear to have been able to meet demand at the official prices. (See chapter 10.) Accordingly, we need not reckon with multiple prices of any consequential sort at this point.

It sometimes is suggested that the ruble price system tends to "favor" the armed forces. Prices supposedly are systematically differentiated so as to reduce military procurement costs. The prices of munitions, of course, "benefit" like other nonconsumption goods from the uneven impact of turnover taxes and subsidies on different commodities. But what is in question here is whether, beyond this, the armed forces and defense

[13] See *SNIP-37*, p. 25, note 5, pp. 60–61; and A. K. Suchkov, *Dokhody gosudarstvennogo biudzheta SSSR*, Moscow, 1945, chap. ii; Suchkov, *Gosudarstvennye dokhody SSSR*, Moscow, 1952, chap. iv; Kondrashev, *op. cit.*, chap. ii.

[14] *SNIP-37*, p. 63.

industries might be able to buy on exceptionally favorable terms through special exemptions from, or special low rates of, the turnover tax, special subsidies, or other discriminating accounting arrangements.

Some examples of such favoritism have indeed been found (see p. 126) but these relate to an early year. For the period of the late thirties, with which we are now concerned, no evidence has been discovered in Soviet sources to suggest that such discrimination still was practiced. Rather, the available information is to the contrary.[15] A price handbook issued in 1940 by the procurement division of the Soviet air force lists petroleum prices which were the same as those given in other sources and which evidently applied in wholesale transactions generally. As for oil, so for grain and various other foods, the armed forces apparently paid the same prices, inclusive of the turnover tax, as wholesale consumers generally. The evidence on this matter is hardly conclusive, but I assume that discrimination of the sort in question was not an important cause of divergence between ruble prices in 1937 and adjusted factor cost.

Wage Differentials in 1937

Soviet wage differentials at the time studied are believed to have corresponded very broadly with the principles of the adjusted factor cost valuation. At this point, therefore, no serious distortion in ruble prices need be reckoned with.

Under socialism, wage differentials conceivably might tend to correspond to productivity and workers' transfer prices under diverse circumstances, but in actuality such a relation seems unlikely unless the following conditions prevail: "Wages," the charge for labor recorded as costs for the employing enterprise, represent at the same time incomes paid out to the workers. The employing enterprise or superior agencies seek systematically to economize money costs. An open market prevails for labor, that is, the worker is free to choose his occupation at the prevailing wage rates. The labor market operates effectively, in the sense that wage differentials vary in response to divergencies between the "demand" and "supply" of labor in the different occupations, as determined by the foregoing circumstances. As between industries, wage differentials are also adjusted so that the supply of labor in different industries tends to meet requirements.

The foregoing conditions concerning the labor market suffice to establish a relation between wages and productivity. For wages to correspond to transfer prices, there must also be an open market for consumers' goods. This has to operate effectively in the sense that at prevailing prices there

[15] See *SNIP-40-48*, pp. 62–63, the sources cited there, and in addition Suchkov, *Gosudarstvennye dokhody SSSR,* Moscow, 1952, pp. 85, 111.

are sufficient goods to meet the demand. As is explained subsequently, these conditions probably were approached in the Soviet Union around 1937. The occupational choices pertinent to wage differentials at any time presumably also reflect circumstances of earlier periods. For this reason, we must consider that in the USSR the open market that prevailed in 1937 had been established only in 1935 and 1936. Prior to these years and indeed from the beginnings of the First Five Year Plan the government distributed consumers' goods to Soviet households primarily through a system of rationing. In determining rations, however, the government systematically discriminated in favor of the more important industries and plants and also the more productive workers. Also, even during the rationing period there was an open market of limited dimensions in the form of the retail collective farm market and also the so-called government commercial shops, where goods were sold in unlimited amounts at high prices.[16] All in all, I am not inclined to attach much weight to the difficulties posed for an adjusted factor cost valuation at this point.

As to the organization of the Soviet labor market, I believe the most essential facts are these:

I have referred often to the *khozraschet* system, according to which the enterprise keeps records in monetary terms of the charges for different factors and the proceeds from sales.[17] One of the charges is that for labor. Moreover, the individual enterprise is expected to economize costs, and premiums are paid to managerial staff in dependence on the economies achieved. At all levels of the planning system, cost reduction is a basis for appraising success.

Under the five year plans, financial controls nevertheless have tended to be lax. Consequently, enterprise managers have often been encouraged to fulfill and overfulfill production targets with only limited regard to costs. Where the financial controls have been at all effective, however, the concern for cost economy presumably has been reinforced by the concern to fulfill and overfulfill the production targets.

The wages charged as costs are paid out to workers as income. Although there is an income tax, until the war for most workers this was very limited in magnitude and only mildly progressive.[18] Moreover, the government introduced a variety of labor controls in 1940, but during practically the entire interwar period until that time there was an open market for labor. Beginning under the First Five Year Plan the government attempted in various ways to restrict the extraordinary labor turn-

[16] Abram Bergson, *The Structure of Soviet Wages,* Cambridge, 1944, pp. 33 ff.

[17] In addition to the sources cited in note 3 of chapter 2, see David Granick, *Management of the Industrial Firm in the USSR,* New York, 1954, particularly chaps. ix to xi; J. S. Berliner, *Factory and Manager in the USSR,* Cambridge, 1957; G. Bienstock et al., *Management in Russian Industry and Agriculture,* New York, 1944, chaps. vi to viii.

[18] Bergson, *op. cit.,* pp. 33 ff.

over, but at least for a time with only limited effect, and while it also took some steps toward labor direction these affected principally only recent graduates of universities, technicums, and factory-apprentice schools. During most of the thirties, therefore, the Soviet worker was largely free to choose his occupation and place of employment at the established wages.[19]

At the time studied, wages were differentiated on much the same basis as under capitalism. Generally, higher wages were paid for more arduous, more complex, and more responsible jobs. On January 1, 1938, 75 percent of the wage earners in "large-scale" industry had their earnings determined by a piece work system of one kind or another.[20] Wage differentials prevailing in the Soviet Union before the war were comparable in magnitude to those prevailing in Tsarist Russia and possibly also in the United States.[21]

Reference is primarily to the differences in wages as between occupations. As between industries, trends in differentials are still to be systematically explored. In terms of the ranking of different industries and the magnitudes involved, such wage differentials on the eve of the five year plans I suspect were again broadly similar to those obtaining under Tsarism. Subsequently, the government revised interindustry wage relations mainly in the interests of industrialization. Most importantly, earnings in basic industries generally tended to increase in relation to those elsewhere.

Essentially, I have repeated here an argument advanced originally in *SNIP-37* and subsequently challenged vigorously by Peter Wiles. For reasons noted, I believe Wiles's objections to my interpretation of ruble wages stem chiefly from a misapprehension regarding the valuation requirements for appraisal of production potential. The limitations for purposes of welfare appraisal, however, of any national income data compiled in terms of ruble wages no doubt are rightly underlined.

Mr. Wiles's critique of "adjusted rubles"[22] is not always easy to follow. Regarding wages, the main contention, I believe, is that, owing to inefficiencies in Soviet planning, ruble wage differentials between industries fail to correspond to differences in marginal value productivity, if the valuation is supposed to be given by consumers' utilities. Also, in Wiles's view, a divergence seemingly persists even if the valuation is supposed to be instead in terms of planners' preferences. Soviet resource allocation is a large and still only partially explored subject, but obviously as Wiles contends interindustrial wage differentials under the five year

[19] See *ibid.*, pp. 143 ff. For another view that stresses the effectiveness of the early controls more than I think is in order, see Solomon Schwarz, *Labor in the Soviet Union*, New York, 1951, chap. iii.

[20] Bergson, *op. cit.*, particularly chaps. xi and xii.

[21] *Ibid.*, chaps. v to viii.

[22] Peter Wiles, "Are Adjusted Rubles Rational?" and "A Rejoinder to All and Sundry," *Soviet Studies* (Oct. 1955, Oct. 1956, respectively).

plans have deviated from differences in marginal value productivities where the valuation is in terms of consumers' utilities. Wiles is less persuasive where planners' preferences are in question, but no doubt there is some divergence from this standpoint as well. As Wiles apparently fails to consider, however, a correspondence of interindustrial wage differentials to differences in marginal value productivity is actually inessential for valuation in terms of adjusted factor cost. For such a valuation, wage differentials within an industry must correspond on the average to relative physical productivities. Both within and between industries they should tend also to reflect workers' transfer prices, but to repeat between industries they need not correspond to differences in marginal value productivities. As Wiles rightly observes, *SNIP-37* fails to establish that ruble wages meet the latter requirement, and this might be said equally of the present work, but in both studies, such a result is neither needed nor assumed.

While in *SNIP-37,* and again here, adjusted factor cost is accepted as a yardstick, the more ultimate desideratum is a theoretically meaningful valuation, and Wiles's criticism must be considered further from this standpoint. Although not entirely explicit, Wiles apparently feels that a lack of correspondence of wage differentials between industries to differences in marginal value productivity is fatal to any attempt at meaningful national income valuation. At least, this is so if the valuation is in terms of any factor cost inclusive of prevailing wages. My answer must be read in conjunction with chapter 3 of this volume. If interindustrial wage differentials fail to conform to differences in marginal value productivity, admittedly a factor cost that is inclusive of such wages must also fail to this extent to conform to the welfare standard. At least this is so unless there are offsetting distortions. If the divergence occurs when productivity is valued in terms of consumers' utilities, the factor cost valuation deviates correspondingly from that called for by the welfare standard defined in the same terms. If the divergence occurs when the valuation is in terms of planners' preferences, the factor cost valuation deviates from that called for by the welfare standard defined in these terms.

On the other hand, a factor cost valuation ordinarily is used where the concern is primarily to measure production potential. Such was the case in *SNIP-37* and is again so here. What is implied in this case? As Wiles seemingly fails to perceive, nothing at all. For purposes of the efficiency standard valuation, the prices finally used to value different commodities must measure marginal rates of transformation. This is fully achieved if the prices correspond to marginal costs. There is no further requirement that the prices that correspond to marginal costs also correspond to marginal utilities or planners' preferences. If the latter relation obtains, this is to the good so far as it permits welfare appraisal, but for purposes of measuring production potential, it is inessential.

The theoretic requirements regarding wages in particular are to be viewed in this light. Wage differentials within any industry must be proportional to marginal productivities. Both within and between industries, wages must correspond to workers' transfer prices. But there is no need at all for wage differentials between industries to correspond also to differences in marginal value productivity. Such a correspondence again is pertinent to the appraisal of welfare but not production potential.

This is one way to formulate the theoretic requirements. It may be of value to put them also in other terms. Within any industry, workers in different occupations are combined so that production takes place at minimum wage cost. There is also no opportunity for workers to improve their lot by changing occupations. As between industries, wage differentials are such as to induce workers to enter different industries in the required numbers. The required numbers depend on the "bill of goods," but the latter need not conform to either consumers' utilities or planners' preferences.

While stressing the divergence of ruble interindustrial wage differentials from marginal value productivities, Wiles, I believe, considers Soviet relative wages to be "irrational" generally. In elaboration, he cites three specific cases. First, the high wages used to induce workers to move to the North and East. The irrationality here arises from the fact that the government's emphasis on the development of the North and East is assertedly uneconomic to begin with. Seemingly what is in question here is a divergence between interregional wage differentials and marginal value productivities. If so, what has been said already on this aspect I believe sufficiently covers this matter. Second, penal labor. I agree that this represents a departure even from adjusted factor cost, although the magnitudes involved probably are not as consequential as might be supposed (see chapter 7). Third, the comparative "real" incomes of industrial and agricultural workers. The "drift from the land has reached frightening proportions, and there is a serious food crisis." A divergence between interindustrial money income differentials and marginal value productivities again seems to be in question here, but I refer below to the special problem of the comparative "real" incomes of industrial and agricultural workers and my reaction to Wiles on this aspect will be evident from what is said there.

In Wiles's view, data showing the inequality of earnings within industries in the USSR to be comparable to that under capitalism must be discounted as evidence that intraindustrial differentials reflect "scarcity relations." I agree that such evidence taken by itself is not especially decisive, but it surely is illuminating when read together with the known facts regarding Soviet wage administration, including the extensive use of piece work and the systematic differentiation of wages according to arduousness, complexity, responsibility, and the like.

For Wiles, the failure to produce relative outputs conforming to consumers' utilities or even to planners' preferences means that resource allocation is essentially "irrational," but the "irrationality" does not end with relative outputs. Wiles is also concerned with methods of production. In terms used here, the community fails to realize production possibilities. In *SNIP-37,* and again here, an attempt is made to allow for the possibility of a significant shortfall from production possibilities. Essentially it is on this account that reference is made to adjusted factor cost rather than to the theoretically ideal efficiency standard. For this reason, the failure to realize production possibilities poses no further problem for us to consider at this point.[23]

Incidentally, Wiles often tends to use "rationality" in a special sense. Apparently, although planners' preferences may be controlling, the failure to produce a bill of goods in accord with consumers' wants is in itself sufficient ground to brand a system "irrational." Wiles is privileged to use this word as he sees fit, but one is entitled to demur against the possible implication that national income data designed to measure welfare are legitimately compiled only in terms of the consumers' utilities variant of the welfare standard.[24]

[23] David Granick, "Are Adjusted Rubles Rational? A Comment," *Soviet Studies,* July 1956.

[24] Donald Hodgman, "Measuring Soviet Industrial Production: A Reply," *Soviet Studies,* July 1956.

Farm Incomes in 1937

The relation between ruble prices and adjusted factor cost in respect of Soviet farm incomes is difficult to appraise. Although this question is seen here in much the same way as in my earlier study, a review will allow me to treat it somewhat more completely than was done previously as well as to take account of revised data.

Since farm income is partly in kind, it is useful to consider separately farm "real" income and farm income in monetary terms. To refer first to farm "real" income, the adjusted factor cost valuation requires that this tend to be the same as the "real" income earned elsewhere by persons of comparable skill. Or rather, this is so if allowance is made for the relative attractions of different fields of work. Available data set forth below are suggestive although hardly conclusive that this may have been broadly true in 1937. At any rate, no basis is found for the familiar assumption that the Soviet government systematically discriminated against the farmer and in favor of the industrial worker. The year studied was a relatively prosperous one for the Soviet farmers. Hence, the finding does not necessarily apply to other periods, but for the moment the circumstances of 1937 are primarily of interest.

Soviet collective farmers in 1937 worked some 33 million man-years on and off the farm. For this, they earned these sums: money payments to collective farmers on a labor day basis, salaries of collective farm executives, and premiums, 7.3 billion rubles; net money income from sale of farm produce, 13.5; income in kind at farm prices, 25.2; and earnings from outside work, 6.7. This totals 52.7 billion rubles. In other words, the collective farmers averaged some 1,600 rubles per man-year. This is a theoretic full-time man-year of 280 days. In fact, able-bodied male collective farmers worked on the average about 270 days in 1937, or somewhat less than the theoretic full-time man-year. The cited figure on collective farm employment is derived from diverse Soviet farm employment statistics. The latter in turn are based on collective farm annual accounts and sample studies. Obviously a calculation of this sort cannot be especially exact.[25]

[25] More precisely, collective farmers are estimated to have worked 32.8 million man-years in 1937. Of this total some 22.5 million man-years were devoted to work on the collective farm, 8.0 million man-years to work on the collective farm subsidiary plot, and 2.3 million man-years to work off the farm. See Appendix K and *SNIP-37,* pp. 146–148.

Soviet households engaged in agriculture in 1937 earned some 15.1 billion rubles from sales of their produce. This was net of their money production expenses. They also retained for their own consumption or for farm investment 28.0 billion rubles of produce, at average realized farm prices. See *SNIP-28–48.* The households in question include not only collective farmers but independent peasants and also wage earners in diverse fields who operated commercial gardens as a secondary occupation. Following *SNIP-37,*

As calculated, collective farm earnings include income in kind valued at average realized farm prices. For purposes of an appraisal of comparative "real" incomes on the farm and elsewhere (although, as I shall explain in a moment, not for purposes of valuation in terms of adjusted factor cost), farm income in kind is more appropriately valued at the retail prices paid by urban workers, or at least at such retail prices less home processing costs. Reflecting the extraordinary turnover taxes, retail prices tend to be far higher than average realized farm prices. As to the magnitudes involved, an alternative computation in terms of urban collective farm market prices is indicative. Collective farm market prices in urban localities in 1937 may have been more or less comparable to the official prices charged for similar goods in the government and cooperative retail shops (see chapter 10). In terms of collective farm market prices, the income in kind of collective farmers rises from 25 to (say) 79 billion rubles.[26] Assuming that home processing costs on produce sold in the collective farm market averaged (say) 5 to 10 percent of the selling price, collective farm income averages about 3,000 rubles per man-year.

Soviet industrial workers in 1937 earned an average wage of 3,005 rubles. This refers to all employees; for ordinary workers of a rank below foreman the corresponding figure was 2,820 rubles.[27] These figures, based on current Soviet statistical reports, are not entirely comprehensive in respect of either the labor force or wage payments. For industrial workers, however, average wages probably are not understated by more than a few percent on this account.

In the late 1930's, the government and cooperative retail network charged, in rural localities, prices for consumers' goods that were perhaps a few percent higher than those charged in urban localities.[28] Food stuffs probably sold at an appreciable discount at rural farm markets. The comparative availability of goods in rural and urban retail shops is not known. The Soviet consumers' goods market generally appears to have functioned effectively in 1937 (see chapter 10).

My figures on both rural and urban incomes omit imputed rents of

---

p. 147, I assume in the text that 90 percent of the total net income in money and in kind accrued to collective farmers. Although the computation on which this percentage is based has been criticized, it should be roughly correct.

Earnings of collective farmers from outside work are from *SNIP-37*, p. 147.

[26] In terms of collective farm market prices, the income in kind of all farm households totaled an estimated 78.3 billion rubles. See Appendix C. This excludes farm investment in kind. Inclusive of the latter, the income in kind of all farm households rises to (say) 88.0 billion rubles. As before, 90 percent of the total is taken to accrue to collective farmers.

[27] *TPP*, pp. 228–229. In Soviet statistics, industry includes manufacturing, mining, and electric power generation.

[28] *SNIP-37*, p. 70.

owner-occupied housing. Owner occupancy was far more important in the country than the city. In a complete account it would be necessary not only to consider owner occupancy but to revalue urban rental housing. The government charges only very low rates for the latter. But in view of the proverbial shortage of housing in the cities under the five year plans, it is questionable whether the industrial worker could have enjoyed any great margin of superiority over the farmer at this point.

Reference has been to "real" income per man-year. I must leave to separate inquiry the related question of the relation of city and country "real" income per capita. Very likely, as is commonly assumed, the city enjoyed a distinct margin of superiority in this regard in the late thirties. Nevertheless, if "real" income per man-year in agriculture did indeed compare favorably with that in industry, this would tend to make understandable otherwise puzzling features of the Soviet labor market. In the thirties, farmers as well as industrial workers enjoyed substantial freedom of choice as to occupation. Among other things, the farmer was more or less free to decide whether to go to the city or not. Moreover, the unemployment that prevailed in the cities in the late twenties was liquidated in the First Five Year Plan and did not reappear thereafter. Such developments might be expected if we may rule out any marked inferiority of rural compared with urban "real" incomes, but not otherwise. Of course, "overt" unemployment in the cities might possibly have been supplanted by "disguised" unemployment in the country. At the prevailing differentials, farmers may have preferred to go to the city but hesitated to do so nevertheless because of the lack of openings there. Such disguised unemployment, however, seems unlikely to have assumed significant dimensions if there were not also an appreciable amount of "overt" unemployment as well. Also, the indications are that, to the contrary, industry was not able to meet its labor recruitment quotas toward the end of the Second Five Year Plan.[29] Possibly the prevailing income differentials were inadequate even to maintain the flow of labor from country to city.

Although the farmer enjoyed considerable freedom of choice of occupation in the thirties, especially in the earlier years, the government found it expedient not to limit themselves to the offering of material induce-

[29] M. Sonin and B. Miroshnichenko, *Podbor i obuchenie rabochikh kadrov v promyshlennosti,* Moscow, 1944, p. 4; S. Trubnikov, "Istochniki komplektovaniia rabochei sily v SSSR," *PE,* 1936, no. 6, p. 150; Schwarz, *op. cit.* p. 61.

In the circumstances of the time studied, I have been unable to find any basis for Wiles's contention that "the drift from the land has reached frightening proportions" ("Are Adjusted Rubles Rational?"). Possibly Wiles had in mind a later date than 1937, although I am unaware that there has been an inordinate drift of the sort he supposes even in recent years.

ments in order to meet industrial labor quotas.[30] Nevertheless, so far as forms of compulsion were used to this end, this tends only to reinforce the conclusions already reached as to the possible inadequacy of material inducements, but the circumstances of the First Five Year Plan and immediately after were very special, and the experience of this period can have little application to later years. Of more interest here perhaps are the labor controls introduced in 1940. These included a draft of urban and farm youths for vocational training and subsequent administrative allocation to industry. But in view of the international situation, circumstances are again complex and interpretation is difficult.[31]

I have compared the "real" incomes of the collective farmer with those of industrial workers. The former compare no less favorably with the "real" incomes of the employees of state farms and the government-owned MTS. Read together with the calculations made above regarding collective farm incomes, the average money earnings of the state farm and MTS workers are an indication.[32] In 1935, average earnings in all government agricultural institutions were 1,566 rubles; in state farms, 1,452 rubles; and in machine-tractor stations, 2,290 rubles. In 1937, average earnings in all government agricultural institutions were 2,121 rubles; figures for state farms and machine-tractor stations are not available. Soviet wage data for state farm employees, however, do not include appreciable supplements to money wages derived from the operation of garden plots. Similarly the reported earnings of MTS employees may or may not include some supplemental income received from the collective farm.[33]

For valuation in terms of adjusted factor cost, farm "real" incomes, so far as they represent labor earnings, must be comparable to the "real" incomes earned by similar skills elsewhere. As mentioned above, Soviet collective farm incomes include some differential rent. They must also include a return on the collective farmers' own capital investments. It would serve little purpose, however, to try to pursue these complexities further here. Hence they are passed by in what follows.

So much for farm "real" income. In monetary terms, as we have already seen, the average collective farmer earned in 1937 1,600 rubles a man-year, or but 60 percent of the annual earnings of the ordinary

[30] Bergson, *op. cit.*, pp. 143 ff.; Schwarz, *op. cit.*, pp. 53 ff.

[31] On the possible rationale of the 1940 legislation, see *SNIP-37,* pp. 72–73.

[32] TSUNKHU, *Trud v SSSR,* 1936 ed., pp. 16–17; *TPP,* pp. 228–229.

[33] In his review of *SNIP-37* (*Journal of Political Economy,* October 1953), Professor Gregory Grossman suggests that the labor services of collective farmers be valued at the average wage of state farm employees. Considering the relatively limited number of the latter workers, as a rule one might hesitate to proceed on this basis, but seemingly for 1937 the resulting value of collective farm labor services might not differ very much from that given them in my calculations.

industrial worker. If we are to adhere in this study to the convention that farm income in kind is to be valued at average realized farm prices, some differential between farm and city money incomes is unavoidable, but the differential is here greater than it might be otherwise so far as in the USSR farm prices differ from urban retail prices not only because of such familiar aspects as transportation, processing, and distribution costs, but because of the notably high turnover taxes on food products. As calculated here, average farm realized prices reflect the high prices realized on sales in the retail collective farm market as well as the low prices obtained on deliveries to the government procurement agencies, but even so we must conclude, I think, that in relation to the services of industrial workers, those of farmers must be undervalued in our accounts.

Granting this, there is perhaps some danger of our being overly logical at this point. While in monetary terms farm incomes are found here to be relatively low, they, I believe, are by no means inordinately so by Western standards. In the United States in 1929, for example, farm money incomes averaged $580 a man-year, or less than 40 percent of the corresponding figure for the employee in manufacturing and mining.[34] Very likely, the moral is that farm labor services are also undervalued in Western countries, and anyhow it must be reckoned that because of the notably rapid tempo of industrialization in the USSR any undervaluation of farm labor services may affect measurements of "real" national income more for that country than elsewhere. But all things considered it may be permissible not to concern ourselves especially with the limitation of ruble prices disclosed at this point. In any event when we come to consider the implications for our calculations of different divergencies of ruble prices from adjusted factor cost, I propose to refer among other things to the incidence of the omission of any systematic charge for agricultural rent. From what is said on this score, the reader will also be able to judge the possible effect of the undervaluation of farm labor services as well.

Curiously, even with the inclusion of rent, farm income per man-year in the United States still averages little more than 55 percent of the average wage in manufacturing and mining. It will still be in order nonetheless to consider the effect on my results for the USSR of the omission of a charge for agricultural rent.[35]

[34] See D. Gale Johnson, "Allocation of Agricultural Income," *Journal of Farm Economics,* November 1948; U. S. Department of Commerce, *National Income, 1954 Edition,* pp. 200, 202.

[35] The foregoing discussion of Soviet farm income it is hoped may clear up some misunderstandings insofar as it makes more explicit than was done in *SNIP-37* that the adjusted factor cost valuation poses requirements regarding farm income in monetary as well as in "real" terms. Also, farm income in kind is here valued initially in current rubles, while in *SNIP-37* it was valued at once in "adjusted rubles."

Ruble Prices in 1950 and 1928

1950: The Soviet price system of 1950, I believe, was much the same as that of the late thirties. For the most part, therefore, what was said about the relation of ruble prices to adjusted factor cost in 1937 applies here as well. On the other hand, there were some interesting differences, and these too must be considered in appraising ruble prices from this standpoint. Essentially, in 1950 as in the earlier year, the turnover tax was an outstanding feature. The rate schedule for 1950 has not been published. No doubt the rates on different commodities still varied widely as they did before the war. In fact, except for oil products and electric power, the government beginning in 1949 ceased altogether to levy the tax on heavy industrial goods. Since in the economy generally the tax was levied at about the same average rate as in 1937, the discrimination against consumers' goods may, if anything, have been even more marked than before.[36] In 1950 as in 1937 the government granted very limited subsidies to economic enterprises. Such grants had been large indeed during and after the war, but through a price reform of January 1949 the government had again been able to curtail this form of aid sharply.

As previously, so in 1950, where enterprises earned profits such revenues generally cannot be identified with factor charges. Also, there was still no charge for interest on fixed capital. Conditions favorable to an understatement of depreciation in the late thirties were also still operative in 1950. As before the war, prices generally seem to have been fixed in relation to average branch cost, even in extractive industries. On the other hand, there were some interesting variants, and the oil industry aside, some use seemingly was made of rent-like charges.[37] Soviet practice in respect of agricultural rent at the time now in question I believe had

[36] On the turnover tax in 1950, see the sources cited in note 2 of this chapter. See also chapter 10.

[37] I refer particularly to lumbering. In this branch the government had instituted in 1949 the practice of charging differential "stumpage fees" (*popennye platy*). Since these were intended to equalize the position of different lumbering sites, they apparently represent in some measure a rental charge of the sort included in adjusted factor cost.

There were also interesting special cases outside of extraction. In connection with the preparatory work for the price reform of January 1949, for example, a calculation reportedly was made to determine how much higher electric power prices would have to be in order to assure profitability to electric power enterprises generally and not merely to those of average or superior efficiency. The Soviet source fails to indicate, however, whether the higher prices were actually established. The reader may judge for himself the possible import of the indicated practice for the relation of prices to adjusted factor cost.

On the government policies in respect of cost variations among enterprises, see the sources cited in notes 9, 10, and 11.

not changed in essentials from that previously described. This is true also in respect of multiple prices.

The government appears to have pursued the same policy on wage differentials since the war as it did in the late thirties. Nevertheless, in appraising the relation of wages to adjusted factor cost in 1950 we must consider that the postwar wage structure has still to be studied systematically. Moreover, diverse regulations restricting the workers' choice of occupation and place of work that had been introduced in 1940 were still on the books a decade later, although apparently often without being enforced.[38] The comparative trends in the "real" incomes of collective farmers and industrial workers from 1937 to 1950 are difficult to judge. Probably there was no very marked change one way or the other. So far as farm labor incomes conform to adjusted factor cost in 1937, therefore, broadly speaking they probably continue to do so in 1950. From 1937 to 1950, however, farm incomes in monetary terms may well have declined in relation to those in industry.[39]

1928: As in later years, ruble prices on the eve of the plans sometimes diverged from and sometimes conformed to adjusted factor cost. Whether in the upshot the degree of conformity was greater or less in 1928 than in 1937 is difficult to say, although no doubt (as is commonly supposed) the price system was more "meaningful" in the earlier year than it often was to be under the plans. Ruble price formation on the eve of the plans has so far been studied little by Western scholars, and hence is not easily appraised here.[40] The turnover tax, so called, had not yet been introduced in 1928 (and was not to be until 1930), but the government was collecting at this time a variety of levies which the turnover tax was to supplant. Among these, several were sales taxes. Accordingly, we must again reckon with a divergence from adjusted factor cost at this point. Most importantly, the "excise tax" (*aktsiz*), which was levied at diverse rates on a number of manufactured consumers' goods, processed foodstuffs and beverages, clearly was a sales tax, and so too, seemingly, was the "business tax" (*promyslovyi nalog*). The latter was levied pri-

[38] Emily C. Brown, "The Soviet Labor Market," *Industrial and Labor Relations Review,* January 1957.

[39] On the comparative trends in farm and industrial "real" incomes from 1937 to 1950, see chapter 13. As to the relative changes in money incomes, from data compiled here and in *SNIP-49-55* we may calculate that, in return for work on the farm, collective farm households earned in 1950 somewhat more than 100 billion rubles. This includes income in kind valued at average realized farm prices. I again assume that 90 percent of the net income from sales of farm produce and of the farm income in kind earned by all farm households accrues to collective farmers. By implication, collective farmers earned about 3,200 rubles per man-year, or twice the corresponding 1937 figure. See Appendix K. In industry, average wages in 1950 were an estimated 273 percent of 1937. See Appendix H.

[40] Appraisal here nevertheless is much facilitated by Dr. Oleg Hoeffding's brief survey in *SNIP-28,* chap. iii.

marily as a percentage of the gross revenues of economic enterprises. To some extent, however, the "business tax" also had the character of a license fee.[41]

The government granted some subsidies to economic enterprises in 1928, but by the standards of the five year plans these were inconsequential.[42] The precise economic nature of such profits as were earned nevertheless is obscure, but as for 1937, it is generally difficult to identify them with a factor charge of the sort called for by adjusted factor cost. In contrast to 1937, the government seems often to have charged public enterprises interest on fixed capital investments, but in the aggregate such charges amounted to only a fraction of 1 percent of the public sector's stock of fixed capital.[43] A divergence from adjusted factor cost, therefore, arises here as well. On the other hand, the sharp inflation that was to undermine Soviet depreciation accounting under the five year plans had not yet become a factor in 1928. For this reason, depreciation charges more nearly conformed to adjusted factor cost in the earlier year than they would later. As far as is known, the government in 1928, as in later years, made no systematic charge for rent in extractive industries.

On the eve of the five year plans, Soviet agriculture still was predominantly in the hands of individual peasants. At the prevailing farm prices, a question is in order nevertheless whether the farmers generally were able to earn any rent on the land they tilled. In fact, as will appear, farm incomes may have been deficient even when viewed as a return to labor services alone.

Prior to collectivization, the peasants sold the bulk of their produce to government agencies at broadly uniform prices but they also sold some products to private middlemen and households at prices which often far exceeded those on sales to official agencies.[44] Such multiple prices must have reflected differences in conditions of sale (for example, bulk purchases at a procurement point versus retail sales at a bazaar), but possibly they often represented some divergence from adjusted factor cost. Although peasant bazaar prices were higher than those realized on sales to government agencies, the "purchasing power of the ruble" for rural workers reportedly was 35 percent greater than for those in urban localities.[45] One inevitably wonders at the economic meaning of this aspect, too. In any event, a breach with adjusted factor cost clearly

[41] On the Soviet tax system on the eve of the five year plans, see *SNIP-28*, pp. 49 ff., and F. D. Holzman, *Soviet Taxation*, Cambridge, 1955, chap. 5.

[42] *SNIP-28*, p. 55.

[43] *SNIP-28*, p. 60.

[44] Jerzy F. Karcz, "Soviet Agricultural Marketings and Prices, 1928–1954," The RAND Corporation, Research Memorandum RM-1930, July 2, 1957, pp. 59 ff.

[45] On the Soviet retail market on the eve of the plans, see chapter 10.

occurs in the urban retail market so far as, because of the growing shortages, the private traders who still functioned on the eve of the plan were able to charge premia above prices prevailing in government and cooperative shops. Multiple prices are also encountered in the industrial sphere, although it is doubtful they are very consequential. Among other things, in contrast to the situation in the late thirties, the government, in fixing prices, sometimes discriminated in favor of the armed forces.[46]

Broadly speaking, Soviet wage differentials on the eve of the plans already were determined in accord with principles such as I have described as prevailing in later years. Although differentials in 1928 bore the imprint of equalitarian policies adopted by the seventh congress of trade unions in December 1926, the leveling that had occurred was very limited.[47] On the eve of the plans as in 1937, I believe wage differentials conform sufficiently well to adjusted factor cost.

If, as has been argued, rural "real" incomes per man-year in 1937 tended to match those in the city, this probably represented a distinct relative improvement in the lot of the farmer in comparison with the situation on the eve of the five year plans. One wonders nevertheless whether the apparent relative inferiority in the position of the peasants' status in 1928 in comparison with 1937 may not have reflected some differences in relative skills, but if we continue as before to take the circumstances of the later year as a benchmark, we must reckon I think with the possibility of some undervaluation of peasants' services at this point. If rural retail prices were also "too" low, in monetary terms the undervaluation would be compounded.[48]

[46] In 1928, the armed forces were allowed a special discount of 5 percent from the going price of Donets coal. See Lynn Turgeon, under the direction of Abram Bergson, "Prices of Coal and Peat in the Soviet Union, 1928–1950," The RAND Corporation, Research Memorandum RM-1423, February 2, 1955, p. 11. In the same year, "privileged consumers" received discounts from the going price of steel. See N. Jasny, *Soviet Prices of Producers' Goods,* Stanford, 1952, p. 59. Presumably the armed forces were among the "privileged consumers."

[47] See Bergson, *Structure of Soviet Wages.*

[48] On the relative trends in farm and nonfarm "real" and money incomes from 1928 to 1937, see chapter 13 and *SNIP-28,* p. 66. The relative position of the peasant in 1928 seems even less favorable than Hoeffding's calculations in *SNIP-28* show, if account is taken of the fact that the Soviet farm employment data he uses are in terms of "adult male equivalent." In estimating employment in these terms, Soviet statisticians discounted the labor of females, minors, and the aged. See Appendix K.

9

NATIONAL INCOME IN RUBLE FACTOR COST

I try now to appraise the effect on the national income figures compiled in ruble prices of divergencies between these prices and adjusted factor cost. Where possible, the national income data are adjusted in this light. These are hardly very tractable tasks, but in order to understand the meaning of our data we must try somehow to grapple with them. The calculations in terms of the ruble prices of 1937 are considered in the first two sections of this chapter and those in terms of the ruble prices of 1950 and 1928 in the third and last section.

National Income at Ruble Factor Cost of 1937

The ruble prices of 1937 deviate from adjusted factor cost on various accounts, among which the chief are turnover taxes, subsidies, profit charges, which are more or less unrelated to adjusted factor cost, and inadequate depreciation charges. Divergencies arise also because of the omission of any systematic charge for agricultural and other rent and for interest on fixed capital. In order to appraise the effect of these distortions on our national income data, I refer in this section to those due to turnover taxes and subsidies. Other causes of the divergence of ruble prices from adjusted factor cost are considered in the section following.

In Table 22 are shown the results of an attempt to adjust my national income data in 1937 rubles for distortions due to turnover taxes and subsidies. This entails recomputation of "real" national income according to this formula:

$$Y_n = \sum_{i=1}^{k} I_i^{on} \times V_i^{37}. \tag{10}$$

Here Y_n is "real" national income for year n; I_i^{on} is the index for the ith use category of "real" outlays in year n, the index being computed with 1937 as the base year, and V_i^{37} represents the value of outlays in the use

TABLE 22

Gross National Product by Use, USSR, 1928–55, in Ruble Factor Cost of 1937
(billions of rubles)

	1928	1937	1940	1944	1950	1955
Household purchases in retail markets						
In government and cooperative shops and restaurants	—	57.7	66.4	35.7	77.9	136.2
In collective farm markets	—	8.4	6.8	0.8	12.1	12.1
Total	55.1	66.1	73.2	36.5	90.0	148.3
Housing; services	10.2	17.2	18.9	13.1	21.3	31.6
Consumption of farm income in kind	39.8[a]	28.0	33.6	20.2	31.4	35.8
Military subsistence	0.6	1.9	3.8	13.1	4.6	7.3
Household consumption outlays	105.7	113.2	129.5	82.9	147.3	223.0
Communal services	6.1	22.6	27.0	20.7	32.8	40.3
Government administration, including NKVD (OGPU; MVD and MGB)	2.8	6.9	10.1	7.9	13.8	9.8
Defense (as recorded in budget)[b]	1.7	17.0	45.2	115.2	41.7	60.9
Gross investment						
Fixed capital	11.0	35.6	39.9	24.5	67.3	113.6
Other	5.6	20.3	10.2	9.8	19.5	17.1
Total	16.6	55.9	50.1	34.3	86.8	130.7
Gross national product	132.9	215.6	261.9	261.0	322.4	464.7

[a] Including farm wages in kind.
[b] Exclusive of pensions to officers et al.

category in question in terms of the prices prevailing in 1937, after certain adjustments. More specifically, the value of outlays in terms of 1937 rubles is reduced by the amount of turnover taxes accruing on such outlays and increased by the corresponding amount of subsidies. An adjustment is also made for farm prices of a nature to be explained below.

The turnover tax was not the only form of sales tax in the USSR at the time studied, but practically speaking it was the only one of any consequence. For this reason, the adjustment of the prevailing values of 1937 for turnover taxes and subsidies in the manner described comes essentially to the same thing as the revaluation of the different use categories and subcategories in terms of the factor charges, including profits, recorded in Soviet accounts in 1937. Since, as will appear, the adjustment for farm prices does not affect this identity, the data in Table 22 are in effect calculated in terms of the ruble factor cost of 1937, and I shall so refer to them henceforth.

The revaluation, however, is only partial. While different use categories and subcategories are now aggregated with weights corresponding to their ruble factor cost in 1937, the different commodities within any category continue as before to be valued relatively to one another in terms of the prevailing prices of that year. I shall consider later to what extent the results of the revaluation might be altered if it were more complete.

The use categories and subcategories in terms of which the revaluation is made are those listed in Table 23. For each category, measures of "real" outlays in 1937 prices were compiled as part of the calculation described in previous chapters of "real" national income in these terms. Where not compiled previously, such measures may readily be derived from the results of the earlier calculations. Accordingly, in applying Formula (10), the necessary index numbers of "real" outlays for different use categories, that is, the magnitudes of I_i^{on} are obtained at once on this basis.[1] In Table 23, I also show for each use category the volume of outlays in 1937 in terms of prevailing prices and the corresponding figures in terms of ruble factor cost, which are needed to complete the formula. The data on outlays in terms of prevailing prices again are taken from calculations already described. The adjustments for turnover taxes, subsidies, and farm prices by which the figures on outlays in terms of ruble factor cost are obtained must now be described.

According to the logic of the revaluation, the turnover taxes to be deducted here should represent for any use category, the total incidence, including amounts paid on materials as well as on final goods. Tax statistics of this sort are not easy to compile, but directly or indirectly

[1] For all use categories other than communal services, the needed measures of "real" outlays are derived in Appendices A to G. For communal services, the necessary series for labor inputs is obtained by aggregating the data compiled in Appendix D on labor inputs to health care and education. I also allow for labor inputs into "other" communal services. The necessary series on nonlabor inputs to communal services is obtained similarly.

TABLE 23

Gross National Product by Use, USSR, 1937 at Prevailing Prices of 1937, Ruble Factor Cost of 1937 and Prevailing Prices of 1928

Outlay category	Value at 1937 prevailing prices		Value at 1937 ruble factor cost		Value at 1928 prevailing prices	
	Billion rubles	Percent	Billion rubles	Percent	Billion rubles	Percent
Household purchases in retail markets						
In government and cooperative shops and restaurants	110.0	39.2	57.7	26.8	—	—
In collective farm markets	16.0	5.7	8.4	3.9	—	—
Total	126.0	44.9	66.1	30.7	21.20	24.7
Housing; services	17.4	6.2	17.2	8.0	4.58	5.3
Consumption of farm income in kind	25.0	8.9	28.0	13.0	4.90	5.7
Military subsistence	2.5	0.9	1.9	0.9	0.42	0.5
Household consumption outlays	170.9	60.9	113.2	52.5	31.10	36.3
Communal services						
Labor inputs	13.4	4.8	13.4	6.2	2.84	3.3
Nonlabor inputs	12.2	4.3	9.2	4.3	3.77	4.4
Total	25.6	9.1	22.6	10.5	6.61	7.7
Government administration, including NKVD (OGPU; MVD and MGB)	7.4	2.6	6.9	3.2	2.01	2.3
Defense						
Military services	4.0	1.4	3.4	1.6	1.23	1.4
Munitions; other	13.4	4.8	13.6	6.3	9.38	10.9
Total	17.4	6.2	17.0	7.9	10.61	12.4
Gross investment						
Fixed capital	35.2	12.5	35.6	16.5	27.45	32.0
Livestock	4.0	1.4	4.4	2.0	0.50	0.6
Inventories						
Trade	3.9	1.4	2.1	1.0	.70	.8
Other	8.6	3.1	6 4	3.0	4.00	4.7
Total	12.5	4.5	8.5	3.9	4.70	5.5
Miscellaneous	7.7	2.7	7.4	3.4	2.70	3.2
Total	59.4	21.2	55.9	25.9	35.35	41.3
Gross national product	280.7	100.0	215.6	100.0	85.68	100.0

Note: Minor discrepancies between sums of individual items and specified totals are due to rounding.

the Soviet turnover tax falls predominantly on household purchases in government and cooperative retail shops, and given this the incidence of the tax I believe was computed fairly accurately in previous SNIP studies. Although the incidence of the tax is recalculated here in order to incorporate some revisions, I rely essentially on previous procedures.

The government collected in 1937, 75.9 billion rubles of turnover taxes. Excluding tax-free components, such as labor inputs to communal services and government administration, and farm income in kind, these taxes were levied on some 229.0 billion rubles of national product. Hence, the average tax rate on taxable final outlays was 33 percent. This represents the indirect as well as direct incidence. For purposes of calculating the incidence of the tax on different use categories, I assume that certain minor categories are subject to the average effective tax rate. This assumption is made for military subsistence, commodity inputs to communal services and government administration, and investments in inventories other than in trade. Collective farm market sales are subject to the turnover tax, but only at nominal rates, taken here to average 2 percent. Taking into account the official tax schedules, including the high rates for petroleum products and the compounding of charges where taxes are levied on intermediate products, I allow for diverse but very limited rates on housing and services, munitions and other military procurement, investment in fixed capital, and miscellaneous investment.

In these ways I account for 12.1 billion rubles of taxes. The balance of 63.8 billions, therefore, falls on household purchases in government and cooperative retail shops and on investments in trade inventories. Allowing for taxes on the latter at the same rate as on the former, the taxes on the household purchases in government and cooperative retail shops amount to 61.6 billion rubles. Since the turnover tax affects collective farm market prices and military subsistence, some taxes are imputed finally to farm income in kind (which has been valued at average realized farm prices) and military services, which as recorded under defense include military subsistence.

In the foregoing calculation, the turnover taxes on household purchases in government and cooperative retail shops are computed as a residual. From the official tax schedules and available data on the structure of household purchases in government and cooperative retail shops, the tax burden on the latter may also be calculated directly. Because of the need to sample from among the many rates applying to different categories of commodities and to allow in some instances for important amounts of taxes levied at early stages (for example, grain products are taxed primarily at the procurement stage), this alternative method is not easy to apply. But in view of the importance of the turnover tax for present purposes, it was felt that the required calculation should be attempted. The result is reassuring. Taxes falling directly or indirectly on household purchases in government and cooperative retail shops amount to 62.5 billion rubles, compared with the 61.6 billion rubles computed initially.

The Soviet government has published for 1937 targets for turnover taxes that were to be paid by different administrative agencies. Although my figures on the incidence of the tax by use category are difficult to compare with these targets, the two sets of data appear broadly consistent.

It does not seem possible to improve here on the admittedly rough calculation made in previous SNIP studies on the incidence of subsidies by use categories. Accordingly, in Table 23 in compiling the data on outlays in terms of ruble factor cost I use essentially the same figures on subsidies as were obtained previously. As for turnover taxes, these supposedly represent indirect as well as direct incidence. In the underlying computation, subsidies are estimated initially by industrial sector and then allocated to use categories in dependence on the assumed distribution of output of different sectors.

Although the attempt to revalue Soviet national income in terms of ruble factor cost calls for the deduction of turnover taxes and the addition of subsidies, these adjustments give rise to a distortion of their own. As was explained, retail collective farm market sales are subject to a turnover tax but only at a nominal rate. Under the heading of consumption, the turnover tax falls almost exclusively on the goods sold in government and cooperative retail shops. Since there is no offsetting difference in the incidence of subsidies, the adjustments for turnover taxes and subsidies mean that the requirement of uniformity in prices in any market area, which initially was met in the retail market, is now violated. As it turns out, values are reduced in both the government and cooperative retail shops, on the one hand, and the collective farm markets, on the other, but far more in the case of the former.

To come to the adjustment of farm prices, this has a twofold basis. On the one hand, in order to repair the deficiency just described I reduce collective farm market prices additionally so that in the upshot they fall proportionately to those in government and cooperative retail shops. On the other, I increase average government farm procurement prices. The reduction in collective farm market prices by itself means a reduction in farm money incomes. In this study, I assume provisionally that farm labor services are correctly valued at the prevailing money incomes earned. Hence the increase in average government farm procurement prices is needed to offset the reduction in farm money incomes resulting from the cut in collective farm market prices.

The adjustment in farm prices measures the incidence on different use categories of these two changes in prices. The cut in collective farm market prices, of course, affects only the value of collective farm market sales. Similarly, the increase in government farm procurement prices falls primarily on household purchases in government and cooperative retail shops, but as in previous SNIP studies an allowance is made for the very limited incidence on other categories where agricultural products are used.[2]

In sum, the adjustment for turnover taxes, subsidies, and farm prices is inexact, but turnover taxes are by far the dominant element, and I believe the computation of the incidence of this aspect is fairly reliable. Thus, turnover taxes totaled 75.9 billion rubles in 1937, or 76.9 billions including imputations, while the corresponding figures for subsidies were but 8.0 and 11.7 billion rubles. The adjustment for farm prices involves a cut of 7.3 billion rubles in the value of collective farm market sales, and offsetting increases in values elsewhere. Under the circumstances, I doubt that the resultant national income data in Table 22 can be very materially affected by errors at this point.[3]

As a result of the revaluation, national income generally grows more or declines less than it did previously (Table 24). This outcome was to be anticipated in view of the greatly reduced weight assigned to household purchases in retail shops. The change in the growth of national income nevertheless is often surprisingly limited, but on closer study this result too seems understandable. To refer only to the more important aspects: The revaluation means that less weight is assigned to household purchases in retail shops, which tend to grow less rapidly than other use

[2] To repeat, the decline in collective farm market prices is taken to be proportional to that in the prices prevailing in government and cooperative retail shops. Ultimately, of course, the latter prices are affected by the adjustments not only for turnover taxes and subsidies but for farm prices, but this complexity may be dealt with by use of simultaneous equations.

In his kind review of *SNIP-37* (*Review of Economics and Statistics,* November 1954), Francis Seton correctly argues that in my adjustment for farm prices the cut in collective farm market prices should be proportional to the cut not in retail shop prices generally but in retail shop prices for foodstuffs alone. In the upshot, however, retail shop prices for foods fall in approximately the same proportion as retail shop prices generally (see Appendix I). Hence, the alternative computation favored by Seton would scarcely affect the results.

Seton apparently feels that "multiple consumer prices" in any case do not pose any special difficulty where the concern is to measure national income in terms of a factor cost standard. I agree if an adjustment for such prices happens to be entirely internal to a particular use category, but where, as in the present case, different use categories are affected, the adjustment yields somewhat more accurate weights for the different categories. Then again, Seton feels that if multiple prices are to be avoided, the desideratum for collective farm market prices is that they be equated to the average prices the government pays for procurements. At this point, I believe Seton is neglecting some material aspects, particularly additional processing, transportation, and distribution costs incurred on the collective farm market sales.

[3] The data on the incidence of turnover taxes, subsidies, and the adjustment of farm prices that are used in calculating outlays in terms of ruble factor cost are presented in Appendix I. I also explain there more precisely than is done in the text the relation of these data to those compiled in previous SNIP studies, particularly *SNIP-28–48.* I referred in the text to an alternative calculation of the incidence of the turnover tax on retail sales. Some further details on this calculation too are set forth in Appendix I, although space forbids a full exposition.

TABLE 24

Gross National Product by Use, USSR, 1928–55, in 1937 Ruble Prices and Factor Cost (1937 = 100)

Outlay category	1928	1937	1940	1944	1950	1955
Household consumption outlays						
1937 prices	88.8	100	114	69.3	133	209
1937 ruble factor cost	93.4	100	114	73.2	130	197
Communal services						
1937 prices	25.8	100	118	91.4	142	174
1937 ruble factor cost	27.0	100	119	91.6	145	178
Government administration, including NKVD (OGPU; MVD and MGB)						
1937 prices	40.5	100	146	115	200	142
1937 ruble factor cost[a]	40.5	100	146	115	200	142
Defense						
1937 prices	10.9	100	263	678	244	356
1937 ruble factor cost	10.0	100	266	678	245	358
Gross investment						
1937 prices	31.5	100	85.7	60.4	153	229
1937 ruble factor cost	29.7	100	89.6	61.4	155	234
Gross national product						
1937 prices	64.8	100	118	108	146	217
1937 ruble factor cost	61.6	100	121	121	150	216

[a] In the calculation of national income in terms of 1937 ruble factor cost, outlays on government administration, including NKVD, are assumed to vary in the same way as in 1937 ruble prices.

outlays, but among the use categories that gain in importance is consumption of farm income in kind (Table 23). The performance of this category is even less favorable than that of household purchases in retail shops. Because of the relatively large share of consumption as a whole in national income in 1928, these conflicting forces do much to determine the final outcome for the period 1928–37, but they also operate during other intervals. Although household purchases in retail shops tend to grow less than other categories, they have not been especially laggard in recent years. Indeed over the intervals 1937–55 and 1950–55, such outlays grow somewhat more rapidly than national income as a whole. Necessarily for this reason too the revaluation tends to have only a limited effect.

While the revaluation means that national income grows more rapidly than previously from 1928 to 1937, the effect is far less than that due to the change in base year from 1937 to 1928 (Table 18). The reasons for this difference I believe are twofold. First, when the base year is shifted from 1937 to 1928, the resultant reweighting appears to be more definitely correlated with the trends in different use categories than is the case where one shifts from 1937 prices to 1937 ruble factor cost. Thus, when the base year is changed from 1937 to 1928, both retail sales and farm income in kind receive much less weight, whereas (as just explained) when the change is from 1937 prices to 1937 ruble factor cost, retail sales receive less and farm income in kind more weight. In Table 23, I reproduce from earlier calculations figures on the value of outlays in different use categories in 1937 in terms of the prevailing prices of 1928. If the reader will bear in mind the general nature of the trends in the physical volume of outlays on different components, he will see at once from these data the difference in the correlation just described. The second reason for the differing results of the different revaluations is the fact that the shift from 1937 prices to 1937 ruble factor cost involves a significant change in price structure but by any standard the corresponding change entailed in the shift in base year from 1937 to 1928 is nothing less than revolutionary. This too may be seen from the data in Table 23 and needs no further demonstration here.

The revaluation affects major components as well as national income as a whole. Suffice it to refer to one outstanding aspect: Consumption generally grows less rapidly than before. This result must be due primarily to the factor referred to above, the reduced weight assigned purchases in retail shops in comparison with farm income in kind.

To repeat, the revaluation in Table 22 is only partial. While physical volume series for different use categories (that is, those in Table 23) are reaggregated with weights corresponding to their 1937 ruble factor cost, within different use categories individual commodities continue as before to be aggregated with weights corresponding to their 1937 market prices. How would the results be affected if the revaluation were more complete? According to a further computation, the answer, if the revaluation is extended to the commodities comprising one major component, retail sales, is this: Household consumption in 1928 rises from the 93.4 percent of 1937 originally computed in Table 22 to 101 percent. Gross national product similarly rises from 61.6 percent of 1937 to 65.4 percent. For two other years for which the recomputations could be made, 1948 and 1954, consumption and gross national product are also affected, but in no case by more than one percentage point.

I referred in chapter 6 to a calculation based mainly on data compiled by Dr. Janet Chapman, of the physical volume of household purchases of different commodities in government and cooperative retail shops. In all, serial data in terms of 1937 prices are compiled for 22 commodity categories, for example, grain products, meat and poultry, textiles, and garments. The changes in my measures of consumption and gross national product described above result from the extension in the scope of the revaluation to embrace the reaggregation of these series. In the reaggregation, each of the 22 series is assigned a weight corresponding to the 1937 ruble factor cost volume of outlays on the commodity in question. Outlays at prevailing prices were determined as part of the computation of the 22 physical volume series. Turnover taxes by commodity category are estimated in the alternative calculation, described earlier in this section, of the incidence of taxes on retail sales. The limited subsidies on agricultural products that accrue to sales by government and cooperative retail shops are allocated by commodity category on the basis of incomplete information on state farm deliveries, prices and costs, and MTS expenses and revenues. In computing ruble factor cost weights for different commodity categories, I also allow different foodstuffs to share in the adjustment for farm prices in proportion to their importance in collective farm market trade.[4]

For the period for which the extension in the scope of the revaluation is at all consequential, 1928–37, the effect is the opposite of that observed in Tables 22 and 24, that is, growth is reduced. Seemingly for commodities for which production grew slowly or declined during this period, the government tended to allow a relatively large share of the selling price to take the form of factor charges. Where output grew rapidly, according to our calculations, the converse was true. If this was indeed the government policy, evidently it was not an unreasonable one, at least if (as seems likely) the varying shares of the market price recorded here as factor charges accrued primarily to ultimate factors, farmers or workers, as the case may be. In effect, the government was simply allowing a relatively greater increase in incentives to ultimate factors in the case of products that increased slowly than in the case of products that increased rapidly.[5] Accordingly, there seems to be no reason to question the results of the revaluation at this point.

The foregoing circumstances also explain why the revaluation in terms of 1937 ruble factor cost has a contrary effect to that resulting from the shift in base year from 1937 to 1928. As a result of the revaluation in terms of ruble factor cost, growth is reduced; as a result of the shift in base year from 1937 to 1928, growth is increased. The latter revaluation

[4] As with the incidence of the turnover taxes by commodity category, so with that of subsidies and the farm price adjustment, some further details are presented in Appendix I. I am indebted to Herbert Levine for aid in making these calculations.

[5] As was explained, as calculated here the ruble factor costs of different products include a share of the adjustment made previously for farm prices. Since by implication the factor costs include incomes earned from sales on the collective farm market, it may be somewhat out of order to speak of the relation of such charges to retail prices as being determined simply by government policy. But in any event, as might be expected, farm earnings from collective farm market sales and accordingly the adjustment here for farm prices were especially great in the case of the scarce animal products. The comparative trends in factor charges and retail prices that are implied in my calculations, therefore, originate partly in this fact.

also causes a somewhat larger change in the growth of retail sales than does the former. The reasons for the latter difference are not easy to summarize, and I shall not pause to explore them here.

With retail sales reaggregated, the revaluation is still only partial, but there are reasons to think that further extensions in its scope would have only a relatively limited effect. With the exception of oil products and Moscow and Leningrad electric power, turnover taxes in 1937 were generally of only a nominal sort for producers' goods, for example, 0.5 percent for coal and steel; 1.0 percent for industrial machinery. While the taxes were high indeed for oil products, and in the aggregate may have yielded the government 6 to 7 billion rubles in 1937,[6] the magnitudes involved for this single industry could not materially affect the larger aggregates of concern here. This I believe is also true for the subsidies which the government still was granting on industrial goods in 1937. Although for some products the subsidies were still important (most notably, perhaps as much as 30 percent of the cost of coal was covered by subsidies in 1937), the several billion rubles involved over-all could again have only very little effect on our global figures. Moreover, both oil products and numerous subsidized articles, for example, coal, are primarily intermediate products. The incidence of price distortions generally should have been widely distributed among the final products totaled in my use categories. Among consumers' goods, the turnover taxes (but not subsidies) are varying and often notably high, and taxed consumers' goods are allocated not only to retail sales but to other final use categories, such as communal services and inventory investment. But the retail sales represent 75 to 85 percent of such goods, and our recalculation for retail sales may be read in this light.[7]

To sum the foregoing, the data in Table 22 represent the results of a partial revaluation of the national product for distortions due to turnover taxes and subsidies, but probably they generally approximate measurements that might be obtained through a more complete revaluation. Household consumption in 1928, however, may well be understated by (say) 7.5 percentage points. There may be a corresponding understatement of (say) 4 percentage points in national income.

[6] A. Bergson, R. Bernaut, and L. Turgeon, "Basic Industrial Prices in the USSR, 1928–1950," The RAND Corporation, Research Memorandum RM-1522, August 1, 1955, p. 85.

[7] For 1928, the extended revaluation described on pages 135–136 applies to all household purchases in retail shops. For other years it applies only to household purchases in government and cooperative shops and restaurants. The cited percentages both relate to 1937, but the higher one represents the share of all household purchases in retail shops to all taxed final outlays on consumers' goods. The lower one represents the share of household purchases in government and cooperative shops to all taxed final outlays on consumers' goods.

National Income at 1937 Ruble Factor Cost, Further Adjusted

In 1937, ruble prices deviated from adjusted factor cost not only because of turnover taxes and subsidies, but because of diverse other aspects. Among these the chief were the inclusion in ruble prices of a charge for profits unrelated to adjusted factor cost, the omission of any systematic charge for agricultural and other rent and for interest on fixed capital, and the inadequacy of bookkeeping charges for depreciation. To revalue Soviet national income in terms of ruble factor cost, therefore, still leaves open the possibility of distortions due to limitations of this standard. To turn to this aspect, I venture to think that the distortions may not be very consequential. At any rate, this seems to be the import of a variety of evidence, some factual, some quite speculative.

The evidence consists partly of data in Tables 25 and 26. In Table 25, column (1), I reclassify Soviet outlays in 1937 as previously computed in ruble factor cost. Under the first of the listed headings I include all final outlays on consumers' goods other than household purchases in the collective farm market and household consumption of farm income in kind. This category, therefore, comprises household purchases in government and cooperative retail shops, military subsistence, consumers' goods inputs to communal services and government administration (taken to be one-half the total commodity inputs in each case) and investments in trade and other consumers' goods inventories. The second, third and fourth of the different sorts of final outlays listed are self-explanatory, and so also is the sixth. Under the fifth heading, I place essentially all final outlays on commodities other than consumers' goods and livestock herds. This category, therefore, includes inputs of such items as fuel and power to communal services and government administration, expenditures on munitions and other military procurement, gross investment in fixed capital, and other investments in basic industrial goods.

In Table 25, columns (2) to (5), are set forth in turn data on the incidence among the foregoing categories of outlays of:

(a) The profits recorded in Soviet accounts in 1937.

(b) A hypothetical charge of 25 billion rubles for agricultural rent, which amounts to about 40 percent of total labor income in agriculture in 1937.[8] According to calculations of Professor Gale Johnson, agricultural land rent in the United States in 1910–14 amounted to 48 percent of farm labor income, including the imputed earnings of self-employed. By 1940–44, the corresponding figure had fallen to 32 percent.[9] The circumstances

[8] In 1937, Soviet farm households earned from all sources 56.0 billion rubles. With income in kind revalued at ruble factor cost, the total comes to 59.4 billion rubles. See *SNIP-28–48,* Table 1, and the present study, Appendix I.

[9] D. Gale Johnson, "Allocation of Agricultural Income," *Journal of Farm Economics,* November 1948. Johnson presents several alternative computations of the functional

TABLE 25

Incidence of Profits, Rent, and Interest by Type of Final Outlay, USSR, 1937
(billions of rubles)

Outlay category	Outlays, ruble factor cost (1)	Profits (2)	Agricultural rent at 40 percent of farm labor income (3)	Interest on fixed capital at 10 percent per annum (4)	Rent plus interest less profits (5)
Final outlays of households and organizations on consumers' goods not elsewhere classified	69.1	14.4	10.0	9.8	5.4
Household purchases in collective farm market	8.4	0.6	2.9	1.0	3.3
Household outlays on housing, utilities, and miscellaneous services	17.2	1.2	—[b]	9.3	8.1
Farm income in kind, including livestock investment	32.4	2.2[a]	11.3	3.8	12.9
Final outlays of households and organizations on producers' durables, munitions, construction, et cetera	66.5	3.4	0.8	12.6	10.0
Labor inputs to communal services and government administration; military services	22.0	0.4[a]	0.3[a]	0.3[a]	0.2[a]
Gross national product	215.6	22.2	25.3	36.8	39.9

[a] Imputed.
[b] — negligible.

affecting agricultural factor charges in the two countries, of course, are very different, and the hypothetical charge for the USSR has to be read accordingly.[10]

distribution of incomes in agriculture. I cite here the results obtained by Method A, which are summarized on p. 742. In Johnson's computations, rent is imputed to land and farm buildings together. For present purposes, rent to land alone is of interest. Accordingly, I assume that Johnson's total is divided between land and buildings in proportion to the relative values of these two forms of property, as given in the *Statistical Abstract of the United States: 1946*, Washington, 1946, p. 573.

[10] On the average, but 1.45 hectares of land were cultivated in the USSR in 1937 per capita of farm population. The corresponding figures for the United States in 1910 and 1940 were 3.86 and 4.39, respectively. We may conclude that only if the marginal productivity of land in relation to that of labor in the USSR were about three times that in the United States would the relation of total rent to labor income be the same in the two countries. On the farm population and cultivated area of the USSR and

TABLE 26

Household Consumption and Gross National Product, USSR, 1928–55, at Specified Valuations (1937 = 100)

	1928	1937	1950	1955
Household consumption outlays				
1937 prices	88.8	100	133	209
1937 ruble factor cost	93.4	100	130	197
1937 ruble factor cost, further adjusted:				
With profits deducted	94.4	100	129	193
With addition of agricultural rent at 40 percent of farm labor income	95.9	100	130	194
With addition of interest at 10 percent of fixed capital	91.3	100	130	197
With profits deducted and rent and interest added	94.7	100	129	191
1937 ruble factor cost, with allowance for nonlabor charges according to U.S. 1947 cost structure	92.5	100	130	192
Gross national product				
1937 prices	64.8	100	146	217
1937 ruble factor cost	61.6	100	150	216
1937 ruble factor cost, further adjusted:				
With profits deducted	60.7	100	150	215
With addition of agricultural rent at 40 percent of farm labor income	65.4	100	147	211
With addition of interest at 10 percent of fixed capital	61.1	100	149	216
With profits deducted and rent and interest added	64.0	100	147	211
1937 ruble factor cost, with allowance for nonlabor charges according to U.S. 1947 cost structure	64.3	100	148	213

(c) A hypothetical interest charge of 10 percent per annum on Soviet fixed capital.

(d) The net of the foregoing, that is, the excess of rent and interest over profits.

In all cases, the cited figures supposedly represent both direct and indirect incidence, that is, charges not only on final goods but on intermediate articles used in their production. Although estimated partly from the planned (as distinct from realized) profits for different industrial commissariats and branches, the incidence of profits by type of final outlay in 1937 probably was more or less as depicted in the table, with

---

USA, see *Narkhoz,* p. 106; Warren Eason, *Soviet Manpower,* Princeton, 1959, p. 97; *Historical Statistics of the United States, 1789–1945,* Washington, 1949, pp. 29, 98.

the chief burden by far borne by processed consumers' goods.[11] In essentials the incidence of rent by type of final outlay may be determined at once from data on the disposition of agricultural output.[12] The incidence of interest on fixed capital is computed from the capital-output ratios shown in Table 27.

[11] Soviet enterprises in 1937 earned some 19.6 billion rubles of profits, including the undistributed earnings before taxes of collective farms. See *SNIP-37,* p. 123 as revised in *SNIP-28–48,* Appendix C. From data in these same sources and from planned targets in A. Smilga, "Finansy sotsialisticheskogo gosudarstva," *PE,* 1937, no. 2, p. 112, these are estimated to have been the earnings in 1937 of different branches: agriculture, including the undistributed earnings of collective farms before taxes, 2.72 billion rubles; heavy industry, 3.22 billion rubles; light and food industry, 3.91 billion rubles; cooperative industry, 1.53 billion rubles; local and other industry, 2.56 billion rubles; government and cooperative trade, 2.40 billion rubles; transport and communications, 1.07 billion rubles; communal economy, 1.19 billion rubles; financial institutions, 1.00 billion rubles. Smilga's planned targets refer to administrative agencies, and the cited estimates of realized earnings have to be read correspondingly, for example, the figure for "heavy industry" refers to the Commissariat of Heavy Industry. The estimates derived here of realized profits for different commissariats seem broadly consistent with corresponding results for 1936, as given in Smilga, p. 112.

As to the incidence of profits by type of final outlay, practically all the profits earned by the commissariats of the light and food industries would have accrued directly or indirectly on outlays of my first sort, that is, final outlays of consumers' goods not classified elsewhere (n.e.c.). Since the government and cooperative trade referred to represents essentially trade in consumers' goods, the profits earned in this sector also accrue on this category of final outlays. The earnings in the communal economy similarly must all have been earned on expenditures classified here as outlays on housing, utilities, et cetera. I allocate agricultural profits between collective farm sales and other marketings in proportion to the ruble factor cost value of the volume of marketings involved (as calculated from data in Appendix I). After making a nominal allowance for agricultural materials used to manufacture producers' goods, profits earned on marketings other than sales in the collective farm market are again allotted to final outlays on consumers' goods n.e.c. For the rest, the allocation of profits by type of final outlay was determined often arbitrarily in the light of diverse information, including chiefly data on the structure of the output of different commissariats and other agencies in Gosplan, *Narodno-khoziaistvennyi plan na 1936 god,* 2nd ed., Moscow, 1936, pp. 392 ff.; *1941 Plan,* pp. 168 ff., 194; N. Kaplan et al., "A Tentative Input-Output Table for the USSR, 1941 Plan," The RAND Corporation, Research Memorandum RM-924, September 2, 1952, p. 73; and information on profits in different industries in L. Vilenskii, "Finansovye voprosy promyshlennosti," *PKh,* 1938, no. 10; and data on the freight rate structure in H. Hunter, *Soviet Transportation Policy,* Cambridge, 1957, chap. xi.

Since profits are earned on sales of farm produce and military subsistence, some earnings are imputed to farm income in kind which is valued at average realized farm prices, and to military services. In Table 25, column (2), the total profits of 22.2 billion rubles exceed profits actually earned by the amount of these imputations.

[12] I first allocate the total charge between farm income in kind, collective farm market sales, and other farm marketings. For each category, the share in the total rental charge corresponds to the relative volume of produce disposed of in 1937 in terms of ruble factor cost. The charges accruing to collective farm market sales and farm income in kind may be recorded at once opposite these headings in Table 25, column (3). After allowance is made for the nominal amount of farm output used in heavy industry, the rent on other marketings is charged to final outlays on consumers' goods n.e.c. Since military subsistence is affected, an appropriate charge must also be imputed to military services.

TABLE 27

Capital-Output Ratios for Different Categories of Final Outlays, USSR, 1937

Outlay category	Ratio, fixed capital to final outlays in ruble factor cost
Final outlays of households and organizations on consumers' goods not elsewhere classified	1.4
Household purchases in collective farm market	1.2
Household outlays on housing, utilities, and miscellaneous services	5.4
Farm income in kind, including farm investment	1.2
Final outlays of households and organizations on such items as producers' durables	1.9
Labor inputs to communal services and government administration; military services	0.0
Gross national product	1.7

Note: Space permits reference only to the bare essentials of the derivation of this table. As is implied in the text, the stock of fixed capital of the USSR in 1937 is assumed to total 365 billion rubles in 1937 prices. In deriving this figure, I take as a point of departure the figure on the Soviet capital stock of 1937 in 1945 prices (564 billion rubles) given in N. Voznesenskii, *Voennaia Ekonomika SSSR . . .* , Moscow, 1947, p. 12. Allowing for a price increase for capital goods of 75 percent from 1937 to 1945 (the price index for 1944 on 1937 as base that is implied by my deflation of fixed capital investment is 167), the corresponding figure in 1937 prices is 322 billion rubles. To this I add livestock herds and private housing which Voznesenskii omits. For present purposes, I also deduct the value of schools and other similar public buildings. From the herd numbers in *Narkhoz*, p. 118, and in N. Jasny, *The Socialized Agriculture of the USSR*, Stanford, 1949, p. 796, and the price data in Appendix G, I calculate that Soviet livestock herds in 1937 were worth some 35 billion rubles. Private housing is estimated at 29 billion rubles on the basis of data in V. L. Kobalevskii, *Organizatsiia i ekonomika zhilishchnogo khoziaistva*, Moscow, 1940, pp. 106–107, and in Appendix B. The value of schools, et cetera, is taken to be 21 billion rubles.

The latter figure is obtained as part of a more general calculation of the industrial structure of fixed capital. Here I proceed primarily on the basis of branch data on capital stocks in Kobalevskii, *op. cit.*, pp. 5, 106–107, and in the processed appendix to N. Kaplan, "Capital Formation and Allocation" in A. Bergson, ed., *Soviet Economic Growth.* Having compiled sector data on capital stocks, I allocate these by type of final outlay mainly by reference to N. Kaplan et al., *A Tentative Input-Output Table for the USSR, 1941 Plan*, The RAND Corporation, Research Memorandum RM-924, September 2, 1952.

Although the Soviet sources of capital stock data are often not explicit regarding the meaning of their figures, the coefficients compiled are believed to represent undepreciated values.

These ratios in turn had to be calculated from diverse untested Soviet data on the volume and industrial structure of the Soviet stock of fixed capital. The underlying figures on capital stocks, I believe, represent undepreciated values, and the interest charges in Table 25, column (4), must be read accordingly.

So far as the data in Table 25, columns (2) to (5), represent the incidence of the different charges described, evidently they provide a basis for corresponding revaluations of national income. In Table 26 I show the results of an attempt to explore this aspect for national income as a whole and for one component, consumption. For both consumption and national income, I first repeat the data already compiled in terms of 1937 prices and 1937 ruble factor cost. For the latter, reference is to the measurements in Table 22. In the next four lines are shown in turn the results of successive reaggregations of the same physical volume series as were summed in the calculation of national income in terms of 1937 ruble factor cost, that is, the physical volume series for the different use categories in Table 23. In each case, the physical volume series for different categories are assigned new base year weights in the light of the data on incidence in Table 25. Thus, on the first line under the heading "1937 ruble factor cost, further adjusted," I show in index number form the results of a reaggregation of series for individual use categories, where each series is valued at its 1937 ruble factor cost, less profits. On the second line, similar figures are shown which were compiled with different series being valued at 1937 ruble factor cost plus agricultural rent. The series on the next two lines were compiled similarly.

In Table 25, the incidence of different charges is calculated only by broad type of outlay. In order to adjust the 1937 values for the different use categories actually reaggregated, that is, the use categories listed in Table 23, I assume that within each broad type of outlay the amount of each charge is distributed among different use categories in proportion to the volume of outlays at ruble factor cost.[13]

The successive revaluations all affect our measures of "real" consumption and "real" national income, but in no case materially (Table 26). This is so even for the period 1928–37. Moreover, as these calculations suggest, even very different charges from those considered might not lead to a different result. For example, suppose that on one account or another, retail sales in 1937 are 10 billion rubles more than the magnitude obtained for them after all revaluations. Suppose all other outlays are unaffected. "Real" consumption in 1928 declines by less than one percentage point in relation to 1937. There is a corresponding and similarly limited increase in "real" national income. These results are among the evidence for the view expressed at the outset that limitations in the ruble factor cost valuation may not be serious for our purposes. I turn now to some other pertinent information.

I do not propose to consider in any systematic way the possible effect of the omission of charges for rent in extractive industries and of the inadequacy of accounting depreciation charges. Judging by the U.S. cost structure, charges for rent for Soviet extractive industries in 1937

[13] In Table 26, in the case of the charges on labor inputs to communal services, et cetera, the totals in each case accrue wholly to military services.

might possibly have been on the order of several billion rubles.[14] As recorded in Soviet accounts in 1937, depreciation charges amounted to 5.8 billion rubles,[15] or 2.7 percent of the national product at ruble factor cost. If, according to a more correct assessment depreciation, charges averaged (say) 4.0 percent of the Soviet stock of fixed capital (perhaps about the same relation as obtained in the United States in 1948), the total charges would rise by but 9 billion rubles.[16] A revaluation of national income on account of these two aspects clearly could not alter our results markedly. Incidentally, in the case of depreciation, the incidence of such a revaluation would be more evenly distributed among different types of outlays than the capital coefficients cited above might suggest. This is because for the most part no depreciation is charged in the USSR on agricultural capital.

In the foregoing, I have made limited reference to American experience as a benchmark. In Table 26, in the final series on household consumption and gross national product, this approach is carried to its logical conclusion. The series are obtained again by the aggregation of indices of physical volume for different use categories. The use categories considered are those listed in Table 28. These physical volume series are once more in terms of prevailing prices of 1937 and hence are taken from previous calculations.[17] In aggregating the series for different use categories, however, I now employ weights given by this formula:

[14] In the mineral industries of the United States in 1919, all nonlabor charges in value added, that is, profits, interest, depreciation, as well as rental charges as such, amounted to 72.7 percent of the wage bill. The corresponding figure in 1939 was 138.4 percent. See *Statistical Abstract of the United States: 1951,* Washington, 1951, p. 682. These data refer to mineral industries, and do not include lumbering. In the Soviet Union in 1937, some 6.0 billion rubles of wages may have been paid in mineral industries and lumbering together. The statement in the text regarding the possible magnitude of rent in extractive industries in the USSR is made in this light. In any accurate appraisal, of course, one might wish also to distinguish pure rent from depletion, although the treatment to be accorded depletion in national income calculations is a subject on which U. S. Department of Commerce practice appears to have varied in the course of time. See *SNIP-37*, p. 24, note 4.

[15] *SNIP-28–48.*

[16] At replacement cost, depreciation charges in the United States totaled $23.0 billions in 1948. See R. Goldsmith et al., *A Study of Savings in the United States,* vol. iii, *Special Studies,* Princeton, 1956, p. 437. This is 5.7 percent of the total value of housing, and producers' structures and durable equipment, $403 billions, as given in R. Goldsmith, "The Growth of Reproducible Wealth in the United States of America from 1805 to 1950," in S. Kuznets, ed., *Income and Wealth of the United States,* Cambridge, 1952, p. 306. Goldsmith's estimate of fixed capital is in depreciated values. In relation to fixed capital at replacement cost, therefore, total depreciation charges would be less.

[17] In the calculation I treat as one use category, communal services and government administration, including the NKVD. Index numbers of physical volume are obtained for this category by aggregating corresponding physical volume series for the two components. The latter are those calculated in terms of ruble factor cost. The same treatment is accorded trade and all other inventories.

$$\bar{V}^{37} = \frac{V_i^{37}}{W_i} \tag{11}$$

Here V_i^{37} represents the outlays on the ith use category in 1937 in terms of ruble factor costs, less profits, and W_i represents the wage cost per dollar of final outlays on the corresponding use category in the United States in 1947.

In their studies of the structure of the American economy, Professor

TABLE 28

Gross National Income by Final Use, USSR, 1937, at Ruble Factor Cost and at Ruble Factor Cost Adjusted According to United States Cost Structure

Outlay category	Value at ruble factor cost[a]: Billion rubles (1)	Value at ruble factor cost[a]: Percent (2)	Wage cost in relation to market value, according to USA cost structure (3)	Value at ruble factor cost, adjusted: Billion rubles [(1) ÷ (3)] (4)	Value at ruble factor cost, adjusted: Percent (5)
1. Household purchases in retail markets					
a. In government and cooperative shops and restaurants	45.7	23.6	0.55	83.1	25.7
b. In collective farm markets	7.8	4.0	0.61	12.8	4.0
c. All	53.5	27.7		95.9	29.6
2. Housing; services					
a. Housing	2.8	1.4	0.13	21.5	6.6
b. Other	13.2	6.8	0.54	24.4	7.5
c. All	16.0	8.3		45.9	14.2
3. Consumption of farm income in kind	26.1	13.5	0.61	42.8	13.2
4. Military subsistence	1.5	0.8	0.55	2.7	0.8
5. Household consumption outlays	97.1	50.2		187.3	57.8
6. Communal services; government administration	28.0	14.5	0.95	29.5	9.1
7. Defense					
a. Military services	3.0	1.6	1.00	3.0	0.9
b. Munitions; other	12.9	6.7	0.62	20.8	6.4
c. All	15.9	8.2		23.8	7.3
8. Gross investment					
a. Producers' durables	13.1	6.8	0.62	21.1	6.5
b. Construction	20.7	10.7	0.67	30.9	9.5
c. All fixed capital	33.8	17.5		52.0	16.1
d. Livestock	4.1	2.1	0.61	6.7	2.1
e. Inventories	7.5	3.9	0.58	12.9	4.0
f. Miscellaneous	7.0	3.6	0.60	11.7	3.6
g. All	52.4	27.1		83.3	25.7
9. Gross national product	193.4	100.0		323.9	100.0

Note: Minor discrepancies between sums of individual items and specified totals are due to rounding.

[a] Less profits.

Wassily Leontief and his associates at Harvard have computed for each of 192 industries in 1947 wage costs per dollar of final outputs. The calculation takes into account not only "direct" wage costs incurred in the industry in question but "indirect" wage costs incurred through the use of intermediate products. Professor Leontief uses for this purpose the Emergency Model "input-output" table compiled by the United States Bureau of Labor Statistics. For any industry, the BLS table also tells us the disposition of the final market value between different final use categories. In applying Formula (11), average wage cost coefficients for different use categories were compiled simply by aggregation from these data of Professor Leontief and the BLS. Although Professor Leontief focuses primarily on the earnings of hired workers, his coefficients have been adjusted to include the imputed service incomes of self-employed farmers. Also, market values in all cases are net of excise taxes on final goods. Compilation of American coefficients that might be applied to Soviet use categories necessarily involved numerous substitutions, most notably use of the American coefficient for investment in producers' durables for Soviet final outlays on munitions. Together with the elements in their calculation, the weights derived by applying Formula (11) are shown in Table 28. Further details on the calculation are in Appendix J.

As computed in this study, outlays in terms of ruble factor cost come to much the same thing as direct and indirect wage costs, including farm and other labor incomes. The latter charges are approached the more closely if Soviet profits charges are omitted. For any use category, therefore, application of Formula (11) tells us what the final outlays would have been in the USSR if market prices were the same in relation to unit wage costs in the USSR in 1937 as in the USA in 1947. So far as excise taxes are omitted from the American market values, the latter relation for the United States comes to much the same thing as that of all primary factor charges to labor charges alone. Hence, by applying the formula we also determine what the Soviet outlays would be at factor cost if nonlabor charges were in the same relation to labor charges as they were in the United States in 1947. Granting that in fact the Soviet experience in this regard could not have duplicated that of the United States, there is perhaps some further reason here to discount the limitations in ruble factor cost as a valuation standard. The revaluation based on Formula (11) again hardly affects our measures of "real" consumption and gross national product (Table 26). Although nonetheless interesting on that account, the result perhaps was predictable, since the Leontief wage cost coefficients vary only to a notably limited degree among different use categories. For example, the coefficients applied to household purchases in retail markets, farm income in kind, investment in producers' durables and construction all range only from $0.55 to $0.67 per dollar of final outlays. See Table 28.[18]

I have been focusing so far on the valuation of broad use categories. On the further question that remains as to the validity of the ruble factor cost valuation for different commodities comprising any one use category, I shall only say that further revaluation within the household retail purchase category in accordance with the Leontief wage cost coefficients appears generally to have only a very limited effect. Interestingly, however, for 1928–37, the impact tends to be the opposite of that resulting from the corresponding adjustment within household retail purchases for such items as turnover taxes and subsidies (see page 135).[19]

To sum the preceding discussion, we do not know with any exactitude to what extent the measures of "real" national income in terms of ruble factor cost are affected by distortions in Soviet factor charges. The supposition seems reasonable nevertheless that the distortions are not

[18] I am much in debt to Herbert Levine for his aid in compiling the necessary wage coefficients, and to Professor Leontief, Dr. E. Gilboy, Dr. A. Conrad, and their associates at the Harvard Economic Research Project for their advice on the many questions that were encountered. Professor Leontief kindly made available unpublished materials needed for the computations.

[19] More particularly, I now take as a point of departure the latter calculation. In other words, the ruble factor cost standard is applied both to different use categories and, within the category of household purchases in government and cooperative retail shops, to different categories of commodities. In aggregating physical volume series for the different commodity categories, however, I now apply weights given by Formula (11). With this change in valuation, "real" household consumption in 1928 is reduced by about two percentage points in relation to 1937. There is a corresponding reduction of "real" national income of one percentage point. For other years considered, "real" outlays in relation to 1937 change by less than one percentage point. For details, see Appendix J.

Among the arguments advanced by Peter Wiles in support of his critique of "adjusted rubles," that is, the ruble factor cost valuation standard, one revolves around the asserted variability of wages as a share of value added in different Western industries. See P. Wiles, "Are Adjusted Rubles Rational?" *Soviet Studies.* From data which Wiles sets forth for the United Kingdom, which represent with equal emphasis ratios for such diverse industries as "blast furnaces" and "vinegar and other condiments," it is not easy to judge the import of the observed variability. At any rate, if Western experience in this regard is to be considered, interpretation appears much facilitated if it is presented in the form employed in the text and in Appendix J. From the calculations made here, one may determine to what extent the observed variation in cost structure affects measures of "real" national income. In the last analysis, of course, this is what we wish to know. Moreover, the value-added ratios such as Wiles cites no doubt are pertinent where the desideratum is a measure of physical volume in terms of value-added weights. In this study, however, we are seeking to compile price-weighted measures of physical volume. For this purpose, direct and indirect wage cost coefficients of the sort cited in the text clearly are the appropriate data to consider. The two sorts of ratios, of course, are not at all the same thing.

From a somewhat different standpoint, Professor Hodgman has also dissented from Wiles's view of the import of variable wage-value added relations. See Hodgman, "Measuring Soviet Industrial Production: A Reply," *Soviet Studies.* See also Moorsteen's review of Hodgman in *ASEER,* February 1956.

likely to be serious. At any rate, I shall proceed tentatively on this basis. Accordingly, the data that have been derived in terms of the ruble factor cost values of 1937 are taken to measure "real" national income where the adjusted factor cost valuation is called for, that is, where the concern is to appraise production potential. Generally, reference is made particularly to the data in Table 22, but these are only partly in terms of ruble factor cost and it will be necessary to consider that for 1928 alternative indices reflecting an extension in the scope of the revaluation within retail purchases very possibly are nearer the mark. Moreover, where the ruble factor cost standard itself is deficient, the consequence particularly in early years is more likely to be an overstatement than an understatement of growth.[20]

National Income at Ruble Factor Cost of 1950 and 1928

Ruble prices diverge from adjusted factor cost in 1950 for essentially the same reasons as in 1937. As was explained, however, the wage structure of 1950 has yet to be studied in any detail, and we are also rather uncertain about the comparative trends in farm and nonfarm incomes from 1937 to 1950. For these reasons, the extent to which there is in 1950 (as there was in 1937) a broad conformity to adjusted factor costs at these points is somewhat conjectural.

In Table 29 I have attempted to adjust the calculations in 1950 prices as I did those in 1937 prices for turnover taxes and subsidies. In other words, I again revalue national income at ruble factor cost. Because of its unimportance, I do not repeat here the adjustment for farm prices that previously was made in association with those for turnover taxes and subsidies, but otherwise the revaluation proceeds in essentially the same way as before. Thus, in the initial computation of "real" national income in 1950 prices, serial data in these terms are compiled for all the use categories in Table 30. I now reaggregate these series

[20] In Table 26, compare with the series in terms of 1937 ruble factor cost these two alternative series: that with profits deducted and rent and interest added and that with allowance for nonlabor charges according to the U.S. 1947 cost structure. As with the series in terms of 1937 ruble factor cost from which they are derived, the latter two series are obtained through a revaluation that is only partial, but in the case of that allowing for nonlabor charges according to the U.S. 1947 cost structure extension of the revaluation in question seems likely to have less rather than more of an impact than that resulting from extension of the initial revaluation in terms of 1937 ruble factor cost (see pages 135 and 147). None of the foregoing series allows for the undervaluation of agricultural labor services (see pages 118 ff.). But, as we may judge from computations involving the addition of agricultural rent at 40 percent of farm labor income, the effect of such an allowance would be to reduce somewhat more the growth of consumption and national income.

assigning to each a weight corresponding to the value of goods and services disposed of in 1950 at the ruble factor cost of that year.[21] The weights applied are calculated in turn from data already compiled on the national income by use in current rubles in 1950 (Table 30) and from

TABLE 29

Gross National Product by Use, USSR, 1928–55, in Ruble Factor Cost of 1950 (billions of rubles)

Outlay category	1928	1937	1940	1944	1950	1955
Household purchases in retail markets	117.4	140.3	150.8	75.1	187.3	316.5
Housing; services	23.7	40.8	44.5	30.5	49.9	75.3
Consumption of farm income in kind	89.6[a]	65.5	74.4	44.0	68.9	77.9
Military subsistence	1.4	4.2	8.3	28.7	10.0	16.0
Household consumption outlays	232.1	250.8	278.0	178.3	316.1	485.7
Communal services	13.8	51.7	61.7	47.3	75.3	92.0
Government administration, including NKVD (OGPU; MVD and MGB)	6.8	16.8	24.5	19.3	33.6	23.6
Defense (as recorded in budget)[b]	4.8	32.0	81.7	210.9	75.6	107.1
Gross investment						
Fixed capital	30.4	87.3	94.5	54.9	155.1	259.0
Other	10.7	39.8	21.3	19.3	38.4	32.9
Total	41.1	127.1	115.8	74.2	193.5	291.9
Gross national product	298.6	478.4	561.7	530.0	694.1	1000.3

[a] Including farm wages in kind.
[b] Exclusive of pensions to officers et al.

estimates of the direct and indirect incidence of turnover taxes and subsidies in 1950. Although the schedule of turnover tax rates effective in 1950 has not been published, except for oil products and electric power, the levy now falls entirely on consumers' goods. Given this, I believe the tax can be allocated by use categories with only limited error by assigning to household purchases in government and cooperative retail shops the vast bulk of the taxes that remain after rather arbitrary allowance is made for levies on consumers' goods, oil products, and electric power used elsewhere. For subsidies, as previously, the allocation by use category is of a rule-of-thumb sort. In these ways I distribute in all 241.3 billion rubles of turnover taxes (including 5.2 billion rubles of

[21] In chapter 6, serial data in 1950 prices are compiled separately for household purchases in government and cooperative retail shops and restaurants, on the one hand, and for household purchases in collective farm markets, on the other. For present purposes, I nevertheless refer only to the aggregate of these two outlay categories and not to each separately. This is done because, with the omission of any adjustment for farm prices, the measures of outlays for the two components that are derived after allowance for turnover taxes and subsidies still fail to reflect relative factor costs.

TABLE 30

Gross National Product by Use, USSR, 1950, at Prevailing Prices and Ruble Factor Cost of 1950

Outlay category	Value at prevailing prices: Billion rubles	Value at prevailing prices: Percent	Value at ruble factor cost: Billion rubles	Value at ruble factor cost: Percent
Household purchases in retail market	375.0	41.1	187.3	27.0
Housing; services	50.4	5.5	49.9	7.2
Consumption of farm income in kind	61.0	6.7	68.9	9.9
Military subsistence	14.1	1.5	10.0	1.4
Household consumption outlays	500.5	54.9	316.1	45.5
Communal services				
Labor inputs	50.9	5.6	50.9	7.3
Nonlabor inputs	34.6	3.8	24.4	3.5
Total	85.5	9.4	75.3	10.8
Government administration, including NKVD (OGPU; MVD and MGB)	36.9	4.0	33.6	4.8
Defense				
Military services	29.1	3.2	25.0	3.6
Munitions	51.7	5.7	50.6	7.3
Total	80.8	8.9	75.6	10.9
Gross investment				
Fixed capital	156.5	17.2	155.1	22.3
Livestock	1.7	0.2	1.4	0.2
Inventories				
Trade	8.0	0.9	3.4	0.5
Other	22.0	2.4	15.5	2.2
Total	30.0	3.3	18.9	2.7
Miscellaneous	19.8	2.2	18.1	2.6
Total	208.0	22.8	193.5	27.9
Gross national product	911.7	100.0	694.1	100.0

Note: Minor discrepancies between sums of individual items and specified totals are due to rounding.

imputations) and 23.7 billion rubles of subsidies (including 8.7 billion rubles of imputations.)[22]

[22] In Table 30, the data on the value of output at prevailing prices are taken from Appendices A to G. For communal services, I aggregate here the data compiled in the appendices on the labor and nonlabor inputs to health care and education. Also outlays on "other" communal services are broken down and distributed.

The turnover tax totaled 236.1 billion rubles in 1950. See *SNIP-49–55*. The effective tax rates on collective farm market sales, housing, and services and miscellaneous investment are taken to be the same as in 1937. Taxes on "munitions, other" and on investments in fixed capital, consisting primarily of taxes on oil products, are taken rather arbitrarily to be 2 and 4 billion rubles, respectively. I have sought to consider here scattered information on the pre-war volume and allocation of oil taxes and on the trends in oil sales to 1950. In the sense understood previously, the average effective tax rate on taxed goods is calculated to be 32 percent. As before, this rate is applied to military

As before, the revaluation has only a relatively limited effect on the trends in the gross national product (Table 31). Usually this is also true for major components. The factors determining the impact of the revaluation are much the same as those that were operative previously. There is no need, therefore, to consider this matter again here.

The revaluation in terms of 1950 ruble factor cost, like that in terms of the ruble factor cost of 1937, is only partial. While I reaggregate serial data on different use categories with weights corresponding to their ruble factor cost values, different commodities within use categories continue as before to be valued at prevailing prices. Moreover, again as in the earlier year, ruble factor cost is one thing and adjusted factor cost another. The revaluation takes us part way but not all the way to our desideratum. Very possibly, however, we have nevertheless approximated the revaluation sought. In respect of the calculations in terms of 1937 prices, when the revaluation in terms of ruble factor cost was made more complete, the results generally were little affected, although household consumption and national income in 1928 rise by a number of percentage points in relation to 1937. Extension of the revaluation to allow for distorting features other than turnover tax and subsidies also appeared to have only a limited effect. The remaining sources of distortion in 1950 are much the same as in 1937. In the case of profits in particular, the total sum involved is somewhat larger in relation to (say) the volume of turnover tax receipts than was so in 1937, but the difference hardly could be very consequential. Profits before taxes amounted to about 82 billion rubles or 35 percent of the turnover tax receipts in 1950. The corresponding figures for 1937 are 19.6 billion rubles and 26 percent. I conclude provisionally that the data in Table 31 are no longer seriously affected by valuation distortions, although a more complete revaluation

---

subsistence; communal services, nonlabor inputs; government administration, nonlabor inputs (taken to be 30 percent of the total; see Appendix D); and investment in inventories, other. In this way I account for 35.6 billion rubles of taxes. After a pro-rata allocation to investments in trade inventories, the balance of 200.5 billion rubles is allotted to household purchases in government and cooperative retail shops and restaurants. Since taxes on military subsistence come to 4.5 billion rubles, a like amount is imputed to military services under defense. Also, in view of the tax on collective farm market prices, I impute 0.7 billion rubles of taxes to farm income in kind, which is valued at average realized farm prices.

Subsidies to economic enterprises totaled an estimated 15 billion rubles in 1950. See *SNIP-49–55*. Account is taken here of the new data in Appendix D of *SNIP-49–55*. Of this total, about 3 billions were paid to industry and some 12 billions to agriculture. Subsidies to industry and agriculture are allocated by use category on the same rule-of-thumb basis as was used previously. Subsidies to agriculture are estimated at 14.1 percent of the value of agricultural marketings. Subsidies are imputed to farm income in kind at the same rate. In order to allow for subsidies on military subsistence, I also impute 0.4 billion rubles of subsidies to military services, under defense.

TABLE 31

Gross National Product by Use, USSR, 1928–55, in 1950 Ruble Prices and Factor Cost (1937 = 100)

Outlay category	1928	1937	1940	1944	1950	1955
Household consumption outlays						
1950 prices	88.2	100	110	67.5	130	207
1950 ruble factor cost	92.5	100	111	71.1	126	194
Communal services						
1950 prices	25.0	100	118	90.9	141	172
1950 ruble factor cost	26.7	100	119	91.5	146	178
Government administration, including NKVD (OGPU; MVD and MGB)						
1950 prices	40.8	100	146	115	201	141
1950 ruble factor cost[a]	40.8	100	146	115	201	141
Defense						
1950 prices	15.7	100	252	659	236	334
1950 ruble factor cost	15.0	100	255	659	236	335
Gross investment						
1950 prices	34.3	100	86.2	57.7	151	225
1950 ruble factor cost	32.3	100	91.1	58.4	152	230
Gross national product						
1950 prices	65.2	100	114	101	143	213
1950 ruble factor cost	62.4	100	117	111	145	209

[a] Assumed to vary in the same way as in prevailing prices of 1950.

might well raise materially the results for 1928 in relation to those for later years.

Although the turnover tax was not yet levied in 1928, ruble prices of that year diverge from adjusted factor cost because of various sales taxes that were then in effect. Subsidies were only nominal and depreciation charges relatively meaningful in 1928, but, as in 1937, prices include profit charges which, I believe, are largely unrelated to adjusted factor cost and little or no interest is charged on fixed capital. At the prevailing farm prices, agricultural labor services seem to be undervalued in comparison with the situation in 1937. The undervaluation is over and above that arising from the absence of any systematic charge for agricultural rent. In 1928, multiple prices are in some respects less and in some respects more of a problem than in 1937. Among other things, while retail prices in different markets are more or less uniform in 1937 there are significant divergencies in 1928.

In Table 32 I have sought to adjust for some of the more important of these distortions. National income as originally calculated in 1928 ruble prices is now recomputed at prices net of sales taxes. Although subsidies are inconsequential, the revaluation also allows for this aspect.

TABLE 32

Gross National Product by Use, USSR, 1928–37, in Ruble Factor Cost of 1928 (billions of rubles)

Outlay category	1928	1937
Household purchases in retail markets	9.41	16.50
Housing; services	2.79	4.60
Consumption of farm income in kind[a]	6.70	4.90
Military subsistence	0.23	0.40
Household consumption outlays	19.13	26.40
Communal services	1.51	6.30
Government administration, including NKVD (OGPU)	0.80	2.00
Defense (as recorded in budget)[b]	0.74	10.60
Gross investment		
Fixed capital	6.15	28.10
Other	1.23	7.90
Total	7.38	36.00
Gross national product	29.56	81.30

[a] Including farm wages in kind.
[b] Exclusive of pensions to officers, et al.

Finally, profits earned by public sector enterprises are redistributed in order to adjust for a wide variation in returns on fixed capital between different sectors, particularly "light" and "heavy" industries. While the latter adjustment takes us beyond a revaluation at ruble factor cost, for convenience I refer to the data in Table 32 as being expressed in terms of the latter standard.

The revaluation again entails the reaggregation of serial data previously compiled for different use categories in prevailing prices, in this case the prices of 1928. The use categories considered are listed in Table 33. Also shown are the weights employed in the reaggregation. For each category, the indicated weight is intended to represent the value of output disposed of in 1928 at prevailing prices, less sales taxes and plus subsidies. A further adjustment, positive or negative, is also made to allow for divergencies within the public sector between actual profit charges and an average rate of 8.9 percent earned on public sector fixed capital generally. Except in minor particulars, the necessary data on the incidence of sales taxes, subsidies, and differentials profits are taken from *SNIP-28*. The government collected 2.67 billion rubles in sales taxes in 1928. Hoeffding was able to estimate the incidence of these charges by major use categories chiefly from information on tax schedules and official data on taxes paid by different sectors. Subsidies, amounting to perhaps 0.05 billion rubles, presumably accrued primarily to invest-

TABLE 33

Gross National Product by Use, USSR, 1928, at Prevailing Prices and Ruble Factor Cost of 1928

Outlay category	Value at prevailing prices: Billion rubles	Value at prevailing prices: Percent	Value at ruble factor cost: Billion rubles	Value at ruble factor cost: Percent
Household purchases in retail markets	12.10	37.5	9.41	31.8
Housing; services	2.79	8.6	2.79	9.4
Consumption of farm income in kind[a]	6.70	20.7	6.70	22.7
Military subsistence	0.25	0.8	0.23	0.8
Household consumption outlays	21.84	67.6	19.13	64.7
Communal services				
Labor inputs	1.02	3.2	1.02	3.5
Nonlabor inputs	0.53	1.6	0.49	1.7
Total	1.55	4.8	1.51	5.1
Government administration including NKVD (OGPU)	0.82	2.5	0.80	2.7
Defense				
Military services	0.40	1.2	0.38	1.3
Munitions; other	0.36	1.1	0.36	1.2
Total	0.76	2.4	0.74	2.5
Gross investment				
Fixed capital	6.00	18.6	6.15	20.8
Livestock	0.20	0.6	0.20	0.7
Inventories				
Trade	0.51	1.6	0.40	1.4
Other	0.31	1.0	0.32	1.1
Total	0.82	2.5	0.72	2.4
Miscellaneous	0.30	0.9	0.31	1.0
Total	7.32	22.7	7.38	25.0
Gross national product	32.29	100.0	29.56	100.0

[a] Including farm wages in kind.

Note: Minor discrepancies between sums of individual items and specified totals are due to rounding.

ment goods. The adjustment for differential profits is made on the basis of official data on public sector profits and fixed capital by industrial origin.[23]

The revaluation hardly affects the trends in either national income or its major components (Table 34). This is due partly to the fact that while sales taxes tend in 1928 as in later years to fall primarily on consumers' goods the rates at which they are levied are generally relatively limited in the early period in question. As a source of distortion, sales taxes in 1928 are compounded by profits which also fall heavily on con-

[23] For purposes of Table 33, it was necessary to elaborate somewhat the more aggregative breakdowns given in *SNIP-28,* chap. iii. The further computations are sometimes rather arbitrary, but errors at this point would be unimportant.

TABLE 34

Gross National Product by Use, USSR, 1928–37, in 1928 Ruble Prices and Factor Cost

Outlay category	1928 ÷ 1937 (percent)
Household consumption outlays	
1928 prices	70.2
1928 ruble factor cost	72.5
Communal services	
1928 prices	23.4
1928 ruble factor cost	24.0
Government administration, including NKVD (OGPU)	
1928 prices	40.8
1928 ruble factor cost[a]	40.8
Defense	
1928 prices	7.2
1928 ruble factor cost	7.0
Gross investment	
1928 prices	20.7
1928 ruble factor cost	20.5
Gross national product	
1928 prices	37.7
1928 ruble factor cost	36.4

[a] Assumed to vary in the same way as in prevailing prices of 1928.

sumers' goods, but even if account is taken of the differential profits on such commodities the overvaluation still does not compare with that caused by the turnover tax alone in 1937. As in later years, the impact of the adjustment is also dampened so far as it results in a higher weight being assigned not only to the fast growing investment and defense sectors but also to the contracting farm income in kind.

The foregoing revaluation is again partial. Since about one-third of the sales tax receipts were collected on sales of vodka and tobacco,[24] both of which grew relatively rapidly, a more complete revaluation might have resulted in a somewhat reduced increase in "real" national income. But considering that such taxes in general were small compared to the turnover taxes of later years, the effect most likely would be less than that observed where valuation is in terms of 1937 ruble factor cost. While adjustments are made for differential profits and by the same token to some extent for the inadequate interest charge on fixed capital, so far as agricultural income was understated initially it remains so in the revaluation. Judging from an illustrative computation, allowance for this aspect too would tend to reduce growth, although only to a relatively limited extent. In the computation in question I arbitrarily increase

[24] *SNIP-28,* p. 51.

agricultural net income by 50 percent or 5.4 billion rubles. This might be viewed as correcting at one and the same time, although probably inadequately, for the undervaluation of the services of agricultural land and labor. This is the effect on the index of "real" national income:[25] The ratio of 1928 to 1937 income in 1928 prices is 37.7 percent; at 1928 ruble factor cost it is 36.4 percent; and at 1928 ruble factor cost, with agricultural net income increased by 50 percent, it is 40 percent. Our calculations for retail trade are supposed to be in terms of the average level of prices prevailing in different markets, but the difficulty in achieving this desideratum for individual commodities may be another source of error in the results.

[25] In 1928 Soviet farmers earned a net income of 10.8 billion rubles. Of this, net income in kind constituted 6.9 billion rubles, while the balance represented money incomes over and above money production expenses. See *SNIP-28,* p. 66; *SNIP-28–48;* and Table 3 of this volume. In order to increase farm net income by 50 percent, therefore, we must raise earnings by 5.4 billion rubles. Taking account of their relative importance in farm production for use and for sale, the implied change in farm prices means that income in kind rises by 3.2 billion rubles and farm marketings by 2.2 billion rubles. For simplicity, I assume that the latter sum accrues entirely to household retail purchases.

The foregoing computation allows only for the undervaluation of farm labor services compared with the situation in 1937. If we wish to adjust also for an undervaluation of such services in the latter year, the adjustment indicated for 1928 is correspondingly increased.

10

HOUSEHOLD CONSUMPTION IN ADJUSTED MARKET PRICES

The task of this chapter is to appraise the effects on my calculations for household consumption of divergencies of ruble prices from the consumers' utility standard. I first consider the relation of the ruble prices of consumers' goods and services to this standard and then explore the possible effect on my calculations of such divergencies as are observed.

CONSUMERS' GOODS PRICES AND THE CONSUMERS' UTILITY STANDARD

Of particular interest in this study is the relation of the prices of consumers' goods and services to the consumers' utility standard in 1937, 1950, and 1928. As in the appraisal of divergencies from adjusted factor cost, so here, I focus especially on my calculations in 1937 prices. Hence, the circumstances of this year must again be given special consideration. I refer first to the prices prevailing for household retail purchases in

1937 and then to the prices at which other categories of household consumption are valued in the same year. Reference is made finally to the prices of consumers' goods and services generally in 1950 and 1928.

Household purchases in retail markets in 1937. In order for retail prices to correspond to consumers' utilities under socialism, two conditions must obtain: Households must be able to buy consumers' goods in an open market, and at established prices they must be free to dispose of their incomes as they please. The open market must be effective in the sense that the government fixes prices which limit demand to the available supply. The first condition was systematically violated in the USSR from early in the five year plans to 1935 and 1936. During this period, the government disposed of consumers' goods primarily although not exclusively by rationing rather than through an open market. But the government discontinued rationing in 1935 and 1936, and from this time until after the Nazi attack it relied instead on the open market in distributing available supplies of consumers' goods. In 1937, therefore, the first condition is met. In the circumstances, there are reasons to think that very broadly the second is also.

As was explained, under the five year plans Soviet collective farmers have been free to dispose of their surplus produce in the retail collective farm market. Since prices in this market are unregulated, they serve at once as a barometer of the availability of supplies at official prices in government and cooperative retail shops, and in this way of the effectiveness of the retail market for consumers' goods generally. If, at the prevailing official prices, the government and cooperative retail shops are unable to meet the demand, very likely similar goods will sell at higher prices on the collective farm market. When supplies in the government and cooperative retail shops are adequate, however, there is no need to pay a premium on the collective farm market. In this case, the collective farm market prices should tend to approach those charged in the government and retail shops.

The functioning of the Soviet retail market in 1937, therefore, may be appraised in this light. The appraisal for a country as large and economically differentiated as the USSR is hardly as simple as my theoretic remarks might suggest. Furthermore, for the time studied, the government has published only meager information of the sort needed. Very likely, however, the retail market functioned more or less effectively at least for a brief interval around 1937.

As might be expected, while rationing prevailed collective farm market prices exceeded the official prices in the government and cooperative shops. Indeed, reflecting the dire circumstances of the time, the margins between the two were often notably great. As late as 1934, for example, collective farm market prices for various foodstuffs were often two to four times the official level.[1] The government discontinued the rationing of foodstuffs, however, in December. In preparation for this step, it also raised sharply official prices of such products. With this, the collective farm market prices tended at once to approach the official prices, as these Soviet data testify. The ratios (in percent) of collective farm market prices to official prices for December 25, 1935, in Moscow,[2] are: beef, 87; pork, 81; potatoes, 137; cabbage, 167; milk, 129; eggs, 97; and butter (melted), 87. The average is 112.

Dr. Karcz has compiled from Soviet sources a good many quotations for prices charged in the collective farm market in 1937.[3] Collating these data with her own statistics on official prices in government and cooperative retail shops, Dr. Janet Chapman reaches these conclusions as to the relation between the two sorts of prices in 1937:[4]

"Of 48 free market quotations for meat in several cities during the period April through December, 1937, most are within the range of official prices for the same type meat in the corresponding price zone. Precise comparisons cannot be made as the quality of the meat is not specified in the case of the free market quotations. All nine located collective farm market prices for various specified grades of flour are below the corresponding official price. For other products the data are less conclusive as there was no uniform centrally established price or set of zonal prices for state and cooperative trade. Official prices of such perishable, seasonal products as milk, eggs, vegetables, and fruit were set locally at that time. For milk, twenty market quotations located by Karcz ranged from 0.55 rubles to 1.70 rubles per liter in various cities during the period April through December. The state shop price in Moscow was 1.60 R. per liter all year; but the Moscow price is probably for bottled, pasteurized milk, while the market prices are undoubtedly for unpasteurized, unbottled milk. In two cases the market price could be compared with the official price in the same city on the same date. In one of these cases the market price was the same as the official price and in the other case the market price was below the official price. Seven quotations for eggs on the Moscow market seem in line with the Moscow official prices. Twenty-seven market quotations for potatoes in several cities ranged from 0.09 rubles to 1.50 rubles per kilogram. Of these five relate to Moscow and range from 0.14 rubles to 0.45 rubles per kilogram during the period October through December, when the state shop price was 0.40 rubles per kilogram. Seventeen quotations for cabbage on the markets of various cities between June and October ranged from 0.10 rubles to 1.50 rubles per kilogram. The latter is a price for early cabbage. During the same period, the state shop price of cabbage in Moscow declined from 2.00 rubles in June to 0.30 rubles per kilogram at the end of August, where it remained through the rest of the year."

These were the circumstances of 1937. Very likely they persisted for a time, but in 1940 even before rationing had been reintroduced, prices in

[1] L. E. Hubbard, *Soviet Trade and Distribution,* London, 1938, p. 148.

[2] TSUNKHU, *Kolkhoznaia i individual'no-krestianskaia torgovlia,* Moscow, 1936, pp. 178 ff.

[3] Jerzy F. Karcz, "Soviet Agricultural Marketings and Prices, 1928–1954," The RAND Corporation, Research Memorandum RM-1930, July 2, 1957, Appendix E.

[4] Janet Chapman, *Real Wages,* chap. ii.

the collective farm market were again above, and in some instances far above those in the government and cooperative retail shops.

In interpreting the available information on the relation of collective farm market and official prices, it is necessary to consider differences in quality, location, and service. As Dr. Chapman suggests, if the collective farm market prices were often below the official level around 1937, the explanation probably is to be found in these facts. Moreover, the collective farm market prices necessarily are more sensitive than the official to seasonal phenomena. While this in itself reflects on effectiveness, premiums that are observable in the collective farm market at particular times may not indicate any persistent deficiency of a sort of interest here in supplies in the government and cooperative retail shops.

The collective farm market has been taken here as a barometer of the functioning of the retail market generally. Actually sales in the former consist predominantly although not exclusively of foodstuffs as distinct from manufacturers. Hence, strictly speaking, prices there provide an immediate basis to judge the functioning of the retail market only for the former products. Where the retailing of foodstuffs is orderly, however, one is inclined to suppose it is more or less so for manufacturers as well.[5]

So far as the retail market tended to function effectively around 1937, this was not accidental. On the one hand, as the calculations made in this study will suggest, by that time a substantial recovery had been achieved from the depressed consumption levels that prevailed at the end of the First Five Year Plan. On the other, as Soviet economists are aware, where consumers' goods are distributed through an open market the proper determination of relative prices is practically important.[6] In fact, the government has not always been especially concerned to act accordingly, but seemingly it was sufficiently so in 1937. This incidentally is among the reasons 1937 has been given special attention in this study.

Other household consumption in 1937. If, in 1937, consumers' goods were sold at retail in a more or less effective open market, this hardly was true of housing. After nearly fifteen years of war, revolution, civil war, and recovery, and a further decade of five year plans, housing was notoriously short by any standard. In 1937, the average city dweller in the USSR occupied but 4.4 square meters of housing space.[7] Despite the acute shortage, the government presumably might still have succeeded in

[5] On a visit to the USSR in the summer of 1937, I had some opportunity to judge first-hand the state of the retail market at the time. Although I found some queuing up in retail shops, particularly in the case of meat stores, I gained the impression that the retail market generally was functioning in an orderly manner, with stocks sufficient to meet requirements at the prevailing prices. I spent most of the summer in Moscow, and my observations refer primarily to the situation there.

[6] Chapman, *Real Wages*, chap. ii.

[7] On the urban housing space, see Appendix B. Some 50.6 million persons lived in urban localities on July 1, 1937.

distributing housing through a market mechanism if it so desired. Rentals, however, would have had to be high indeed. In fact, under a complex formula that was applied, the government charged notably low rents for housing. Typically an industrial family of four might have paid in 1937 for public housing an annual rental of (say) 150 rubles, or but 5 percent of the average Soviet wage of the time. In relation to family income, the rental would have been still lower. Although Western eyes must view this low figure in the light of the proverbial qualitative as well as quantitative deficiencies in Soviet housing, a material divergence from the consumers' utility standard must be reckoned with at this point.

Just how the Soviet housing market functioned in the absence of an adequate rental charge is still to be studied systematically. An account by one who served as an official in Soviet prewar housing administration tends only to confirm the impression as to the inadequacy of the charges to effectively limit demand:[8]

". . . the term vacant apartment is virtually unknown in the Soviet Union. Housing has been such a scarce commodity that it almost might be characterized as a luxury; no matter how poor accommodations may be they are still sought after. Not only are there long waiting lists for every room or corner of a room long before they are to become vacant, but individuals as well as organizations often take arbitrary possession of apartments or other buildings before construction has been completed, in direct violation of existing law."

The legal norm of housing space has long been nine square meters per person. The nature of the rationing procedures by which the space actually occupied has been restricted to an average level far below this norm are not known.

On the degree to which the prices charged for utilities and miscellaneous services limited demand to the available supply in 1937, little is known. From 1928 to 1937 the prices of different services for the most part rose far less than retail prices, and one is led to suspect that the market for services could not have been especially effective. Supply often increased sharply, however, and the relatively limited increase in prices must have been partly a reflection of this fact (Table 35). In trying to value consumption in terms of the consumers' utility standard, clearly a range of possibilities must be considered regarding the prices of services.

For purposes of the consumers' utility valuation, consumption of farm income in kind seemingly is appropriately valued more or less at retail prices, provided the latter reflect consumers' utilities. If conventional principles of national income accounting are to be observed, a deduction nevertheless must be made for transportation and distribution charges not incurred. So far as home processing is to be omitted from national income, the retail prices applied must also be net of processing charges. In my

[8] T. Sosnovy, *The Housing Problem in the Soviet Union,* New York, 1954, p. 109.

TABLE 35

Indices of Physical Volume and Prices of Household Retail Purchases and Selected Services, USSR, 1928
(1937 = 100)

	Volume 1928	Prices 1928
Household purchases in retail shops	83.3	11.5
Electricity, urban	19.2	90.0
Water, urban	30.1	100
Urban passenger transport	28.6	73.3
Railroad passenger service	27.0	34.3

Note: For household purchases in retail shops, the physical volume index is that in 1937 prices. Correspondingly the price index is that given by Formula (5). The other physical volume data represent for electricity, all municipal power consumed; for water, probably all urban consumption; urban passenger transport, supposedly the number of passengers carried by trams and trolley busses, and for railroads, total passenger miles. The data were all compiled by Dr. Janet Chapman. See Appendix B. For prices, I also cite figures compiled by Dr. Chapman in *Real Wages* from incomplete information, e.g., for electric power, reference is to rates charged for lighting private apartments in Moscow and Leningrad.

computations in terms of 1937 rubles, income in kind is valued in terms of the average realized farm prices of that year. Although some of the prices considered in the average refer to the retail market, that is, the prices prevailing in the collective farm market, obviously such computations do not conform with the consumers' utility standard. Accordingly, when we come to revalue consumption in terms of this standard, we must allow for a distortion in ruble values at this point.

Although somewhat arbitrary, the estimates of military subsistence in 1937 supposedly represent the value of food and other supplies provided military personnel at current wholesale prices gross of turnover taxes. I assume provisionally that military subsistence is correctly valued in terms of the consumers' utility standard.[9]

[9] Since in *SNIP-37,* the concern was only to compute national income in terms of adjusted factor cost, the consumers' utility standard is applied for the first time in the present study. Moreover, so far as ruble prices accord with the consumers' utility standard, I shall of course retain these prices in computing household consumption in terms of this standard. To this extent, therefore, the present approach to the valuation problem may possibly mollify Peter Wiles ("Are Adjusted Rubles Rational?" and "A Rejoinder to All and Sundry," *Soviet Studies*). But if I understand Wiles correctly, he comes finally to feel that Soviet national income generally, and not merely consumption, may be computed in terms of the consumers' utility standard. He also seems to argue that calculations in terms of prevailing rubles may serve for this purpose. If the aim is valuation in terms of consumers' utilities, no doubt the use of unadjusted rubles as an alternative to adjusted factor cost shifts the comparative weights of consumption and nonconsumption in the right direction. But, as Holzman points out ("The Adjusted Factor Cost Standard of Measuring National Income: Comment," *Soviet Studies,* July 1957), except by coincidence the results still could hardly reflect accurately the utilities of Soviet consumers. After all, the chief cause of the divergence between unadjusted rubles

Consumption generally in 1950 and 1928. The functioning of the consumers' market around 1950 has as yet been little explored. At this time, as before the war, consumers' goods were distributed through an open market system. In fact this has been the situation ever since December 1947, when the government finally abandoned the rationing system which was introduced after the German attack. Moreover, the market may well have functioned with some effectiveness in 1950. As we have seen, one indication of the effectiveness of the open market in 1937 was the tendency at that time for prices in the uncontrolled collective farm market to be more or less in line with those prevailing in the government and cooperative retail shops. Prices in the two markets probably were similarly related in 1950. Thus, prices in government and cooperative retail shops in 1950 averaged 222 to 244 percent of 1937. The corresponding index for collective farm market prices may have been on the order of 208 percent. Because of the uncertainties regarding trends in collective farm market prices, little significance can be attached to the fact that the latter are found to rise less than the official prices.

If housing was undervalued in 1937, this certainly was still true in 1950. At this time, the average city dweller occupied 4.6 square meters of housing space, or about the same amount as in 1937. While the average rental rate in 1950 was perhaps 85 percent above that of the earlier year, retail prices as we have just seen were more than double the previous level. In relation to retail prices, the prices for utilities and services generally may have been about the same in 1950 as in 1937, although for different items there are nevertheless very diverse trends in both volume and prices. In any event, we must continue as before to allow for a range of possibilities so far as the valuation of these goods is concerned. So far as farm income in kind is valued at the average realized prices of 1950, clearly we must again reckon here with a departure from the consumers' utility standard. As for 1937, the valuation of military subsistence

---

and adjusted factor cost is the turnover tax. The magnitude of this tax reflects many factors, but obviously it does not bear any meaningful relation to the premium that Soviet consumers might wish to apply to consumers' goods in valuing them in relation to (say) investment goods. Moreover, as has been mentioned, even within the consumption sector, the prevailing ruble prices leave something to be desired from the standpoint of a consumers' utility valuation.

I have felt, nevertheless, that the deficiencies in such prices are not irreparable if the aim is to value in these terms household consumption alone, but one hesitates to try to extend such a computation to national income generally. At any rate, it is not attempted here. As was explained, the calculation in terms of adjusted factor cost may possibly be indicative of welfare understood in terms of planners' preferences. So far as national income is also measured in terms of the consumers' utility-factor cost standard (see chapter 3, note 3), the data may help us appraise welfare in terms of a mixture of consumers' utilities and planners' preferences. None of the national income computations made, however, enables us to appraise welfare in terms of the consumers' utility standard alone.

at wholesale prices gross of turnover taxes is taken to conform sufficiently well to the latter formula.

In 1928, the government still maintained the open market for consumers' goods that had been introduced under the New Economic Policy, but as the First Five Year Plan was getting under way the market hardly functioned very effectively.[10] As a means of exercising pressure on the still existing private trade, the government fixed prices in its own and in the cooperative shops at a relatively low level, but the fact that the partly controlled prices in private trade nevertheless persisted at levels averaging almost 40 percent above the official level already testifies that the government had insufficient supplies to meet the demand in its own outlets. Then too, toward the end of 1928 the government had already found it expedient to introduce a rationing system of bread distribution in some major cities, although it was not until 1929–30 that this system was to be applied on a relatively extensive scale. In 1928, it should be noted, private trade accounted for 23 percent of all retail sales. This refers to trade conducted by "intermediaries" in "stationary" shops and does not take account of sales made directly to households by peasants and other producers. Much of the latter trade took place in rural farm markets, where prices seemingly tended to be below the average urban levels. All in all, retail prices in 1928 must be considered as diverging markedly from the consumers' utility standard.

In 1928, accelerated industrialization and the concomitant mushrooming of cities were still in the future, but even so the average city dweller had at his disposal but 5.7 square meters of housing space. Considering that a family of four might have had to pay but 55 rubles a year or less than 8 percent of the current average wage, we see that the housing very likely was also undervalued, although not by as much as it was to be in the period under the five year plans.

The degree to which the prices of utilities and services conformed to the consumers' utility standard in 1928 is conjectural. As was explained, the government in 1928 levied diverse sales taxes on consumers' goods sold in the retail market. It also earned differential profits from the operations of its enterprises in "light" industry. If only for these reasons we see that in valuing farm income in kind at average realized farm prices we tend in 1928 as in later years to diverge from the consumers' utility standard. For 1928 as for later years the prices at which military subsistence is valued are considered as conforming to this formula.

Consumption Outlays in Adjusted Market Prices

Among consumers' goods and services purchased by households in 1937, prices diverge from the consumers' utility standard chiefly because of

[10] See Chapman, *Real Wages,* chap. ii: Bergson, *Structure of Soviet Wages,* pp. 36 ff.

the undervaluation of farm income in kind and housing in relation to the prices prevailing in government and cooperative retail shops. The prices charged for utilities and other services may also diverge from the consumers' utility standard, although little is known about this aspect.

The different series in Table 36 may help to appraise the import of

TABLE 36

Household Consumption Outlays, USSR, 1928–55, in Prevailing and Adjusted Market Prices of 1937 (1937 = 100)

Year	In prevailing prices of 1937	In prevailing prices of 1937, with farm income in kind, housing and services revalued	In prevailing prices of 1937, with farm income in kind, housing and services revalued, alternative computation
1928	88.8	94.1	91.7
1937	100	100	100
1940	114	113	113
1944	69.3	70.1	70.4
1950	133	126	126
1955	209	190	190

these limitations. In the first column, I repeat the series on household consumption previously derived in terms of the prevailing ruble prices of 1937. The elements of the calculation of the series in the second column appear in Table 37. Household retail purchases and military subsistence

TABLE 37

Household Consumption Outlays, USSR, 1928–55, in Adjusted Market Prices of 1937 (billion rubles)

Outlay category	1928	1937	1940	1944	1950	1955
Household purchases in retail markets	105.0	126.0	140.0	70.0	171.0	283.0
Housing; services	25.5	40.4	45.0	32.2	51.0	73.2
Consumption of farm income in kind	86.9[a]	63.0	71.8	43.1	64.3	75.0
Military subsistence	0.8	2.5	5.0	17.2	6.0	9.6
Household consumption outlays	218.2	231.9	261.8	162.5	292.3	440.8

[a] Including farm wages in kind.

are included as previously computed in terms of 1937 prices. I also use the same physical volume series as before for housing and services, but in each case total outlays in the base year are revalued. As recorded in our accounts initially, housing outlays in 1937 amount to 2.8 billion rubles. I now increase these fourfold to 11.2 billion rubles. After this adjustment, the implied rental rate for urban dwelling space is related to retail prices for food and manufactures in more or less the same way as rental rates for ordinary urban apartments in the United States were related to the corresponding prices in this country in 1950. I rely here on ruble-dollar price comparisons made by Kaplan and Wainstein.[11] By applying a similar logic to utilities and miscellaneous services, I find that the value assigned them in 1937 conservatively must be increased at least twofold. Accordingly, total outlays on utilities and services in 1937, calculated initially at 14.6 billion rubles, are revalued at 29.2 billion rubles.[12]

In calculating the data in the second column of Table 36, farm income in kind is recomputed. The physical quantities of different products constituting income in kind are the same as before, but I now reaggregate these in terms of the prices prevailing in the collective farm market in 1937.[13] At the same time, while new index numbers of physical volume are obtained in this way, I record consumption of farm income in kind as having a value in 1937 of 63 billion rubles. In terms of collective farm

[11] In 1950, in terms of retail food prices, one dollar was worth 20.0 rubles. The corresponding magnitude for retail prices of manufactured consumers' goods was 14.1 rubles, and for dwelling space, 2.9 rubles. See N. Kaplan and E. S. Wainstein, "A Comparison of Soviet and American Retail Prices in 1950," *Journal of Political Economy*, December 1956, as revised in *Journal of Political Economy*, December 1957. I cite the ruble-dollar ratios which Kaplan and Wainstein compute in terms of Soviet 1937 weights, which are more relevant here than alternative although very similar ratios they compile in terms of 1950 weights. From data compiled for the present study, I find that these were the corresponding purchasing-power-equivalents for rubles in 1937 and dollars in 1950: food, 8.3 rubles per dollar; manufactured consumers' goods, 5.7 rubles per dollar; and dwelling space, 1.6 rubles per dollar. The necessary deflators for foodstuffs and manufactured consumers' goods are interpolated from Janet Chapman's calculations in the manner described in Appendix A. On the trends in rental rates from 1937 to 1950, see Appendix B. Given the assumed fourfold increase in the value of housing in 1937, therefore, one 1950 dollar is worth 6.4 rubles of 1937 in respect of dwelling space. This is somewhat above the calculated purchasing power equivalent of a ruble in respect of manufactured consumers' goods but still below that in respect of foods.

[12] For all services, including rent, Kaplan and Wainstein find that one 1950 dollar is worth 4.8 1950 rubles. From their data, I believe the corresponding relation excluding rent was 5.9 rubles to one dollar. Taking this result together with data on service prices compiled by Chapman, I find that for services other than rent one 1950 dollar was worth 2.6 rubles of 1937. This relation may be compared with those cited above for food and manufactures.

[13] For 1928, the figure on farm income in kind in terms of collective farm market prices of 1937 that is obtained by the method of aggregation is reduced by 13.5 percent in order to make it correspond in scope to the SNIP measures on farm income in kind derived from Soviet global data on farm output and its disposition. In calculating farm income in kind for 1928 in the present study, I generally have relied on the latter measures. See Appendix C. For 1944, farm income in kind in collective farm market prices is taken to be 60 percent of that of 1940, or the same relation as prevails where the data are in average realized farm prices.

market prices, the corresponding figure is 78 billion rubles. As was explained, collective farm market prices in 1937 probably tended to approach the levels of the prices prevailing in government and cooperative retail shops. The value assigned consumption of farm income in kind nevertheless is reduced below that in terms of collective farm market prices in order to exclude marketing costs not incurred on farm income in kind. In the light of the experience in government and cooperative retail shops, a 15 percent deduction made on this score must be conservative.[14] Also, by convention, we wish to omit from farm income in kind such home processing as occurs on goods sold in the collective farm market. I arbitrarily deduct on this account another 5 percent from the 1937 value of consumption in kind in terms of collective farm market prices.

Reliable data on collective farm market prices are especially difficult to compile, and the calculations of farm income in kind in these terms must be judged accordingly. Interestingly, however, the trends in this category are not markedly affected in comparison with those shown by the previous calculation in terms of average realized farm prices (see Table 38).

TABLE 38

Consumption of Farm Income in Kind, Alternative Valuations, USSR, 1928–55 (1937 = 100)

Year	In collective farm market prices of 1937	In average realized farm prices in 1937
1928	138	142[a]
1937	100	100
1940	114	120
1944	68.4	72.0
1950	102	112
1955	119	128

[a] Including farm wages in kind

In revaluing housing and services in the manner described, in effect I apply to Soviet household outlays U.S. dollar price relations. This is, of course, a dubious expedient. Accordingly, in the third column of Table 36, I repeat the foregoing calculation, but in order to appraise the import of the valuation for housing and services I experiment with alternative weights. The rental rate for housing is increased fivefold instead of fourfold. The prices of utilities and services are now increased three instead of two times.

[14] See Appendix D.

As might be expected in view of the greatly increased weight of farm income in kind (outlays on this category in 1937 rise from 25.0 to 63.0 billion rubles), the initial revaluation of household consumption reduces the growth in this category over the years studied. With the further revaluation of housing and services, growth tends to increase, but the further effect is perceptible only for the period 1928–37, and even here amounts to only a few percentage points. I conclude that within limits the precise values assigned housing and services are not very material for our purposes.

As recomputed here, household consumption is far above the figure obtained for it earlier in terms of ruble factor cost; that is, according to Table 37 household consumption is 232 billion rubles in 1937, and the corresponding figure in terms of ruble factor cost is 113 billion rubles. It will be seen at once that this discrepancy poses no special problem. Concerned as we are to measure "real" outlays, we are free to choose as we please the average level of prices in terms of which national income is finally valued. In the calculation in terms of ruble factor cost, this was most conveniently determined by the implied decision to take as a datum the average level of money wages. In the present calculation, the average level of prices in government and cooperative retail shops is appropriately taken as given. The divergent absolute magnitudes of household consumption follow at once from these decisions.

As it turns out, the alternative measures of household consumption in Table 39 also differ in respect of the resultant trends over time. Such

TABLE 39

Household Consumption, Alternative Valuations, USSR, 1928–55 (1937 = 100)

Year	In prevailing prices of 1937, as adjusted in Table 36	In 1937 ruble factor cost, Table 22
1928	94.1	93.4 (101)[a]
1937	100	100
1940	113	114
1944	70.1	73.2
1950	126	130
1955	190	197

[a] Index in parentheses represents result of extending the ruble factor cost valuation to different commodities comprising retail trade. See page 135.

divergencies are to be expected, however, in view of the different standards applied and different purposes served, and what perhaps must excite comment instead is that the divergencies are no greater than is observed. Seemingly, such differences as prevail in the USSR between relative values in terms of ruble factor costs and relative utilities are not as consequential for national income calculations as might be supposed. Actually, for major components, the relative values themselves do not differ widely (Table 40).

TABLE 40

Household Consumption by Type of Outlay, Alternative Valuations, USSR, 1937 (percent)

Outlay category	In prevailing prices of 1937, as adjusted in Table 36	In 1937 ruble factor cost, Table 22
Household purchases in retail markets	54.3	58.4
Housing; services	17.4	15.2
Consumption of farm income in kind	27.2	24.7
Military subsistence	1.1	1.7
Total	100.0	100.0

Apparently, the sharp reduction in the value of household retail purchases that results from their revaluation at factor cost has much the same effect on relative values as the sharp increase in the values of housing, services and farm income in kind that results when these are revalued in terms of the consumers' utility standard.

The alternative series in the second and third columns of Table 36 are intended to provide a basis for the appraisal of consumption from the standpoint of the consumers' utility standard. I shall refer to them, however, as being in "adjusted market prices." Even with the adjustment made here, it would be misleading to speak of such imperfect data (as one might be tempted to do) as being in terms of consumers' utilities. As between the two series, priority henceforth will be accorded that in the second column.

As was explained, for purposes of this study serial data on housing were compiled by the aggregations of data taken from the SNIP studies on public, private urban, and private rural housing space. In the aggregation, the latter two kinds of space are discounted in the light of comparative data on depreciated values and costs. While this calculation obviously was crude in any event, I have sought in effect to discount the private urban and private rural housing space in the light of the relation of the corresponding service costs to those of public housing. As was not sufficiently considered previously, in proceeding in this way, I am probably more or less in step with national income calculations generally. The procedure clearly is also the appropriate one to follow in this study where output generally is being valued at ruble factor cost. But a question is in order as to whether and to what extent valuation in terms of service costs can also be taken as an approximation (as in effect I have taken it to be) to the valuation in terms of the consumers' utility standard that is in order where (as here) the concern is to measure household consumption as it bears on welfare. Unhappily the question is also utterly speculative, but it may be of interest to see how my measures of household consumption in adjusted market prices are affected if instead of the housing series described use is made of an alternative one where I make no discount at all for inferior value of either private rural or private urban housing (1937 = 100):

Year	Household consumption as calculated in Table 36	Same, except that use is made of alternative series on housing
1928	94.1	94.5
1937	100	100
1950	126	126
1955	190	188

For 1950 as for 1937, prices diverge from the consumers' utility standard due to the undervaluation of farm income in kind and housing. Moreover, a question is again in order regarding the prices of utilities and other services. Together with the series compiled originally in 1950 rubles, the results of the attempt to adjust for these distortions are shown in Table 41, in which I repeat the original indices in 1950 rubles. In ad-

TABLE 41
Household Consumption, 1928–55, in Prevailing and Adjusted Market Prices of 1950
(1937 = 100)

Year	In prevailing prices of 1950	In prevailing prices of 1950, with farm income in kind, housing and services revalued
1928	88.2	91.0
1937	100	100
1940	110	108
1944	67.5	68.1
1950	130	120
1955	207	184

justing these data, I proceed in essentially the same way as was done regarding the measures in 1937 prices. Household retail purchases and military subsistence have the same magnitudes as they had originally in 1950 rubles. For housing and services, I use the same physical volume series as was employed in the initial computation in 1950 rubles, but as recorded originally housing outlays amounted to 7.2 and outlays on services to 43.2 billion rubles. Again taking the dollar price structure of 1950 as a benchmark, I increase the former figure sixfold to 43.2 billion rubles and the latter threefold to 129.6 billion rubles.[15] Farm income in kind is again recomputed in terms of collective farm market prices, although 1950 (rather than 1937) is now the year to which the prices pertain. As before, the totals given by valuation in collective farm market prices are reduced by 20 percent in order to exclude marketing and processing costs.[16]

These indices may clarify the effects of divergencies of ruble prices from the consumers' utility standard in 1928: The ratio of 1928 to 1937 household consumption outlays in prevailing prices of 1928 is 70.2 percent and with farm income in kind revalued, 75.4 percent. The first index is the one derived previously in 1928 prices. In the computation of the second, all use categories are as before except for farm income in kind. While housing and services may have been undervalued in 1928 as in later years, as far as can be judged from the American price structure the undervaluation is unlikely to be consequential here.[17] As to farm income in kind, physical volume varies as before in terms of average realized farm prices of 1928, but at these prices this category totalled 6.7 billion rubles in that year. I now raise this figure to 10.3 billion rubles. In relation to retail prices, the implied level of farm prices is the same as that obtaining in 1937 after adjustment.[18]

After as well as before the recomputation, household retail purchases supposedly are valued at average retail prices of 1928. So far as there were multiple prices, evidently, the average prices of different com-

[15] See note 11.

[16] On the calculation in terms of 1950 collective farm market prices, see Appendix C. As before, the figure for 1928 obtained in Appendix C by the method of aggregation is adjusted to correspond in scope to SNIP measures on farm income in kind derived from Soviet global data on farm output and its disposition. The old and new weights for all the different categories considered in the recomputation of household consumption, with figures for selected revaluations in parentheses, are as follows (billions of rubles): household retail purchases, 375.0 (375.0); housing, services, 50.4 (172.8); consumption of farm income in kind, 61.0 (150.0); military subsistence, 14.1 (14.1); and household consumption outlays, 500.5 (711.9).

[17] By extending to 1928 the computations described in note 11, I obtain these purchasing-power-equivalents between 1928 rubles and 1950 dollars: food, 0.86 ruble per dollar; manufactured consumers' goods, 0.82 ruble per dollar; housing, 0.58 ruble per dollar, and services, 0.75 ruble per dollar. Adjustment for divergencies in purchasing power parities of these sorts would hardly affect our measures of household consumption.

[18] In Table 37, farm income in kind amounts to 86.9 billion rubles in 1928. This is in terms of 1937 collective farm market prices, less a 20 percent allowance for marketing costs not incurred and also less home processing costs. Urban retail food prices in 1928 averaged about 11.8 percent of 1937. See Chapman, *Real Wages*.

The revaluation entails an increase of 54 percent in the prices at which farm income in kind is valued. Interestingly, in *SNIP-28,* p. 65, Hoeffding estimates from scattered data that urban retail prices were on the average 50 percent above average realized farm prices.

modities might diverge materially from the consumers' utility standard. Regrettably there seems to be no way to allow for this aspect. The computations in terms of 1928 prices may err significantly on this account.[19]

As in the case of the adjusted data referring to 1937 as a base year, I refer to those based on 1950 and 1928 as being in adjusted market prices.

[19] For further discussion of the possible import of the limitations in 1928 retail prices, see Chapman, *Real Wages,* chap. iii.

PART IV

CONCLUSIONS

11

OTHER COMPUTATIONS OF SOVIET "REAL" NATIONAL INCOME

In this concluding part, I compare my results with those obtained in other calculations, summarize findings, and explore implications. In earlier chapters, national income data were compiled for the benchmark years 1928, 1937, 1940, 1944, 1950, and 1955. As was explained, I have also compiled annual figures for the period 1948–55. In this part, where it is in order, I refer to the annual data as well as to those for benchmark years. Hoeffding and Nimitz explain that the attempt in *SNIP-49–55* to measure gross investment and hence national income in current rubles in 1954 encountered special difficulties. In this study I take their calculations on these aspects as a point of departure but I consider alternative data as well. Alternative figures that are presented below on national income in 1954 in terms of each base year and formula result from this procedure. Regrettably it does not seem possible to select between the different computations; indeed still other results are not precluded. The annual data for 1949–54 that are considered in this and succeeding chapters are set forth in full in the Addendum.[1]

[1] On the alternative current ruble figures considered for 1954, see Appendix G.

Comparisons with other calculations are the subject of this chapter and results and implications, of the chapters following.

The "real" national income of the USSR has been the subject of a number of inquiries. Over a long period, the Soviet government itself has compiled and published serial data on this category. A number of calculations have also been made by non-Soviet scholars. Among these the best known are the calculations of Dr. Naum Jasny, Colin Clark, and the late Dr. Julius Wyler. In appraising my results, it is useful to compare them with those obtained in these previous studies.

Comparisons are in order, of course, regarding not only global totals but measures of components. In this study, however, I have calculated national income by type of final outlay. This procedure is often employed also in the computations to be considered, but some use is made too of the familiar alternative, involving the calculation of national income by economic sector of origin. In such cases, the comparison of components perhaps is still not precluded, but necessarily they are difficult to make and difficult to interpret. In any event, if only to limit my task to feasible dimensions I have felt impelled to proceed here provisionally by comparing, in addition to global totals, measures of components only where these refer as here to final outlays. It may be doubted that further comparisons with such data as have been compiled on the output of individual branches would materially affect the outcome, but this question must be left for separate inquiry.

By the same token, no attempt can be made either to relate my results to diverse measures of the output of different economic sectors in the USSR that have been compiled independently and not as a part of a national income computation. Some of these data, however, probably are among the more reliable that have been derived on Soviet economic trends, and considering this some interest may attach to the results of a very tentative attempt that was made to compile on this basis still another series of measures of national income as a whole (see Table 42) which might be compared with those derived in previous pages.

In the first column I repeat measures of the gross national product by use that have been compiled in this study in terms of ruble factor cost of 1937. Essentially, for purposes of deriving the corresponding measures in the second column I have aggregated available serial data on the physical volume of production on different economic sectors. In the aggregation, each sector is assigned a weight corresponding to its net product in terms of 1937 ruble factor cost. For sake of completeness, computations on the output of different sectors made by others have had to be supplemented here by data compiled in this study (in 1937, sectors for which the latter figures are employed account for about 30 percent

TABLE 42

National Product of USSR, 1928–55, Alternative Computations
(1937 = 100)

Year	Gross national product (Bergson) in ruble factor cost of 1937	Net national product as aggregate of selected series on physical volume of different industrial sectors[a]
1928	61.6	59.7
1937	100	100
1940	121	117
1950	150	144
1955	216	204

[a] The different branches considered in the compilation of the measures of net national product by economic sector and the serial data taken to represent their respective contributions are as follows: (1) Agriculture. Net product of agriculture in terms of official purchase prices of 1958, as calculated in D. Gale Johnson and Arcadius Kahan, "Soviet Agriculture: Structure and Growth," Joint Economic Committee, Congress of the United States, *Comparisons of the United States and Soviet Economies*, Part I, p. 205. (2) Civilian Industries. Net output of civilian industrial goods in ruble prices of 1950, as calculated in a forthcoming study of Norman Kaplan and Richard Moorsteen. The authors employ wage bill weights as between and price weights within major components. (3) Munitions industries. Military procurement of munitions in ruble prices of 1937 as calculated in this study, Appendix E. For 1928–37, procurement of finished munitions is taken to vary proportionately with procurements of munitions and miscellaneous supplies taken together. (4) Construction. Materials inputs to construction in ruble prices of 1937, as calculated in Raymond P. Powell, "A Materials Input Index of Soviet Construction, 1927/28 to 1955." Part I. The RAND Corporation, Research Memorandum RM-1872, February 14, 1957 and "A Materials Input Index of Soviet Construction, Revised and Extended." The RAND Corporation, Research Memorandum RM-2454, September 28, 1959, p. 6. (5) Transport and communications. All transport freight ton-kilometers plus railway passenger-kilometers as given in TSU, *Narodnoe khoziaistvo SSSR v 1958 godu*, Moscow, 1959 (hereafter *Narkhoz-1958*), pp. 539, 541. On Soviet railways before the war, a passenger-kilometer appears to have cost about the same amount as a freight ton-kilometer. (6) Trade. All retail sales in 1937 ruble factor cost, as calculated in this study, Appendix A. (7) Services, including government. The aggregate volume in 1937 rubles of housing services, entertainment, miscellaneous services purchased by households, trade union and other dues, and employment in government administration, communal services and defense, all as calculated in this study.

In aggregating the different sectors, I assign to each a weight corresponding to its net product in terms of ruble factor cost of 1937. Data on the latter aspect are taken from *SNIP-37*, p. 76, as revised in *SNIP-28–48*. In the latter source, the net national product of industry and construction is given as 75.9 billion rubles in adjusted prices. I assume that of this total, civilian industries account for 60.4 billion rubles, munitions industries for 5.0 billion rubles, and construction for 10.5 billion rubles. This would seem to be a reasonable breakdown considering data compiled in this study on final outlays on munitions and construction, and diverse information on the structure of costs in these and related branches.

of the national product). The resulting measures, therefore, are not independent of those of national income by use that have been derived in previous chapters. But all things considered the broad agreement that is evident is reassuring.

Comparisons with the Soviet official data are made in the first three sections of this chapter. I then relate my results first to those of Jasny and then to those of Clark and Wyler.

Soviet Official Data: General

For all years considered in this study the Soviet government has published statistics on "real" national income as a whole. In contrast to this study, which computes "real" national income by final use, Soviet statisticians appear to calculate this category primarily although not exclusively by industrial origin. At any rate, while the government has released some percentage figures on the disposition of national income between "accumulation" (*nakoplenie*) and "consumption" (*potreblenie*) or other similar categories and while these sometimes appear to represent base year values, I believe the underlying calculations in all cases are in current rubles. On the other hand, the government has published some serial figures of an outlay sort in terms of constant prices. Among these probably the most interesting are index numbers in unspecified prices of the physical volume of retail sales in government and cooperative shops and data declaredly in terms of the prices of July 1955 on investments in fixed capital. How, if at all, these figures are related to published official statistics on "real" national income is not known, but in this study I have made calculations for outlay categories of this sort as well as for national income as a whole. Hence, a comparative appraisal is possible in respect of both sorts of data. Nevertheless, I must focus here primarily on the relation of the global measures but in conclusion I also consider briefly the comparative results on government and cooperative retail sales and fixed capital investment.

Under the five year plans, the Soviet government has published two sorts of data on "real" national income. For most years up to 1950, it has released measures of this category in terms of the ruble prices of the fiscal year, 1926–27. For the period since 1950, the official measures have been compiled in terms of the ruble prices of 1951. Regrettably, in view of the importance of this matter, Soviet authorities have not been entirely clear on it, and while there is little doubt that the 1926–27 base year has finally been abandoned, the calculations for 1950 and after may possibly have been made in terms of January 1, 1952 prices instead of the prices of 1951.[2] Since the government for years has released only

[2] On Soviet national income methodology generally, see the writings cited in note 5 of chapter 1. As to the base year employed in recent calculations, in the 1952 edition of his statistics text, A. I. Petrov informs us that the prices of January 1, 1952 are the ones used. See *Kurs ekonomicheskoi statistiki,* Moscow, 1952, pp. 434–435. In the 1954 edition, he is equally definite that valuation is in terms of 1951 prices. See *ibid.,* 1954 ed., p. 406. According to A. I. Gozulov, *Ekonomicheskaia statistika,* Moscow, 1953,

percentage figures on the change in "real" national income over time and no absolute magnitudes, the precise nature of the change in base year cannot be established by inspection of the data themselves.

Table 43 gives the two sorts of official data for years considered here. I also list the corresponding measures of "real" national income compiled in this study. According to the Soviet concept, national income represents the value of output at prevailing prices, including turnover and other indirect taxes.[3] Although, as will appear, in the calculation of "real" national income this concept has been modified in interesting ways, the Soviet official data are best compared with mine in terms of prevailing rubles as distinct from those in terms of ruble factor cost or "adjusted market prices." Accordingly, in the table I cite only the former.

In computing national income, Soviet statisticians focus on "material production." According to what is thought to be a Marxian view, services generally are considered as unproductive, at least for the purposes of national income accounting. The corresponding earnings, therefore, are viewed essentially as transfer incomes, and omitted from national income. Although not without some misgivings, the statisticians omit not only personal services, such as those of doctors, teachers, lawyers, domestics, and the like, but services of diverse other sorts, including those of government employees and housing. Passenger transportation is also omitted, and at least in recent years, so too seemingly are communications services to households. In order to facilitate comparisons, in Table 43 I show not only measures of "real" national income compiled in previous chapters but alternative data obtained by a recomputation. In the recomputation, as far as possible, services of sorts excluded from Soviet calculations of national income have been omitted here as well.[4]

---

pp. 379–380, valuation is in terms of January 1, 1952 prices. Actually while Gozulov explains that that standard is applied in the calculation of the gross output of industry, he is not entirely definite that it is applied to national income. In his illuminating article, "'1926/27' and All That," *Soviet Studies,* October 1957, p. 125, A. Nove informs us that for the period since 1950 valuation has been in terms of 1951 prices.

Whether the new base date is 1951 or January 1, 1952, it should be observed that it applies only to the period of the Fifth Five Year Plan, that is, only until 1955. For the period of the Sixth Five Year Plan, reportedly the base date for valuation purposes has again been changed, this time to July 1, 1955. See *ibid.,* p. 125.

[3] On the nature of the prices in terms of which income is valued, see especially A. Bergson, *National Income of the Soviet Union,* CEIR A-5, November 1954, pp. 11–12; A. Nove, "Soviet National Income Statistics," *Soviet Studies,* January 1955, pp. 250 ff.

[4] The omitted items are household outlays on housing; railway and urban passenger transport; entertainment and miscellaneous services; and trade union and other dues; also labor inputs to communal services and government administration, including the NKVD, and military services. In terms of 1937 prices, household outlays on housing, passenger transport, entertainment and miscellaneous services, and trade union and other dues are derived in Appendix B. Labor inputs to health care and education are given in Appendix D, while labor inputs to other communal services are taken to be about one-half the total outlays on this category. Labor inputs to government administra-

TABLE 43

"Real" National Income of the USSR, 1928–55 (Bergson's and Soviet Official Data)

Year	Bergson			Bergson, Soviet concept			Soviet official	
	In 1928 rubles[a]	In 1937 rubles	In 1950 rubles	In 1928 rubles[a]	In 1937 rubles	In 1950 rubles	In 1926–27 rubles[b]	In 1951 rubles[c]
					(1937 = 100)			
1928	37.7	64.8	65.2	36.4	67.8	68	25	—
1937	100	100	100	100	100	100	100	—
1940	—	118	114	—	116	111	133	—
1944	—	108	101	—	102	89	—	—
1948	—	117	114	—	113	108	154	—
1949	—	129	126	—	126	122	181	—
1950	—	146	143	—	145	140	219	—
1951	—	161	157	—	160	155	—	—
1952	—	175	170	—	174	167	—	—
1953	—	186	182	—	187	181	—	—
1954	—	196 (199)	194 (197)	—	197 (200)	194 (197)	—	—
1955	—	217	213	—	221	216	—	—
					(1950 = 100)			
1950	—	100	100	—	100	100	—	100
1951	—	110	110	—	111	110	—	112
1952	—	119	119	—	120	119	—	125
1953	—	127	127	—	129	129	—	136
1954	—	134 (136)	136 (137)	—	136 (139)	138 (140)	—	153
1955	—	148	149	—	153	154	—	171

[a] Figures for 1940 to 1955 are not available.
[b] Figures for 1944 and for 1951 to 1955 (1937 = 100) and for 1950 to 1955 (1950 = 100) are not available.
[c] Figures for 1928 to 1955 (1937 = 100 only) are not available.

In 1928 the omitted services were of only limited importance in the USSR, accounting for 10.0 percent of the gross national product (western concept) in 1937 prices. Subsequently, they increased in volume but in 1955 they still accounted for but 12.4 percent of the total output in 1937 prices. If, as is evident, the recomputation has hardly any effect on the trends in "real" national income, this is because of these circumstances.

My results nevertheless diverge markedly from the Soviet data. This is still true after the recomputation of my measures in accord with the Soviet national income concept. We may usefully consider first the period 1928–37. I then refer more briefly to the period 1937–55. Finally I summarize the findings regarding the national income data generally.

Soviet Official Data: 1928–37

As might be expected, my calculations for 1928–37 in terms of 1937 prices show a far smaller increase in "real" national income than do the official figures in terms of 1926–27 prices. But there is also a divergence, albeit a much reduced one, when reference is to my data in terms of 1928 prices. As has been explained, my revaluation of national income in 1928 prices is not entirely complete. For this reason, my measure of "real" national income for 1928 may well be overstated in relation to 1937 by several percentage points (p. 93). If so, the divergence between the official data and my own is further reduced but it still persists. What is the explanation?

Apart from the incompleteness in the revaluation, my calculations in 1928 prices are inexact. Very possibly, the divergence in some measure is due to this fact. The Soviet calculations, however, also have their limita-

---

tion, including the NKVD, are taken to be 70 percent of the total outlays on this category. See Appendix D. On defense services in terms of 1937 rubles, see Appendix E.

In deriving corresponding data in terms of 1950 and 1928 prices, I proceed similarly but use here the previous calculations of different national income components in terms of these rather than of 1937 prices. Household outlays on passenger transport, entertainment, and miscellaneous services were not calculated previously in terms of 1950 and 1928 prices. I assume that in relation to the corresponding total of household outlays on "services," the expenditures on these items in terms of 1950 and 1937 rubles are the same as in terms of 1937 prices.

On the Soviet concept of national income, see the writings cited in note 5 of chapter 1, especially Studenski, "Methods of Estimating National Income in Soviet Russia," *Studies in Income and Wealth,* vol. iii, pp. 199–202; Bergson, *National Income of the Soviet Union,* CEIR A-5, p. 11; Nove, "Soviet National Income Statistics," *Soviet Studies,* pp. 246–250. In addition to the Soviet sources cited in these studies, reference may be made to M. Bor, "O nekotorykh voprosakh natsional'nogo dokhoda sotsialisticheskogo obshchestva," *VE,* 1954, no. 10; V. Belkin, "Tak li nado traktovat' natsional'nyi dokhod?" *VE,* 1956, no. 5, and M. V. Kolganov, "O metodike perescheta natsional'nogo dokhoda SSHA," *VE,* 1955, no. 11.

On the alternative index numbers shown for each series compiled here for 1954, see Appendix G.

tions. As my results testify, these probably are not as serious as many Western students of the Soviet economy (including the writer) have assumed, but an upward bias in the official data hardly is precluded. On this familiar theme there is now a voluminous and sometimes controversial Western literature.[5] I must limit myself to bare essentials.

Soviet scholars too have written a good deal on their national income data. Regrettably, they are not always incisive on vital methodological aspects, and they are also notably reticent on statistical details. Arguably, in view of these facts alone, the official data must be discounted, but the information released permits a partial appraisal. Since Soviet statisticians apparently calculate "real" national income primarily by industrial origin, in their methodological writings they also focus on methods used in this sort of computation. The official data have to be appraised, therefore, chiefly by reference to these methods.

To refer first to the procedures used in respect of the important industrial sector, if Western scholars have erred in their appraisal of the official data, I suspect the reason is chiefly the overestimation of the bias introduced by the Soviet treatment of "new" products. Possibly on this matter M. Dobb after all has hit nearer the mark than his critics (including the writer). On the other hand, the calculations obviously are crude, generally, and while the resultant errors are difficult to appraise, it is easy to believe that the official national income data begin to be inflated at this point. Let us first consider the aspects of the problem apart from the question of "new" products. While the essentials, I believe, are not especially controversial, it may be in order to summarize and elaborate somewhat previous Western discussions. To begin with, there are the special procedures used to derive the "real" net product of industry from its "real" gross product. Correct practice, of course, calls for the deduction from "real" gross product of independently determined "real" production expenses. Soviet statisticians nevertheless have held differing opinions on the merits of this procedure.[6] In any event, their actual practice is not clear, but some use probably has been made of two dubious alternatives: "Real" net product is assumed to vary proportionately with "real" gross product, and "real" net product is obtained by deflation, the deflator being given by the computation of "real" gross product, that is, in effect, the price trends for goods entering into gross output are assumed to apply to net output. As may not always be considered by Western scholars, in the case of these particular procedures, the probability seems to be more that growth is understated than that it is

[5] See note 5 of chapter 1.

[6] See A. I. Rotshtein, *Problemy promyshlennoi statistiki SSSR,* Part I, Leningrad, 1936, pp. 304 ff.; A. I. Gozulov, *Ekonomicheskaia statistika,* Moscow, 1953, p. 379 ff.; Nove, "Soviet National Income Statistics," *Soviet Studies,* January 1955, p. 267.

overstated, but the contrary is not precluded. So far as the first method is used, the likelihood of understatement is suggested by familiar considerations revolving around the high value added (in relation to gross output) of the fast growing machinery industries. Similarly, if the second method is the one applied, one thinks first of the probability that the prices of goods entering into production expenses might tend to rise more than those entering into gross output (as will readily be seen, if this is so the second method necessarily understates growth). Nevertheless, value added is by no means low in many branches, for example, garments, textiles, and the like, which in Soviet conditions have grown only slowly. Moreover, the relation of value added to gross output depends in any case on organization, particularly the degree of integration. Finally, under the Soviet five year plans comparative price trends are especially difficult to judge *a priori*. For all these reasons, in the case of both methods one hesitates to rule out the possibility of overstatement of growth.[7]

As to the "real" gross product of industry, this is calculated by the "factory method," and hence depends on the state of economic organization.[8] It increases if there is any trend away from integrated operations, for example, if a tractor plant ceases to produce its own engines and buys them instead from another plant, and it decreases in the reverse case. Correctly computed, of course, "real" production expenses should also be

[7] According to the Soviet official data, "real" gross output in 1937 was 446 percent of the 1928 level. *Narkhoz-1956,* p. 52. If it is assumed, as I think is likely, that the underlying calculation refers in 1928 as well as 1937 to industry as it has come to be understood in the USSR in the course of time, that is, inclusive of most if not all forestry and fishing, the corresponding official index of "real" net output is about 467 percent. See Bergson, *National Income of the Soviet Union,* pp. 19, 58–59. In his *Soviet Economy during the Plan Era,* p. 32, Naum Jasny cites a higher index, 585 percent, for net output, but I believe the underlying calculations for 1928 omit and those for 1937 include forestry and fishing. At any rate, we may conclude that if the Russians used the first method in calculating "real" net output, they did not do so exclusively. In some measure they also used the second method or perhaps also the more correct conventional procedure described in the text.

As to the nature and extent of the error resulting from the application of the different procedures, I assume in the text that so far as the first and second methods are used they are applied to industry as a whole. This is implied in Rotshtein, *op. cit.,* pp. 304 ff, but one wonders nevertheless whether at least for the first method the procedure may not have been to apply this instead to individual industries; that is, "real" net output is taken to grow proportionately to "real" gross output in individual industries rather than to industry as a whole. If so, no doubt the results would tend to be more accurate than they might be otherwise.

On the question of the comparative trends of "real" net and gross product, one might wish to refer to comparative statistical data on these two categories for other countries. To my knowlege, such data are unavailable.

Here and elsewhere Soviet statistical procedures that are criticized, I fear, are none the less dubious if (as the reader will readily perceive) they have a precedent in the present volume so far as they are employed in the tentative calculation of national income by sector of origin described on pp. 176 ff.

[8] Donald Hodgman, *Soviet Industrial Production, 1928–1951,* Cambridge, 1954, pp. 2–5.

affected by such reorganizations and in the same way. Hence, "real" net product should not be changed one way or the other. If use is made of either of the two short-cut procedures described above, however, "real" net product is affected. Under the first method, the bias is in the same direction as that for the "real" gross product. Under the second method, the outcome is more difficult to predict. In any case, the trends in Soviet industrial organization in the period in question are complex and not easily summarized. This factor too, therefore, might affect "real" net product in either direction, but Western scholars no doubt have been right to speculate whether it may not be a cause of the rapid growth shown by the official national income data.

As Hodgman points out,[9] such a result only seems the more likely when it is considered that some intraplant turnover is included in gross output, for example, completed production of the enterprise's shops devoted to its own capital construction. For this reason, "real" gross output is also affected by any changes that may have occurred in definition in this respect. Furthermore, "real" net product might be changed in this case even if a conventional calculation (rather than the first method or the second) were used.

For cooperative industry, gross output is valued at the prices not of 1926–27 but of 1932.[10] If (as may well be so) the resulting measures are used without adjustment in the calculation of net industrial output in 1926–27 prices, this too would inflate the official data. A good deal of the output of the cooperatives consists of consumers' goods, the 1932 prices of which probably were significantly above the 1926–27 level.

To come to the proverbial Soviet treatment of "new" industrial products, the "real" gross output of industry is calculated by the method of aggregation (as distinct from that of deflation). For articles introduced for the first time after 1926–27, the base year prices required for this computation necessarily are unavailable. Under the circumstances, Soviet statisticians value these products not at some "synthetic" base year prices (as one might wish) but simply at the prices prevailing at the time the products are introduced.[11] This rather was the procedure until 1936. Under a statistical reform of that year, the government revised the procedures used to calculate gross output in 1926–27 prices. As a result, it has been held, the government "removed criticism on this particular score." [12] According to another and I believe more accurate

[9] *Ibid.*, pp. 3–4.

[10] L. M. Volodarskii, *Statistika promyshlennosti i voprosy planirovaniia*, Moscow, 1958, p. 109.

[11] For an article not produced in 1926–27, the 1926–27 price is taken as the "price prevailing at the time when mass production of the article began, or at the average price prevailing in the first three months of its production": Rotshtein, *op. cit.*, p. 241.

[12] M. Dobb, "Further Appraisals of Russian Economic Statistics," *Review of Economics and Statistics*, February 1948, p. 36.

interpretation, the reform left unchanged the data already published for years prior to 1936. For 1936 and after, a major aim was simply to substitute all-union 1926–27 prices for regionally varying ones previously used. The reform also provided for the use of correction coefficients to translate the prices of new products introduced after 1935 to the 1926–27 level, but apparently the "old" products the price trends for which were taken as a standard for this purpose themselves might have been introduced after the base year. Hence the translation might only be made to a date later than 1926–27. Then too, the instructions on valuation were in any case often disregarded.[13]

What is the import of this aspect of Soviet methodology? Although the matter may be more complex than is often supposed, I believe there is some theoretic support for the common-sense view that so far as the initial costs and hence prices of new products tend to be high, these products tend to be overvalued in the Soviet calculations. In any case, other things equal, this would clearly be the effect of the pervasive wage inflation of the period of the five year plans. But other things were not equal, and in trying to appraise the values attached to new products we must consider also the government policy of subsidizing heavy industrial goods. Until 1936, this necessarily limited the impact of rising wages on prices generally. Furthermore, as a result of the introduction of serial methods the government succeeded in sharply reducing "real" costs of production in many industrial branches. The mastery of mass production methods generally must have affected the costs even of new products, and the more so where (as was often the case) the latter represented essentially new models rather than wholly new activities.

Stressing factors favoring overvaluation, many critics of the official data have argued that the statistics on the "real" gross and net product of industry are subject to a substantial upward bias. This is not only a result of the overvaluation of new products at the time of their introduction. Since the new products tend to grow rapidly thereafter the official data are further inflated on this account.[14] Stressing rather the offsetting factors of subsidies and cost reduction, at least one defender of the Soviet data feels that "any upward bias thereby introduced . . . is much smaller than the critics imply."[15]

As was stated, between these two theories, I now believe Dobb's may

[13] See Rotshtein, *op. cit.*, pp. 247 ff.: Gerschenkron, *A Dollar Index of Soviet Machinery Output*, The RAND Corporation, Report R-197, April 6, 1951, pp. 3 ff.; Hodgman, *op. cit.* pp. 6 ff.; Nove, "'1926/27' and All That," *Soviet Studies*, pp. 118 ff.

[14] See, for example, Gerschenkron, *op. cit.*, chap. i; Hodgman, *op. cit.*, pp. 5 ff.; Nove, "'1926/27' and All That," *Soviet Studies*, pp. 118 ff.

[15] M. Dobb, "Comment on Soviet Statistics," *Soviet Studies*, June 1949, p. 21. See also Dobb's, "Further Appraisals of Russian Economic Statistics," *Review of Economics and Statistics*, February 1948.

be the more nearly correct. I am guided in this chiefly by the price data shown in Table 44, which were compiled for this study. New products were especially important in machinery branches. Yet Moorsteen finds the price level rose in these branches only when the calculation is in

TABLE 44

Index Numbers of Prices, Selected Products, USSR, 1928–37 (1937 = 100)

Year	Prices of machinery, USSR (Moorsteen)		Prices of basic industrial products, USSR (Bergson, Bernaut, Turgeon), 1937 weights		Retail prices (Chapman)	
	1927/28 weights	1937 weights	Including oil products	Excluding oil products	1928 weights	1937 weights
1928	70	140	45	57	11.5	16.8
1935	84	93	69	59	—	—
1937	100	100	100	100	100	100

terms of 1927/28 weights, representing the output of old products alone. If the calculation is made instead in terms of 1937 weights, where the new products are represented, prices on the average tended to fall. Any serious overvaluation of new products under these circumstances is hardly likely. Many new articles were also produced in other branches of heavy industry, but here too one wonders whether a major overvaluation could have occurred. Excluding oil products, which were subject to heavy turnover taxes, prices generally hardly rose perceptibly until 1936, when the government largely abandoned subsidies.[16] It remains to refer to manufactured consumers' goods. As Dr. Janet Chapman's retail price data suggest, wholesale prices for such goods tended sharply upward. The price increases, however, reflect in part the introduction in 1930 and the subsequent boosts of turnover taxes, and apparently "new" products were valued at prices net of such taxes.[17] Moreover, new products were less numerous here than elsewhere.

While the overvaluation of new products during 1928–37 probably is less important than many Western scholars have supposed, a rarely considered aspect may be consequential. Even after the 1936 reform, repair work (which apparently is included in some measure in industrial pro-

[16] In Table 44, I cite index numbers calculated in terms of 1937 weights. In contrast to the index numbers for machinery, those for basic industrial goods appear to be little affected by shifts in the base year.

[17] Rotshtein, *op. cit.*, pp. 245–246.

duction) was valued at current planned costs.[18] Since such costs were especially affected by the inflationary trends in wages, this procedure must have tended to inflate the official data. A question arises also regarding the immediate effect of the statistical reform of 1936. According to the official data, "real" gross output increased 29 percent in 1936. In view of this increase, high even by Soviet standards, it is permissible to wonder whether, at least at the time of its initiation, the 1936 unification of 1926-27 prices may not have increased the bias in the official data rather than the reverse.[19]

So much for the calculations for industry. Although less is known about computations for most other sectors, questions must be raised on some aspects. Again I do little more than summarize previous Western discussion. As A. Nove informs us, for the computation of the "real" net product of transport Soviet statisticians adopted an even simpler expedient than for industry. The net product in the base year is inflated by the trends in freight turnover in terms of ton-miles carried. Since passenger service is omitted from the official data, the measurement of this aspect poses no problem.[20] If a short-cut has to be used, this one is probably as good as any, as Nove argues, but it must be recorded nevertheless as still another source of error in the official data. Again, however, the nature of the bias is conjectural. The methods used for agriculture appear to be broadly conventional, but calculated as it is by the method of aggregation (as distinct from the method of deflation) "real" gross product apparently is affected by the shift from the "barn" to "biological" concept of the harvest which was initiated in 1933. In the absence of any evidence in Soviet sources to the contrary, Jasny speculates that this shift has been allowed illegitimately to affect the "real" net product as well. The latter seemingly is computed by deducting "real" production expenses from the "real" gross product. If the "real" net product is affected, the error would tend to be inflationary.[21]

In terms of current prices the calculation of the net product of trade and construction also appears to be generally of a conventional sort, but little is known regarding that in terms of 1926–27 prices, and the reliability of the official data for these sectors therefore must be in doubt. In view of the inherent difficulties of calculating the "real" net product of construction, a question seems in order especially regarding the official computation for this sector.

Moreover, reference has been made to the Soviet treatment of new industrial products. New products are also a problem in other sectors.

[18] *Ibid.*, pp. 248–249.

[19] Nove, " '1926/27' and All That," *Soviet Studies*, p. 120.

[20] On the Soviet calculation of the "real" net product of transport, see Nove, "Soviet National Income Statistics," *Soviet Studies*, January 1955, p. 270.

[21] Jasny, *The Socialized Agriculture of the USSR*, Stanford, 1949, chap. xxviii.

Indeed, in construction much if not all output might properly be viewed as new. Soviet sources nevertheless have little to say about the treatment accorded new products outside industry, and Western writers also usually devote little attention to this problem. Very possibly, however, the procedure was the same as that used for industry. If so, at least in the case of construction, there is a further cause of inflation at this point, for whatever economies were realized in this branch could not have matched those in heavy industry. Hence, the generally rising wages necessarily would have left an imprint on prices and costs. As Powell has pointed out, this helps explain an otherwise puzzling phenomenon: as given by the official data, "real" net output of construction tends to move generally with available statistics on net output of this branch in current rubles.[22]

Soviet Official Data: 1937–55

The official figures for years after 1937 may be compared with mine in terms of 1937 and 1950 rubles (Table 43) and also with these further calculations in 1928 rubles: Taking the national income, Soviet concept, for 1937 as 100 percent, the corresponding index for 1940 is 127; and for 1950, 170. For the period 1928–37, my revaluation of Soviet national income in terms of 1928 prices was relatively although not entirely complete. No similar calculations have been made for years since 1937, but for purposes of appraising the Soviet official data I have again resorted to a procedure used previously. Within each of 25 final use categories, "real" outlays are measured in terms of 1937 rubles. As between these use categories, valuation is in terms of 1928 rubles. The data cited above were obtained in this way.[23]

Apparently, the official data show greater increases than mine for both 1937–40 and 1937–50 (see Table 43). In view of the difference in base year, of course such a divergence is to be expected when reference is to my data in 1937 and 1950 rubles. But the divergence persists when reference is to the results of the partial revaluation in terms of 1928 rubles. Moreover, the gap is especially pronounced for the period 1937–50; that is, compared with the official index of 219 percent, mine is 170 percent. Since the revaluation is only partial, my calculations probably un-

[22] Raymond P. Powell, "A Materials Input Index of Soviet Construction, 1927/28 to 1955," Part II, The RAND Corporation, Research Memorandum RM-1873, February 14, 1957, pp. 498 ff. See also Nove, "Soviet National Income Statistics," *Soviet Studies,* January 1955, pp. 268–269, "'1926/27' and All That," *Soviet Studies,* October 1957, pp. 122–123.

[23] More specifically for each of the 25 use categories use is made of index numbers of "real" outlays in terms of 1937 rubles with 1937 as 100 percent. In aggregating these index numbers, I assign to each category a weight corresponding to the volume of outlays on it in 1937 in terms of 1928 prices.

derstate the rise in national income in 1928 rubles during the years in question. Furthermore, my calculations are imprecise generally, but for 1937–50 Soviet statisticians appear to have applied much the same methodology as before, and clearly this may again be a factor in the divergence in results. As before, I suspect the bias in the official data, at least for 1937–40, is less than Western critics have supposed. As may not have been sufficiently considered, once the 1936 reform was introduced, it may possibly have resulted at least for a time in a more correct valuation of new products. Possibly also there have again been misapprehensions regarding the underlying economic trends. But if the reform of 1936 were at all ineffective, circumstances probably were more favorable than previously to the introduction of an upward bias on this account. This is true of the period 1937–40 but more so of the period 1937–50. In the munitions sector where new products became especially important, it is true that the government managed to cut prices during the war, but these could never have fallen to anything like the 1926–27 level (whatever that means in this case), and both before and after the war prices rose. Elsewhere, new products perhaps were less important than during 1928–37, but from 1937 on, industrial prices generally as well as wages tended to rise. The inflation extended even to the newer branches of the machinery sector. As a result of the reintroduction of subsidies on a progressively increasing scale, the government managed to limit industrial price increases after the German attack, but some increases occurred nonetheless, and finally when large-scale subsidies were again abandoned in 1949, industrial prices rose far above the previous level. I refer to the prices of machinery and basic industrial goods. For manufactured consumers' goods, prices also rose before the war, were probably stable during the war, and then increased sharply soon after. These diverse circumstances may help explain not only the high official national income indices for years after 1937, but the relatively great inflation observed in the index for 1950.[24]

The official data for 1950–55 supposedly are in terms of 1951 prices. Even so, the indicated growth in "real" national income still exceeds that shown by my data in terms of either 1937 or 1950 prices. The import of this divergence is not easy to judge. Since Soviet statisticians continue to be reticent regarding methods and statistical details, uneasiness as to the reliability of their results must persist. So far as their present methods are known, however, they apparently differ at some points from those used previously. Some of the changes clearly represent improvements, but probably not all do. In contrast to the official data in 1926–27 rubles, those in terms of 1951 prices do not appear as yet to be especially controversial, but Western research on the latter is still at an early stage and

[24] On industrial price trends after 1937, see Appendices A, E, and F.

as it proceeds no doubt we shall be better able than we are now to appraise the recent Soviet data.

As to the changes in methods: Although Russian sources are still not entirely explicit, Soviet statisticians may now be calculating the "real" net product of industry as good practice requires by deducting from "real" gross output the independently determined magnitude of "real" production expenses. This method would be used in place of the dubious procedures described earlier. Possibly, the correct method of calculating "real" net product has also supplanted similar expedients which had been employed in some other sectors.[25] Since Stalin's death, the government has reverted to the "barn" (as distinct from the "biological") concept of agricultural crops. At least this is the concept to which published crop data refer. For recent years, therefore, harvest losses presumably are no longer included in the net output of agriculture; if indeed this was the practice previously.

Industrial prices in the USSR lately have been declining. Perhaps not surprisingly then the Soviet statisticians have finally abandoned the discredited procedure used previously to value "new" products. Presently, the new products may still be valued in terms of their initial prices, but only if in the industrial branch concerned prices generally have been stable. If they have not been, the initial prices apparently are adjusted in the light of price trends in the branch concerned.[26] While this evidently corresponds more or less to preferred Western practice, some misgivings must remain if (as is likely) the initial prices that are taken as a point of departure refer as before to a very early stage of production. In effect, many fast growing products would still be valued at relatively high prices. Although new products are less numerous than at earlier periods, they are still important, especially in civilian machinery and munitions branches.

Soviet statisticians still consider national income as representing the value of output at prevailing prices, including indirect taxes, but in calculating the "real" gross product of industry different commodities are valued initially at "factory prices" which are net of turnover taxes.[27] As is understood, heavy industrial goods in consequence receive a higher weight in relation to consumers' goods than they would otherwise. While the procedure is nevertheless not without merit (in effect it represents a resort to something like a factor cost standard), the results become difficult to interpret when it is considered that in all probability the resulting

[25] A. I. Petrov, *Kurs ekonomicheskoi statistiki,* Moscow, 1954, pp. 405–406; D. V. Savinskii, *Kurs promyshlennoi statistiki,* 4th ed., Moscow, 1954, p. 111; Nove, "Soviet National Income Statistics," *Soviet Studies,* January 1955, pp. 267–268.

[26] N. Liubimov, "Voprosy primeneniia optovykh tsen dlia opredeleniia ob"ema valovoi i tovarnoi produktsii promyshlennosti," *VS,* 1955, no. 4, pp. 29 ff.

[27] *Ibid.,* p. 22 ff.

index numbers of industrial output as a whole are still incorporated in the official national income calculations at prices gross of the turnover tax. The period 1950–55 witnessed a rapid expansion of the production of consumers' as well as heavy industrial goods, but some distortion in the official data is unavoidable.

Soviet Official Data: Conclusion

As computed here, Soviet national income grows less than is shown by official data in 1926–27 rubles. For the period 1928–37, this is true even when reference is to my results in terms of an "early" base year, 1928. If my calculations in terms of 1928 rubles were extended to later years, some divergence of the sort observed for the period 1928–37 probably would persist. Although my figures are inexact, I believe the Soviet official data are subject to an upward bias, and the divergence in results is to be read partly in this light. If the official figures are biased in this way, the distortion nevertheless appears to be less than Western critics of these data have often supposed. In appraising the limitations of the Soviet calculations, the latter no doubt have underestimated the role of cost reductions as a factor limiting the overvaluation of new products in the official series.

But while the official data are not as defective as has been assumed, there is no lack of confirmation for the further contention of Western critics that Soviet results are also affected by the choice of an early base year. In 1937, national income is found here to be 265 percent of 1928 when the measurement is in 1928 rubles. When measurement is in 1937 rubles, the index falls to 154 percent! Base year relativity does not preclude useful applications of the national income figures (see chapter 3) and from a purely technical standpoint the choice of an early base year is always admissible, as Dobb, for example, has argued. But evidently such a procedure can easily give rise to misunderstandings, and as the Soviet statisticians and Dobb must be aware such misunderstandings have not been avoided in the case of the Soviet official data. Criticisms of these figures may have been somewhat misdirected but they are hardly groundless.

Although for 1950–55, the Soviet calculations supposedly are in terms of 1951 prices, national income is still found here to grow less than is shown by the official figures. This is so according to my calculations in either 1937 or in 1950 rubles. As between the Soviet and my results, it is presently difficult to say where the error lies. Because of the still limited information available on the underlying Soviet procedures and details, however, uneasiness regarding the resulting data necessarily persists.

It remains to refer to the Soviet official figures on government and cooperative retail sales and fixed capital investment. To begin with the former, these have been published only in index number form, and Soviet sources do not specify the prices in terms of which they were calculated, but reference I suspect is made to a contemporary base year or alternatively to several such years, the published series being obtained in this case by the chaining of successive links. In any event, my calculations for household purchases in government and cooperative retail shops are more or less in accord with the official data for benchmark years (Table 45). This is so whether reference is to my computations in 1937

TABLE 45

Government and Cooperative Retail Trade in the USSR, 1940–55, Alternative Indices (1950 = 100)

Year	Sales of consumers' goods to households (Bergson): In 1937 rubles	Sales of consumers' goods to households (Bergson): In 1950 rubles	All sales (Soviet official)
1940	85.8	83.8	90.9
1948	63.5	64.0	64.1
1950	100	100	100
1955	176	178	189

rubles or to those in 1950 rubles. The official series differs in scope from mine. The limited divergence for 1955, I believe, is due largely to this fact. My calculations for 1940, however, are less reliable than for other years, and there may be further reason at this point to think that my indices for that year are somewhat low.[28]

[28] With 1940 as a percentage base, the Soviet index numbers for 1950 and 1955 are given in *Sovtorg,* p. 9. For 1948, see *Pravda,* January 18, 1950 and January 26, 1951.

My data differ in scope from the Soviet indices in several ways. For all years, I omit, and the Soviet series includes, sales to institutions and sales of farm producers' goods and building materials to households. For 1955, I also omit and the Soviet data include repair work and the like (I classify such activities throughout with services) and the newly organized "commission trade" of the cooperatives (classified here with collective farm market sales). When the Soviet series is adjusted to correspond in scope to mine, the index for 1955 falls to 182 percent. The indices for 1940 and 1948, however, are only slightly affected.

As was stated, the sources of the official indices fail to explain how they were calculated. Moreover, discussions of computations of this sort in Soviet statistics texts focus exclusively on comparisons of two years and for this reason are not especially illuminating on the important question of the choice of base year in the compilation of serial indices. But I believe the serial indices may in fact be obtained by the chaining of successive links. If so, each link in turn probably is calculated in terms of an "early"

In contrast, my calculations for investments in fixed capital are quite at odds with recently published Soviet data on this category. According to my computations either in 1937 prices or in 1950 prices, such investments systematically increase less than is shown by the *Narkhoz* figures, and often markedly so (Table 46). Since the base year in the case of the latter is stated to be 1955, the different series, if anything, should be in the reverse relation. The *Narkhoz* statistics are not fully comprehensive of Soviet investments in fixed capital, but in Table 46 I have adjusted my measures so that they are of more or less similar scope. For this reason, divergence at this point probably is not very material.[29] But *Narkhoz*

TABLE 46

Investments in Fixed Capital, Excluding Livestock and Capital Repairs, USSR, 1937–55, Alternative Calculations

Year	Bergson, 1937 rubles	Bergson, 1950 rubles	*Narkhoz,* 1955 rubles
		(1937 = 100)	
1937	100	100	100
1940	109	104	129
1944	68.9	62.7	97.5
1948	114	104	187
1950	179	166	268
1955	302	277	462
		(1950 = 100)	
1948	63.6	62.8	69.8
1950	100	100	100
1955	169	167	172

base year. In any event, a difference in methodolgy at this point seems unlikely to be a further significant cause of the divergencies observed between the official indices and mine in terms of 1937 and 1950 rubles.

On the Soviet methodology of compiling index numbers of the physical volume of retail sales, see N. Riauzov i. N. Titel'baum, *Kurs torgovoi statistiki,* Moscow, 1956, pp. 143 ff; Petrov, *Kurs ekonomicheskoi statistiki,* Moscow, 1952, pp. 402 ff; Gozulov, *Ekonomicheskaia statistika,* Moscow, 1953, pp. 356 ff.

[29] In Table 46, the index numbers attributed to *Narkhoz* are calculated here from corresponding absolute figures. The latter in turn are obtained by aggregating two series given in *Narkhoz,* pp. 158–159, one for the volume of investments in fixed capital "on account of funds assigned by the state plan, and also on account of funds of enterprises and other non-centralized means," and the other representing investments of the collective farms. These data, like mine, omit investments in livestock herds. The *Narkhoz* figures also omit capital repairs and apparently private investment. Finally, they exclude outlays on "planning-exploratory and prospecting" activities. In Table 46, I have adjusted my figures to exclude capital repairs (the repairs for machinery are given in Appendix F; for construction, the necessary data were estimated from figures on all capital repairs in current rubles compiled by Norman Kaplan in *Fixed Capital,* the figures on capital repairs to machinery in current rubles in Appendix F, and the

fails to explain how the valuation in 1955 prices was made, and while the precise procedure is conjectural the published data almost certainly are not what they seem in this regard. Indeed, for reasons noted, it is difficult to view the *Narkhoz* figures as measuring physical volume in any conventional sense. The observed divergencies, therefore, are not considered as reflecting in any serious way on my calculations. Because of the manner of their compilation, the *Narkhoz* data probably vary in reliability at different times. Probably this explains the relatively limited gap between the alternative calculations for years since 1948 (Table 46). At any rate, such a gap must be within the range of error of my calculations.[30]

---

index numbers of the prices of construction inputs in Raymond P. Powell, "A Materials Input Index of Soviet Construction, Revised and Extended," The RAND Corporation, Research Memorandum RM-2454, September 28, 1959, p. 85). Further adjustments for private investments and "planning-exploratory and prospecting" activities probably would not be very consequential.

[30] In an interview at GOSSTROI on July 12, 1956, Hans Heymann, Jr., was informed that in compiling the *Narkhoz* figures, use was made of the method of deflation. The deflation was accomplished by reference to index numbers of the prices of construction materials, equipment, and hourly wages. Admittedly, the calculation was controversial. Heymann has summarized his interview in a communication to me, dated July 31, 1956. Somewhat in contrast, as Richard Moorsteen informs me, he was told at TSU in August 1956 that the *Narkhoz* figures were obtained by chaining links for successive periods. For 1937–55 use was made of calculations for different intervals that had been made previously in terms of the so-called "estimating prices," that is, prices of materials, equipment, and labor prevailing in a year taken as base for the purposes of accounting for construction. Thus, the published series was compiled in this way from previous calculations for 1937–45 in terms of 1936 "estimating prices"; for 1945–50 in terms of 1945 "estimating prices"; and for 1950–55 in terms of 1950 "estimating prices." Calculations of this sort, I believe, are usually made to a great extent by the method of aggregation rather than by the method of deflation, but Moorsteen reports that for years up to 1937 the necessary index numbers of physical volume were compiled for *Narkhoz* by deflation.

But whatever the general procedure used to derive the *Narkhoz* figures, the actual calculations could hardly have been reliable. According to *Narkhoz,* for example, investments in fixed capital, including those by collective farms, totaled 36.5 billion rubles in 1937 in terms of 1955 prices. The corresponding figure in terms of current prices might have been on the order of 29.5 billion rubles (see note 29; Appendix F; and Kaplan, *Fixed Capital*). By implication, investment goods prices in 1955 were 124 percent of 1937. According to data compiled for this study, money wages in Soviet industry in 1955 (after allowing for the increase in hours) averaged 271 percent of 1937. Similarly, the prices of construction materials in 1955 were 239 percent of the 1937 level, while the corresponding figure for machinery prices was 146 percent. Since the *Narkhoz* data supposedly are valued in terms of the prices of July 1, 1955, I cite corresponding indices of the prices of construction materials and machinery. With due allowance for errors in these calculations, and for increases in productivity, it is difficult to see how the *Narkhoz* figure could be at all near the mark. On the trends in money wages, see Appendix H. The cited index of the prices of construction materials is from Raymond P. Powell, "A Materials Input Index of Soviet Construction, Revised and Extended," The RAND Corporation, Research Memorandum RM-2454, September 28, 1959, p. 80. On machinery prices, see Moorsteen, *Machinery*.

Again, according to *Narkhoz,* investments in fixed capital in 1939 in 1955 prices were 176 percent of 1934. The corresponding figure in terms of current rubles was 184 per-

Jasny's Computations in "Real" 1926–27 Rubles

As with the Soviet statisticians, Dr. Naum Jasny computes Russia's national income in terms of the ruble prices of the fiscal year 1926–27.[31] Since the limitations of the Soviet valuation procedure supposedly are avoided, the calculation is described as being in terms of "real" 1926–27 rubles. For simplicity I shall refer to them without repeating the qualification. As computed here, Soviet national income increases distinctly more than is found by Jasny. Jasny calculates Soviet national income both by final use and by industrial origin. According to the former computation "real" national income in 1928 is 54.8 percent of 1937; according to the latter, 46.2 percent. Referring to my calculations in 1928 rubles, which evidently are the appropriate ones to consider, "real" national income in 1928 is 37.7 percent of 1937 (Table 47). In addition to 1928 and 1937, Jasny calculates Soviet national income for 1940 and 1948. Depending on the nature of the computation, "real" national income in 1940 is either 120 or 122 percent of 1937. The corresponding figures for 1948 are 120 and 115 percent. No systematic computation in terms of 1928 rubles is made here for years after 1937, but according to the partial revaluation described earlier "real" national income in 1940 is 128 percent of 1937. For 1948, the corresponding figure is somewhat higher, 134 percent. With a more complete revaluation of my data, very likely the difference between Jasny's results and mine would be greater.

---

cent. Hence the implied price index is 105 percent. In 1939, money wages in construction were 192 percent of 1934. The corresponding index for construction materials was 137 percent and for machinery prices 99 percent. For investments in fixed capital in current rubles, the available data are inclusive of some types of investment that are omitted from the *Narkhoz* figures, but it is unlikely that this difference in scope would go far to explain the evident incongruity between the price index implied by the *Narkhoz* figures and the others cited above. On the trends in money investments and also in machinery prices, see Moorsteen, *Machinery*. The indices of money wages in construction and of the prices of construction materials are from Raymond P. Powell, "A Materials Input Index of Soviet Construction, Revised and Extended," The RAND Corporation, Research Memorandum RM-2454, September 28, 1959, pp. 78, 80.

On the basis of a comparison of the *Narkhoz* measures with available data on investments in current rubles, Norman Kaplan has concluded that in compiling the former Soviet statisticians for a protracted period up to the forties may actually have relied on trends given by current ruble statistics. Seemingly, however, calculations are in some sort of constant prices for later years. See also Raymond P. Powell, "A Materials Input Index of Soviet Construction, 1927–28 to 1955," The RAND Corporation, Research Memorandum RM-1873, February 14, 1957, pp. 504 ff.

[31] Naum Jasny presents his national income calculations in *The Soviet Economy During the Plan Era,* Stanford, 1951. This volume, however, has to be read together with two others he has published dealing with related topics: *Soviet Prices of Producers' Goods,* Stanford, 1952, and *The Soviet Price System,* Stanford, 1951. Jasny is often complex and elusive on the details of his calculations. In trying to understand his procedures, I have found of value the detailed critique by Norman Kaplan, "Arithmancy, Theomancy and the Soviet Economy," *Journal of Political Economy,* April 1953.

TABLE 47

"Real" National Income of the USSR (Bergson's and Jasny's Data) (1937 = 100)

Year	Bergson		Jasny, in 1926/27 rubles	
	In 1928 rubles	In 1937 rubles	By final use	By industrial origin
1928	37.7	64.8	54.8 (52.3)	46.2
1937	100	100	100	100
1940	—	118	120 (119)	122
1948	—	117	120 (119)	115

As Jasny has recognized, in calculating "real" national income by use in *The Soviet Economy During the Plan Era* he erred in the treatment of depreciation. Although the data compiled there purportedly measure net national product, for the years 1937, 1940, and 1948, they actually represent gross national product. Jasny has since corrected accordingly his figures for these years. In Table 47, for purposes of facilitating comparison with my data on gross national product, I nevertheless continue to cite outside parentheses his results for gross national product for 1937, 1940, and 1948. His corresponding measures of net national product appear in parentheses. For 1928, Jasny compiles a measure of net national product only. This again is in parentheses. Outside parentheses I take the liberty to insert the measure of gross national product that is implied if depreciation is allowed for as Jasny allows for it in later years. In his calculation "by industrial origin," Jasny compiles measures on the net national product throughout. These are the measures cited in Table 47.[32]

[32] For Jasny's initial and erroneous data on net national product by use and his final data on net national product by industrial origin, see *The Soviet Economy During the Plan Era,* p. 85. Jasny has circulated his revised figures on the net national product by use in a separate errata sheet. In index number form, these appear in parentheses in Table 47. For 1937–48, the corresponding indices outside parentheses are derived from Jasny's final data on the net national product by use by the addition to the latter of Jasny's allowance for depreciation as given in the errata sheet: for 1937, 2.0 billion rubles; for 1940, 2.9 billion rubles; and for 1948, 2.7 billion rubles. For 1928, depreciation is taken here to total 2.4 billion rubles, or the amount computed in *SNIP-28–48,* exclusive of depreciation on private housing. The index of "real" gross national product for 1928, given outside parentheses in Table 47, is obtained by adding this sum to Jasny's total for the net national product in 1928.

In relation to Jasny's figures for 1937–48, the cited figure for depreciation for 1928 will seem large. Possibly it is, but it is hardly likely that Jasny's figures are reliable. Jasny does not explain his estimates in any detail. By unstated procedures, depreciation in current rubles is for 1940 and 1948 reduced to depreciation in 1926–27 rubles. As to depreciation in current rubles, Jasny takes as a point of departure Soviet bookkeeping charges. On the amounts of these charges, apparently data were at hand only for 1940; for 1948, the corresponding figure is obtained by extrapolation. In any event,

National income as computed by me includes government administration and the NKVD and as computed by Jasny omits it. This incongruity is immaterial for 1928–37. For later years, particularly 1948, my totals are raised somewhat in relation to Jasny's.[33] Since with this exception the two calculations appear to be of essentially the same scope and since additionally prices in 1928 varied little from those of 1926/27,[34] the difference in our measures of growth must be due to statistical deficiencies. As has been explained, my computations are subject to error, but obviously so also are Jasny's. Of chief interest here are his data on national income by final use, particularly for the period 1928–37, for which I have made systematic parallel calculations in terms of an "early" base year. At least in respect of these data there are reasons to think the difference between Jasny and me may be due very largely to miscalculations on his part.

If account is taken of the limited differences in base year and scope, the two computations may be compared regarding not only indices of growth but absolute magnitudes, and regarding not only national income but components. While there are many divergencies and these are sometimes offsetting (Table 48),[35] the systematic tendency in all consequential

no allowance seems to be made for the fact that these bookkeeping figures represent original cost rather than current values. Moreover, Jasny erroneously, I believe, deducts from the bookkeeping depreciation charges Soviet bookkeeping allowances for capital repairs. These procedures are used to estimate depreciation for 1940 and 1948. On the volume of depreciation in 1926–27 rubles for 1937, it is only stated that the "estimate" of the 1937 investment probably needs a comparable reduction.

In Jasny's calculation of national income by industrial origin, the allowance for depreciation is not sufficiently explicit to permit an independent appraisal.

[33] Jasny's treatment of government administration and the NKVD in his calculation by industrial origin is not entirely clear, but these activities clearly are omitted from the calculation by use. Moreover, so far as wage payments are concerned, the omission is made on methodological grounds but I believe not very defensible ones: such payments apparently are felt to represent a form of double counting (*ibid.*, p. 85). On the same erroneous reasoning, Jasny also considers that pay and upkeep of the armed forces and pay of personnel in education and health services "represent duplications" which must be deducted from national income, but in Table 47, I cite the totals he derives inclusive rather than exclusive of these "duplications."

[34] In *ibid.*, pp. 62, 110, Jasny assumes that the prices of goods and services entering into household consumption were "slightly lower" in 1927–28 than in 1926–27. The relation of 1928 prices to those of 1926–27 is not specified, but presumably it would have been about the same. For investment goods, prices in 1928 are taken to be 96 percent of 1926–27. According to Soviet official data, wholesale prices of agricultural products in 1927–28 averaged 100 percent of 1926–27 and of industrial goods 95.4 percent. For retail prices generally, the corresponding index was 100 percent and for farm prices, 105 percent. Within these broad categories, price changes for different products also appear generally to have been limited. See Gosplan, *Kontrol'nye tsifry narodnogo khoziaistva SSSR na 1928–1929 god,* Moscow, 1929 (hereafter *KTS 1928–29*), pp. 501 ff.

[35] In Table 48, I cite Jasny's constant ruble data as given in *The Soviet Economy During the Plan Era,* pp. 66, 85, 108. Account is taken of revisions made in a separately circulated errata sheet. For military subsistence in 1937, Jasny apparently miscopies in his summary tables in *ibid.*, pp. 66, 85, the result derived in *ibid.*, p. 110. I cite the

cases I believe is for Jasny's final measure of growth to be reduced relatively to mine. Moreover, all relate to 1937 and seemingly revolve about a limited number of features of the two computations for this year. For purposes of appraising the conflicting measures, it may suffice to consider each of these in turn.

Jasny generally derives his constant ruble figures as I do by deflation. Among other things, this method is applied by him as well as by me in the case of investment other than in fixed capital. In current prices, however, he takes such outlays to be but 12 billion rubles in 1937 (Table 48). Very possibly my corresponding figure of 24.2 billion rubles is too high, but for purposes of comparison I have summed Jasny's estimates for "owned variable capital" of government economic organizations and "all others." As computed, neither category includes farm investments in kind. Moreover, the investments in "owned variable capital" are extrapolated from 1938 while as Jasny acknowledges his figures for "all others" for all years are "wild guesses." In the light of more substantial evidence assembled in this study, I believe Jasny markedly underestimates at this point investments in inventories, stock piles and possibly other categories.

In order to translate into 1926/27 rubles household money outlays on consumption in 1937, Jasny deflates by a cost of living index compiled especially for this purpose.[36] In the present study, the corresponding constant ruble figure has also been obtained mainly by deflation, although for some components I apply instead the method of aggregation of physical indices. For the category as a whole, however, my implied deflator is but 556 percent (1928 = 100), while in 1937 Jasny finds the cost of

latter figure outside and the figure from the summary tables inside parentheses. For investment in 1937 I cite Jasny's figure gross of depreciation. As was explained he derives a figure for net investment only for 1928. I raise this by 2.4 billion rubles in order to allow for depreciation. See note 32. Similarly the cited figures on gross national product correspond to Jasny's on the net national product. For 1937, I simply add to the latter Jasny's allowance for depreciation. For 1928, I add 2.4 billion rubles.

For Jasny's figures in current rubles, see *ibid.,* pp. 40 ff, 108 ff, 110 ff. For communal services, Jasny does not state the current ruble figures that correspond to the revised constant ruble data in his errata sheet. I assume that in relation to the original data in *ibid.,* p. 80, they change in proportion to the change in the constant ruble data. For 1928, Jasny estimates net investment at 4.7 billion rubles. The corresponding gross investment is taken here to be 2.4 billion rubles greater. For 1937, I cite Jasny's data on investment gross of depreciation.

Jasny's deflators either are taken from *ibid.,* pp. 63, 110, or are computed from his current and constant ruble data on different sorts of final outlays.

In Table 48, in relating Jasny's results to mine I take his category "Education and Health" to correspond to my "Communal services." Also, his "Capital investments, state" and "Kolkhoz investments" together are compared with my "Gross investment, in fixed capital." Similarly, his "Owned variable capital of state organizations" and his "All others" are taken to correspond to my "Gross investment, other."

On the comparative level of prices in 1928 and 1926–27, see note 34.

[36] Jasny, *The Soviet Economy During the Plan Era,* pp. 57 ff., 97 ff.

TABLE 48

Calculation of Soviet "Real" National Income by Final Use, 1928–37 (Bergson and Jasny)

Outlay category	Outlays in billion 1928 rubles (Bergson) and 1926–27 rubles (Jasny): 1928	1937	Outlays in current rubles, billions: 1928	1937	Deflators, percent: 1937 ÷ 1928	1937 ÷ 1926/27
Household consumption outlays other than farm income in kind, military subsistence						
Bergson	14.89	25.78	14.89	143.4	556	—
Jasny	—[a]	19.9	—	149	—	750[f]
Consumption of farm income in kind						
Bergson	6.70[b]	4.90	6.70	25.0	510	—
Jasny	—	2.9	—	—	—	—
Military subsistence						
Bergson	0.25	0.42	0.25	2.5	595	—
Jasny	—	0.3 (.5)[c]	—	2.2	—	750[f]
Household consumption outlays						
Bergson	21.84	31.10	21.84	170.9	550	—
Jasny	21.0	23.3	—	—	—	—
Communal services						
Bergson	1.55	6.61	1.55	25.6	387	—
Jasny	1.6	4.7	1.6	26.3[e]	—	560
Government administration, including NKVD						
Bergson	0.82	2.01	0.82	7.4	368	—
Jasny	—	—	—	—	—	—
Defense						
Bergson	0.76	10.61	0.76	17.4	164	—
Jasny	0.7	5.7	0.7	17.5	—	307
Gross investment						
In fixed capital						
Bergson	6.00	27.45	6.00	35.2	128	—
Jasny	—	18.4	—	34.0	—	185
Other						
Bergson	1.32	7.90	1.32	24.2	306	—
Jasny	—	3.6	—	12.0	—	333
All						
Bergson	7.32	35.35	7.32	59.4	168	—
Jasny	7.2[d]	22.0	7.1[d]	46.0	—	209
Gross national product						
Bergson	32.29	85.68	32.29	280.7	328	—
Jasny	30.5[d]	55.5 (55.7)[c]	—	—	—	—

[a] — = not available or not applicable.
[b] Including 0.30 billion rubles of farm wages in kind.
[c] Figures in parentheses are Jasny's final summary data. Figures outside parentheses correct for copying error. See text.
[d] Jasny estimates net investment at 4.84 billion rubles in 1926–27 prices and 4.66 billion rubles in 1928 prices. In addition, I allow for depreciation charges of 2.4 billion rubles. See text.
[e] Implied. See text.
[f] Jasny's rounded figure. The implied deflator differs slightly.

living to be 750 percent of 1926/27. The difference in the percentage base is immaterial. Jasny compiles his measures of the cost of living from a relatively limited sample of commodity prices (for example, all of clothing is represented by calico; all potatoes and vegetables, by potatoes), and possibly this is a factor in the conflicting results. Then too, neither computation is exact in any case, but the explanation of the divergence I believe is nevertheless to be found largely elsewhere. Jasny compiles his index numbers in terms of 1926–27 weights. As he fails to consider, use of such a deflator yields a measure of "real" outlays in 1937 that nominally is of the desired sort in terms of 1926/27 rubles but in fact still reflects the 1937 price structure (see chapter 3). So far as I deflate household money outlays on consumption I have sought to apply instead, as is logically correct, index numbers of prices compiled in terms of 1937 weights. For the category as a whole, therefore, my implied deflator very largely represents the change in prices in terms of such weights. As to the import of this difference in methodology, a basis for judgment is provided by my calculations in terms of 1937 rubles. Here the implied deflator for household money outlays on consumption, which represents the change in prices in terms of 1928 weights, is in 1937, 774 percent (1928 = 100), or nearly the same as Jasny's index.

Jasny employs his cost of living index, 750 percent, to deflate not only household money outlays on consumption but military subsistence (as recorded under consumption), the wage component of outlays on communal services, and military pay and subsistence (as recorded under defense). I deflate military subsistence (as recorded under consumption) by an index of retail prices: 595 percent (1928 = 100). Again, reference is made as is proper to an index compiled in terms of 1937 weights. In the deflation of the wage component of outlays on communal services, logic calls for the use not of an index of the cost of living but of one of average wages. Accordingly, wage payments to workers engaged in health care and education are here reduced to 1928 rubles by reference to indices of average money wages (for workers in health care, 385 percent of 1928; for educational employees, 508 percent). Similarly, where "real" outlays on military pay and subsistence (as recorded under defense) are computed by deflation, the correct procedure is to deflate by an index of average military pay (including the money value of subsistence). In this study, however, such military service inputs are calculated instead, as is also permissible, by reference to data on the size of the armed forces. The implied deflator for 1937 is 325 percent (1928 = 100).[37]

For Jasny an index number calculated for machinery prices is an important constituent of a more comprehensive one derived for "capital investments, state," which in turn is a "mainstay" in the deflation of investments generally. Here are the essentials:[38] Price data are compiled for individual machinery items. For six of these, for which there are comparable data for 1927 and 1936, prices in the later year range from

[37] The discrepancy between Jasny and me at this point is the greater since in respect of outlays on military pay, Jasny uses as a deflator not the cost of living index cited, but an alternative index supposedly referring to urban workers. Moreover, this is taken to be 1000 percent, although if I rightly understand Jasny's computations, the correct figure would be 820 percent.

On Jasny's calculations for military subsistence (as recorded under consumption), the wage component of outlays on communal services and military pay and subsistence (as recorded under defense), see *ibid.*, pp. 49 ff., 66, 76 ff., 110.

[38] See Jasny's *Soviet Prices of Producers' Goods,* and Kaplan, "Arithmacy, Theomancy and the Soviet Economy," *Journal of Political Economy.*

80 to 270 percent of the 1927 levels. Apparently relying chiefly on these data, Jasny assumes "quite arbitrarily" that domestic machinery prices in 1936 were 130 percent of 1927. On a similar basis, it is felt that "the general revision of machinery prices in 1937 may have raised the percentage increase to 50." For unexplained reasons, the prices of imported machinery in 1926/27 are assumed to be one-third below those of similar domestic machinery. Considering this and the volume of imports in 1928, the prices of all machinery, domestic and imported, in 1937 turn out to be 165 percent of 1926/27. One wonders whether here as for the cost of living Jasny mistakenly took as a desideratum an index employing "early" weights. Remarkably enough his rule-of-thumb index turns out to be almost identical with the one compiled by Moorsteen in terms of 1928 weights: 166 percent (1928 = 100). But to repeat such a desideratum would be mistaken. For Jasny's purposes, here as elsewhere, what is called for rather is an index employing 1937 weights. If Moorsteen's systematic computations are at all reliable, the distinction as for the cost of living is by no means academic. In terms of 1937 weights, Moorsteen finds machinery prices in 1937 to be but 83 percent of 1928. In reducing investments in machinery in 1937 to 1928 rubles, I employ the latter index as a deflator.

For munitions, prices in 1937 are held to have been 250 percent of 1926–27.[39] This is chiefly on the ground that "armaments were moderately more expensive than civilian machinery until and including 1941 . . ." For miscellaneous defense procurements other than military pay and subsistence, the appropriate deflator is "more or less an enigma," but prices in 1937 are taken to be 350 percent of the base year. Jasny is undoubtedly right in assuming in this early period that the munitions sector did not experience economies from mass production on anything like the scale characteristic of machinery production, but so far as he misjudges machinery price trends in terms of the "late" year weights that are pertinent, very likely he also misjudges the trends in munitions prices. At all events, with due allowance for relatively limited technological progress in munitions, the prices of these goods in 1937 in terms of 1937 weights are held in the present study to be 143 percent of 1928. Taking account of price data for basic industrial goods as well as machinery, I consider this index as an appropriate deflator for all defense outlays other than military pay and subsistence.

While generally deriving constant ruble data by deflation, Jasny calculates "real" farm income in kind in 1937 by complex procedures, involving among other things the aggregation of physical data in terms of base year prices. But as he has acknowledged since the appearance of *The Soviet Economy During the Plan Era,* the calculation is also in

[39] Jasny, *The Soviet Economy During the Plan Era,* pp. 49 ff., 110.

error. In any case, in place of the incredibly low figure derived there of 2.9 billion 1926/27 rubles (amounting according to his own computations to but 24 percent of farm output available for sale and home consumption), Jasny now favors an estimate of 4.7 billion 1926–27 rubles. Moreover, this refers to the income in kind of the farm population, and if income in kind from rural workers' gardens and the like is included, as in my calculation, Jasny's total rises to 5.2 billion 1926/27 rubles. This is almost the same as my estimate in terms of 1928 rubles.[40] Farm prices rose a few percent from 1926/27 to 1928, but Jasny's revised figure on farm income in kind may include some investments in kind. Hence, the essential agreement in results is unaffected. Jasny has not explained his revision, however, so it is difficult to judge the import of this accord.

I have been comparing my calculations of national income by final use with Jasny's corresponding data for 1928–37. When the comparison is extended to 1940 and 1948, a divergence seemingly persists, although in the case of my computations reference must be to data that only very partially reflect the 1928 price structure. As a limited inquiry makes clear, Jasny's computations for 1940 and 1948 are of much the same quality as those for 1928 and 1937. For this reason, and because of the partial nature of the revaluation made here in 1928 rubles, no attempt is made to explore the conflicting results for the later years. In the space available, I must refrain from comment also on Jasny's figures on national income by industrial origin. In his view, the agreement between his alternative computations may be taken as corroboration. Considering the manifest deficiencies in the computation by final use, this is hardly possible.

In the preceding paragraphs Jasny's data have been reviewed by the author of a competing compilation. Nevertheless, in the light of a searching critique, which I have found a valuable guide, Norman Kaplan also considers "it impossible to share this belief" of Jasny's that his data are "of sufficient validity to yield a reasonably trustworthy and reasonably comprehensive picture of the results of Soviet Plans."[41] As to the import of the agreement between Jasny's alternative computations, "the nature of the calculations of national product by industrial origin suggests that the correspondence between the national product totals obtained by Jasny's two methods must be considered fortuitous."[42]

Anyone seeking seriously to understand the Soviet economy must be indebted to Naum Jasny, especially for his monumental work on the

[40] Jasny apparently considers the inclusion of farm income in kind of nonfarmers as illegitimate, but as far as I can see in his calculation of national income he fails to record this item anywhere else either. For his revision of his estimate of farm income in kind, see his "On the Wrong Track," *Soviet Studies,* July 1956, p. 61.

[41] Kaplan, *op. cit.,* p. 94.

[42] *Ibid.,* p. 107.

agricultural sector. Regarding national income, he is properly critical of the Soviet official data in 1926/27 rubles. Nevertheless, at least for the period 1928–37, it is difficult to avoid the conclusion that in this sphere he may be further from the mark in one direction than the official data are in the other.

Calculations of Clark and Wyler in U.S. Dollar Prices

Colin Clark calculates Soviet national income by use. The measurements are intended to be in terms of "international units." Nominally, one "international unit" has the same purchasing power as a U.S. dollar had on the average during 1925–34, but the data compiled are supposed nevertheless to be "on a geometric mean base," that is, apparently they must correspond to measurements that would be obtained if Soviet ruble figures had been deflated by index numbers given by Professor Irving Fisher's "ideal" formula.[43]

Among years considered in this study, Clark has compiled figures for 1928, 1937, 1940, 1951, and 1953. According to my calculations, Soviet national income grows from 1928 to 1937 by somewhat more than is indicated by Clark's figures (Table 49). For years after 1937, however,

TABLE 49

"Real" National Income of the USSR, 1928–40
(According to Bergson, Clark, and Wyler)
(1937 = 100)

Year	Bergson: In ruble prices of 1937	Bergson: In ruble prices of 1950	Bergson: In ruble prices of 1928	Clark, in "international units"	Wyler, in U.S. dollar prices of 1940
1928	64.8	65.2	37.7	72.5 (75.1)	61.1
1937	100	100	100	100.0	100
1940	118	114	—	121.6 (120.8)	126
1951	161	157	—	162.1 (159.4)	—
1953	186	182	—	186.9 (182.0)	—

the two computations show more or less similar trends. I refer to my data in terms of 1937 rubles. Where reference is to my calculations in terms of 1950 rubles, the comparative trends are much the same as before, but output for 1940 which was already relatively low in my computation in terms of 1937 rubles is now somewhat lower. In terms of

[43] Colin Clark, *The Conditions of Economic Progress,* 3rd ed., London, 1957, chaps. ii and iv. See also 2nd ed., London, 1951, pp. 16 ff. and chap. iv.

1928 rubles, I found that national income increases from 1928 to 1937 even more than it does when the calculation is in terms of 1937 rubles. The former measurements, therefore, diverge more than the latter from Clark's data.

TABLE 50

Selected "Real" Outlays, USSR, 1928–53
(According to Bergson and Clark)
(1937 = 100)

	1928	1937	1953
Household consumption			
Bergson, in 1937 rubles	88.8	100	175
Bergson, in 1950 rubles	88.2	100	173
Bergson, in 1928 rubles	70.2	100	—
Clark	105.5	100.0	137.2
Communal services			
Bergson, in 1937 rubles	25.8	100	151
Bergson, in 1950 rubles	25.0	100	150
Bergson, in 1928 rubles	23.4	100	—
Clark	33.8	100.0	306.9
Defense			
Bergson, in 1937 rubles	10.9	100	341
Bergson, in 1950 rubles	15.7	100	328
Bergson, in 1928 rubles	7.2	100	—
Clark	18.5	100.0	229.5
Investment			
Bergson, in 1937 rubles	31.5	100	189
Bergson, in 1950 rubles	34.3	100	187
Bergson, in 1928 rubles	20.7	100	—
Clark	22.4 (20.8)	100.0	264.2 (260.4)

Note: Clark omits government administration from his calculations. Accordingly, no data are set forth on this aspect.

As may be seen in Table 50, from the comparative results for three years, 1928, 1937, and 1953, the relative trends that are observed by Clark and me for different use categories are sometimes similar to those for output as a whole but more often very different.

Clark focuses generally on the calculation of net investment and net national product, but in Table 49 and Table 50, for purposes of comparison with my data, I cite outside parentheses measurements of gross investment and gross national product that are given or implied by him. His measurements of net investment and net national product are shown inside parentheses.

I propose to discuss, in chapter 12 following, the question of index number relativity. Although attention is focused on the effects of historical shifts in base year for a single country, in the light of what is said there the reader may wish to consider a related question that is posed by Clark's and my computations: Given the differing valuation standards applied, how in general might the results be expected to compare? But whatever is concluded on this score (and in view of Clark's concern with a "geometric mean base" I fear the question is more complex than it might at first appear) any conformity that is observed of the actual results to expectations one suspects must often be fortuitous. In any case, in appraising the comparative measurements, the reader will wish to consider not only the differences in valuation standards but statistical limitations. Deficiencies of the latter sort that affect my measurements have already been explained. It is difficult to avoid the conclusion that those affecting Clark's must often be far more consequential than he seems to assume.

To refer only to a few of the more significant aspects: through a complex calculation entailing use of diverse estimates, household monetary outlays on nonfood commodities (excluding housing) are found to total 120 billion rubles in 1951. From Soviet official data of a sort that Clark generally accepts, we may ascertain that in fact for such goods retail sales alone amounted to 160.3 billion rubles in that year.[44] While perhaps 10 to 15 billion rubles of this consists of sales to institutions (rather than households), Soviet households in 1951 spent their money incomes not only in retail shops but elsewhere, and among other things paid more than 30 billion rubles for utilities and other services not included in retail sales.[45] By a largely undocumented computation, "real" household outlays on nonfoods (excluding housing) in 1953 are found to be 213 percent of those of 1951. For "real" retail sales of nonfoods the Soviet government itself claims an increase for this period of but 31 percent.[46] Household consumption generally is calculated initially in terms of "international units" unadjusted to "a geometric mean base," but corresponding adjusted figures are then obtained by application of different coefficients in different years, including one of 1.075 for 1928 which "is found from experience of the countries so far covered to give a good approximation to the true geometric mean price level." [47] It is permissible to wonder how applicable experience elsewhere in this regard is to Soviet Russia.

Ruble expenditures on health care and education in postwar years are translated directly into "international units" at the rate of 10 rubles

[44] See *Sovtorg*, pp. 24, 39.
[45] See *SNIP-49–55*.
[46] *Sovtorg*, p. 11.
[47] Clark, *The Conditions of Economic Progress*, 3rd ed., p. 32.

to a dollar. This is the same rate as is felt to apply for "other services," that is, apparently utilities and other services purchased by households. For prewar years, defense outlays in "international units" are assumed to vary with the corresponding expenditures in U.S. dollar prices of 1940, as calculated by Dr. Julius Wyler. Reference is made to a computation which Wyler later revised; in any event, Wyler never explained his data in any detail. For postwar years, ruble expenditures on defense, including munitions, like those on education and health care, are translated into "international units" at the rate that is supposed to apply to "other services," that is, again utilities and other services purchased by households! Although depreciation is estimated independently, for purposes of calculating net investment in prewar years Jasny's computation serves as a point of departure. As Clark fails to consider, while Jasny's data nominally are in 1926/27 rubles, those for investment have only a rule of thumb character. But no attempt is made in any event to make the results conform to the "international unit" price structure, either unadjusted or adjusted to "a geometric mean base." Apparently because of an arithmetic error, investment in 1940 is overstated by 11 percent. For 1951, investment in "international units" is inferred from the fact that Nove "advances circumstantial evidence for an 80 percent increase between 1940 and 1951."[48]

To Colin Clark belongs the distinction of being one of the first Western scholars to attempt an independent computation of Soviet national income. One can only regret that at a late stage he has still seen fit to lend his name to patent statistical crudities such as have been described.

For three years 1928, 1937, and 1940, the late Dr. Julius Wyler calculated Soviet national income in terms of American dollar prices of 1940.[49] As computed by me in terms of 1937 and 1950 rubles, national income grows in broadly the same way as it does according to Wyler. Nevertheless, especially for 1937–40, the increase is found by me to be less than it is by Wyler (Table 49). As measured in this study in terms of 1928 rubles, national income grows much more rapidly than Wyler calculates. As for the comparison with Clark, so here, the relative trends observed must be appraised in the light of both the different valuation standards applied and statistical deficiencies. In the light of the discussion of index number relativity that is to follow, I believe the reader will be able to judge the possible import of the former aspect more easily where the comparison is with Wyler than where it is with Clark. As to statistical

[48] *Ibid.*, p. 227.

[49] "Die Schätzungen des sowjetrussischen Volkseinkommens," *Schweizerische Zeitschrift für Volkswirtschaft und Statistik*, 1951, nos. 5 and 6. Wyler revised here the data published originally in "The National Income of Soviet Russia," *Social Research*, December 1946.

deficiencies, from the few details Wyler released on his calculations, one must suppose that as with Clark these must often be consequential in his case. It may suffice to cite one example: the determination of the value of a 1937 ruble in terms of 1940 dollars in respect of investment goods. On this aspect we are told that ". . . Wyler took as a point of departure the purchasing power parity for retail sales. Account was taken first of the fact that the relative burden of indirect taxes on consumers' goods considerably exceeds that on investment goods; second, of the fact that the greater burden of indirect taxes on consumers' goods is partly compensated by the extremely low government procurement prices for farm products; and third, productivity in investment goods production is comparatively high. The quantitative measurement of these different elements was as complicated as it was uncertain. Finally, a parity of 14 cents per 1937 ruble was considered appropriate." [50]

[50] "Die Schätzungen. . . ." p. 26.

12

INDEX NUMBERS AS MEASURES OF GROWTH

The task undertaken in this study was complex, and so also are the computations that have been presented. Since the five year plans brought notable changes in economic structure, the possibility had to be considered that national income measurements might be affected materially by the choice of base year. It seemed in order, therefore, to try to compile measurements in terms of alternative base years. More particularly, while focusing especially on computations based on 1937, I have also sought to compile data based on two other years, 1950 and 1928.

Because of the peculiarities of ruble prices, special attention also had to be given the problem of valuation. Thus, while calculating national income initially in terms of prevailing prices, the results have also been revalued in terms of ruble factor cost. National income statistics in terms of ruble factor cost are supposed to provide a basis (as national income data generally are taken to do) for the appraisal of production potential. Possibly they also lend themselves to some extent to another familiar theoretic application, the appraisal of welfare, but in this case welfare must be understood in terms of planners' preferences rather than in terms of the more conventional consumers' utilities. The revaluation in ruble factor cost may facilitate applications not only of global figures on national income but of data on its disposition among final uses. Finally, as a contribution to the appraisal of welfare defined by consumers' utilities, household consumption is also recomputed in terms of adjusted market prices. As it turns out, the different revaluations are rarely very consequential, but this could not have been anticipated.

In this and the remaining chapters of Part IV, I must summarize findings and explore economic implications. A recurring question in the empirical study of economic growth is that concerning the character of the measurements themselves. Where use is made of index numbers of production, how are the results affected by a change in base year? If, in the light of my calculations for different base years, I consider this topic in the present chapter, the inquiry may be of interest for its own sake. It will also serve as a preliminary to the discussion that follows. In chapter 13, the calculations in terms of ruble factor cost and adjusted market prices provide the basis for an examination of various aspects of the Soviet growth process under the five year plans. I confine myself here to Soviet experience, but as far as my calculations and available data for the United States permit, chapter 14 compares Soviet growth trends with those that have prevailed in this country. The final chapter (15) is devoted to brief comment on the prospects for future Soviet development.

In his study of Soviet machinery production, Professor Gerschenkron formulates an interesting hypothesis regarding index number relativity: Under industrialization, measurements of the physical volume of production depend on the base year. More particularly, output grows more rapidly where the computation is in terms of an "early" than where it is in terms of a "late" base year.[1] The hypothesis presupposes, of course, that prices behave in a certain way: Generally, they must rise less or fall more for more rapidly expanding than for more slowly expanding products. In Professor Gerschenkron's view, this will indeed be the case:

". . . one way of describing industrialization is to define it as a process of changing scarcity relationships. At early stages of industrialization, the value of output of certain commodities or groups of commodities constitute a *relatively* small sphere of the value of aggregate industrial output, while prices of these commodities are *relatively* high in relation to prices of commodities composing the bulk of industrial output . . . in the course of the industrialization process it is precisely these commodities whose output expands at a particularly high rate; and this expansion is accompained by a cheapening of these commodities in terms of the rest of industrial output."[2]

[1] Alexander Gerschenkron, *A Dollar Index of Soviet Machinery Output, 1927–28 to 1937*, The RAND Corporation, Report R-197, April 6, 1951, pp. 46 ff.

[2] *Ibid.*, p. 47.

One need not feel that the hypothesis is as impelling as this might suggest in order to take it as a point of departure for an empirical inquiry into index number relativity.

Professor Gerschenkron refers especially to industrial production. According to my calculations, his principle applies no less to national income, at least for the USSR. Thus, Soviet national income is found here to grow less in terms of 1937 than in terms of 1928 ruble factor cost (Table 51).[3] Where valuation is at 1950 ruble factor cost, growth generally is less than where valuation is at 1937 ruble factor cost.

TABLE 51

Gross National Product by Use, USSR, 1928–55, in Ruble Factor Cost (1937 = 100)

Outlay category	1928	1937	1940	1944	1950	1955
Household consumption outlays						
Ruble factor cost of 1937	93.4 (101)[a]	100	114	73.2	130	197
Ruble factor cost of 1950	92.5	100	111	71.1	126	194
Ruble factor cost of 1928	72.5	100	—	—	—	—
Composite, 1937 base	72.5	100	114	71.1	126	194
Communal services						
Ruble factor cost of 1937	27.0	100	119	91.6	145	178
Ruble factor cost of 1950	26.7	100	119	91.5	146	178
Ruble factor cost of 1928	24.0	100	—	—	—	—
Composite, 1937 base	24.0	100	119	91.5	146	178
Government administration, including NKVD						
Ruble factor cost of 1937	40.5	100	146	115	200	142
Ruble factor cost of 1950	40.8	100	146	115	201	141
Ruble factor cost of 1928	40.8	100	—	—	—	—
Composite, 1937 base	40.8	100	146	115	201	141
Defense (as recorded in budget)[b]						
Ruble factor cost of 1937	10.0	100	266	678	245	358
Ruble factor cost of 1950	15.0	100	255	659	236	335
Ruble factor cost of 1928	7.0	100	—	—	—	—
Composite, 1937 base	7.0	100	266	659	236	335
Gross investment						
Ruble factor cost of 1937	29.7	100	89.6	61.4	155	234
Ruble factor cost of 1950	32.3	100	91.1	58.4	152	230
Ruble factor cost of 1928	20.5	100	—	—	—	—
Composite, 1937 base	20.5	100	89.6	58.4	152	230
Gross national product						
Ruble factor cost of 1937	61.6 (65.4)[a]	100	121	121 (108)[c]	150	216
Ruble factor cost of 1950	62.4	100	117	111 (98.6)[c]	145	209
Ruble factor cost of 1928	36.4	100	—	—	—	—
Composite, 1937 base	36.4	100	121	111 (98.6)[c]	145	209

[a] Figures in parentheses result from extension of revaluation at ruble factor cost within household retail purchases. See pp. 135 ff.

[b] Exclusive of pensions to officers, et al.

[c] Figures in parentheses are exclusive of Lend-Lease.

[3] The "composite, 1937 base" series in Table 51 is explained and discussed subsequently.

In the light of Professor Gerschenkron's principle, these results must also be reassuring regarding the reliability of the calculations. Moreover, as he implies, prices are likely to behave in the required manner only if to begin with they correspond in some degree to scarcity relations. With all their limitations, therefore, this must also be true of ruble prices as adjusted here. Actually, the calculations tend more or less to conform to Professor Gerschenkron's hypothesis even before adjustment (Table 18), and as we have seen the adjustment itself has only a limited effect on growth. By implication, the requirement regarding correspondence of prices to scarcity relations cannot be very stringent. But requirement there is, and to this extent the positive outcome here is all to the good.

While conforming to Professor Gerschenkron's principle, index number relativity is found here to vary widely at different times. As a result of the shift in base year from 1928 to 1937, growth is radically reduced. With the further shift to 1950, the increase in national income generally is again diminished, but only to a relatively limited extent. For 1950–55, growth actually is increased, albeit only slightly. Professor Gerschenkron makes no prediction regarding the comparative degree of index number relativity at different times. Nevertheless, does not the striking discontinuity observed at this point in itself suggest that my calculations are not all they should be? As was explained, the recomputations in terms of alternative base years are to some extent partial. Since this is more true of the calculations in respect of 1950 than of those in respect of 1928, this may in itself tend to limit somewhat the relative impact of the shift in base year from 1937 to 1950. Very possibly the varying relativity also reflects in some degree deficiencies in the calculations at other points. Nevertheless, the degree of index number relativity depends on the extent of and correlation between structural changes in production and prices. Judging from my constant ruble data on different final outlays (Table 51), the variation in relativity that we observe probably is due in good part to a dampening of structural changes in production. As will appear in chapter 13, the period studied seems also to have witnessed a dampening in structural changes in prices. At least, if scarcity relations are given by planners' preferences, it is not easy to see why such dampening is in any sense economically precluded and hence necessarily indicative of limitations in the computations. This I believe holds not only for limitations generally but for valuation distortions in particular. Nevertheless, in appraising the import of the observed discontinuity in relativity and indeed of the relativity generally, one might wish to scrutinize more closely the comparative trends in production and prices. Such an inquiry could quickly take us beyond the limits of this study, but structural changes are considered further in chapter 13 and while the concern there is somewhat different from the present one, in the light of the facts to appear the reader will agree I think that there is still little reason to find any serious fault with my computations.

Although I focused in this study on the compilation of data in 1928 rubles for two years, 1928 and 1937, a very partial revaluation in these terms was also made for the years 1940 and 1950. Interestingly, despite their limitations these calculations too illustrate the Gerschenkron principle:[4] The national income in 1937 prices (1937 = 100) was for 1940, 118 percent; and for 1950, 146 percent. As partially revalued in 1928 prices, it was for 1940, 128 percent; and for 1950, 169 percent.

Reference so far has been to national income as a whole. When we turn to individual use categories, we observe diverse results. For household consumption, as for national income, a change in base year generally has a distinct impact and moreover one in accord with Professor Gerschenkron's principle. Considering that for a major element, retail sales, the adjusted prices generally still include varying sales taxes, we see again that the requirement regarding conformity of prices to scarcity relations cannot be very stringent, but as before the results can only be considered as favorable from all standpoints. For communal services and government administration, the shifts in base year have no effect to speak of one way or the other. Very likely in these instances such shifts could not have any marked impact in any event, but the results remind us of the limitations of the computations, particularly the very restricted scope of the revaluations involved. For both defense expenditures and gross investment, Professor Gerschenkron's principle is again manifest. While in the case of defense expenditures the measures are not especially reliable, the positive result is again to the good for both categories.

As for national income so for individual use categories, where the change in base year has any impact to speak of, the effect tends to be less where the shift is from 1937 to 1950 than where it is from 1928 to 1937. While the particular circumstances responsible for the declining relativity must differ for different categories, I believe what was said regarding this aspect in the case of national income applies broadly here as well. For this reason, no further comment is made on it at this point.

For household consumption alone I have calculated "real" outlays in terms of adjusted market prices as well as ruble factor cost. Interestingly, these measures too fall in with Professor Gerschenkron's principle so far as concerns the shift from 1928 to 1937 (Table 66, p. 252). Generally this is true also of the further shift to 1950, but sometimes the impact tends

[4] The slight differences between the indices cited here and those cited in chapter 11 arise because the present ones refer to national income according to the concept employed generally in this study. The indices cited in chapter 11 represent national income according to the Soviet concept.

to be the reverse of that which Professor Gerschenkron calls for. Considering the partial nature of the revaluation at 1950 prices, these varying results are not surprising. On the other hand, one wonders whether in principle the sort of revaluation attempted might not be expected to limit the applicability of Professor Gerschenkron's hypothesis. I refer particularly to the fact that the revaluation, while tending to make prices conform to the consumers' utility standard, divorces them even more than they were initially from ruble factor cost. Presumably the less related prices are to costs the less likely they are to behave as Professor Gerschenkron assumes.

In judging the import of the patterns of the index number relativity that have been observed, it should be considered that physical volume data in terms of alternative base years have been compiled previously for different Soviet economic branches, including different sectors of industry and also agriculture generally. Moreover, Professor Gerschenkron's hypothesis seems generally to hold here also, although perhaps not surprisingly the relativity is quite weak in the case of agriculture.[5] Among the calculations referred to, only those of Dr. Moorsteen for machinery production employ a succession of base years for the period of the five year plans. While the result is already more or less implied in Moorsteen's corresponding measurements of machinery prices which have been employed in this study, as was found here for national income, a shift in base year has a distinctly smaller impact at "late" than at "early" stages.

In appraising the patterns of relativity observed in my Soviet national income data, the reader will also wish to consider that as will appear in chapter 14 little is known about the relativity of American national income measurements for early years. Nevertheless, the Gerschenkron principle most likely prevails here as well as for the USSR under the five year plans. Then too, while the degree of relativity hardly can compare with that seen in the latter case, it may well be consequential. For more recent times in the United States, the Gerschenkron principle is known to obtain, but as for the USSR since the mid-thirties the relativity is limited. At a later point there will also be occasion to refer to some computations in terms of alternative base years that have been made of the physical volume of production in different American sectors. These include data on machinery production compiled by Professor Gerschenkron himself. Apparently these computations too generally

[5] See Moorsteen, *Machinery,* chapter viii; Nutter, "Measuring Production in the USSR," *American Economic Review,* May 1958, no. 2; D. Gale Johnson and Arcadius Kahan, "Soviet Agriculture: Structure and Growth," in Joint Economic Committee, Congress of the United States, *Comparisons of the United States and Soviet Economies,* Part I, Washington, 1959.

tend to conform to the Gerschenkron hypothesis, although the relativity is sometimes hardly perceptible. Interestingly, in the case of machinery production for the USA as for the USSR, a shift in base year is decidedly more consequential at "early" than at "late" stages.

As we have seen, index number relativity depends in part on the extent of the changes in the structure of prices and production. While illuminating the applicability of Professor Gerschenkron's hypothesis to the USSR, therefore, my calculations would also seem to underline the violence of the structural changes that occurred under the first two five year plans. I refer particularly to the notable relativity manifest here when the base year is shifted from 1928 to 1937. So far as may be judged from the impact of the further shift to 1950, however, the subsequent changes in structure were relatively limited in character, perhaps more so than might be supposed. But while index numbers measure structural changes, they do so only in a highly summary way. Moreover, the results depend not only on the extent of the changes in prices and production but on their correlation. For these reasons, the question of structural changes perhaps is more easily appraised by observing directly the relative trends shown by data such as those in Table 51 on "real" outlays on different use categories. I shall refer at a later point to the trends that these data indicate.

13

GROWTH TRENDS

Data that have been compiled on national income in terms of ruble factor cost and on household consumption in terms of adjusted market prices are to provide the basis here for a brief inquiry into various aspects of the Soviet growth process under the five year plans. Measurements of "real" national income such as have been made in terms of ruble factor cost are supposed to be indicative of production potential. They may also bear on welfare in terms of planners' preferences. I first consider in the light of these data the growth of "real" national income viewed as an indicator of production potential. From the discussion of this aspect, I believe what might be said additionally on the related question of the growth of "real" national income viewed as a measure of welfare will be sufficiently evident. As far as available data on employment permit, the subsequent section explores implications regarding trends in "real" gross national product per employed worker. In calculating "real" national income in terms of ruble factor cost, I have also compiled corresponding data on its disposition among different final uses. Such statistics, of course, have an interest of their own. I turn next to consider some results and implications of these calculations.

My measurements of household consumption in terms of adjusted market prices should bear on welfare in terms of consumers' utilities. As a contribution to the appraisal of the latter aspect, therefore, a final section examines trends in per capita consumption in terms of adjusted market prices. From available information on employment, we may also be able to gauge the main trends in consumption in these terms in relation to the volume of employment. Considering that the period studied witnessed significant changes in the "participation rate," it will also be of interest to do so.

Growth of National Income

Under the five year plans, Soviet Russia expanded her national product to a notable extent. Despite the war, total output in 1955 was 3.5 times that of 1928. Correspondingly, over the entire period, production grew at an average annual rate (compounded) of 4.7 percent. The year 1928 marked the initiation of the First Five Year Plan; in 1955, the Russians were completing the fifth such program. For purposes of illuminating production potential, I cite the results of my calculations in terms of ruble factor cost. The particular figures mentioned are given by the computation on which I have concentrated especially, that in terms of the ruble factor cost of 1937 (Tables 51 and 52). This series, of course, is the conventional sort where output is calculated throughout in terms of the values prevailing in a single year taken as base. As we have seen (chapter 3), if the concern is to appraise production potential, such a series is always of interest, but for this purpose serial data of a somewhat different sort are no less so. Indeed, regarding capacity to produce the product mix of the base year, the alternative series is often more reliable than the former. I refer to serial measures where each comparison with the base year is made in terms of the values prevailing in the given year. In a way that will become clear, I believe it is possible to approximate from calculations already made such a given year weighted series with 1937 as base year. If so, the result is that national income grows even more than where the weights are those of the base year: In 1955, total output is now 5.7 times the 1928 level. Correspondingly, growth is at an annual average rate of 6.7 percent. (In Tables 51 and 52, see the "composite, 1937 base" series.)

In previous chapters, national income was measured not only in terms of the ruble factor cost of 1937 but in terms of that of 1950. For two years, 1928 and 1937, output was also valued at 1928 ruble factor cost. Moreover, just as we are able to compile from such data serial measures in terms of given year ruble factor cost with 1937 as base, we can also to a limited extent compile corresponding data with 1950 and 1928 as base. The two series based on 1937, however, have an interest of their own. Furthermore, in exploring the effects of a change in formula when 1937 is base, we evidently shall also be involved by implication with the

TABLE 52

Average Annual Rates of Growth of Gross National Product and Different Use Categories, USSR, 1928–55, in Ruble Factor Cost
(Percent per annum)

Outlay category	1928–55	1928–37	1937–40	1940–44	1944–50	1950–55
Household consumption outlays						
Ruble factor cost of 1937	2.8 (2.5)[a]	0.8 (−0.1)[a]	4.6	−10.6	10.1	8.7
Ruble factor cost of 1950	2.8	0.9	3.5	−10.5	10.0	9.0
Ruble factor cost of 1928	—	3.6	—	—	—	—
Composite, 1937 base	3.7	3.6	4.6	−11.2	10.0	9.0
Communal services						
Ruble factor cost of 1937	7.2	15.7	6.1	−6.4	8.0	4.2
Ruble factor cost of 1950	7.3	15.8	6.1	−6.4	8.1	4.1
Ruble factor cost of 1928	—	17.2	—	—	—	—
Composite, 1937 base	7.7	17.2	6.1	−6.5	8.1	4.1
Government administration, including NKVD						
Ruble factor cost of 1937	4.8	10.6	13.4	−5.8	9.7	−6.6
Ruble factor cost of 1950	4.7	10.5	13.5	−5.8	9.7	−6.8
Ruble factor cost of 1928	—	10.5	—	—	—	—
Composite, 1937 base	4.7	10.5	13.4	−5.7	9.7	−6.8
Defense (as recorded in budget)[b]						
Ruble factor cost of 1937	14.2	29.2	38.5	26.3	−15.6	7.9
Ruble factor cost of 1950	12.2	23.5	36.7	26.8	−15.7	7.2
Ruble factor cost of 1928	—	34.4	—	—	—	—
Composite, 1937 base	15.4	34.4	38.5	25.5	−15.7	7.2
Gross investment						
Ruble factor cost of 1937	7.9	14.4	−3.6	−9.0	16.7	8.5
Ruble factor cost of 1950	7.5	13.4	−3.1	−10.5	17.3	8.6
Ruble factor cost of 1928	—	19.3	—	—	—	—
Composite, 1937 base	9.4	19.3	−3.6	−10.2	17.3	8.6
Gross national product						
Ruble factor cost of 1937	4.7 (4.5)[a]	5.5 (4.8)[a]	6.7	−0.1 (−2.9)[c]	3.6 (5.6)[c]	7.6
Ruble factor cost of 1950	4.6	5.4	5.5	−1.4 (−4.3)[c]	4.6 (6.6)[c]	7.6
Ruble factor cost of 1928	—	11.9	—	—	—	—
Composite, 1937 base	6.7	11.9	6.7	−2.3 (−5.1)[c]	4.6 (6.6)[c]	7.6

[a] Figures in parentheses result from extension for 1928–37 of ruble factor cost valuation within household retail purchases. See pp. 135 ff.
[b] Exclusive of pensions to officers, et al.
[c] Figures in parentheses refer to the gross national product of 1944 exclusive of Lend-Lease.

effects of a shift from this to other base years. Indeed, when viewed in this light, the two series based on 1937 are seen to contain practically all the information that has been compiled in this study on Soviet production potential. Accordingly, for purposes of this summary survey, it may suffice if for the most part I focus on these two series.

The figures cited on the growth of output during 1928–55 are affected by territorial changes. The following measurements allow in an approximate way for this aspect:[1]

	Growth of gross national product, 1928–55, after adjustment for territorial changes	
	1955 ÷ 1928	Average annual increase (percent)
With output in 1937 ruble factor cost	3.2	4.4
With output as composite, 1937 base	5.2	6.3

Except during the war, output rose continuously over the years studied, but at varying rates. As for the entire period, so for different intervals, the tempo also depends on the nature of the measurement. During the first two five year plans, 1928–37, national income in terms of 1937 ruble factor cost is calculated to grow at 5.5 percent annually. Where given year weights are employed, the corresponding figure is twice as great: 11.9 percent. As is proper where the latter formula is in question, I cite here the rate given by the computation that was made previously in terms of 1928 ruble factor cost. Throughout this summary survey it must be considered that my calculations are inexact, but they are especially so for the period 1928–37, and probably the tendency is more to overstate than to understate growth. Although the cited figures must be read accordingly, with either of the two sorts of measurement the tempo during the early years in question was rapid.

So far as errors in my calculations are systematic, they appear to originate primarily in two sorts of deficiencies in the ruble factor cost valuation: the partial nature of the revaluation in these terms and the fact that this standard itself leaves something to be desired. Where valuation is at ruble factor cost of 1937, there is some basis to appraise these two sorts of deficiencies not only for 1928–37

[1] Changes in Soviet boundaries that have occurred since 1939 affect not only the measurements just presented but still others that are yet to be set forth, but in all cases this is because one or another of two sorts of comparisons is entailed: (a) As with the measurements just presented, a pre-1940 year is compared with 1955. (b) As with measurements that will appear, a pre-1940 year is compared with 1940. For purposes of adjusting for the boundary changes, I assume that both in 1940 and in 1955 the new territories incorporated in the USSR produce a total output amounting to 10 percent of that produced within the pre-1939 boundaries. At the time of their inclusion in the USSR, the territories in question had a population amounting to about 12 percent of that in the pre-1939 USSR. Whether and to what extent they were correspondingly productive is uncertain, but no doubt output was reduced in 1940 as a result of the Soviet take-over itself, and for present purposes we must consider that in any case my output data for that year may not fully reflect the territorial expansion. As to 1955, the supposition that output of the new territories is less than proportional to their population still seems plausible when we consider well known facts regarding comparative economic trends in different regions of the USSR, but use of an alternative hypothesis hardly would affect my results significantly in any case.

but to some extent for the period 1928–55 generally. To refer first to the incomplete revaluation in terms of ruble factor cost, in Tables 51 and 52, I have inserted parenthetically alternative data which are indicative of the possible import of a major extension of the revaluation, that is, within household retail purchases, for the period 1928–37. Further computations for 1937–48 and 1937–54 indicate that where the revaluation is extended in the same way for these intervals the measures of "real" national income are little affected.

As to the second sort of deficiency, the alternative series compiled in Table 26 may be suggestive. In the table, the series in question are given in index number form. For convenience I set forth in Table 53 for two of the more interesting

TABLE 53

Average Annual Rate of Growth of Gross National Product, USSR: Alternative Computations for Various Periods, 1937 Ruble Factor Cost

Computation	1928–55	1928–37	1950–55
With output in 1937 ruble factor cost	4.7	5.5	7.6
With output in 1937 ruble factor cost, with profits deducted and rent and interest added	4.5	5.1	7.5
With output in 1937 ruble factor cost, with allowance for nonlabor charges according to U.S. 1947 cost structure	4.5	5.0	7.6

series and selected intervals corresponding rates of growth. For purposes of comparison, I also show the corresponding figures where valuation is in 1937 ruble factor cost (all figures in percent). As with the series at 1937 ruble factor cost from which they are derived, the two alternative series shown rest on revaluations that are only partial, but in the case of that where ruble factor cost is adjusted according to the U.S. cost structure, an extension of the revaluation within household retail purchases seems likely to have less rather than more of an impact than that resulting from extension within this category of the revaluation at 1937 ruble factor cost (see p. 147).

As has been explained (pp. 122–123, and p. 148, note 20), if agricultural labor services are undervalued in the USSR, probably this is no less true of other countries, but the undervaluation means that here too the "real" national income data, particularly in early years, are subject to a perceptible upward bias. Moreover, because of the relatively rapid tempo of Soviet industrialization, the bias often may be somewhat greater for the data compiled for the USSR than for corresponding figures that might be compiled elsewhere, although just how the Soviet data are affected relatively to those for any other country presumably would depend on the stage of development of the latter.

Reference has been made to deficiencies in ruble factor cost valuation. It should also be recalled here that in some degree, especially in early years, my calculations are also affected by an upward bias as a result of the omission of home processing. Judging from available data on this aspect (see chapter 7), it is perhaps not as important as might have been supposed, and in any event home processing usually is omitted from national income data for other countries, but here again one inevitably wonders whether the import of the limitation may not be greater for the USSR than often is so elsewhere, particularly if the comparison is with another country at a late stage of development.

For 1937–40, national income in terms of 1937 ruble factor cost grows at 6.7 percent annually if no allowance is made for territorial changes. But within the pre-1939 boundaries, the corresponding figure probably was on the order of 3.4 percent, or appreciably less than the tempo indicated by the same sort of measurement for the period 1928–37. Most likely the tempo did indeed decline as these inexact data would suggest. For the interval 1937–40, use of the alternative given year weighted formula hardly could affect the results significantly; in any event, with this formula, the tempo during 1937–40 is far below the corresponding figure for 1928–37.

Valued at 1937 ruble factor cost, output in 1944 is found to equal that in 1940. Where the computation is in terms of ruble factor cost of the given year, output declines but probably not very much: approximately 10 percentage points. In gauging the trend that obtains where given year weights are employed, I believe I am not far from the mark in taking as a guide at this point my previous calculation in terms of 1950 ruble factor cost. As computed, national income includes Lend-Lease. If the latter goods are omitted, income declines in both instances, although the reduction still amounts to but (say) 13 to 22 percentage points, depending on the formula.[2] The reader should recall at this point, however, that following the usual procedure in national income accounting, the gross national product here includes the services of military personnel. Exclusive of this item, as well as Lend-Lease, the gross national product in 1944 is 22 to 31 percentage points below prewar.

During the six years of war, demobilization, and reconstruction that followed 1944, output seems to grow only at a relatively limited rate. If the Lend-Lease is omitted from the 1944 total, however, the tempo compares favorably with that prevailing during the prewar period 1928–37. Moreover, the 1950 output in any case is already well above the prewar level. These are the trends where valuation is in terms of 1937 ruble factor cost. According to the given year weighted formula, output during 1944–50 grows at about the same rate and to about the same level as where base year weights are employed. However, the tempo is below the corresponding one that prevailed during 1928–37. In appraising growth according to the given-year weighted formula, the index

[2] In terms of the ruble prices of 1937, Lend-Lease Aid may have amounted to some 30 to 35 billion rubles in 1944, or 10 to 12 percent of the gross national product of that year (see chapter 7). Translated into ruble factor cost of 1937 according to methods described previously, the volume of aid seems to have been about the same magnitude in relation to the gross national product. Probably this is so also where valuation is in terms of 1950 ruble factor cost.

employed for 1950 is necessarily that previously calculated in terms of 1950 ruble factor cost.[3]

Under the Fifth Five Year Plan (1950–55), the tempo accelerates. Valued at 1937 ruble factor cost, national income actually grows more rapidly during this period than it did under the first two five year plans. So far as I am guided again by my computations in terms of 1950 ruble factor cost, I probably overstate somewhat the 1950–55 tempo that results where valuation is in terms of given year weights, but the rate of growth under the alternative formula must be as found here about the same as when base year weights are employed. In comparison with the corresponding figure for 1928–37, however, measurement in terms of given year weights means that the 1950–55 tempo is reduced. Hence, to the interesting question of whether relatively to the earlier period growth during 1950–55 accelerates or slows, the answer awkwardly depends on the formula.

I have been focusing on selected benchmark years. When we consider the annual data compiled for 1948–55, we see that the prewar level of output already was reattained in 1948. Depending on whether valuation is in terms of 1937 or given year ruble factor cost (I continue to take the latter as being represented for this period by the measurements in terms of 1950 ruble factor cost), output in 1948 either exceeds 1940 by three or falls short of 1940 by two percentage points. Also, the rate of growth during the four years 1944–48 is below, and during 1948–50 well above the average for the entire 1944–50 period. During 1950–55, growth fluctuates notably, as shown in Table 54, but there is no clear trend one way or the other.

As was explained, in calculating "real" national income in 1954, I take as a point of departure current ruble figures for this year computed in *SNIP-49–55* but I also consider variants. In Table 54 I cite outside parentheses annual increases in "real" national income during 1953–55 which are indicated where use is made of the *SNIP-49–55* current ruble figures. The measures given in parentheses correspond to the alternative current ruble figures that were considered.

Regrettably, no calculation could be made for 1932, the last year of the First Five Year Plan. Considering the circumstances, particularly the

[3] In Table 52, for 1940–50 I cite inside parentheses rates of growth where national income in 1944 is exclusive of Lend-Lease. Lend-Lease is assumed to total 11 percent of the disposable national income of 1944.

As calculated for 1950, national income includes reparations receipts, but while such revenues no doubt were of significant value to the Russians they seemingly were of a relatively limited magnitude. For this reason, the rate of growth would be little affected if they were omitted. I refer below to the annual data on national income that I have compiled for the period 1948–55. To the extent that any were received, reparations are included in national income throughout this period, but as for 1950 so for other years they do not appear to be very consequential.

TABLE 54

Gross National Product, USSR, 1951–55, Alternative Valuations

Year	Ruble factor cost of 1937	Ruble factor cost of 1950
	(Percent increase over previous year)	
1951	9.2	9.0
1952	8.6	7.8
1953	5.0	5.5
1954	4.2 (5.6)	6.0 (7.3)
1955	11.2 (9.7)	9.7 (8.4)

vicissitudes of agriculture under the impact of collectivization, one wonders whether under the First Five Year Plan the rate of growth may not have been below, and under the Second Five Year Plan above, the average observed for the two plans taken together.

I cited at the outset measurements of the average rate of growth of national income during 1928–55. What would the tempos have been if there had been no war? Depending on the more specific assumptions, the question presumably might be answered variously, but during the war the Russians suffered notable economic losses and after its close they did not regain until 1948 their 1940 level of national income. The expansion of output both to the pre-war level and beyond, it is true, was facilitated by reparations and by the fact that for a time there were partially damaged plants which might be renovated and restored to full use with only limited investments. But we surely may arrive at one interesting answer to the question that has arisen if we suppose that but for the war the Russians might have achieved the actual growth of 1928–55 in no more than 23 years, that is, the actual number of years in the period less the four war years. By implication, but for the war, output might have grown by at least these rates:

	Gross national product, average annual rate of growth, 1928–55 (percent)	Gross national product, average annual rate of growth, 1928–55, after adjustment for territorial changes (percent)
With output in 1937 ruble factor cost	5.6	5.2
With output as composite, 1937 base	7.9	7.5

Following Professor Gregory Grossman,[4] measurements such as these which impute to nonwar years Soviet growth for periods spanning the

[4] G. Grossman, "Thirty Years of Soviet Industrialization," *Soviet Survey*, October 1958.

war will be referred to as representing the average rate of growth for "effective years."

In sum, Soviet national income grew rapidly under the five year plans. This is indicated by both computations that have been considered. Nevertheless, the tempo and in some degree the pattern of variation over time depend on the formula. On the average for the entire period studied, the tempo is higher where output is calculated in terms of given year values than where use is made of the more conventional base year weights. In either case, but especially in the former, growth is at a rapid rate during 1928–37. Discounting for territorial changes the tempo subsequently declines, particularly where the calculation is in terms of given year values, and during the war output falls absolutely. The wartime loss, however, is soon made good thereafter. Finally, a relatively rapid tempo again prevails during 1950–55, although with given year weights this is below and with base year weights above the corresponding rate observed during 1928–37.[5]

Despite their limitations, my alternative measurements referring to different base years have been seen to conform to a plausible pattern (chapter 12). In some degree, therefore, the observed divergencies assuredly are statistically significant. Where this is so, theory suggests that as between the two sorts of serial data compiled, the one in terms of base year weights and the other in terms of given year weights, the latter is often more indicative of production potential in respect of the base year mix. Is this in fact the case here? The period studied was one of continual change in Soviet production structure. As my divergent computations suggest, structural variations were especially pronounced under the first two five year plans. Under such circumstances,

[5] I said earlier that the two series based on 1937 contained practically all the information at hand on Soviet production potential. It may nevertheless be of interest to see a complete inventory of the available data on the "real" gross national product for three benchmark years for which the information at hand seems most plentiful (1937 = 100):

	Based on 1937		*Based on 1950*		*Based on 1928*	
	With base year weights	With given year weights	With base year weights	With given year weights	With base year weights	With given year weights
1928	61.6	36.4	62.4	—	36.4	61.6
1937	100	100	100	100	100	100
1950	150	145	145	150	—	143

All indices employing base year weights are taken from Table 51. All indices employing given year weights are derived from those employing base year weights.

Although no index was calcualted for 1950 in terms of 1928 ruble factor cost, no doubt it would be higher than the others cited for this year. As is readily seen, this means that the given year weighted index for 1928 where 1950 is base would be even lower than the index for 1928 in terms of 1928 ruble factor cost.

as theory also teaches, even ideal data are often inaccurate regarding production potential, and possibly very much so. This is true regardless of the formula. On the other hand, in the period studied, the structure of prices changed along with that of production. The variation was marked indeed from 1928 to 1937; from 1937 to 1950 the further change appears to have been relatively limited (Table 63, p. 238). As was explained, the calculation in terms of given year weights is more reliable whenever prices in the given year are more indicative than those of the base year of the possibilities in the given year of transforming the given year mix into that of the base year. The conclusion is difficult to avoid that this is true for the USSR in comparisons between 1928, on the one hand, and 1937 and later years, on the other. Possibly it is also true for comparisons between the late thirties, on the one hand, and 1944 and postwar years, on the other, but this is more conjectural.

For purposes of appraising Soviet production potential, I conclude that where the concern is with capacity to produce the mix of 1937, at least for the years 1928–37, we must be guided more by the measurements in terms of given year than by those in terms of base year weights. It is only in regard to the early years, of course, that the choice is especially material. By implication, relatively to the situation during 1928–37, the growth of capacity to produce the 1937 mix during 1950–55 may have accelerated somewhat, but more likely there was some retardation.

If measurements in terms of given weights are to be favored in the appraisal of capacity regarding the 1937 mix, they must be also where the concern is with the mixes of 1950 and 1928. By the same token, however, the serial data in terms of 1937 ruble factor cost have their place after all. While not so pertinent where the concern is to appraise capacity regarding the 1937 composite, they provide at once a partial basis to appraise capacity regarding mixes of other years. Thus, from these data, we see among other things that at least over the period 1937–50 capacity to produce the mix of 1950 may well have grown in much the same way as that to produce the mix of 1937. At least during 1928–37, however, capacity regarding the 1937 mix probably grew more rapidly than that regarding the mix of 1928. Considering the relatively industrial (as distinct from agricultural) nature of the 1937 mix as compared with that of 1928, the latter conclusion is surely plausible.[6]

[6] The stated conclusions are the only ones regarding capacity to produce the 1950 and 1928 mixes that may be drawn from the two series based on 1937. If we consider not only these two series but my calculations generally (see note 5), however, we may perhaps go somewhat beyond these findings. More particularly, during 1928–37 capacity to produce the 1950 mix may have grown more rapidly than that to produce the 1937 mix, although this is quite conjectural. Also, if capacity regarding the 1928 composite grew relatively slowly from 1928–37 there is no evidence here that this was also true from 1937–50.

In the light of considerations set forth in the text, I believe there is indeed as I have

Reference thus far has been to aggregate national income. In per capita terms, the trends of course are similar to those observed in the aggregative data, but necessarily the rate of growth is reduced (Tables

TABLE 55

Gross National Product by Use per Capita, USSR, 1928–55, in Ruble Factor Cost (1937 = 100)

Outlay category	1928	1937	1940	1944	1950	1955
Household consumption outlay						
Ruble factor cost of 1937	102 (110)[a]	100	96.9	69.1	119	166
Ruble factor cost of 1950	101	100	93.8	67.1	116	163
Ruble factor cost of 1928	79.1	100	—	—	—	—
Composite, 1937 base	79.1	100	96.9	67.1	116	163
Communal services						
Ruble factor cost of 1937	29.4	100	101	86.5	133	150
Ruble factor cost of 1950	29.1	100	101	86.4	134	150
Ruble factor cost of 1928	26.2	100	—	—	—	—
Composite, 1937 base	26.2	100	101	86.4	134	150
Government administration, including NKVD						
Ruble factor cost of 1937	44.2	100	124	108	183	120
Ruble factor cost of 1950	44.5	100	124	109	184	119
Ruble factor cost of 1928	44.5	100	—	—	—	—
Composite, 1937 base	44.5	100	124	109	184	119
Defense (as recorded in budget)[b]						
Ruble factor cost of 1937	10.9	100	225	640	225	302
Ruble factor cost of 1950	16.4	100	216	622	217	282
Ruble factor cost of 1928	7.6	100	—	—	—	—
Composite, 1937 base	7.6	100	225	622	217	282
Gross investment						
Ruble factor cost of 1937	32.4	100	75.9	58.0	142	197
Ruble factor cost of 1950	35.2	100	77.1	55.1	140	194
Ruble factor cost of 1928	22.4	100	—	—	—	—
Composite, 1937 base	22.4	100	75.9	55.1	140	194
Gross national product						
Ruble factor cost of 1937	67.2 (71.3)[a]	100	103	114 (102)[c]	137	182
Ruble factor cost of 1950	68.0	100	99.4	105 (93.1)[c]	133	176
Ruble factor cost of 1928	39.7	100	—	—	—	—
Composite, 1937 base	39.7	100	103	105 (93.1)[c]	133	176

[a] Figures in parentheses result from extension of revaluation at ruble factor cost within household retail purchases.

[b] Exclusive of pensions to officers, et al.

[c] Figures in parentheses are exclusive of Lend-Lease.

55 and 56). With the recalculation, the data are in a sense adjusted not only for population growth but also for territorial changes. For this

---

assumed a presumption in favor of my serial data in terms of given year ruble factor cost where the aim is to appraise the change in capacity regarding the base year mix. The case for these data, however, only seems to gain in force if one considers also the theoretic analysis in chapter 3, pp. 31 ff.

TABLE 56

Average Annual Rates of Growth per Capita Gross National Product by Use, USSR, 1928–55, in Ruble Factor Cost
(Percent per annum)

Outlay category	1928–55	1928–37	1937–40	1940–44	1944–50	1950–55
Household consumption outlays						
Ruble factor cost of 1937	1.8 (1.5)[a]	−0.2 (−1.0)[a]	−1.0	−8.1	9.5	6.8
Ruble factor cost of 1950	1.8	−0.1	−2.1	−8.0	9.5	7.1
Ruble factor cost of 1928	—	2.6	—	—	—	—
Composite, 1937 base	2.7	2.6	−1.0	−8.8	9.5	7.1
Communal services						
Ruble factor cost of 1937	6.2	14.6	0.4	−3.8	7.4	2.4
Ruble factor cost of 1950	6.3	14.7	0.3	−3.8	7.5	2.3
Ruble factor cost of 1928	—	16.0	—	—	—	—
Composite, 1937 base	6.7	16.0	0.4	−3.9	7.5	2.3
Government administration, including NKVD						
Ruble factor cost of 1937	3.8	9.5	7.3	−3.2	9.2	−8.2
Ruble factor cost of 1950	3.7	9.4	7.4	−3.2	9.1	−8.4
Ruble factor cost of 1928	—	9.4	—	—	—	—
Composite, 1937 base	3.7	9.4	7.3	−3.1	9.1	−8.4
Defense (as recorded in budget)[b]						
Ruble factor cost of 1937	13.1	27.9	31.1	29.8	−16.0	6.0
Ruble factor cost of 1950	11.1	22.2	29.3	30.3	−16.1	5.4
Ruble factor cost of 1928	—	33.2	—	—	—	—
Composite, 1937 base	14.3	33.2	31.1	29.0	−16.1	5.4
Gross investment						
Ruble factor cost of 1937	6.9	13.3	−8.8	−6.5	16.2	6.7
Ruble factor cost of 1950	6.5	12.3	−8.3	−8.0	16.8	6.7
Ruble factor cost of 1928	—	18.1	—	—	—	—
Composite, 1937 base	8.3	18.1	−8.8	−7.7	16.8	6.7
Gross national product						
Ruble factor cost of 1937	3.8 (3.5)[a]	4.5 (3.8)[a]	1.0	2.7 (−0.3)[c]	3.1 (5.1)[c]	5.8
Ruble factor cost of 1950	3.6	4.4	−0.2	1.3 (−1.6)[c]	4.1 (6.1)[c]	5.8
Ruble factor cost of 1928	—	10.8	—	—	—	—
Composite, 1937 base	5.7	10.8	1.0	0.4 (−2.5)[c]	4.1 (6.1)[c]	5.8

[a] Figures in parentheses result from extension for 1928-37 of ruble factor cost valuation within household retail purchases.
[b] Exclusive of pensions to officers, et al.
[c] Figures in parentheses refer to the gross national product of 1944 exclusive of Lend-Lease.

reason, we see more clearly than before the retardation in the growth of national income that occurred during 1937–40.[7]

At the outset of this section I cited measurements of the average rate of growth of national income for the period 1928–55. Corresponding per capita figures are shown in Tables 55 and 56. If where the computation is in per capita terms we allow as before for the war, output during 1928–55 grows at an average annual rate of 4.4 percent when valuation is at 1937 ruble factor cost. When valuation is at ruble factor cost of the given year, the corresponding figure is 6.7 percent.

[7] In calculating national income per capita, I employ population data centered on July 1. For the population figures in question, I rely chiefly on computations of Dr. John Kantner and his associates of the U. S. Bureau of Census. See Appendix K.

Output per Employed Worker

To turn to implications as to gross national product per employed worker: The data set forth in Tables 57–59, represent the results of the attempt that is called for to relate my measurements of the gross national product to corresponding measurements of total employment. For an economy where agriculture is still a major sector, the latter aspect

TABLE 57

Gross National Product, Employment and Product per Employed Worker, USSR, 1928–55

	1955 ÷ 1928 (percent)	Average annual rate of growth (percent)
Gross national product		
In 1937 ruble factor cost	350	4.7 (4.5)[a]
Composite 1937 base	574	6.7
Employment, all sectors	183	2.3
Gross national product per employed worker		
With gross national product in 1937 ruble factor cost	192	2.4 (2.2)[a]
With gross national product as composite, 1937 base	315	4.3

[a] Figures in parentheses result from extension for 1928–37 of ruble factor cost valuation within household retail purchases.

TABLE 58

Gross National Product, Employment and Product per Employed Worker, USSR, Selected Intervals
1937=100

	1928	1937	1940	1950	1955
Gross national product					
In 1937 ruble factor cost	61.6 (65.4)[a]	100	121	150	216
Composite, 1937 base	36.4	100	121	145	209
Employment, all sectors	71.9	100	119	122	131
Gross national product per employed worker					
With gross national product in 1937 ruble factor cost	85.7 (91.0)[a]	100	102	122	164
With gross national product as composite, 1937 base	50.6	100	102	119	159

[a] Figures in parentheses result from extension of ruble factor cost valuation within household retail purchases.

TABLE 59

Gross National Product, Employment and Product per Employed Worker, USSR, Average Annual Rates of Growth, Selected Intervals (Percent per annum)

	1928–37	1937–40	1940–50	1950–55
Gross national product				
In 1937 ruble factor cost	5.5 (4.8)[a]	6.7	2.1	7.6
Composite	11.9	6.7	1.8	7.6
Employment, all sectors	3.7	5.8	0.3	1.4
Gross national product per employed worker				
With gross national product in 1937 ruble factor cost	1.7 (1.1)[a]	0.8	1.8	6.1
With gross national product as composite, 1937 base	7.9	0.8	1.5	6.1

[a] Figures in parentheses result from extension of ruble factor cost valuation within household retail purchases.

hardly could lend itself to accurate calculation in any event; the figures on it that are used here I fear are the less reliable since within the limits of this study I could do little more at this point than collate available incomplete and sometimes quite imperfect data. The resulting measurements of the gross national product per employed worker, however, may provide a better basis to appraise the trends in this important category than has been available hitherto. Although everyone agrees that the usage is dubious, one can hardly refrain from employing also for this aspect the more familiar designation of productivity of labor.

This study has resulted in the compilation of a variety of series of national income data. For purposes of measuring productivity, I focus again on the two series which were singled out previously: that where national income is valued in terms of the ruble factor cost of 1937 and that where comparisons with 1937 are made in terms of ruble factor cost of the given year. The two series (for convenience, repeated in Tables 57–59) are considered in turn in the comparison of output with employment. In this way, two alternative sets of measurements are obtained on output per employed worker.

As to employment, essentially the data compiled on this matter (Tables 57–59) are obtained by aggregating:[8]

(a) Average employment during the year in nonfarm civilian occupations, as determined chiefly from Dr. Warren Eason's careful computations.

(b) Agricultural employment in terms of "full-time" equivalent as

[8] I summarize here details on sources and methods set forth in Appendix K.

estimated for 1928 from a Soviet official calculation of a related sort. For 1937–55, I rely on estimates compiled from diverse Soviet data of uneven quality by Nancy Nimitz.

(c) The penal labor force, which was negligible in 1928 and is taken rather arbitrarily to number 3.0 millions in 1937, 3.5 millions in 1940 and 1950, and 2 millions in 1955 (as so fixed, the penal labor force at its peak in 1940 accounts for 4.3 percent of total employment in all sectors).

(d) The armed forces as determined elsewhere in this study.

Although my measures of employment are inexact, when seen in relation to the changes in population the resultant trends shown in Table 60 do not seem implausible. When familiar facts about the sharp increase in industrial employment of women are considered, the comparative increase in employment may not be as great as some expected.[9] Moreover, because of the fall in the birth rate during the war and the resultant decline in the relative numbers of children in the population, employment expands even less when compared to the adult population than when compared to the population generally. On the other hand, women already worked extensively in agriculture on the eve of the five year plans. As the urban population grew, a marked increase in the industrial employment of women was needed in order to assure that total employment would simply keep pace with total population. Furthermore, the period studied also witnessed both a decline in the employment of children and a sharp increase in the numbers of persons of 16 years and over attending school and these developments too tended to limit the relative increase in employment generally.

While the precise form of measurement varies somewhat as between sectors, employment is calculated here in terms of physical units. This of course is the usual procedure in the measurement of labor productivity, but for this purpose employment arguably should be computed instead in index number form, that is, through the aggregation of appropriately valued components. If this were done, I believe employment generally would increase more and output per worker less than has been shown. So far as employment is calculated in index number form, conceivably one might also compile alternative series corresponding to the two different national income series considered. The further results of recourse to such a procedure are difficult to gauge. Possibly, the marked divergence between the alternative measures of output per employed worker during 1928–37 that are given by the comparison of employment with the two different national income series would be reduced.

[9] In trying to appraise the comparative trends observed regarding Soviet employment and population I have benefited from the illuminating discussion of the related question of the developments regarding the Soviet labor force and population in Warren Eason, *Soviet Manpower,* Princeton, 1959, chap. iii.

TABLE 60

Population and Employment, USSR, 1928–55

Year	Population, all ages	Population, 16 years and over	Employment all sectors
	(1937 = 100)		
1928	91.7	89	71.9
1937	100	100	100
1940	118	119	119
1950	109	118	122
1955	119	132	131

Note: On the population data, see Appendix K.

In comparison with the calculation in physical units, that utilizing index numbers of course must indicate a greater increase in employment if employment tends to increase more in the case of high paid than in the case of low paid workers. In fact, an outstanding feature under the five year plans is the sharp increase in nonfarm relatively to farm employment. As we have seen, in monetary terms the nonfarm workers are also more highly paid. Within the nonfarm and farm sectors, trends under the five year plans are more complex but very likely the effect of the shifts between sectors is here compounded.

In judging how the alternative measures of output per employed worker are affected where output in each case is compared with employment computed according to a corresponding index number formula, we must consider that the relative incomes of nonfarm workers were especially high on the eve of the five year plans. As is readily seen, given this, adoption of the indicated procedure should mean a reduced divergence between the alternative measures of productivity. On the other hand, the alternative measures might be affected in a contrary way by the tendency of many skilled workers and of workers generally in priority industries to receive increased income differentials in the course of time.

As was explained earlier (see chapter 8), differences in the earnings of different occupations in the USSR probably tend broadly to correspond to differences in "productivity." As between industries, there is perhaps some tendency also for differences in earnings to reflect workers' transfer prices. Under the circumstances, by computing employment in index number form, we in effect allow for changes in average skill or "disutility" that occur because of changes in the structure of employment. In calculating national income as an indicator of production potential, I believe I undervalued the services of agricultural labor (chapter 8). If so, the computation of employment in index number form would have the further merit that the services of agricultural labor might be discounted correspondingly at this point. In this way, one would obtain measures of labor productivity which are unaffected by the initial undervaluation of agricultural labor.

Because of the nature of the data considered, the physical units in terms of which employment has been calculated tend broadly to be man-years, but the measurements of productivity that are compiled fail to reflect changes in working time. In trying to gauge how the results might be affected if account were taken of this aspect, the reader may find the data in Table 61 of value. I repeat here from Tables 57 and 59 the data that have been compiled on output per worker, and I give corresponding figures where for civilian nonfarm workers employment has been adjusted for changes in nonfarm hours. For civilian nonfarm workers generally, hours of employment are assumed to vary as they do for workers in industry alone.[10] As the cited figures imply, hours of work in Soviet industry tended generally to increase over the period studied. They initially decrease slightly, however, while the over-all increase originates chiefly in a government decree of June 26, 1940. Although during the war, hours of work increased still more, this boost proved to be temporary. After the war, the working day initiated by the decree of June 26, 1940 was re-established. Trends in the agricultural workday in the USSR have been the subject of conflicting opinions, the appraisal of which I must leave to separate inquiry. Possibly there was no change to speak of; possibly as a result of collectivization the workday was reduced.[11] Trends in output per labor hour for the working force as a whole might vary accordingly.

Let us now consider the trends in productivity that are indicated. For the period 1928–55, the gross national product per employed worker is found to increase at an average annual rate of 2.4 percent. This is the result where output is measured in a conventional way in terms of ruble factor cost of a single base year. According to the alternative computation where output is measured instead in terms of ruble factor cost of the given year, the gross national product per employed worker increases at an average annual rate of 4.3 percent (Tables 57–59). During 1928–37, output per employed worker is shown by the former calculation to have grown at a somewhat lower rate than was realized during the entire period 1928–55. As measured by the latter, the tempo is much higher than the over-all average: 7.9 percent. If, as was explained, my calculations on national income are especially crude for 1928–37, this is also true of those on labor productivity; and as before, the result is more apt to be an upward than a downward bias.[12] Whether and to what extent, where valuation is at 1937 ruble factor cost, output per worker during 1937–40 grew less rapidly than in previous years, as my

[10] See Appendix H.

[11] Naum Jasny, *Socialized Agriculture of the USSR,* Stanford, 1949, p. 419; Arcadius Kahan, "Changes in Labor Inputs in Soviet Agriculture," *Journal of Political Economy,* October 1959, p. 451.

[12] On possible causes of an upward bias in my national income data, particularly for the early years, see above, p. 218. On the import of one aspect for the measurements of output per worker, see the parenthetic figures in Tables 57, 58, and 59. Like the data on national income, those on employment probably are relatively crude for early years, but in the latter case the direction of error is conjectural.

TABLE 61

Output per Worker, and per Worker Adjusted for Nonfarm Hours, USSR, Average Annual Rates of Increase for Selected Intervals (Percent)

Year	Output per worker—		Output per worker, adjusted for nonfarm hours—	
	With output in terms of 1937 ruble factor cost	With output as composite, 1937 base	With output in terms of 1937 ruble factor cost	With output as composite, 1937 base
1928–37	1.7	7.9	1.8	8.0
1937–40	0.8	0.8	−0.4	−0.4
1940–50	1.8	1.5	1.3	1.0
1950–55	6.1	6.1	6.0	5.9
1928–55	2.4	4.3	2.1	4.0

data show, is therefore a conjectural question. Where valuation is at ruble factor cost of the given year, however, the rate of increase clearly declines, and indeed markedly so. For the decade 1940–50, the tempo is found to be 1.8 percent where output is in terms of 1937 ruble factor cost and 1.5 percent where it is in terms of ruble factor cost of the given year. With either computation, output per worker grows by 6.1 percent annually during 1950–55. Thus, where valuation is at 1937 ruble factor cost, the tempo is above the corresponding rate for 1928–37. Where valuation is at ruble factor cost of the given year, the tempo probably is about the same as or somewhat below that prevailing during the earlier interval.

No computation could be made of output per employed worker for 1944. From scattered data one may conjecture that from 1940 to 1944 this aspect increased little, if at all. In fact, if as has been done for other years employment in 1944 is taken as inclusive of military personnel, output per employed worker probably declined. The gains in productivity realized during 1940–50, therefore, must have originated in the postwar reconstruction years.[13]

As for national income, so here, it is interesting to calculate rates of growth for "effective years" during the period 1928–55, that is, rates adjusted for the war on the supposition that the entire gains of the period are realized in peacetime years. Where output is valued at 1937

[13] The change in output per worker during 1940–44 may be gauged from these data: The ratio of the gross national product, composite 1937 base (ex. Lend-Lease), for 1944 to that for 1940 is 81.5 percent; for the same category (ex. military services), the corresponding figure is 70.5 percent; for employment (civilian nonfarm, plus armed forces), 91.8 percent; and for employment (civilian nonfarm), 65.2 percent.

ruble factor cost, the rate of growth of output per worker for effective years is 2.9 percent annually. The corresponding figure with output valued at ruble factor cost of the given year is 5.1 percent.

In measuring labor productivity, we also provide a basis to appraise the part of the increase in output that is "accounted for" by the increase in this aspect as distinct from the part "due to" the increase in the volume of employment. Thus, taking the period studied as a whole, about one-half of over-all growth is explicable in terms of the increase in productivity. This is so if output is valued at 1937 ruble factor cost. With output valued at given year factor cost, some two-thirds of the over-all growth is due to the increase in productivity. During 1928–37, productivity is in the former case less important than, and in the latter case about as important as, it usually is. For both calculations it becomes less consequential during 1937–40, and accounts for the bulk of the increase in output during 1940–50 and again during 1950–55.

In calculating labor productivity, we seek in effect to appraise the sources of growth of production potential. As we have seen, however, where the concern is with production potential both sorts of calculations of gross national product that have been considered are of interest but a calculation in given year prices probably is more indicative than one in base year prices of changes in capacity to produce the base year mix. Considering that the base year here is 1937, the implication seemingly is that per employed worker Soviet capacity to produce the mix of that year during 1928–37 probably grew more rapidly than the calculation where output is measured in a conventional way in terms of 1937 ruble factor cost might suggest. In years after 1937, the tempo of capacity per employed worker is little affected by the choice of formula, but if productivity is conceived in this way there is now more reason than before to think that the rate of increase of this feature declined during 1937–40. Then too the tempo during 1950–55 is now seen to be relatively high, and possibly on a par with that of 1928–37.

Since I must leave to separate inquiry the important question of the trends in inputs other than of labor, it is not easy to appraise the foregoing tentative findings on output per worker. Nevertheless, from data compiled in this study something may be surmised regarding inputs of one factor, fixed capital, and when we consider these the observed trends in productivity are not implausible.[14] Thus, the five year plans saw

[14] If the data considered in Table 27 are at all reliable, the Soviet stock of reproducible fixed capital, net of depreciation, in 1937, probably was not far in excess of the national product of that year. In commenting below on possible trends in the stock of fixed capital, I consider mainly this fact, the data compiled in this study on the rate of investment in reproducible fixed capital, and information on depreciation on fixed capital in N. Kaplan, "Capital Formation and Allocation," in A. Bergson, ed., *Soviet Economic Growth,* Evanston, 1953, p. 47. Account is also taken of the wartime destruction of fixed capital.

many developments adverse to productivity, most notably the dislocations of collectivization and war, but if in the course of time the Russians were able to increase markedly output per employed worker this is hardly surprising when we consider that the period also witnessed an increase in fixed capital in sharp disproportion to the increase in employment, and together with this an unprecedented transformation of technology. The novel institution of central planning was in its infancy at the beginning of the period. Very likely productivity was also raised as this system tended to become more efficient in the course of time.

While collectivization and the attendant losses occurred during 1928–37, I find that per employed worker capacity to produce the 1937 mix probably grew relatively rapidly in these years, but this result seems understandable since under the early five year plans fixed capital hardly lagged even in relation to employment, and technological progress must have been particularly marked at this time. In trying to explain the decline in the growth of productivity during 1937–40, one thinks especially of the sharp expansion in the armed forces and the mounting defense preparations generally which were an outstanding feature of this period. Since military personnel are included in my employment figures, the increase in their numbers necessarily tended to limit the calculated increase in productivity. No doubt this result was only compounded by dislocations associated with the defense preparations generally. Although not an important part of the story for the entire period 1928–55, presumably the wholesale purges also played a part at this point. My calculations for 1940 supposedly refer to the enlarged Soviet territory of the time. The observed trends are affected, therefore, although it is difficult to say how, by any differences in productivity between the USSR within its previous boundaries and the areas that were taken over during 1939–40.

While the war brought dislocations, in the munitions sector it also brought further technological progress and greater efficiency, and technological progress generally must have been rapid during reconstruction. But all things considered there seems little basis to question that for the decade 1940–50 as a whole productivity increased at only a modest rate such as has been found here. If, as has been suggested, such gains were realized wholly in the reconstruction period, this too does not seem surprising. In economic affairs, the years 1950–55 are notable especially for the great agricultural measures initiated after Stalin's death, but in 1955 some of the most important of these, particularly the "new lands" program, had still had little chance to bear fruit. If per employed worker capacity to produce the 1937 mix grew rapidly in these years, and perhaps about at the peak tempo of 1928–37, probably the chief explanation is that fixed capital grew especially rapidly in relation to the limited increase in labor and that with this the transformation of technology continued apace. No doubt the government was also able to make good in these years inefficiencies that had developed in the previous decade of war and reconstruction.

Reference has been to trends in output per worker. Because of uncertainties about changes in the agricultural workday, the corresponding trends in output per man-hour are conjectural, but most likely the gains in the latter generally paralleled and were at least nearly as great as those in output per worker. During 1937–40, however, the performance regarding output per man-hour probably was markedly less favorable even than that regarding output per worker. By the same token, where reference is to the former rather than the latter, trends in productivity usually are still broadly explicable in terms of the forces that have been described, but during 1937–40 it must be supposed that those impeding productivity gains were even more powerful than seemed so previously.

Trends in Relative Shares

The disposition of Soviet national income was discussed in the SNIP studies. More particularly, in the light of data compiled there in terms of current ruble factor cost, an attempt is made to measure and interpret trends in relative shares of the gross national product accruing to different use categories. In the present study, I have again compiled data on the disposition of national income but these are now in terms of the ruble factor cost of different base years. If from measures of this sort one calculates the relative shares of the national income going to different use categories, the results, of course, may often diverge from those indicated by measures such as are derived in the SNIP studies. Indeed, a divergence must occur whenever factor cost per unit of output varies differently for the goods and services disposed of in diverse use categories. As must often be so, costs in turn vary differently whenever there are divergent trends in either factor productivity or in factor prices.

Moreover, whether the two sorts of calculation diverge or not, each I believe has an interest of its own. From data on relative shares in terms of current values, one may gauge how in any given period the community in question allocates available resources and material values between alternative uses. There is also a basis to judge the possible gains and losses to different use categories that might result from resource reallocations. From data on relative shares in terms of base year values, one is able to appraise the comparative trends in the volume of goods and services disposed of in successive intervals. Such trends reflect the changes that occur in resource allocation, but they diverge from the latter so far as factor productivity and prices vary disproportionately for different use categories. Measurements of trends that so diverge from those in resource allocation are of interest from different standpoints. As is rarely considered, for example, where as in the study of the growth process one wishes to integrate serial measurements of the rate of investment with serial measurements of the capital stock in constant prices, the former data too are appropriately compiled only in constant prices.

The task of this section is to discuss summarily results and implications of my calculations of national income disposition in terms of the ruble factor cost of different base years. Data of this sort might be examined from different standpoints but I believe much that is of interest here may best be brought out if, in the light of these measures together with the corresponding ones compiled in the SNIP studies, I review the trends in relative shares. The review perhaps is the more in order since in *SNIP-49–55* national income is measured by use only in terms of prevailing rubles, and Hoeffding and Nimitz are able on this basis to comment only very tentatively on trends in relative shares. For purposes of this study, corresponding data have now been compiled in terms of current ruble factor cost, and recent trends in relative shares may now be examined in the light of these computations as well as of those on disposition in terms of base year ruble factor cost which were made in previous chapters. I turn, therefore, to the trends in relative shares.

The pertinent SNIP data as elaborated here are set forth in Table 62.[15] Also shown there are corresponding figures compiled in terms of the ruble factor cost of 1937, 1950, and 1928. In examining the trends in relative shares in the light of these figures, we may usefully consider at the same time the index numbers of ruble factor cost per unit of output that they imply (Table 63).[16] Among the different data on disposition

[15] For 1928 and 1937 I cite somewhat revised figures derived in chapter 9. For 1940 and 1944 the cited figures are taken from *SNIP-28–48,* except that I have now revised them slightly to make them comparable to those for other years. As was explained, in *SNIP-49–55,* national income is calculated only in prevailing rubles. For 1950, corresponding figures in terms of current ruble factor cost are here taken from chapter 9 of this volume. For 1955, data in terms of current ruble factor cost have been compiled for use in the present study by Nancy Nimitz. Miss Nimitz takes as a point of departure the *SNIP-49–55* current ruble figures as revised here and employs procedures that are essentially the same as those applied in chapter 9 in calculating national income for 1950 in terms of current ruble factor cost. Later, I shall also cite data on the national income by use in terms of current ruble factor cost for 1948, 1949, and 1951–54. It may be just as well to explain here that the figures for 1948 are taken from *SNIP-40–48*. The data compiled in the latter study, however, are revised somewhat here in order to make them comparable to corresponding figures for other years. For 1949 and 1951–54 I again rely on computations made by Miss Nimitz on the basis of the *SNIP-49–55* current ruble figures as revised in this study.

[16] In each case, the index number cited for any use category and year is obtained as the quotient for the use category and year in question of an index of outlays in terms of current ruble factor cost and a corresponding index of outlays in terms of the

TABLE 62

Relative Shares of Final Uses in Gross National Product, Alternative Valuations, USSR, 1928–55
(Percent)

Outlay category	1928	1937	1940	1944	1950	1955
Household consumption outlays						
In current ruble factor cost	64.7	52.5	51.0	36.1	45.5	49.2
In 1937 ruble factor cost	79.5	52.5	49.4	31.8	45.7	48.0
In 1950 ruble factor cost	77.7	52.4	49.5	33.6	45.5	48.6
In 1928 ruble factor cost	64.7	32.5	—	—	—	—
Communal services						
In current ruble factor cost	5.1	10.5	9.9	9.1	10.8	10.0
In 1937 ruble factor cost	4.6	10.5	10.3	7.9	10.2	8.7
In 1950 ruble factor cost	4.6	10.8	11.0	8.9	10.8	9.2
In 1928 ruble factor cost	5.1	7.7	—	—	—	—
Government administration, including NKVD						
In current ruble factor cost	2.7	3.2	3.8	3.7	4.8	2.6
In 1937 ruble factor cost	2.1	3.2	3.9	3.0	4.3	2.1
In 1950 ruble factor cost	2.3	3.5	4.4	3.6	4.8	2.4
In 1928 ruble factor cost	2.7	2.5	—	—	—	—
Defense (as recorded in budget)[a]						
In current ruble factor cost	2.5	7.9	16.1	36.8	10.9	10.3
In 1937 ruble factor cost	1.3	7.9	17.3	44.1	12.9	13.1
In 1950 ruble factor cost	1.6	6.7	14.5	39.8	10.9	10.7
In 1928 ruble factor cost	2.5	13.0	—	—	—	—
Gross investment						
In current ruble factor cost	25.0	25.9	19.2	14.3	27.9	27.9
In 1937 ruble factor cost	12.5	25.9	19.1	13.1	26.9	28.1
In 1950 ruble factor cost	13.8	26.6	20.6	14.0	27.9	29.2
In 1928 ruble factor cost	25.0	44.3	—	—	—	—

[a] Excluding pensions to officers, et al.

compiled here, I first focus on those in terms of ruble factor cost of 1937 and then consider briefly how the results are affected if we refer instead to the data based on other years. We must consider in each case the corresponding implied index numbers of factor cost per unit of output.

1928–37. An outstanding finding of the SNIP studies is that at the end of the first two five year plans the "money" rate of investment is the same as it was at the beginning.[17] Although such investment might well

ruble factor cost of the base year considered. Although all index numbers are expressed as percentages of 1937, the base year in effect is the same as that to which the data on "real" outlays refer. On the other hand, as is readily seen, all index numbers correspond to Formula (3); that is, they reflect variable weights of the given year.

[17] For convenience, unless otherwise indicated, I shall use the term "rate" in this section as synonymous with "relative share." It is also helpful to speak of outlays in terms of current ruble factor cost as "money" outlays, and of outlays in terms of ruble factor cost of one or another base year as "real" outlays. The corresponding rates of expenditure are referred to similarly.

TABLE 63

Index Numbers of Ruble Factor Cost per Unit of Output Implied by National Income Computations, USSR, 1928–55 (1937 = 100)

	1928	1937	1940	1944	1950	1955
Household consumption outlays						
Implied by outlays in 1937 ruble factor cost	18.1	100	136	161	215	216
Implied by outlays in 1950 ruble factor cost	18.3	100	140	166	222	219
Implied by outlays in 1928 ruble factor cost	23.3	100	—	—	—	—
Communal services						
Implied by outlays in 1937 ruble factor cost	24.7	100	126	162	230	242
Implied by outlays in 1950 ruble factor cost	25.0	100	126	162	229	242
Implied by outlays in 1928 ruble factor cost	27.8	100	—	—	—	—
Government administration, including NKVD						
Implied by outlays in 1937 ruble factor cost	28.6	100	131	175	244	263
Implied by outlays in 1950 ruble factor cost	28.6	100	131	174	244	266
Implied by outlays in 1928 ruble factor cost	28.4	100	—	—	—	—
Defense						
Implied by outlays in 1937 ruble factor cost	44.0	100	123	118	181	165
Implied by outlays in 1950 ruble factor cost	29.3	100	128	122	188	176
Implied by outlays in 1928 ruble factor cost	62.9	100	—	—	—	—
Gross investment						
Implied by outlays in 1937 ruble factor cost	44.4	100	132	154	223	208
Implied by outlays in 1950 ruble factor cost	40.9	100	130	162	227	212
Implied by outlays in 1928 ruble factor cost	64.4	100	—	—	—	—
Gross national product						
Implied by outlays in 1937 ruble factor cost	22.2	100	132	142	215	210
Implied by outlays in 1950 ruble factor cost	22.0	100	136	155	222	217
Implied by outlays in 1928 ruble factor cost	37.6	100	—	—	—	—

have already been high on the eve of the plans, the introduction of the five year plan in 1928 meant the initiation in the USSR of the famous Policy of Industrialization, and under the circumstances one inevitably wondered at the reliability of the SNIP calculations. But as we now see, the moral is, as some surmised, not that the SNIP data are unreliable but simply that under the first two plans "money" investments are one thing and "real" investments quite another. In any event, from data now at hand we see that with the same "money" rate of investment the government actually was able to achieve a major increase in the "real" rate of investment. While construction is a major component, industries producing investment goods ordinarily seem to experience significant relative cost reductions in the course of industrialization. In the USSR under the first two five year plans, such relative economies by implication were marked indeed, and some may feel surprisingly so, but the result must be read in the light of the radical technological transformation that occurred at this time in heavy industrial branches.

The SNIP studies calculate Soviet defense outlays from budgetary data which admittedly may represent understatements, although probably less so before than during and after the war. The "money" rate of defense expenditures is found on this basis to increase sharply from 1928 to 1937. At the earlier date, however, such outlays still were quite limited, and the subsequent increase must be read in this light. As calculated in the present study, the rate of defense expenditures increases over the period in question much more in "real" than in "money" terms. By implication, unit costs of defense goods and services, like those of investment goods, including construction, rose appreciably less than costs generally.

The SNIP studies did not pause to consider the import of the significant increase observed under the first two five year plans in the "money" rate of outlays on communal services. Such expenditures, of course, in a sense supplement household consumption, but, as students of development have come increasingly to realize, they can also be an important supplement to investment as a source of growth. The Soviet government too has hardly been oblivious of the latter aspect. The experience under the first two plans must be viewed accordingly. The increase in the "money" rate of outlays may signify a concern for consumers' welfare but presumably it testifies chiefly to the government's belief in the importance of such expenditures for the success of industrialization. The rate of expenditure on communal services is found here to rise somewhat more in "real" than in "money" terms. Since much of the outlays in question go for labor services, factor productivity here presumbly tends to lag behind that elsewhere, but while my calculations on communal services throughout could easily be somewhat in error costs may have declined relatively as implied as a result of a relative decline in the money incomes of the workers in question. The rate of expenditure on government administration, including NKVD, also increases over the period in question, and again somewhat more in "real" than in "money" terms, but here too while much of the outlays are for labor services the results may reflect a relative decline in money incomes.[18] Under the first two five year plans, given the relative shares in "money" terms for other use categories, that for household consumption necessarily is found to decline in the SNIP studies. Where the calculation is in "real" terms, we now see that under the Policy of Industrialization this share declines still more.[19]

[18] Actually, in the case of both communal services and governmental administration, a relative decline in earnings almost certainly is at least a partial cause of the disproportionate increase in costs that is observed. Note, however, that what counts is the trend of earnings in these sectors in relation to that prevailing not merely among hired employees generally but among all workers, including farmers. On this aspect, see chapter 8 and Appendices D and H.

[19] As before, I have been focusing on measuerments obtained through a partial revaluation, but if instead reference is made to those obtained by extending the revaluation within household retail purchases (pp. 135 ff), the trends in relative shares are little affected. Thus, in terms of 1937 ruble factor cost, the share of household consumption was found initially to decline from 79.5 in 1928 to 52.5 percent in 1937. With the more extended revaluation, the corresponding figures are 80.7 and 52.5 percent.

Neither in the SNIP studies nor here could national income be calculated for any date between 1928 and 1937. If such a computation were made for 1932, for example, the final year of the First Five Year Plan, I suspect that the rate of investment would be found to be above and the rate of household consumption outlays below the corresponding magnitudes in both 1928 and 1937. The comparison with 1937 would hold where the relative shares are in "money" although possibly not where they are in "real" terms.

1937–40. The SNIP calculations provided a basis to appraise the recurring question as to the degree to which the Russians mobilized before the German attack. The mobilization seemingly was on a sizable scale. In 1940, the government spent on defense 16 percent of the national income in "money" terms. This is twice the corresponding rate of expenditure in 1937. With the data now at hand, we can also appraise the scale of mobilization in "real" terms. Apparently, as so calculated, the rate of defense outlays increases fully as much as or indeed even more than in "money" terms. If, by implication, unit costs of defense goods rose during this period nearly as much as unit costs generally, this perhaps is not especially surprising in view of the rapid expansion of outlays at this still early stage of heightened defense preparation.

For various reasons the SNIP studies felt it to be plausible that the increased defense outlays should have been financed, as was calculated, in good part at the expense of "money" investments and only to a limited extent at the expense of "money" consumption outlays. While I believe the mobilization program was more complex than was supposed previously, there still is little basis to question this SNIP finding.[20] As calculated here, the rate of investment from 1937 to 1940 varies in the same way in "real" as in "money" terms. For household consumption, the rate of expenditure in "real" terms falls somewhat more than that in "money" terms. During this period, therefore, the costs of investment goods vary commensurately with, while the costs of consumption goods rise somewhat more than in proportion to, costs generally. If these trends are rather in contrast with those observed under the first two five year plans, this does not seem surprising when we consider among other things the purges and the rapid mobilization that was occurring.

From 1937 to 1940 the rate of expenditure on communal services

[20] As was not considered before, in cutting investments the government seemingly sacrificed first of all investments in inventories in the consumers' goods sector. See Appendices F and G. Seen in this light, the government policy on resource allocation during the mobilization period is not as paradoxical as it appears at first sight. On the other hand, the government undoubtedly also reduced sharply at this time the rate of investment in fixed capital in civilian industries, and so far as this was done I feel the explanation probably is broadly the one given previously. See *SNIP-40–48*, pp. 92–93.

declines somewhat in "money" but does not change perceptibly in "real" terms. Although a limited cost decrease thus is again implied for this use category, as before, the workers employed here may have suffered a relative decline in money incomes. In any event, in appraising the implied cost trend for communal services, we must consider that labor productivity in the economy generally increased only to a limited extent during the period in question. For government administration, including the NKVD, the rate of outlays now increases somewhat in both "money" and "real" terms.

1940–44. As calculated in the SNIP studies, defense expenditures in 1944 account for 37 percent of the national income in "money" terms. From what is generally known about the Soviet defense effort, this may appear an implausibly low figure, but we are now able to corroborate the suggestion in the SNIP studies that the war is another period where "money" and "real" outlays are two quite different things. This is especially so for defense outlays. Thus, where relative shares are calculated in "real" terms the share of defense in 1944 rises to 44 percent. The calculations regarding "real" defense expenditures are among the less reliable I have made. This is true for the entire period 1928–55, but perhaps more so during the war than at other times. Nevertheless, there can hardly be any doubt that as large-scale serial production of munitions became the order of the day the Russians did indeed achieve for defense goods and services generally a marked relative reduction in costs such as my calculations imply.

In appraising the SNIP finding on military outlays, as was pointed out previously, we must also consider that in addition to such expenditures the government apparently continued during the war to make sizable investments. Moreover, much of such expenditures in 1944 must have been made in support of defense activities. From the SNIP calculations it was possible to measure the "money" rate of investment in wartime. As we now see, investments are also on a sizable scale in "real" terms, but as so calculated the rate is somewhat below that in "money" terms. In effect, therefore, costs of investment goods are found to rise during the war slightly more than costs generally.

The government during the war reduced fractionally the "money" rate of expenditure on communal services. That on government administration, including the NKVD, was left unchanged. The corresponding rates in "real" terms, however, fall in both cases. Thus, in relation to costs generally, costs in these sectors now revert to a more "normal" pattern.

Of the total national income in "money" terms, according to the SNIP calculations but 36 percent remains for household consumption in 1944. This includes military subsistence. For civilians alone the share of consumption is but 30 percent. Where national income is in "real" terms, the corresponding figures are calculated here to be 32 and 27 percent. Here, too, therefore costs rise disproportionately during the war.

1944–50. From the SNIP calculations we could also appraise the familiar question as to the extent to which after the war the government demobilized its wartime military establishment. Apparently the demobilization was on a sizable scale, but thereafter defense expenditures continued to be notably high by prewar standards. Thus, at the end of the Fourth Five Year Plan in 1950, such outlays accounted for 11 percent of the national income. This was far below the corresponding figure for 1944, but before the war it was only exceeded in the years immediately preceding the Nazi attack. In the SNIP studies, however, the disposition of the national income was calculated in "money" terms, and, as we may now observe, demobilization is still on a sizable scale where the calculation is in "real" terms, but with such measurements the 1950 rate of expenditures in comparison with prewar years is even higher than before. The costs of defense goods and services, therefore, are found here to have risen over the demobilization period a little more but over the decade 1940–50 less than costs generally.

Having determined defense outlays, the government after the war still had to choose between investment and household consumption. Apparently, despite the wartime privations, the decision was to continue with the Policy of Industrialization. Thus, in 1950 the government was once more devoting to investment a share of national income fully comparable to that realized in prewar years before mobilization. Concomitantly, it could also raise the share of income going to household consumption above the abysmal level of 1944, but as late as 1950 the rate of household consumption was still much below that of prewar years. These trends could be observed from the SNIP calculations on the disposition of national income in "money" terms, and we now see that in essentials they also prevail where such measurements are made in "real" terms.

As was explained, under the first two five year plans, the costs of investment goods rose less, and of consumption goods more, than costs generally. By implication, in the period of reconstruction, costs of the two sorts of goods rose in step. One perhaps can surmise the reasons for this change in pattern. Most importantly, in scope and intensity, the technological revolution that occurred in heavy industry under the first two five year plans probably was of a more or less unique sort. The further technological gains realized in this sector in the reconstruction period hardly could be commensurate. Moreover, under reconstruction the trend to modernization no doubt was extended on some scale to previously neglected areas.[21] For this reason, the possibility of realizing

[21] I am indebted to Professor Gerschenkron for this observation.

superior gains in productivity in the priority sectors became the more limited.

Although during reconstruction the relative shares of investment and household consumption in "real" terms vary in much the same way as they do in "money" terms, there are divergencies. More particularly, the "real" relative share of household consumption is in 1944 below, and in 1950 about the same as, the corresponding "money" share. For investment, the "real" rate in both years is below the money rate. In the reconstruction period, therefore, not only is there no longer a relative reduction in the costs of investment goods such as occurred under the first two five year plans, but to a degree, there is now a relative reduction in the costs of consumption goods, In view of the deficiencies of my calculations, one hesitates to stress limited variations of this sort but if my data are reliable at this point, the observed trends no doubt could have been produced by factors such as have just been discussed.

Under reconstruction, the rate of "money" expenditure rises for both communal services and government administration, including the NKVD. As a result, however, the share of the national income going to the former in 1950 is about the same as that devoted to the same uses in the premobilization year 1937. For government administration, the rate of expenditure in 1950 is well above prewar levels. The latter trend results almost entirely from the disproportionate postwar increase in NKVD outlays. The possible import of this aspect was discussed previously, and there is no need to dwell on it again here.[22] For both communal services and government administration, the rate of outlay in "real" terms during the reconstruction period varies closely with that in "money" terms. In appraising the implied cost trends, it should be recalled that from 1944 to 1950 productivity rose to only a relatively limited extent in the economy generally (see pp. 227 ff).

1950–55. The Korean War began in June 1950. Stalin died on March 5, 1953. The year 1955 marked the close of the Fifth Five Year Plan. In surveying trends in relative shares, one turns with particular interest to consider the impact of these events. Seemingly, the impact was rather limited. Although the government's pronouncements might easily be read otherwise, in 1955 it was devoting to defense about the same share of the national income as it did in 1950. Stalin's successors themselves have been explicit that they are continuing the Policy of Industrialization, but in their pronouncements their emphases have varied at different times. On the vital question of the comparative allocations of income to investment and household consumption, we see that in the third year after Stalin's death they were in fact proceeding in broadly the same way

[22] See *SNIP-40–48,* p. 95.

as he had in his last years. In 1955, they allotted to investment a share of the national income as large as Stalin had in 1950. The share of household consumption in 1955, however, was somewhat above the notably low level at which Stalin had left it.

As could be surmised from the prevailing ruble figures computed in *SNIP-49–55* but as is seen more clearly from corresponding figures now at hand in terms of current ruble factor cost, the foregoing trends prevail where reference is to "money" shares. From my calculations in terms of base year ruble factor cost, we see that essentially they also prevail where reference is instead to "real" shares. From 1950 to 1955, costs generally fell, but only to a limited extent. From the computations on national income disposition, we also see that cost trends were broadly similar for different major use categories. The pattern of cost variation, thus, differed somewhat from that prevailing under reconstruction, but the further and more significant divergence that is observed from the pattern prevailing under the first two five year plans was in essentials already anticipated in the reconstruction period, and seemingly is to be understood in much the same terms as the similar divergence from the prewar pattern that was seen at that time.

In *SNIP-49–55* no comment is made on recent trends in communal services and government administration, including the NKVD. For the former, the "money" rate of expenditure in 1955 seems perceptibly below that of 1950. Presumably this result must be read in the light of the relative decline of the school population due to the decline in births during and after the war. Since the corresponding "real" rate declines more noticeably, costs for the goods and services in question are again found to vary according to the "normal" pattern. For government administration, including the NKVD, the "money" rate of expenditure declines sharply over the period considered. The reduction affects both governmental administration generally and the NKVD in particular, but especially the latter. Internal security agencies, I believe, found their responsibilities, which had been greatly expanded immediately after the war, significantly curtailed even under Stalin. Since the dictator's death, his successors by all accounts have curtailed them still further. The cited trends in expenditures must also be viewed in the light of the vigorous campaign that has been waged recently to curtail the staffs of governmental agencies generally. Again illustrating the "normal" pattern of cost variation, the "real" rate of expenditure is found here to decline even more than that in "money" terms.

I have been considering trends in relative shares between benchmark years. For 1948–55, data on relative shares in "money" terms are compiled in the SNIP studies for all years, and while recent annual as well as benchmark year figures are in prevailing rubles, if we translate the former as we did the latter into current ruble factor cost (Table 64) we see that the events of the period left more of an imprint than the data for benchmark years might suggest. Most notably, the "money" rate of defense expenditures which was relatively stable from 1948 to 1950 rises

TABLE 64

Relative Shares of Final Uses in Gross National Product, Alternative Valuations, USSR, 1948–55
(Percent)

Outlay category	1948	1949	1950	1951	1952	1953	1954	1955
Household consumption outlays								
In current ruble factor cost	43.0	42.6	45.5	43.3	44.4	46.8	51.2	49.2
In 1937 ruble factor cost	39.4	42.5	45.7	44.5	44.3	47.0	50.8	48.0
In 1950 ruble factor cost	39.9	42.8	45.5	44.1	44.2	47.1	50.5	48.6
Communal services								
In current ruble factor cost	12.1	11.0	10.8	10.3	10.1	9.9	10.0	10.0
In 1937 ruble factor cost	12.5	10.9	10.2	9.5	9.0	8.8	9.2	8.7
In 1950 ruble factor cost	13.5	11.8	10.8	10.1	9.6	9.4	9.6	9.2
Government administration								
In current ruble factor cost	5.9	4.9	4.8	4.6	4.2	3.3	3.0	2.6
In 1937 ruble factor cost	6.0	4.6	4.3	3.9	3.5	2.7	2.5	2.1
In 1950 ruble factor cost	6.9	5.2	4.8	4.4	4.0	3.1	2.9	2.4
Defense (as recorded in budget)[a]								
In current ruble factor cost	11.5	10.6	10.9	11.6	12.7	12.0	10.3	10.3
In 1937 ruble factor cost	14.9	13.8	12.9	13.3	15.2	14.5	12.5	13.1
In 1950 ruble factor cost	12.1	11.2	10.9	11.5	12.9	12.2	10.7	10.7
Gross investment								
In current ruble factor cost	27.4	30.9	27.9	30.2	28.7	28.0	25.5	27.9
In 1937 ruble factor cost	27.2	28.2	26.9	28.8	28.1	27.0	25.0	28.1
In 1950 ruble factor cost	27.6	29.2	27.9	29.8	29.3	28.1	26.2	29.2

[a] Excluding pensions paid to officers, et al.

perceptibly in the next two years and then declines to the 1955 level already referred to. In the years in question, the rate of investment seems to vary erratically although within narrow limits, but one wonders whether he cannot read in the decline in 1954 and subsequent rise the rapidly varying policy emphasis of Stalin's successors immediately after his death. As allocations to other major categories varied, those to household consumption had to vary reciprocally. In this way among other things household consumption seemingly bears much of the adjustment to Korea but subsequently it recoups its losses in 1953 and after, and momentarily (in 1954) the rate of outlay is at a new (although still notably low) postwar peak. The rate of expenditure on communal services tends to decline throughout the period considered. So also does that on government administration, including NKVD.

These are the trends in "money" shares. From annual data in terms of base year ruble factor cost that are also at hand (Table 64), we see that "real" shares generally tend from year to year to vary closely with "money" shares. Nevertheless this is not always so, but I can hardly pursue here such divergencies as are observed, and accordingly will say no more on this aspect.

In Table 64, both the figures in terms of current ruble factor cost and those in terms of constant ruble factor cost for 1954 conform to current ruble data compiled in *SNIP-49–55*. If instead use is made of alternative current ruble data that also have been considered in this study (see p. 175), the share of gross investment is somewhat larger than is shown, for example, in the case of the computation in terms of 1937 ruble factor cost, 26.0 instead of 25.0 percent. Concomitantly the shares of other outlays are reduced in proportion.

In surveying trends in relative shares, I have focused thus far on "real" shares given by calculations in terms of the ruble factor cost of 1937. We must now consider how the results are affected if reference is made instead to corresponding data based on 1950 and 1928. To refer first to the former, evidently the trends in this case are essentially unchanged throughout (Tables 62 and 63). While there are nevertheless some divergencies, I don't think these are sufficiently important to detain us here. Data on relative shares in terms of 1928 ruble factor cost are at hand for two years, 1928 and 1937. For these years, we again observe much the same trends as before, but interestingly the disparity in the trends of investment and consumption observed previously is here magnified.

As for national income, so for different use categories, from our calculations of the physical volume of goods and services disposed of in terms of the ruble factor cost of different years it is possible to compile corresponding measures still based on one or another year but in terms of given year ruble factor cost. Indeed, with 1937 taken as a base, this has been done here (Tables 51 and 52). For purposes of appraising comparative trends in relative shares, however, I believe we need not go beyond the serial data already considered. From measures in terms of given year ruble factor cost, as is readily seen, we may compare relative shares in the given year only with those in the base year. Moreover, the trends that might be observed in this way are already more or less manifest from the discussion of trends indicated by data in ruble factor cost of different base years.

A recurring theme in the literature on economic growth is that concerning the variation in the relative shares of a country's output devoted to different uses that occurs in the process of industrialization. Seemingly very diverse patterns may prevail, but theoretically a distinction is usefully made between two successive phases. The first is the "take-off" where a backward country, previously stagnant, finally manages to accelerate growth. In this phase, the rate of investment might be expected to rise and that of consumption correspondingly to decline. In the second phase, that of "self-sustained" growth, the country continues to expand output at a relatively rapid rate. Here the rate of investment may well continue to increase at the expense of that of consumption, but such further shifts in allocation as do occur, it appears, should be of a comparatively limited sort. On the eve of the five year plans, the Soviet economy already had taken far too many steps in the direction of industrialization to permit any easy identification with the backward economy of economic theory, but very likely the five year plans did indeed bring about an acceleration in growth. At least, this must be so if we discount the previous performance under the NEP (New Economic Policy) to allow for the fact that notably rapid growth occurred at that time only from abysmally low levels. Then too, as we saw, growth recently has continued at a high rate, although in a meaningful sense there may have been some retardation in comparison with the experience under the first two five year plans.

All things considered, therefore, it is interesting to observe that in the USSR of the five year plans, the relative shares of investment and consumption indeed vary broadly as theory suggests. From interval to interval, the disposition of national income varies in special ways in response to special circumstances, but in the first instance the rate of investment rises and that of consumption falls. In both cases, the shifts are of the marked sort expected in a "take-off." More recently, there is still a drift in favor of investment and against consumption, but as is characteristic of "self-sustained" growth this does not compare in degree with the shift in relative shares occurring during the "take-off."

I refer, however, to trends in shares in "real" terms. As appears not to have been considered in theoretic writings, shares may vary differently, depending on whether they are in "money" or in "real" terms. Indeed, in the process of industrialization they are apt to do so, and among other things, so far as investment goods are cheapened in relation to other goods, a shift from consumption to investment may be observable for "real" but not nearly so much for "money" shares. In effect, the dynamics of the process in the latter case are obscured by the process itself. We may view in this light, I think, the fact that while in "money" as in "real" terms investment under the five year plans tends to increase at the expense of consumption, the shift in shares that occurs is in the former case relatively limited. Also, we can no longer distinguish two phases as we could previously.

Actually, under the Policy of Industrialization the "real" rate of investment in the USSR rises to a notable degree. But under the same policy, investment goods probably are also cheapened in an extraordinary way. As a result, in "money" terms the trend toward higher investments is even more limited than it might ordinarily be.

In relating the Soviet experience to the economics of growth, we must consider that in the Soviet case output is divided not merely between investment and consumption as is usually envisaged in theory but also between these and still other major use categories. Thus, under the five year plans the rate of defense expenditures tends to rise far more even than the rate of investment. Although the increase occurs from an initially low level, the growth in defense outlays necessarily means a further reduction in the share of consumption. From one standpoint, communal services might be viewed as a supplement to the private consumption of households, but for the USSR it is probably more a testimonial to the requirements of growth itself that the former too increased disproportionately. For this reason, the relative share of household consumption declines still more.

Finally, under collectivization the Russians lost a major part of their agricultural capital. During the war, they lost a good fraction of their capital generally. For these reasons, in order to achieve the observed expansion in output over the entire period, the rate of investment on the average has had to be higher than it might have been otherwise. By the same token, the share of consumption has had to be reduced the more on this account.

The concern of this section, to repeat, is to comment summarily on the results and implications of calculations made on the disposition of national income in terms of the ruble factor cost of different years. Thus far I have focused especially on trends in relative shares. From the data that have been compiled on national income disposition, however, one may appraise not only relative shares but also the magnitude of the variation in "real" outlays on different use categories. Indeed, calculations of the sort in question seem to lend themselves most naturally to the latter sort of application. Nevertheless, from this standpoint different use categories are of varying interest, and once we have considered trends in relative shares, probably for only two sorts of outlays is such a further inquiry merited. Moreover, for one of these, household consumption, trends in "real" outlays are to be examined in the section following in the light of more significant and yet very similar measurements in terms of adjusted market prices. For present purposes, therefore, it may suffice if I confine myself here to brief comment on the trends in "real" outlays on the other use category in question, defense.

If the calculations on defense are generally among the less reliable made, we can hardly hope to have measured with any exactitude the impact on "real" outlays on this category of a shift in base year. Nevertheless, in considering trends in such expenditures we may usefully refer to two series: One is that obtained from the main calculation made in terms of the ruble factor cost of 1937; the other is the corresponding series in terms of the ruble factor cost of the given year (Tables 51 and 52).

As we saw, the government under the first two five year plans raised sharply from an initially very low level the share of "real" national income devoted to defense. From 1937 to 1940 it raised such allocations again, and during the war they increased still more. After the war, the share of defense outlays was much reduced, but in 1950 it still was on about the same level as that realized in late prewar years. In 1955, defense expenditures accounted for about the same share of the "real" national income as they did in 1950. The comparative levels of "real" defense outlays at different times necessarily reflect these changing allocations, but they also are affected by changes in the magnitude of "real" national income. Thus, as "real" national income rises under the first two five year plans, "real" defense outlays increase sharply indeed (Tables 51 and 52). From 1937 to 1940, total output expanded at only a limited rate, but "real" outlays in 1940 are nevertheless 2.7 times as large as those of 1937. This index is given by either of the two series in question. Seen in these terms, therefore, the prewar mobilization seems even more impressive than before. We must be the more impressed too when we consider that, while total output fell during the war, the government succeeded by 1944 in increasing the volume of goods and services devoted to defense to 6.6 to 6.8 times the 1937 level. The particular index depends on the series. As we may now see, the postwar demobilization meant that by 1950 "real" defense outlays were less than two-fifths those of 1944. According to either computation, however, they still were nearly as great as they had been in 1940. As total output rose substantially, even without any increase in the share of defense, "real" outlays on this category increased under the Fifth Five Year Plan by no less than 42 to 46 percent, depending on the series.

For years since 1948, we may also observe year to year changes as shown in Table 65.

Although I shall not comment here on trends in "real" outlays on use categories other than defense, the reader may observe the variation in "real" outlays on all categories from data in Tables 51 and 52. Corresponding figures in per capita terms may be found in Tables 55 and 56.

Consumption Per Capita and Per Employed Worker

Earlier in this study I calculated household consumption in terms of adjusted market prices. Such computations are intended to serve as a basis for appraisal of welfare in terms of consumers' utilities. I turn now

TABLE 65

"Real" Defense Expenditures, Alternative Computations, USSR, 1948–55 (1937 = 100)

Year	In 1937 ruble factor cost	Composite, 1937 base
1948	235	216
1949	235	216
1950	245	236
1951	276	271
1952	342	328
1953	342	328
1954	307	306
1955	358	335

to consider trends in per capita consumption, as so computed. The period studied witnessed significant changes in the "participation rate," that is, the relative number of breadwinners in the population. Under the circumstances, an attempt is usefully made also to gauge the trends in consumption in relation to the volume of employment.

Alternative computations of household consumption have been made at the adjusted market prices of different years. Here, as in the appraisal of the growth of national income, it may suffice to refer to a series based on 1937 and to a composite of indices drawn from this series and two others compiled with 1950 and 1928 as base years. The composite is obtained in the same way as the corresponding series on national income and like the latter may be broadly indicative of trends prevailing where valuation is at given year prices.[23] For purposes of appraising welfare, the case for measurement at given year prices seems less weighty than where the concern is with production potential, but the two series on which I focus summarize in a convenient way the available data on household consumption in terms of adjusted market prices.

If welfare is understood in terms of consumers' utilities, prices ideally conform to the corresponding valuation standard. In considering my measures in terms of adjusted market prices, the reader should recall that I take as a datum government and cooperative retail prices which probably are broadly in accord with consumers' utilities in 1937 but which may or may not be so related to this standard in 1950. In 1928, they very possibly diverge significantly from the desideratum. Moreover, the revaluations in terms of the prices of different years are often only

[23] More particularly, with 1937 as percentage base, the index for 1928 is that in terms of adjusted market prices of 1928, while the index for 1940 is that in terms of adjusted market prices of 1937. For 1944, 1950, and 1955 I use indices compiled in terms of adjusted market prices of 1950.

partial, while the computations generally are subject to statistical error. In sum, the two series on which I focus are both inexact, but the series in terms of adjusted market prices of 1937 probably is more reliable than that obtained as a composite.

Although the valuation standards are different, the trends in aggregate household consumption at adjusted market prices are already more or less implied by the trends considered previously in national income at ruble factor cost and in the share in national income, as so measured, that accrues to household consumption. Moreover, the corresponding developments regarding per capita consumption might also be surmised from broadly familiar facts concerning Soviet population growth. Nevertheless, we may usefully record explicitly that Soviet per capita consumption, which was notably low on the eve of the five year plans, must still have been so at the end of the second such plan in 1937. My two series, however, are appreciably in conflict at this point. Valued at the adjusted market prices of 1937, per capita consumption in 1937 is 3 percent below the 1928 level. Valued at adjusted market prices of the given year, this category shows a gain of 22 percent over the same period (Table 66).[24]

Over the next three years, as defense preparations mounted, the two computations merge to show a limited decline in standards. During the war, they decline further and indeed drastically so. With either valuation, per capita consumption in 1944 is about one-third below the prewar level. At the end of the Fourth Five Year Plan, in 1950, I find that the prewar standards had been exceeded. This appears in either computation. According to both computations, too, the Fifth Five Year Plan brings a sharp improvement in this sphere. Also, the final standard is substantially above that of 1928. Again, however, the two series are in conflict regarding magnitudes. Valued at adjusted market prices of 1937, per capita consumption in 1955 is 55 percent above that of 1928. With valuation at adjusted market prices of the given year, the less reliable of the two calculations, the corresponding gain is 89 percent.

From annual data at hand for the period 1948–55 (Table 67) we see that material gains from relatively low levels were already being realized in regard to per capita consumption in Stalin's last years. Nevertheless, a significant part of the improvement realized over the entire period 1928–55 occurs under his successors during the years 1953–55.

Although no computation has been made for 1932, the final year of the First Five Year Plan, per capita consumption at that time must have been below the level of either 1928 or 1937. Very likely such a trend would be revealed by measurements in terms of given year values as well as by measurements in terms of 1937 values.

Unimpressive as the record in regard to per capita consumption was

[24] On the population data employed here and elsewhere in this section, see Appendix K.

TABLE 66

Household Consumption per Capita and per Employed Worker, USSR, 1928–55 (1937 = 100)

	1928	1937	1940	1944	1950	1955
Household consumption per capita						
In adjusted market prices of 1937	103	100	95.6	66.0	116	160
In adjusted market prices of 1950	99.2	100	91.8	64.3	110	155
In adjusted market prices of 1928	82.2	100	—	—	—	—
Composite, 1937 base	82.2	100	95.6	64.3	110	155
Household consumption per employed worker						
In adjusted market prices of 1937	131	100	95.2	—	103	145
In adjusted market prices of 1950	127	100	91.4	—	97.9	140
In adjusted market prices of 1928	105	100	—	—	—	—
Composite, 1937 base	105	100	95.2	—	97.9	140

under the first two five year plans, apparently it was possible to achieve it only through a marked increase in the "participation rate." Thus, according to either computation, consumption per employed worker in 1937 is below what it was in 1928. With valuation at adjusted market prices of 1937, the standard falls by nearly one-fourth (Table 66). In calculating household consumption per employed worker, I make use of data on employment which were described in a previous section.

From 1937 to 1940 I find no change to speak of in the "participation rate," one way or the other. Accordingly, consumption per employed worker declines by the same amount as consumption per capita. This appears in both computations, which merge at this point. Since no esti-

TABLE 67

"Real" Household Consumption per Capita, Alternative Computations, USSR, 1948–55 (1937 = 100)

Year	In adjusted market prices of 1937	Composite, 1937 base
1948	86.3	84.3
1949	98.7	95.3
1950	116	110
1951	120	113
1952	127	121
1953	138	132
1954	153	147
1955	160	155

mate could be made of the volume of employment in 1944, the change in consumption per employed worker during and after the war is conjectural. Over the decade 1940–50 the "participation rate" apparently again increases. Consequently, while consumption per capita rises modestly in this period, consumption per employed worker in 1950 is only slightly above the low prewar level. These trends again are manifest with either of the two sorts of valuation being considered. Moreover, at the end of the Fourth Five Year Plan consumption per employed worker is below the level prevailing at the beginning of the First. Where valuation is at adjusted market prices of 1937, it is 21 percent below the earlier level.

Under the Fifth Five Year Plan the "participation rate" declines but only slightly. Like consumption per capita, therefore, that per employed worker increases sharply in this period. The gain is again manifest whether valuation is at adjusted market prices of 1937 or at adjusted market prices of the given year. In the case of consumption per capita, however, we saw that the 1955 level is substantially above that of 1928 according to either computation. Reflecting the increase in the "participation rate" over the entire period, consumption per employed worker in 1955 is still not much above the 1928 level where valuation is at 1937 adjusted market prices. With valuation at adjusted market prices of the given year, consumption per employed worker rises over the 27 year period but the gain — 33 percent — is still not comparable to that realized in consumption per capita with the corresponding valuation.

Although annual data on consumption are at hand for the period 1948–55, no corresponding figures could be compiled for employment. Accordingly, we are not able to determine year-to-year changes in consumption per employed worker. If consumption per capita in 1932 was below the levels of 1928 and 1937, probably this was true also of consumption per employed worker.

In order to make my calculations in terms of adjusted market prices conform to conventional national income accounting, I valued farm income in kind at retail collective market prices less an allowance for marketing costs not incurred. Nevertheless, such a deduction means that farm income in kind is undervalued in relation to similar goods sold in the cities, and hence for purposes of appraisal of welfare is not especially logical. In any event, in gauging gains from this standpoint we may usefully consider not only measurements of the conventional sort but alternative data obtained when farm income in kind is valued at collective farm market prices with no deduction (see Table 68). The revaluation, however, has only a rather limited effect.

Appraisal of another deficiency of a conventional sort in my calculations, the omission of home processing, is more difficult. Nevertheless, from

TABLE 68

"Real" Household Consumption per Capita, with Alternative Valuations of Income in Kind, USSR, 1928–55
(1937 = 100)

Year	In adjusted market prices of 1937	In adjusted market prices of 1937, but with farm income in kind at collective farm market prices
1928	103	106
1937	100	100
1950	116	114
1955	160	156

data compiled previously (chapter 7), we see that the inclusion of a number of the more important home processing activities would tend to reduce the growth in per capita consumption but again to a relatively limited extent. Actually, in valuing farm income in kind initially, I not only excluded marketing costs not incurred, but considering the data compiled on home processing I also made a limited deduction for such fabrication as occurs for goods sold on the collective farm market. Since, in the recomputation just referred to, farm income in kind is valued at collective farm market prices with no deduction on either account, the results to some extent reflect the inclusion of home processing.

I have been referring here only to private consumption and hence have passed by communal services. In an important sense, outlays on the latter might properly be viewed as investment rather than consumption, but an attempt to show the effect of their inclusion on my results in Table 69 may nevertheless be of interest.

I cite again here my indices of household consumption in terms of the adjusted market prices of 1937. Also, these same indices have been recomputed to allow for communal services. I assume that in terms of adjusted market prices communal services are in the same proportion to household consumption as in terms of ruble factor cost.

Reference thus far has been to the experience of the whole population. Taken together with other data at hand, my calculations also provide a partial basis to gauge a significant structural aspect: the comparative experience of the industrial worker and the peasant (see Table 70). More particularly, in terms of consumption per employed worker, the industrial population probably fared worse than that on the farms. The

TABLE 69

"Real" Household Consumption per Capita, and "Real" Household Consumption per Capita Adjusted for Communal Services (1937 = 100)

Year	Household consumption per capita in adjusted market prices of 1937	Household consumption per capita, in adjusted market prices of 1937 including communal services
1928	103	90.5
1937	100	100
1950	116	118
1955	160	158

relative deterioration in the position of the former was most marked under the first two plans.

In Table 70 I cite again the data compiled here on household consumption per employed worker. These figures refer to all employed workers, including those on as well as off the farm. In her study on "real" wages, Dr. Janet Chapman measures this category for nonfarm workers in various variants; I cite her data on "real" wages excluding taxes and bond deductions and including pensions and allowances. Except that a limited amount of voluntary savings is still included, the resultant measures in effect represent nonfarm household consumption per employed worker.[25] Dr. Chapman calculates real wages by deflation. According to reasoning explained elsewhere (see chapter 3), the series she obtains by applying cost of living indices based on 1937 but using given year weights in effect measures real wages in terms of the prevailing ruble prices of 1937. By deflating by alternative cost of living indices using 1937 weights, she obtains measures in terms of the prevailing rubles prices of the given year. Her data in terms of prevailing rubles tend slightly to overstate growth in comparison with mine in terms of adjusted market prices.

The five year plans saw a radical increase in industrial compared to farm employment. Depending on the comparative levels of consumption in the two sectors, therefore, the data set forth above on consumption per employed worker for the gainfully engaged population generally and on the net real wages of nonfarm workers alone are consistent with

[25] For present purposes, it seemed in order to modify somewhat Dr. Chapman's data. In the pertinent series, Dr. Chapman allows not only for pensions and allowances but for communal services. I here exclude the latter.

rather diverse trends in farm consumption per employed worker. Nevertheless, if we read the cited figures together with the comparison made earlier (see chapter 8) between industrial and farm "real" incomes in 1937, we see that nonfarm very likely deteriorated relative to farm standards. More specifically, on the eve of the plans, household consumption per employed worker probably was higher in industry than on the farm. Subsequently the differential in favor of the former tended to diminish. For the ordinary industrial worker, very possibly there was none to speak of by the end of the first two five year plans. Perhaps the relative position of the industrial worker was at least maintained at its reduced level in later years, although this is conjectural.

What of the comparative trends in consumption per capita? When this question has been studied more carefully than has been possible here, I suspect that here, too, the industrial worker will be found to have experienced a relative decline in standards, although how it compares with that regarding consumption per employed worker is difficult to judge. On the eve of the plans, the industrial worker, I believe, was better off than the farmer regarding consumption per capita as well as consumption per employed worker (p. 8). At least in the former respect he very likely continued to enjoy some margin of superiority under the plans, but in the period studied the "rate of participation" undoubtedly increased markedly in agriculture as well as industry; at least this is so if (as in order here) agricultural employment is measured in terms of full-time equivalent. For this reason, in comparison with the farmer the industrial worker must have suffered under the plans regarding consump-

TABLE 70

Household Consumption per Employed Worker and "Real" Wages of Nonfarm Workers, USSR, 1928–55

(1937 = 100)

Year	Household consumption per employed worker: In adjusted market prices of 1937	Household consumption per employed worker: Composite, 1937 base	Real wages of nonfarm workers, net (Chapman): In prevailing rubles of 1937	Real wages of nonfarm workers, net (Chapman): Composite, 1937 base
1928	131	105	180	123
1937	100	100	100	100
1940	95.2	95.2	93.3	89.5
1948	—	—	70.5	63.3
1950	103	97.9	—	—
1952	—	—	116	107
1954	—	—	145	137
1955	145	140	—	—

tion per capita as regarding consumption per employed worker, although the extent of the disparity is uncertain.

In sum, the Russian people hardly prospered under the five year plans, although perhaps they did not fare quite as badly as is sometimes supposed. Consumption per capita, which was already notably low in 1928, was still lower at the close of the First Five Year Plan. Toward the end of the thirties, however, the Russians at least were again enjoying something like their initial standard. In withstanding the German attack, the populace had to make great sacrifices indeed, but after the war even under Stalin there were significant gains, and in the dictator's last years the low 1928 standard was finally left well behind. The brief interval from Stalin's death to the final year studied saw further marked gains, with the result that for the period as a whole there was actually a substantial improvement. If the record regarding per capita consumption during much of the interval studied is nevertheless hardly impressive, it would have been still less so but for the increase in the "rate of participation." Through the increase in the relative volume of employment, the Russians were able throughout to enjoy higher standards than their earnings would otherwise have permitted. Thus, consumption per employed worker declined initially even more than consumption per capita. It subsequently rose, then declined during the war, and then rose again, but the Russians did not again reattain the 1928 standard per employed worker until around the time of Stalin's death. In fact, according to one of two computations made — that in adjusted market prices of 1937 — consumption per employed worker at that time was still below the 1928 level. In 1955, however, both of my computations show an improvement over that faraway date, although only for the less reliable of two computations considered is the gain especially marked.

Contrary to a common supposition, the industrial worker fared no better than the peasants under Stalin's five year plans. Indeed, he seemingly fared worse, although I believe he was able to maintain in some degree the margin he enjoyed initially in respect of consumption per capita. According to many indications, the peasant under Stalin's successors has again gained ground in relation to the industrial worker, but in the brief period since Stalin's death that has been considered in this study and with the limited data at hand, it is not easy here to appraise this aspect.

Students of growth wish to know whether industrialization at Soviet tempos can be consistent with progressively rising consumption standards. If the Soviet experience is any indication, the answer must be in the negative. Moreover, limited as the Soviet achievements have been regarding consumption standards, they would have been still more so but for the notable increase in the "rate of participation." Nevertheless, the achievements differ in two phases. In the "take-off," as the "real" rate of investment increased, progress was limited indeed. In fact, at the outset, standards actually declined. In the period of "self-sustained growth," the "real" rate of investment has remained at a high level but consumption has grown rapidly with the expansion of total output. In fact, in the final years studied, the gains were notable by any standard.

14

USSR VERSUS USA

Introduction

In this chapter, the task is to contrast Soviet growth trends, as measured in this study, with corresponding trends that have prevailed in the United States. From available data for the latter country, it may be of interest to try to gauge relative developments in each of the different spheres considered previously for the USSR alone: "real" gross national product, gross national product per employed worker, disposition of the "real" gross national product among different uses and "real" household consumption per capita and per employed worker.

In comparing Soviet and American growth, one might seek light on diverse issues, but among these not least is the familiar one regarding the relative economic efficiency of the two competing social systems. In judging the import from this standpoint of the trends described, the reader will wish to consider that while the Soviet performance is compared with that of the United States in both early and recent times relative developments are affected in each case by factors more or less beyond the reach of social systems. Furthermore, if the more outstanding aspects are at all indicative, one wonders whether at least in the comparison with the United States in recent years the USSR may not have been favored at this point. Thus, especially in relation to the United States at an early stage, the Russians have been handicapped by limitations in agricultural resources in relation to population. But the Soviet population has also been relatively large compared with the capital stock. For this reason, returns to additional capital investments should have been greater than they might otherwise have been. At one time, of course, the United States was also assured of a plentiful labor supply through immigration, but this ceased long ago to be a material factor. Then too, in relation to the United States at any stage, the Russians have had the notable advantage that in industrializing late they have been able to borrow advanced technology abroad on an unprecedented scale. Although the United States too was able to borrow technology abroad in early stages, this hardly was of comparable importance.

Apart from differences in circumstances such as the foregoing, the two economies must still have evolved differently in some degree not because of differences in efficiency but simply because of the divergence in prevailing preferences. Most importantly, as one of the comparisons made may clarify, Soviet socialism has shown a marked disposition to favor "nonconsumption," including investment, over "consumption." Consequently, in the USSR total output and output per capita and per employed worker should have grown more than would have been the case if preferences had been of a more conventional sort. This should have occurred without economic efficiency being any the greater in the Soviet case. By implication too, consumption should have grown less, but as may not always be considered this occurs only so far as the share of "nonconsumption" is rising and not simply because it is high. As will appear, the distinction is quite important to an understanding of the comparative Soviet performance at different times.

Then too, so far as the comparisons made reflect on economic efficiency, they necessarily bear more on "dynamic" efficiency (where reference is to the *change* in output over time under changing circumstances) than on efficiency in the "static" sense familiar in economic theory (where reference is to the *absolute level* of output at any one time under given circumstances), although the two, of course, are closely related. The comparisons made, therefore, must be read in this light too.

All things considered, I venture to think that if Soviet socialism is nearly as efficient economically as its proponents hold, this has yet to be demonstrated. On the other hand, it seems no less clear that this system has been much underrated by many Western critics. But, in the light of the facts presented, the reader will wish to judge for himself what may be concluded on this weighty theme.

The reasons for the decision where possible to compare the Soviet performance under the five year plans with that of the United States in both recent and early times will I think be generally understood. But the appropriateness of this procedure may be more evident if it is considered that on the eve of the five year plans the USSR was producing annually an output on the order of $170 per capita. This in terms of dollar prices of 1929.[1] In the United States we already had surpassed this level in the first decade after the Civil War.

Growth of National Income

For information on the "real" national income of the United States, one turns first of all to the calculations of Professor Kuznets and the

TABLE 71

Rates of Growth of "Real" Gross National Product, USSR and USA, Selected Periods

USSR[a]			USA[b]		
	Average annual rate of growth (percent) with output—			Average annual rate of growth (percent) with output—	
Year	In ruble factor cost of 1937	As composite series, 1937 base	Year	In 1929 dollars	In 1954 dollars
1928–1937	5.5 (4.8)[c]	11.9	1869/78–1879/88	6.6 (6.1)[d]	—
1937–1940	3.4	3.4	1879/88–1889/98	3.3	—
1928–1940	5.0 (4.5)[c]	9.7	1889/98–1899/1908	4.6	—
1940–1950	2.1	1.8	1869/78–1899/1908	4.8 (4.6)[d]	—
1950–1955	7.6	7.6	1899/1908–1929	3.4	—
1928–1955	4.4 (4.1)[c]	6.3	1929–1948	—	2.5
1928–1955 "effective years"[e]	5.2 (4.9)[c]	7.5	1948–1957	—	3.7
			1929–1957	—	2.9

[a] Where in order, Soviet data have been adjusted for territorial changes.

[b] For a period defined in terms of decade intervals, the cited rates of growth are calculated on the basis of the corresponding average annual outputs. In each case the average annual output is centered on the middle of the decade in question.

[c] Data for USSR in parentheses result from extension for 1928–37 of ruble factor cost valuation within household retail purchases.

[d] The figures in parentheses represent rates of growth after adjustment for probable under-coverage in initial estimates for 1869/78.

[e] Growth during 1928–55 imputed to peacetime years.

Department of Commerce. In Table 71 are shown comparative data on the growth of this category in the USA and the USSR that have been

[1] See Table 55, and note 9 of this chapter.

compiled on the basis of the Kuznets and Commerce Department computations together with those made in previous pages for the USSR. More particularly, for the USSR I cite rates of growth derived from alternative measurements of the Soviet gross national product compiled in this study. For the United States the cited rates of growth for years since 1929 are computed from data on our gross national product published by the Department of Commerce. In their latest revision these data are in terms of dollar prices of 1954. For years prior to 1929 I rely on the corresponding calculations of Professor Kuznets in terms of dollar prices of that year.[2]

In the present study I have sought to pattern my calculations for the USSR after those made for the United States by the Commerce Department. Gross national product is understood here, therefore, in much the same way as it is by that agency. Professor Kuznets on the other hand diverges from the Commerce Department in certain well known particulars, but I limit my use of his data to selected years where I believe comparisons can be made that are not consequentially affected by this feature.[3]

As will be recalled, the ruble factor cost standard of national income valuation that is used in my calculations has its limitations, and my data are inexact in any case. The prevailing dollar prices which the Commerce Department and Professor Kuznets use in their calculations must also be something less than ideal for purposes of national income valuation, although they are surely more satisfactory in this regard than ruble factor cost, to say nothing of prevailing ruble prices. The Commerce Department data, one suspects, are statistically among the most reliable of the national income measurements presently available for any country, but necessarily they too are subject to a margin of error. As Professor Kuznets may not stress sufficiently, while his calculations generally are in terms of dollar prices of 1929, because of the nature of the computation they may often significantly reflect also dollar prices of the "given" year. On the other hand, for reasons to appear this may not be

[2] For the Commerce Department data, see *U. S. Income and Output,* pp. 118–119. With Professor Kuznets' kind permission, I refer in his case to the results of a forthcoming revision of computations previously published in various works, including for example Simon Kuznets, "Long Term Changes in the National Income of the United States of America Since 1870," in Simon Kuznets, ed., *Income and Wealth of the United States — Trends and Structure,* Cambridge, 1952, pp. 29 ff. Professor Kuznets compiles his revised measures in three variants. I use here his Variant III, which is statistically most comparable to the Commerce Department calculations.

[3] While the Commerce Department includes in gross national product all government expenditures on currently produced goods and services, Professor Kuznets endeavors to limit the government outlays that are included to those representing either "direct services" to consumers or additions to stocks of durable war goods. Although the difference in concept sometimes results in materially divergent trends, apparently this is not so for years for which use is made here of Professor Kusznets' data. See *ibid.,* p. 32.

an unmixed evil for our purposes.[4] Professor Kuznets is explicit that especially in early years his calculations are often inexact in any case.

In addition to measures of the rates of growth of the gross national product, I have also compiled corresponding figures on the gross national product per capita (Table 72). For the USSR I again rely on computations made in this study. For the United States, use is made of available population data, including decade averages compiled by Professor Kuznets. In Table 73, are shown the serial data from which the USA rates of growth in Tables 71 and 72 are compiled. For convenience, Professor Kuznets' figures have been raised throughout as I think is permissible by 3 percent, or the amount by which the Commerce Department total for 1929 in current dollars exceeds his in the same terms. The discrepancy results from the difference in concept described previously.

For purposes of appraising relative trends in "real" national income in the two countries, we are able to refer to any of several sorts of serial data for the USSR. Furthermore, although each of the two inquiries considered for the United States provides us with only one set of measures for that country, as will appear something is known about alternatives here as well. Which sorts of measures are appropriately compared in the two countries? While the pertinent methodological issue is rarely explored, I think it will be evident that all possible comparisons might be interesting, but that some are apt to be more interesting than others. Moreover, data permitting, one might wish to make still others now precluded. In any event, there will probably be no occasion for dissent if I proceed here on these suppositions: Comparisons may usefully be

[4] As has been explained, in order to compile by deflation serial data on physical volume in terms of prices of some "base" year, use is properly made of deflators compiled in terms of "given" year weights. If one employs instead deflators with "base" year weights, the serial data turn out to be such that, in each comparison with the "base" year, valuation is in terms of the "given" year price structure. Granting this, as is generally understood, deflators with base year weights often may still be employed without any consequential distortion if prior to the deflation the output data are broken down into sufficiently detailed categories. In his calculations, Professor Kuznets evidently assumes that this desideratum has in fact been achieved, but one wonders nevertheless especially in early years whether there may not be significant departures from it. Thus, extensive use is made throughout of measurements of the physical volume of different sorts of finished goods compiled by Shaw by deflation. In deflating, Shaw uses index numbers of prices calculated in terms of "base" year weights. Thus, for years since 1919, the indices are calculated in terms of weights pertaining to the 1920's. For earlier years, use is made of weights pertaining to 1909. While Shaw generally deflates only within rather detailed categories, some of the categories seem comparatively broad (for example, "7. Clothing and personal furnishings"; "25a. Industrial machinery and equipment"). For early years, use in any event has often to be made of "surrogate" price index numbers. See on this whole question, Simon Kuznets, *National Product Since 1869,* New York, 1946, pp. 59 ff.; Kuznets, "Long Term Changes in the National Income of the U.S.A." in Kuznets, ed., *Income and Wealth of the U.S.——Trends and Structure,* pp. 44 ff.; W. H. Shaw, *Value of Commodity Output Since 1869,* New York, 1947, pp. 287 ff.

TABLE 72

Rates of Growth of "Real" Gross National Product per Capita, USSR and USA, Selected Periods

USSR			USA		
	Average annual rate of growth (percent) with output—			Average annual rate of growth (percent) with output—	
Year	In ruble factor cost of 1937	As composite series, 1937 base	Year	In 1929 dollars	In 1954 dollars
1928–1937	4.5 (3.8)[a]	10.8	1869/78–1879/88	4.1 (3.6)[b]	—
1937–1940	1.0	1.0	1879/88–1889/98	1.2	—
1928–1940	3.6 (3.1)[a]	8.3	1889/98–1899/1908	2.6	—
1940–1950	2.9	2.6	1869/78–1899/1908	2.6 (2.5)[b]	—
1950–1955	5.8	5.8	1899/1908–1929	1.7	—
1928–1955	3.8 (3.5)[a]	5.7	1929–1948	—	1.5
1928–1955			1948–1957	—	1.9
"effective			1929–1957	—	1.7
years"[c]	4.4 (4.2)[a]	6.7			

[a] Data in parentheses result from extension for 1928–37 of ruble factor cost valuation within household retail purchases.

[b] The figures in parentheses represent rates of growth after adjustment for probable under-coverage in initial estimate for 1869/78.

[c] Growth during 1928–55 imputed to peacetime years.

made where, as here, the measurements for each country are in local prices. The data compared preferably are obtained by application of the same index number formula in the two countries, although one may also wish to know how the results are affected if for both countries an alternative formula is applied. Measurements considered for each country as a rule are preferably compiled in terms of prices that are more or less contemporaneous with, rather than distant from, the period considered. Then too, especially if the periods considered are felt to be at all "comparable," the base years considered for the two countries might well be similarly located in the respective periods. However, where feasible, one also wishes to know how the results might change if the base years were shifted.

If properly compiled, national income data may bear on one or both of two abstract ultimates: welfare and production potential. Although neither Professor Kuznets nor the Commerce Department is explicit in this regard, I believe their calculations pertain to the former as well as to the latter of these two categories. But as we have seen my calculations relate mainly to the latter. The comparisons that are to be made here, therefore, presumably are most readily construed as relating to this aspect.

Where it is not already so, I think the logic of the suppositions set forth in the preceding paragraph will become sufficiently clear when in the latter part of this section I come to consider the import of the relative trends observed regarding production potential.

Let us turn to the relative trends themselves. With the data available, we may compare the Soviet performance, as is desirable, with that of the United States both in recent and in relatively early times. Considering the methodological suppositions that are to be guiding, in undertaking each comparison we may usefully inquire I think as to the relative trends prevailing in each of two cases: (a) Output is valued for the USSR at 1937 ruble factor cost and for the USA similarly at the dollar prices of some intermediate year in the period considered. (b) For the USSR, with 1937 as base, output is valued at ruble factor cost of the given year. For the USA with the selected intermediate year as base, output is valued at dollar prices of the given year. Inquiry into the trends given by these measures will be no less in order if sometimes they can only be speculative. If we must speculate, I believe this is due chiefly to limitations in available information on the effects of revaluations on measures of American growth. It may be hoped that before long this deficiency in the otherwise impressive American data will be repaired.

I shall begin by comparing the Soviet with the recent U.S. performance and shall refer first to case (a). Apparently the USSR here tends systematically to grow more rapidly than does the United States. Thus, in terms of dollar prices of 1954, the gross national product of the United States during 1929–57 is found to increase at an annual average rate of 2.9 percent (Table 71). If (as is desired) output were valued instead at dollar prices of the late thirties, the corresponding tempo would be higher but I believe by only a fraction of a percentage point. On this matter, I am guided chiefly by the results of alternative computations of our gross national product made in elaboration of a version of the Department of Commerce calculations previous to the one referred to in this study.[5] Valued at 1937 ruble factor cost, Soviet output during 1928–55 grows in contrast at an average annual rate of 4.4 percent.[6] This

[5] The computations refer to the period 1929–49. Among those made, only a few are now pertinent but others will also be of interest momentarily. Accordingly, I set forth here all that were made and indicate in each case the corresponding average annual rate of growth for the period in question: With gross national product valued in terms of dollar prices of 1929, average annual rate of growth was 2.6 percent; of 1933, 2.7; of 1939, 2.6; of 1947, 2.5; and of 1949, 2.5 percent. See George Jaszi and John W. Kendrick, *Problems and Techniques of Measuring the Volume of Output,* 1953.

[6] In this section, unless otherwise indicated, cited rates of growth of the Soviet gross national product refer to the increase in output after adjustment for territorial changes (see Table 71).

TABLE 73

Gross National Product of the United States by Final Use, 1869/79–1957

Year	Gross national product	House-hold con-sumption	Gross invest-ment	Other outlays	Gross national product per capita	House-hold con-sumption per capita	Gross invest-ment per capita	Other outlays per capita
	(In billions of 1929 dollars)				(In 1929 dollars)			
1869–1878	11.0	8.2	2.5	0.3	253	189	57	7
1879–1888	20.8	15.4	4.5	0.9	379	281	82	16
1889–1898	28.7	20.5	7.1	1.1	425	303	105	16
1899–1908	44.9	32.8	10.3	1.8	552	403	127	22
1929	104.4	79.0	20.9	4.5	857	649	172	37
	(In billions of 1954 dollars)				(In 1954 dollars)			
1929	181.8	128.1	43.2	10.5	1493	1052	355	86
1948	293.1	199.3	59.1	34.7	1999	1359	403	237
1957	407.0	270.3	77.2	59.5	2377	1579	451	348

is an average for all years during the period in question. If (as clearly should be done) reference is made instead to the average for "effective years," the Soviet tempo is still higher: 5.2 percent.[7]

Referring now to the corresponding measures in terms of given year values [case (b)], from alternative computations of the American gross national product just mentioned, we may infer that the American rate of growth in this case is again only slightly higher than where the calculation is in dollar prices of 1954. For the USSR, however, the gross national product now grows at an annual rate of 6.3 percent. This again is an average for all years in the period 1928–55. For "effective years," the corresponding rate of growth is 7.5 percent. I conclude that where measures are in terms of given year values the Soviet margin over us is even greater than it was before.

Although an attempt has been made to adjust the Soviet rate of growth for the war, this is necessarily a speculative enterprise. Furthermore, quite apart from the war one inevitably wonders at the import of a summary figure for a period which in the case of the USSR saw in its

[7] Here and elsewhere in this survey we must consider that some of the deficiencies in my calculations for the USSR apparently tend to cause an upward bias. While the bias is present chiefly in early years, data on growth for the entire period 1928–55 are also affected. Some of the deficiencies must also be operative regarding the data considered for the USA, but particularly where for that country reference is to recent years the comparisons made may well be distorted somewhat favorably to the USSR. (See chapter 13 and the parenthetic data for the USSR in Tables 71 and 72. The parenthetic figures for the USA in Tables 71 and 72 are also of interest, although they pertain to a special aspect). On the other hand, as was explained, in the case of the USSR the adjustment made for the war must be conservative, and this is at least a partial offset.

early years the first important applications of novel techniques of central planning and also an extraordinary reorganization of agriculture with attendant extraordinary losses of capital and skill. By the same token, it may be of interest that if for the USSR we consider the postreconstruction years the margin in favor of that country increases. This is so rather where output is calculated at values of an intermediate year. Where calculations are instead in terms of given year values, the Soviet margin over us is little affected. But in any case the record at hand for the postreconstruction period in the USSR is very brief and the Soviet performance during this interval must be discounted in some degree for this reason.

For the United States too, the interval considered is certainly complex, but curiously, as will appear, the average rate of growth realized fits in well enough with the trend established previously over a lengthy period. Considering that the Great Depression may well have been a unique episode, one might still wish to distinguish our performance since the war from that of prewar years, but the tempo prevailing during 1948–57 is not markedly higher than that prevailing during the entire period 1929–57.

Turning to the comparison with the American performance at an earlier period, I think it will not be amiss here to focus, in the case of the United States, on the period 1869/78 to 1899/1908. Also we may again refer first to case (a). For the USSR, the average rate of growth for all years during 1928–55 now as before is 4.4 percent. For "effective years," the corresponding tempo is 5.2 percent. For the United States, we are now interested in the rate of growth that obtains for 1869/78 to 1899/1908, when output is valued at the dollar prices of (say) the late 1880's. This is not known, but when valued at dollar prices of 1929, output during this period grows at an average rate of 4.8 percent. Moreover, as we have seen, while Professor Kuznets' calculations are generally in terms of 1929 dollars they may also significantly reflect prices of the "given" year. Then too we may also refer here to a variety of somewhat conflicting evidence on index number relativity at early stages in the United States.[8] In sum, I venture to think that with the

[8] Briefly the evidence in question is as follows:

(a) If for American machinery production for the period 1899–1923 we shift the base year from 1923 to 1899, we obtain an index for 1923 (1899 = 100) 3.6 times as high as it was initially. This calculation refers to selected machinery production including automobiles. If automobiles are excluded, the corresponding figure is 2.8. See Alexander Gerschenkron, *A Dollar Index of Soviet Machinery Output, 1927–28 to 1937,* The RAND Corporation, Report R-197, April 6, 1951, p. 54. With automobiles omitted, the degree of relativity is still fully comparable to that observed by Moorsteen for Soviet machinery production for the period 1928–37 when the base year is shifted from 1937 to 1928.

(b) For American durable consumers' goods for the period 1899–1923, a shift in base

desired valuation our rate of growth would be higher than that given by Professor Kuznets' calculations but probably not markedly so. By implication, neither country much outpaces the other at this point.

Now for case (b), that is, with the same base years as before, measurements are in terms of given year values. For the USSR, the average rate of growth for all years during the period 1928–55 in this case again rises to 6.3 percent. The corresponding tempo for "effective years" is 7.5 percent. How rapidly the American gross national product grows in the present case is conjectural indeed. Considering aspects such as were just set forth regarding the effect on American output measurements of a change in base year at early stages, presumably our rate of growth would be appreciably higher than that indicated by Professor Kuznets' data (4.8 percent annually) but one wonders whether it could equal that of the USSR.

---

year from 1923 to 1899 has no effect to speak of on the observed increase in output. See Ira O. Scott, Jr., "The Gerschenkron Hypothesis of Index Number Bias," *Review of Economics and Statistics,* November 1952.

(c) For American finished goods generally for the period 1869–1928, partial revaluations appear to have only a limited effect on measurements of the growth of output (1869 = 100):

	1869	*1899/1908*	*1903*	*1919/1928*	*1928*
In 1913 dollars	100	530		1128	
In 1929 dollars	100	535		958	
In 1889 dollars	100		537		1386

The indices in terms of 1913 dollars are compiled from Shaw's data as collated by Kuznets. For reasons already suggested (note 4), Shaw's calculations may to a significant extent reflect the price structure of the "given" year rather than that of 1913. The alternative figures in 1929 dollars result from a reaggregation of Shaw's data by Kuznets. In the reaggregation, 1929 values are employed as weights as between but not within detailed commodity categories. The alternative figures in 1889 dollars were derived similarly by the writer. For Shaw's calculations, see Shaw, *Value of Commodity Output Since 1869,* New York, 1947. For Kuznets' collation and reaggregation, I refer to the unpublished study previously cited.

(d) As calculated by Professor Robert Gallman (in his "Commodity Output in the U. S.," *Studies in Income and Wealth,* forthcoming), the aggregate value added by agriculture, mining, manufacturing, and construction in the United States increased from 1869 to 1899 at an annual average rate of 4.4 percent. Because of the nature of the procedures employed, I fear Professor Gallman's data in part are only nominally in terms of the prices on which he focuses, that is, those of 1879, but clearly this valuation has been realized to an appreciable extent. In Professor Gallman's view, the "real" gross national product after 1869 "increased only slightly faster than commodity output." Reference is to "commodity output" as calculated in his study. Professor Gallman's kindness in permitting me to refer to his forthcoming study is appreciated.

(e) Judging from data on relative shares of the gross national product devoted to different major uses (see pp. 276 ff), the United States even over protracted intervals has not experienced in peacetime since the Civil War a change in the physical structure at all comparable to that experienced by the USSR under the five year plans.

Interestingly, whether measurements are in base year or in given year values, the Russians during 1950–55 probably grew more rapidly than we did during 1869/78 to 1899/1908. On the other hand, for a decade or so after the Civil War, we grew nearly as rapidly as the Russians did during 1950–55, although subsequently our tempo fell sharply.

In view of the terminal dates considered, we may, I think, reasonably assume that the growth rates calculated for the United States generally reflect (as one would wish here) secular trends as distinct from the ups and downs of business cycles. Curiously, despite the fact that the terminal figures in this case are decade averages, we see that for early years there are significant decade-to-decade fluctuations in growth rates. One inevitably wonders whether business cycles may not be a factor at this point, but if so this aspect must become less important where reference is to protracted periods.

I have been considering relative trends in "real" national income. What may be concluded regarding relative trends in production potential? Even for one country, inferences from the former to the latter are apt to be inexact, to say the least, and where we compare two countries the uncertainties are only compounded. But, as I believe the reader will agree if he recalls the pertinent methodology (chapter 3), the presumption must be that since 1928 the Russians have tended to expand capacity regarding commodity mixes they produced in the late thirties more rapidly than we have done regarding commodity mixes we produced at that time. We may also compare the growth of Soviet capacity since 1928 regarding Soviet mixes of the late thirties with the growth of our capacity in the latter decades of the last century regarding the mixes we produced in (say) the late 1880's. Perhaps the Russians still match or surpass us at this point, although this is conjectural.

Having said this much I must say more. With the same change in a country's production potential there may be different changes in its capacity to produce different mixes. With the same change in its capacity to produce different mixes, there may be different changes in its production potential. Granting that each country increased its production capacity in the manner described, therefore, must we not consider still that production potential may have varied incommensurately? Indeed, in view of the Russians' notable concentration on industry at the expense of agriculture and services, is this not likely to have been so? Thus, could not the Russians have often outpaced us regarding output without their doing so regarding production potential and simply because the gains realized in the latter respect in both countries allowed larger increases in the production of the Soviet mixes than in that of ours?

When these familiar questions can be examined with the care they deserve, the conclusion presumably will be that in some degree the two countries have indeed experienced disproportionate changes of the sort assumed in capacity to produce different mixes. One wonders whether the degree to which under industrialization "technological progress" has favored industry over agriculture and services is not often overestimated, but as production potential has increased in each country very likely the corresponding increase in capacity to produce any mix has often tended, as is assumed, to be greater the larger the share of industrial goods and the smaller that of agricultural products and services in the mix in question. In fact, as the reader will recall, regarding the USSR we have already been led to substantially this view by the calculations of this study.

Probably, however, it will also be found that the disproportionalities are not so clearly favorable to the Russians as is suggested. At least, I venture to think this will be so where the comparison is between contemporary performances. What is in question here is primarily the comparative structure of the Soviet mixes of the late thirties and of ours of the same time. Referring therefore to these mixes, as even a limited inquiry makes clear, those of the USSR contain relatively fewer services than ours do but seemingly they also contain relatively fewer industrial goods. In comparison with ourselves, therefore, the Russians should have found that their expansion of capacity was facilitated on the former account and inhibited on the latter. As to the comparison between the Soviet performance since 1928 and that of the United States in the later decades of the last century, perhaps there is at this point some basis to discount any apparent Soviet superiority. In any event, of concern here is the comparative structure of the Soviet mixes of the late 1930's and of ours of the late 1880's. Here, as we may see from available data, the share of services in the USSR is no longer markedly below that in the USA, but the share of industrial goods in the USSR probably is greater than that in the USA.[9]

[9] Of all gainfully employed persons in the USSR, those engaged in service branches (such as trade; health care; education; government, including the armed forces; finance; domestics) probably constituted somewhat less than 20 percent in 1937. In the United States, the corresponding figure in 1890 was also about 20 percent but in 1940 it was on the order of 37 percent. For the USSR, see Appendix K and *Narkhoz-1956,* pp. 204–205. For the United States, see Kuznets, "Long Term Changes in the National Income of the USA Since 1870" in Simon Kuznets, ed. *Income and Wealth of the United States — Trends and Structure,* p. 107, and Daniel Carson, "Changes in the Industrial Composition of Manpower Since the Civil War," in Conference on Research in Income and Wealth, *Studies in Income and Wealth,* vol. xi, New York, 1949, p. 47. As to the share of industry in total output in the two countries perhaps it suffices to observe that the USSR in 1937 produced only 1.5 times the grain but over 4 times the steel that we did in 1890. On the other hand, the corresponding ratios to our 1940 production were 0.83 and 0.29, respectively. See Joint Economic Committee, United States Congress, *Soviet Economic Growth,* Washington, 1957, pp. 32–33, 62; *Historical Statistics of the United States, 1789–1945,* Washington, 1949, pp. 106 ff.

Reference thus far has been to comparative trends in gross national product. If instead we consider gross national product per capita, we see that the comparison generally although not always becomes somewhat more favorable to the USSR. Moreover, where the Soviet performance under the five year plans is contrasted with ours during the last century the Russians now seem more clearly than before to enjoy an advantage (Table 72).

Output per Employed Worker

For purposes of comparing trends in gross national product per employed worker, the data in Table 74 may serve as a point of departure.

TABLE 74

Gross National Product, Employment, and Gross National Product per Employed Worker, USSR and USA, Average Annual Rates of Growth for Selected Periods (Percent per annum)

	USSR[a]						
	1928–1955	1928–1955, "effective years"	1928–1940	1928–1937	1937–1940	1940–1950	1950–1955
Gross national product:							
In 1937 ruble factor cost	4.4 (4.1)[b]	5.2 (4.9)[b]	5.0 (4.5)[b]	5.5 (4.8)[b]	3.4	2.1	7.6
Composite, 1937 base	6.3	7.5	9.7	11.9	3.4	1.8	7.6
Employment, all sectors	1.9	2.2	3.4	3.7	2.5	0.3	1.4
Gross national product per employed worker:							
With output in 1937 ruble factor cost	2.4 (2.2)[b]	2.9 (2.6)[b]	1.5 (1.0)[b]	1.7 (1.1)[b]	0.8	1.8	6.1
With output as composite, 1937 base	4.3	5.1	6.0	7.9	0.8	1.5	6.1

	USA				
	1869/78–1899/1908	1899/1908–1929	1929–1957	1929–1948	1948–1957
Gross national product:					
In 1929 dollars	4.8 (4.6)[c]	3.4	—	—	—
In 1954 dollars	—	—	2.9	2.5	3.7
Employment, all sectors	2.9	1.7	1.3	1.0	2.0
Gross national product per employed worker:					
With output in 1929 dollars	1.9 (1.7)[c]	1.6	—	—	—
With output in 1954 dollars	—	—	1.6	1.6	1.7

[a] Where in order, Soviet output and employment data are adjusted for territorial changes. For simplicity, I assume somewhat erroneously that employment is affected in the same way as output by the changes in question. On this assumption, no adjustment need be made in the measures of output per worker.

[b] Figures in parentheses result from extension for 1928–37 of ruble factor cost valuation within household retail purchases.

[c] Figures in parentheses represent rates of growth after adjustment for probable undercoverage in output total for 1869/78.

For the USSR, I cite the results of calculations described in chapter 13. As before, there are alternative measurements of the gross national product per employed worker depending on whether the gross national product is valued at ruble factor cost of 1937 or at ruble factor cost of the given year with 1937 as base. For the pertinent series on the gross national product and for the series on employment that were considered, I cite in Table 74 rates of growth corresponding to those compiled for output per employed worker.

In order to obtain corresponding measurements of labor productivity for the United States, I relate the series on the American gross national product that were described in the previous section with measures of employment which for years prior to 1929 are derived by summing: (a) the labor force in nonagricultural branches after allowance for unemployment; and (b) the number of farmers, together with the number of agricultural employees in terms of their assumed full-time equivalent.[10] For convenience, I rely here mainly on Professor J. Schmookler's adaptation of the basic Fabricant data. For 1929 and after, in the light of calculations of Kuznets and the Department of Commerce, employment is measured in all sectors in terms of its full-time equivalent. Rates of growth given by the series on the gross national product and employment that are considered are shown in Table 74.

As was explained, the data on employment that are used in the computation of output per employed worker for the USSR are rather tentative. Obviously, at least for early years, the corresponding figures used in calculating output per worker for the United States also leave something to be desired. In any event, from the standpoint of reliability

[10] These are the data on employment in the United States on which the computation of productivity rests: 1869/78, 12.4 millions; 1879/88, 17.4; 1889/98, 22.3; 1899/1908, 29.1; 1929, 44.9; 1948, 54.0; and 1957, 64.5 millions. While not needed here, the figures for 1879/88 and 1889/98 are to be used subsequently. For these intervals and for 1869/78 and 1899/1908, the cited figures are decade annual averages obtained in each case by summing: (a) The average annual number of farmers for the decade in question as given in J. Schmookler, "The Changing Efficiency of the American Economy," *Review of Economics and Statistics,* August 1952, pp. 218–219. (b) The average annual full-time equivalent employment during the decade of hired farm labor. In *ibid.,* pp. 218–219, Schmookler compiles for the decades in question data on the average annual employment of hired farm labor. In order to express these figures in terms of their full-time equivalent, I discount them by 35 percent, or approximately the amount by which the actual average earnings of farm employees in 1929 fell short of their estimated full-time earnings. See *ibid.,* p. 218. (c) The average annual nonagricultural labor force during the decade, less the corresponding amount of unemployment as given in *ibid,* p. 219. For 1929, the cited figure is obtained by summing the volume of employment of employees in full-time equivalent units and the number of entrepreneurs, as given in S. Kuznets, *National Income and Its Composition 1919–1938,* vol. 1, New York, 1941, pp. 314, 316. For 1948 and 1957, I assume that the percentage change from 1929 is as indicated by the Commerce Department data on total employment in full-time equivalent units. See *National Income, 1954 Edition,* pp. 202–203; *U.S. Income and Output,* p. 214.

the comparative figures compiled on productivity are inferior to those considered previously for total output.

For both the USSR and the USA, the figures compiled on output per worker do not take account of variations in working hours. Although in what follows I shall accordingly focus primarily on corresponding trends, some notion of how these might be affected if allowance were made for changes in hours may be provided by the data in Table 75. These are obtained by making for both countries the sort of adjustment in output per worker that was made previously for the USSR alone. More particularly, for each country the cited figures correspond to those in Table 74 except that for nonfarm employment allowance is made for changes in working hours.[11]

TABLE 75

Output per Worker Adjusted for Nonfarm Hours, USSR and USA, Average Annual Rates of Growth (percent)

USSR			USA		
Year	With output in 1937 ruble factor cost	With output as composite, 1937 base	Year	With output in 1929 dollars	With output in 1954 dollars
1928–55	2.1	4.0	1869/78–1899/1908	2.0	—
1928–55, "effective years"	2.5	4.8	1899/1908–1929	2.2	—
			1929–1957	—	2.1

As was explained before, working hours for Soviet nonfarm employees tended to increase over the period studied. The adjusted figures on output per worker reflect this fact. For the United States, however, the corresponding adjusted figures are affected by a contrary trend. In the course of time, nonfarm working hours have tended systematically to decline. In trying to appraise comparative trends in output per man hour, it should also be considered that in Soviet agriculture the working day may or may not have decreased in the interval in question. In the United States,

[11] The needed figures on U.S. working hours are either taken from or interpolated from estimates in J. F. Dewhurst and Associates, *America's Needs and Resources, A New Survey,* New York, 1955, p. 1073.

the farm working day reportedly has tended to decline during periods considered.

As for national income, so for productivity we may compare the Soviet performance during 1928–55 with that of the United States both during 1929–57 and during 1869/78 to 1899/1908. In each comparison let us inquire as to the relative trends prevailing in each of two cases corresponding to those on which we focused previously. To refer first to the comparison with the United States during 1929–57, during this period American output per worker grew at an average annual rate of 1.6 percent (Table 74). Production is valued here at dollar prices of 1954 but if, as is in order in the first of two cases in question, it is valued instead at dollar prices of the late thirties, productivity would grow at only a slightly higher rate (here and later, on the effect of a shift in base year or formula on measures of U.S. output per worker, see above pp. 265 ff.). If, as is also in order, output in the USSR is valued at ruble factor cost of 1937, output in that country grows during 1928–55 at 2.4 percent annually. This is the average tempo for all years during the period considered. For "effective years," output per worker grows at 2.9 percent a year. Although these data leave much to be desired, I conclude that in the case in question productivity probably tends to grow more rapidly in the USSR than in the USA.[12]

In case (b), the Russians apparently again outpace us but by a greater margin than before. Thus, if as is appropriate in this case we retain for the United States a base year in the late thirties but value output at dollar prices of the given year, output per worker still should grow at an annual rate of little more than 1.6 percent. For the USSR, however, with 1937 as base, output must now be valued at ruble factor cost of the given year. With such a computation, productivity grows during 1928–55 at an average annual rate of 4.3 percent for all years or of 5.1 percent for "effective years."

For both calculations for the USSR, but more so if they are in base year rather than in given year values, productivity in the USSR grows more rapidly during 1950–55 than during 1928–55. In the USA, output per worker during 1948–57 grows at about the same rate as during 1929–57. The Soviet margin over us is still greater, therefore, if the comparison is made for recent postwar years.

I turn to the comparison with the American performance during 1869/78 to 1899/1908. Here in the first of the two cases of interest, output per worker in the USSR grows during 1928–55 at 2.4 percent annually

[12] As with national income so here, particularly where reference is to the USA in recent years, the comparative data compiled appear more likely to err in favor of the USSR than of the USA, although in the case of the USSR the adjustment made for the war probably is again conservative and hence as before something of an offset.

when we average all years and at 2.9 percent annually when we average "effective years." As is required, I refer again to the calculation where production is valued at 1937 ruble factor cost. For the United States, reference must be to the corresponding calculation where output is valued at dollar prices of the late 1880's. If as so computed, American output grows at an unknown rate during 1869/78 to 1899/1908, its growth in relation to employment must also be conjectural. But from Professor Kuznets' calculations of the gross national product in 1929 dollars we see that our output per worker over the interval considered grows at 1.9 percent annually. While with valuation at dollar prices of the late 1880's the corresponding figure would be higher, the presumption must be, I think, that the Russians either match or surpass us at this point.

In case (b), that is, where reference is to the corresponding measurements in given year values, productivity in the USSR grows (as we saw before) at 4.3 percent annually when we average all years in the period considered and at 5.1 percent annually when we average "effective years." Although the corresponding American tempo is again conjectural, as I believe the reader will agree, our conclusion must be much the same as in case (a).

If we have succeeded at all in measuring output per worker in the two countries, there is also a basis to appraise the interesting question of the comparative roles of productivity changes and of increases in employment in the observed relative trends in total output. Thus, if in recent years the Russians have tended to expand total output more rapidly than we, a more rapid increase in employment in their case probably has been a factor but a more rapid increase in their productivity has been one also. This I believe is so even where output measurements are in terms of base year values. Where calculations are made instead in terms of given year values, the Soviet margin over us regarding the rate of growth of total output is increased. Furthermore, a higher Soviet tempo in respect of productivity is now very decidedly a factor. Depending on which of the two sorts of measurements is considered, comparison of the rate of growth of total output in the USSR during 1928–55 and in the USA during 1869/78 to 1899/1908 appears to lead to somewhat different conclusions, but in either case it is now the USA which experiences the more rapid increase in employment. As a source of increase in total output, gains in productivity are at least as consequential in the USSR as they are in the USA. Possibly they are more so.

As was explained, in recent years the Russians probably have expanded their capacity regarding commodity mixes which they produced in the late thirties more rapidly than we have expanded ours regarding mixes which we produced at the same time. As we now see, if this is indeed so, the higher Soviet tempo may be due partly to the more rapid expansion of employment in their case but the Russians benefited also from a more rapid expansion of productivity. Previously I also ventured to speculate about the comparative growth of Soviet capacity during 1928–55 regarding the Soviet mixes of the late thirties and of American capacity during 1869/78 to 1899/1908 regarding American mixes of that time. The Russians may well match or surpass us at this point, although this is uncertain. In any event, the contribution of productivity gains to the expansion of capacity may have been at least as great in the USSR as in the USA.

I have been considering throughout relative developments in output per worker. If reference is made instead to output per man-hour the comparison probably becomes distinctly more favorable to the United States, although the precise trends are uncertain.

Trends in Relative Shares

From data that were compiled on the disposition of the "real" gross national product, I sought in the previous chapter to appraise trends in relative shares of total output accruing to different final uses in the USSR. On the basis of the figures in Table 76 we may be able now to gauge the comparative developments in this regard in the two countries. For the USSR, essentially I repeat here data compiled previously. For the USA, the cited percentage figures are computed from corresponding absolute data in Table 73. I have already explained the sources and methods used in compiling the figures on the American gross national product in the latter table. For the most part, the corresponding figures cited there on outlays on different use categories are obtained on the same basis.

In compiling the data on relative shares in Table 76, I sought to assure that the different use categories considered would be similar in scope for the two countries, but inevitably there are incongruities. Most importantly, in both countries household consumption includes household outlays on education and health care, but because of the difference in institutional arrangements, the share of such services privately paid for is quite limited in the USSR but consequential in the USA. For this reason, Soviet household consumption tends to be somewhat understated here in relation to the corresponding American category. Since Soviet outlays on education and health care have increased disproportionately in the course of time, the relative understatement probably tends to be greater in recent than in early years. By the same token, the comparative data compiled on "other outlays" are subject to a contrary bias, for in the case of both countries, this category includes all public outlays on education and health care.

TABLE 76

Relative Shares of Final Uses in "Real" Gross National Product, USSR and USA
(Percent)

USSR					USA				
Year	Gross national product	Household consumption[a]	Gross investment	Other	Year	Gross national product	Household consumption[a]	Gross investment	Other
	In ruble factor cost of 1937					In 1929 dollars			
1928	100.0	79.5	12.5	8.0	1869–78[b]	100.0	74.5	22.7	2.7
1937	100.0	52.5	25.9	21.6	1879–88[b]	100.0	74.0	21.6	4.3
1940	100.0	49.4	19.1	31.5	1889–98[b]	100.0	71.4	24.7	3.8
1944	100.0	31.8	13.1	55.0	1899–1908[b]	100.0	73.1	22.9	4.0
1950	100.0	45.7	26.9	27.4	1929	100.0	75.7	20.0	4.3
1955	100.0	48.0	28.1	23.9		In 1954 dollars			
					1929	100.0	70.5	23.8	5.8
					1948	100.0	68.0	20.2	11.8
					1957	100.0	66.4	19.0	14.6

[a] Including education and health care privately paid for.
[b] Averages for the decade indicated.

For both countries, "other outlays" also include expenditures on government administration and defense as these categories have been understood in this study. Nevertheless, especially in postwar years, "other outlays" for the USSR may tend to be understated relatively to those for the USA. Among other things, unlike the latter, the former may omit certain kinds of defense outlays, for example expenditures for additions to atomic weapon stock piles.[13]

[13] In Table 76, the Soviet data are taken from Table 62. For other outlays I aggregate the figures given previously for "communal services," "government administration," and "defense" (as recorded in the budget). For the USA, as was explained, the cited percentages were computed from the data in Table 73. The figures on the gross national product in the latter table were discussed previously. As to the corresponding figures for outlays on different use categories, to refer first to those in 1954 dollars for the period 1929–57, these are obtained as follows:

Household consumption. "Personal consumption expenditures" in U.S. Department of Commerce, *U.S. Income and Output,* pp. 118–119.

Gross investment. This item comprises gross private domestic investment, net exports of goods and services, civilian public construction, and government purchases of civilian producers' durables. In 1929, gross private domestic investment was 35.0 billions of 1954 dollars; in 1948, 49.8 billions; and in 1957, 57.8 (*ibid.,* pp. 118–119). In 1929, net exports of goods and services were 0.2 billion of 1954 dollars; in 1948, 2.0; and in 1957, 3.9 (*ibid.,* pp. 118–119). Civilian public construction totaled, for 1929, 5.3 billions of 1954 dollars; for 1948, 5.4 billions; and for 1957, 11.5 billions. For 1929, according to U.S. Department of Commerce, *National Income, 1954 Edition,* p. 208, outlays on "new public construction activity" other than on "military facilities" totaled $2.5 billion in terms of current prices. For public construction, prices in 1929 were 47.6 percent of 1954. See U.S. Department of Commerce, *U.S. Income and Output,* p. 225. For 1948 and 1957, corresponding figures on construction in 1954 dollars are given in *ibid.,* p. 191. Government purchase of civilian producers' durables, as independently estimated for 1929 amounted to 2.7 billions of dollars; for 1948, 1.9; and for 1957, 4.0 billions.

Other. Calculated as a residual.

In Table 73, the data on different use categories for 1929 and earlier years in dollar prices of 1929 are obtained as follows:

Household consumption. For all years I take as a point of departure unpublished calculations of Simon Kuznets on the "flow of goods to consumers" in dollar prices of 1929. As measured by Kuznets, this category differs somewhat in scope from the Commerce Department category "Personal consumption expenditures." Thus, unlike the latter, it includes "direct services by government" and omits "services furnished without payment by financial intermediaries except insurance companies." For 1929, Kuznets' figure consequently is 101.6 percent of the corresponding Commerce Department total: $79.0 billion in 1929 dollars. See *ibid.,* pp. 118–119. For purposes of compiling measures which throughout are comparable in scope to the Commerce Department data, I believe I have erred little in assuming that the 1929 relation between the two categories also prevails in earlier years.

Gross investment. This is "gross capital formation," as determined by Kuznets in his unpublished calculations. In order to obtain figures comparable in scope to the gross investment data compiled above for recent years in 1954 dollars, I deduct from Kuznets' totals expenditures on "durable war goods," as estimated by him.

Other. Calculated as a residual.

As for national income, so for individual use categories where use is made of Kuznets' unpublished calculations, I refer to his variant III.

I discussed briefly in the text the question of the comparability of the data compiled there for the two countries on the relative shares of different use categories. For further details on this aspect, see *SNIP-40–48,* pp. 98 ff.

If as before we compare Soviet trends under the five year plans with those in the United States during a contemporary and an early period, the more interesting relations emerging from the foregoing data are fairly evident: (a) The period of five year plans witnessed a radical increase in the share of the Soviet gross national product devoted to investment. The increase occurs primarily under the first two five year plans, and the upward trend is actually reversed immediately before and during the war, but it is resumed thereafter. At the end of the period, investment seems to constitute an even larger share of the gross national product than in the mid-thirties. In the United States, the share of the gross national product devoted to investment shows no trend one way or the other in the period 1869/78 to 1899/1908. Then too, while the share of investment appears to vary secularly to a limited extent after 1928, in contrast to the experience in the USSR, the trend here is downward.

(b) In the USSR, the five year plans also saw a sharp increase in relative allocations to "other outlays." These allocations, which include defense, of course rose most notably before and during the war, but these years apart, a pronounced upward trend is still manifest. As was so for gross investment, the increase is most marked under the first two five year plans but the share of other outlays in the late fifties is perceptibly above that of 1937. For the United States, available data on the share of the gross national product going to "other outlays" in early years are rather arbitrary, but if this category increased at all at this time, no doubt the increase was limited, as is shown in Table 76. For the two benchmark years 1948 and 1957, however, other outlays absorb a markedly higher share of the gross national product than in 1929.

(c) In association with the foregoing trends, over the period 1928–55 the share of household consumption in the gross national product of the USSR tends sharply to decline. While the low point reached during the war is not maintained thereafter, in postwar years the share of consumption remains below the reduced levels of the thirties. For the United States, household consumption tends to absorb a nearly constant share of the gross national product in the last decades of the last century. More recently, this share apparently has tended to decline, but only to a limited extent.

I have been considering comparative trends in relative shares indicated by calculations of the disposition of the "real" gross national product which for the USSR are in terms of 1937 ruble factor cost. For the USA, the corresponding computations referred to for early years are in terms of 1929 dollar prices and for recent years in terms of dollar prices of 1954. For the USSR, data on relative shares have also been compiled where the gross national product is calculated by use in terms of 1950 ruble factor cost. For the two years, 1928 and 1937, such figures have been compiled additionally from corresponding computations in terms of 1928 ruble factor cost. Considering these alternative sorts of data, we may conclude that in the comparison between the USSR under the five year plans and the USA in a contemporary period the contrasting trends in relative shares in the two countries would be little affected if we considered for the USSR computations not in 1937 ruble factor cost but in ruble factor cost of, for example, a "late" year in the period in question. This would also be true, I believe, if alternatively we considered for the USA computations in terms not of 1954 dollars but of dollars of, for example, the late thirties. If in each country reference is made to computations in terms of an "early" base year in the period in question, however, the divergencies in trends observed initially presumably would be somewhat magnified. In the case of the United States, I assume throughout that as for the increase in total product so for the shares devoted to different use categories the effect on our measurements of a shift in base year within the period since 1928 must be very limited.

In the comparison between the USSR under the five year plans and the USA in an early period, we do not know how the relative trends might be altered if for the United States we considered computations not in 1929 dollars but in dollars of, for example, the late 1880's. Very possibly developments in the United States would tend to approach more nearly to the Soviet pattern, but it hardly seems possible that the differences observed would be obliterated. One suspects this would also be the result if for each country one considered alternatively data compiled in terms of a base year that is either "early" or "late" in the period in question.

For purposes of appraising comparative trends in relative shares, I believe the foregoing are the more interesting cases to consider. In previous sections, I referred to still another case where for both countries output is calculated in values of the given year, but such measurements do not provide a satisfactory basis for appraisal of trends in relative shares.

In considering the comparative disposition of the gross national product in the USSR and USA, I have been treading on ground explored earlier in the SNIP studies, but I do so now with different data and as is readily seen the present inquiry is complementary rather than competitive with that made previously. Thus, while in the SNIP studies reference was made to calculations which for each country were in terms of current values, I have been considering here measurements which for each country are in terms of values prevailing in some base year. From the former data, one may gauge relative trends in "resource allocation" in the two countries. From the latter, one may appraise relative trends in shares of total output devoted to different uses. These trends diverge from those in "resource allocation" where prices of goods and services devoted to different uses vary differently in relation to each other in the two countries.

Granting the difference in the nature and meaning of the two sorts of measurements in question, the trends observed above may usefully be compared with those indicated by the SNIP figures. As elaborated here, the latter data are shown in Table 77.[14] Interestingly, the results are broadly similar, but there are divergencies. Most notably, for the USSR investment rises to only a limited degree where measurements are in current values but sharply where measurements are in constant values. Correspondingly, the decline in consumption is less in the former case than in the latter. These divergent trends have no counterpart in the United States in either early or recent times. By implication, there is also no counterpart in the United States of the sharp relative cut in the prices of investment goods (including construction) that occurred in the USSR under the first two five year plans.

From comparative data on national income shares in terms of current values, it is possible not only to appraise trends in "resource allocation" in the two countries but to compare "resource allocation" in one country with "resource allocation" in the other at specific times. As may not always be considered, the corresponding data in constant values provide a basis to appraise relative trends over time in shares of total output devoted to different uses but not for the comparison of such shares in the two countries at particular times. For the latter sort of appraisal, output rather must be valued in terms of the same prices in both countries: preferably, the prices prevailing in one or the other of the two countries compared. Only in this way do the comparative shares show (as is desired) the comparative physical volume of goods and services devoted to different uses in the two countries. As the measurements considered here suggest, I venture to think that the Russians lately have devoted a larger share of total output to investment than we have. Correspondingly, their allocation of goods and services to household consumption probably is distinctly smaller than ours. But this aspect is properly the subject of a separate inquiry, and cannot be pursued here.

Whether the concern is to appraise relative trends over time or comparative magnitudes at particular times, it should be observed that for the United States for the period 1928 I refer in Tables 76 and 77

[14] For the USSR, see Table 62. For the USA the data in Table 77 are compiled by use of essentially the same sources and methods as those employed in the derivation of the corresponding figures in constant prices.

TABLE 77

Relative Shares of Final Uses in Gross National Product, USSR in Current Ruble Factor Cost, and USA in Current Dollars
(Percent)

USSR					USA				
Year	Gross national product	Household consumption[a]	Gross investment	Other	Year	Gross national product	Household consumption[a]	Gross investment	Other
1928	100.0	64.7	25.0	10.3	1869–78[b]	100.0	77.0	20.3	2.7
1937	100.0	52.5	25.9	21.6	1879–88[b]	100.0	77.0	19.5	3.5
1940	100.0	51.0	19.2	29.8	1889–98[b]	100.0	73.5	22.1	4.4
1944	100.0	36.1	14.3	49.6	1899–1908[b]	100.0	74.0	21.7	4.3
1950	100.0	45.5	27.9	26.5	1929	100.0	75.7	20.0	4.3
1955	100.0	49.2	27.9	22.9	1948	100.0	68.7	20.4	10.9
					1957	100.0	64.6	19.8	15.6

[a] Including education and health care privately paid for.
[b] Average for the decade indicated.

to relatively prosperous years. If, as might have been desirable, reference had been made instead to decade averages such as are considered for early times, presumably the share of investment would have been less and that of household consumption greater than is observed.

It was said that my calculations are patterned after those of the U.S. Department of Commerce. At a late stage, partly as a result of discussions with Dr. Richard Moorsteen, I have come to feel that in scope my measurements of the gross national product probably differ somewhat from those of both Professor Kuznets and the Department of Commerce because of the inclusion in the former of "capital repairs." Depending on their specific nature and on the kind of underlying data employed, outlays of the sort classified in my calculations for the USSR as "capital repairs" apparently are treated variously in those of Kuznets and the Commerce Department for the USA, but in the upshot I believe that while expenditures of this sort often find their way into the gross national product, they also often do not. In effect, in the latter case such outlays are viewed as representing "intermediate" rather than "final" products.

This difference in treatment of capital repairs, however, hardly affects the comparisons that have been made of the growth of total output and of output per worker in the two countries. Thus, if in order to make my data for the USSR comparable in scope with those of Kuznets and the Commerce Department for the USA we omit from the former, for example, one-half of the total capital repairs, the average rate of growth of the gross national product for effective years during 1928–55 falls by but 0.1 percent, that is, from 5.2 to 5.1 percent a year. As to the comparative trends over time in relative shares, the principal effect of the same adjustment in the Soviet data is to dampen somewhat the increase that is observed in the rate of investment (both in my calculations for the USSR and, so far as such outlays are included in the gross national product, in those of Kuznets and the Commerce Department for the USA, capital repairs are classified in this final use category):

Year	Gross investment as share of gross national product in terms of 1937 ruble factor cost, USSR (Percent): As initially computed (Table 76)	With one half of capital repairs omitted
1928	12.5	12.1
1937	25.9	25.2
1950	26.9	25.6
1955	28.1	26.6

The foregoing deals with the way in which my comparisons might be affected if my data for the USSR are adjusted to correspond in scope to those of Kuznets and the Commerce Department for the USA. Arguably, a more appropriate procedure would be to adjust the latter figures in order to make them comparable in scope to the former. Regrettably, information on the volume of capital repairs in the United States that is needed for such an adjustment is not at hand, but the adjustments made above in my Soviet data reflect a sharp increase under the five year plans in capital repairs in relation to the gross national product. In either of the two periods considered for the United States, it hardly seems possible that in relation to gross output capital repairs would have increased nearly as sharply. For this reason, I suspect that an adjustment in the American data of the sort in question would have even less effect on the comparative trends of interest here than does that which I have made in the Soviet data.

With the kind permission of Professor R. Powell and Dr. Moorsteen, use has been made here of estimates of capital repairs in the USSR that they have compiled as part of a study they are preparing on Soviet capital formation.

Household Consumption Per Capita and Per Employed Worker

For purposes of appraising comparative developments in household consumption per capita and per employed worker, reference is made to the data in Tables 78 and 79. For the USSR, I cite rates of growth corresponding to alternative measurements of these categories that were derived previously. For the USA, the cited rates of growth for household consumption per capita correspond to the serial data on this aspect in Table 73. For household consumption per employed worker, the necessary serial data for the USA are obtained by reference to the figures on aggregate household consumption in Table 73, and the figures on employment in the USA derived previously.

Because of the omission of home processing, the data considered tend to exaggerate gains in household consumption for both countries, but probably more so for the USSR than for the USA, at least where in the

TABLE 78

Rates of Growth of "Real" Household Consumption per Capita, USSR and USA, Selected Periods

USSR			USA		
	Average annual rate of growth (percent) with output—			Average annual rate of growth (percent) with output—	
Year	In adjusted market prices of 1937	As composite series, 1937 base	Year	In 1929 dollars	In 1954 dollars
1928–1937	−0.3	2.2	1869/78–1879/88	4.0	—
1937–1940	−1.5	−1.5	1879/88–1889/98	0.8	—
1928–1940	−0.6	1.3	1889/98–1899/1908	2.9	—
1940–1950	1.9	1.4	1869/78–1899/1908	2.6	—
1950–1955	6.7	7.1	1899/1908–1929	1.9	—
1928–1955	1.7	2.4	1929–1948	—	1.4
1928–1955 "effective years"[a]	2.0	2.8	1948–1957	—	1.7
			1929–1957	—	1.5

[a] Growth for entire period imputed to peacetime years.

case of the latter reference is (as it will be in one of two comparisons to be made) to recent years. On the other hand, as before, household consumption includes in both countries private but not public outlays on education and health care. Since the latter have been not only predominant but increasingly large in the USSR, the growth of household consumption in that country tends on this account to be somewhat understated compared with the increase in this category in the United States. The net of these two conflicting biases is uncertain; nevertheless one surmises that on balance the USSR probably is favored little if at all. The adjusted market prices in terms of which Soviet household consumption is valued are conceptually less than ideal generally, but those for 1928 are particularly dubious. If only for this reason the serial measures in terms of adjusted market prices of the given year are less reliable than those in terms of adjusted market prices of 1937, although the latter are also inexact. Like the measures of the gross national product to which they are related, the American data on household consumption also have their limitations.

As was done for national income, we may compare Soviet developments during 1928–55 with American developments both during 1929–57 and during 1869/78 to 1899/1908. In making each comparison, I shall consider these cases: (a) Consumption for the USSR is valued at adjusted market prices of 1937 and for the USA at the dollar prices prevailing at some intermediate date in the period considered. (b) With the base year as in (a), consumption in each country is calculated in terms of given year values, either ruble factor cost or dollar prices, as the case may be. These two cases, of course, correspond to those on which I focused in the appraisal of trends in national income. The data on Soviet household consumption at adjusted market prices are intended primarily to illuminate welfare as given by consumers' utilities. The corresponding measures cited for the United States, I believe, are pertinent to production potential as well as to welfare as given by consumers' utilities, but evidently the relative trends observed in the two countries are best read as bearing on the latter category. By the same token, the theoretic ultimate of chief interest here is different from that where the concern was with national income. Furthermore, the sort of measurements called for in case (b) are consequently no longer as impelling as before, but we may usefully refer here to this case as well as to case (a).

The relative trends regarding household consumption to some extent are already implied in those considered previously in total output and in relative shares. In the United States during 1929–57 (to begin with the comparison with this interval), household consumption per capita increased at an average annual rate of 1.5 percent (Table 78). This rate obtains where output is valued at dollar prices of 1954, but in the case

TABLE 79

Rates of Growth of "Real" Household Consumption per Employed Worker, USSR and USA, Selected Periods

USSR			USA		
	Average annual rate of growth (percent) with output—			Average annual rate of growth (percent) with output—	
Year	In adjusted market prices of 1937	As composite series, 1937 base	Year	In 1929 dollars	In 1954 dollars
1928–1937	−3.0	−0.5	1869/78–1879/88	3.0	—
1937–1940	−1.6	−1.6	1879/88–1889/98	0.4	—
1928–1940	−2.6	−0.8	1889/98–1899/1908	2.1	—
1940–1950	0.8	0.3	1869/78–1899/1908	1.8	—
1950–1955	7.1	7.4	1899/1908–1929	1.8	—
1928–1955	0.4	1.1	1929–1948	—	1.4
1928–1955 "effective years"[a]	0.4	1.3	1948–1957	—	1.4
			1929–1957	—	1.4

[a] Growth for entire period imputed to peacetime years.

of household consumption, index number relativity for obvious reasons should be little if at all greater than in the case of total output. Indeed, one might ordinarily expect it to be less. If, as is in order in case (a), therefore, output were valued instead at dollar prices of the late thirties, the tempo of increase in American household consumption should at most be only slightly greater than 1.5 percent per annum. If, for the USSR, output is valued in adjusted market prices of 1937 — as is also in order in case (a) — the corresponding tempo for that country during 1928–55 is 1.7 percent. This is the average for all years in this period. For "effective years," the corresponding figure is 2.0 percent. Considering the limitations in these calculations, I conclude that with measurements as in case (a), household consumption per capita probably has increased at about the same rate in the two countries. Possibly the Soviet tempo exceeds that in the USA.

If, as in case (b), reference is made to corresponding measurements in terms of given year values, the American tempo presumably would again be no more than slightly above 1.5 percent a year. For the USSR, however, household consumption per capita now increases at an average annual rate of 2.4 percent, or of 2.8 percent for "effective years." Although my serial data for the USSR in terms of adjusted market prices of the given year are not very reliable, in case (b) very possibly the Soviet tempo is higher than ours.

Although when seen in these summary terms the Soviet performance compares favorably with ours, presumably it has not been a matter of indifference to the Soviet population that the recorded gains in consumption to a great extent were realized only in the final years of the period in question, and that for a protracted initial interval standards rose to only a relatively limited extent. In fact, according to the more reliable of the two sorts of measures considered, the initial trend was downward. On the other hand, one need not consult statistics to be aware that in the period 1929–57 the rise of consumption standards in the United States too was by no means uninterrupted, and this fact also must be considered in an appraisal of comparative trends in the two countries.

Turning to the comparison with the United States during 1869/78 to 1899/1908, the conclusion in a case (a) must be that the two countries again are not very far apart, but probably it is now we who experienced the greater progress. Thus, during 1928–55, household consumption per capita in the USSR is found to increase at an annual rate of 1.7 percent when we average all years or of 2.0 percent when averaging "effective years." As is appropriate in case (a), I cite again rates of growth that prevail where output is valued in adjusted market prices of 1937. With output as calculated by Professor Kuznets in terms of dollar prices of 1954, American household consumption per capita increases during 1869/78 to 1899/1908 at an average annual rate of 2.6 percent. With output valued as is now in order at dollar prices of the late 1880's, the corresponding tempo might be appreciably higher.

As we have seen, with 1937 as base and with output valued at adjusted market prices of the given year, Soviet household consumption per capita grows during 1928–55 at 2.4 percent annually when we average all years and at 2.8 percent annually when we average "effective years." To repeat: this computation is less reliable than that in terms of adjusted market prices of 1937. When we consider these facts and also the fact that for the United States during 1869/78 to 1899/1908 the rate of growth of per capita consumption (where the base year is in the late 1880's and valuation is in given year prices) very possibly would again be materially above 2.6 percent, I believe we may conclude that in case (b) the American progress still matches or surpasses that of the USSR.

As before, we must consider that in the case of the USSR much of the progress achieved during the interval studied was realized only in its final years. For the United States, too, progress was seemingly uneven, but there hardly was any near counterpart in the interval studied of the Soviet experience regarding consumption under the first two five year plans.

Reference thus far has been to household consumption per capita. Regarding household consumption per employed worker, it may suffice to say that, in relation to population, employment in the USSR for "effective years" during 1928–55 grew more rapidly than in the United States during 1928–57. For this reason, the comparison of consumption per employed worker in these recent intervals is decidedly more favorable to the USA than is that of consumption per capita (Table 79). If, in the case of the United States, we consider not recent years but the period 1869/78 to 1899/1908, employment in the USSR still tends to grow more rapidly in relation to population than in the USA, although not as much so as before. By the same token, the comparison of consumption per employed worker is again somewhat more favorable to the USA than that of consumption per capita. No calculations have been made of consumption per man-hour. Whether we consider the United States in early or recent times, a comparison of this aspect most likely would be still more favorable to the USA than is that of consumption per employed worker.

Under the five year plans, especially in early years, the industrial worker in the USSR in comparison with the farmer experienced a relative decline in household consumption per employed worker. Possibly the former also suffered in comparison with the latter regarding household consumption per capita. I must leave it to a separate inquiry to consider whether and to what extent there has been any parallel to these developments in the USA.

In sum, trends in consumption standards in the two countries have been complex, and alternative measurements on even a single aspect are somewhat conflicting, but the Soviet performance probably appears here as better than has often been supposed. Nevertheless, much of the over-all progress that is observed in the Soviet case results from an exceptional spurt in the final years of the period studied, and for a protracted previous period the lot of the consumer could not have been especially appealing. Moreover, such sacrifices as were made in the early years were none the lighter because per capita consumption at the outset probably did not exceed some $160.[15] This is in terms of 1929 prices. In the United States, the corresponding figure as early as 1869/78 was about $190. The more recent Soviet economic performance under a relatively mature planning system, however, has an interest of its own, and for consumption particularly one wonders whether the progress achieved with total output already growing at a high rate may not signify more for the future than that achieved previously when the rate of growth of total output had to be increased. But this is a subject for comment in chapter 15, so I shall say no more about it here.

[15] See Table 66, and note 10 of chapter 15.

15

PROSPECTS

Since she initiated her First Five Year Plan, Soviet Russia has been expanding economically at notable tempos. As measured in previous pages, her total and per capita gross national product have grown at these rates:

	Average annual rate of growth	
	1928–55 "effective years,"	1950–55
	(percent per annum)	
Gross national product		
With output at 1937 ruble factor cost	5.2[1]	7.6
With output as composite, 1937 base	7.5[1]	7.6
Gross national product per capita		
With output at 1937 ruble factor cost	4.4	5.8
With output as composite, 1937 base	6.7	5.8

Despite the war, output in 1955 was 3.2 to 5.2 times that of 1928. For per capita production, the corresponding indices are 2.7 to 4.4. What are

[1] After adjustment for territorial changes.

the prospects for the future? The calculations that have been made may provide a partial basis to appraise this important theme.

In this study, I have focused on the period 1928–55. As a preliminary, it should be observed that since 1955 production has continued to expand at a high tempo. Indeed, if we may judge from a tentative computation, the rate of growth during 1955–58 is practically the same as it was during 1950–55. This is true for both total and per capita output.[2] As a result, total output in 1958 was nearly one-fourth greater than in 1955. Correspondingly, per capita production during the same interval increased by more than 15 percent.

TABLE 80

Gross National Product, USSR, Alternative Projections

	Average annual rate of growth, 1959–75	Total as percent of 1959			
		1959	1965	1970	1975
With output per worker increasing annually by:					
4 percent	5.0	100	134	171	218
5 percent	6.0	100	142	190	254
6 percent	7.0	100	150	210	295

Turning to prospects, the hypothetical figures in Table 80 may suggest some of the more interesting possibilities regarding the gross national product.

During 1928–55, employment in the USSR increased at the estimated rates cited below. For comparison, I set forth also the corresponding tempos for the population of working age, that is, 16 years and over. For employment, the average annual rate of growth for 1928–55 ("effective years") was 2.7 percent and for 1950–55, 1.4; for the population 16

[2] In chapter 11 reference was made to a computation of the net national product of the USSR by industrial origin. The computation involves the aggregation of diverse series that are available on the physical volume of production of different economic sectors. For the period 1950-55, I find on this basis that the net national product grows at 7.3 percent a year. This is approximately the same rate as has been given by either of the two alternative computations referred to in the text. By use of sources and methods similar to those employed previously, I have also attempted to extend the computation of the net national product by industrial origin to the period 1955-58. On this basis, I find that the net national product in these years grows at 7.0 percent annually or about the same rate as prevailed during 1950–55.

During 1955–58, population grew only slightly more rapidly than it did during 1950–55.

On the extrapolation of national income to 1958, see also pp. 58–59.

years of age and over, the average annual rate of growth for 1928–55 ("effective years") was 1.7 percent and for 1950–55, 2.3 percent.

The change in employment during 1955–58 is not known. Most likely it was at much the same rate as prevailed during 1950–55. If so, this would mean that as before employment grew more slowly than the population of working age.[3]

In all three of the hypothetical cases considered I assume that in the future employment will grow at but 1 percent annually. Especially in the later years in question, this may turn out to be somewhat conservative. It is true that as a result of the wartime decline in the birth rate the population of working age is expected in the coming decade and a half to grow at but 1.5 percent annually, and that in the course of time such persons will consist increasingly of the aged. On the other hand, while women are already participating in the labor force to a notable degree, the government hopes in diverse ways to induce them to work still more. Moreover, to a significant degree, the low rate of growth in employment during 1950–55 was due to the disproportionate increase in youths of 16 and over who were still going to school. Through the educational reform law of 1958, such persons momentarily are now entering the labor market in increasing numbers.[4]

Although the three cases rest on a common assumption as to the future growth of employment, they differ regarding the supposed increase in output per worker. The different suppositions are suggested by the past trends in this aspect as calculated in this study:

[3] On the average during 1958 some 54.6 million persons were employed in the USSR as wage earners and salaried workers. This represents a gain of 6.2 millions over the corresponding figure for 1955. See *Narkhoz-1958,* p. 656. From data in *ibid.,* p. 655, one may also infer that in the same interval there was little if any change in employment on the collective farm. From data in Khrushchev's speech before the Supreme Soviet of January 14, 1960, seemingly the armed forces on the average numbered but 3.6 millions in 1958, or 1.9 millions less than in 1955. By implication, if there had also been no change in employment elsewhere, employment in all sectors in 1958 would have totaled 94.5 millions, or 104.8 percent of 1955. See Appendix K. Very possibly, however, there has been a decline since 1955 in the number of persons engaged in penal labor. Considering this, we must conclude, I think, that during 1955–58, employment grew by little if at all more than (say) 1.5 percent a year, or about the same rate as prevailed during 1950–55.

During 1955–58, the population of 16 years and over grew by 2.0 percent yearly. I rely here on unpublished data of the U. S. Bureau of the Census corresponding to those on the population of working age that have been employed elsewhere in this study. See Appendix K.

[4] On the future growth of the Soviet population I rely here on an unpublished projection of the U.S. Bureau of the Census. This represents an elaboration of data in John F. Kantner, "Population and Labor Force," in Joint Economic Committee, Congress of the United States, *Comparisons of the United States and Soviet Economies,* Part I, Washington, 1959. See also Warren Eason, *Soviet Manpower,* Princeton, 1959. These two sources also discuss the prospects for the Soviet labor force.

	Average annual rate of growth of output per worker (percent)	
	1928–55, "effective years"	1950–55
With output at 1937 ruble factor cost	2.9	6.1
With output given by composite, 1937 base	5.1	6.1

Apparently the assumption of the first case is that productivity will increase at a rate falling between my two conflicting measures for 1928–55. In the third case, the future tempo of output per worker corresponds essentially to that which according to both measures prevailed during 1950–55. In the second case, an intermediate rate of growth is considered.

If I am right that since 1955 employment has increased at about the same rate as during 1950–55, this would also be true of output per worker. Hence, the tempo assumed in the third case still prevails in recent years.

For the nonfarm labor force, hours of work in 1955 were somewhat longer than they had been in 1928, but for farmers they may or may not have been shorter. Since the net of these conflicting changes is not known, the trends during 1928–55 in employment in terms of man-hours and in output per man-hour are uncertain. During 1950–55, there was no change to speak of in the work-week in industry and probably none either in agriculture. For this reason, employment in terms of man-hours during this period varied in the same way as employment in terms of physical persons. Similarly, output per man-hour varied proportionately to output per worker.[5] Since 1956, however, the government has been shortening hours for nonfarm workers, and very possibly it will complete by 1960 the shift that it has projected for these persons from an 8- to a 7-hour day. As nonfarm employees account for about one-half of the labor force, during 1955–58 man-hours of employment increased significantly less than employment in physical persons. Correspondingly, output per man-hour increased more than output per worker. By implication, such relations must continue to prevail from 1958 to 1960. Then too, the government avowedly plans to reduce hours still more after 1960, and during 1964–68 a transition is also to be made to a 35-hour week. Whether and to what extent these ambitious aims will be implemented remains to be seen. If they are, man-hours of employment must continue to grow more slowly than employment in physical persons and output per man-hour must continue to grow more rapidly than output per worker. The alternative hypothetical cases regarding output per worker that have been listed must be viewed accordingly.

[5] Actually, the data on employment compiled in this study refer not to physical persons but more or less to man-years. Correspondingly, my measures of productivity come to much the same thing as measures of output per man-year.

What are the prospects that output per worker will tend to vary in accord with one or another of the hypothetical cases? In trying to appraise this complex question, one should first consider the fact that while the USSR generally is well endowed with natural resources, especially in agriculture the endowment probably is not as generous as is often assumed. In any case, in seeking to increase labor productivity in the past, the Russians have been materially impeded so far by limitations in this aspect, and one must suppose that this will only be the more true in the future. The reduced grain harvest of 1959 is only the most recent reminder of this fact. Then, too, trends in the Soviet stock of fixed capital have been left here for separate inquiry, but almost certainly this category is presently growing appreciably more rapidly than output.[6] By implication, the USSR currently must devote an increasing share of its output to capital replacement needs; and so far as these needs encroach on the resources available for new capital formation, this too tends to impede somewhat the growth of labor productivity.

I have already recorded my opinion that if the Russians thus far under their five year plans have achieved notable increases in labor productivity, not the least of the reasons is their ability to borrow industrial techniques and processes abroad on an unprecedented scale. Yet, presumably, the opportunities for borrowing should diminish with the very advances that are realized, and considering this, one is tempted to think that here, too, circumstances will be less favorable to progress in the future than they have been previously. But, with an output per worker in 1955 of no more than (say) 30 percent of that in the United States, the USSR must still have opportunities enough for fruitful borrowing from abroad.[7] Moreover, the Russians now have a corps of 1,750,000 professionally trained scientists and engineers, or 200,000 more than we have. Currently they are graduating from their universities 180,000 of such persons, or 75,000 more than we are graduating from ours.[8] The Russians hardly will experience again a technological revolution like that of the early thirties, but all things considered, one wonders whether in the coming years progress in techniques is apt to be any less rapid than it has been in the very recent past.

It was suggested, too, that the swift growth achieved to date probably does not signify any notable degree of economic efficiency on the part of the Soviet planning system. Nevertheless, if the Russians have not been especially efficient thus far, there should be opportunities for future

[6] See above, pp. 223 ff.

[7] In 1955, about 70 percent as many man-years were gainfully employed in the USA as in the USSR. See chapter 14, and Appendix K. The ratio of output per worker in the two countries is computed from this relation and from their relative outputs, as given on p. 295.

[8] These unpublished figures were kindly supplied me by N. DeWitt.

gains in this regard, and one need not be especially conversant with the Soviet planning system to be aware that this is indeed the case. Besides, opinions may differ on the merits of one or another of the recent notable measures affecting economic organization — such as the reform in agricultural procurement prices, industrial reorganization, and liquidation of the "machine-tractor" station (MTS) — but I think it will be agreed that on balance they will be favorable to efficiency. Furthermore, political circumstances are more propitious than they were previously to the discovery and introduction of additional rationalization measures in the future. By the same token, there may be an offset here to forces elsewhere that are adverse to productivity. Of course, if as was implied above, the Russians henceforth become increasingly self-reliant regarding technology, this in itself would have to be viewed as a gain in economic efficiency on their part, but what is suggested is that there may be gains on other accounts as well, among other things in the "static" realm familiar in economic theory where technology is viewed as given.

Last but not least, in achieving a high rate of growth of productivity, the government lately has raised little if at all the rate of investment; at least this was so until 1955. Nevertheless, in the future, the government can increase such allocations. Indeed, if circumstances require, it can increase them materially. Of course, such a policy would have to be pursued at the expense of consumption, but with total output growing as it now is at more than 7.0 percent yearly, and with the population growing at but 1.8 percent yearly, the government is able to increase the rate of investment and yet at the same time to raise not only aggregate but per capita consumption. While the latter might not continue to grow at the extraordinary rates of recent years, the increment might still be material. For example, if data on national income disposition for 1955 are at all indicative of the current situation, the government in the coming years might increase the physical volume of capital investment annually by as much as 10 percent. While doing so, it might still allow consumers a yearly increase of as much as 2.8 percent in their per capita standards. Such a policy, it is true, would be feasible only if the Russians succeed in maintaining a high rate of growth of total output. The policy itself, however, might make continued high-tempo growth possible.

Of course, if other forces affecting productivity are not especially adverse, the government may be able to assure continued rapid progress in this sphere by increasing only slowly or not at all the rate of investment. By implication, consumption standards might then continue to rise at rates approaching those realized in the recent past. But apparently, even if other forces are relatively adverse, the government in some degree may be able to counter them in the manner described; and the more successful it is in this regard the greater the prospects of further successes.

I have been assuming implicitly that as total output expands defense expenditures increase commensurately. If, on the contrary, military outlays increase less than total output, the possibilities of achieving continued rapid growth in both total output and per capita consumption could only be enhanced. They would be enhanced still more if at long last defense expenditures could be curtailed.

It is not easy to gauge the net of the opposing forces that have been described. In the coming years, the rate of growth of Soviet Russia's output per worker may decline below its recent high level, but if so one hesitates to assume that the reduction will soon be very consequential.

As measured in this study, however, the tempo of increase in output per worker in the USSR under the five year plans matches but may not markedly exceed that prevailing in the USA during three decades 1869/78 to 1899/1908. Is the Soviet tempo not more likely, therefore, to decline much as ours has done and in due course to our more recent levels? That the Soviet rate of growth exceeds ours during 1869/78 to 1899/1908 can no longer be considered very doubtful if in the case of the USSR we consider not the period of the five year plans as a whole but years since 1950. In any event, as in the USA so in Soviet Russia the increase of productivity depends on diverse opposing forces, but if Soviet output per worker has grown thus far at notable rates, this is due consequentially to the presence there of one factor which apparently has no clear American counterpart: the political control over the rate of investment. This factor presumably will continue to prevail in the USSR in the future. If only for this reason, there is little basis to suppose that the Russians must repeat our experience.

From a recent computation of Dr. Morris Bornstein, it would appear that Soviet Russia in 1959 produced a gross national product on the order of nearly one-half of that of the United States.[9] If the hypothetical

[9] M. Bornstein finds that for 1955 the gross national product of the USSR is 26.8 percent of that of the United States when the calculation is in terms of ruble prices and 53.4 percent of that of the United States when the calculation is in dollar prices. The geometric average of the two ratios is 37.8 percent. See M. Bornstein, "National Income and Product," in Joint Economic Committee, Congress of the United States, *Comparisons of the United States and Soviet Economies,* Part II, p. 385. In order to obtain a corresponding figure for 1959, I take the gross national product of the USSR in that year to be 130.0 percent of that for 1955. See note 2 of this chapter. For the United States, output in 1959 is about 108.0 percent of that of 1955. See U.S. Department of Commerce, *U.S. Income and Output,* pp. 118–119; *Survey of Current Business,* November 1959, p. 11. By implication, the Soviet gross national product in 1959 is 45.5 percent of that of the United States in the same year. This ratio should be raised to 47.5 percent in order to allow for an understatement resulting from Bornstein's use of prevailing rubles rather than ruble factor cost in his comparison of total output in terms of ruble values. An understatement of at least the assumed magnitude is suggested by a partial recomputation in terms of ruble factor cost.

Perhaps it is not seriously amiss if for simplicity I follow Bornstein here in averaging the two conflicting index numbers. It is evident that as for comparisons of different

TABLE 81

Gross National Product, USSR and USA, Alternative Projections (USA 1959 Output = 100)

	USA			USSR		
	with annual increase of—			with annual increase of—		
Year	2.0 percent	3.0 percent	4.0 percent	5.0 percent	6.0 percent	7.0 percent
1959	100.0	100.0	100.0	47.5	47.5	47.5
1965	112.6	119.4	126.5	63.6	67.4	71.2
1970	124.3	138.4	153.9	81.2	90.2	100.0
1975	137.3	160.5	187.3	103.7	120.6	140.2

cases that have been considered for the USSR are at all indicative of prospects for its total output, they also provide a basis to project the future course of the relation of total output in the two countries (see Table 81). All figures in Table 81 for both the USA and the USSR

dates in one country, so for comparisons between countries, each of the divergent indices that is obtained has an analytic interest of its own, and properly each should be considered in any attempt such as is to be made in the pages following to project the future relations between countries.

Because of its late appearance I regret it was not possible to take Dr. Bornstein's interesting paper fully into account in this study. As a preliminary to his comparison of total output in the two countries, Bornstein compiles data on the 1955 gross national product of the USSR by final use in "adjusted prices," that is, prevailing ruble prices less indirect taxes plus subsidies. Bornstein's results differ significantly from the corresponding figures compiled here for 1955 in terms of current ruble factor cost.

In the 1955 Soviet gross national product, according to my figures, household consumption (including communal services) constitutes 59.2 percent; government administration, 2.6; defense, 10.3; and gross investment, 27.9. According to Bornstein's calculations, the corresponding figures are for household consumption (including communal services), 58.9 percent; government administration, 2.9; defense, 13.0; and gross investment, 25.2. The divergencies at all points, I believe, are due chiefly to Bornstein's attempt to adjust Soviet budgetary defense data for omissions. In the absence of any detailed explanation of sources and methods, it is difficult to appraise the reliability of this aspect.

Having calculated the Soviet gross national product by final use in "adjusted prices," Bornstein translates the results into dollar prices of 1955. The measurements so derived tend to confirm the speculation advanced earlier (chapter 14) that in recent years the Russians have been allocating to investment a relatively large share not only of their total resources but also of the total goods and services produced.

Finally, by aggregating physical volume series on the net product of different industrial branches, Bornstein also compiles data on the "real" national product of the USSR for 1950–58. The results seem to correspond reasonably well to those derived in this study. The average rate of growth according to my calculation by use for 1950–55 is 7.6 percent and according to my calculation by origin, 7.3. For the 1955–58 period, no calculation was made by use. According to my calculation by origin, the average rate of growth is 7.0 percent. According to Bornstein's figures, the average rate of growth for 1950–55 is 6 to 7 percent and for 1955–58, 7 to 8 percent.

are expressed as percentages of the American gross national product of 1959. Of the three cases considered for the United States, the intermediate one assumes that in the future our output will grow at the same rate as has prevailed over long periods in the past.

The cited figures refer to total output. In per capita terms, the Russians are now producing about 40 percent as much goods and services as the United States. With Soviet output growing yearly by 6.0 percent and ours by 3.0 percent, the corresponding figure in 1975 might be on the order of 65 percent.

Under the five year plans, the Soviet consumer has experienced many vicissitudes, but in the upshot, per capita consumption during 1928–55 grew at these rates:

	Average annual rate of growth (percent)	
	1928–55, "effective years"	1950–55
With output valued at adjusted market prices of 1937	2.0	6.7
With output as composite, 1937 base	2.8	7.1

What are the prospects regarding this aspect? The trends in standards during 1955–58 are uncertain. Very possibly they have continued, as they did during 1950–55, to rise at a relatively high rate. As to the future, what might be said here I believe is already evident from what was said regarding total output. Depending on the future rate of growth of total output and on the investments required to assure it, per capita standards may possibly continue to increase at rates comparable to those prevailing in the recent past. Alternatively they may henceforth increase at slower tempos. In any event, the government should be able to assure continued progress. Under Stalin the Russian people paid heavily for an acceleration in the rate of growth of total output. Now that a high tempo has been achieved there should be no need for them to pay any comparable price in order to maintain the tempo of increase under Stalin's successors.

In 1955 the average Russian consumed about one fourth as much goods and services as the average American.[10] Evidently, even if Soviet standards continue to rise at relatively high tempos, they still will be far below those of the United States for many years to come.

Khrushchev is seeking as Stalin did to "overtake and surpass" the

[10] According to M. Bornstein, *op. cit.*, p. 385, aggregate consumption in the USSR in 1955 is 20.8 percent of that in the United States in the same year where the calculation is in terms of ruble prices and 39.0 percent of that in the United States where the calculation is in terms of dollar prices. The geometric average of the two ratios is 28.5 percent. Since in 1955 the Soviet population was some 19 percent larger than ours, the corresponding ratio for consumption per capita is 23.9 percent.

United States economically. This aim is to be achieved largely if not entirely by 1970. This will represent a "universal-historical victory for socialism in peaceful competition in the international arena." [11] Khrushchev's plans for the future may often be overoptimistic, but they have some basis in fact.

[11] Khrushchev is somewhat ambiguous regarding his long-term goals. Clearly, the Russians by 1970 are to outdo the United States regarding not only total but per capita industrial output. But declaredly this will "assure [them] the highest living standards in the world." Khrushchev may mean by this that in 1970 Soviet consumption per capita is also to exceed that of the United States but then again he may not. See *Pravda,* November 15, 1958; January 28, 1959.

ADDENDUM: ANNUAL DATA, 1948–55

The text presented the results of my calculations for the years 1928, 1937, 1940, 1944, 1950, and 1955. For the period 1948–55, data have also been compiled for years other than 1950 and 1955. Together with the corresponding SNIP figures in current rubles, these further results are set forth in Tables 82–86. For purposes of comparisons, I repeat the figures presented previously for 1950 and 1955.

In Table 82 are shown the SNIP data in current rubles as revised in this study. In Tables 83 and 84 are the data that have been compiled in terms of 1937 and 1950 rubles. For the most part, I simply extend here to 1948–49 and 1951–54 procedures used previously to derive data in the same terms for other years. Accordingly, the further results now set forth require no systematic explanation at this point. In any event, details on sources and methods are given in the appendices.

Data in terms of ruble factor costs of 1937 (Table 85) are again obtained through the reaggregation of physical volume series for different use categories in terms of the prevailing ruble prices of 1937. As before, the use categories considered are those listed in Table 23, while the necessary measures of "real" outlays in 1937 rubles for each category are

TABLE 82

Gross National Product of the USSR by Use, 1948–55, in Current Rubles
(billions of rubles)

Outlay category	1948	1949	1950	1951	1952	1953	1954		1955
Household purchases in retail markets									
In government and cooperative retail shops and restaurants	283.0	305.0	328.0	339.0	350.0	382.0	426.0		442.0
In collective farm markets	34.0	43.0	47.0	48.0	51.0	46.0	49.0		51.0
Total	317.0	348.0	375.0	387.0	401.0	428.0	475.0		493.0
Housing; services	44.7	47.9	50.4	52.2	55.9	58.4	64.0		65.7
Consumption of farm income in kind	55.0	58.0	61.0	54.0	61.0	65.0	74.0		85.0
Military subsistence	13.0	12.0	14.1	16.5	19.4	18.1	17.7		17.2
Household consumption outlays	429.7	465.9	500.5	509.7	537.3	569.5	630.7		660.9
Communal services									
Health care	23.4	24.5	25.0	25.7	26.8	27.4	31.9		34.0
Education	58.4	60.2	59.0	59.2	59.9	61.7	66.1		69.3
Other	1.5	1.5	1.5	1.5	1.5	1.5	1.7		1.7
Total	83.3	86.2	85.5	86.4	88.2	90.6	99.7		105.0
Government administration, including NKVD (OGPU; MVD and MGB)	39.1	36.5	36.9	37.0	36.3	29.9	29.6		27.6
Defense (as recorded in budget)[a]	64.3	77.2	80.8	91.9	106.6	105.8	99.8		105.4
Gross investment									
In fixed capital	92.0	156.8	156.5	174.8	176.5	195.7	224.5		239.6
Other	68.0	81.2	51.5	71.2	71.5	50.3	9.5	(23.5)	45.4
Total	160.0	238.0	208.0	246.0	248.0	246.0	234.0	(248.0)	285.0
Gross national product	776.4	903.8	911.7	971.0	1,016.4	1,041.8	1,093.8	(1,107.8)	1,183.9

[a] Exclusive of pensions to officers et al.

TABLE 83

Gross National Product of the USSR by Use in 1937 Prices, 1948–55
(billions of rubles)

Outlay category	1948	1949	1950	1951	1952	1953	1954	1955
Household purchases in retail markets								
In government and cooperative retail shops and restaurants	94.0	114.0	148.0	165.0	177.0	212.0	251.0	260.0
In collective farm market	10.0	17.0	23.0	23.0	25.0	24.0	23.0	23.0
Total	104.0	131.0	171.0	188.0	202.0	236.0	274.0	283.0
Housing; services	19.2	20.8	21.6	23.1	24.9	26.3	30.1	32.1
Consumption of farm income in kind	26.0	27.0	28.0	26.0	28.0	28.0	28.0	32.0
Military subsistence	4.1	4.3	6.0	7.6	9.3	9.6	9.9	9.6
Household consumption outlays	153.3	183.1	226.6	244.7	264.2	299.9	342.0	356.7
Communal services								
Health care	10.6	10.4	11.0	11.4	12.0	12.5	14.7	15.8
Education	26.9	24.2	24.6	24.7	24.9	25.5	27.0	28.1
Other	.7	.7	.7	.7	.7	.7	.7	.7
Total	38.2	35.3	36.3	36.8	37.6	38.7	42.4	44.6
Government administration, including NKVD (OGPU; MVD and MGB)	17.4	14.3	14.8	14.7	14.2	11.6	11.4	10.5
Defense (as recorded in budget)[a]	40.5	40.5	42.4	48.0	59.5	59.4	53.6	62.0
Gross investment								
In fixed capital	44.2	55.5	66.5	73.7	78.7	87.3	98.8	112.2
Other	34.9	33.1	24.2	35.1	35.6	25.2	2.5 (10.5)	23.8
Total	79.1	88.6	90.7	108.8	114.3	112.5	101.3 (109.3)	136.0
Gross national product	328.5	361.8	410.8	453.0	489.8	522.1	550.7 (558.7)	609.8

[a] Exclusive of pensions to officers et al.

TABLE 84

Gross National Product of the USSR by Use in 1950 Prices, 1948–55
(billions of rubles)

Outlay category	1948	1949	1950	1951	1952	1953	1954		1955
Household purchases in retail markets									
In government and cooperative retail shops and restaurants	210.0	254.0	328.0	365.0	389.0	473.0	567.0		585.0
In collective farm markets	20.0	35.0	47.0	47.0	51.0	49.0	47.0		47.0
Total	230.0	289.0	375.0	412.0	440.0	522.0	614.0		632.0
Housing; services	44.8	48.4	50.4	54.0	58.5	62.1	71.0		76.2
Consumption of farm income in kind	55.0	58.0	61.0	55.0	60.0	60.0	59.0		69.0
Military subsistence	9.6	10.1	14.1	17.8	21.9	22.6	23.3		22.6
Household consumption outlays	339.4	405.5	500.5	538.8	580.4	666.7	767.3		799.8
Communal services									
Health care	24.1	23.6	25.0	25.9	27.2	28.5	33.3		35.9
Education	65.3	58.3	59.0	59.0	59.5	60.7	64.5		66.9
Other	1.5	1.5	1.5	1.5	1.5	1.5	1.5		1.5
Total	90.9	83.4	85.5	86.4	88.2	90.7	99.3		104.3
Government administration, including NKVD (OGPU; MVD and MGB)	43.5	35.1	36.9	36.9	35.9	29.4	28.9		25.9
Defense (as recorded in budget)[a]	73.4	73.4	80.8	92.9	112.6	112.6	105.2		114.6
Gross investment									
In fixed capital	103.2	131.5	156.5	174.7	187.1	205.5	231.5		261.1
Other	73.0	70.7	51.5	73.2	76.5	52.6	4.2	(20.1)	49.2
Total	176.2	202.2	208.0	247.9	263.6	258.1	235.7	(251.6)	310.3
Gross national product	723.4	799.6	911.7	1,002.9	1,080.7	1,157.5	1,236.4	(1,252.3)	1,354.9

[a] Exclusive of pensions to officers et al.

TABLE 85

Gross National Product by Use, USSR, 1948–55, in Ruble Factor Cost of 1937
(billions of rubles)

Outlay category	1948	1949	1950	1951	1952	1953	1954	1955
Household purchases in retail markets								
In government and cooperative retail shops and restaurants	49.3	60.0	77.9	86.6	92.9	111.4	131.6	136.2
In collective farm markets	5.3	8.9	12.1	12.1	13.1	12.6	12.1	12.1
Total	54.6	68.9	90.0	98.7	106.0	124.0	143.7	148.3
Housing; services	18.9	20.6	21.3	22.9	24.6	26.0	29.8	31.6
Consumption of farm income in kind	29.1	30.2	31.4	29.1	31.4	31.4	31.4	35.8
Military subsistence	3.1	3.3	4.6	5.8	7.1	7.3	7.5	7.3
Household consumption outlays	105.7	123.0	147.3	156.5	169.1	188.7	212.4	223.0
Communal services	33.6	31.7	32.8	33.4	34.3	35.4	38.4	40.3
Government administration, including NKVD (OGPU; MVD and MGB)	16.2	13.3	13.8	13.7	13.2	10.8	10.6	9.8
Defense (as recorded in budget)[a]	40.0	40.0	41.7	46.9	58.2	58.1	52.2	60.9
Gross investment								
In fixed capital	44.9	56.2	67.3	74.4	79.7	88.3	100.0	113.6
Other	28.2	25.5	19.5	27.1	27.6	19.9	4.3 (10.0)	17.1
Total	73.1	81.7	86.8	101.5	107.3	108.2	104.3 (110.0)	130.7
Gross national product	268.6	289.7	322.4	352.0	382.1	401.2	417.9 (423.6)	464.7

[a] Exclusive of pensions to officers et al.

TABLE 86

Household Consumption Outlays, USSR, 1948–55, in Adjusted Market Prices of 1937 (billions of rubles)

Outlay category	1948	1949	1950	1951	1952	1953	1954	1955
Household purchases in retail market	104.0	131.0	171.0	188.0	202.0	236.0	274.0	283.0
Housing; services	45.8	49.2	51.0	54.2	58.0	61.0	69.0	73.2
Consumption of farm income in kind	57.8	61.0	64.3	57.5	63.6	60.6	60.4	75.0
Military subsistence	4.1	4.3	6.0	7.6	9.3	9.6	9.9	9.6
Household consumption outlays	211.7	245.5	292.3	307.3	332.9	367.2	413.3	440.8

taken from the prior calculation of national income in these terms. In the reaggregation, the index numbers of "real" outlays for each category are assigned a weight corresponding to the volume of outlays on it in 1937 in terms of ruble factor cost. The weights, therefore, are the same as those used previously in calculating national income in terms of ruble factor costs of 1937, that is, those in Table 23.

Similarly, in calculating household consumption outlays in adjusted market prices of 1937 (Table 86), I again aggregate physical volume series for the use categories listed in Table 37. The index numbers of physical volume series used for the years now considered are of the same sort and are obtained by the same methods as those employed previously, while the weights applied in aggregating them are those applied in the compilation of the series on household consumption outlays in adjusted market prices in Table 37.

Annual data compiled by similar methods on the gross national product in terms of 1950 ruble factor cost and on household consumption in terms of adjusted market prices of 1950 are not here reproduced.

APPENDIX A

Household Purchases in Retail Markets in Constant Prices

Purchases in Government and Cooperative Shops and Restaurants, 1937–55

Scope of category. Data compiled on this category for 1937–55 are intended to represent the volume of household purchases of consumers' goods from government and cooperative trade outlets, including such places as retail shops of all sorts, restaurants and (insofar as they are patronized by households) warehouses, and supply bases. In calculating the volume of such purchases in terms of constant rubles, I take as a point of departure corresponding data in terms of current rubles that were derived from and are broadly similar in scope to statistics that the Soviet government has published on the retail sales of government and cooperative trade outlets. The official statistics cover sales to households by all trade outlets, but they also embrace diverse sales by the trade networks to enterprises and institutions. During much if not all the period studied, procurement of foods by certain organizations (primarily of a "social-cultural" sort) from such places as restaurants, shops, and warehouses were reported as retail sales; purchases of some other consumers' goods (furniture and office supplies, for example) by most enterprises and institutions, and last but not least, collective farm purchases of producers' goods from practically any source were also classified as retail sales. On the basis of incomplete information, sales to enterprises and institutions have been excluded from the current ruble series considered here. The latter series is also supposed to omit household purchases of building materials and farm producers' goods that are included in the official statistics for all years; and repair services and certain custom work that are included in the official statistics beginning in 1951.

The use of a current ruble series so restricted in scope will be seen to be appropriate here when it is considered that in the present study retail sales to institutions either become a production expense or appear under other final use categories (for example, communal services and government); similarly, household purchases of building materials are here treated as investment and household purchases of farm producers' goods as a production expense. Repair services and custom work of the sort that began to be included in the official data in 1951 are classified in the present study under "Housing; services."

Since 1951, the Soviet government has also classified as retail sales, sales of houses to private owners and certain retail sales of produce by state farms and farms subordinate to industrial enterprises, et cetera. The magnitudes of these items are believed to be very small, and for practical purposes, the rather arbitrary adjustment made for repairs and custom work may be considered as allowing for them as well. So far as concerns retail sales by state and subsidiary farms, of course, these might properly be included here in household purchases, if only they could be included throughout, but this is not feasible.

Late in 1953, "commission sales" were instituted as a new trade channel in the USSR. These are sales to consumers that are made by consumers' cooperatives on behalf of collective farms and farmers. Such sales are included in the official data on retail sales by government and cooperative trade outlets. In the present study, they are classified instead as collective farm market sales.

Soviet sources are not fully clear regarding the coverage of the official data on retail sales during the period studied. Apparently, the government has sought throughout to increase the coverage of its data, and there are reasons to think it may have succeeded in doing so in respect of still other household purchases of a very minor sort in addition to those just described. The scope of the current ruble data used here would vary correspondingly.

Both the official data and my current ruble series include throughout sales of second-hand clothing and the like that are made by government and cooperative shops. For present purposes, of course, such sales properly should be omitted.

On the scope of household purchases in government and cooperative shops and restaurants and of the official series on retail sales, see *SNIP-28–48; SNIP-49–55;* Pisarev, Riauzov, and Titel'baum, 1938, chapters iii-v; Tenenbaum and Riauzov, 1939, chapters iv, v, xiii; Margolin, 1939, pp. 100–102; Margolin, 1940, pp. 88–89; Riauzov and Titel'baum, 1947, chapters iv-vi; Riauzov and Titel'baum, 1951, chapters iv-vi; Riauzov and Titel'baum, 1956, chapters iv-vi.

Purchases in terms of 1937 rubles. The elements in the calculation of household purchases of consumers' goods in government and cooperative outlets in terms of 1937 rubles are shown in Table A-1, columns (1), (2), and (3). In column (1), the data on household purchases in terms of current

TABLE A-1

Calculation of Household Purchases in Government and Cooperative Shops and Restaurants, in 1937 Prices, USSR, 1937–55

Year	Household purchases, current prices (bil. rubles) (1)	Official prices, Chapman Formula (5) (1937 = 100) (2)	Household purchases, 1937 rubles (bil. rubles) (1) ÷ (2) (3)	Official prices, Chapman Formula (6) (1937 = 100) (4)	Household purchases in terms of "given year" price structure and 1937 average price level (1) ÷ (4) (5)
1937	110	100	110	100	110
1940	160	126	127	132	121
1944	111	(143; 330; 1850)[a]	68.0	(143; 330; 1850)[a]	68.0
1948	283	300	94.0	333	85.0
1949	305	(268)	114	—	—
1950	328	(222)	148	—	—
1951	339	(206)	165	—	—
1952	350	198	177	216	162
1953	382	(180)	212	—	—
1954	426	170	251	180	237
1955	442	(170)	260	—	—

[a] Ration prices, increased rural prices, and commercial shop prices, respectively.

rubles for 1937–48 are from *SNIP-28–48*. Those for 1949–55 are from *SNIP-49–55*. The data have the scope described above.

In Table A-1, column (2), I show outside parentheses the index numbers of the prices prevailing in government and cooperative shops that Dr. Janet Chapman has computed according to Formula (5). See Chapman, *Real Wages,* Appendix E, particularly her series on "official prices, given year weights." For 1944, the index numbers in parentheses were obtained from the same source. They refer, respectively, to the prices prevailing for ration goods distributed mainly in urban localities, the higher prices prevailing for manufactured goods distributed in rural localities, and the astronomic prices charged in the so-called "commercial shops," where scarce goods might be purchased without ration coupons. All three index numbers are very crude, and cannot readily be identified with any conventional index number formula.

In Table A-1, column (2), I also show in parentheses the results of an attempt to extend Dr. Chapman's calculations to years of interest here that she does not cover. The manner in which this was done may be explained by reference to Table A-2. In Table A-2, the Soviet official index numbers of retail prices prevailing before and after the annual spring price cuts are calculated from corresponding figures based on the fourth quarter 1947 in *Sovtorg,* p. 132. The corresponding annual averages are calculated by me from these indices and quarterly and monthly data on retail sales in *ibid.,* pp. 29–30. The annual average for 1955 is taken to be the same as that for 1954. See *ibid.,* p. 132. In Table A-2, I again list outside parentheses Dr.

TABLE A-2

Soviet Official and Chapman Index Numbers of Retail Prices, 1948–55
(1948 = 100)

	Soviet official	Chapman Formula (5)
1948	100	100
1949		
Precut	100	
Postcut	85.5	
Average	(87.7)	(89.5)
1950		
Precut	85.5	
Postcut	68.7	
Average	(71.1)	(73.9)
1951		
Precut	68.7	
Postcut	63.9	
Average	(64.6)	(68.5)
1952		
Precut	63.9	
Postcut	60.2	
Average	(61.1)	66.0
1953		
Precut	60.2	
Postcut	54.2	
Average	(55.5)	(60.0)
1954		
Precut	54.2	
Postcut	51.8	
Average	(52.4)	56.7
1955	(52.4)	(56.7)

Chapman's Formula (5) indices, but now with 1948 as 100. Taking account of the changing ratios of Dr. Chapman's indices to the corresponding official indices, I also extend Dr. Chapman's series to the years 1949–51, 1953, and 1955. The Formula (5) indices for these years in the second column of data in Table A-1, are calculated on this basis.

In their statistical manuals, Soviet writers appear to favor the given-year weighted aggregative formula for price indices, but the question remains whether the indices in *Sovtorg,* which are expressed in terms of the fourth quarter 1947 = 100 percent, were originally computed on this base or whether alternatively the published series was obtained by shifting to this base indices originally computed on some other bases. I suspect the latter, and more particularly that the original data were obtained as annual links, but this is uncertain. On the Soviet approach to index number calculations, see Riauzov and Titel'baum, 1947, pp. 143 ff.; Petrov, 1952, pp. 402 ff.; Gozulov, 1953, pp. 356 ff.

To come back to Table A-1, the data on household purchases in terms of 1937 rubles in column (3) are obtained by dividing column (1) by column (2). For 1944, the different index numbers listed are applied separately to the corresponding household sales, as follows: urban trade, subject to ration prices, 77.5 billion rubles; rural sales, subject to ration prices, 14.0; rural sales, subject to higher prices, 13.5; and commercial sales, 6.0. All sales amounted to 111.0 billion rubles. Essentially, I rely here on Chapman, *Real Wages,* Appendix E.

Purchases in terms of 1950 rubles. I first calculate household purchases in government and cooperative shops and restaurants in terms of 1952 ruble prices for the years 1937, 1940, 1948, 1952, and 1954. See the first column of data in Table A-3. The 1952 figure is taken directly from the first column of Table A-1. For the other four years, these data are obtained as follows: in *Real Wages,* Dr. Chapman compiles Formula (5) price indices for twenty-two categories of consumers' goods, for example, such items as grain products and legumes, meat and poultry, textiles, and garments. She also computes for different years the percentage shares of retail sales to households that these products represent. See her Appendix E. From the percentage shares, I compute corresponding absolute data on sales of different categories by reference to the figures on the total volume of household purchases in all groups in Table A-1, column (1). Deflating the sales data for a given category by the corresponding Formula (5) price indices, I obtain measures of the volume of sales for that category in terms of 1937 prices expressed in terms of 1952 = 100. This computation is repeated for each of the twenty-two categories. Dr. Chapman's index numbers of prices for different categories for 1952 and 1954 are for price-cut years, I translate these to a calendar year basis by use of data in *Sovtorg,* p. 132. Finally, the twenty-two series are then aggregated in terms of their respective sales volumes in 1952.

While the resultant series is designated as being in terms of 1952 rubles, evidently it is in terms of mixed weights. Within each of the twenty-two categories, individual products are aggregated in terms of their 1937 prices. The resultant twenty-two physical volume series are weighted by their 1952 sales values.

In relative terms, the series obtained in this way is taken to represent the "real" volume of household purchases in 1950 prices. Corresponding absolute figures in 1950 prices, therefore, are obtained simply by applying to the entire series in the first column of data in Table A-3 the following factor:

Retail sales in 1950 in terms of 1950 prices ÷ retail sales in 1950 in terms of 1952 prices = 328.0 ÷ 295.0 = 111.2 percent. The results appear in the second column of data in Table A-3.

Dr. Chapman compiles index numbers of prices and data on percentage shares in retail sales for the 22-commodity categories for 1937, 1940, 1948,

TABLE A-3

Calculation of Household Purchases in Government and Cooperative Shops, Alternative Price Weights, USSR, 1937–55

Year	Household purchases, 1952 prices (billion rubles)	Household purchases, 1950 prices (billion rubles)
1937	223	248
1940	247	275
1944	—	(147)
1948	189	210
1949	228	254
1950	295	328
1951	328	365
1952	350	389
1953	425	473
1954	510	567
1955	526	585

1952, and 1954. Accordingly, the calculation described above could be made only for these years. In order to complete the series in terms of 1950 rubles, I assume that from 1940 to 1944 the percentage change in household purchases in these terms is the same as in terms of 1937 rubles. Similarly, the magnitudes of household purchases in terms of 1950 rubles in 1949–51, 1953, and 1955 are interpolated and extrapolated from the magnitudes de-

TABLE A-4

Household Purchases in Government and Cooperative Shops, Alternative Price Weights, USSR, 1937–55 (1937 = 100)

Year	In 1952 prices: Table A-3 (1)	In 1937 prices: Table A-1 (2)	In terms of "given year" price structure: Table A-1 (3)
1937	100	100	100
1940	111	115	110
1944	—	62	62
1948	85	86	77
1949	102	104	—
1950	132	135	—
1951	147	150	—
1952	157	161	147
1953	191	193	—
1954	229	228	215
1955	236	236	—

rived for other years. In this computation, the trends in household purchases in terms of 1937 rubles serve as a benchmark.

In Table A-4, column (1), the series compiled in terms of "1952 rubles" is set forth again with 1937 as 100 percent. These index numbers may usefully be compared with two alternative series that have been derived on the "real" volume of household purchases in government and cooperative outlets. In Table A-4, column (2), I repeat in percentage terms the measures in 1937 rubles given in Table A-1, column (3). In Table A-4, column (3), are set forth corresponding percentage figures obtained by using as a deflator Dr. Chapman's Formula (6) price indices. See Table A-1, columns (4) and (5). In effect, these index numbers reflect for each comparison with 1937 the price structure of the "given year." See chapter 3, note 2. Although such a series is difficult to interpret, the comparison between 1937 and 1952 is of special interest, since it is indeed in terms of 1952 prices. The difference between the index number for 1952 in column (3) and that in column (1), therefore, serves as a measure of the degree to which the column (1) series reflects the 1937 as distinct from the 1952 price structure. As has been argued in the text, however, the failure of the column (1) series fully to reflect 1952 prices may be to the good here, since the ultimate concern is to obtain a series in terms of 1950 prices. Computed as it is in terms of mixed 1937–1952 weights, the column (1) series probably is closer to a true 1950 weighted series than it would be if it reflected the 1952 price structure alone. In any event, considering all three series in Table A-4, we may at least conclude that shifts in base year must be of only limited consequence in the period studied.

Purchases in Collective Farm Markets, 1937–55

Scope of category. This refers to household purchases in collective farm markets in the USSR. The current ruble series that is deflated is derived from Soviet official data or corresponding estimates on the volume of sales in collective farm markets. The official figures are inclusive of sales to institutions and exclusive of the so-called "commission sales" that were organized in late 1953. The current ruble figures that I deflate are supposed to be exclusive of the former and inclusive of the latter, but otherwise they correspond in scope to the official data. This means that they include some household purchases of producers goods, especially livestock, which properly should be omitted from our calculation at this point. Official figures available for 1940 and 1950–55 are said to refer to "extra rural" (*vnederevenskii*) trade. Apparently, such trade is understood to include village sales by farmers to the nonfarm population. The current ruble data used here for 1940 and 1950–55 are believed to correspond in scope to the official figures for these years. For 1937, the current ruble figure considered also represents "extrarural" trade but whether and to what extent village sales to the nonfarm population are included is not known.

On the scope of household purchases in collective farm markets, see

SNIP-28–48; SNIP-49–55; J. T. Whitman, *Soviet Studies,* April 1956; J. Karcz, RAND RM-1930, Appendix B.

Purchases in terms of 1937 and 1950 rubles. The elements of the calculation in terms of 1937 rubles are shown in Table A-5. The figures on household purchases in current rubles are from *SNIP-28–48* and *SNIP-49–55.* For 1950–55, Soviet official index numbers of collective farm market prices have been published with 1940 as 100 percent. See *Sovtorg,* p. 182. In a manner explained in *Real Wages,* chapter vi, Appendix E, Dr. Chapman has extended the official index numbers to obtain the series shown in Table A-5. In column (3) the figures on household purchases in 1937 rubles are obtained by dividing column (1) by column (2). In index number form, the resultant series is also taken to represent household purchases in 1950 rubles. Accordingly, the corresponding absolute magnitudes in 1950 rubles are obtained as the product of column (3) and the following expression: purchases in 1950 in 1950 prices ÷ purchases in 1950 in 1937 prices = 47.0 ÷ 23.0 = 204.3 percent.

TABLE A-5

Calculation of Household Purchases in Collective Farm Markets, in 1937 Prices, USSR, 1937–55

Year	Household purchases, current prices (billion rubles) (1)	Collective farm market prices Chapman-Soviet official (1937 = 100) (2)	Household purchases, 1937 prices (billion rubles) (1) ÷ (2) (3)
1937	16.0	100	16.0
1940	26.0	200	13.0
1944	30.0	1850	1.6
1948	34.0	350	10.0
1949	43.0	250	17.0
1950	47.0	208	23.0
1951	48.0	210	23.0
1952	51.0	208	25.0
1953	46.0	194	24.0
1954	49.0	214	23.0
1955	51.0	222	23.0

Purchases in All Retail Markets, 1928

Scope of the category. The current ruble figure that is deflated (12.10 billion rubles) represents the sum of sales to households of industrial goods and extravillage retail sales of agricultural products, both exclusive of producers' goods and building materials, 10.44 billion rubles; restaurant sales, 0.66; and allowance for cash intravillage sales of agricultural produce, exclusive of farm producers' goods, 1.00. As with the corresponding totals compiled for later years, therefore, the cited figure for 1928 is exclusive of institutional purchases and of household purchases of producers' goods and building materials. For 1928, all producers' goods are excluded, but for practical purposes a comparable result is achieved for 1937–55 by the exclusion of agricultural producers' goods. The inclusion of an allowance for intravillage sales of agricultural produce in 1928 seems to be in conflict with the practice adopted for 1937–55, since for the latter years intrarural sales on the collective farm market are excluded. For 1937–55, however, rural sales of the government and cooperative shops are included in total household purchases, and in the course of time these shops very likely took over some of the intravillage trade that formerly was conducted privately. Moreover, at least for 1940 and after, village collective farm market sales to the nonfarm population are classified in Soviet statistics as "extrarural" and hence also find their way into my retail trade figures. As it stands, therefore, the current ruble figure on household purchases that is considered for 1928 is perhaps more comparable to the corresponding figures considered for 1937–55 than it would be if the intravillage sales were omitted. In any event, because of the nature of the underlying calculations, all intrarural trade in the USSR in 1928 is accounted for in this study under either household purchases or farm income in kind. This seems to be largely true also for later years, although the later data are more difficult to interpret in this regard than are those for 1928. See below, Appendix C.

On the scope of household purchases in 1928, see *SNIP-28,* pp. 114 ff.; *SNIP-28–48.*

Purchases in terms of 1937, 1950, and 1928 rubles. The current ruble figure that is deflated, 12.10 billion rubles, is from *SNIP-28–48.* For purposes of translating this in terms of 1937 rubles, I deflate by the Formula (5) index for retail prices in all markets in 1928 that is compiled in Chapman's *Real Wages,* Appendix E: 11.5 (1937 = 100).

The calculation in terms of 1950 rubles is made in essentially the same way as those in the same terms made above for the period 1937–55. Dr. Chapman compiles Formula (5) price indices for 1928 for each of twenty-two categories of consumers' goods and corresponding percentage data on the shares that the different products represent of household purchases in all categories. By reference to the figure above for the latter total (12.10 billion rubles), corresponding absolute figures may be computed on household purchases in the different categories. Applying Dr. Chapman's Formula (5) price indices to these figures, measures are compiled on the volume of sales in the different categories in terms of 1937 rubles. Restated in index number form with 1952 as 100 (the corresponding measures for 1952 in terms of 1937 prices were compiled above), the measures are aggregated in terms of the 1952 sales values for the different categories. Finally, the results are translated in terms of 1950 rubles in the manner described above.

In *Real Wages,* the figures Dr. Chapman compiles on the structure of household purchases in retail markets in 1928 refer to urban workers' purchases only. In the foregoing calculation, I use corresponding unpublished data that Dr. Chapman has compiled relating to all household purchases, including those in rural localities. Dr. Chapman's price indices for the twenty-two categories of consumers' goods refer to official prices, Moscow. For all categories of goods taken together, the index of official prices, Moscow, is 107.8 percent of the corresponding index of all retail prices in Soviet retail markets generally. Therefore, the magnitude that is obtained by the calculation just described for household purchases in all retail markets in 1928 in terms of 1950 rubles is finally increased by 7.8 percent.

To recapitulate, household purchases in all retail markets in 1928 are found to total 196.0 billion rubles in terms of 1952 prices. In terms of 1950 rubles, this comes to 218.0 billion rubles. This reflects the use of index numbers of official prices, Moscow, in deriving the component measures of "real" household purchases for the twenty-two categories of consumers' goods. Allowing for the average difference between these prices and prices in all markets, household purchases in terms of 1950 rubles total 235.0 billion rubles.

Purchases in All Retail Markets, 1937

Scope of category. This comprises household purchases in government and cooperative shops and restaurants and in collective farm markets.

Purchases in terms of 1928 prices. The total purchases in current rubles in 1937 amounted to 126.0 billion rubles. See Tables A-1 and A-5. As a deflator, I use the inverse of a Formula (6) index of retail prices in all markets in 1928 (with 1937 as 100) that Dr. Chapman compiles in *Real Wages,* Appendix E. Thus, applying Formula (6), Dr. Chapman finds that retail prices in all markets in 1928 averaged 16.8 percent of 1937. Household purchases in 1937, therefore, amount to 21.20 (that is, 126.0 × 0.168) billion rubles in terms of 1928 prices.

APPENDIX B

Housing and Services in Constant Prices

Housing

Scope of category. This represents the total of the rents paid by households on government housing and of the imputed rents earned on private urban and rural housing. The data also include imputed rents earned on "cooperative" housing for years when the cooperatives functioned (that is, up to 1937). Imputed rents are supposed to represent the value, at the average rental charged on government housing, of the government housing equivalent of the occupied space.

Rents in current rubles. In the SNIP calculations, rents are imputed to nongovernmental housing without any allowance being made for differences in the character of the different types of housing. As a preliminary to my computation of actual and imputed rents in constant rubles, I felt it in order to revise the SNIP data to allow for such differences in quality. The elements of the revision appear in Table B-1.

In columns (1), (2), and (3), the data on the stocks of different kinds of housing in million square meters are from *SNIP-28–48* and *SNIP-49–55*. The figures on public housing include cooperative as well as government housing. The figures on the total housing stock in column (4) are obtained by totaling columns (1), (2), and (3). In column (5) I show the corresponding figures in terms of government housing equivalent. These data are derived by applying to the different kinds of housing the following adjustment factors: for one square meter of government and cooperaitve housing, 1.0; of urban private housing, 0.6; and of rural private housing, 0.4.

The average value of a square meter of private urban housing in 1936 was about one-third of the average value of a square meter of public housing. See the data in Kobalevskii, 1940, pp. 106–107; however, Kobalevskii is not especially explicit about the nature of the values in question. Very

TABLE B-1

Housing Space, and Actual and Imputed Rent, in Current Rubles, USSR, 1928–55

Year	Public housing (mil. m²) (1)	Private housing, urban (mil. m²) (2)	Private housing, rural (mil. m²) (3)	All housing (mil. m²) (4)	All housing, public housing equivalent (mil. m²) (5)	Assumed rental rate (rubles per m²) (6)	Actual and imputed rent (bil. rubles) (7)
1928	76	87	375	538	278	3.09	0.86
1937	140	85	350	575	331	8.50	2.8
1940	180	100	400	680	400	12.00	4.8
1944	135	80	350	565	323	15.00	4.8
1948	212	111	380	703	431	15.84	6.8
1949	222	115	380	717	443	15.84	7.0
1950	232	119	380	731	455	15.84	7.2
1951	244	123	380	747	470	15.84	7.4
1952	255	128	380	763	484	15.84	7.7
1953	267	133	380	780	499	15.84	7.9
1954	281	138	380	799	516	15.84	8.2
1955	295	143	380	818	533	15.84	8.4

likely they are intended to represent depreciated 1936 reproduction costs. According to data compiled in Berliner, CEIR, A-47, pp. 48–59, especially in recent years private urban housing might contrast more favorably with public housing than Kobalevskii's data indicate if the comparison were made in terms of new construction costs. In any case, I felt that the comparative rental value of the detached private homes would be markedly higher than their comparative depreciated reproduction costs. The coefficient applied to private rural housing (on the eve of the plans, predominantly log houses with thatched roofs and no amenities to speak of) is quite arbitrary.

In column (6) in Table B-1, the assumed rental rates are intended to represent the average rental rates charged for government-owned housing. See *SNIP-40–48, SNIP-28–48,* and *SNIP-49–55.* For 1928, the average rental rate charged for government housing was taken to be 2.90 rubles per m². In column (6), the somewhat higher figure that is cited represents the average rental value of all housing in terms of its government housing equivalent. In computing the average, I follow the SNIP calculations in assuming that half of the urban private housing space (43 million m²) was rented at a rate of 2.90 rubles per actual square meter, which is equal to a rent of 4.83 rubles per square meter in terms of public housing equivalent. All other space is assigned a value of 2.90 rubles per square meter in terms of public housing equivalent. Column (7) is a product of column (5) and column (6).

Rents in constant rubles. Actual and imputed rent in terms of 1937 rubles is obtained as the product of the total housing stock in terms of government housing equivalent (Table B-1, column (5)) and the average rental rate for government housing in 1937, that is, 8.50 rubles per m². The corresponding data in terms of 1950 and 1928 rubles are calculated similarly.

Utilities, et cetera

Scope of category. Reference is made here to the outlays of households for diverse services, including electricity, water, and other utilities; transportation and entertainment; tuition fees; personal services, such as domestics and barbering; repair services and custom work; and custom processing of farm products. On the scope of this category, see the SNIP studies and the sources cited therein.

Utilities, et cetera, in constant prices. The elements of the calculation of this category in 1937 rubles appear in Tables B-2 and B-3. In Table B-2,

TABLE B-2

Indicators of Selected Services Consumed by Households, USSR, 1928–55 (1937 = 100)

Year	Railway passenger kilometers	Electric power for municipal services (kw hours)	Urban water consumption	Urban transport, passengers carried	Movie attendance, USSR
1928	27.0	19.2	30.1	28.6	25.9
1937	100	100	100	100	100
1940	108	131	144	117	101
1944	73	119	123	56	70
1948	82	167	184	91	113
1949	89	—	—	—	—
1950	97	206	208	112	131
1951	108	—	—	—	147
1952	119	298	239	143	154
1953	128	—	—	—	—
1954	142	392	271	186	266
1955	156	—	293	213	285

are shown the various indicators that Dr. Chapman compiles in *Real Wages,* Appendix B. Serial data in the latter source, for selected years, are here extended to other years partly on the basis of unpublished calculations by Dr. Chapman. The figures for electricity probably include power-supplied street lighting and possibly other municipal services as well as household consumption. Similarly, the data on water consumption probably represents total urban consumption for all purposes. The series on urban transportation is intended to represent the number of passengers carried by trains, trolley-buses, and autobuses.

In Table B-3, the constant ruble data on household outlays on each of the different services listed are obtained as the product of the household outlays in 1937 on the service in question and corresponding indicators of the trends in the physical volume of such outlays over time. Soviet households spent in 1937 13.5 billion rubles on services classified here as "Utilities,

TABLE B-3

Selected Services Consumed by Households, in 1937 Prices, USSR, 1928–55 (billions of rubles)

Year	All specified services (1)	Railway passenger services (2)	Electricity (3)	Water (4)	Urban transport (5)	Entertainment (6)	Repairs, custom work, et cetera (7)
1928	7.3	0.81	0.13	0.09	0.72	0.52	5.0
1937	13.5	3.0	0.7	0.3	2.5	2.0	5.0
1940	14.4	3.2	0.9	0.4	2.9	2.0	5.0
1944	9.2	2.2	0.8	0.4	1.4	1.4	3.0
1948	13.9	2.5	1.2	0.6	2.3	2.3	5.0
1949	(14.6)	2.7	—	—	—	—	5.0
1950	15.3	2.9	1.4	0.6	2.8	2.6	5.0
1951	(16.7)	3.2	—	—	—	2.9	5.0
1952	18.1	3.6	2.1	0.7	3.6	3.1	5.0
1953	(19.4)	3.8	—	—	—	—	5.0
1954	22.7	4.3	2.7	0.8	4.6	5.3	5.0
1955	(24.6)	4.7	—	0.9	5.3	5.7	5.0

et cetera." See *SNIP-28–48*. According to an unpublished memorandum of James Blackman, railway passenger revenues totaled 2.8 billion rubles in 1937. I round this to 3.0 billion rubles in order to allow for miscellaneous railway passenger charges, particularly baggage charges. This leaves 10.5 billion rubles for household expenditures on other services classified here as "Utilities, et cetera." Of their total outlays on these remaining services in 1937, Soviet workers may have spent about 60 percent on electricity, water, urban transportation, and entertainment. See Chapman, *Real Wages,* Appendix B. I assume that for the population generally, the outlays on urban electric power, water, and transportation and on entertainment constituted a smaller share of total outlays on the "Utilities, et cetera," exclusive of railway transport, say 5.5 billion rubles. At the same time, the breakdown of this total between the different services covered may be judged from Dr. Chapman's data on their comparative importance in workers' budgets in 1937.

In Table B-3, for each service listed other than "repairs, custom work, et cetera," the trends in "real" household outlays over time are taken as given by the corresponding indicators in Table B-2. Motion picture attendance is allowed to represent entertainment generally. "Real" household outlays on "repairs, custom work, et cetera" are assumed constant throughout the period studied, except during 1944 when they fall sharply with household consumption generally. In Table B-3, column (1), figures on all specified services for the years 1928–48, 1950, 1952, and 1954 are obtained by totaling columns (2) to (7). For other years, the corresponding totals are obtained by interpolation and extrapolation.

In Table B-4, I show the elements in the alternative calculation of house-

TABLE B-4

Calculation of Household Outlays on "Utilities, et cetera," by Deflation

Year	Outlays in current prices (billion rubles) (1)	Services prices, Chapman (1937 = 100) (2)	Outlays in 1937 prices (billion rubles) (3)
1928	1.79	33.8	5.3
1937	13.5	100	13.5
1940	19.8	142	13.9
1944	13.5	179	7.5
1948	34.8	220	15.8
1952	42.2	235	18.0
1954	48.8	217	22.5

hold outlays on "Utilities, et cetera" in 1937 prices by deflation. The figures in column (1) are from *SNIP-28–48* and *SNIP-49–55*. I also list index numbers of the prices of services, excluding housing, which Dr. Chapman has compiled by use of Formula (5). These indices are unpublished components of index numbers of prices of services, including housing, which are derived in *Real Wages*. Data in column (3) are obtained by dividing figures in column (1) by those in column (2).

For purposes of calculating "Utilities, et cetera" in terms of 1950 and 1928 prices, I assume that in index number form "real" household outlays in terms of these prices are the same as they are in terms of 1937 prices. The index numbers with 1950 taken as 100 are applied to the 1950 household outlays on "Utilities, et cetera" of 38.2 billion rubles. With 1928 as 100, they are applied to the 1928 total outlays of 1.79 billion rubles. On the outlays of households on "Utilities, et cetera" in current rubles, see *SNIP-28–48* and *SNIP-49–55*.

TABLE B-5

Trade Union and Other Dues and Average Money Wages, USSR, 1928–55

Year	Dues in current prices (billion rubles)	Average money wages, USSR (1937 = 100)	Dues in 1937 prices (billion rubles)
1928	0.14	22.4	0.63
1937	1.1	100	1.1
1940	1.6	122	1.3
1944	1.8	139	1.3
1948	3.1	195	1.6
1949	5	203	2.4
1950	5	209	2.4
1951	5	216	2.4
1952	6	223	2.7
1953	6	227	2.7
1954	7	233	3.0
1955	7	237	3.0

Trade Union and Other Dues

In Table B-5, the figures on household payments of dues to trade unions and other organizations in current rubles are taken from *SNIP-28–48* and *SNIP-49–55*. Indices of average money wages, which are used here as a deflator, are also shown. On the cited indices, which represent average wages after adjustment for changes in working hours, see Appendix H. "Real" outlays are assumed constant during 1949–51 and during 1952–53, although the deflation indicates they declined slightly. Percentage changes in trade union and other dues in terms of 1950 and 1928 rubles are assumed to be the same as those in terms of 1937 rubles.

APPENDIX C

"Real" Farm Income in Kind

Scope of category. Broadly speaking, this category is intended to represent the total amount of farm produce consumed by its producers. For the period 1937–55, the magnitudes involved are generally computed by aggregating the amounts of different products available for human consumption that remain to the farm population after allocations to production expense and marketings. As given in Soviet sources, or estimated, marketings data for 1937–55 reflect the Soviet statistical practice of the time. Soviet sources are not entirely explicit about the nature of this practice, but the marketings data that have been compiled nevertheless are known to refer primarily to extrarural marketings, and to omit throughout most intrarural sales. Such sales, therefore, must be included in my data on income in kind. On the other hand, marketings include and income in kind omits government and other procurements used to supply rural government and cooperative retail shops. Similarly, the marketings include and income in kind omits supplies (mainly grain) made available from centralized procurements for "return sales" to rural deficit areas. Finally, at least for the fifties, the marketings include and income in kind omits rural sales by collective farmers to the nonfarm population, for example, industrial workers and teachers.

Although the Soviet concept of marketings appears to have been broadly stable since the mid-thirties, the concept currently in use differs in important particulars from one that is reflected in official marketings data of the late twenties. In the case of the basic data appearing in *KTS 1929–30,* for example, reference is as it was to be later to extrarural sales, but apparently "return sales" to rural deficit areas are omitted, at least in the case of grain. As with the marketings data for recent years, intrarural trade among farmers is also omitted, but so also are rural farm sales to the nonfarm population. Moreover, some of the intrarural trade of the late twenties was to some extent an antecedent for the government procurements that later were used to supply local rural government and cooperative retail shops. In these ways too, therefore, the 1928 definition of marketings tends to be more restrictive than that of later years. It follows also that when calculated from official marketings data, income in kind in 1928 tends to be inflated in relation to the magnitude obtained for this category by our calculations for later years.

Therefore, although I make such a calculation for 1928, I rely instead on an alternative computation. This involves the inflation of the SNIP figure on farm income in kind in 1928 in terms of current rubles. The SNIP figure is derived from Soviet global data in monetary terms on the output and disposition of farm goods. Such Soviet data, it is true, reflect the narrow official concept of marketings of the time, but the *SNIP-28* computation adjusts for this by assuming that one-half of the officially reported intrarural trade in farm produce is for cash; moreover, this share is treated as marketings and omitted from farm income in kind. It is not possible to equate such intrarural cash sales to the "return sales" and other trade that are omitted from the official marketings data of 1928 and included in the corresponding figures of later years, but the *SNIP-28* computation is believed to yield a result more nearly comparable to our estimates for 1937–55 than does that obtained by the method of aggregation.

Calculated by the method of aggregation, farm income in kind in 1928 comes to 39.9 billion rubles in terms of 1937 prices. Calculated by inflating the SNIP figure for 1928, farm income in kind comes to 34.5 billion rubles. The intrarural cash sales that are considered as marketings in the latter calculation, however, amount to 5.4 billion rubles in 1937 prices. Moreover, an equal amount of intrarural barter sales is considered as income in kind in both computations. The practical import of any differences in scope between the 1928 figure on income in kind that is relied on and the data compiled for later years should be judged in this light.

Even though my data on farm income in kind vary in scope in different years, this need not lead to any corresponding variation in the scope of household consumption generally. This is because the figures on farm income in kind are more or less complementary to the data compiled in this study on retail sales. For 1928, for example, all intrarural trade in farm products (other than producers' goods) is classified either as retail trade or as farm income in kind. While the division between these two categories is arbitrary, total household consumption is unaffected. Similarly, my income-in-kind data for 1937–55 appear to include much intrarural collective farm market trade, but such trade is omitted from my data on retail sales. Again, government and other procurements to supply rural government and cooperative retail outlets are omitted from income in kind but included in marketings.

The concern here is to compute consumption (as distinct from investment) of farm income in kind, but for 1937–55 no deductions are made from output for investments in kind. The calculations are limited, however, to products used for human consumption, and only very limited amounts of investment in kind in the form of changes in stocks of produce available for human consumption (for example, grain stocks) are likely to be included. The same procedure is used in the calculation of farm income in kind for 1928 by the method of aggregation. In the alternative computation for this year based on Soviet global data in monetary terms, the current ruble figure that it considered is net of livestock investments. For all years, I include in gross investment a separately computed allowance for the latter investments.

To repeat, farm income in kind is obtained here as a residual, after the deduction of production expense and marketings. In the case of production expense, where possible an allowance is also made for losses on the farm due to spoilage, et cetera.

The foregoing brief comments scarcely exhaust the complex question concerning the meaning and scope of the Soviet official statistics on farm marketings. On this whole question, I have been guided chiefly by Karcz, RAND RM-1930. For further details the reader is referred to this report. Also of value was an interview which Dr. Joseph Kershaw and I had with Professor V. Starovskii, Director of TSU, in Moscow on August 5, 1959.

Agricultural versus calendar year. The SNIP figure for 1928 that is derived from Soviet global data in monetary terms refers to the calendar year 1928. In calculating farm income in kind by the method of aggregation, I use for all years official figures on output and marketings which often also refer to the calendar year. But often, too, reference is instead to the agricultural year (that is, the year beginning July 1) or to some variant thereof. Moreover, the Soviet and western sources used are not always explicit regarding the dating of the statistics presented, and as a result we are sometimes not clear as to the nature of the year to which reference is made. Although when viewed as calendar year data our measurements of income in kind may often be in error on these accounts, I doubt that the resulting distortions can be very consequential. On the dating of the data used in this study, see, in addition to the Soviet statistical sources to be referred to, *SNIP-28,* pp. 99 ff.; Karcz, RAND RM-1930, Appendix D; and Gozulov, 1959, pp. 255–61.

Average Realized Prices, 1926/27, 1928, 1937, 1950

The price data used for the purposes of valuation of income in kind are presented in Table C-1. In addition to prices for benchmark years, 1928, 1937, and 1950, I also present 1926/27 prices which are needed to supplement the benchmark year data.

The 1926/27 prices, from Soviet sources, are suitable for our purposes conceptually, being average prices realized in all forms of marketings in that year. An issue might be raised about the prices of grain and oil seed. The basic source (*KTS 1929–30,* pp. 581–82) quotes one price for the valuation of gross output and another for the valuation of marketings. (In the case of grain, the former is 51.3 and the latter 55.5 rubles per ton. Incidentally, the source itself is not very consistent in its use of prices. A gross output of grain of 73.6 million tons is reported as having a value of 3.592 million rubles. The implied price is 48.8 rubles per ton.) In valuing

TABLE C-1

Average Realized Prices of Farm Products, USSR, 1926/27, 1928, 1937, 1950
(rubles per ton)

Product	1926/27 (1)	1928 (2)	1937 (3)	1950 (4)
Grain	55.5	70	150	400
Potatoes	25.0	37	190	430
Flax fiber	368.5	480	1,050	4,270
Milk	59.8	75	520	855
Meat, live weight	229	220	1,900	4,160
Eggs[a]	30.5	33	320	545
Food vegetables, excluding melons	50	—	340	1,535
Melons	27	—	510	—
Sunflower seed	66.5	—	550	1,360
Wool	1,079	—	7,500	11,300
Hides, large[a]	10,500	—	11,850	—
Hides, small[a]	2,450	—	5,500	—
Fruit	100	—	680	—
Hemp fiber	370	—	2,000	—
Flax seed	94.6	—	1,125	—
Hemp seed	86.1	—	1,550	—
Other oilseed	73.3	—	1,640	—
Poultry meat	725.0	—	6,000	—

[a] Rubles per thousand.

income in kind, I use the prices which refer to marketings, although no doubt the alternative would also be defensible.

Soviet price quotations for 1928 are available for agricultural years 1927/28 and 1928/29 but not for the calendar year 1928. For six products Karcz estimates average realized prices for the calendar year 1928 as weighted averages of prices prevailing in the four quarters of 1928, quarterly marketings being used as weights. See RAND RM-1930, Appendix G. I cite Karcz's results in Table C-1. Average prices for the calendar year 1928 for other products are lacking.

For 1937 and 1950, I cite estimates derived chiefly by Karcz and Nimitz; these again are supposed to represent average prices realized in all marketings.

The sources and methods for Table C-1 follow:

Column (1). 1926/27 prices. All prices are from *KTS 1929–30,* pp. 581–82, except the following:

Meat. Karcz, RAND RM-1930, Appendix G, p. 340.

Food vegetables. Jasny, 1949, p. 600.

Fruit. The 1926/27 price of fruit other than grapes was 93.3 rubles per ton, that of grapes 125.1 rubles per ton. See *KTS 1929–30,* p. 582. In the absence of marketings data, it is asumed that the ratio of marketings of fruit to those of grapes was about 5 to 1.

Other oilseed. I cite the average price of all oilseed. See *KTS 1929–30,* p. 581.

Column (*2*). *1928 prices.* These are Karcz's estimates referring to the calendar year 1928. See his RAND RM-1930, p. 33.

Column (*3*). *1937 prices.*

Grain; potatoes; flax fiber; milk; meat; eggs. See Karcz, RAND RM-1930, p. 33.

Vegetables; melons. The average realized prices of vegetables and melons are computed from price data in an unpublished memorandum of Jerzy Karcz, July 11, 1957.

Sunflower seed. Computed from price and quantity data in unpublished memorandum of Jerzy Karcz, June 29, 1957.

Wool; hides. Prices paid for centralized procurements of these products are assumed equal to average prices. I cite the results of unpublished calculations of Jerzy Karcz.

Fruit. The change in price from 1926/27 is assumed identical with that for vegetables.

Hemp fiber. I assume that the average price corresponds to the price (including premiums) paid for contract deliveries, as estimated independently.

Flax seed; hemp seed; other oilseed. Computed from price and quantity data in unpublished memorandum of Jerzy Karcz, June 29, 1957.

Poultry meat. The change from 1926/27 is taken to be identical with that for meat.

Column (*4*). *1950 prices.* Estimates of Nancy Nimitz. The estimates are derived as part of a revision of calculations of farm income in kind made initially in *SNIP-49–55*. On the nature of the revision, see page 334.

Farm income in kind in current prices. In Table 3, I cite data on the consumption of farm income in kind for 1928–55 in terms of current rubles. The figures for 1928–48 are taken from *SNIP-28–48*. As is explained there, the current ruble figures are derived from the constant ruble calculations that are being presented in this study. In Table 3, for 1949–55 I cite estimates of consumption of farm income in kind that have been derived by Miss Nimitz. The estimates represent the results of the revision of calculations made initially in *SNIP-49–55*.

Farm Income in Kind in Constant Prices: 1928

To refer first to the calculation by the method of inflation, consumption of farm income in kind in 1928 amounted to 6.4 billion rubles in terms of current prices (see *SNIP-28–48*). As is explained in a moment, according to the method of aggregation, consumption of farm income in kind in 1928 amounts to 7.4 billion rubles in 1928 prices and 39.9 billion rubles in 1937 prices. By implication, average realized farm prices in 1937 are 539 percent of 1928. By the method of inflation, therefore, farm income in kind in 1928 comes to 34.5 billion rubles in terms of 1937 prices, that is, 6.4 billion rubles × 5.39.

The SNIP figure for farm income in kind, to repeat, is 6.4 billion rubles in terms of 1928 prices. This figure, which is computed from Soviet global data on farm output and its disposition, evidently falls 1.0 billion rubles short of the corresponding figure derived here by the method of aggregation. The latter figure, however, includes some 1.0 billion rubles of intrarural cash sales of farm produce available for human consumption (see *SNIP-28*, pp. 100 ff., 114 ff.) which are omitted from the former. Allowing for this, the method of aggregation actually yields a figure exactly equal to the SNIP figure. Such agreement was not to be expected but is nevertheless reassuring.

The foregoing deals with the derivation of the estimate that is adopted of income in kind in terms of 1937 prices. The corresponding figure in terms of 1928 prices is, of course, the *SNIP-28* figure itself. By the method of inflation, it may also be calculated that in terms of 1950 prices income in kind is 75.6 billion rubles. I again use here a price index implied by data on income in kind compiled by the method of aggregation.

To come then to the calculation by the method of aggregation: the elements of this computation appear in Table C-2. The sources and methods follow:

Column (1). Gross output. For the most part, the cited figures are from *Narkhoz-1958*, pp. 418, 467. For meat, hides, fruit, hemp fiber, oilseed other than sunflower, and poultry meat, however, see *KTS-1929–30*, pp. 532–533. The figure in this source on the output of meat in terms of slaughtered weight is converted to live weight on the assumption that one ton of the former corresponds to 1.85 tons of the latter.

Column (2). Marketings. See *KTS 1929–30*, pp. 538–9. For food vegetables, marketings on the average during 1923–27 amounted to 1.7 million tons. See *Narkhoz-1958*, p. 351. I assume that the corresponding figure for 1928 is somewhat greater. For sunflower seed, see *SKh 1935*, p. 386, as quoted in Jasny, 1949, p. 80. Jasny's figures refer to state procurements which are here assumed to be identical with marketings. For flax, see *Piatiletnii plan*, vol. II, part 1, p. 332.

Column (3). Production expenses in kind; losses. For grain, milk, and eggs, see Jasny, 1949, pp. 751, 766. Jasny's figures are partly from Soviet sources and partly independent estimates. For potatoes, flax fiber, and wool see Johnson and Kahan in *Comparisons of United States and Soviet Economies*, Part I, pp. 231–237. For food vegetables, I allow for fodder allocations of 1.7 million tons. See Jasny, 1949, p. 596. The total allocation to production expense is raised to 2.4 million tons in order to allow for losses.

For sunflower seed, production expenses and losses are estimated at 3.5 percent of gross output, or allowing for the difference in yields roughly the same relation as prevailed in the fifties. See Johnson and Kahan, *op. cit.*, pp. 231–237. Losses of fruit are estimated at 10 percent of income in kind including losses. For hemp fiber, production expenses and losses are in the same proportion to gross output as for flax fiber. For oilseed other than sunflower, the amount used in production and losses is assumed to account for the same percentage of gross output as for sunflower seed.

Column (4). Residual: Column (1) less columns (2) and (3).

Columns (5) to (8). Income in kind in 1926/27, 1928, 1937, and 1950

TABLE C-2

Farm Income in Kind, USSR, 1928, in Constant Prices of 1926/27, 1928, 1937, 1950

Product	Gross output (mil. tons) (1)	Marketings (mil. tons) (2)	Production expenses in kind; losses (mil. tons) (3)	Residual (mil. tons) (4)	Income in kind: In 1926/27 prices (mil. rubles) (5)	Income in kind: In 1928 prices (mil. rubles) (6)	Income in kind: In 1937 prices (mil. rubles) (7)	Income in kind: In 1950 prices (mil. rubles) (8)
Grain	73.3	8.33	32.5	32.47	—	2,273	4,870	12,988
Potatoes	46.4	2.91	29.7	13.79	—	510	2,620	5,930
Flax fiber	0.32	0.12	0.02	0.18	—	86	189	769
Milk	31.0	6.29	2.45	22.26	—	1,670	11,575	19,032
Meat (beef, mutton, pork)	7.58[a]	2.39[a]	. . .	5.19[a]	—	1,142	9,861	21,590
Eggs	10.8[b]	3.97[b]	1.08[b]	5.75[b]	—	190	1,840	3,134
Food vegetables, excluding melons	10.5	2.0	2.4	6.1	305	1,160 (food vegetables through poultry meat combined)	2,074	9,364
Sunflower seed	2.13	1.07	0.07	0.99	66		544	1,346
Wool	0.18	0.05	0.04	0.09	97		675	1,017
Hides, large	13.4[c]	11.2[c]	. . .	2.2[c]	23		26	7,983 (hides, large through poultry meat combined)
Hides, small	68.9[c]	34.0[c]	. . .	34.9[c]	86		192	
Fruit	2.6	1.0	0.2	1.4	140		952	
Hemp fiber	0.50	0.11	0.03	0.36	133		720	
Oilseed other than sunflower	1.17	0.66	0.04	0.47	40		677	
Poultry meat	0.29	0.11	. . .	0.18	131		1,080	
All itemized products						7,031	37,895	83,153
All products						7,400	39,900	87,500

[a] Live weight.
[b] Billion units.
[c] Million units.
Note: Throughout, . . denotes negligible or not applicable and — denotes not available.

prices. In column (5), the residuals for nine products are valued in terms of the 1926/27 prices given in Table C-1. Oilseed other than sunflower is valued at 84.7 rubles per ton, an unweighted average of the prices of flax seed, hemp seed, and other oilseed. In column (6), for all except these nine products, the residuals are valued in terms of the 1928 prices given in Table C-1. In terms of 1926/27 prices, the residual amounts of the remaining nine products were worth 1,021 million rubles. According to calculations of Jerzy Karcz, farm prices in 1926/27 averaged 88 percent of 1928. This index obtains where use is made of 1928 weights. See RM-1930, p. 42. In terms of 1928 prices, therefore, the residuals of the remaining nine products were worth 1,160 million rubles. Income in kind from miscellaneous products not covered in the computation, such as melons and honey, is assumed to amount to 5.0 percent of that from all products, both covered and uncovered.

In column (7), the residuals are valued in terms of the 1937 prices given in Table C-1. Oilseed other than sunflower is valued at 1,440 rubles per ton, an unweighted average of the prices of flax seed, hemp seed, and other oilseed. Miscellaneous products not covered are allowed for as above.

In column (8), the residuals are valued in terms of the 1950 prices given in the Table C-1. For commodities for which 1950 prices are unavailable, income in kind is assumed to account for 9.6 percent of the income in kind derived from all itemized products taken together, or the same proportion of the total that they account for when valued at 1937 prices. Miscellaneous products not covered are again allowed for as in the calculation in 1928 rubles.

Farm Income in Kind in Constant Prices: 1937

The elements in the calculation are in Table C-3. The sources and methods follow:

Column (1). Gross output. With exceptions to be noted, the figures are from *Narkhoz-1958,* pp. 418–419. For basic meats, the figure in terms of slaughtered weight in Nimitz, RAND RM-1250, is converted to live weight on the assumption that one ton of the former equals 1.9 tons of the latter. For food melons, see the data on sown area and yields in Jasny, 1949, pp. 599–602. For hides, see United Nations, *Economic Survey of Europe in 1953,* p. 268. For hemp fiber, the figure on "biological" harvest in *ibid.,* p. 268, is reduced by 37 percent in order to obtain the corresponding "barn" crop. Compare the relation of the "biological" and "barn" crop for flax fiber in *Narkhoz-1958,* p. 418, and Johnson and Kahan, *op. cit.,* p. 232. On flax, hemp, and other oilseed, the data are taken from an unpublished memorandum of Karcz, June 29, 1957.

Column (2). Marketings. For grain, potatoes, flax fiber, milk, meat, and eggs, see Karcz, RAND RM-1930, pp. 26 and 218. For vegetables and melons, I rely on an unpublished memorandum of Karcz, July 11, 1957. On sunflower seed and wool, see *TPP,* pp. 83, 89–90. On hides, the official data are from *TPP,* p. 232. According to *TPP,* p. 89, centralized procurements of hemp fiber amounted to 0.049 million tons. Such procurements are assumed

TABLE C-3

Farm Income in Kind, USSR, 1937, in Constant Prices of 1928, 1937, 1950

Product	Gross output (mil. tons) (1)	Marketings (mil. tons) (2)	Production expenses in kind; losses (mil. tons) (3)	Residual (mil. tons) (4)	Income in kind: In 1928 prices (mil. rubles) (5)	Income in kind: In 1937 prices (mil. rubles) (6)	Income in kind: In 1950 prices (mil. rubles) (7)
Grain	97.4	37.97	34.5	24.93	1,745	3,740	9,988
Potatoes	58.7	11.70	35.5	11.5	426	2,185	4,945
Flax fiber	0.36	0.32	0.02	0.02	10	21	85
Milk	26.1	8.02	2.0	16.08	1,206	8,362	13,748
Meat (beef, mutton, pork)	4.50[a]	2.80[a]	...	1.70[a]	374	3,230	7,072
Eggs	8.2[b]	3.34[b]	0.82	4.04[b]	133	1,293	2,202
Food vegetables	15.4	4.4	3.1	7.9		2,686	12,126
Melons	3.9	2.2	1.2	0.5		255	768
Sunflower seed	1.76	1.28	0.06	0.42		231	571
Wool	0.106	0.079	0.007	0.020		150	226
Hides, large	10.8[c]	10.3[c]	...	0.5[c]		6	
Hides, small	32.0[c]	31.2[c]	...	0.8[c]	839 (Food vegetables through Poultry meat)	4	
Hemp fiber	0.118	0.058	0.01	0.05		100	
Flax seed	0.62	0.36	0.02	0.24		270	4,843 (Hides, large through Poultry meat)
Hemp seed	0.26	0.10	0.01	0.15		232	
Other oilseed	0.51	0.40	0.02	0.09		148	
Fruit	—	—	—	1.4		952	
Poultry meat	—	—	—	0.06		360	
All itemized products					4,733	24,225	56,574
All products					4,900	25,000	58,300

[a] Live weight.
[b] Billion units.
[c] Million units.
... = negligible or not applicable.

to account for 85 percent of all marketings, as in the case of flax fiber. See Karcz, RAND RM-1930, Appendix D. For the different oilseeds, I again rely on an unpublished memorandum of Jerzy Karcz, June 29, 1957.

Column (3). Production expenses in kind; losses. For grain, potatoes, milk, and meat, see the estimates in Jasny, 1949, p. 765. For grain, I raise Jasny's estimate (34.0 million tons) somewhat in view of the higher figure used here for gross output. For potatoes, Jasny takes feed and seed to amount to 34.2 million tons. I reduce this by 10 percent to make it conform to the lower figure used here for gross output, but I also assume that an additional 10 percent of the amount on the farm is lost.

For flax fiber, eggs, and sunflower seed, production expenses and losses are taken to constitute the same share of gross output as in 1928. For food vegetables, production expenses and losses are taken to amount to 20 percent of the gross output, or again approximately as was the case in 1928. In view of the greater feed use for melons, the corresponding figure for these is taken to be 30 percent. For wool, see Johnson and Kahan, *op. cit.*, pp. 231–237. As for flax fiber, production expenses and losses for hemp fiber are taken to amount to about 6 percent of gross output. For the different sorts of oilseed other than sunflower seed, the experience for sunflower seed serves as a benchmark.

Column (4). Residual. Column (1) less columns (2) and (3). For fruit, income in kind is assumed to be the same as in 1928. For poultry meat, income in kind declines from 1928 as it does for basic meats.

Column (5). Income in kind in 1928 prices. For grain, potatoes, flax fiber, milk, meat, and eggs, the residuals are valued at the 1928 prices in Table C-1. For all other itemized products, the residuals are worth 711 million rubles in terms of 1926/27 prices. For 1928, farm prices generally averaged 118 percent of 1926/27. This index obtains where use is made of 1937 weights. See Karcz, RAND RM-1930, p. 42. In terms of 1928 prices, therefore, the remaining itemized products are worth 839 million rubles (that is, 711 × 1.18). Income in kind from miscellaneous products not covered is taken to amount to 3.0 percent of all income in kind.

Column (6). Income in kind in 1937 prices. The residuals are valued at the 1937 prices in Table C-1. Miscellaneous products not covered are allowed for as above.

Column (7). Income in kind in 1950 prices. For all products listed through wool, the residuals are valued at the 1950 prices in Table C-1. Food melons are valued at the 1950 price of food vegetables. Other itemized commodities for which 1950 prices are not available account for 8.56 percent of income in kind of all itemized products valued in terms of 1937 prices. I assume that they account for the same share in terms of 1950 prices. Miscellaneous products not covered are allowed for as in the calculation in terms of 1928 rubles.

Farm Income in Kind in Constant Prices: 1940

The elements in the computation are in Table C-4. The sources and methods follow:

TABLE C-4

Farm Income in Kind, USSR, 1940, in Constant Prices of 1937 and 1950

Product	Gross output (mil. tons) (1)	Marketings (mil. tons) (2)	Production expenses in kind; losses (mil. tons) (3)	Residual (mil. tons) (4)	Income in kind: In 1937 prices (mil. rubles) (5)	Income in kind: In 1950 prices (mil. rubles) (6)
Grain	95.5	38.3	33.8	23.4	3,510	9,360
Potatoes	75.9	12.9	45.9	17.1	3,249	7,353
Flax fiber	0.349	0.330	...	0.019	20	81
Milk	33.6	10.8	5.0	17.8	9,256	15,219
Meat (beef, mutton, pork)	7.1[a]	4.0[a]	...	3.1[a]	5,890	12,896
Eggs	12.2[b]	4.9[b]	1.2[b]	6.1[b]	1,952	3,324
Food vegetables	13.7	6.1	2.7	4.9	1,666	7,522
Sunflower seed	2.64	1.87	0.09	0.68	374	925
Wool	0.161	0.120	0.006	0.035	262	396
Hemp fiber	0.132	0.044	...	0.088	176	—
All itemized products					26,355	57,076
All products					29,900	65,500

[a] Live weight.
[b] Billion units.
. . . = negligible or not applicable.

Column (*1*). *Gross output.* Except for meat and hemp fiber, see *Narkhoz-1958,* pp. 418–419, 467. The output of all meats, including poultry and other minor meats, was 7.5 million tons of live weight. See *ibid.,* p. 467. From data in *Zhiv-59,* pp. 157, 159, I estimate that poultry and minor meats amounted to 0.4 million tons. Hence, the output of basic meats was 7.1 million tons. For hemp fiber, see Korneev, 1957, p. 259.

Column (*2*). *Marketings.* All figures except those for eggs and hemp fiber are from *Dostizheniia,* p. 154. The figure for all meats cited in this source is reduced slightly in order to exclude poultry and other minor meats. For eggs, marketings are taken to amount to about 40 percent of gross output as in 1937. On hemp fiber, see Korneev, 1957, p. 259.

Column (*3*). *Production expenses in kind; losses.* For grain, potatoes, and sunflower seed, these dispositions are taken to account for the same share of gross output as in 1937. For flax fiber and hemp fiber, the very limited production expenses and losses are neglected. For milk, production expenses and losses are taken to account for 15 percent of gross output, or about the same share as in the fifties. For eggs, the corresponding relation is taken to be 10 percent, or about the same as that of 1928 and 1937. For food vegetables, I believe production expenses and losses may have amounted to about 20 percent of gross output. For wool, see Johnson and Kahan, *op. cit.,* pp. 231–237.

Column (*5*). *Farm income in kind in 1937 prices.* For the ten itemized products, the residuals are valued in terms of the 1937 prices in Table C-1. The ten products accounted in 1937 for 88 percent of all income in kind valued at 1937 prices. I assume that the itemized products accounted for the same share of income in kind in 1940, valued at 1937 prices.

Column (*6*). *Farm income in kind in 1950 prices.* For itemized products, except hemp fiber, the residuals may be valued in terms of the 1950 prices in Table C-1. In 1937, the nine products in question accounted for about 87 percent of all income in kind in terms of 1950 prices. I assume that they account for the same share of income in kind in 1940 in terms of 1950 prices.

Farm Income in Constant Prices: 1944

This is assumed to have amounted to 60 percent of the 1940 figure. Although this estimate is arbitrary, I take into account a variety of evidence including chiefly the data on farm output and marketings in 1940 and 1945 in Table C-5. Data for 1940 are from Table C-4. For 1945, gross output of grain is from Jasny, 1949, p. 546. On the gross output of potatoes, wool, milk, meat, and eggs, see Johnson and Kahan, *op. cit.,* p. 232; their meat figure is here reduced by 0.1 million tons to allow for poultry and other minor meats. The cited figure for the gross output of food vegetables is a rule-of-thumb estimate. For marketings of all products except eggs, see *Dostizheniia,* p. 154. The figure on all meats cited in this source is reduced somewhat in order to exclude poultry and other minor meats. Egg marketings in 1945 are assumed to be half of those of 1940, as was the case for milk.

TABLE C-5

Gross Output and Marketings of Selected Agricultural Products, USSR, 1940 and 1945
(millions of tons)

Product	Gross output		Marketings	
	1940	1945	1940	1945
Grain	95.5	50.0	38.3	23.2
Potatoes	75.9	58.3	12.9	11.8
Milk	33.6	26.43	10.8	5.4
Meat (beef, mutton, pork)[a]	7.1	4.6	4.0	2.3
Eggs[b]	12.2	4.88	4.9	2.4
Food vegetables	13.7	13.9	6.1	4.8
Sunflower seed	2.64	1.6	1.87	0.62
Wool	0.161	0.111	0.120	0.073

[a] Live weight.
[b] Billion units.

For the eight products considered, in terms of 1937 prices total output in 1945 was 69 percent of 1940. Judging from diverse information, including data in Johnson and Kahan, *op. cit.*, p. 232, I believe the corresponding figure for 1944 might have been about 55 percent. In terms of 1937 prices, marketings of the eight products considered were in 1945 some 60 percent of those of 1940. For 1944, the corresponding figure may have been about 50 percent. I consider here an unpublished calculation of Jerzy Karcz, according to which government procurements in 1944 were on the order of 50 to 55 percent of those in 1940.

Little is known about production expenses in 1944. If, for the eight products in question, we may assume that they declined in relation to 1940 in much the same proportion as gross output, income in kind in 1944 may be calculated as follows:

	1944 ÷ 1940 (percent) (1)	1940 (bil. rubles) (2)	1944 (bil. rubles) (3)
Gross output	55	71.0	39.0
Marketings	50	27.0	13.5
Production expense and losses	55	17.8	9.8
Residual		26.2	15.7

The figures in the first column have been explained above. Those in the second column are calculated from data compiled previously for 1940. Those in the third column are implied. By implication, too, income in kind in 1944 is 60 percent of 1940.

The foregoing calculations relate to eight products which in 1940 accounted for 90 percent of all income in kind. I assume that the same relation prevailed in 1944. As we have seen, gross output for the eight crops in 1945 was 69 percent of that of 1940. For all crops, gross output in 1945 according to

Soviet official data was 61 percent of 1940. See *Narkhoz-1958,* p. 350. The latter figure covers many technical crops, however, which do not enter significantly into income in kind, and the output of which no doubt declined more sharply during the war than did that of nontechnical products.

Farm Income in Kind in Constant Prices: 1948 and 1949

Because of the lack of information, it seems possible to calculate farm income in kind for 1948 and 1949 only by a rule-of-thumb extrapolation from 1950. The extrapolation takes into account the following information:

Farm production. Soviet agricultural output according to official data varied as follows from 1948 to 1950 (1950 = 100): In 1948, all products, 97.1; crops, 104.6; and animal products, 81.4. In 1949, all products, 100.0; crops, 103.3; and animal products, 92.4 The cited indices are implied by Soviet official data on gross agricultural output. See *Narkhoz-1958,* p. 350.

Marketings. As far as can be judged from very meager evidence, marketings outside the collective farm market probably increased little if at all during this period. According to rule-of-thumb estimates (*SNIP 1928–48, SNIP 1949–55*), sales by collective farms and farmers to procurement agencies increased sharply in current rubles: In 1948, they amounted to 15 billion rubles; in 1949, 20; and in 1950, 25 billion rubles. The prices realized on these deliveries, however, rose by about 70 percent from 1948 to 1952 (letter of Karcz to Bergson, July 6, 1957). The increase probably materialized chiefly during the year 1949.

On the other hand, the physical volume of sales in the urban collective farm market rose sharply from 1948 to 1950: Sales on collective farm market for 1948 amounted to 11 billion 1937 rubles; for 1949, 18; and for 1950, 24 billion 1937 rubles. I deflate here total sales as distinct from sales to households. Otherwise the calculations are the same as in Appendix A. If these figures, nevertheless, are at all trustworthy, I believe all marketings (including deliveries to procurement agencies as well as sales on the collective farm market) increased appreciably during the years in question.

The upshot of these trends is conjectural. I assume that farm income in kind increased appreciably from 1948 to 1950. Account is taken of the fact that in 1950 animal products accounted for 60 to 70 percent and crops for 30 to 40 percent of all income in kind.

Farm Income in Kind in Constant Prices: 1950–55

Elements of the calculations for these years appear in Tables C-6 to C-11. All data on physical quantities were computed by Nancy Nimitz and represent revisions of the estimates presented in *SNIP-49–55.* Four types of revisions were made. First, estimates of output and the various types of marketings were corrected for new Soviet data from various sources, principally the following: *Narkhoz-1958; TSU, SSSR v tsifrakh; Sel'skoe khoziaistvo SSSR; Zhiv-1959.*

TABLE C-6

Farm Income in Kind, USSR, 1950, in 1937 and 1950 Prices

Product	Gross output (mil. tons) (1)	Marketings (mil. tons) (2)	Production expenses in kind; losses (mil. tons) (3)	Residual (mil. tons) (4)	Income in kind[d]: In 1937 prices (mil. rubles) (5)	Income in kind[d]: In 1950 prices (mil. rubles) (6)
Grain	81.2	37.3	28	15.9	2,380	6,360
Potatoes	88.6	14.0	51	23.6	4,480	10,150
Flax fiber	0.255	0.182	...	0.073	80	310
Milk	35.3 (31.3)[a]	11.4	5.3 (4.7)[a]	18.6 (15.2)[a]	9,670 (7,900)[a]	15,900 (13,000)[a]
Meat (beef, mutton, pork)	7.7[b]	4.1[b]	...	3.6[b]	6,840	14,980
Eggs	11.70[c]	3.64[c]	1.17[c]	6.89[c]	2,200	3,760
Food vegetables	9.3	4.2	1.4	3.7	1,260	5,680
Sunflower seed	1.80	1.33	0.05	0.42	230	570
Wool	0.180	0.138	...	0.042	320	470
Total, nine itemized products					27,460 (25,690)[a]	58,180 (55,280)[a]
All income in kind					30,500 (28,500)[a]	64,600 (61,400)[a]

[a] Figures in parentheses are based upon adjusted milk output (see text).

[b] Live weight.

[c] Billion eggs.

[d] Value figures for the nine itemized products have been rounded to the nearest 10 million rubles. Value figures for all income in kind have been rounded to the nearest 100 million rubles.

... = negligible or not applicable.

TABLE C-7

Farm Income in Kind, USSR, 1951, in 1937 and 1950 Prices

Product	Gross output (mil. tons) (1)	Marketings (mil. tons) (2)	Production expenses in kind; losses (mil. tons) (3)	Residual (mil. tons) (4)	Income in kind[d]: In 1937 prices (mil. rubles) (5)	Income in kind[d]: In 1950 prices (mil. rubles) (6)
Grain	78.8	39.3	26	13.5	2,020	5,400
Potatoes	70	11.8	38	20.2	3,840	8,690
Flax fiber	0.194	0.166	...	0.028	30	120
Milk	36.2 (32.3)[a]	12.4	5.4 (4.8)[a]	18.4 (15.1)[a]	9,570 (7,850)[a]	15,730 (12,910)[a]
Meat (beef, mutton, pork)	7.1[b]	3.9[b]	...	3.2[b]	6,080	13,310
Eggs	13.25[c]	4.46[c]	1.32[c]	7.47[c]	2,390	4,070
Food vegetables	8.5	4.3	1.3	2.9	990	4,450
Sunflower seed	1.74	1.44	0.05	0.25	140	340
Wool	0.192	0.160	...	0.032	240	360
Total, nine itemized products					25,300 (23,580)[a]	52,470 (49,650)[a]
All income in kind					28,100 (26,200)[a]	58,300 (55,200)[a]

[a] Figures in parentheses are based upon adjusted milk output (see text).
[b] Live weight.
[c] Billion eggs.
[d] Value figures for the nine itemized products have been rounded to the nearest 10 million rubles. Value figures for all income in kind have been rounded to the nearest 100 million rubles.
... = negligible or not applicable.

TABLE C-8

Farm Income in Kind, USSR, 1952, in 1937 and 1950 Prices

Product	Gross output (mil. tons) (1)	Marketings (mil. tons) (2)	Production expenses in kind; losses (mil. tons) (3)	Residual (mil. tons) (4)	Income in kind[d]: In 1937 prices (mil. rubles) (5)	Income in kind[d]: In 1950 prices (mil. rubles) (6)
Grain	91.8	40.4	34	17.4	2,610	6,960
Potatoes	75	12.5	40	22.5	4,280	9,680
Flax fiber	0.212	0.196	...	0.016	20	70
Milk	35.7 (32.0)[a]	13.2	5.4 (4.8)[a]	17.1 (14.0)[a]	8,890 (7,280)[a]	14,620 (11,970)[a]
Meat (beef, mutton, pork)	7.8[b]	4.4[b]	...	3.4[b]	6,460	14,140
Eggs	14.40[c]	5.24[c]	1.44[c]	7.72[c]	2,470	4,210
Food vegetables	9.5	4.4	1.4	3.7	1,260	5,680
Sunflower seed	2.21	1.60	0.06	0.55	300	750
Wool	0.219	0.179	...	0.040	300	450
Total, nine itemized products					26,590 (24,980)[a]	56,560 (53,910)[a]
All income in kind					29,500 (27,800)[a]	62,800 (59,900)[a]

[a] Figures in parentheses based upon adjusted milk output (see text).
[b] Live weight.
[c] Billion eggs.
[d] Value figures for the nine itemized products have been rounded to the nearest 10 million rubles. Value figures for all income in kind have been rounded to the nearest 100 million rubles.
... = negligible or not applicable.

TABLE C-9

Farm Income in Kind, USSR, 1953, in 1937 and 1950 Prices

Product	Gross output (mil. tons) (1)	Marketings (mil. tons) (2)	Production expenses in kind; losses (mil. tons) (3)	Residual (mil. tons) (4)	Income in kind[d]	
					In 1937 prices (mil. rubles) (5)	In 1950 prices (mil. rubles) (6)
Grain	82.5	35.8	32	14.7	2,200	5,880
Potatoes	72.6	12.1	42	18.5	3,520	7,960
Flax fiber	0.162	0.153	...	0.009	10	40
Milk	36.5 (32.8)[a]	13.7	5.5 (4.9)[a]	17.3 (14.2)[a]	9,000 (7,380)[a]	14,790 (12,140)[a]
Meat (beef, mutton, pork)	8.5[b]	4.9[b]	...	3.6[b]	6,840	14,980
Eggs	16.06[c]	6.07[c]	1.61[c]	8.38[c]	2,680	4,570
Food vegetables	11.4	5.1	1.7	4.6	1,560	7,060
Sunflower seed	2.63	2.07	0.06	0.50	280	680
Wool	0.235	0.198	...	0.037	280	420
Total, nine itemized products					26,370 (24,750)[a]	56,380 (53,730)[a]
All income in kind					29,300 (27,500)[a]	62,600 (59,700)[a]

[a] Figures in parentheses are based upon adjusted milk output (see text).
[b] Live weight.
[c] Billion eggs.
[d] Value figures for the nine itemized products have been rounded to the nearest 10 million rubles. Value figures for all income in kind have been rounded to the nearest 100 million rubles.
... = negligible or not applicable.

TABLE C-10

Farm Income in Kind, USSR, 1954, in 1937 and 1950 Prices

Product	Gross output (mil. tons) (1)	Marketings (mil. tons) (2)	Production expenses in kind; losses (mil. tons) (3)	Residual (mil. tons) (4)	Income in kind[d] In 1937 prices (mil. rubles) (5)	Income in kind[d] In 1950 prices (mil. rubles) (6)
Grain	85.6	39.1	32	14.5	2,180	5,800
Potatoes	75.0	13.0	45	17.0	3,230	7,310
Flax fiber	0.218	0.198	...	0.020	20	90
Milk	38.2 (34.5)[a]	14.5	5.7 (5.2)[a]	18.0 (14.8)[a]	9,360 (7,700)[a]	15,390 (12,650)[a]
Meat (beef, mutton, pork)	9.0[b]	5.4[b]	...	3.6[b]	6,840	14,980
Eggs	17.18[c]	6.53[c]	1.72[c]	8.93[c]	2,860	4,870
Food vegetables	11.9	5.8	1.8	4.3	1,460	6,600
Sunflower seed	1.91	1.34	0.07	0.50	280	680
Wool	0.230	0.186	...	0.044	330	500
Total, nine itemized products					26,560 (24,900)[a]	56,220 (53,480)[a]
All income in kind					29,500 (27,700)[a]	62,500 (59,400)[a]

[a] Figures in parentheses are based upon adjusted milk output (see text).
[b] Live weight.
[c] Billion eggs.
[d] Value figures for the nine itemized products have been rounded to the nearest 10 million rubles. Value figures for all income in kind have been rounded to the nearest 100 million rubles.
... = negligible or not applicable.

TABLE C-11

Farm Income in Kind, USSR, 1955, in 1937 and 1950 Prices

Product	Gross output (mil. tons) (1)	Marketings (mil. tons) (2)	Production expenses in kind; losses (mil. tons) (3)	Residual (mil. tons) (4)	Income in kind[d] In 1937 prices (mil. rubles) (5)	Income in kind[d] In 1950 prices (mil. rubles) (6)
Grain	106.8	41.9	40	24.9	3,740	9,960
Potatoes	71.8	12.7	41	18.1	3,440	7,780
Flax fiber	0.381	0.352	...	0.029	30	120
Milk	43.0 (39.1)[a]	17.1	6.4 (5.9)[a]	19.5 (16.1)[a]	10,140 (8,370)[a]	16,670 (13,770)[a]
Meat (beef, mutton, pork)	9.2[b]	5.5[b]	...	3.7[b]	7,030	15,390
Eggs	18.48[c]	7.00[c]	1.85[c]	9.63[c]	3,080	5,250
Food vegetables	14.1	6.8	2.1	5.2	1,770	7,980
Sunflower seed	3.80	2.62	0.09	1.09	600	1,480
Wool	0.256	0.201	...	0.055	410	620
Total, nine itemized products					30,240 (28,470)[a]	65,250 (62,350)[a]
All income in kind					33,600 (31,600)[a]	72,500 (69,300)[a]

[a] Figures in parentheses are based upon adjusted milk output (see text).

[b] Live weight.

[c] Billion eggs.

[d] Value figures for the nine itemized products have been rounded to the nearest 10 million rubles. Value figures for all income in kind have been rounded to the nearest 100 million rubles.

... = negligible or not applicable.

Second, the interpretation of market output data was revised. When the original *SNIP-49–55* estimates were made, it was not clear whether data on total marketings included or excluded sales on the rural collective farm market. Therefore alternative calculations were shown, the preferred one of which made rule-of-thumb adjustments to total marketings data to exclude the presumed rural component. It has now been established, through a conversation with the head of the Central Statistical Administration, Professor V. Starovskii, that marketings data for the fifties do include some sales on rural markets, but only those to workers and employees not engaged in farming (the volume of such sales is estimated from sample budget investigations). Therefore no adjustment to marketings data on this score is required. The revised interpretation affected particularly estimates of collective farm market sales, which were derived in part as a residual (after accounting for other components of total market output).

Third, allowances for production expenses and losses were slightly modified in the light of improved output and marketings data, including new data on the share of marketings in output of state and institutional farms (where "market output" comprehends virtually all human consumption).

Fourth, reconsideration of the official series for milk output raised the possibility that data for the 'fifties were exaggerated. The main reason for suspecting exaggeration is the trend implied in private sector milk yields, which apparently increased from about 1,300 kg/yr in 1940 to 1,500 from 1950 on. It is not easy to reconcile such an increase with the reported deterioration in feed supply in the early 'fifties, and with the fact that collective farm milk yields did not rise significantly above the 1940 level (1,000 kg) until 1955. Accordingly, it seemed advisable to make alternative calculations of income in kind of milk, one using the official output series and the other adjusted figures. The adjusted figures were obtained by reducing private sector milk output (*Zhiv-1959,* p. 163) by 15 percent, or roughly 4 million tons each year; this is tantamount to assuming that private yields in the 'fifties remained close to their 1940 level. The adjustment is a token one, in the sense that other sources of exaggeration (besides bias in the Soviet estimates of private sector output) exist for which I do not attempt to discount.

In the course of revising the *SNIP-49–55* estimates of physical quantities, as described above, current price estimates were also slightly revised for new information and second thoughts. Both price and quantity revisions are reflected in the series for farm income in kind in current prices in the text tables, and in the average realized prices for 1950 shown in Table C-1.

The nine products itemized in Tables C-6 to C-11 are assumed to account for 90 percent of all income in kind (compared with about 88 percent in 1937 and 1940).

Farm Income in Kind, 1928–55, in Terms of 1937 and 1950 Collective Farm Market Prices

The value of farm income in kind of selected products at 1937 and 1950 collective farm market prices is calculated in Tables C-12 and C-13. The

TABLE C-12

Farm Income in Kind, Selected Products, in 1937 Collective Farm Market Prices, USSR, 1928–55

Product	Collective farm market prices, 1937 (rubles per ton)	Value of farm income in kind (million rubles)[c]								
		1928	1937	1940	1950	1951	1952	1953	1954	1955
Grain	1,000	32,470	24,930	23,400	15,900	13,500	17,400	14,700	14,500	24,900
Potatoes	600	8,274	6,900	10,260	14,160	12,120	13,500	11,100	10,200	10,860
Milk	1,200	26,712	19,296	21,360	18,240[b]	18,120[b]	16,800[b]	17,040[b]	17,760[b]	19,320[b]
Meat (beef, mutton, pork)	4,200	21,798	7,140	13,020	15,120	13,440	14,280	15,120	15,120	15,540
Eggs	400[a]	2,300	1,616	2,440	2,760	2,990	3,090	3,350	3,570	3,850
Food, vegetables	850	5,185	6,715	4,165	3,140	2,460	3,140	3,910	3,660	4,420
Sunflower seed	3,500	3,465	1,470	2,380	1,470	880	1,920	1,750	1,750	3,820
Total, seven itemized products		100,204	68,067	77,025	70,790	63,510	70,130	66,970	66,560	82,710
All income in kind		119,700	78,300	88,900	79,800	71,400	79,000	75,300	75,100	93,200

[a] Rubles per 1,000.
[b] Based on adjusted milk output.
[c] Figures for itemized products for the years 1950–55 have been rounded to the nearest 10 million rubles. Figures for all income in kind in all years have been rounded to the nearest 100 million rubles.

TABLE C-13

Farm Income in Kind, Selected Products, in 1950 Collective Farm Market Prices, USSR, 1928–55

Product	Collective farm market prices, 1950 (rubles per ton)	Value of farm income in kind (million rubles) [c]								
		1928	1937	1940	1950	1951	1952	1953	1954	1955
Grain	3,080	100,007	76,784	72,072	48,970	41,580	53,590	45,280	44,660	76,690
Potatoes	900	12,411	10,350	15,390	21,240	18,180	20,250	16,650	15,300	16,290
Milk	2,620	58,321	42,130	46,636	39,820[b]	39,560[b]	36,680[b]	37,200[b]	38,780[b]	42,180[b]
Meat (beef, mutton, pork)	9,000	46,710	15,300	27,900	32,400	28,800	30,600	32,400	32,400	33,300
Eggs	910[a]	5,232	3,676	5,551	6,270	6,800	7,030	7,630	8,130	8,760
Food vegetables	4,000	24,400	31,600	19,600	14,800	11,600	14,800	18,400	17,200	20,800
Sunflower seed	6,150	6,088	2,583	4,182	2,580	1,540	3,380	3,080	3,080	6,700
Total, seven itemized products		253,169	182,423	191,331	166,080	148,060	166,330	160,640	159,550	204,720
All income in kind		301,800	209,900	221,400	187,000	166,200	186,700	180,100	179,300	230,300

[a] Rubles per 1,000.
[b] Based on adjusted milk output.
[c] Figures for itemized products for the years 1950–55 have been rounded to the nearest 10 million rubles. Figures for all income in kind in all years have been rounded to the nearest 100 million rubles.

1937 prices are estimates derived by Karcz either in RAND RM-1930, Appendices B and E, or (in the case of vegetables and sunflower) in his unpublished memoranda of June 29, 1957 and July 11, 1957. The 1950 prices are revisions by Nancy Nimitz of the *SNIP-49–55* estimates.

The prices shown in the first columns of data of Appendix Tables C-12 and C-13 are multiplied by the residuals derived in previous sections of this Appendix to obtain the values given in the second to tenth columns of data.

The seven products itemized in Tables C-12 and C-13 are assumed to account for the same proportion of total income in kind at 1937 and 1950 collective farm market prices as in terms of 1937 and 1950 average realized prices, respectively. The proportions are as shown in Table C-14.

TABLE C-14

Share of Seven Itemized Products in Total Income in Kind at Average Realized Prices, 1928–55 (percent)

Year	1937 prices	1950 prices
1928	83.7	83.9
1937	86.9	86.9
1940	86.6	86.4
1950	88.7	88.8
1951	89.0	89.1
1952	88.7	89.1
1953	88.9	89.2
1954	88.6	89.0
1955	88.7	88.9

APPENDIX D

Communal Services; Government Administration in Constant Prices

Health Care

Scope of category. In delimiting the scope of "health care" I necessarily fall in with Soviet budgetary practice, but the activities that are included seem generally to be of a conventional kind, that is, doctors' services; upkeep of clinics, hospitals, and sanatoriums; public health measures; et cetera. Also included here are the small outlays on "physical culture" which are usually reported under a separate heading in the government budget.

Various related expenditures are classified elsewhere: (a) Military medicine that is financed out of the government budget appropriation to defense is recorded under that use category. (b) Administrative expenditures of the highest organs of health care are classified under government administration. (c) Outlays on medical education and research, I believe, are largely classified under education. (d) The very limited expenditures by households on private medical services and drugs fall under household consumption. (e) Capital construction is classified under investment.

The category includes expenditures from the government budget appropriation to "health care," and also expenditures of similar sorts financed from other sources, including the social insurance budget (which of course has for many years been represented by a separate expenditure heading in the government budget) and funds of the trade unions, cooperatives, collective farms, et cetera.

The foregoing comments apply to 1937 and essentially, I believe, also to more recent years. Information on the scope of the current ruble figure that is taken as a point of departure in 1928 is meager. As for later years, however, extrabudgetary as well as budgetary outlays on "health care" are included, and a deduction has been made for investments.

On the scope of "health care," see Narkomfin SSSR, *Klassifikatsiia raskhodov i dokhodov edinogo gosudarstvennogo biudzheta na 1936 g.;* Pomanskii, 1949, pp. 355 ff; Rovinskii, 1951, pp. 288 ff; and the SNIP studies and other sources cited therein.

Outlays in terms of 1937 rubles. The elements in the calculation are in Table D-1. I comment on each column in turn.

(1) *All outlays (billions of current rubles).* See *SNIP-28–48* and *SNIP-49–55.*

(2) *Wage earners and salaried workers engaged (1937 = 100).* The underlying absolute figures, representing employment in "health care" (*zdravookhranenie*), are taken from *Narkhoz,* p. 190. I assume these figures cover the very small number of workers employed in physical culture activities. Employment in 1944 is assumed to be 90 percent of that for 1945 (which is 126 percent of 1937). This is approximately the relation of government budget appropriations to health care in the two years. See Plotnikov, 1948, p. 329. Wages and prices probably did not change significantly from 1944 to 1945, so the budget appropriations should indicate the comparative employment in the two years. Employment for 1948 is interpolated from figures for 1945 and 1950 on the basis of the increase in Soviet employment generally. Employment in 1954 is assumed to be about 4 percent less than in 1955 (which is 233 percent of 1937). The government budget appropriation for 1954 was 93 percent of that for 1955 (see *SNIP-49–55*), but money wage rates lately have been tending slightly upward, so the "real" outlays and hence employment in 1954 should have been greater than this in relation to 1955.

(3) *Average annual wage (1937 = 100).* The underlying absolute figure for 1928, 638 rubles, is from TSUNKHU, *Trud v SSSR,* 1936 ed., pp. 16–17. That for 1937, 2455 rubles is from *TPP,* pp. 228–229. For 1940, average earnings of all Soviet workers were 133 percent of 1937. According to data in *1941 Plan,* p. 512, the goal for 1941 for the earnings of workers engaged in health care was 3122 rubles, or 127 percent of 1937, but, I believe, the *1941 Plan* figures may tend to overstate the increase over previous years. Accordingly the 20 percent increase allowed from 1937 to 1940 may if anything be high. I assume average earnings in 1944 were 160 percent of 1937, and in 1948, 220 percent of 1937. According to Yanowich, *ASEER,* April 1955, the starting salaries of teachers in elementary and secondary schools in August 1943 were 146 to 148 percent of rates introduced in April 1936, and in 1948, 197 to 240 percent of the latter rates. Apparently the 1936 rates still prevailed in 1940. This seems inconsistent with known facts on the increase in earnings of educational workers from 1937 to 1940, and also would imply wartime increases much in excess of that reported for industrial workers, 42 percent. See Appendix H. Base and actual earnings of education workers generally could have risen, however, while the starting salaries of elementary and secondary school teachers were constant. I assume nevertheless that the Yanowich data indicate the over-all increase in earnings of

TABLE D-1

Calculation of Outlays on Health Care in 1937 Prices, USSR, 1928–55

Year	All outlays (bil. current rubles) (1)	Wage earners and salaried workers engaged (1937 = 100) (2)	Average annual wage (1937 = 100) (3)	Wage bill (1937 = 100) (4)	Wage bill (bil. current rubles) (5)	Nonlabor outlays (bil. current rubles) (6)	Wage bill (bil. 1937 rubles) (7)	Nonlabor outlays (bil. 1937 rubles) (8)	Total outlays (bil. 1937 rubles) (9)
1928	0.54	35.4	26.0	9.2	0.29	0.25	1.1	1.0	2.1
1937	7.9	100	100	100	3.2	4.7	3.2	4.7	7.9
1940	11.6	134	120	161	5.2	6.4	4.3	5.2	9.5
1944	12.6	113	160	181	5.8	6.8	3.6	5.2	8.8
1948	23.4	161	220	354	11.3	12.1	5.2	5.4	10.6
1949	24.5	—	—	—	—	—	(5.5)	(4.9)	10.4
1950	25.0	182	231	420	13.4	11.6	5.8	5.2	11.0
1951	25.7	—	—	—	—	—	(6.1)	(5.3)	11.4
1952	26.8	—	—	—	—	—	(6.4)	(5.6)	12.0
1953	27.4	—	—	—	—	—	(6.8)	(5.7)	12.5
1954	31.9	225	253	569	18.2	13.7	7.2	7.5	14.7
1955	34.0	233	257	599	19.2	14.8	7.5	8.3	15.8

educational workers from 1937 to 1944 and 1948, and I take the trend in earnings of health workers to have been similar. Before the war, earnings of workers engaged in health care varied closely with those of educational workers. I allow for an increase of about 15 percent in earnings from 1948 to 1954, or somewhat less than the increase in the earnings of all workers (19.3 percent) during this period. See Appendix H. Indices for 1950 and 1955 are also estimated from the trends in wages for workers generally as given in Appendix H.

It may be of interest to compare the resulting series on the earnings of workers engaged in health care with available data on the earnings of wage earners and salaried workers generally (see Table D-2). On the earnings of all workers, see Appendix H.

TABLE D-2

Average Annual Wages, All Workers and Health Care Workers, USSR, 1928–55
(1937 = 100)

Year	All workers	Health care workers
1928	23.1	26.0
1937	100	100
1940	133	120
1944	181	160
1948	230	220
1950	247	231
1954	275	253
1955	280	257

(4) *Wage bill (1937 = 100)*. This is the product of columns (2) and (3).

(5) *Wage bill (billions of current rubles)*. Derived from column (4) and an independent estimate of the 1937 wage bill. The government budget appropriation for health care (including physical culture and capital investments) in 1937 was 7.0 billion rubles. See *SNIP-28–48*. Of this sum 2.4 billion rubles, or 34 percent, were paid out in wages. See Narkomfin SSSR, *Raskhody na sotsial'nokulturnye meropriiatiia* . . . p. 50. Assuming the same relation obtained in the case of "other outlays," including capital investments, which amounted to 1.9 billion rubles, total wage payments for health care in 1937 come to 3.0 billion rubles. I raise this figure to 3.2 billions in order to allow for charges which are proportional to wages, particularly social insurance contributions. See SNK decree no. 493, March 23, 1937, and *SZR*, no. 22, April 17, 1937, on the social insurance rates for medical personnel.

The cited figure for the total wage bill exclusive of the latter charges, 3.0 billion rubles, may be compared with that given for "health care" in *TPP*, pp. 228–229: 2.7 billion rubles. This *TSUNKHU* figure, I believe, is not fully comprehensive. Probably it omits many workers where health care activities are secondary to some other activities.

(6) *Nonlabor outlays (billions of current rubles)*. Calculated as a residual.

(7) *Wage bill (billions of 1937 rubles)*. The product of the 1937 wage bill, 3.2 billion rubles, and column (2). The figures for 1949 and 1951–53 are obtained by interpolation.

(8) *Nonlabor outlays (billions of 1937 rubles)*. The nonlabor outlays in current rubles are reduced to constant rubles by reference to the deflator derived in Table D-3. The total nonwage outlays of 1937, 4.7 billion rubles, are assumed to have been constituted as follows: food, 40 percent; drugs, 20; small-valued equipment not included in fixed capital, 10; building materials, 5; fuel and power, 15; and miscellaneous materials and supplies, 10 percent (totaling 100).

For purposes of deriving a deflator for nonlabor outlays, I combine with the weights given by this breakdown the following price indices:

(a) *Food*. The weight for this category is assigned to Dr. Janet Chapman's given year weighted index numbers of the state and cooperative shop retail prices of food. See her *Real Wages*. For years since 1948, Dr. Chapman compiles food price index numbers for 1952 and 1954 only. I extend the series to other years on the basis of data on official prices in *Sovtorg*, p. 132. Here and elsewhere, where in order, I adjust Dr. Chapman's price indices for 1952 and 1954, which refer to post-cut levels, to obtain indices for the respective calendar years.

(b) *Drugs*. The index numbers to which this weight is assigned are obtained as follows:

1928–40. An average of indices of the wholesale prices of inorganic chemicals and the retail prices of soap. The indices are: for inorganic chemicals for 1928, 57 and for 1940, 118; for soap for 1928, 12.4 and for 1940, 105. See Bergson, et al., RAND RM-1522, p. 18; Chapman, *Real Wages*.

1948. In 1948, the retail price of castor oil tablets was the same as in 1937, while the retail price of aspirin had been reduced. On the other hand, such articles as absorbent cotton, gauze bandages, and thermometers had increased by 29 to 247 percent. See Chapman, RAND RM-803-1, p. 11, and letter of Janet Chapman to Abram Bergson, August 1956. I assume that drug prices generally were somewhat above 1937.

1949–1952. According to Dr. Chapman's letter of August 1956, the prices of drugs were unchanged from 1948 to 1952.

1953–55. From data in *Pravda*, April 1, 1953 and April 1, 1954, I estimate that the prices of drugs in 1953 and 1954 averaged 89 and 75 percent respectively of 1952. For 1955, drug prices are assumed unchanged. There was no change to speak of in retail prices generally from the 1954 level.

(c) *Small-valued equipment*. I arbitrarily assign the weight for this category to an unweighted average of the given year weighted index numbers of wholesale machinery prices, compiled in Moorsteen, *Machinery*, and the index numbers of the retail prices of housewares in Chapman, *Real Wages*. Housewares include metal utensils, electric goods, and various other wares (samovars, serving machines, and primus stoves). Dr. Chapman's indices for

TABLE D-3

Assumed Indicators of Prices of Nonlabor Inputs to Health Care, USSR, 1928–55 (1937 = 100)

Year	Food (1)	Drugs (2)	Small-valued equipment (3)	Building materials (4)	Fuel and power (5)	Miscellaneous materials and supplies (6)	Average (7)
1928	11.2	35	48	57	48	14	27.7 (25)
1937	100	100	100	100	100	100	100
1940	125	112	113	108	135	129	122
1944	—	—	—	124	138	—	130
1948	313	125	186	124	146	280	225
1949	276	125	249	382	350	265	258
1950	223	125	196	313	348	230	225
1951	202	125	188	300	348	222	214
1952	187	125	175	292	334	218	204
1953	164	111	167	292	334	202	189
1954	158	94	163	292	334	185	182
1955	158	94	156	287	324	185	179

1952 and 1954 refer to the post-cut levels. Housewares I believe were unaffected by the April 1952 price cut. For 1954, the yearly average prices for consumers' goods generally were 101.2 percent of the post-cut prices (see Table A-2). I assume this was so for housewares as well. For purposes of calculating an index of nonlabor inputs price indices for housewares for years for which Dr. Chapman's price indices for this category are unavailable, 1940, 1949–51, and 1953, are adapted roughly from indices for all consumers' goods in Table A-1 and corresponding data that have been compiled for manufactured consumers' goods alone.

(d) *Building materials*. The pertinent price indices are compiled from wholesale price index numbers given in Bergson, et al., RAND RM-1522, and in Turgeon and Bergson, RAND RM-1919, for lumber products, nonmetallic minerals, and paint products. The different series are weighted roughly in accord with their 1937 marketed outputs.

(e) *Fuel and power*. The weight for this category is assigned to an unweighted average of the following indices:

Electric power. On the household rates, see Chapman, *Real Wages*. Electric power rates charged institutions appear to have been slightly below those charged households for lighting in 1928, but in the first half of 1937 the lighting rates for institutions, I believe, were 150 percent of those for households. During the second half of 1937, the relation varied from 150 to 200 percent. I assume that on the average for 1937 the institutional rates were 162 percent of those for households and that for more recent years the relation prevailing during the second half of 1937, averaging (say) 175 percent of the household rate, has continued to prevail.

On institutional rates, see Leningradskoe ob'edinenie gosudarstvennykh stantsii "Elektrotok," *Statisticheskii spravochnik, 1913–1928,* p. 100; Moskovskii oblastnoi ispolnitel'nyi komitet sovetov R.K. i. K.D., *Sbornik postanovlenii moskovskogo oblastnogo ispolnitel'nogo komiteta R.I. i. K.D.*, p. 170; Levitini and Fal'kovich, p. 190, 1935; *SZR,* no. 36, June 4, 1937, pp. 337–339.

Coal; peat; fuelwood. An average of price relatives for these three products given in Bergson, et al., RAND RM-1522, and Turgeon and Bergson, RAND RM-1919.

(f) *Miscellaneous materials and supplies.* The weight for this category is assigned the given year weighted index numbers of state and cooperative shop prices of manufactures compiled in Chapman, *Real Wages.* For years since 1948, Dr. Chapman compiles indices only for 1952 and 1954. I interpolate roughly on the basis of trends in official prices. See Appendix A and *Sovtorg,* p. 132.

The foregoing calculations yield price index numbers for nonlabor inputs for all benchmark years covered in Table D-3 except 1944. According to Chapman, *Real Wages,* the ration prices of food and manufactures in 1944 averaged 143 percent of 1937. I take the average prices of all nonlabor inputs to be 130 percent of 1937.

To come to the breakdown of nonlabor outlays given above, the underlying calculations are complex and it may suffice to say that rough estimates of the relative expenditures on foods, drugs, small-valued equipment, and all other materials taken together could be derived from data on the yearly expenditure norms for different types of outlays in Miterev, 1944, p. 280; and budgetary data in Grin'ko, 1937, p. 45. I also considered unpublished information supplied by Marvin Hoffenberg on the structure of inputs to health care in the United States in 1947. The distribution of other expenditures between fuel and power, building materials, and miscellaneous supplies is of a rule-of-thumb character. Miterev's norms refer to 1935; I allow rather arbitrarily for the effects of changes in the price structure from 1935 to 1937.

As was indicated, the electric power rates considered in compiling our deflator for nonlabor outlays are special institutional rates, but I believe I am right in assuming (as I have) that on the whole the medical institutions pay the same prices as wholesale consumers generally. Aside from electric power, I know of no instance of special pricing for institutional buyers. Possibly, nevertheless, there are other cases, but there is positive evidence that the Russians do not make a general practice of arranging special prices for particular purchasers. See pp. 112–113.

Of course, the medical institutions very likely are able to buy at wholesale prices, and the deflator has been compiled in good part from retail prices. Moreover, Dr. Chapman's data for retail prices refer to Moscow alone. For 1937–55, Dr. Chapman finds that retail price trends in Moscow closely parallel those for the USSR generally. Similarly, trade margins declined during this period, but only by a few percent. For this reason, Dr. Chapman's indices of retail prices may be taken to measure the trends in wholesale prices since 1937.

On the other hand, Dr. Chapman finds that with 1937 as a base, retail prices in the USSR in 1928 average but 93 percent of those in Moscow. Then too, Soviet data on trade margins for early years are difficult to compare with those for the period 1937, but the gap between wholesale and retail prices probably narrowed before as well as after 1937, and possibly more in the earlier than in the later period. Under the circumstances, the deflator for nonlabor outlays for 1928 is reduced to about 90 percent of the average of the index numbers of the prices of different inputs. In Table D-3, the computed average for 1928 is shown outside and the deflator finally used inside parentheses.

On the relation between Moscow and average Soviet retail prices, see chapter 4 of this volume and Chapman, *Real Wages*. As to the trade margins, account has been taken of these facts: the *nalozhenie* for goods handled by the "socialized trade apparatus" in the late twenties reportedly was 22.9 percent. It is not easy to be sure what this figure means. Apparently, reference is to the costs incurred in the wholesale and retail distribution of consumers' goods, but the costs of agricultural procurements may also be included. The costs include profits and probably taxes paid by trade outlets. In the base of the percentage, goods handled are counted only once, and very likely are valued at retail prices in the case of processed goods. In 1937, the operating costs of retail outlets amounted to 10.5 percent of retail sales. Inclusive of the costs of wholesale outlets for consumers' goods, and profits of most (although not all) trade outlets in both retail and wholesale trade, the margin rises to 15 percent. For purposes of comparison with the *nalozhenie* of 1928, allowance must be made also for turnover taxes levied on retail outlets, which amounted to about 3.5 percent of retail sales. In retail trade, costs fell from 10.5 percent of retail sales in 1937 to 9.7 percent in 1940. The corresponding figures for 1950 and 1955 were 7.6 and 7.0 percent. Inclusive of wholesale costs and profits generally but exclusive of turnover taxes on retail outlets, the trade margin fell from 15 percent in 1937 to 13.9 percent in 1940, 10.8 percent in 1950, and 11.3 percent in 1955. The foregoing figures are taken from or compiled from data in *Piatiletnii plan,* Vol. II, part 2, pp. 143–144; *KTS 1928–29,* pp. 321–322; *Sovtorg,* pp. 20, 117–119, 124–125; *SNIP-37,* p. 138.

By use of the deflator derived in Table D-3, and the current ruble data on nonlabor outlays in Table D-1, I obtain measures of nonlabor outlays in terms of 1937 rubles for all years except 1949 and 1951–53. Figures for the latter years are computed from the data on total money outlays for health care in column (1); the interpolated figures on labor outlays in 1937 rubles in column (7); assumed indices of money wage changes; and the deflator derived in Table D-3.

The data in column (9) are obtained by totaling the figures in columns (7) and (8).

Outlays in terms of 1950 and 1928 rubles. In index number form, labor and nonlabor outlays in terms of 1950 and 1928 rubles are assumed to correspond to the measures derived above in terms of 1937 rubles.

EDUCATION

Scope of category. As may be judged from the breakdown available for 1937 (Table D-4: see Narkomfin USSR, *Raskhody na sotsial'no-kul'turnye meropriiatiia* . . . , pp. 21–22, 36; *Kul'tstroi,* 1940 ed., p. 33) this category is of broad scope. The current ruble data taken as a point of departure

TABLE D-4

Expenditures on Education, USSR, 1937

Budgetary Expenditures	Million rubles
"General education" (*massovoe prosveshchenie*)	
For children	
General schools	6,481.9
Pioneer movement, children's homes, kindergartens, et cetera	1,723.7
For adults, including libraries, clubs, "houses of culture" (*doma kul'tury*), "red corners," et cetera	1,081.7
Theater, radio, press, et cetera	696.2
Other	46.1
All	10,029.6
Training of cadres	
Technicums, rabfaki and other secondary vocational schools	1,567.0
Universities and other institutions of higher education	2,145.7
Other, including "special courses" (*kursovye meropriiatiia*)	1,859.6
All	5,572.3
"Science" (*nauka*) including Academy of Sciences, research institutions, libraries, museums, et cetera	852.5
All	16,454.7
Other Expenditures	
By government economic organizations	
For training of cadres	498.7
Research	242.6
Capital investments	602.8
Other	196.6
All	1,540.7
By social insurance agencies	243.5
By trade unions	1,156.8
By collective farms, industrial cooperatives, et cetera	1,208.8
All	4,149.8

embrace expenditures not only on schools, universities, and the like but on libraries, museums, scientific research, the pioneer movement, "red corners," and diverse other cultural activities. Some expenditures on the theater, press, et cetera (probably chiefly subsidies) are also covered, as are some expenditures on research and workers' training by government economic organizations. Additional outlays by the trade unions, collective farms and the like, the precise nature of which is not clear, are also covered.

In Table D-4, the budgetary and extrabudgetary expenditures on education total 20.6 billion rubles. For 1937, education in the present study amounts to but 17.0 billion rubles. The difference represents stipends and scholarships, tuition payments, and capital construction. Stipends and scholarships are treated here as a transfer. Tuition payments are included under household outlays on services, and capital construction for education is classified under investment. Both the totals cited above (that is, 20.6 and 17.0 billion rubles) probably omit outlays on the higher government administrative organs concerned with education. Such outlays, then, would fall instead under government administration.

The current ruble figure used in this study for 1928 includes outlays on "general education" (*sotsial'noe vospitanie*); training of cadres; institutions of political education (*politprosvetitel'nye ucherezhdeniia*); cinema, radio, and press; and scientific institutions. Extrabudgetary as well as budgetary outlays are included, while a deduction has been made for capital construction. Since 1937, the current ruble data used here are believed to be essentially of the same scope as the corresponding 1937 figure, although extrabudgetary outlays had to be extrapolated from prewar relations, and information on the scope of the budgetary figures is incomplete.

On the scope of "education," see also the references cited above for health care. See also *Kul'lstroi,* 1936 ed., p. 73.

Outlays in terms of 1937 rubles. The elements in the computation are shown in Table D-5. I comment on each column in turn.

(1) *All outlays* (*billions of current rubles*). See *SNIP-28–48* and *SNIP-49–55.*

(2) *Wage earners and salaried workers engaged* (*1937 = 100*). The series refers to workers in "education" (schools, educational institutions, scientific-research and cultural-educational institutions). This apparently is "education" in the broad Soviet sense that is observed here. Underlying absolute data are from *Narkhoz,* p. 190. For 1944, employment is assumed to be 80 percent of 1945 (which is 110 percent of 1937). This is approximately the relation of government budget appropriations to education in the two years. See Plotnikov, 1948, p. 329. See also the comment above on the corresponding figure for education. Employment for 1948 is interpolated between 1945 and 1950. Employment in 1954 is assumed to be somewhat below 1955 (which was 197 percent of 1937). The budget appropriation for education in 1954 was 65.6 billion rubles and in 1955, 69.2 billion rubles (see *SNIP-49–55*). See also the comment on the corresponding figure for health care.

(3) *Average annual wage* (*1937 = 100*). The underlying absolute figure for 1928, 678 rubles, is from TSUNKHU, *Trud v SSSR,* 1936 ed., pp. 16–17. That for 1937, 3442 rubles, is from *TPP,* pp. 228–9. For 1940, average earnings of all Soviet workers were 133 percent of 1937. According to possibly inflated data in *1941 Plan,* p. 512, the goal for the earnings of educational workers for 1941 was 4331 rubles, or 126 percent of 1937. I assume a 20 percent increase to 1940. For 1944–55, see the discussion above of the corresponding figures for workers engaged in health care.

TABLE D-5

Calculation of Outlays on Education in 1937 Prices, USSR, 1928–55

Year	All outlays (bil. current rubles) (1)	Wage earners and salaried workers engaged (1937 = 100) (2)	Average annual wage (1937 = 100) (3)	Wage bill (1937 = 100) (4)	Wage bill (bil. current rubles) (5)	Nonlabor outlays (bil. current rubles) (6)	Wage bill (bil. 1937 rubles) (7)	Nonlabor outlays (bil. 1937 rubles) (8)	Total outlays (bil. 1937 rubles) (9)
1928	0.87	34.0	19.7	6.7	0.66	0.21	3.3	0.6	3.9
1937	17.0	100	100	100	9.8	7.2	9.8	7.2	17.0
1940	23.8	126	120	151	14.8	9.0	12.3	7.6	19.9
1944	20.9	88	160	141	13.8	7.1	8.6	5.5	14.1
1948	58.4	143	220	315	30.9	27.5	14.0	12.9	26.9
1949	60.2	—	—	—	—	—	(14.9)	(9.3)	24.2
1950	59.0	162	231	374	36.7	22.3	15.9	8.7	24.6
1951	59.2	—	—	—	—	—	(16.6)	(8.1)	24.7
1952	59.9	—	—	—	—	—	(17.3)	(7.6)	24.9
1953	61.7	—	—	—	—	—	(18.0)	(7.5)	25.5
1954	66.1	190	253	481	47.1	19.0	18.6	8.4	27.0
1955	69.3	197	257	506	49.6	19.7	19.3	8.8	28.1

(4) *Wage bill (1937 = 100)*. The product of columns (2) and (3).

(5) *Wage bill (billions of current rubles)*. Derived from column (3) and an independent estimate of the wage bill for 1937. The government budget appropriation to education in 1937 was 16.5 billion rubles. Of this sum, 6.9 billion rubles, or 41.8 percent, were paid out in wages to educational workers. See Narkomfin SSSR, *Raskhody na sotsial'no-kulturnye meropriiatiia . . .* , p. 50. The cited figure on wage payments excludes wage expense incurred in the training of "mass cadres." The precise nature of this omission is not clear, but I believe we will be about right if we assume that all wages constituted 45.0 percent of the budget expenditures. Assuming the same proportion obtained in the case of "other outlays," the total wages paid from all sources come to 9.3 billion rubles. I raise this to 9.8 billion rubles in order to allow for charges that are proportional to wages, particularly social insurance contributions. See SNK decree No. 493, March 23, 1937, *SZR*, no. 22, April 17, 1937 for the social insurance contribution rates.

According to *TPP*, pp. 228, 229, 7.9 billion rubles of wages were paid to workers engaged in education in 1937. As with the comparable figure for health care, this TSUNKHU figure must omit many educational workers whose activities are of a secondary nature to their employing establishment.

(6) *Nonlabor outlays (billions of current rubles)*. Calculated as residual.

(7) *Wage bill (billion of 1937 rubles)*. The product of column (2) and the 1937 wage bill, 9.8 billion rubles. For 1949 and 1951–53, the figures are interpolated.

(8) *Nonlabor outlays (billion 1937 rubles)*. The nonlabor outlays in current rubles are reduced to constant rubles by reference to the deflator derived in Table D-6. The deflator is obtained as an unweighted average of the following price indices:

Fuel, power. See Table D-3.

Building materials. See Table D-3.

Housewares; cultural-sport goods. An unweighted average of the Chapman indices for housewares used in deriving Table D-3, column (3) and corresponding indices that Dr. Chapman has compiled of "cultural-sport goods." The latter includes such items as cameras, gramophones, accordions, pianos, bicycles, pencils, penholders. See Chapman, *Real Wages*. Dr. Chapman's indices for 1952 and 1954 refer to post-cut prices. Cultural and sport goods were unaffected by the price cut of April 1952. For 1954, I assume that average prices were 101.2 percent of the post-cut prices, as with retail prices generally. See Table A-2. Indices for cultural-sport goods for 1940, 1949–51, and 1953 and 1955 are adapted roughly from Dr. Chapman's indices for all manufactures and corresponding indices in *Sovtorg*, p. 132.

Reading matter. Index numbers of retail prices for 1928–48 and post-cut 1952 and 1954 are from Chapman, *Real Wages*. Reading matter apparently was unaffected by the 1952 and 1954 price cuts. For 1949–51, I interpolate as for cultural and sport goods. The prices of manufactures generally in 1955 remained unchanged at the 1954 level.

(While for present purposes use is supposed to be made here of Dr. Chapman's given-year weighted index numbers, at a late stage it was found

TABLE D-6

Assumed Indicators of Prices of Nonlabor Inputs to Education, USSR, 1928–55
(1937 = 100)

Year	Fuel, power (1)	Building materials (2)	House-wares; cultural, sport goods (3)	Reading matter (4)	Food (5)	Average (6)
1928	48	57	41	48	11.2	41 (37)
1937	100	100	100	100	100	100
1940	135	108	124	105	125	119
1944	138	124	—	—	—	130
1948	146	124	260	227	313	214
1949	350	382	238	215	276	292
1950	348	313	202	190	223	255
1951	348	300	192	187	202	246
1952	334	292	186	183	187	236
1953	334	292	175	183	164	230
1954	334	292	166	183	158	227
1955	324	287	166	183	158	224

that for reading matter for 1948 her base-year weighted index was employed instead. If in place of the latter index for 1948 of 227 (Table D-6), reference is made to the former, which is 194, my index of the prices of nonlabor inputs to education for 1948 falls from 214 to 207. Correspondingly, for 1948 nonlabor outlays on education rise from 12.9 to 13.3 billion 1937 rubles, and total outlays from 26.9 to 27.3 billion 1937 rubles. Because of the change in the 1948 price index for reading matter, the corresponding interpolated figures for 1949–51 are also affected, and consequently there are changes also in the index numbers of prices of all nonlabor inputs for these years, but my final results regarding nonlabor and total outlays for these years are hardly affected.)

Food. See above, Table D-3.

For 1944, Dr. Chapman finds that the ration prices of food and manufactured goods averaged 143 percent of 1937. The corresponding figure for 1940 was 132 percent. I assume that the index of the prices of all nonlabor inputs rose from 119 in 1940 to 130 in 1944.

The comments made in the section on health care on the appropriateness of index numbers of retail prices to measure the trends in prices to institutions apply here as well. As before, the index I use as a deflator for 1928 is reduced 10 percent below the computed average of the index numbers of input prices. In Table D-6, the computed average is outside and the index used as a deflator is inside parentheses.

The various series in Table D-6 are intended to be representative of the more important nonlabor inputs to education. These, I believe, include power and fuel; materials for the repair and maintenance of equipment and buildings; such furniture and equipment as are not considered as fixed capital investments in Soviet statistics; books, miscellaneous teaching supplies; office supplies and food. A search of Soviet sources has yielded only scattered and often conflicting information on the structure of nonlabor inputs to education. Although Dr. Marvin Hoffenberg kindly supplied some I-O (input-output) data for the United States, which provided some guidance, it did not seem possible to construct a set of weights for the available indicators of input prices. Food is the major constituent of expenditures of nursery schools, children's homes and probably also of the pioneer movement, which together totaled 1.3 billion rubles in 1937.

By deflating the current ruble data on nonlabor outlays in Table D-5, I obtain corresponding constant ruble figures for all years except 1949 and 1951–53. "Real" outlays for the latter years are also obtained by deflation. The current ruble figures are computed as residuals from the data on total outlays in Table D-5, column (1), the interpolated figures on the "real" wage bill in column (7) of the same table, and indices of money wage changes interpolated from the data in column (3).

The data in column (9) are obtained by totaling the figures in columns (7) and (8).

Outlays in 1950 and 1928 Rubles

In index number form, labor and nonlabor outlays in terms of 1950 and 1928 rubles are assumed to correspond to the measures derived above in terms of 1937 rubles.

Other Communal Services

In relation to the total outlays on health care and education, the expenditures on these services (such as social security administration) in terms of constant rubles are taken to be more or less proportional to their magnitudes in current rubles.

Government Administration

Scope of category. In the Soviet budgetary sources from which the current ruble data on this category are taken, the figures usually are cited as representing "expenditures on the maintenance of government organs of administration and judicial institutions" or some similiarly designated outlays. Such expenditures are for the maintenance of all higher and local organs of governmental authority, executive, legislative, and judicial, except the NKVD and its predecessors and successors, and of the defense departments. Expenditures of superior organs for the administration of health care and education probably are included. Among agencies administering the economy, the *glavki* or departments of ministries (prior to 1946, commissariats) are included if they do not operate on a *khozraschet* basis but are excluded if they do operate on this basis. This means among other things that supply and procurement departments of industrial ministries that were placed on *khozraschet* operations in 1936 are included in "government administration" prior to but not after that year. Moreover, some agencies which might conventionally be considered government organs probably have been supported at one time or another out of government appropriations to "financing the national economy," under the heading "operational outlays" rather than out of appropriations to "government administration." For example, this has been so in the case of agencies administering the weather service, geodetics, resettlement, and weights and measures.

See above, p. 18; the SNIP studies and the source cited therein; Narkomfin SSSR, *Klassifikatsiia raskhodov i dokhodov edinogo gosudarstvennogo biudzheta na 1936* g; D'iachenko, 1940, pp. 417 ff.

Expenditures in 1937, 1950, and 1928 rubles. In Table D-7, column (1), the figures on outlays in current rubles are from *SNIP-28–48* and *SNIP-49–55.*

TABLE D-7

Calculation of Expenditures on Government Administration, in 1937 Rubles, 1928–55

Year	Total outlays (billion current rubles) (1)	Assumed annual wage, (1937 = 100) (2)	Assumed prices of nonlabor inputs (1937 = 100) (3)	Prices of all inputs (1937 = 100) (4)	Total outlays (billion 1937 rubles) (5)
1928	0.73	22.9	37	27.1	2.7
1937	4.4	100	100	100	4.4
1940	6.8	133	119	129	5.3
1944	7.4	181	130	166	4.5
1948	13.1	230	214	225	5.8
1949	13.5	239	292	255	5.3
1950	13.9	247	255	249	5.6
1951	14.0	255	246	252	5.6
1952	14.3	263	236	255	5.6
1953	13.9	268	230	257	5.4
1954	13.6	275	227	260	5.2
1955	12.6	280	224	263	4.8

In column (2), the indices of average annual earnings of government workers for 1928 and 1937 are based on corresponding absolute figures in TSUNKHU, *Trud v SSSR,* 1936 ed., pp. 16–17, and *TPP,* pp. 228–229. The earnings data in these sources probably represent the average wages of workers not only in "government administration" but also in certain related branches, especially intermediate organs of economic administration that operate on a *khozraschet* basis, for example, trusts and syndicates, and the trade unions and possibly the Communist Party. For 1937–55, the indices are taken to be the same as for all workers, as given in Appendix H. For the period 1928–37, earnings in the branches covered by the *Trud v SSSR* and *TPP* data increased by the same amount as the earnings of all workers. Thus, the average annual wage in government administration and related branches in 1928 was 22.9 percent of 1937; the average annual wage of all workers in 1928 was 23.1 percent of 1937.

In column (3) of Table D-7, the indices of nonlabor input prices are the same as those derived in Table D-6 for nonlabor inputs to education.

In calculating the indices of the prices of all inputs in Table D-7, column (4), I assign the wage indices a weight of 0.7 and the nonlabor input price indices a weight of 0.3. According to D'iachenko, 1940, p. 420, wages constitute "about 70 percent" of the total outlays on government administration. For 1937, a similar relation seems to be obtained if one starts with the wage bill data for government administration and related branches in *TPP,* pp. 228–229, and deducts an allowance for the earnings in related branches.

The figures in column (5) are obtained as the quotient column of (1) and column (4). In terms of 1950 and 1928 rubles, "real" outlays on government administration vary in the same way as in terms of 1937 rubles.

NKVD

Scope of category. The current ruble figure for 1928 that is deflated represents the budgetary expenditures of the Unified State Political Administration (OGPU), the chief agency concerned with "internal affairs" at the time, and of the People's Commissariat of Internal Affairs (NKVD), which then administered certain "special purpose militia." In 1937 and 1940 the then existing commissariat of the latter name apparently was in charge of "internal affairs" generally. For these years, therefore, the current ruble figure deflated represents the budgetary expenditures of that agency. For more recent years, the SNIP figures represent the budgetary expenditures of various successor agencies to the 1937–40 NKVD: from 1944 to 1953 the Commissariats (after 1946 Ministries) of Internal Affairs and State Security (NKVD and NKGB); in 1953–54, the Ministry of Internal Affairs (MVD), and in 1954 and 1955, the Ministry of Internal Affairs (MVD) and the Committee on State Security (KGB).

The precise scope of the "NKVD" expenditures is not entirely clear. In addition to its main concern, internal security, the NKVD, at least at one time or another has performed a variety of other activities such as fire protection, civil registration, forest guards, automobile inspection, and inspection of weights and measures. So far as its responsibilities have varied in these regards, this need not affect the comparability of our data on government administration, including the NKVD, for when the tasks in question were not performed by the NKVD they may have been performed by other agencies financed out of the budgtary appropriation to "government administration." Some of such outlays, however, have also been financed, out of "Financing the national economy," under "operational expenditures." To this extent, comparability may be affected.

As part of its internal security activities, the NKVD also maintains quasi-military detachments. These have performed such services as military police, POW guards, and convoy escorts. In other countries such services usually fall to the military establishment proper, and in national income calculations such as mine would be classified below under "Defense."

The figure cited for 1940 is known to be exclusive of an appropriation for "various construction work of the NKVD." This appropriation was made under the heading "Financing the national economy," and in my calculations finds its way (as it properly should) into "Gross investment." Very possibly capital construction outlays of the NKVD were also financed this way in other years. On the other hand, so far as they were not they presumably would be included in NKVD expenditures as recorded in our calculations. Since in the SNIP studies "Gross investment" is calculated as a residual, there would be a corresponding understatement of this category.

In its use of "penal labor," the NKVD, I believe, operates substantially on a *khozraschet* basis. This means that penal subsistence is largely financed out of sales receipts rather than out of the budgetary appropriation to the NKVD. Since penal subsistence may not be included anywhere else in my calculations, there may be a resultant understatement of both household consumption and national income.

The foregoing remarks are taken largely from *SNIP-40–48,* pp. 198–199.

TABLE D-8

Calculation of NKVD Expenditures in 1937 Rubles, 1928–55

Year	Outlays (billion rubles) (1)	Assumed prices of inputs (1937 = 100) (2)	Outlays (billion 1937 rubles) (3)
1928	0.09	27.1	0.33
1937	3.0	100	3.0
1940	7.1	129	5.5
1944	6.6	166	4.0
1948	26	225	11.6
1949	23	255	9.0
1950	23	249	9.2
1951	23	252	9.1
1952	22	255	8.6
1953	16	257	6.2
1954	16	260	6.2
1955	15	263	5.7

Expenditures in 1937, 1950, and 1928 rubles. In Table D-8, column (1), the current ruble figures are from *SNIP-28–48* and *SNIP-49–55.* On the price indices in column (2), see Table D-7, column (4). The figures in column (3) represent the quotient of columns (1) and (2). In terms of 1950 and 1928 rubles, NKVD outlays are assumed to vary in the same way as they do in 1937 rubles.

APPENDIX E

"Real" Defense Outlays

Scope of category. As recorded in the government budget, defense outlays represent the appropriation to the department or departments administering the Soviet armed forces: in 1928 the Commissariat of War and Naval Affairs; in 1937–44 the Commissariat of Defense, so-called, and (after July 1937) the Commissariat of the Naval Fleet; in 1948–50 the Ministry of the Armed Forces; in 1950–53 the Ministries of War and Navy; and in 1953–55 the Ministry of Defense. The appropriations cover military pay and subsistence, munitions procurement, and presumably expenditures for diverse other commodities and services of a conventional sort, principally petroleum and other nonmunitions needed for current operations, labor and materials needed for military construction, and transport. Outlays on military and civilian administrative employees of the defense departments are also included.

In the USSR, munitions production is the responsibility not of the military establishment but of economic agencies — since the mid-thirties, of agencies specialized to this end. Accordingly, the budget defense appropriation (as is usually the case also in the United States) includes munitions costs at the procurement stage, but omits any stocks held by the defense production agencies. Although outlays for the construction of military facilities, for example, camps and fortifications, are included in the defense appropriation, investments in defense plant construction are classified instead under "Financing the National Economy." Under this heading they are included in the appropriation to the defense production agencies.

What has been said of munitions and defense plant construction generally, it is believed, applies also to atomic weapons and atomic weapon plant construction. Stock piles of atomic weapons in the USSR, as in the United States, may be held by agencies other than the defense departments. If so, the stock-piling of such weapons would not be financed by the budget defense appropriation. Some expenditures on military research, including atomic research, may be included under the budget appropriation for education rather than under that for defense.

As has been noted, the NKVD is engaged in some activities which in other countries would generally be performed by the military establishment as such. Accordingly, the budget appropriation to the latter is correspondingly restricted.

Some premilitary training is given in common schools, and as such is financed by budget appropriations to education. Paramilitary training is provided by various "voluntary" societies as assistance to the armed forces.

I do not know how the Russians accounted in their budget for requisitions and occupation charges levied since the war in Eastern Europe and Germany. No doubt some of these do not show up in the budget at all, and accordingly are also omitted from the recorded expenditures of the military establishment. It is not known either how the Russians account for military assistance to China and the satellites. They may or may not include it in the budget defense appropriation.

Most military pensions in the USSR have long been paid out of the budget appropriation to "social assistance," and are thus omitted from that to defense. On the other hand, under arrangements dating at least from 1941, pensions are paid to officers, certain other personnel, and their dependents out of the budget defense appropriation. In the present study, an allowance for such pensions has been deducted from the budget appropriation.

In the present study, defense plant construction falls under gross investment. Any additions to weapon stock piles not financed from the defense appropriation might also find its way into gross investment here. Civilian research and development expenditures are included under education. The support of NKVD military activities falls here under NKVD outlays. Premilitary training presumably is included in education, while paramilitary training may not be represented anywhere in my data. Similarly, if requisition and occupation charges are not cleared through the government budget, they do not show up in my calculations at all. If Soviet military assistance to the Orbit is omitted from Soviet defense outlays, it may fall under gross investment.

The foregoing is taken largely from *SNIP-40–48,* pp. 198–201. See also the sources cited therein and the other SNIP studies.

Expenditures in current rubles. The current ruble data on defense expenditures that are taken as a point of departure are assembled in Table E-1. The figures on all outlays correspond to the sums recorded in the budget as defense expenditures after deduction from the latter of an allowance for pensions paid to officers, et al. In the table, the figures on total outlays are from *SNIP-28–48* and *SNIP-49–55.* For 1953 and 1955 the *SNIP-49–55* figures are revised in the light of late budgetary data in *Narkhoz-1958,* p. 900.

The data on pay and subsistence are also taken from the SNIP studies,

TABLE E-1

Defense Expenditures, USSR, 1928–55
(billions of rubles)

Year	All expenditures	Military pay	Military subsistence	Munitions and other procurement
1928	0.76	0.15	0.25	0.36
1937	17.4	1.5	2.5	13.4
1940	56.5	4.1	6.6	45.8
1944	135.7	14.2	25.7	95.8
1948	64.3	10.2	13.0	41.1
1949	77.2	10.5	12.0	54.7
1950	80.8	15.0	14.1	51.7
1951	91.9	19.0	16.5	56.4
1952	106.6	23.2	19.4	64.0
1953	105.8	23.6	18.1	64.1
1954	99.8	24.1	17.7	58.0
1955	105.4	23.4	17.2	64.8

but in the latter the estimates for these categories for 1948–55 rest on a rather arbitrary supposition that throughout this period the Soviet armed forces were of a constant size, 4.0 million men. In Table E-1, I have revised the SNIP figures for military pay and subsistence in order to make them conform instead to these data on the size of the armed forces:

In 1948, there were 2.9 million men; in 1949, 2.9; in 1950, 4.0; in 1951, 4.9; in 1952, 5.8; in 1953, 5.8; in 1954, 5.8; and in 1955, 5.5 million men.

In his speech before the Supreme Soviet of January 14, 1960 (*Pravda*, January 15, 1960), Khrushchev reports that "by 1948" the Soviet armed forces had been reduced from their wartime strength to 2,874,000 men. I assume that this is also the number of men who were under arms *on the average* during 1948. Khrushchev also indicates that prior to a cut initiated in the latter part of 1955, the armed forces had numbered 5,763,000 men. Considering that the cut was to have involved 640,000 men, I take the average strength for 1955 to have been 5.5 millions. Khrushchev does not reveal when the increase to the 1955 pre-cut strength was realized. Most likely it occurred mainly at the time of the Korean War and immediately after.

In the SNIP studies, military pay and subsistence for 1937 are computed on the supposition that the armed forces during that year averaged 1,750,000 men. In his speech before the Supreme Soviet, Khrushchev reports that "by 1937" the armed forces had been increased to 1,433,000. Considering the ambiguity of Khrushchev's language, it did not seem worthwhile to revise the SNIP figures on pay and subsistence at this point. Similarly, while the SNIP data for 1944 assume that the armed forces in that year averaged 12.0 million men, no revision seemed indicated in order to take account of Khrushchev's statement that "by May 1945" the armed forces had been increased to 11,365,000 men.

To complete the story, in the SNIP studies the armed forces were taken to number 562,000 in 1928 and 3,500,000 in 1940. These figures would seem to be reasonably consistent with further data reported by Khrushchev: The armed forces reached 586,000 men "by 1927" and 4,207,000 men "by 1941."

In Table E-1, expenditures on munitions and other procurement are obtained as a residual.

Some further information is available regarding the structure of expenditures on munitions and other procurement. The data pertain to the annual plan for 1941. The government expected to spend on defense in that year 71 billion rubles. Of this sum, some 15.5 billion rubles might have been allotted to military pay and subsistence, leaving a balance of about 55 billions for munitions and other procurement. See Kaplan, et al., RAND RM-924, pp. 131 ff. In this report, the Soviet armed forces were assumed to have been planned to average 5.5 million men in 1941. I reduce the resultant estimates of troop pay and subsistence by about 15 percent in order to make them conform more nearly to Khrushchev's report that the armed forces had come to number 4.2 millions "by 1941." Furthermore, in order to make the estimate of military subsistence consistent with revised data on this item in *SNIP-28–48,* subsistence per man is taken here to have been worth 2200 rubles a year in terms of January 1941 prices.

On the disposition of the planned outlays on munitions and other procurement, there are these data:

(a) The defense industry commissariats were to produce in 1941 a "marketed output" (*tovarnaia produktsiia*) of 40.3 billion rubles in current wholesale prices. See *1941 Plan,* p. 11. This includes additions to the finished goods inventories of the munitions factories, such secondary products of munition factories as are produced for the market, and some additional products which are so classified in the USSR, that is, principally finished goods and productive services (power, water, et cetera) allocated to the enterprises' own construction work, to capital repair, and to housing, et cetera. The Russians, I believe, do not classify as marketed industrial output construction activities as such. The cited figure on the output of the munitions industries apparently is part of a breakdown of industrial output. Almost certainly the cited figure was calculated by the "factory method," and includes sales by one munitions plant to another within any given commissariat. The foregoing all tend to inflate the *1941 Plan* figure in relation to actual munitions transfers to the military establishment (which are the ultimate interest here), but some munitions probably were produced by commissariats other than those specialized to munitions production, and this would have been an offset.

On the Soviet concept of *tovarnaia produktsiia,* see NKTP, *Formy kontrol'nykh tsifr tiazheloi promyshlennosti na 1937 god,* pp. 6 ff; TSUNKHU, *Slovar — spravochnik po sotsial'no-ekonomicheskoi statistike,* 2nd ed., pp. 112–113, 117; Savinskii, 4th ed., pp. 86 ff.

(b) The target for military construction to be carried out by the defense commissariats in 1941 may have totaled 3.0 to 3.5 billion rubles. See *1941 Plan,* pp. 3, 483–485, Kaplan, RAND RM-735, pp. 155–156.

(c) Planned petroleum procurements may be estimated at 1.5 billion rubles. See the data on tonnage procurements in Kaplan, et al., RAND RM-924, pp. 34 ff. and the price data in Nimitz, RAND RM-1497, p. 73.

Of special interest here is the breakdown of munitions and other procurements between the two major components. Although this is difficult to gauge, we probably shall not be far in error in assuming that munitions constituted (say) 70 percent of the total in 1941 or about 38 billion rubles. Other procurements, therefore, account for 30 percent, or 17 billion rubles. Two main uncertainties concern the volume of sales between different munitions factories and the amount of munitions produced by nonspecialized agencies. In the United States in wartime, sales between munitions factories were important. Possibly this has been true for the USSR as well, but if so production by nonspecialized factories probably was significant also. I find that construction and petroleum procurements totaled but 4.5 to 5.0 billion rubles. Hence, on the assumed breakdown some 10 billion rubles are still left for transportation and other miscellaneous procurements. It is difficult to believe that the actual figure could have been much larger. In exploring the possible structure of Soviet procurements, I have considered also the wartime experience of the United States in the light of information supplied by S. A. Haggart of The RAND Corporation.

To recapitulate, I am led to some such breakdown as the following of the 71 billion rubles of planned defense outlays for 1941: military pay and subsistence, 16 billion rubles or 22.5 percent of the total; munitions, 38 billion rubles or 53.5 percent; and other, 17 billion rubles, 23.9 percent.

Military services in 1937 prices. In Table E-2, column (2), the data on

TABLE E-2

Defense Expenditures in 1937 Prices, USSR, 1928–55
(billions of rubles)

<table>
<tr><th>Year</th><th>All expenditures (1)</th><th>Military services (2)</th><th>Munitions (3)</th><th>Other (4)</th></tr>
<tr><td>1928</td><td>1.9</td><td>1.3</td><td colspan="2">0.6</td></tr>
<tr><td>1937</td><td>17.4</td><td>4.0</td><td colspan="2">13.4</td></tr>
<tr><td>1940</td><td>45.8</td><td>8.0</td><td>26.8</td><td>11.0</td></tr>
<tr><td>1944</td><td>118.0</td><td>27.4</td><td>70.6</td><td>20.0</td></tr>
<tr><td>1948</td><td>40.5</td><td>6.6</td><td>25.9</td><td>8.0</td></tr>
<tr><td>1949</td><td>40.5</td><td>6.6</td><td colspan="2">33.9</td></tr>
<tr><td>1950</td><td>42.4</td><td>9.1</td><td>25.3</td><td>8.0</td></tr>
<tr><td>1951</td><td>48.0</td><td>11.2</td><td>27.8</td><td>9.0</td></tr>
<tr><td>1952</td><td>59.5</td><td>13.3</td><td>36.2</td><td>10.0</td></tr>
<tr><td>1953</td><td>59.4</td><td>13.3</td><td>36.1</td><td>10.0</td></tr>
<tr><td>1954</td><td>53.6</td><td>13.3</td><td>30.3</td><td>10.0</td></tr>
<tr><td>1955</td><td>62.0</td><td>12.6</td><td>39.4</td><td>10.0</td></tr>
</table>

TABLE E-3

Index Numbers of Prices, Munitions and Related Series, USSR, 1928–55 (1937 = 100)

Year	Munitions procurement prices, assumed (1)	Domestic civilian machinery, wholesale prices (Moorsteen) (2)	Munitions materials inputs, wholesale prices (3)	Average annual wages, adjusted, industrial workers (4)
1928	60[a]	70	60	27
1937	100	100	100	100
1940	120	106	126	128
1944	96	110	144	154
1948	106	130	144	208
1949	—	273	286	219
1950	127	191	206	231
1951	123	186	206	243
1952	109	165	185	254
1953	109	165	185	259
1954	109	165	185	266
1955	101	153	179	271

[a] Including other procurement.

military services in terms of 1937 rubles are obtained as the product of the outlays on military pay and subsistence per man in 1937 (2286 rubles) and the size of the armed forces in the respective years. The armed forces vary, as has been explained.

Military pay and subsistence represent in effect the value of military services in the defense budget. The foregoing calculation, therefore, tells us the value of military services in different years in terms of the average pay (in money and kind) of the armed forces in 1937. It will readily be seen that this is what is desired at this point. The alternative procedure that might be considered, involving the deflation of military pay and subsistence, would be logically inappropriate.

Index numbers of prices; related series. In deriving the measure of "real" outlays on munitions and other procurement in Table E-2, columns (3) and (4), use is made of a number of series of index numbers of prices that might indicate defense price trends. The series are set forth in Table E-3, columns (2), (3), and (4), and in Table E-4, columns (2), (3), and (4). I comment below on each series in turn. The price series for munitions in Table E-3, column (1), and that for other procurements in Table E-4, column (1), are explained later.

Domestic civilian machinery, wholesale prices. These are Formula (5) index numbers compiled in Moorsteen, *Machinery*. They refer to domestically produced machinery, and do not reflect the prices of imports. The

TABLE E-4

Index Numbers of Prices, Other Procurement and Related Series, USSR, 1928–55 (1937 = 100)

Year	Other procurements, prices assumed (1)	Basic industrial goods, wholesale prices (Bergson, Bernaut, Turgeon) (2)	Average annual wages, adjusted, industrial workers (3)	Average RR revenue per ton/km (Blackman) (4)
1928	—	45	27	73
1937	100	100	100	100
1940	125	121	128	156
1944	140	128	154	196
1948	170	128	208	151
1949	—	303	219	277
1950	245	256	231	262
1951	247	251	243	—
1952	245	236	254	253
1953	248	236	259	259
1954	250	236	266	—
1955	250	228	271	—

latter were of some importance in 1928 and again (under Lend-Lease) in 1944. In 1928, Moorsteen finds that the prices of all machinery, domestic and imported, averaged 60 percent of the domestic prices of 1937.

Munitions materials inputs, wholesale prices. An average of Formula (6) index numbers for quality steel, nonferrous metal rolled products, and inorganic chemicals compiled in Bergson, Bernaut, and Turgeon, RAND RM-1522, and in Turgeon and Bergson, RAND RM-1919. Considering the U.S. wartime experience, J. C. DeHaven and Robert Grosse of The RAND Corporation advised me to assign weights of 4:1:1 to these different series, the larger weight being assigned to quality steel.

Average annual wages, adjusted, industrial workers. See Appendix H. For 1944, the cited index involves the discounting of the wartime overtime hours on the ground that they were of inferior quality. Without the discount, the 1944 index would be 138.

Basic industrial goods, wholesale prices. These are Formula (6) index numbers but partial recomputation in terms of Formula (5) yield the same index for 1928 and nearly the same index (a few percent lower) for 1955. See Bergson, Bernaut, and Turgeon, *Journal of Political Economy,* August 1956, Turgeon and Bergson, RAND RM-1919.

Average RR revenue per ton/km. From an unpublished memorandum of James Blackman. Since railways are the predominant Soviet carrier, the series may indicate very roughly the trends in freight charges generally. For present purposes, it is difficult to interpret nevertheless because actual freight payments depend partly on the length of haul. Moreover, the average charge for all freight is determined largely by the freight charges on bulk cargoes. There are indications that munitions tariffs may have moved quite differently from tariffs generally.

In Table E-5, the index numbers in Table E-3 have been recomputed in a form convenient for present purposes.

Munitions and other procurement in 1937 prices: 1928. The assumed price index, 60 percent of 1937 (Table E-3), is somewhat below that for civilian machinery and somewhat above that for basic industrial goods. Defense outlays as a whole, including military pay and subsistence, constituted but a few percent of the national income in 1928. For this reason, and because of the inherent limitations in any calculation for 1928, it did not seem worth while to treat munitions and other procurements separately for this early year.

Munitions and other procurement in 1937 prices: 1940–55. It may be well to explain first that I assume that there was no change in the "real" volume of defense outlays in 1949. While this was the year of a major price reform, Zverev (*PKh,* 1949, no. 2, p. 49) informs us that defense outlays remained on the level of the previous year if account is taken of increases in these outlays in connection with the increase in wholesale prices and RR rates. Prior to adjustment for officers pensions, defense expenditures in 1948 amounted to 66.3 billion rubles. See *SNIP-28–48.* The corresponding target for 1949 was 79.1 billion rubles while the realized outlays amounted to 79.2 billion rubles. See Zverev, *op. cit.,* p. 49 and *SNIP-49–55.* Exclusive of military pay, subsistence, and pensions, therefore, expenditures in 1949 both planned and realized were 33 percent above 1948. Wages probably rose only a few percent in 1949 but the prices of the chief munitions materials inputs doubled (Table E-5). In order for "real" defense outlays to have been constant in 1949, the government probably would have had to impose some reduction in profit margins on munitions enterprises, but without further information it seems best to rely on Zverev at this point nevertheless.

Turning to years other than 1949, essentially munitions and other procurements are calculated separately by deflation for 1940. For later years, other procurements are estimated directly in 1937 rubles by a free hand extrapolation. The results, taken together with assumed price index numbers for other procurements, provide the basis for the calculation of such procurements in current rubles for 1944 and after. From the data in Table E-1, munitions procurements in current rubles are computed as a residual. Using assumed index numbers of prices, corresponding constant ruble data are obtained by deflation. Although the figures used for other procurements in terms of 1937 rubles for 1944 and after are arbitrary, I believe my calculation of defense outlays as a whole is more reliable than it would have been if this lesser component had not been treated separately.

To refer in more detail to the calculations for years other than 1949, of the 45.8 billion rubles spent on munitions and other procurements in 1940, I take 30 percent or 13.7 billion rubles as representing outlays on the latter. See above, the breakdown of defense expenditures planned for 1941. The corresponding sum in 1937 rubles (Table E-2) is computed by deflation. I explain in a moment the index number of prices that is used as the deflator. In

TABLE E-5

Index Numbers of Prices, Munitions and Related Series, USSR, 1928–55
(bases of percentages as indicated)

Year	Munitions procurement prices, assumed (1)	Domestic civilian machinery, wholesale prices (Moorsteen) (2)	Munitions materials inputs, wholesale prices (3)	Average annual wages adjusted, industrial workers (4)
1928 ÷ 1937	60[a]	70	60	27
1940 ÷ 1937	120	106	126	128
1944 ÷ 1940	80	104	114	120
1948 ÷ 1944	110	118	100	135
1949 ÷ 1948	—	210	199	105
1950 ÷ 1948	120	147	143	111
1951 ÷ 1950	97	97	100	105
1952 ÷ 1951	89	89	90	105
1953 ÷ 1952	100	100	100	102
1954 ÷ 1953	100	100	100	103
1955 ÷ 1954	93	93	97	102

[a] Including other procurement.

extrapolating "real" outlays on other procurement to later years, and first of all to 1944 (Table E-2), I consider that military construction ordinarily might have declined considerably after the actual initiation of conflict, but the Red Army must have had a good deal of construction work to do in the devastated areas it was reoccupying, for example, air bases and transport installations. Furthermore, there must have been a considerable increase in petroleum procurements, transportation, civilian services, et cetera. As it turns out, the assumed increase in other procurements still leaves it a smaller proportion of total "real" defense outlays in 1944 than in 1940.

In terms of 1937 prices, other procurements in 1948 are taken to fall below the 1940 level. The armed forces of 1948 probably were somewhat smaller than those of 1940. Moreover, military construction and diverse other kinds of procurement must have been much less than before the war. The extrapolation from 1948 takes into account the rising strength of the armed forces. As will appear, munitions procurement also rose after 1948. Very possibly, other procurements rose more than is assumed. If "real" outlays on other procurements in 1955 were 12.5 billion rubles (instead of the 10.0 billion rubles that is assumed in Table E-2), "real" outlays on defense generally would fall from 62.0 to 58.3 billion rubles.

To repeat, use is made of assumed index numbers of the prices of other procurements in order to deflate the current ruble figure derived above for 1940 and to inflate the constant ruble data extrapolated for later years. In Table E-4, the index numbers of the prices of other procurements are obtained simply by averaging with roughly equal weights the indices of the prices of basic industrial goods and of adjusted average wages in industry. Considering that the former indices include petroleum prices with a weight equal to nearly one-third of the total, I believe they may properly represent other procurements of industrial goods generally. Average industrial wages may be taken to represent the wages of civilian employees of the military establishment in administrative, construction, and other work. For a number of years from 1940 on, basic industrial prices move fairly closely with industrial wages, so the precise weights used in aggregating these two series are not so consequential. On the other hand, there are marked divergencies, especially in 1948, and the computations inevitably become more arbitrary at this point.

Given the foregoing calculations, total current ruble outlays on munitions and other procurements are divided between these two components as shown in Table E-6. The figures on munitions and other are from Table E-1. That on other procurements alone for 1940 is derived above. Those on other procurements for later years are obtained as the product of the index numbers of the prices of other procurements (Table E-4) and the "real" outlays on these procurements (Table E-2). Current ruble outlays on munitions are obtained as a residual.

Corresponding constant ruble data for munitions (Table E-2) are obtained by reference to assumed index numbers of munitions (Table E-3). To come finally to the latter, I assume that munitions prices rose 20 percent from 1937 to 1940. The prices of civilian machinery rose 6 percent from 1937 to 1940. Although the output of machinery tended to fall in this period, the Russians probably realized significant economies in this sector, for the prices of quality rolled steel, a principal material input, rose 14 percent, while average industrial wages rose 28 percent, allowing for changes in hours. In contrast to machinery, munitions production expanded sharply from 1937 to 1940, but in view of the abrupt increase from a low level the effects on costs is problematic. However, the assumed 20 percent increase still allows for some cost economies. This is seen when one considers that the prices of nonferrous metals rolled products rose 82 percent from 1937–40. Chiefly on this account the prices of munitions materials inputs increased by 26 percent. Moreover, wages in munitions probably rose more than in industry generally during this period.

The commissariats of defense industry reportedly produced these amounts of goods in the period in question: in 1926/27 prices for 1937, 8.4 billion rubles; for 1938, 11.5; for 1939, 16.9; and for 1941 (Plan), 31.9 billion rubles. Judging by budgetary defense appropriations, the corresponding Soviet official figure for 1940 was perhaps 28 billion rubles, or 3.3 times those of 1937. As computed here, munitions procurements may have been on the order of 2.8 times those of 1937. Although Soviet official production data in terms of 1926/27 rubles are probably not as fallible as is generally supposed (see chap. 11), my calculations should not understate the increase in output.

On the Soviet official data for 1937–41, see Sorokin, 1946, p. 41; Kurskii,

TABLE E-6

Expenditures on Munitions and Other Procurement in Current Rubles, USSR, 1940–55 (billions)

Year	Munitions and other	Munitions	Other
1940	45.8	32.1	13.7
1944	95.8	67.8	28.0
1948	41.1	27.5	13.6
1949	54.7	—	—
1950	51.7	32.1	19.6
1951	56.4	34.2	22.2
1952	64.0	39.5	24.5
1953	64.1	39.3	24.8
1954	58.0	33.0	25.0
1955	64.8	39.8	25.0

1940, p. 98; and *1941 Plan*. According to Sorokin, the Soviet output of munitions in 1938 was 36.4 percent above 1937. I believe Sorokin is referring to the output of the then existing Commissariat of Defense Industry. Munitions output in 1937, therefore, may be computed from Sorokin's figure and the corresponding absolute figure on the 1938 output of the Defense Industry Commissariat in Kurskii. The target for 1941 represents the aggregate output of the several commissariats responsible for munitions production in that year. The defense industry commissariats do not produce all Soviet munitions, but they are responsible for the vast bulk of the output. The figures cited, therefore, represent the trends in Soviet munitions production generally, as far as these are revealed by Soviet official data.

The Russians were engaged in munitions production on a vast scale in 1944. Although the prices of materials and wages rose during the war (Table E-3), a 20 percent cut is assumed in munitions prices. This takes into account these Soviet claims:

(a) The wholesale prices of the "output of war industry" in 1942 were 72 percent of the prewar level. See Voznesenskii, 1947, p. 127. Voznesenskii clearly refers to the prices of munitions rather than of industrial goods generally. The underlying computation is unexplained. On the other hand, Voznesenskii also cites 1942 price indices for the following additional sectors: industry generally, 98 percent; machine construction, 87 percent; other heavy industry, 98 percent; light and food industry, 120 percent. The index for other heavy industry is roughly consistent with the 4.5 per cent increase for basic industrial products computed by Bergson, Bernaut, and Turgeon. The index for machine construction seems in conflict with Moorsteen's computations which show machinery prices rising during the war years, but probably Voznesenskii's index covers munitions as well as civilian machinery.

(b) From 1941 to 1943, the number of labor hours expended on different kinds of munitions declined as shown in Table E-7. See Turetskii, 1949, p. 8.

(c) The costs of production of "mass forms of war equipment" were reduced 30 to 50 percent during the war. See Belov, *VE*, 1950, no. 5, p. 13; Man'kov and Pupanov, *VE*, 1955, no. 5, p. 19.

(d) According to *ibid.*, p. 19, the cost economies realized during the war permitted a reduction in the prices of the "most important forms of military equipment" by 2 to 3 times (that is, presumably by 50 to 67 percent). As a result, the "economy" in 1943 outlays alone was 35 billion rubles. Apparently, this refers to the total economy in outlays in 1943 due to the price cuts occurring during that and previous war years. See also Belov, *VE*, 1950, No. 5, p. 13. By conjectural calculations not worth reproducing here, I find that a wartime reduction in munitions prices of 25 to 40 percent may be implied.

Chiefly as a result of wage increases, costs rose during the war in the civilian machinery and basic industrial branches. By means of budget subsidies, the government nevertheless succeeded in severely limiting price increases. The assumed price cut in munitions evidently is in no way inconsistent with rising costs of machinery and basic industrial goods.

J. P. Miller, 1949, pp. 283–284, cites the indices shown in Table E-8 of "contract price changes" for U.S. War Department procurements. The indexes record "changes in contract prices negotiated with individual companies and not changes in average prices negotiated or changes in average prices paid." (p. 205). The indexes "probably tend on balance to understate the total decline in average contract prices from 1942 to 1945." (p. 205). The price reductions were realized despite an increase in average weekly earnings in U.S. manufacturing from $36.65 in 1942 to $55.39 in 1945. Hourly earnings increased from $.85 to $1.02.

In view of the Soviet claims and Miller's price data for the United States, the assumed reduction in Soviet munitions prices may be conservative, but considering the great many new products introduced during the war, undocumented claims regarding price and cost reductions cannot be taken at face value. Besides, the Soviet claims refer to 1942 and 1943. In view of the government's reticence about 1944, one hesitates to assume that the downward price trend that prevailed to 1943 persisted a year later.

Voznesenskii, 1947, informs us that ". . . the war production of the eastern and central regions of the USSR alone in the period of the Patriotic War increased 2.5 times in comparison with the level of production in the whole territory of the USSR in 1940." Voznesenskii means by this, I believe, that the munitions production of the "eastern and central regions" in wartime reached 2.5 times the total Soviet output of 1940. The scope of the "central and eastern regions" is not clear; probably the areas in question produced in wartime the predominant part, if not all, of Soviet munitions. According to the Soviet calculations, therefore, Soviet munitions output at its wartime peak was more than 2.5 times the 1940 level. "Real" outlays on munitions in 1944 are found in the present study to be 2.6 times 1940. Exclusive of Lend-Lease (chapter 7 of this volume), the corresponding figure might be about 2.3.

TABLE E-7

Reduction in Labor Expenditure, Selected Munitions, USSR, 1941–43

	Reduction in expenditures (percent of 1941)
Airplane IL-4	37.5
Airplane IL-3	38
Airplane PE-2	48
Tank T-34	53.8
Tank kv	50.7
155-mm howitzer	46.7
76-mm regimental cannon	33.4
Division cannon	72.7
High-caliber machine gun	48.5

Under the wartime conditions of declining prices, Soviet official data in 1926/27 ruble prices should be less prone to an upward bias than they might otherwise be (see chapter 11). My calculations nevertheless should not seriously understate the wartime munitions outlays. Some pertinent Soviet releases on the wartime increases in output of different kinds of munitions must also be considered (Table E-9). Figures on steel consumption in ammunition production (in thousands of tons) are from Voznesenskii, 1947, p. 80; indices on ammunition, planes, and tanks are from Gotovskii, 1946, p. 91; monthly rates of production for planes and tanks are from Sherwood, 1948, pp. 336–7; and indices on guns are from Stalin in *Pravda,* February 10, 1946.

An increase in munitions prices from 1944 to 1948 of (say) 10 percent (Table E-5) seems in order in view of the changes in input prices during

TABLE E-8

Contract Price Changes, U.S. War Department Procurements, 1942–45 (October 1942 = 100)

	January 1942	August 1945
War Department	108.6	75.4
Army Air Forces	112.1	64.0
Ordinance	107.1	80.3
Signal Corps	119.4	72.7
Corps of Engineers	102.2	94.5
Chemical Warfare	104.4	80.3
Medical Department	114.2	57.8
Quartermaster Corps	94.9	107.5
Transportation Corps	99.3	94.1

this period. Judging from data for the metal working industries, materials, fuels, and power may have constituted three-fifths or more of the production expenses of munitions industries at this time. Wages and related payments perhaps constituted about one-third of the total. See Turetskii, 1948, p. 105. From 1944 to 1948, the prices of materials inputs and of basic industrial goods generally were unchanged. Allowing for postwar cuts in hours, average wages in industry may have increased by about 35 percent. Workers in munitions whose earnings had risen greatly during the war probably did not benefit as much as workers in other industries from the postwar increases. Munitions production was sharply curtailed after the war, but the government may have avoided productivity losses by concentrating output in the superior factories. Possibly there were some gains.

Civilian machinery prices rose 18 percent in this period. In part, this increase may have been intended to bring prices more nearly in line with costs than they were under the wartime practice of subsidization.

The further 20 percent increase in munitions prices assumed for 1948–50 again reflects chiefly the trends in input prices. The prices of material inputs rose 43 percent while industrial wages may have increased by about 10 percent (Table E-5). Very possibly, some gains in productivity were realized during this period. In order to re-establish profitable operations, the government drastically increased the prices of civilian machinery and basic industrial goods generally in 1949. Finding that the 1949 increases overshot the mark, the government cut these prices in 1950, but civilian machinery prices in the latter year were still 147 percent of the 1948 level. The prices of basic industrial goods were 200 percent of 1948. It will readily be seen that there is no reason to suppose any parallel increase in munitions prices.

Since 1950, the government has fixed the prices of civilian machinery more or less in accord with costs. Munitions prices are assumed to vary with civilian machinery during this period.

Pricing of defense goods; machinery prices and costs. The armed forces procure many products which are purchased by civilian agencies as well, for example, food, clothing, and petroleum. In the SNIP calculations of military subsistence in current rubles, it is assumed that in making these purchases, the military establishment pays the same prices as civilian agencies. In other words, the armed forces are not favored by any special tax exemptions, special subsidies, et cetera. Similarly, this has been assumed here in my calculations regarding other procurements. The evidence for this assumption is presented on pp. 112–113. My calculations also assume that for benchmark years the armed forces have had to pay for munitions prices that are more or less in accord with costs. With exceptions noted, machinery prices are also taken to correspond to costs.

Defense expenditures in 1950 and 1928 prices. In recalculating defense outlays in terms of 1950 prices, the different major components (services, munitions, other procurements) are taken to vary in the same way as they did in 1937 prices. In calculating munitions in terms of 1937 prices, I made limited use of Moorsteen's Formula (5) indices of civilian machinery prices. From

TABLE E-9

Munitions Production in the USSR, 1940–44, Soviet Series

	Steel consumption in ammunition production, thous. tons (1)	Ammunition, percent (2)	Planes, monthly rate (3)	Planes, percent (4)	Tanks, monthly rate (5)	Tanks, percent (6)	Guns, percent (7)
"Prewar"		100		100		100	100
1940	830						
July 1941			1800		1000		
1942	1838						
1943	2437						
1942–44			3300		2500[a]		
"End of 1944"		"almost 400"		400		700 to 800	600 to 700

[a] Including self-propelled guns and armored cars.

Moorsteen's calculations, it is possible to derive corresponding indices applying Formula (8), p. 87. Theoretically, for purposes of reducing munitions to 1950 rubles, it might be in order to take the Formula (8) indices as benchmarks. In this way, one might hope to reflect in some measure the 1950 price structure within the munitions component. This has been done in deflating munitions (and other procurements) for a single year 1928, where the two formulas give widely different indices (with 1937 as 100, the Formula (5) index is 70 percent; the Formula (8) index is 47 percent). For the rest, however, the indices move closely together, and since the machinery prices are used only to a very limited extent as a benchmark anyhow it did not seem worth while to recalculate the munitions deflator for the period 1940–55 in order to take the Formula (8) indices as a benchmark.

My series for munitions for the years 1937–55, therefore, is the same as that used previously, except that 1950 is taken as a base year. For 1928 (with 1937 as 100), the index of the prices of munitions and other procurement is now taken as 50 percent instead of 60 percent.

In the recalculation in terms of 1928 prices, services vary in the same way as in terms of 1937 prices. The prices of munitions and other procurements in 1928 are 70 percent of 1937. This index is intended to correspond to Formula (6). I take into account the following index numbers for 1928 (1937 as 100): for civilian machinery, wholesale prices (Moorsteen), using Formula (5), 70 and using Formula (6), 140; for basic industrial goods, wholesale prices (Bergson, Bernaut, and Turgeon), using Formula (6), 45. See Moorsteen, *Machinery*. As has been explained, a partial recomputation of the index numbers of the prices of basic industrial goods in terms of Formula (5) leaves the result for 1928 unchanged. Moorsteen's very high Formula (6) index reflects the great decreases that occurred during 1928–37 in the prices of types of civilian machinery which were produced on a limited scale or not at all in 1928 and subsequently were placed in mass production. I hesitate to suppose that there were any corresponding decreases in the prices of munitions and other procurements in this period, although I allow for more limited increases than were previously assumed in terms of Formula (5), that is, my assumed Formula (6) index for 1928 is 70. Previously I assumed a Formula (5) index of 60.

As was explained, the Commissariat of Defense Industry in 1937 reportedly produced 8.4 billion rubles of goods in terms of 1926/27 prices. Judging from the structure of defense expenditures planned for 1941, procurements of munitions in 1937 may have been on the order of 9.5 billion rubles, while the "marketed output" of the Commissariat of Defense Industry was (say) 10 billion rubles. These sums are in terms of 1937 prices. By implication, munitions prices in 1926/27 were from 80 to 90 percent of 1937. This result is far too conjectural to be relied on here, even as an indication of the price index implied by official production data in 1926/27 rubles, and this says nothing of the dubious nature of the latter measures. But the implied index corresponds to Formula (6), and serves as still another benchmark, albeit a very nebulous one.

APPENDIX F

"Real" Investments in Fixed Capital

Scope of category. This corresponds broadly to the Soviet statistical category *kapital'nye vlozheniia.* This is to say that it includes:

(a) Purchases of machinery and equipment

(b) Assembly and installation of machinery and equipment

(c) Construction

(d) Design and research work and geological and prospecting work connected with particular investment projects

(e) Expenditures on land improvement measures, including drainage and irrigation

(f) Other expenditures, including expenditures on the training of labor cadres for enterprises under construction; maintenance of the management of such enterprises; certain exploratory and prospecting work not connected with specific investment projects; certain resettlement expenditures, et cetera.

In Soviet statistical usage, investments in fixed capital include some investments in livestock herds. In the present study, such investments are classified with gross investments other than those in fixed capital.

The line of demarcation between investments in fixed capital and in inventories in Soviet statistics has evolved in the course of time. In a decree of July 29, 1936, the Council of Commissars ordered that after August 1, 1936, expenditures for "short-lived, small-value durables" be omitted from accounts of fixed capital investments. Instead, they were to be included in inventories. The durables in question are stated to be those having an expected service life of less than one year or a value of less than 200 rubles. Prior to August 1, 1936, durables of this sort apparently were classified as fixed capital investments. In 1954, the limiting value for assets to be classified as fixed capital was changed to 300 rubles. I attempt to observe here the line of demarcation that was introduced in 1936, but no adjustment is made for the further change in statistical practice that was made in 1954.

As part of a series of administrative changes that were introduced in 1950, "project-making" organizations which previously were attached to ministries were separated from these agencies and financed directly from the government budget. Accordingly, the Russians began to publish in the following year data on fixed capital investments which were exclusive of these appropriations. Probably this was a matter of statistical convenience rather than a change in principle in the Soviet concept of fixed capital investments. In any case, the appropriations in question had been included in reported totals of fixed capital investments prior to 1951, and on the whole it seems just as well to try here to conform throughout to the pre-1951 practice.

In Soviet statistics on fixed capital investment, this category sometimes includes and sometimes omits certain investments-in-kind, particularly labor participation in farm construction work by collective farm members and labor services contributed to road building by farm population by "self-taxation." Such activities are omitted here throughout.

Insofar as I adhere to Soviet methodology, I include in fixed capital investments some rather dubious items, especially those included under "other expenditures." It is open to question whether such expenditures ought to be considered investments of any sort, and the Russians themselves recognize that many of these expenditures as well as those for land improvement do not result in an addition to the *stock* of fixed capital (*osnovnye fondy*). With the data available, however, it is not possible to separate these outlays systematically from other investments. Moreover, from scattered data it appears that such outlays are material but by no means a major part of the total.

In Soviet accounting practice a distinction generally is drawn between capital repairs and current repairs: Capital repairs (*kapital'nyi remont*) involve relatively substantial renovations that are intended to restore an asset to full working power. Significant parts may be replaced. Outlays of this sort are treated as representing additions to assets or, what comes to the same thing, as offsets to the balance in the depreciation account. Current repairs (*tekushchii remont*) involve less significant repairs that are intended to keep an asset in normal working condition and are treated as a current expense. In accord with these accounting practices, the Russians prior to 1938 generally included capital repairs in their data on capital investment. Since 1938 they usually have reported the repairs separately from other capital investments, but apparently they still are considered as properly included in any comprehensive total of capital investments.

I am guided by Soviet methodology at this point as previously. In other words, "capital repairs," as these are understood in the USSR, will be considered a part of capital investments. The Soviet accounting and statistical practices in this regard, I believe, are broadly similar to those used in the West, but (as will appear) the outlays for capital repairs seemingly have become sizable in the course of time, and some further inquiry probably is in order as to how the Russians apply the indicated principles in practice.

In the sense described, I consider all investments in fixed capital by the socialist sector, that is, state and cooperative enterprises and collective farms. An allowance is also made for private investments in housing. For 1928, private investments in other forms of fixed capital are also included.

On the demarcation in Soviet statistics between fixed and working capital investment, see Moorsteen, *Machinery*. On the Soviet concept of fixed capital investment generally, see D'iachkov and Kiparisov, 1948, pp. 9 ff.; TSUNKHU, *Slovar'-spravochnik po sotsial'no-ekonomicheskoi statistike*, 2nd ed., pp. 73 ff., 345 ff.; and Plotnikov, et al., 1954, pp. 48 ff.; Zhebrak, 1950, chap. ii. For further citations and a detailed discussion, see Kaplan, RAND RM-735, pp. 1 ff.

Investments in current rubles. The current ruble data on the volume and structure of fixed capital investments that I take as a point of departure may be explained by reference to Table F-1. In the table, the different series listed are obtained as follows:

(1) *Investments in socialist sector*. These figures are intended to represent the aggregate value of investments in state-owned, cooperative and collective farm fixed capital, including capital repairs. The figures, however, are exclusive of labor participation in road building and in collective farm investment. For 1951–55, as well as for earlier years, the data include project making expenditures. The data are preliminary estimates taken from Kaplan, *Fixed Capital*.

However, I revise the 1928 figure of 4.083 billion rubles given by Kaplan. This is a Soviet figure representing the Soviet concept of the time, and includes investments in short-lived and small-value equipment which were later classified as working capital. Such investments have been estimated at 0.068 billion rubles in Moorsteen, *Machinery*. Accordingly, I deduct this sum from the Soviet figure of 4.083 billion rubles.

(2) *Livestock acquisitions, socialist sector*. Column (1) includes investments in livestock herds. In column (2), an attempt is made to estimate these investments in order that they may be deducted from the total.

The data in column (2) more specifically are supposed to represent outlays on the acquisition of productive and working livestock. The figures probably refer to the acquisition of "basic" herds, as distinct from animals purchased exclusively for fattening and slaughter, but the precise scope of the figures in this regard is not very clear. In any event, the figures are often crude estimates of such acquisitions, while (as will be explained presently) such acquisitions in turn may or may not correspond fully to the livestock investments which are included in column (1). All this is to say that when I come to deduct livestock investments from total investments, I shall be deriving a residual which is not precisely what is desired, but the errors involved are necessarily very small in relation to the balance of investments. The series in column (2), therefore, may serve well enough for present purposes.

The data in column (2) are obtained as follows:

TABLE F-1

Investments in Fixed Capital in Current Rubles, USSR, 1928–55
(billions of rubles)

Year	Investments in socialist sector (1)	Livestock acquisitions, socialist sector (2)	Investments in socialist sector other than in livestock acquisitions (3)	Private investments other than in housing, livestock (4)	Allowance for private housing construction (5)	All investments other than in livestock (6)	Machinery other than capital repairs (7)	Capital repairs to machinery (8)	Construction (9)	Other (10)
1928	4.015	0.032	3.983	0.869	1.147	6.00	1.21	0.29	4.38	0.12
1937	35.4	0.88	34.5	—	0.7	35.2	11.0	1.4	21.5	1.3
1940	55.0	1.56	53.4	—	0.5	53.9	11.8	2.6	33.9	5.6
1944	40	1.64	38.4	—	0.5	38.9	9.8	1.6	24.5	3.0
1948	92	2.74	89.3	—	2.7	92.0	—	6.2	—	—
1949	157	3.44	153.6	—	3.2	156.8	50.5	7.6	87.5	11.2
1950	157	3.72	153.3	—	3.2	156.5	46.3	10.1	90.1	10.0
1951	175	3.07	171.9	—	2.9	174.8	47.4	11.3	103.7	12.4
1952	176	3.07	172.9	—	3.6	176.5	41.4	12.5	109.4	13.2
1953	192	2.40	189.6	—	6.1	195.7	46.5	13.6	121.0	14.6
1954	221	2.92	218.1	—	6.4	224.5	55.8	14.8	137.2	16.7
1955	236	2.50	233.5	—	6.1	239.6	63.3	15.6	144.1	16.6

1928; 1937; 1940; 1944. See Moorsteen, *Machinery.* The cited figure for 1928 apparently includes some outlays involved in the erection of buildings to house livestock herds. See Kaplan, RAND RM-735, pp. 102 ff.

1948–54. For 1950, 1952–54, acquisitions of working and productive herds by collective farms for investment purposes are stated by Golev, *Finansy SSSR,* 1956, no. 2, p. 58, to have been as follows: 1950, 3.235 billion rubles; 1952, 2.672; 1953, 2.085; and 1954, 2.539 billion rubles. I assume acquisitions by the whole socialist sector totaled 115 percent of these sums. From data in *Narkhoz,* pp. 119–120, I calculate that the productive livestock herds of the whole socialist sector in January 1951 and again in January 1953 had an aggregate value equal to about 115 percent of the herds in collective farms alone. I value the different kinds of animals tabulated in *Narkhoz* mostly at their estimated average slaughter values in 1952. The estimates are Karcz's and are of a very crude sort to be described below. This calculation refers to productive herds only, but presumably there was very little investment either by collective or by state farms in draft animals.

Collective farm investments of all sorts varied as follows, in comparison with 1950: 1948, 73.7 percent and 1949, 92.6 percent. I rely here on unpublished preliminary calculations of Norman Kaplan. Somewhat different percentages are implied by data in Kaplan, RAND RM-1733, p. 29. Livestock acquisitions in the whole socialist sector are taken to vary with total investments by collective farms. For 1951, Kaplan finds collective farm investment to be about the same as in 1952. I take the 1951 livestock acquisitions to equal those of 1952. In 1955, collective farm investment is almost 20 percent greater than in 1954. I believe this increase consisted primarily of construction and other forms of investment rather than of livestock. According to Golev, *op. cit.,* p. 59, long-term credits to collective farms for livestock purchases fell sharply in 1955. While in previous years these had dwindled in relation to total acquisitions, they tended nevertheless to move with these acquisitions. Data in *Narkhoz,* pp. 119–120 on livestock herds held on the state and collective farms are also illuminating. They are as follows: October 1, 1954, cattle, 36.3 million head; hogs, 28.4; sheep, 93.2; and goats, 3.6. October 1, 1955, cattle, 35.3 million head; hogs, 29.8; sheep, 94.9; and goats, 2.7. Socialist livestock acquisitions in 1955 are assumed here to have declined to about the 1953 level.

To come to the scope of the livestock investments that are included in data on total fixed capital investments in the socialized sector, there appears to be a general agreement in the pertinent Soviet methodological writings that investments in fixed capital in the form of livestock herds consist of outlays for the acquisition and breeding of "basic" herds of productive and working animals. Apparently outlays on the fattening of livestock for slaughter are not considered as fixed capital investments. See D'iachkov and Kiparisov, 1948, p. 11; Kaplan, RAND RM-735, p. 1.

Insofar as fixed capital investments in livestock include breeding, this category is more comprehensive than that to which the data in column (2) refer. The latter, it will be recalled, refer to acquisitions alone. I have been considering, however, the concept of fixed capital investments that is advanced in Soviet methodological writings. In respect of livestock investments, the data in column (1) conform rather to the actual usage in Soviet statistics, and this is not necessarily the same thing as that in methodological writings. On the contrary, this has varied, but very often livestock acquisitions alone are included. For this reason many if not all the data cited in column (1) include as fixed capital investments livestock acquisitions alone. To be more specific, this is true of the data for 1928 (apparently, as with the figure for 1928 in the second column of data in Table F-1, some outlays on buildings are included). See Kaplan, RAND RM-735, pp. 104 ff., and p. 214. According to *ibid.*, pp. 115, 214, this is also true of 1937, so far as investments in enterprises other than collective farms are concerned. It appears to be so again for the data on collective farm investments that are included in total fixed capital investments for the years 1950–54, although the inclusion of very small breeding outlays is not precluded. See Kaplan, RAND RM-1733, pp. 22 ff.

For other categories and other years, the precise scope of the fixed capital investment data in the first column of figures is not known, and they may include breeding outlays. If so, the deduction of the second column still would leave these outlays in the remainder in some years, but the amounts involved must be very small in relation to the total fixed capital investments, and for present purposes the error at this point is unimportant.

(3) *Investments in socialist sector other than in livestock acquisitions.* Column (1) — column (2).

(4) *Private investments other than in housing, livestock.* The cited figure for 1928 is obtained as the sum of private investments in industry, 0.018 billion rubles; private investments in machinery and equipment in industrial enterprises in agriculture, 0.045; private investments in agriculture construction, other than housing, 0.584; and private investments in agricultural machinery, 0.222 billion rubles. The first three figures listed are from *Narkhoz-1932,* pp. 142–143, 294–295. The figure on private investments in agriculture machinery is a rough estimate derived in Moorsteen, *Machinery.*

(5) *Allowance for private housing construction.* For 1928, total private housing construction, as given in *Narkhoz-1932,* p. XXX. For 1937 and after, I sum the rather arbitrary allowances made in *SNIP-28–48* and *SNIP-49–55* for household purchases of building materials and services. The purchases of materials and services include outlays for maintenance as well as fixed capital investments, but they do not include the households' own labor. The cited series can have no independent interest and is inserted here only to round out the calculation of fixed capital investments.

(6) *All investments other than in livestock.* Sum of columns (3), (4), and (5).

(7) *Machinery other than capital repairs.* This is intended to represent the total investments in fixed capital that consist of machinery and equipment, exclusive of capital repairs. Because of changes in the underlying Soviet statistical categories, the scope of the cited data varies somewhat in the course of time. Expenditures for heating and plumbing equipment, for

example, are included in machinery as computed in the mid-thirties, but at least since the war they have been omitted (they are included instead under "construction." (See below.) These expenditures, however, amount to only 1/2 percent of the total investment in equipment in 1937. The data cited in column (7) are from Moorsteen, *Machinery.*

(8) *Capital repairs to machinery.* See *ibid.* For 1948 I take capital repairs to machinery as equal to 39 percent of 16 billion rubles, a preliminary estimate of all capital repairs, as given in Kaplan, *Fixed Capital.* The indicated fractional relation is obtained from *1941 Plan* and is assumed by Moorsteen to hold also for most of the period 1937–1955.

(9) *Construction.* This represents construction including assembly and installation. It also includes capital repairs to structures. The cited data are derived as follows:

1928. This is the sum of: construction, socialist sector, 2.64 billion rubles; private housing, 1.15; private agricultural construction, 0.58; and private industrial construction, 0.01. These make a total of 4.38 billion rubles.

Construction (including installation), socialist sector, is from Powell, RAND RM-1873, p. 419. Private housing is from Table F-1, column (5). Private agricultural construction is given above. Private industrial construction is calculated from data in Moorsteen, *Machinery* and the figure on all private industrial investment given above.

1937. This is the sum of: construction, socialist sector, other than collective farm, 19.9 billion rubles; collective farm construction, 0.9; and private housing, 0.7. These make a total of 21.5 billion rubles. Total collective farm money investments amounted to 3.1 billion rubles in 1937. See Kaplan, RAND RM-1733, p. 29. Hence, money investments in the socialist sector other than collective farms amounted to 32.3 billion rubles. Construction, socialist sector other than collective farm, is taken as 61.5 percent of socialist money investments other than collective farm investments. See Moorsteen, *Machinery.* Construction constituted about 30 percent of collective farm investments in 1937. See TSUNKHU, *Kolkhozy vo vtoroi stalinskoi piatiletke,* p. 127. Private housing is from column (5).

1940. This is the sum of: construction, socialist sector, other than capital repairs, 29.4 billion rubles; capital repairs to structures, 4.0; and private housing, 0.5. These make a total of 33.9 billion rubles.

Capital investments in the socialist sector other than capital repairs amounted to 48.4 billion rubles. See Kaplan, *Fixed Capital.* Of this, construction constituted 60.8 percent. See Moorsteen, *Machinery.* Capital repairs to machinery and structures totaled 6.6 billion rubles. See Kaplan, *op. cit.* Capital repairs to machinery amounted to 2.6 billion rubles. See Table F-1, column (8). Private housing is from the same table, column (5).

1944. This is the sum of: construction, socialist sector, other than capital repairs, 21.6 billion rubles; capital repairs to structures, 2.4; and private housing, 0.5. These make a total of 24.5 billion rubles. Sources and methods are the same as for 1940.

1949–55. The totals comprise the elements shown in Table F-2.

Construction, socialist sector, other than capital repairs and collective farm construction, is calculated by disaggregating total fixed capital investment in the socialist sector. Thus, from the data on the latter given in Table F-1, I deduct project making, capital repairs, and collective farm investment as given in Kaplan, *Fixed Capital*. A deduction is also made for noncollective farm machinery investment. Data on all machinery investments, inclusive of those by collective farms, are given in Table F-1, column (7). Corresponding figures on machinery investments exclusive of those by collective farms are compiled in the light of incomplete data on the latter in Golev, *Finansy SSSR,* 1956, no. 2, p. 58. In addition to outlays on new construction by socialist enterprises other than collective farms, the balance remaining after these deductions includes diverse other investments by such enterprises. From percentage data on the structure of investments in *Narkhoz,* pp. 159–160, we may infer that during 1949–55 outlays of the former sort constituted about 90 percent of the total residual in question. The *Narkhoz* percentages are based on calculations in terms of July 1, 1955 prices and the underlying absolute figures are rather dubious (see chapter 11), but they should be roughly indicative of relative magnitudes of the different kinds of current ruble investments that are of concern at this point.

Capital repairs to structures are calculated as the difference between all capital repairs, as given in Kaplan, *Fixed Capital,* and capital repairs to machinery, as given in Table F-1, column (8). Collective farm construction is estimated from incomplete data in Golev, *Finansy SSSR,* 1956, no. 2, p. 58. Private housing construction is from Table F-1, column (5).

(10) *Other*. These figures are calculated as a residual, and should include diverse outlays of a sort refered to earlier: design and research work and geological and prospecting work not connected with specific projects; expenditures on land-improvement measures; expenditures for the training of labor cadres for enterprises under construction and maintenance of the management of such enterprises; certain resettlement expenditures, et cetera. In the aggregate, outlays of the foregoing sorts probably were limited in 1928, but they are understated in Table F-1 because of their possible partial inclusion in other categories, particularly machinery.

Investment in 1937 prices. In Table F-3, column (1), are shown Moorsteen's variable weight, that is, Formula (5), index numbers of the prices of new machinery. See Moorsteen, *Machinery*. In Table F-4, column (2), the data on new machinery outlays in 1937 rubles are obtained by the use of these indices as deflators.

In Table F-3, I cite Moorsteen's index numbers for the prices of domestically produced machinery. For 1928 and 1944, I deflate instead by corresponding index numbers shown in parentheses that are supposed to represent the trends in the prices of domestic and imported machinery taken together.

Current ruble data on the volume of outlays on machinery are not available for 1948. I assume that in terms of 1937 rubles, machinery outlays in 1948 amount to 63.0 percent of the volume of construction in the same terms, as derived below. The corresponding relation for 1949 is 63.8 percent. Judging from percentage data on the structure of investments in

TABLE F-2

Construction Outlays by Type in Current Rubles, USSR, 1949–55
(billions)

	1949	1950	1951	1952	1953	1954	1955
Construction, socialist sector, other than capital repairs and collective farm construction	66.7	67.5	78.7	81.5	86.9	98.7	101.2
Capital repairs to structures	14.4	15.9	17.5	19.2	21.4	23.2	24.4
Collective farm construction	3.2	3.5	4.6	5.1	6.6	8.9	12.4
Private housing	3.2	3.2	2.9	3.6	6.1	6.4	6.1
Total	87.5	90.1	103.7	109.4	121.0	137.2	144.1

Narkhoz, p. 160, in relation to the "real" volume of construction the "real" volume of machinery outlays should have been slightly smaller in 1948 than in 1949.

In Table F-3, column (4), I show Moorsteen's series of indices of the prices of inputs to capital repairs to machinery. These indices are obtained by averaging the indices for machinery prices, shown in Table F-3, column (1), with corresponding indices of the wages of machinery workers. In

TABLE F-3

Index Numbers of Prices of New Machinery and of Capital Repairs to Machinery, USSR, 1928–55
(1937 = 100)

Year	New machinery, variable weights of the given year in relation to 1937 (1)	New machinery, variable weights of the given year in relation to 1950 (2)	New machinery 1937 weights (3)	Capital repairs, variable weights of the given year in relation to 1937 (4)	Capital repairs, variable weights of the given year in relation to 1950 (5)
1928	70 (60)	47 (40)	140	57	42
1937	100	100	100	100	100
1940	106	112	106	118	122
1944	110 (114)	131 (136)	123	132	146
1948	130	144	138	166	176
1949	273	285	282	265	273
1950	191	197	197	214	218
1951	186	192	192	212	216
1952	165	176	175	198	205
1953	165	176	175	200	207
1954	165	176	175	203	210
1955	153	162	163	197	203

averaging the two series, machinery prices are rather arbitrarily given a base year weight of 2 and wages a base year weight of 1. Moorsteen calculates no index for 1948. Those shown in the table were obtained, however, by his methods and from his data on prices and wages.

In Table F-4, column (3), the data on capital repairs in terms of 1937 rubles are obtained by using as deflators these indices of the prices of capital repairs inputs.

In Table F-4, column (4), the data on construction in terms of 1937 prices are obtained by multiplying Powell's indices of the physical volume of construction by the figure derived here on the volume of construction in current rubles in 1937. I use here the indices which Powell derives by valuing construction materials inputs in terms of 1937 ruble prices. See Powell, RAND RM-1872, p. 6; RAND RM-2454, p. 3.

Powell was unable to compile an index of construction materials inputs for 1944. He has compiled for this and other years, however, rough indices of construction input prices, and from these he derives a more complete series of physical volume indices; RAND RM-1872, p. 57; RAND RM-2454, p. 9. These are shown in Table F-5. For comparison I also show his indices of the volume of construction materials inputs. Powell's indices of the prices of construction inputs refer to labor and materials prices. The indices cited are based on 1937 weights; the use of given year weights does not appear to affect the results materially for years after 1937.

In Table F-4, the figure for the "real" volume of construction for 1944 is obtained on the assumption that the change from 1940 is the same as is indicated by Powell's deflated value of outputs, that is, 1944 is 57.5 percent (58.6 ÷ 102) of 1940. Because of the greater reliability of the indices for 1940, extrapolation from that year seemed preferable to an alternative computation employing the indices for 1945 as a base.

In Table F-4, "construction" includes capital repairs to construction. As computed it is also supposed to represent assembly and installation. In other words, I assume assembly and installation, together with construction generally, move proportionately with Powell's materials input indices. According to a very rough calculation, this may result in an understatement of the volume of fixed capital investment in 1944 by as much as one billion rubles, or 4 percent. For other years studied, the margin of error is probably much smaller than this. Insofar as assembly and installation have to be estimated from indirect evidence, it might be suggested that "real" outlays on machinery would be a better indicator of this aspect than Powell's measures of the "real" volume of construction. The machinery outlays, however, include large and variable sums expended on acquisitions (tractors, RR rolling stock, et cetera) which do not require assembly and installation, and such evidence as there is on this matter demonstrates only that any procedure adopted must yield crude results. In appraising the reliability of alternative treatments of assembly and installation, including that adopted in this study, I take into account incomplete data on outlays on this category in terms of current rubles in Moorsteen, *Machinery*.

TABLE F-4

Investments in Fixed Capital, in 1937 Prices, USSR, 1928–55
(billions of rubles)

Year	All investments in fixed capital (1)	New machinery outlays (2)	Capital repairs to machinery (3)	Construction (4)	Other (5)
1928	10.9	2.02	0.51	7.89	0.45
1937	35.2	11.0	1.4	21.5	1.3
1940	39.4	11.1	2.2	21.7	4.4
1944	24.2	8.6	1.2	12.5	1.9
1948	44.2	14.4	3.7	22.8	3.3
1949	55.5	18.5	2.9	29.0	5.1
1950	66.5	24.2	4.7	33.3	4.3
1951	73.7	25.5	5.3	37.8	5.1
1952	78.7	25.1	6.3	42.1	5.2
1953	87.3	28.2	6.8	46.7	5.6
1954	98.8	33.8	7.3	51.4	6.3
1955	112.2	41.4	7.9	56.8	6.1

To come finally to other investments in fixed capital, current ruble data are available for a number of years. See Table F-1. I reduce these to constant (1937) prices by using as a deflator indices of adjusted average money wages in Soviet industry. See Appendix H. "Other" may be calculated in this way for all years except 1948, for which no current ruble figure is at hand. For this year, I assume that in terms of 1937 rubles "other" amounts to 8.0 percent of the sum of investments in machinery, capital repairs, and construction. For other years studied, "other" has varied as shown in Table F-6 in relation to the sum of the latter investments.

The reason for the exceptionally large figure for 1940 is unknown. Possibly

TABLE F-5

"Real" Construction Outlays, Alternative
Computations, USSR, 1928–54
(1937 = 100)

Year	Construction materials inputs	Deflated value of outputs
1928	36.7	45.0
1937	100	100
1940	101	102
1944	—	58.6
1945	42.9	69.2
1950	155	143
1954	239	225

TABLE F-6

Other Investments in Fixed Capital in Relation to Investments in Machinery, Capital Repairs, and Construction, USSR, 1928–55

Year	Percent
1928	4.3
1937	3.8
1940	12.5
1944	8.5
1949	10.1
1950	6.9
1951	7.4
1952	7.1
1953	6.9
1954	6.8
1955	5.7

it reflects exceptionally large outlays for training of workers and the like in connection with the expanding defense program. Reasons for the variation observed in other years are also conjectural.

Investments in 1950 prices; 1928 prices. In Table F-3, column (2), the index numbers listed for the prices of new machinery, although for convenience expressed as percentages of 1937, are intended to correspond to Formula (8), p. 87. In Table F-7, column (2), the figures on investments in new machinery in 1950 prices are obtained by use of these index numbers as deflators.

The Formula (8) index numbers of machinery prices are computed from a variety of fixed weight index numbers of new machinery prices compiled in Moorsteen, *Machinery*. As calculated initially, with 1950 as 100 percent, the indices for 1928, 1937, and 1955 correspond strictly to the formula. The index for 1940 reflects the *1941(Plan)* rather than 1940 weights. For lack of an alternative, the index for 1944 is computed in the same way. For 1948–54, the initially computed index numbers all reflect 1955 rather than true "given year" weights.

For 1928 and 1944, I deflate by index numbers shown in parentheses that represent the prices of imported as well as domestic machinery. These numbers were obtained by multiplying the 1928 and 1944 indexes for domestic machinery alone by 60/70 and 114/110, respectively (see column (1) of Table F-3).

In Table F-7, column (2), the figure on new machinery outlays in 1950 ruble prices for 1948 is derived as the following product:

$$\Sigma P_{37}Q_i \times \frac{\Sigma \frac{P_{50}}{P_i} P_iQ_i}{\Sigma P_iQ_i} \times \frac{\Sigma P_iQ_i}{\Sigma \frac{P_{37}}{P_i} P_iQ_i}.$$

TABLE F-7

Investment in Fixed Capital in 1950 Prices, USSR, 1928–55
(billions of rubles)

Year	All investments in fixed capital (1)	New machinery outlays (2)	Capital repairs to machinery (3)	Construction (4)	Other (5)
1928	30.7	5.86	1.53	22.3	1.04
1937	88.1	21.6	3.0	60.5	3.0
1940	95.3	20.7	4.6	59.8	10.2
1944	55.4	14.2	2.4	34.4	4.4
1948	103.2	25.6	7.6	62.3	7.7
1949	131.5	34.9	6.1	78.6	11.9
1950	156.5	46.3	10.1	90.1	10.0
1951	174.7	48.7	11.4	102.7	11.9
1952	187.1	46.4	13.3	115.3	12.1
1953	205.5	52.1	14.3	126.1	13.0
1954	231.5	62.6	15.4	138.8	14.7
1955	261.1	76.9	16.8	153.2	14.2

As may be readily seen, this reduces to $\Sigma P_{50}Q_i$, which is what is desired. Of the three expressions, the values of the first are given in Table F-4, column (2); the values of the second are computed from Table F-3, column (2), the "given year" being taken equal to 100 percent; and the values of the third are given in Table F-3, column (1). The results of the foregoing calculations are the same as those that would be obtained by the use of Formula (8) indices (or rather their reciprocals) as deflators if current ruble data were available.

The price indices for capital repairs to machinery in Table F-3, column (5), are obtained by averaging the indices of machinery prices given by Formula (8) with the indices of the wages of machinery workers in Moorsteen, *Machinery*. In averaging the two sets of indices, machinery prices are assigned a weight of 2 and wages a weight of 1. In Table F-7, column (3), the figures on capital repairs in terms of 1950 rubles are derived simply by deflation. The foregoing indices are used as deflators.

Powell (RAND RM-1872, p. 27; RAND RM-2454, p. 3) has compiled construction materials input indices in terms not only of 1937 prices but also of July-December 1950 prices. I take these indices as a basis for translating construction into 1950 prices. The total volume of construction in terms of average prices for the year 1950, that is, 90.1 billion rubles, is the point of departure. The Powell indices are used to derive corresponding figures for other years. The 1944 index is taken to be in the same relation to 1940 as in the previous calculation of the physical volume of construction in 1937 prices, that is, 57.5 percent.

In Table F-7, column (5), the figures on other investments in 1950 prices for different years are taken to be the same in relation to 1950 as they were in terms of 1937 prices.

To come to the recalculation in terms of the 1928 price structure, the elements in this and the results are shown in Table F-8. Essentially the

TABLE F-8

Investments in Fixed Capital in 1928 Prices, USSR, 1928–37
(billions of rubles)

Year	All investments in fixed capital	New machinery outlays	Capital repairs to machinery	Construction	Other
1928	6.00	1.21	0.29	4.38	0.12
1937	27.5	13.3	1.5	12.3	0.35

calculation proceeds in the same way as that in terms of the 1950 price structure. In Table F-1, column (7), outlays on new machinery in current rubles in 1928 are 1.21 billion rubles. This represents the total outlays at average investors' prices, including domestic and import prices. The corresponding figure for 1937 is 11.0 billion rubles. In Table F-3, column (3), I cite a Formula (6) index compiled in Moorsteen, *Machinery*. With 1928 as 100, the index for 1937 is 71 percent. Using this as a deflator, investments in new machinery in 1937 come to 15.5 billion rubles. The cited price index number refers to the prices of domestically produced machinery. In order to obtain a figure on investment outlays for 1937 that is comparable to the one cited for 1928, I reduce the figure just derived to 0.857 × 15.5 billion rubles where 0.857 is the ratio of investors' to producers' prices in 1928.

An index for the reduction of capital repairs in 1937 to 1928 prices is obtained from the indices of machinery prices in Table F-3, column (3), taken together with the indices of the average earnings of machinery workers, in Moorsteen, *Machinery*.

For purposes of calculating construction in 1937 in terms of 1928 prices, use is made of materials input indices in terms of 1928 prices compiled by Powell, RAND RM-1872, p. 27; RAND RM-2454.

APPENDIX G

Other Gross Investment in Constant Prices

In terms of constant prices, this is computed as the sum of: investments in livestock herds; investments in inventories in wholesale and retail trade; investments in inventories in government and cooperative enterprises in sectors other than trade; and miscellaneous investments (Table G-1). As a preliminary to comment on these computations, it is advisable to explain the current ruble data on other gross investments that are set forth in Tables

TABLE G-1

Other Gross Investments in 1937 Prices, USSR, 1928–55
(billions of rubles)

Year	Other gross invest- ments, all (1)	Invest- ment in livestock herds (2)	Invest- ment in inventories, all sectors (3)	Inventory invest- ments in trade (4)	Other inventory invest- ment (5)	Miscel- laneous (6)
1928	7.8	1.5	5.4	4.43	0.98	0.86
1937	24.2	4.0	12.5	3.9	8.6	7.7
1940	11.5	3.0	4.0	...	3.5	4.5
1944	11.7	1.5	6.0	—	—	4.2
1948	34.9	3.7	17	10.0	6.8	14.2
1949	33.1	3.6	22	9.7	12.2	7.5
1950	24.2	.6	14	3.6	10.4	9.6
1951	35.1	2.0	20	11.2	8.4	13.1
1952	35.6	−0.3	20	12.1	8.3	15.9
1953	25.2	0.8	16	4.4	11.4	8.4
1954	2.5 (10.5)	1.8	−4 (4)	−4.1	... (7.6)	4.7
1955	23.8	1.7	18	8.2	9.3	4.1

... = negligible.

3 and 82. The latter figures are computed simply as residuals, that is, from gross investment, I subtract fixed capital investments, as given in the same tables. At the same time, the data on gross investment for 1928–48 are taken from *SNIP-28–48*. Those for 1949–55 are taken from *SNIP-49–55*, but as is explained below the present study revises somewhat the data compiled in *SNIP-49–55* on investments in livestock herds. This leads to a coresponding revision of the *SNIP-49–55* figures on gross investments. For 1953 and 1955, the latter figures also had to be revised because of revisions made in the *SNIP-49–55* data on defense expenditures.

Investment in Livestock Herds

Scope. The data compiled are supposed to represent the value of the increment in herds in any year. Reference is to the net increment in herds, after the deduction of all dispositions, including slaughtering, "normal" attrition, losses due to disease, et cetera. Generally, in this study I am concerned to calculate *gross* investments in fixed capital. In the case of livestock, the measures derived clearly refer more to net than to gross investment. In the case of livestock, however, the distinction between gross and net investment is difficult to make theoretically. In any event, there was no possibility with the data available to derive a series on anything like gross investments.

In calculating the value of the increment in livestock herds, I consider only the numerical changes. No allowance can be made for changes in quality (for example, age and weight) during the year. Such changes, I believe, might be significant.

These remarks refer primarily to the calculations made for 1937–55. For 1928, the calculation rests on a Soviet official figure that may possibly reflect changes in the quality as well as numbers of herds during the year.

The calculations refer to herds of cows, other cattle, hogs, and sheep and goats. For 1928 and 1937, horses are also included.

Investments in current rubles. In Table 3, the livestock investments that are included in gross investments in terms of current rubles for the years 1928–48 are taken from *SNIP-28–48*. As is explained there, these data are derived from the corresponding constant ruble figures that are being explained here: that is, those in Table G-1, column (2). For 1949–55, however, the livestock investments that are included in gross investment in terms of current rubles in Table 3 represent a revision of the corresponding current ruble figures in *SNIP-49–55*. The revision was necessary in order to make the current ruble figures consistent with my constant ruble data for 1949–55. There is a corresponding difference in gross investments as a whole.

Investments in constant prices. The data compiled in terms of 1937 prices appear in Table G-1, column (2). To refer first to the years 1937–55, data were compiled on the increments (decrements) of the following categories of livestock herds: cows, cattle other than cows, hogs, and sheep and goats. See *Narkhoz,* p. 118. I value the different herds at the following prices per head: cows, 500 rubles; other cattle, 350; hogs, 250; and sheep and goats, 75 rubles. These are Karcz estimates of the average prices realized in 1937 in marketings of the animals in question. The estimates are based on Karcz's calculations in RAND RM-1930 of the average prices of cattle, hogs, and sheep per kilogram of liveweight that were realized in marketings in 1937 and on the data in Jasny, 1949, p. 798 on the average slaughter weight of different kinds of animals in 1937. The price of cows is fixed on the basis of data on premiums paid for these animals. Goats are believed to be of about the same value per head as sheep.

For 1937, data are also available on the increment in horse numbers. See Jasny, 1949, p. 797. Valued at (say) 400 rubles per head, the increment in herds in 1937 was worth 120 million rubles. This sum is included in the estimate of investments for that year. Data of this sort, however, are not available for years since 1937, and no allowance could be made for changes in horse herds for these years.

I comment below on special problems that arose regarding particular years in the period 1937–55:

1940; 1944. I assume arbitrarily that total investments in 1940 were somewhat below 1937, that is, 3 billion rubles, and that in 1944 they were well below 1940: say 1.5 billion rubles. A calculation based on changes in livestock numbers for 1940 indicates total investments of 5.5 billion rubles, but the livestock counts used presumably reflect boundary changes and I felt it inadvisable to rely on them. No data are at hand on the changes in livestock numbers during 1944. I cited in Table F-1 the following estimates of livestock acquisitions by socialist enterprises: for 1937, 0.88 billion rubles; for 1940, 1.56; and for 1944, 1.64 billion rubles. Because of uncertainties about the prices in terms of which these acquisitions are valued and about the concomitant changes in private holdings, it was not possible to rely on these data either, but they are suggestive.

1953; 1954; 1955. For 1954, I cite the value of the increment in herds from October 1953 to October 1954. For 1953, reference is made to an average of this figure and another one representing the value of the increment in herds during the calendar year 1952. For 1955, I cite the increment from October 1954 to October 1955. No information is at hand on the changes in livestock numbers during calendar years after 1952.

It remains to explain the calculation for 1928. The figure cited in Table G-1 is calculated from statistics on investments in livestock given in *Narkhoz-1932,* pp. XXVI–XXVII. According to data in this source, gross investments in livestock in 1928 amounted to 0.933 billion rubles in terms of current prices. On a basis to be explained, I find that 1937 prices were eight times 1928 prices, so in terms of 1937 prices gross investment amounts to 7.5 billion rubles.

The precise nature of these gross investments is not clear. Apparently they represent investments before certain deductions which are made under the heading of "depreciation" and losses due to disease, et cetera. Probably they represent increments in quality as well as in numbers, but for present purposes, an investment figure sufficiently comparable to those I have cited for 1937–54 probably is obtained if I simply correct the gross investments for depreciation and other losses, which I estimate at 6.0 billion rubles.

The relation of 1937 and 1928 livestock prices is computed as follows. According to *KTS 1929–30*, pp. 448–449, the total fixed capital in the form of livestock, fowl, and apiaries at the beginning of 1928–29, that is, October 1, 1928, amounted to 9.036 billion rubles in 1926–27 prices. From data in the same source, pp. 448–449, 454, prices in 1928 were 104.44 percent of 1926–27, so in terms of 1928 prices the total fixed capital in the form of livestock, fowl, and apiaries on October 1, 1928 amounted to 9.437 billion rubles. I assume the corresponding figure, exclusive of fowl and apiaries, was 9.00 billion rubles.

Soviet livestock herds on October 1, 1928 probably were not very different from the June 1928 counts given in Jasny, 1949, p. 797, and which I find were worth 72.58 billion rubles in terms of 1937 prices. In 1937, therefore, prices were eight times (that is, 72.58 ÷ 9.00) as high as in 1928. In this connection, I recomputed the 1937 livestock prices given above in order to allow for the differences in average slaughter weights in 1928 and 1937. See Jasny, p. 798.

The calculated index of livestock prices, 1928–37 is crude, but all things considered, it agrees notably with a corresponding index of farm prices for livestock and meat that Karcz has computed independently: 1937 = 863 percent of 1928. See RAND RM-1930, p. 33.

According to *Narkhoz-1932* "depreciation" and losses due to disease, et cetera, amounted to 0.805 billion rubles. This is in terms of mixed, probably acquisition, prices, but the cited figure is 9.41 percent of the January 1, 1928 value of herds in terms of much the same prices. In terms of 1937 prices, Soviet livestock herds were worth 63.31 billion rubles as of January 1, 1928. For the January 1, 1928 herds, see *Narkhoz*, p. 118. In the case of horses, I use the spring 1928 count given in *KTS 1929–30*, pp. 530 ff. In terms of 1937 prices, depreciation and other losses are taken equal to 6.0 billion rubles, that is, 0.0941 × 63.31 billion rubles.

The foregoing rather involved calculation of 1928 investments in livestock, I should explain, was necessary because of the lack of a January 1, 1929 livestock count. Without this, the 1928 investments could not be computed by the methods used for 1937–54.

I have been describing the calculation of livestock investments in terms of 1937 prices. According to Karcz's unpublished calculations, the average realized prices per kilogram of different kinds of livestock in 1952 varied as follows in relation to 1937: for cattle, 210 percent; for hogs, 203; and for sheep, 179 percent. Prices in 1950, I believe, were about the same as in 1952. Livestock investments in terms of 1950 prices are obtained, therefore, simply by multiplying by two the corresponding figures in terms of 1937 prices.

The figures for 1928 and 1937 on investment in 1928 prices are derived from those in 1937 prices by reference to the index derived above of the relation of 1937 to 1928 prices: 800 percent.

Inventory Investments in Trade

Scope. The figures in Table G-1, column (4), are computed from and correspond in scope to current ruble statistics on inventories in *Sovtorg.* The latter data represent the stocks of consumers' goods held by government and cooperative wholesale and retail trade organizations in the USSR. The precise nature of the wholesale organizations is not specified. Apparently, inventories held by the sales agencies of industrial ministries are included. Possibly the data also cover stocks of finished consumers' goods held by industrial enterprises, although this seems unlikely. Agricultural products held by procurement agencies are believed to be omitted.

The *Sovtorg* data refer to inventories of consumers' goods. Stocks of packaging materials, et cetera, held by trade organizations for their own use probably are omitted.

I have been referring to my figures for 1937–55. For 1928, the figure in Table G-1, column (4), essentially is computed from and corresponds in scope to data on investments in inventories in "trade" in Rozentul, *PKh,* 1929, No. 1. Investments by private as well as government and cooperative agencies are included. Otherwise, the scope of the Soviet data is conjectural. Presumably investments in such items as fuel and packaging materials, are included, but investments by procurement agencies may or may not be.

The scope of the *Sovtorg* data must be inferred from *ibid.,* pp. 79 ff. On the Soviet data used in calculating inventory investments in trade in 1928, see Rozentul, *PKh,* 1929, No. 1, and below.

Investments in current rubles. For 1928, investments amount to 0.509 billion rubles. This is computed from corresponding figures for the fiscal years 1927/28 and 1928/29 in *ibid.,* pp. 314–315. Rozentul's figures for trade, I believe, include cooperative industry. The investments involved, estimated at 0.004 billion rubles, are here deducted. Rozentul's data for inventory investments generally do not include 0.068 billion rubles of public investment in short-lived, small-valued equipment that were classified as fixed capital according to the Soviet statistical practice of the time. Of this sum, 0.023 billion rubles are assumed to have been invested in trade. On Rozentul's inventory investment figures, see above, p. 378, and below, pp. 402 ff.

The elements in the calculation of investments in current rubles for 1937–55 are shown in Table G-2, columns (1) to (8).

Columns (1) to (3). Except for figures in parentheses, these data are taken from *Sovtorg,* pp. 79, 84. The data in column (1) represent inventories of consumers' goods held by state and cooperative shops in the USSR, while the figures in column (3) represent inventories held both in these shops and in wholesale trade organizations. The inventories, I believe, are valued in terms of prices prevailing at the date to which the inventories refer, that is, the prices prevailing at the end of the year concerned. See on this the note in *Sovtorg,* p. 85.

The figures in parentheses in column (3) are calculated from the corre-

TABLE G-2

Calculation of Inventory Investments in Trade, in Current Rubles, USSR, 1937–55

Year	Inventories in retail trade, in current rubles, end of year (billion rubles) (1)	Inventories in retail trade ÷ inventories in all trade (percent) (2)	Inventories in all trade, in current rubles, end of year (billion rubles) (3)	Prices, end of previous year ÷ prices, end of given year (percent) (4)	Inventories in all trade, in prices of end of previous year (billion rubles) (5)	Increment in inventories, in all trade, in prices of end of previous year (billion rubles) (6)	Prices average for year ÷ prices, end of previous year (percent) (7)	Increment in inventories, in all trade, average prices of year (billion rubles) (8)
1936	11.7	(61)	(19.2)	—	—	—	—	—
1937	13.6	61	22.5	103	23.2	4.0	98	3.9
1938	12.9	—	—	—	—	—	—	—
1939	12.9	(56)	(23.0)	—	—	—	—	—
1940	16.4	56	29.3	80	23.4	0.4	122	0.5
1941	7.3	—	—	—	—	—	—	—
1942	5.7	—	—	—	—	—	—	—
1943	10.0	—	—	—	—	—	—	—
1944	13.7	—	—	—	—	—	—	—
1945	19.1	—	—	—	—	—	—	—
1946	27.8	—	—	—	—	—	—	—
1947	38.7	(55)	(70.4)	—	—	—	—	—
1948	59.5	(60)	(99.2)	102	101.2	30.8	99	30.5
1949	72.3	(65)	(111.2)	116	129.0	29.8	88	26.2
1950	64.1	67	96.3	125	120.4	9.2	83	7.6
1951	76.9	69	111.7	108	120.6	24.3	94	22.8
1952	93.2	72	128.8	106	136.5	24.8	96	23.8
1953	94.3	76	123.9	111	137.5	8.7	92	8.0
1954	90.0	81	110.9	105	116.4	−7.5	97	−7.3
1955	98.9	79	124.6	100	124.6	13.7	100	13.7

sponding figures in column (2), while the latter in turn are extrapolations. The extrapolations take into account the data compiled in Table G-3 from information in *Sovtorg,* p. 87, on the structure of inventories in cooperative trade, although in view of the limited importance of the latter (they constituted about one-fifth of all trade inventories in 1937 and one-fourth in 1950) they could not be taken as controlling.

TABLE G-3

Inventories in Retail Trade as Share of Inventories in All Trade, End of Year, USSR, 1936–55

Year	All trade organizations, Table G-2, column (2) (percent)	Cooperative shops, *Sovtorg,* p. 87 (percent)
1936	(61)	60.5
1937	61	60.4
1939	(56)	60.4
1940	56	61.7
1947	(55)	53.5
1948	(60)	56.3
1949	(65)	60.9
1950	67	63.3
1951	69	63.8
1952	72	61.6
1953	76	64.8
1954	81	66.5
1955	79	65.7

In contrast to the experience of the cooperative network alone, inventories in state and cooperative retail shops taken together tended to decline before the war in relation to trade inventories generally (that is, their share in the total fell from 61 percent at the end of 1937 to 56 percent at the end of 1940). On this basis, it might have been in order to assume that the share of retail inventories in the total at the end of 1939 was greater than at the end of 1940, but according to a foreign observer's report, the retail inventories of many goods were already much depleted at the end of 1939. See *MLR,* May 1940, pp. 1272 ff.

In view of the extraordinarily large inventory investments that are calculated for 1948 and 1949, I experimented with various alternative assumptions as to the share of retail shops in total trade inventories in these years, but while perhaps even larger investment figures are possible, I doubt that those accepted are appreciably too high. I shall return to this later.

Column (4). Retail food prices are assumed to have increased 1 percent during 1937. Food prices generally were constant during the year, but there were limited changes, mainly increases, for some articles. See Chapman, RAND RM-707–1, pp. 49 ff. According to Prokopovich, *Quarterly Bulletin of Soviet Russian Economics,* May 1941, p. 130, food prices on July 1, 1938 were 103.1 percent of the July 1, 1936 level. From data in Chapman, RAND RM-803–1, pp. 45 ff., and in *Sovtorg*, pp. 96 ff., I calculate that the retail prices of manufactures declined by about 6 percent during 1937. When the inventory data in *Sovtorg*, pp. 96 ff. are used as weights, this indicates that retail prices generally declined by about 3 percent during 1937.

Retail prices generally are assumed to have risen on the order of 25 percent during 1940. According to calculations in Zaleski, *Etudes et Conjuncture*, No. 4, April 1955, p. 343, retail prices in Moscow in July 1940 were 131 percent of July 1939, and in January 1941, 133 percent of July 1939. Some of this increase probably occurred in 1939, but prices rose primarily during 1940. See Prokopovich, *op. cit.*, p. 126; *MLR*, November 1939, pp. 1276 ff.; May 1940, pp. 1272 ff.; August 1940, pp. 500 ff.; February 1941, pp. 474 ff. In interpreting the foregoing materials, I have been aided by Janet Chapman (letter of May 24, 1957).

The small change in prices shown for 1948 is intended to allow for the decreases in the prices of a number of articles reported in the *New York Times*, July 18, 1948. Price changes during the years 1949–54 are calculated from the official price indices in *Sovtorg*, p. 132. The retail price level did not change significantly in 1955. See *Sovtorg*, p. 131.

Column (*5*). The product of columns (3) and (4).

Column (*6*). For any given year, column (5) minus the previous year, column (3).

Column (*7*). The price cuts that took place during 1937 occurred primarily in June and July. I assume the average price level for the year is about midway between the January 1 and December 31 levels.

From data in *Sovtorg*, pp. 131–2, it may be calculated that end of year prices were 102.8 percent of the average level for 1940. In relation to the January 1, 1940 level, the average level for the year, therefore, is 125 ÷ 102.8.

For 1948, I interpolate between the beginning and end-of-year levels. For 1949–54, the relation between average prices for the year and prices prevailing at the end of the previous year is calculated from the official indices in *Sovtorg*, p. 132. Indices of the average prices for the year are calculated by a procedure described in Appendix A. For 1955, the index is taken to be 100 percent.

Column (*8*). The product of columns (6) and (7).

In view of the fluctuating and often extraordinarily large magnitudes calculated for investment in trade inventories, further comment is in order regarding the meaning and reliability of the results.

The *Sovtorg* data from which the calculation begins, I believe, represent the values of consumers' goods stocks in terms of retail prices. Stocks held by both wholesale and retail organizations are valued in these terms. According to the current Soviet accounting practice, many consumers' goods are valued in the books of wholesale trade organizations in these terms to begin with and apparently the practice is universal in retail trade, although in both cases there are offsetting accounts which assure that the net values correspond to costs. See Il'in, 1954, pp. 191, 221, 227 ff. Reason to think that the inventory data in *Sovtorg* reflect retail values generally is to be found in the corresponding data published on the number of days retail turnover that the stocks (wholesale and retail) represent. Although I have been unable to reproduce precisely the underlying calculations, the latter data presumably could be computed only because the stocks are in terms of retail prices.

Given this valuation, indices of retail prices may properly be used as I have used them to translate the stock values into alternative price levels. On the same basis, I shall use them later to reduce the estimates of inventory investments to 1937 rubles. On the other hand, for purposes of national income accounting, wholesale and retail trade inventories are more correctly valued at their respective acquisition prices than at retail selling prices. An allowance might be made for distribution costs incurred in acquiring and holding the inventories, but valuation at retail prices tends to inflate the calculated investments in trade by unearned trade margins and turnover taxes paid by trade organizations. The overstatement on the former account probably does not exceed several percent, but substantial turnover taxes are paid by wholesale trade organizations in the USSR and considering this the inventory investment data may be overstated in all by (say) 10 to 20 percent.

Nevertheless, in this study national income is computed in prevailing rubles only as a preliminary to a further computation in "adjusted rubles." Since turnover taxes are omitted from the latter, the final valuation of inventory investments in trade errs little after all. The initial overstatement nevertheless affects the magnitudes of the current ruble investments of miscellaneous sorts, which are computed as a residual, but an attempt to correct accordingly this dubious calculation did not seem in order.

The estimated inventory investments in trade in 1948 and 1949 are notably large — the increases over the initial stocks are 44 and 30 percent; see Table G-2, columns (3) and (6) — and warrant special consideration. The calculation of these magnitudes involved a rather arbitrary extrapolation of the share of retail trade inventories in all trade inventories. While these extrapolations may err, I doubt that they result in any important overstatement of inventory investments in 1948 and 1949. For example, if the share of retail trade in all trade inventories rises evenly from 61 percent in 1947, for example, to 67 percent in 1950, the alternative estimates of inventory investment shown in Table G-4 result.

TABLE G-4

Investment in Inventories, All Trade,
Average Prices for the Year

Year	As calculated in Table G-2	Alternative calculation
1948	30.5	32.6
1949	26.2	30.4
1950	7.6	7.6

The extrapolations are needed in order to estimate inventories in wholesale trade, but inventories in cooperative wholesale trade are given in *Sovtorg*, p. 87, so the one unknown is the amount of inventories in *all other* wholesale trade. As it turns out, the calculation made actually allows only rather limited sums for investments in this sector as shown in Table G-5. At the end of 1950, other wholesale organizations had 70 percent of all inventories held in wholesale trade.

TABLE G-5

Investments in Inventories, Average Prices for the Year

Year	All trade	All retail shops	Cooperative wholesale organizations	Other wholesale organizations
1948	30.5	21.8	4.4	4.3
1949	26.2	21.5	2.8	1.9
1950	7.6	6.5	0.5	0.6

The estimates of inventory investments in trade often seem especially large when compared with the annual targets for the increase in "own working capital" for the entire public sector (Table G-6).

Moreover, as we shall see, in the postwar period industry was to receive the lion's share of the planned increase in "own working capital" for the "public sector." For 1949, the projected increase in "own working capital" for trade, together with procurement, was but 0.84 billion rubles. See Zverev, *PKh,* 1949, no. 2, p. 45. The corresponding figures for other years are not known; presumably they were very small.

What is the explanation? Is there not further reason to suspect the estimates of inventory investments in trade? These estimates seem relatively firm to me. Accordingly, I am inclined to explain the discrepancy between the small planned increment in "own working capital" that is implied for trade and the calculated inventory investments in these terms: (a) In formulating the plan for inventory investment, the government may have underestimated the increase in inventories in trade that resulted from its own price and fiscal policies and (b) the expansion could have been financed primarily by bank credits, as distinct from "own working capital." Credits normally are the main source of finance in the case of trade; the reliance on credits may have been especially heavy in some of the postwar years.

Investments in constant prices. For all years I deflate by Dr. Chapman's Formula (5) index numbers of retail prices. See Appendix A. For 1928, my inventory investment figure in current rubles refers to private as well as government and cooperative trade. I deflate by Dr. Chapman's corresponding index. For the years 1937–55, the inventory investment figures in current rubles refer to government and cooperative trade. In this case, I deflate by Dr. Chapman's indices for this sector. As was noted at a late stage, for

TABLE G-6

Inventory Investment in Public Sector and Trade, in Current Rubles, USSR, 1937–55

Year	Planned increase in "own working capital," "public sector" (billion rubles)	Inventory investment, trade (billion rubles)
1937	11	3.9
1940	10.3	...
1944	4.5	—
1948	17.1	30
1949	23.6	26
1950	16.3	8
1951	11.3	23
1952	10.7	24
1953	15.1	8
1954	15.9	−7
1955	12	14

... = negligible.

all years use inadvertantly was made not (as might have been desirable) of the unrounded current ruble figures in Table G-2, column (8), but of corresponding rounded figures.

In terms of 1950 rubles, inventory investments in trade are assumed to vary in the same way as in terms of 1937 rubles. For purposes of computing 1937 investments in terms of 1928 prices, I use as a deflator the reciprocal of Dr. Chapman's Formula (6) index of retail prices in 1928, that is, 16.8 (1937 as 100).

Inventory Investments Other Than in Trade

Scope. For 1937–55 the figures in Table G-1, column (5), were computed mainly from two sorts of Soviet financial data of somewhat differing scope. Except that I omit trade, my computations tend to reflect the scope of both sorts of statistics. I refer, on the one hand, to Soviet statistics on the "own working capital" (*sobstvennye oborotnye sredstva*), hereafter OWC. These figures refer generally to *khozraschet* organizations, but not I believe such organizations in construction. Consumers' and industrial cooperatives appear to be included, at least until recent years, but collective and individual farms are omitted throughout. For the most part, I believe the MTS are omitted but they may have been included to some extent in 1937 (before they were fully transferred to the budget in the following year) and they may again be represented in the OWC data for recent years.

The second main type of Soviet financial statistics employed are the data on State Bank credits outstanding (hereafter GD). These data embrace all organizations covered by the OWC figures, but cooperatives definitely are included. Some short-term credits have also been extended to other organizations, including the MTS and collective farms.

Although the OWC and credit statistics differ in scope, for convenience I shall refer to both as applying to the public sector.

For 1928, the figure cited in Table G-1 refers to all government and cooperative enterprises. Collective and private farms are omitted.

The general scope of the Soviet statistics on OWC and bank credit may be inferred from the nature of the *khozraschet* system. On the coverage of the construction agencies, cooperatives, MTS, and collective farms, see Zverev, 1946, p. 19; Campbell, "Notes on Trip to the Soviet Union," p. 11; *VS,* 1957, no. 2, pp. 94–96; D'iachenko, 1940, p. 523. On the scope of the 1928 figure on inventory investment, see below.

Investments in current rubles: all sectors. In Table G-7, column (1), the figure cited for 1928 on total inventory investments is calculated from corresponding figures for the fiscal years 1927/28 and 1928/29 in Rozentul, *PKh,* 1929, no. 1, pp. 314–315. Omitting collective and private farms, the

TABLE G-7

Inventory Investments in Sectors Other than Trade, USSR, 1928–55
(billions of rubles)

Year	All sectors (1)	All industry (2)	Producers' goods industries (3)	Consumers' goods industries (4)	Transport and communications (5)	Agriculture (6)	Other (7)
1928	0.313	0.234	0.140	0.094	0.023	0.061	−0.005
1937	8.6	6.0	3.0	3.0		2.6	
1940	5	3	5	−2		2	
1944	7[a]	—	—	—		—	
1948	11	8	5	3		3	
1949	32	27	23	4		5	
1950	22	18	13	5		4	
1951	17	13	9	4		4	
1952	16	12	9	3		4	
1953	21	17	12	5		4	
1954	... (14)	... (10)	... (10)	...		... (4)	
1955	17	13	9	4		4	

[a] Including trade.
... = negligible.

Rozentul data indicate total investments in physical working capital for the calendar year 1928 of 0.754 billion rubles. To this sum I add 0.068 billion rubles in order to allow for public investment in short-lived, small-value equipment which were not classified with working capital under the Soviet practice of the time. Investments in trade estimated above at 0.509 billion rubles are deducted. Rozentul's data are apparently estimates, but I believe they reflect the change in physical inventories in terms of current prices, which is what is desired here. The physical volume of inventory investment apparently was about the same in 1927/28 as in 1928/29, so we should not be too far off in deriving a figure for the calendar year as an average (with weights of 3 to 1, respectively) of the investments in these two years. Prices rose sharply in 1928/29, however, and possibly my calendar year figure does not reflect very accurately the average prices of 1928, which is what is desired here.

The data on inventory investments in sectors other than trade for 1937–55 are rather impressionistic. It may suffice if I outline the essentials. The calculations utilize Soviet financial statistics, including chiefly the data in Table G-8. As a preliminary, it is necessary to explain these figures.

In Soviet accounting practice, the physical assets that are of interest to us form part of a larger accounting category which appears to come to much the same thing as "current assets" in U. S. practice, and which may be so designated here (the Soviet term is *oborotnye sredstva*). The Soviet category, therefore, embraces not only short-lived physical assets, for example, such items as raw materials and goods-in-process but also various

TABLE G-8

Own Working Capital (OWC), Gross Short-term Indebtedness to the State Bank (GD), and Settlement Accounts (SA) of Economic Enterprises, USSR, 1936–55 (billions of rubles)

Year	OWC, Jan. 1 (1)	GD, Jan. 1 (2)	SA, Jan. 1 (3)	Annual increment of OWC: Planned (4)	Annual increment of OWC: Actual (5)	Annual increment of GD: Planned (6)	Annual increment of GD: Actual (7)
1936	27.4	26.9	5.4	9.2	9.9	—	7.3
1937	37.3	34.2	6.4	11	8.4	5.6	6.5
1938	45.7	40.7	7.5	8.9	6.5	—	4.3
1939	52.2	45.0	8.7	10.1[a]	8.6	—	2.9
1940	60.8	47.9	—	10.3	7.6	—	7.1
1941	68.4	55.0	—	10.2	—	—	—
1942	—	—	—	—	—	—	—
1943	—	—	—	—	—	—	—
1944	—	—	—	4.5	—	—	—
1945	59.2	—	—	6.8	—	—	—
1948	—	—	—	17.1	—	—	—
1949	—	—	—	23.6	—	—	—
1950	—	—	—	16.3	—	—	—
1951	—	163	—	11.3	—	—	—
1952	—	—	—	10.7	—	—	—
1953	—	203	—	15.1	—	—	5
1954	—	208	—	15.9	—	—	—
1955	—	—	—	12	—	—	—
1956	—	199	—	—	—	—	—

[a] State enterprises only.

monetary assets, including principally accounts receivable, cash, and funds held at an enterprise's disposal in its "settlement account" (*raschetnyi schet*, to be abbreviated here as SA) at the State Bank. The firm's holdings of current assets are financed from several sources: (a) government budget appropriations, accumulated profits, and certain other funds that are permanently at the disposal of the enterprise, for example, minimum sums of accrued wages; (b) Gosbank short term credits; and (c) credits extended by other enterprises and other "passives."

According to a practice originating in the credit reform of 1930–32, funds of the first sort are supposed to be used only to finance minimum balances of a number of types of assets the amounts of which are controlled by established norms. The assets in question comprise practically all the short-term physical assets of the enterprise, including such items as inventories of raw materials, work in process, finished goods, and miscellaneous supplies, and with minor exceptions these consist only of such assets. Funds of the first sort, which the enterprise has permanently at its disposal, are called "own working capital" (*sobstvennye oborotnye sredstva*), abbreviated here as OWC. In Soviet accounting practice, minimal sums of accrued wages and similar funds are considered as formally distinct from OWC but for practical purposes they come to the same thing and I believe are treated as such in most published statistical reports on OWC.

To repeat: funds of the first sort are used to finance minimal holdings of most short-term physical assets. For purposes of financing holdings of these assets in excess of the minimum requirements, especially to meet seasonal peak needs, the enterprise normally obtains funds through State Bank credits (GD). Such credits are also used to finance holdings of certain physical assets other than those controlled by norms, most importantly goods in transit. Although Soviet sources are not explicit on this, Gosbank credits may also provide the enterprise with cash and funds held at the enterprises' disposal in its settlement account (SA) at Gosbank.

A principal aim of the Credit Reform was to limit the previous practice according to which enterprises extended credit to one another on a substantial scale. Subject to legal restriction on their duration and other aspects, however, interenterprise credit still continued and, accordingly, such credits are still another source of finance to the Soviet enterprise, although of course the enterprises' financial requirements may be the greater as a result of the same practice. Holdings of current assets may also be financed to some extent from various other sources (for example, there may be such items as debts to individuals and accrued wages over and above the normal minimum), but again these may offset corresponding assets.

I have been describing the typical accounting and financial procedure. In the course of time, special arrangements have come to be used in several branches, especially in trade and machinery. In most cases, these arrangements provide for the use of credit to finance not only seasonal peak short-term capital requirements but some minimal needs.

On the scope of the Soviet accounting category *oborotnye sredstva* and on the Soviet arrangements regarding the financing of the assets it embraces, see Kondrashev, 1937, pp. 11 ff.; NKTP, *Formy kontrol'nykh tsifr tiazheloi promyshlennosti na 1937 god;* Katsenellenbaum, 1945, chaps. 1, 2; Bachurin, 1953, chap. xi; Kontorovich, 1953, chap. 8; Gusakov and Dymshits, 1951, pp. 226 ff.

In Table G-8, all data refer to "public sector" enterprises as was explained.

It is not entirely clear how the Russians value physical assets which are reflected in published data on OWC and GD such as are in the table. (On Soviet procedures in valuing inventories, the most illuminating account I have found which refers to the recent practice in industry is that of Shchenkov, 1955, pp. 8–9, 75, 296–297, 308–309. See also Rozentul, *PKh,* 1929, no. 1, p. 203; NKTP, op. cit., pp. 59, 134, 137 ff.; Nikolaev, 1936, pp. 125, 145, 158 ff.; Kondrashev, 1937, pp. 11–26; Dolgov, 1937, pp. 15 ff., 46; Efimov and Aleksandrov, *DiK,* 1940, no. 1, p. 16; Atlas, 1947, p. 305.) The cardinal principle governing inventory valuation is the conventional one: valuation at cost. This does not preclude valuation in alternative terms, for example, as where consumers' goods purchases by retail shops are recorded at retail prices, but apparently the use of such alternatives is usually associated with the use of offset accounts, so that net asset values still correspond to costs. The published data on OWC and GD no doubt also correspond to costs, and the figures in Table G-8 may be read accordingly. This means among other things that inventories of finished goods are valued finally at prices net rather than gross of turnover taxes, a salient fact for our purposes.

What if prices or costs change after the asset is acquired? As a rule, at least in the case of general price reforms, I believe asset values and hence the OWC and GD are adjusted to take into account price changes. Not only materials and finished products but work in process are revalued; as assets are revalued, the OWC and GD are adjusted correspondingly.

Soviet sources, especially Shchenkov, are quite clear that this is the recent Soviet practice, at least for the more important price reforms. I am less sure that this was also the practice in the thirties, and in the absence of fully explicit statements in Soviet sources, one inevitably wonders for both recent and early years to what extent revaluations are undertaken in response not only to general price reforms but also to changes in individual prices and to the almost continual change in costs which an enterprise must experience. It is hardly possible that revaluations would be made in response to any and all such changes in prices and costs.

Of particular concern for present purposes are the values which the published OWC and GD figures for January 1 in the table reflect. To what extent do the figures reflect the prices and costs of the date in question, as distinct from the prices and costs of acquisition? What has just been said about the book values of OWC and GD generally applies also to the figures published for January 1, although there is perhaps some additional reason to think that these figures reflect current values. At any rate, it is difficult to see how the Russians could avoid compiling figures in such terms for purposes of budget and credit planning. In order to determine the enterprise's financial needs for the plan year, the initial and closing stocks would have to be valued at planned prices, and as it turns out these have often been the prices prevailing on January 1 of the plan year.

Under Soviet conditions, it should be observed also, there are limits in any case to the extent to which book values at a given moment might deviate from current values. On the one hand, price changes to a great extent take the form of wholesale revision which the book values apparently do reflect. On the other, Soviet inventories generally have a high velocity, so most stocks on hand at any moment should have been acquired recently. Inventories in industry on January 1, 1941, for example, may have totaled 75 to 100 billion rubles. At the output planned for 1941 (*1941 Plan,* p. 11), the average turnover would have been four to five times per year.

All this does not settle the question of the values to which the published January 1 figures on OWC and GD relate, but I make only limited use of the January 1 data and it may be permissible to assume tentatively that the figures used are more or less indicative of current values.

What of the data on planned ΔOWC and ΔGD? Soviet plans are formulated in terms of planned prices and costs, and presumably this applies to supplements to working capital. As a practical expedient, I believe plans have often been drawn up in terms of prices prevailing at around the beginning of the plan year, and where price changes have occurred during the year the reported targets for inventory investment may represent initial rather than average prices for the year. For present purposes, however, I believe this limitation on the planned investment figures is not very important.

The volume of credits needed to finance certain physical assets, particularly goods in transit, are not planned for individual enterprises, but apparently they are planned for the economy as a whole. See Gusakov and Dymshits, 1951, pp. 280–283. For this reason, a published target for ΔGD must be comprehensive in this regard, which makes it more useful for our purposes than it would be otherwise.

The sources and methods for Table G-8 follow:

Column (*1*). *1936; 1937*. Smilga, *PE,* 1937, no. 2, pp. 118–119; Grin'ko, 1937, pp. 38–39. Bogolepov, *PKh,* 1937, no. 3, p. 115, states that OWC was 42 billion rubles on January 1, 1937. I have been unable to explain the discrepancy between this and the figure cited in Table G-8, but accept the latter because it fits in more easily with the data for other years.

1938. Zverev, 1946, p. 19.

1939. OWC increased 8.6 billion rubles during 1939. See D'iachenko, 1940, p. 405.

1940. Zverev, 1946, p. 80.

1941. Zverev, 1946, pp. 80, 108; *SNIP-40–48,* pp. 202–203.

1945. Zverev, 1946, p. 154, cites this figure for 1944 but I believe he means the end of the year.

Column (*2*). *1936; 1937*. Grin'ko, 1937, pp. 7, 30.

1938. Gusakov and Dymshits, 1951, p. 146.

1939. Livshits, 1948, p. 245.

1940. Ikonnikov, 1954, p. 277.

1941. Gusakov and Dymshits, 1951, p. 146.

1951. Usoskin, 1956, p. 100.

1953. ABM, 1953.

1954. Atlas, *DiK,* 1955, no. 2, p. 25.

1956. Usoskin, 1956, p. 100. By September, 1956, the total was 230 billion rubles. *DiK,* 1956, no. 11, p. 6.

Column (*3*). *1936; 1937.* Ikonnikov, *Ekonomicheskaia zhizn',* February 6, 1936.

1938; 1939. Atlas, 1952, p. 207.

Column (*4*). *1936.* Grin'ko, 1936, p. 43.

1937. Smilga, *PE,* 1937, no. 2, pp. 118–119; Grin'ko, 1937, pp. 38–39. Bogolepov, *PKh,* 1937, no. 3, p. 115 cites a figure of 15 billion rubles.

1938–1941; 1944; 1945. Zverev, 1946, pp. 19, 51, 80, 108, 133, 154.

1948–1952. ABM, 1948–52.

1953. Plotnikov, 1954, p. 507.

1954. PKh, 1954, no. 3, p. 18.

1955. PKh, 1955, no. 2, p. 39.

Column (*5*). For all years calculated from column (1).

Column (*6*). The 1937 figure is from Grin'ko, 1937, p. 30.

Column (*7*). Calculated from column (2).

To come to the inventory investment figures for 1937–55, these represent the results of a rather freehand reading of the figures in Table G-8. So far as it may be inferred from these figures, I take as a benchmark the magnitude

$$\Delta WC = \Delta OWC + \Delta GD.$$

For a single enterprise, inventory investments may diverge from ΔWC owing to a change in the net balance with other enterprises of accounts receivable and payable, indebtedness to individuals, and any other short-term debt and accruals incurred. Insofar as OWC and GD are used to finance holdings of SA and cash, there is a further source of divergence. Among these items, accounts receivable and payable with other enterprises are the most important, and for sufficiently large sectors, these in good part should tend to cancel.

Nevertheless inventory investments probably have diverged from ΔWC for industry and for the public sector generally, but the possible magnitudes involved may be judged from the relation of physical inventories to WC (that is OWC + GD) in industry. On January 1, 1951, the former amounted to 87 percent of the latter; for January 1, 1956, the corresponding figure was 86 percent. See *VS,* 1957, no. 2, pp. 94–96. The cited figures I believe include "goods in transit." These recently constituted 10 percent of the current assets of union industrial enterprises. See *DiK,* 1957, no. 7, p. 28. For the public sector as a whole, physical inventories amounted to 87 percent of total WC on January 1, 1951 and 88 percent on January 1, 1956. According to scattered information, these relations have varied in the course of time but generally to a limited extent.

In estimating inventory investment, in addition to the magnitudes of ΔWC implied by the data in Table G-8, I take into account the estimates already made of investments in trade, the magnitude of other gross investments as a whole, the trends in prices which affect the meaning of the statistics on OWC and GD as shown chiefly by the index numbers of retail prices in Table G-2, data on the prices of other goods used below in the deflation and unpublished information on machinery prices (in a letter of Moorsteen to Bergson, May 29, 1957), and diverse other pertinent information.

For 1937–44, inventory investment is estimated initially for the public sector as a whole. From this I deduct investments in trade as already computed in order to determine investments in sectors other than trade. For 1940, ΔOWC was planned to be 10.3 billion rubles. Presumably, there was also to be an increase in credit, so that an increase in inventories of more than 10.3 billion rubles must have been projected. Reason to think that in fact only a very limited increase occurred is to be found partly in the calculation already made for trade. I find that there was no increase in inventories to speak of in this sector during 1940. Also illuminating were some data on the increase in GD for different branches. Considered together with concomitant price increases, these suggest that inventories in consumers' goods industries and possibly also in trade decreased. See below, p. 415. Finally, other gross investments as a whole are quite limited for 1940. (See Table 3.)

For 1948–55, inventory investment for sectors other than trade is computed as the sum of the corresponding magnitudes for industry and for miscellaneous branches. See Table G-7, columns (2) and (5) to (7). For industry for 1949–53 and 1955 (I consider 1948 and 1954 separately below), planned targets for inventory investment are assumed to have been realized. Planned inventory investment is taken to be 140 percent of planned ΔOWC. Physical inventories on hand in industry totaled 143 percent of all OWC on January 1, 1951 and 141 percent on January 1, 1956. See *VS*, 1957, no. 2, pp. 94–96. Finally, the planned ΔOWC for industry varies as follows: in 1949, 19.5 billion rubles; in 1950, 13.0; in 1951, 9.0; in 1952, 8.6; in 1953, 12.1; and in 1955, 9.6 billion rubles. For 1949 and 1955 I cite the reported targets for ΔOWC for industry. See Zverev, *PKh*, 1949, no. 2, p. 45; ABM, 1955. For 1949 and 1955, industry's share in the ΔOWC planned for the entire public sector (Table G-8) was 83 and 80 percent respectively. For the years 1950–53, I assume that the planned ΔOWC in industry was 80 percent of the planned ΔOWC for the public sector.

The figures on the planned ΔOWC for the public sector in Table G-8 and hence the derived figures for the planned and realized inventory investment for industry presumably are in planned prices and costs. They may also be taken, I believe, as representing inventory investment approximately in average prices for the year. Of interest here are the prices at which inventories are recorded in the books of Soviet industrial enterprises. A divergence between the plan and actuality regarding these prices might arise in part because of unanticipated changes in wages and labor productivity, but wages increased only slowly in this period (an average of about 3 percent annually), and while the Russians tend to be optimistic regarding labor costs, I doubt that divergencies at this point could be important.

For the rest, the period witnessed a series of changes in wholesale industrial prices, retail and probably wholesale prices of consumers' goods, and farm procurement prices. For the most part, however, I believe the price changes were taken into account in the annual financial plans. Insofar as they were not, the resulting divergence between the planned prices in terms of which the targets for OWC in industry were expressed and average yearly prices I believe generally would have been on the order of only a few percent. For 1955, the divergence perhaps was somewhat higher. The extent to which the price changes were considered in the annual financial plans may be inferred from annual budget messages. In considering the possible magnitude between planned and actual prices, I consider mainly the index numbers of prices that are used later to deflate inventory investments in industry.

The foregoing calculations yield estimates for inventory investment in industry for 1949–53 and 1955. For 1954, the same procedures yield an estimate of 18 billion rubles. In Table G-7, column (2), I assume that in fact there was no investment to speak of. This assumption seems unavoidable in view of the extremely limited magnitude of "other gross investment" (exclusive of livestock investments, but 4.6 billion rubles) in 1954. But "other gross investment" is calculated here as a residual in total gross investment, and as Hoeffding and Nimitz make clear (RAND RM-2101, pp. 128 ff., 179 ff.) their estimate of total gross investment for 1954, on which essentially I rely here, may well represent a significant understatement. For this reason, as an alternative to the hypothesis just mentioned, I have felt it in order to consider also the case where investment in industrial inventories in 1954 amount to (say) 10 billion rubles. Assuming (as seems reasonable in view of the concomitant depletion of trade inventories) that such industrial inventory investment as took place in 1954 all occurred in producers' goods industries and accordingly that none occurred in consumers' goods industries, the implied level of investment in the former branches turns out under the alternative hypothesis to be about midway between the corresponding levels of 1953 and 1955. The division of total industrial inventory investment between producers' and consumers' goods industries in the different years studied is considered below.

When price and production trends are taken into account, inventory investments in industry in 1948 may have been less than half those of 1949. I assume that in fact the investments were but 8 billion rubles, in view of the Zverev statement (*PKh,* 1949, no. 2, p. 46) that "on October 1, 1948, the inventories of material values in all union industry . . . were lower than the corresponding balances on January 1, 1947 and 1948." Possibly there was no inventory investment in industry to speak of in 1948. Considering that Zverev limits himself to the period up to October 1 and to "union" enterprises (which produced 67 percent of the total industrial output in 1950) and considering also the total of "other" gross investments that has to be accounted for, I hesitate to assume that anything like this was the fact.

The accepted figure, 8 billion rubles, is taken to be in terms of current prices and costs. Owing to the widespread subsidization of producers' goods industries at the time, the costs at which goods in process and finished goods were recorded on the books no doubt were quite out of line with final selling prices.

Because of the violent change in price structure and in view of Zverev's statement, it was not possible to calculate industrial inventory investment for 1948, as was done for 1949–55, on the basis of the planned ΔOWC for the public sector (17.1 billion rubles in 1948), and the 1949 share of industry in the total.

The total physical inventories of industry on January 1, 1956 may be estimated at some 220 billion rubles, of which 145 billion rubles were held by producers' goods industries and 75 billion rubles by consumers' goods industries (GD of each sector is calculated from data in Table G-8 and Popov, 1956, p. 19. The relation of physical assets to GD is calculated from data in *VS,* 1957, no. 2, pp. 94–96). On the assumption that the physical volume of inventories in the two sectors of industry varied proportionately to the Soviet official production indices (*Narkhoz-1956,* p. 53), and that inventory price trends are measured by deflators compiled below, it is possible to derive alternative data on inventory investments in industry. The results of this calculation are shown in Table G-9, together with the estimates we have derived mainly from financial statistics.

TABLE G-9

Inventory Investments in Industry, Average Prices of the Current Year, USSR, 1948–55

Year	Estimated from financial data (billion rubles)	Estimated from price and production trends (billion rubles)
1948	8	12
1949	27	26
1950	18	23
1951	13	18
1952	12	17
1953	17	21
1954	. . . (10)	24
1955	13	24

. . . = negligible.

On the face of it, the alternative calculation might seem preferable to the one that has been used. I have hesitated to rely on it nevertheless in view of the dubious nature of the underlying official production indices. Beyond this, the Russians claim increases in the "velocity of turnover" during the period in question (see ABM, pamphlet edition, 1951, 1952), and while the claims are difficult to interpret, there is further reason to doubt that inventories varied proportionately with output in the manner assumed.

The alternative figures tend to be higher than those I accept. The latter data may represent an underestimation of Soviet inventory investments, but the alternative data may also be too high. If the official production statistics are subject to an upward bias, as is usually assumed, and the "velocity of turnover" has increased, the alternative calculation would tend to understate the volume of inventories on hand in the earlier years. The current percentage increments, however, would be overstated. The net of these opposing biases is conjectural for early years, but most likely investments would be overstated in years near 1956.

In Table G-7, inventory investments in sectors other than industry and trade for 1948–55 are guesses. The data in Table G-8 and a published breakdown of the planned ΔOWC for the public sector in 1949 provided a point of departure. See Zverev, *PKh,* 1949, no. 2, p. 45. As for industrial inventories, so here, for 1954 I consider alternative hypotheses.

Investments in current rubles: by sector and type. As a preliminary to the deflation of investments in sectors other than trade, it was necessary to try to disaggregate in some degree the global current ruble data compiled. In Table G-7, the sector breakdown for 1928, except for the division of industrial investments between those of producers' goods and consumers' goods industries, is again calculated from fiscal year data in Rozentul, *PKh,* 1929, no. 1, pp. 314–15. Rozentul's figures for trade, I believe, include cooperative industry. I transfer this sum, estimated at 0.004 billion rubles, to my industrial sector. Although the concern here is generally with the public sector, I include in industry private investments as given in Rozentul. As noted, investments in collective farm and private agriculture are omitted. In order to round out Rozentul's tabulation, I assume that of the 0.068 billion rubles of small-valued or short-lived assets not covered by him 0.030 billion are invested in industry, and 0.015 in transport and the balance of 0.023 billion rubles was assigned above to trade.

The further breakdown of inventory investments in 1928 as between producers' and consumers' goods industries as shown in Table G-7, columns (3) and (4), and by type as shown in Table G-10, is estimated mainly from the data on inventory investments by industrial branch and type in 1926/27 and the corresponding draft targets for 1927/28 and 1928/29 in VSNKH, *Kontrol'nye tsifry piatiletnego plana . . . SSSR,* pp. 163–165, and in VSNKH, *Svodnyi proizvodstvennogo-finansovyi plan . . . na 1926–27.* Some gaps are completed by reference to the corresponding breakdowns for 1937.

The latter, as shown in Table G-7 and Table G-10, seem broadly plausible in the light of Soviet financial and related statistics, including chiefly the figures on January 1, 1937, OWC by sector, and corresponding 1937 targets for ΔOWC in Smilga, *PE,* 1937, no. 2, pp. 118–119; the corresponding sector data on GD on January 1, 1937 and January 1, 1938 in Grin'ko. 1937, pp. 10–11, and *Finansy SSSR za XXX let,* p. 127; and the data on

TABLE G-10

Investments in Inventories by Sector and Type, in Current Rubles, USSR, 1928 and 1937 (billions of rubles)

	1928	1937
Machinery industries		
Finished goods	0.005	0.3
Goods in process	0.015	0.4
Other producers' goods industries		
Finished goods	0.025	0.9
Goods in process	0.025	0.4
All producers' goods industries: other investments		
Raw materials		0.6
Instruments, et cetera	0.070	0.3
Other		0.1
All producers' goods industries: all investments	0.140	3.0
Consumers' goods industries		
Finished goods	0.021	0.7
Goods in process		0.7
Raw materials	0.073	1.1
Instruments, et cetera		0.2
Other		0.3
All	0.094	3.0
All industry	0.234	6.0
Transport and communications	0.023	
Agriculture	0.061	2.6
Other	−0.005	
All sectors	0.313	8.6

SA in Atlas, *PKh,* 1937, no. 9–10, pp. 121–124; *Ekonomicheskaia zhizn',* July 30, 1937; TSUNKHU, *Socialist Construction in the USSR,* 1936 ed., pp. 516–517; and figures on the structure of inventories on October 1, 1935, January 1, 1936, and January 1, 1939 in Omel'chenko, 1938, pp. 10–11; Khromov, *PE,* 1937, no. 1, pp. 70–72; Katsenellenbaum, 1945, p. 26. The calculations take into account the estimated investments in inventories in trade (Table G-2).

In Table G-7, the sector data for 1940 are guesses. I take into account the sector data on GD on January 1, 1940 and 1941 in Atlas, 1947, pp. 338–339; D'iachenko, 1940, p. 523; Gusakov and Dymshits, 1951, p. 147; and pertinent price trends.

For 1948–55, the estimated inventory investments in industry and in miscellaneous branches were explained above. I also referred previously to an alternative computation of the volume of inventory investments in industry for these years. The calculation leads to estimates not only of total

TABLE G-11

Inventory Investments in the USSR, Other Than in Trade, in 1937 Prices, 1928–55
(billions of rubles)

	1928	1937	1940	1944	1948	1949	1950	1951	1952	1953	1954	1955
Producers' goods industries	0.269	3.0	4.3	—	3.2	7.8	5.4	3.8	4.1	5.5	. . . (4.6)	4.3
Consumers' goods industries	0.482	3.0	−1.8	—	1.6	1.9	2.5	2.1	1.7	2.9	. . .	2.0
All industries	0.751	6.0	2.5	—	4.8	9.7	7.9	5.9	5.8	8.4	. . . (4.6)	6.3
Transport and communications	0.046	}										
Agriculture	0.203	} 2.6	1	—	2	2.5	2.5	2.5	2.5	3	. . . (3)	3
Other[a]	−0.015	}										
All sectors	0.98	8.6	3.5	6.0[b]	6.8	12.2	10.4	8.4	8.3	11.4	. . . (7.6)	9.3

[a] Procurement probably is in "trade" in 1928. It is allowed for under "Other" from 1937 to 1955.
[b] Including trade.
. . . = negligible.

inventory investments in industry but also of investments in producers' goods industries and consumers' goods industries separately. Although I have hesitated to use the over-all figures, in Table G-7 the breakdown of investments in industry as between the two sectors for the years 1948–55 is based generally on the breakdown given by the alternative computation. For 1954, I have assumed previously that investments in industrial inventories are either null or 10 billion rubles. In the former case, I now assume further that such investments are null in both producers' and consumers' goods industries. In the latter case, it seems just as well to suppose that all of the investments occur in producers' and none in consumers' goods industries.

Investments in constant prices. In Table G-11 are shown the results of the deflation of inventory investments in sectors other than trade. My current ruble figures on inventory investments are taken throughout to be in average prices of the year to which they relate. Accordingly, the various components are deflated by price indices which are supposed to measure the average prices of the year. The calculations for all years except 1944 are described below by major components; 1944 is referred to separately. The standards of reliability achieved in the deflation are hardly higher than those set in the calculations of the current ruble data. The limitations are sufficiently evident not to require comment.

Producers' Goods Industries

1928. The deflation proceeds in terms of the items in Table G-10.

(a) *Machinery industries: finished goods.* Deflated by Moorsteen's Formula (5) index number of machinery prices. See Table G-12, column (1), and Moorsteen, *Machinery.* Unless otherwise noted, references to Moorsteen's index numbers will be to his Formula (5) indices.

(b) *Machinery industries: goods in process.* Deflated by an average of Moorsteen's index number of machinery prices (70) and the index of metals prices with 1928 weights (58) computed by Bergson, Bernaut, and Turgeon in RAND RM-1522, p. 69b. Although the values of goods in process depend on wage rates and labor productivity, it seems reasonable to assume that they would move closely with the prices of the principal raw material and the finished product.

(c) *Other producers' goods industries: finished goods and goods in process.* Deflated by the Bergson, Bernaut, and Turgeon index of the prices of basic industrial products, 1937 weights: 45. With only partial reweighting, the 1928 index with 1928 weights turns out to be the same as that based on 1937 weights. See *ibid.*, p. 69b. In Table G-12, column (2), I cite the 1937 weighted series for all years from RAND RM-1522, p. 69a, and Turgeon and Bergson, RAND RM-1919, p. 13.

(d) *All producers' goods industries: other goods (raw materials, instruments, et cetera).* Taking into account the Moorsteen index (70) and the Bergson, Bernaut, and Turgeon index (45), I take the pertinent deflator to be 55.

1940–1955. For all producers' goods taken together, I deflate by an

TABLE G-12

Selected Price Indices Used in the Deflation of Inventory Investment
(1937 = 100)

Year	Machinery prices, variable weights of given year (Moorsteen) (1)	Prices of basic industrial goods, 1937 weights (Bergson, Bernaut, Turgeon) (2)	Machinery and basic industrial prices (3)	Retail prices, given year weights (Chapman extended) (4)	Retail prices adjusted for turn-over taxes (5)	Prices of industrial inventories of finished consumers' goods (6)	Realized farm prices, (Karcz)[a] (7)	Retail prices of grain products (Chapman) (8)	Prices of all inventories in consumers' goods industries (9)
1928	70	45	51	11.5	18	14	21	8.5	—
1937	100	100	100	100	100	100	100	100	100
1940	106	121	117	126	122	124	100	103	111
1944	110	128	124	—	—	—	105	—	—
1948	130	128	128	300	234	267	105	270	189
1949	273	303	296	268	217	242	140	240	209
1950	191	256	240	222	198	210	180	180	197
1951	186	251	235	206	183	194	180	150	186
1952	165	236	218	198	180	189	180	132	180
1953	165	236	218	180	175	178	180 (225)	118	174 (191)
1954	165	236	218	170	183	176	180 (270)	111	172 (206)
1955	153	228	209	170	181	176	270	109	205

[a] Other than CFM, institutional deliveries and grain.

average of the Moorsteen index numbers of machinery prices and the Bergson, Bernaut, Turgeon Formula (6) index numbers of the prices of basic industrial goods. See Table G-12, column (3). The two component indices are assigned weights of 1 to 3, respectively. These weights are suggested by the breakdown of inventory investments in producers' goods industries in 1937. I allow to some extent for an increase in the importance of elements reflecting machinery price trends in later years, but while machinery production has increased in relation to producers' goods generally (*Narkhoz,* pp. 47, 74), the relatively more limited increases in machinery prices tend to be an offset. For 1948, the deflator is arbitrarily increased by one-fifth in order to allow for the subsidized costs of goods in process and finished goods.

Consumers' Goods Industries

1928. The components in Table G-10 are considered in turn.

(a) *Finished goods.* Dr. Chapman's Formula (5) index for retail prices in 1928 is 11.5 percent. See her *Real Wages.* The 1937 prices on which this index is based include sizable turnover taxes which were paid on processed consumers' goods, and which were only partly reflected in the book values of finished goods inventories held by industry. The latter, it will be recalled, are generally in terms of costs, and hence would reflect the taxes paid where one producer (for example, a clothing manufacturer) uses as a material another's taxed product (for example, textiles), but would not reflect the taxes on the manufacturer's own product, levied at the processing and retail stages. If all turnover taxes paid by processers and trade organizations were deducted, the 1928 index might rise to about 18 percent. Taking into account that some turnover taxes were included in book values and that some excise taxes were levied in 1928, I use as a deflator an index of 14 percent.

(b) *Consumers' goods industries: goods in process, raw materials, instruments, et cetera.* The index used, 22 percent, takes into account, to begin with, the book price index just derived, 14. I also consider an index of realized farm prices for marketings other than in the collective farm market, 32, compiled by Jerzy Karcz in an unpublished memorandum. Allowing for turnover taxes levied at the procurement stage in 1937 (which Karcz's index does not reflect), selling prices to processers in 1928 may have been about 16 percent or less of the 1937 level (calculated from tax data in *SNIP-37,* p. 138 and the estimated value of procurements in 1937 at realized farm prices, 17.4 billion rubles, as given in *SNIP-28–48,* Appendix E). The book price index and the adjusted Karcz index together are allowed to stand for goods in process and the adjusted Karcz index alone for raw materials. An average of the Moorsteen index of machinery prices and the Bergson, Bernaut, and Turgeon index of the prices of basic industrial goods as shown in Table G-12, stands for instruments and other stocks.

1940–1955. In order to derive a deflator for all inventory investment in consumers' goods industries, I aggregate three indices:

(a) Assumed indices of book prices of manufacturers' inventories of finished goods. See Table G-12, column (6). This indicates finished goods price trends and in part stands for the price trends for goods in process.

Although retail and industrial book price trends are less divergent after 1937 than before, it seemed in order to try to adjust the Chapman retail price indices for the entire period studied in order to appraise the trends in industrial book prices of finished consumers' goods. In Table G-12, column (4), are shown Dr. Chapman's Formula (5) index numbers of retail prices. See Appendix A and her *Real Wages*. The indices in Table G-12, column (5), are intended to show the trends in retail prices after the deduction of all turnover taxes paid by processers of and traders in finished consumers' goods. For 1937 and 1940, I estimate that such taxes amounted respectively to 59 and 63 percent of all turnover taxes. See *SNIP-37*, p. 138, and *SNIP-40–48*, p. 221. The corresponding figure for 1948 is taken to be 63 percent and for 1949–55 (after taxes were eliminated on most heavy industrial goods) 65 percent. The relation of the taxes to retail prices is then computed from familiar data on total turnover tax receipts and the volume of retail trade. In Table G-12, column (6), the assumed indices of industrial book prices of finished consumers' goods for all years other than 1928 are obtained simply by averaging the adjusted and unadjusted retail price indices in columns (4) and (5). I believe I am right in assuming that as a result of processers' purchases of taxed products from other processers their book prices of finished goods would include significant turnover taxes, but one-half the total levied on processers and trading organizations may be too high a figure for the sum involved, for many sales between processers are exempted from the tax. On the turnover tax structure, see Suchkov, 1945, chap. ii; Suchkov, 1949, chap. iv; Suchkov, 1955, chap. xiii. On the exemptions, see especially *ibid.*, pp. 178–179. For 1928, as noted, my assumed index is reduced somewhat below the average of columns (4) and (5) to take account of the excise taxes of that year. See Holzman, 1955, pp. 112 ff.

(b) A series of indices obtained by averaging indices of farm prices compiled by Karcz for the purposes of this study and index numbers of the retail price of grain products compiled in Chapman, *Real Wages*. For 1952 and 1954, the latter have been adjusted from a post-cut to calendar year basis. Also, indices for years not covered are interpolated. The average indices are intended to show the trends in agricultural raw material prices paid by processers and in part to stand for the trends in the prices of goods in process. Farm products generally are delivered to processers more or less at farm prices, but some sales are gross of sizable turnover taxes. The chief case in point is grain, where the wholesale price to processers actually is tied to the retail price of bread, with allowance for trade and milling markups. The excess of the resultant price over the farm price yields a sizable part of the total turnover tax revenues in the Soviet government budget. The Karcz indices used here refer to marketings outside the collective farm market. In order to exclude a large increase in accounting prices on "institutional" farm deliveries, which would not affect consumers' goods industries, Karcz has recomputed for me the indices given in his RAND RM-1930 to exclude such deliveries. In the recomputation, he also excludes grain. Indices for years other than those covered in Karcz's calculations are interpolated. I tentatively assume that the government held the line on prices to processers in the face of the farm price increases of 1953–54. In Table G-12, column (7), I show outside parentheses constant indices, which are used in my calculation and in parentheses the original Karcz indices of farm prices. On January 1, 1937, inventories in food processing probably were roughly comparable to those in other consumers' goods industries. In view of the government's pricing practices, grain products must have constituted a sizable part of the food processing inventories. In aggregating the Karcz and retail grain indices, I use weights of 3 to 1.

(c) An equal weighted average of the Moorsteen index numbers of machinery prices and the Bergson, Bernaut, and Turgeon index numbers of the prices of basic industrial goods. This stands for the prices of instruments, fuel, and miscellaneous inventories.

In the light of the breakdown of the 1937 investments, I aggregated (a), (b), and (c) with the weights of 3 to 4 to 1, respectively. In Table G-12, column (9), the indices in parentheses correspond to those in parentheses in column (7).

Transport and Communications; Agriculture; Other

For 1928, I obtain a deflator of 50 percent for transport by aggregating the Moorsteen index of machinery prices and the Bergson, Bernaut, Turgeon index numbers of the prices of basic industrial products and of coal. In agriculture, I believe the inventory investment consisted primarily of immature livestock, seed and other farm products, and unfinished production (all to be considered here only insofar as a money investment was involved), and to a limited extent of industrial products, such as fuel, spare parts, et cetera. An average deflator of 30 percent is used taking account of the Karcz farm price index (32 percent), the index of average wages in agriculture (15 percent; see TSUNKHU, *Trud v SSSR,* 1936 ed., pp. 16–17; *TTP,* pp. 228–229), the Moorsteen index of machinery prices, and the Bergson, Bernaut, and Turgeon index of the prices of basic industrial goods. "Other" is deflated arbitrarily.

For 1940–55, my constant ruble figures for these sectors represent mainly freehand projections from 1937. Since the current ruble figures are arbitrary, no systematic deflation was attempted.

In current prices, inventory investment in all sectors in 1944 is taken to be 7 billion rubles. I assume that the pertinent deflator was on the order of 120 percent. Probably a major part of the investment was in munitions and basic industrial factories. Munitions prices in 1944 may have been somewhat below 1937 (Appendix E) but basic industrial prices stood at 128 percent, and in view of the extensive subsidies, book costs in industry must have been considerably higher. Any appreciable investments in consumers' goods and trade would also have been at relatively high prices. While farm prices were stable from 1937–44, ration prices of consumers' goods in 1944 were 143 percent of the 1937 level. See Appendix A.

In terms of 1950 prices, inventory investments in each branch (Table G-11) are assumed to vary throughout as in terms of 1937 prices. For purposes of computing 1937 inventory investments in 1928 prices, I use essentially the same procedures as were used above to translate inventory investments in 1928 in terms of 1937 prices. Where possible, use is made of Formula (6) price index numbers instead of the Formula (5) indices employed previously. These measures result: The 1937 inventory investment in 1928 rubles, for all sectors, was 4.0 billion; for all industry, 3.0; of which producers' goods industries were 2.2; consumers' goods industries were 0.8; and other, 1.0 billion.

Miscellaneous Investments

Scope. This residual category is supposed to comprise a variety of outlays not elsewhere accounted for, including inventory investments other than in the "public sector" (for example, such money inventory investments in the MTS and collective farms as are not included in my public sector data; money inventory investments in private agriculture); increments in stockpiles; certain "operational expenditures" of the investment type not elsewhere classified; and the net foreign balance on commercial account.

Investments in current and constant rubles. In Table G-13, the data in

TABLE G-13
Miscellaneous Money Investments in the USSR, 1928–55
(billions of rubles)

1928	0.30
1937	7.7
1940	5.1
1944	5.1
1948	20.3
1949	15.8
1950	19.8
1951	27.1
1952	32.4
1953	18.9
1954	11.6
1955	9.9

current rubles are computed as a residual, that is, from gross investments other than fixed capital I deduct livestock and inventory investments. In order to compute the corresponding figures in 1937 rubles (Table G-1), I use as a deflator an equal-weighted aggregate of the previously derived composite of index numbers of machinery and basic industrial goods prices, as shown in Table G-12, column (3); the Karcz index numbers of farm prices realized outside the collective farm market; and index numbers of average money wages for all workers in the USSR, adjusted for changes in hours (Appendix H).

APPENDIX H

Average Money Wages in the USSR

This appendix sets forth and explains some data on money wages which are utilized at various points in this study. The data are assembled in Table H-1. I comment first on the figures for all workers and then on the figures for industrial workers.

All Workers

The data cited in column (1) refer to the average annual earnings of wage earners and salaried workers in the USSR. Although the Soviet sources are not especially explicit, the figures probably refer throughout to the so-called TSUNKHU labor force, which excludes military personnel, forced labor, and probably some other special categories of hired labor. The figures also exclude cooperative and independent artisans and collective farmers. See Bergson, *Review of Economic Statistics,* November 1947, and the sections on money wages in the SNIP studies. The sources and methods for the figures in column (1) follow:

1928. TSUNKHU, *Trud v SSSR,* 1936 ed., pp. 16–17.

1937. TPP, p. 228. A figure of 3047 rubles is given in *PKh,* 1939, no. 5, p. 170. According to Liapin, 1951, p. 104, the figure is 3093 rubles.

1940. See Lifits, 1948, p. 52, cited in Yanowich, *ASEER,* April 1955, p. 219. A figure of 4069 is implied by prewar Soviet data on labor force and wage bill. See Bergson, *Review of Economic Statistics,* November 1947, p. 236.

1944. I assume a 35 percent increase over 1940. In Voznesenskii, 1947, p. 118, the average monthly wages of ordinary workers (*rabochie*) in industry are reported to have increased 42 percent over 1940. In Stepanov, 1945, p. 10, average monthly wages "in all industry" in 1944 are said to have

TABLE H-1

Average Money Wages in the USSR, 1928–55

	All workers					Industrial workers				
	Average annual wages			Assumed indices, industrial working hours (1937 = 100)	Average annual wages adjusted for hours (1937 = 100)	Average annual wages			Assumed indices, industrial working hours (1937 = 100)	Average annual wages adjusted for hours (1937 = 100)
	Rubles (1)	Rubles, rounded (2)	Percent (1937 = 100) (3)	(4)	(5)	Rubles (6)	Rubles, rounded (7)	Percent (1937 = 100) (8)	(9)	(10)
1928	703	703	23.1	103	22.4	843	843	28.1	103	27.3
1937	3038	3038	100	100	100	3005	3005	100	100	100
1940	4054	4054	133	109	122	4207	4210	140	109	128
1944	5473	5500	181	144	139	5974	5970	199	144	154
1948	7000	7000	230	118	195	7362	7360	245	118	208
1949	—	7250	239	118	203	—	7780	259	118	219
1950	—	7500	247	118	209	—	8200	273	118	231
1951	—	7750	255	118	216	—	8620	287	118	243
1952	7989	7990	263	118	223	9032	9030	300	118	254
1953	8149	8150	268	118	227	9213	9210	306	118	259
1954	8351	8350	275	118	233	9443	9440	314	118	266
1955	8518	8520	280	118	237	9632	9630	320	118	271

been 54 percent above 1940. This is probably for "union industry." Voznesenskii (p. 117) reports an increase of 53 percent in the latter branch.

1948. I round down here the estimate of 7116 rubles given in *SNIP-40–48,* p. 135. The rounded figure like the previous estimate is arbitrary but some downward revision of the latter seems in order. In *SNIP-40–48,* it is calculated that the Soviet labor force increased from 31.2 millions in 1940, to 33.4 millions in 1948. The average wage figure follows from this and a corresponding calculation of the change of the wage bill. For purposes of calculating the change in average wage, I now feel it is more in order to use a figure of 30.4 millions for the 1940 labor force. While 31.2 millions is now cited in many Soviet sources, 30.4 millions is the figure that Voznesenskii cites in the source from which the wage bill figures are taken. Also, in an unpublished study, Warren Eason estimates the 1948 labor force at 34.6 millions. Using these figures, a calculation based on the same methods as were used previously indicates an average annual wage in 1948 of as little as 6700 rubles. The underlying logic of this calculation is open to question, however, and all in all it seems just as well to settle for a figure of 7000 rubles.

1952. Money wages in 1953 were 2 percent higher than in 1952. *PFR,* 1953.

1953. This is 201 percent of 1940. See Akademiia Nauk SSSR, *Politicheskaia ekonomiia,* 1954 ed., p. 462.

1954. This is 206 percent of 1940. See Akademiia Nauk SSSR, *Politicheskaia ekonomiia,* 1955 ed., p. 483, cited in *SNIP-49–55.*

1955. Wages increased 4.5 percent from 1952 to 1954. I assume a further increase of 2 percent in 1955.

In column (2), the figures from column (1) for years after 1940 have all been rounded. The average money wage for the years 1949–51 is determined by interpolation. In column (3), the data from column (2) are expressed as percentages of 1937. The derivation of the indices of working hours in column (4) is explained below. The indices in column (5) are obtained by dividing those in column (3) by those in column (4). If working hours in 1944 had remained at the level of the second half of 1940, the index of hours for 1944 would have been 118 and the adjusted wage index would have been 153. Assuming the wartime overtime hours were not as "good" as peacetime hours, I compute the adjusted wage index for 1944 as an average of 126 (the index of adjusted wages implied by the index of actual hours, 144) and 153 (the index of adjusted wages implied by prewar hours). The reader should recall that the adjusted wage indices are used in this study as deflators. The wartime hours must be discounted from this standpoint.

Industrial Workers

The data cited in column (6) are the counterpart for industrial workers of those cited in column (1). The workers covered probably vary in scope in the course of time. Among other things, lumber workers are omitted in 1928 but included during the years 1937–55. The sources and methods for column (6) follow:

1928. Computed from the following wage fund and employment data for large-scale and small-scale industry from TSUNKHU, *Trud v SSSR,* 1936 ed., pp. 11, 20:

	Wage bill (billion rubles)	Employment (millions)
Large-scale	2.695	3.096
Small-scale	0.260	0.408
Total	2.955	3.504

1937. *TPP*, p. 228.

1940. Assumed arbitrarily to be 140 percent of 1937 in view of several conflicting items of information:

(a) When it is assumed that average wages in industry increased from 1937 by the same percentage as did average wages in the whole economy, that is, by 33 percent, the average industrial wage in 1940 is about 4000 rubles.

(b) According to *1941 Plan,* pp. 512–513, a total wage bill of 52.230 billion rubles was to be earned in 1941 by 11.092 million industrial workers. This implies an industrial average wage for 1941 of 4709 rubles. This was to be 106.5 percent of 1940, so the 1940 average industrial wage should have been 4422 rubles, or 147 percent of 1937. The cited figure for the industrial wage bill for 1941 is part of a tabulation of which the total for the entire economy, 175.3 billion rubles, is the so-called "full" wage bill. The cited figure for industrial employment, however, is part of a tabulation of which the total for the entire economy, 31.6 million, is the so-called TSUNKHU labor force corresponding to the restricted TSUNKHU wage bill. See Bergson, *Review of Economic Statistics,* November 1947. There are reasons to think, nevertheless, that the cited targets for the *industrial* labor force and wage bill may both be part of the TSUNKHU totals and hence be comparable. For example, taking together the eleven economic sectors that are itemized in the *1941 Plan* tabulations, average wages may be computed at 4266 rubles. This is about 5 percent above the 1940 level for all workers covered by the TSUNKHU series. See Table H-1, column (1). The eleven sectors were to employ 26.457 million workers. If the balance of the TSUNKHU labor force of 31.6 million were to earn 4266 rubles, the implied TSUNKHU wage bill would be 134.8 billion rubles, or 77 percent of the "full" wage bill given in *1941 Plan,* that is, 175.3 billion rubles. This is about the same relation as prevailed in other years. But granting that the *1941 Plan* targets for the industrial wage bill and labor force may be comparable, the evidence is not conclusive, and I hesitate to rely solely on these data.

(c) According to Maslova, 1949, p. 120, the average annual wage "in socialist industry" in 1940 was 4054 rubles. Maslova links this figure with figures for 1928 and 1932 which are known to refer to large-scale industry. At the same time, the same figure is cited by Lifits, 1948, p. 52 as representing the average wage of *trudiashchiesia* and he links it to a 1929 figure for the economy as a whole. I believe the Maslova-Lifits figure does in fact refer to the economy as a whole rather than to industry alone.

1944. The average monthly wage of ordinary workers (*rabochie*) in industry in 1944 was 42 percent above 1940. Voznesenskii, 1947, p. 118.

1948. Assumed to be 175 percent of 1940. For all workers, the corresponding increase was taken to be 172.7 percent.

1952. I assume an increase of 2 percent from 1952 to 1953. For all workers, the increase was 2 percent. The implied wage is 9125 rubles.

1953. The average industrial wage in 1953 was 2.19 times the 1940 level. *Pravda,* April 27, 1954. The implied figure is 9308.

1954. 102.5 percent of 1953, as with all workers.

1955. A further increase of 2 percent, as for all workers.

In column (7) the figures from column (6) have been rounded. For 1949–51, the figures on average wages are obtained by interpolation. In column (8), the data on average wage are expressed as percentages of 1937. I repeat in column (9) the indices of working hours which are given in column (4) and which are explained below. The indices of adjusted wages in column (10) are obtained by dividing column (8) by column (9). As before, for 1944 I take an average of two adjusted wage indices: an index of 138 implied by the index of actual working hours, 144; an index of 169, implied by an index of hypothetical working hours, 118, corresponding to the working hours of the second half of 1940.

Hours of Work in Industry

The derivation of the indices of industrial working hours cited above may be explained by reference to Table H-2.

TABLE H-2

Hours of Work in Industry, USSR

Year	Normal hours per calendar week (1)	Average hours actually worked per calendar week, allowing for overtime, vacations, absenteeism, et cetera (2)	Assumed indices of working hours (1937 = 100) (3)
1928	46.8	37.3	103
1937	40.8	36.1	100
1940	44.4	—	109
1944	—	52	144
1948–55	48	—	118

Columns (1) and (2)

1928. The following information is at hand on working day of the time: The 8-hour day was the legal maximum but the 7-hour day began to be introduced in industry late in 1927. See Schwarz, 1951, pp. 259 ff. The "length of normal working day for adult workers in large scale industry" was 7.8 hours in 1928: TSUNKHU, *Socialist Construction in the USSR*, 1936 ed., p. 386. "Average daily hours including overtime" of industrial workers were 7.37 hours in 1928: Markus, *International Labor Review*, July 1936, p. 7. See also Manya Gordon, 1941, p. 257.

As understood in Soviet statistics, the "normal length of working day" is the number of hours the worker is obliged to work by law. For industry generally, an average is obtained by aggregating the pertinent figures for different branches. TSUNKHU, *Slovar'-spravochnik po sotsial'no-ekonomicheskoi statistike*, 2nd ed., p. 396. Markus probably is referring to the "factual length of the working day" which is obtained by dividing the number of hours worked during a calendar period by the number of days worked. Markus' figure oddly is lower than the "normal" day, but overtime was low at the time (about 3 percent of the actual hours: see Manya Gordon, 1941, p. 257), and his figure presumably reflects the shorter hours that were customary at the time on the eve of Sundays and holidays (hours were cut by 2 hours from an 8-hour day and one hour from a 7-hour day: see Schwarz, 1951, p. 270) and also idleness due to machine stoppages.

The figure in column (1) is obtained as the product of 6×7.8. The normal work week at the time was 6 out of 7 days.

During 1928, the average worker (*rabochii*) in "census industry" spent his year as follows: total days, 365; free days or holidays, 62.3; vacation, 14.2; full-time year, 288.5; stoppages, 1.9; and illnesses, et cetera, 23.6. Days actually worked amounted to 263. See *Narkhoz-1932*, pp. 444–446.

For column (2):

$$\frac{263 \times 7.37}{52} = \frac{1938}{52}.$$

I assume that the stoppages (1.9 days) refer to whole day stoppages and are not included in the calculation of 7.37 hours actually worked.

1937. In 1937, the bulk of Soviet industrial workers were employed on a 5-days-out-of-6 work week. In July 1935, 80.4 percent of the workers in large-scale industry worked at this work week, while 9 percent worked 4 days out of 5 and another 11 percent on other schedules. See TSUNKHU, *Trud v SSSR*, 1936 ed., p. 80. The percentage on 5 days out of 6 probably had increased by 1937.

Working hours for those employed 5 days out of 6 were 7 hours a day. In some dangerous and arduous trades, hours were reduced to 6. The hours worked on the 4-day-out-of-5 schedule were 7 and 8 when this arrangement was first introduced in 1929. Whether this continued to be the case in 1937 is not clear. See Schwarz, 1951, pp. 270–271, 276–277.

For the 7-hour 5-day-out-of-6 schedule, working hours in a calendar week normally would come to 40.8. For the 7- and 8-hour 4-day-out-of-5 schedule, the corresponding figures are 39–45.

The "normal length of the working day" for the adult industrial worker in 1934 averaged 6.98 hours. TSUNKHU, *Socialist Construction in the*

USSR, 1936 ed., p. 386. For the 5-day-out-of-6 schedule, normal working hours per calendar week on this basis would be 40.7 hours.

The "average daily hours, including overtime" of Soviet industrial workers in 1935 was 7.06. Markus, *op. cit.,* p. 7. Again, this probably represents the "factual length of the working day" as defined above.

For column (1), I take the normal hours for all workers to be 40.8. While this may be slightly high, I shall be using this figure only in comparisons with corresponding figures for later years which are also slightly on the high side.

On the way in which the worker (*rabochii*) in large-scale industry spent his year there are the following data for 1934 and 1935:

	1934	1935
Total days	365	365
Free days or holidays	65.8	—
Vacation	14.3	—
Full time year	284.9	—
Full day stoppages	1.8	1.6
Illness, et cetera	17.7	—
Actually worked	265.4	266.2

See TSUNKHU, *Trud v SSSR,* 1935 ed., p. 142; 1936, p. 78. Markus, *op. cit.,* p. 7, cites a figure of 267 days worked for 1934 and a provisional figure of 268 days worked for 1935. These figures may include full-day stoppages, but this apparently was not the case in respect of a figure Markus cites for 1928, which is the same as that cited above for 1928 exclusive of full day stoppages.

For column (2):

$$\frac{266.2 \times 7.06}{52} = \frac{1879}{52}$$

1940. During the first half of the year, the industrial worker normally worked five 7-hour days out of 6. This was the general rule, although again there were 6-hour days in some dangerous and arduous trades, and probably there were other special schedules for some workers. By the decree of June 26, 1940, a 6-day-out-of-7 work week was re-established, with a normal day of 8 hours. Shorter hours were retained in dangerous and arduous trades. See Schwarz, 1951, pp. 298–299; Gsovski, vol. I, 1948, p. 826.

For column (1), I take the average of 40.8 and 48 hours, or 44.4 hours. 40.8 is the average number of hours worked per 7-day week on a schedule calling for five 7-hour days out of 6; 48 is the average number of hours worked per 7-day week on a schedule calling for six 8-hour days out of 7. No allowance is made in either case for persons on shorter hours in special trades or on special schedules, but the resulting average is comparable to 40.8 cited for 1937, column (1).

1944. In principle, normal hours remained as fixed by the decree of June 26, 1940, but by the decree of June 26, 1941, the management of an enterprise was authorized to introduce up to 3 hours of overtime per day, and reportedly 60- and 66-hour weeks became the rule. The decree of June 26,

1941, also canceled regular vacations for the duration. See Gsovski, vol. I, 1948, p. 826; Schwarz, 1951, p. 300.

According to Voznesenskii, 1947, p. 114, the average number of hours worked per month by an industrial worker increased 22 percent "during two years of the Patriotic War." Voznesenskii indicates that the change in hours reflects the increase in overtime and the reduction in stoppages and absenteeism. Probably he also is allowing for the cancelation of vacations. If so, his figure is comparable to those I have compiled for 1928 and 1937 in column (2). If the 1937 relation between columns (2) and (1) prevailed in the second half of 1940, the actual hours worked in the second half of 1940, allowing for holidays, vacations, absenteeism, et cetera, would have been 42.5 hours (that is, $\frac{36.1}{40.8} \times 48$). The corresponding figure for 1943 (and I assume 1944) would be 52 hours (that is, 42.5×1.22). This is entered in column (2).

1948–55. The Russians returned after the war to the working week introduced on June 26, 1940, that is, six 8-hour days out of 7, with reduced hours for dangerous and arduous trades. See Schwarz, 1951, p. 302. This continued to be the established working week through the Fifth Five Year Plan (1951–55). I take the figure in column (1) to be 48 hours. Although this does not allow for the shorter hours in special trades, it is comparable to the corresponding figure for 1937.

Column (3)

For 1928–37 and 1937–44, based on column (2). For other years, based on column (1).

APPENDIX I

National Income by Final Use in 1937, at Ruble Factor Cost

The purpose of this appendix is to explain further the calculations, described in chapter 9, of the national income by final use in 1937 in terms of ruble factor cost. Some additional comment is also in order concerning the corresponding calculation referred to for household purchases in retail markets in 1937 by commodity category. To refer first to the former calculation, the results are shown together with the elements in their derivation in Table I-1. In column (1), the data on outlays in 1937 in terms of prevailing rubles again are taken from Appendices A to G. For communal services, it is again necessary to aggregate for labor and nonlabor inputs the corresponding inputs to health care and education as given in Appendix D. Under each heading, I also include an appropriate share of the outlays on "other" communal services.

In deriving the data on the turnover tax in column (2), I employ much the same procedures and assumptions as were used in *SNIP-37,* as revised in *SNIP-28–48*. However, the present calculation differs from that in *SNIP-28–48* in these respects: (a) The underlying data on the gross national product in *SNIP-28–48* have here been slightly revised. (b) The average effective tax rate is applied to the same use categories as before, except for "gross investment, other." For the latter category, I still apply the average rate to investment in inventories other than trade, but taxes on investment in inventories in trade are calculated as a residual along with taxes on household purchases in government and cooperative retail shops and restaurants. Also, I now assume arbitrarily an effective rate of 10 percent for miscellaneous investment. (c) As just explained, taxes on inventories in trade are computed as a residual, along with taxes on retail purchases. The

TABLE I-1

Gross National Product by Use, USSR, 1937, Adjusted for Turnover Taxes, Subsidies, and Farm Prices
(billion rubles)

	Value at prevailing prices (1)	Turnover taxes (2)	Subsidies (3)	Adjustment for farm prices (4)	Value at ruble factor (5)
Household purchases in retail markets					
In government and cooperative shops and restaurants	110.0	61.6	4.0	5.3	57.7
In collective farm markets	16.0	0.3	...[a]	−7.3	8.4
Total	126.0	61.9	4.0	−2.0	66.1
Housing; services	17.4	0.2	...	...	17.2
Consumption of farm income in kind	25.0	0.2	3.2	...	28.0
Military subsistence	2.5	0.8	0.1	0.1	1.9
Total outlays for consumption	170.9	63.1	7.3	−1.9	113.2
Communal services					
Labor inputs	13.4	...	...	...	13.4
Nonlabor inputs	12.2	4.0	0.4	0.6	9.2
Total	25.6	4.0	0.4	0.6	22.6
Government administration, including NKVD	7.4	0.7	0.1	0.1	6.9
Defense					
Military services	4.0	0.8	0.1	0.1	3.4
Munitions; other	13.4	0.7	0.7	0.2	13.6
Total	17.4	1.5	0.8	0.3	17.0
Gross investment					
Fixed capital	35.2	1.8	1.8	0.4	35.6
Livestock	4.0	...	0.4	...	4.4
Inventories					
Trade	3.9	2.2	0.2	0.2	2.1
Other	8.6	2.8	0.4	0.2	6.4
Total	12.5	5.0	0.6	0.4	8.5
Miscellaneous	7.7	0.8	0.3	0.2	7.4
Total	59.4	7.6	3.1	1.0	55.9
Gross national product	280.7	76.9[b]	11.7[c]	0.1[d]	215.6

[a] ... = negligible or not applicable.

[b] Turnover taxes totaled 75.9 billion rubles in 1937. Excess of 1.0 billion recorded here represents in part imputed taxes on farm income in kind. Also taxes on military subsistence are recorded twice, once under consumption and again under defense.

[c] Subsidies totaled 8.0 billion rubles in 1937. Excess of 3.7 billion rubles is due to imputation of subsidies on farm income in kind and recording of subsidies twice on military subsistence.

[d] The adjustment would total zero if it had not been recorded twice for military subsistence.

residual is distributed between these two categories in proportion to the volume of outlays involved.

In the third column, the data on the incidence of subsidies are taken from *SNIP-28–48*. In the latter study, subsidies on "gross investment, other" are estimated at 0.9 billion rubles. Of this sum, I take 0.2 billions as applying to investment in trade inventories (implying the same subsidy rate here as is calculated for household purchases in government and cooperative retail shops). The distribution of the balance between investment in other inventories and miscellaneous investment is arbitrary. For purposes of calculating the incidence of the adjustment for farm prices in column (4), I repeat the calculation that was made in *SNIP-28–48*. Because of the slightly changed estimate here of the turnover taxes accruing to household purchases in government and cooperative retail shops, k_{37}, the reduction in retail prices after all adjustments is now found to be 47.6 percent, compared with the previous 46.8 percent. Given this, all proceeds as before. Of the total adjustment, 0.6 billion rubles accrues to "gross investment, other." I distribute this by components in the same way as I allocated the corresponding figure for subsidies. In Table I-1, column (5) is obtained as the sum of columns (1), (3), and (4), less column (2).

In Table I-2 are the elements in the calculation in terms of ruble factor cost of household purchases in government and cooperative shops and restaurants in 1937 by commodity category. In column (1), data on outlays in terms of prevailing prices are calculated from corresponding percentage figures in Chapman, *Real Wages,* chapter v and Appendix E. These data are also used in Appendix A for the estimation of household purchases in 1950 rubles. For definitions of the different categories, reference may be made to Dr. Chapman's discussion. Dr. Chapman omits from her calculations several categories of consumers' goods purchased by households in government and cooperative retail shops. The chief omissions are furniture and fuels, other than kerosene. In column (1), the outlays on omitted categories are imputed to those that are included.

In Table I-2, column (2), the estimates of the turnover taxes accruing to different commodity categories are obtained by an involved calculation. Essentially, from official tax schedules an average tax rate is calculated for each category. The official rates are given in diverse sources, chiefly Narkomfin SSSR, *Stavki naloga s oborota po prodovol'stvennym tovaram,* 1937 ed.; Narkomfin SSSR, *Alfavitnyi perechen' promtovarov po stavkam naloga s oborota i biudzhetnykh natsenok,* 1938 ed.; Narkomfin SSSR, *Spravochnik po stavkam naloga s oborota i biudzhetnoi raznitse po prodovolstvennym tovaram,* 1944 ed.; and various issues of *FKhZ.*

For any commodity category, the tax rate varies depending on the particular commodity that is taxed; for example, for "grain products and legumes" there are different taxes for rye bread, wheat bread, et cetera. Very often the tax also varies with the quality or grade and sometimes even the zone. In calculating the average rate for any commodity category, reference is made here only to the commodities and grades which Dr. Chapman takes as representative in her cost of living calculations. Where the tax varies regionally, we follow Dr. Chapman in focusing on Moscow. Use is made of the preliminary version of Dr. Chapman's calculations in RAND RM-707–1 and RAND RM-803–1. The Soviet turnover tax is quoted in various terms. For present purposes the tax was translated in all cases as a percentage of retail price. Among other things this entailed adjusting for trade margins taxes quoted as a percentage of wholesale prices. Similarly, taxes quoted in rubles per physical unit are related to the corresponding retail prices. Data on prices and price margins are obtained from numerous sources,

TABLE I-2

Household Purchases in Government and Cooperative Retail Shops, USSR, 1937, by Commodity Category, Adjusted for Turnover Taxes, Subsidies, and Farm Prices (billion rubles)

	Value at prevailing prices (1)	Turnover taxes (2)	Subsidies (3)	Adjust-ment for farm prices[a] (4)	Value at ruble factor cost (5)
Foods					
Grain products and legumes	27.07	19.41	2.02	0.95	10.63
Meat and poultry	6.32	2.12	0.20	1.29	5.69
Fish	2.92	1.35	...[b]	...	1.57
Sugar and confectionary	11.52	7.93	0.54	...	4.13
Fats (including butter)	4.23	2.92	...	...	1.31
Milk and milk products	1.39	0.58	0.19	1.02	2.02
Eggs	0.49	0.20	...	0.26	0.55
Vegetables and fruit	3.96	0.72	0.17	1.69	5.10
Salt	0.21	0.14	...	...	0.07
Tea and coffee	0.83	0.62	...	...	0.21
Alcoholic beverages	10.48	7.80	...	...	2.68
All foods	69.41	43.79	3.12	5.21	33.96
Manufactured goods					
Textiles	8.40	4.08	0.18	...	4.50
Garments	7.23	2.59	...	...	4.64
Knitwear	2.44	0.85	...	...	1.59
Shoes	5.15	1.44	...	...	3.71
Haberdashery, notions	2.19	0.85	...	...	1.34
Soap, drugs, et cetera	2.96	1.38	...	...	1.58
Housewares	2.56	0.96	...	...	1.60
Reading matter	1.54	0.03	...	...	1.51
Cultural, sport goods	3.37	0.73	...	...	2.64
Kerosene, matches	1.01	0.79	...	...	0.22
Tobacco products	3.73	2.99	...	...	0.74
All manufactures	40.59	16.69	0.18	...	24.07
All commodities	110.00	60.48	3.30	5.21	58.03

[a] Minor discrepancies between indicated totals and sums of items are due to rounding.
[b] ... = negligible or not applicable.

principally the studies of Dr. Chapman and Soviet price handbooks that she cites. For grain products, clothing, and shoes it was necessary also to translate taxes on raw materials into taxes on finished products. In translating grain into final products, reference is made to data in Suchkov, 1945, p. 41, and Coogan, 1952. For garments and shoes, a rule-of-thumb translation is made on the basis of various cost and price data.

According to the foregoing calculations, turnover taxes on household purchases in government and cooperative retail shops total 60.5 billion rubles. In comparing this sum with the corresponding figure in Table I-1, 61.6 billion rubles, it should be observed that the former omits while the latter supposedly includes taxes on oil products used in agriculture to produce foods sold in government and cooperative retail shops. Such taxes, I believe, may have totaled (say) 2.0 billion rubles. See Bergson, Bernaut, and Turgeon, RAND RM-1522, pp. 84 ff.

In Table I-1, column (3), subsidies on household purchases in government and cooperative retail shops and restaurants amount to 4.0 billion rubles in 1937. Of this sum, subsidies on agricultural products account for 3.3 billion rubles. In Table I-2, column (3), the latter subsidies alone are allocated by commodity category. In *SNIP-28–48,* subsidies on all agricultural products in 1937 are estimated at 4.5 billion rubles. Of this sum, perhaps 1.0 billion rubles represents subsidies to state farms (see Karcz, RAND RM-1930, p. 50), leaving a balance of 3.5 billion rubles to the MTS. The subsidies to state farms are allocated by commodities on the basis of data in *ibid.,* pp. 28, 50–51, on state farm prices, costs, and deliveries. In estimating the corresponding breakdown of MTS subsidies, we refer to data in *ibid.,* pp. 28, 34, 87, on MTS receipts in kind and on the bookkeeping prices at which these were recorded in MTS accounts, and on data in TSUNKHU, *Itogi raboty mashino-traktornykh stantsii za 1933 i 1934 gg,* p. 68, on the volume of MTS work by products. On the basis of these data, we estimate the distribution of all state farm and MTS subsidies by product. In order to determine the corresponding distribution for subsidies on products purchased by households from government and cooperative retail shops, we adjust the estimated subsidies for each product in proportion to the relation of the total subsidies on agricultural products purchased in such shops (3.3 billion rubles) to the total subsidies on agricultural products wherever sold (4.5 billion rubles).

In Table I-2, column (4), we distribute by commodity category the adjustment for farm prices that accrues to household purchases in government and cooperative retail shops and restaurants. (We use here an earlier total of 5.21 billion rubles instead of reworking our calculations to make them conform to the revised estimate of 5.3 billion rubles shown in Table I-1.) This adjustment offsets the reduction in collective farm market prices which is needed to assure that the latter are on a par with prices prevailing in government and cooperative retail shops. Accordingly, the adjustment is allocated by commodity category in accord with the shares of different commodities in collective farm market sales. On the latter aspect, see Karcz, RAND RM-1930, pp. 317–320. In Table I-2, column (5) is obtained as the sum of columns (1), (3), and (4), less column (2).

APPENDIX J

National Income by Final Use in 1937, at Ruble Factor Cost Adjusted According to the United States Cost Structure

In chapter 9, I refer to a calculation of Soviet national income applying an adjusted ruble factor cost standard of valuation. The adjustment is made in the light of the United States cost structure. "Real" outlays for different use categories are measured in terms of prices prevailing in the USSR in 1937. In aggregating the resultant physical volume series for different use categories, I assign to each a weight corresponding to the outlays on the use category in question in 1937. The outlays are calculated initially in terms of ruble factor cost, less profits, but are then adjusted in accord with the United States cost structure. The adjustment entails the application to the volume of outlays for any use category of a coefficient of direct and indirect wage cost per dollar of final outlays that obtains for the corresponding use category in the United States. The latter coefficient is calculated from data that have been compiled for the United States in 1947 by Professor Wassily Leontief and his associates at the Harvard Economic Research Project. This appendix explains further the calculation of these adjusted ruble factor cost weights for different use categories in 1937. I also describe the sources and methods used in deriving similar data for different categories of commodities purchased by households in government and cooperative retail shops. The latter data are used as weights in the reaggregation of physical volume series for the different commodity categories. This in turn is part of the further recalculation of national income in terms of an adjusted ruble factor cost standard that is described in chapter 9. I refer first to the derivation of the adjusted ruble factor cost weights for different use categories and then to the derivation of the corresponding data for different categories of commodities purchased by households in government and cooperative retail shops and restaurants.

Together with the resulting weights, the elements in the former calculation are shown in Table 28. In column (1), the data on outlays at ruble factor cost less profits are obtained as explained in chapter 9. In chapter 9, housing and services are treated as a single use category and so also is fixed capital investment. In terms of ruble factor cost, less profits, the separate outlays given in Table 28, for housing and services and for producers' durables and construction are calculated by the same procedures as are used to derive such data on use categories generally.

In Table 28, column (3), are shown the coefficients of direct and indirect wage cost per dollar of final outlays that are applied in adjusting the data in terms of ruble factor cost, less profits. In each case, the wage cost coefficient represents the relation obtaining for the corresponding use category in the United States as given by calculations of the Harvard Economic Research Project for 1947. Professor Leontief compiles wage cost coefficients for 192 industries in the United States. He uses in this connection the 192-industry (Emergency Model) "input-output" table compiled by the United States Bureau of Labor Statistics. For any industry, the BLS table also tells us the disposition of the final market value between different final use categories. In column (3), the cited coefficients are obtained from these data essentially by aggregation.

The wage cost coefficients that Professor Leontief and his associates have compiled appear in Harvard Economic Research Project, *Report on Research for 1953,* and Harvard Economic Research Project, *Report on Research for 1954.* Use is made of these privately circulated reports with Professor Leontief's kind permission. Similar coefficients in terms of man years are presented and explained in W. Leontief, *Proceedings of American Philosophical Society,* September 28, 1953; W. Leontief, *Review of Economics and Statistics,* November 1956. The BLS circulates its 192-industry (Emergency Model) input-output table on request. For a discussion of the underlying methodology, see W. D. Evans and M. Hoffenberg, *Review of Economics and Statistics,* May 1952.

In compiling wage cost coefficients, the Harvard Economic Research Project in a number of instances omits from wage costs the value of the services of self-employed persons. As a preliminary to our use of the data, it was felt advisable to adjust these coefficients in order to take account of one such omission of special interest here, self-employed farmers. In the Harvard Economic Research Project calculations, direct wage costs in agriculture are taken to be \$0.1923 per dollar of gross output. This represents the value of the services of hired and unpaid family labor. On the basis of the calculations of Professor Gale Johnson referred to in chapter 9, this figure is raised to \$0.332 per dollar of gross output. The latter figure includes the services of self-employed farmers. By implication, the adjustment assumes that labor income constitutes 65 percent of the net income of agriculture. So far as any industry uses agricultural raw materials, the revision of the direct wage cost coefficient in agriculture requires a corresponding revision of the direct and indirect wage cost coefficient for that industry.

In view of the concern here to apply national income methodology, it was also necessary to make some adjustments in the BLS "input-output" table. In the BLS table, payments of the federal government to households, totaling $23,407.2 millions, include transfers. For present purposes, this is reduced to $9,687.0 millions, which represents compensation to employees, including contributions to social security funds. In other words, we exclude interest, subsidies and other transfers. Some business expense recorded as payments to households, particularly travel allowances, are also excluded and are recorded instead as payments to the transportation industry. On the structure of the federal government payments to households, see National Bureau of Economic Research, *Input-Output Analysis, Technical Supplement, Studies in Income and Wealth,* vol. 18, chap. 2, p. 52. Similarly, from the payments to households by state and local governments, recorded at $5,818.7 millions by the BLS, we deduct $2,571.0 millions of net interest payments and other transfers. See Harvard Economic Research Project, *Input-Output Study No. 9020* (unpublished), p. 29. We also add $317.1 millions of social security payments. See *ibid.* Hence the resultant total, $3,564.7 millions, represents compensation to employees, including government social security contributions.

In the BLS table, household payments to transport industries (railroads, air transport, and local and highway transport) include 575.0 of travel allowances paid by the federal, state, and local governments. See National Bureau of Economic Research, *op. cit.*, chap. 2, p. 49, and Harvard Economic Research Project, *Input-Output Study No. 9020* (unpublished), p. 29. We deduct one-third of these allowances from each of the transport industries affected. Corresponding adjustments are made in purchases by the federal, state, and local governments from the same industries.

In the BLS calculations, new and maintenance construction are treated as industries producing only final products, but the corresponding final outlays are distributed among various use categories, particularly "Gross Private Capital Formation," "Federal Government," "State and Local Government," and "Households." For present purposes, new and maintenance construction are considered simply as a final use category. Accordingly, outlays on the products of these industries are excluded from the BLS final use categories.

In the BLS table, stock piles of by-products are treated as a separate industry (267), but when the wage cost coefficients were calculated the by-products were distributed instead among producing industries. The latter treatment is accorded them here.

As calculated by the BLS, final outlays for processing industries represent essentially the value of goods finally disposed of at processers' f.o.b. prices. Correspondingly, as calculated by Professor Leontief, direct and indirect wage cost for the same industries represents wage costs incurred at all stages short of the shipment and distribution of the final products. By suitable aggregation of coefficients for processing industries, transport, and trade, however, it is possible to obtain coefficients that relate wage costs at all stages to final market values inclusive of transport and distribution charges, and this has been done here. Evidently, the more comprehensive coefficients are the ones to be applied in our calculations for the USSR. The final outlays to which Professor Leontief relates wage costs are also net of excise taxes on final products, but from the present standpoint this omission is all to the good. Accordingly there is no need to repair it.

Quite apart from the inclusion of trade and transport where appropriate, the coefficients in Table 28, column (3), are obtained in all cases by the aggregation for one or more use categories of coefficients for different BLS industries. Essentially, this entails only application of this formula:

$$W_i = \left(\sum_{j=1}^{n} \overline{W}_j P_j\right) \div \left(\sum_{j=1}^{n} P_j\right).$$

For given BLS use categories, final outlays on BLS industries $j = 1, \ldots, n$ are taken to be equivalent to the ith Soviet use category. In the formula, W_i represents the wage cost coefficient for the ith Soviet use category; $\overline{W}_j$ represents the Leontief wage cost coefficient for the jth BLS industry, and P_j represents the final outlays on this industry in the use categories in question.

I list below the Soviet use categories considered and indicate in each case the BLS use categories and industries that are taken to be equivalent. Cited numbers are those assigned different use categories and industries in the BLS table.

1. *Household purchases in retail markets:* a. *In government and cooperative retail shops and restaurants.* Purchases by 200, Households, from 11–164, comprising mining and manufacturing industries producing among other things processed foodstuffs and manufactured consumers' goods; from 176, 177, representing wholesale and retail trade margins on the foregoing; and from 180, Eating and Drinking Places. Also included is one-half of purchases by Households from 169–175, comprising transportation industries such as railroads, trucking, et cetera. This is after the deduction explained above is made for travel expense on government account recorded under household purchases. After the deduction, the total purchases represent freight out on consumers' goods and passenger travel other than on government account. I arbitrarily assume the two components are of the same magnitude. Omitted from the above list of BLS activities are unprocessed foods of a sort included in the Soviet use category, but the average wage coefficient is not significantly affected. Also omitted are purchases by Households from 225 Foreign Trade. These consist partly of transfers, while for the rest no wage cost coefficient is available for the inclusion of this sector in the calculations. b. *In collective farm markets.* Purchases by Households from 1–4, 7–10, representing consumption of farm income in kind and nonfarm household purchases of unprocessed food.

2. *Housing; services:* a. *Housing.* Purchases by Households from 183, Real Estate and Rentals. Unlike the Soviet category, this includes utilities paid for by landlords, the services of Real Estate Agencies, and nonresidential

farm rentals. b. *Other.* Purchases by Households from industries 167 and 168, representing expenditures on electricity and gas (apparently, however, much of the household consumption of these items falls under 183); one-half the purchases by Households from 169–175, after the deduction for business travel expense (see above use category 1.a.); purchases by Households from 178, Local and Highway Transportation, and from 179, Telephone and telegraph; and Household purchases from 190, Motion Pictures and Other Amusements, from 184, Laundries and Dry Cleaning, and from 185, Other Personal Services. Taken together, it is doubtful that the foregoing industries can be especially comparable in scope to the Soviet use category.

3. *Consumption of farm income in kind.* See use category 1.b.

4. *Military subsistence.* See use category 1.a.

6. *Communal services; government administration:* A wage cost coefficient of $0.95 per dollar of final outlays is cited for this category in the light of these facts. For final outlays in all BLS use categories on 192, Nonprofit Institutions, the wage cost coefficient is $0.98 per dollar of final outlays. For purchases by 215, Federal Government, and 220, State and Local Government, from all domestic industries, excluding new and maintenance construction, and from households, excluding transfers, the average U.S. wage cost coefficient is $0.87. Among other things, however, this includes government purchases of producers' durables, munitions, and military services. Such expenditures are omitted from the USSR use category. For completeness, it should also be observed that the cited coefficient for purchases by Federal Government and State and Local Government refers to purchases from industries other than the governmental branches themselves. In the BLS table, the latter purchases consist partly of Social Security contributions which are treated here as compensation to employees. The purchases also include excise taxes, which we wish to omit. For the rest, they consist primarily of transfers. In calculating the cited coefficient for purchases by Federal Government and State and Local Government, we also omit purchases from 225, Foreign Trade, which consist partly of transfers and partly of outlays for which no wage cost coefficient is available. Because of the lack of a wage cost coefficient, we also omit purchases from 951, Small Arms, and 961, Small Arms Ammunition.

7. *Defense:* a. *Military services.* The appropriate coefficient evidently is $1.00. b. *Munitions; other.* See use category 8.a.

8. *Gross investment:* a. *Producers' durables.* I cite the average coefficient for all 205, Gross Private Capital Formation, excluding outlays for new and maintenance construction. Also omitted are purchases from 215, Federal Government and 220, State and Local Government. The latter represent excise taxes. b. *Construction.* The average coefficient for all purchases from other industries by 211, New Construction and 212, Maintenance Construction. Omitted are purchases from 215, Federal Government and 220, State Government, which represent excise taxes, and from 961, Small Arms Ammunition, 265, Waste Products, Metal, and 266, Waste Products, Nonmetal, for which no wage cost coefficients are available. d. *Livestock.* See use

category 1.b. e. *Inventories.* The average coefficient for all "purchases" by 230, 231, 235, 236, representing changes in inventories. We omit purchases from 215, Federal Government, and 220, State Government, representing excise taxes, and also from these industries for which no wage cost coefficient is available: 225, Foreign Trade, 951, Small Arms, 961, Small Arms Ammunition, 265, Waste Products, Metal, and 266, Waste Products, Nonmetal. f. *Miscellaneous.* The cited coefficient is arbitrary.

Together with the elements in their calculation, the adjusted ruble factor cost weights for different categories of commodities purchased by households in government and cooperative retail shops are shown in Table J-1. In column (1), the data on outlays at ruble factor cost are taken from Table I-2, column (5). Ruble factor cost here is inclusive of profits. Data are not available to permit the exclusion of the latter. In column (3) are shown

TABLE J-1

Household Purchases in Government and Cooperative Retail Shops, USSR, 1937, at Ruble Factor Cost and at Ruble Factor Cost Adjusted According to United States Cost Structure

	Value at ruble factor cost		Wage cost in relation to market value, according to USA cost structure	Value at ruble factor cost, adjusted	
	Billion rubles (1)	Percent (2)	(3)	Billion rubles [(1) ÷ (3)] (4)	Percent (5)
Foods:					
1. Grain products and legumes	10.63	18.3	0.537	19.80	18.6
2. Meat and poultry	5.69	9.8	0.647	8.79	8.2
3. Fish	1.57	2.7	0.735	2.14	2.0
4. Sugar and confectionary	4.13	7.1	0.488	8.46	7.9
5. Fats (incl. butter)	1.31	2.3	0.577	2.27	2.1
6. Milk and milk products	2.02	3.5	0.577	3.50	3.3
7. Eggs	0.55	0.9	0.781	0.70	0.7
8. Vegetables and fruit	5.10	8.8	0.461	11.06	10.4
9. Salt	0.07	0.1	0.534	0.13	0.1
10. Tea and coffee	0.21	0.4	0.534	0.39	0.4
11. Alcoholic beverages	2.68	4.6	0.417	6.43	6.0
12. All foods	33.96	58.5	—	63.67	59.7
Manufactured goods:					
13. Textiles	4.50	7.8	0.576	7.81	7.3
14. Garments	4.64	8.0	0.605	7.67	7.2
15. Knitwear	1.59	2.7	0.605	2.63	2.5
16. Shoes	3.71	6.4	0.539	6.88	6.4
17. Haberdashery, notions	1.34	2.3	0.560	2.39	2.2
18. Soap, drugs, et cetera	1.58	2.7	0.500	3.16	3.0
19. Housewares	1.60	2.8	0.604	2.65	2.5
20. Reading matter	1.51	2.6	0.577	2.62	2.5
21. Cultural, sport goods	2.64	4.5	0.572	4.62	4.3
22. Kerosene, matches	0.22	0.4	0.280	0.79	0.7
23. Tobacco products	0.74	1.3	0.420	1.76	1.7
24. All manufactures	24.07	41.5	—	42.98	40.3
25. All commodities	58.03	100.0	—	106.65	100.0

the wage cost coefficients which are applied in adjusting the outlays at ruble factor cost. The wage cost coefficients supposedly represent the average relation between direct and indirect wage costs and market values for household purchases of corresponding categories of commodities in the United States in 1947. In contrast to the coefficients in Table 28, those cited here have the scope of the Leontief coefficients from which they are compiled. This is in respect of the treatment accorded wage costs incurred and market values generated in transport and distribution of final goods. Accordingly, the coefficients relate direct and indirect wage costs incurred at stages short of these activities to producers' market values. As before, however, the market values are net of excise taxes. Moreover, the coefficients again take into account the imputed wages of self-employed farmers.

In compiling the coefficients in Table J-1, as far as possible in the case of each Soviet use category I select the Leontief coefficient for a BLS industry of more or less similar scope. Where the coefficients for different BLS industries are aggregated, the household outlays on the different industries serve as weights. Where necessary, I also resort to "substitutions." The different Soviet commodity categories are listed below. In each case, I indicate the BLS industry or industries that are taken to be equivalent.

1. *Grain products and legumes.* 24, Grain Mill Products, and 25, Bakery Products.

2. *Meat and poultry.* 21, Meat Packing and Wholesale Poultry.

3. *Fish.* 10, Fisheries, Hunting, and Trapping.

4. *Sugar and confectionary.* 27, Sugar.

5. *Fats (incl. butter).* 22, Processed Dairy Products.

6. *Milk and milk products.* 22, Processed Dairy Products.

7. *Eggs.* 2, Poultry and Eggs.

8. *Vegetables and fruit.* 8, Vegetables and Fruit.

9. *Salt.* The cited coefficient is an average for 21 to 28, and 180, representing all processed foods.

10. *Tea and coffee.* See 9, *Salt.*

11. *Alcoholic beverages.* 28, Alcoholic Beverages.

12. *All foods.*

13. *Textiles.* 30, Spinning, Weaving, and Dying.

14. *Garments.* 34, Apparel.

15. *Knitwear.* 34, Apparel.

16. *Shoes.* 69, Footwear (excluding rubber).

17. *Haberdashery, notions.* The cited coefficient is an average for 11–20, 29–164, representing all consumers' goods manufacturing other than of processed foods and beverages.

18. *Soap, drugs, et cetera.* 54, Drugs and Medicines, and 55, Soap and Related Products.

19. *Housewares.* An average for 94, Cutlery, 96, Hardware, n.e.c., 101, Metal Stampings, 135, Electrical Appliances, and 138, Electric Lamps.

20. *Reading matter.* 47, Printing and Publishing.

21. *Cultural, sport goods.* An average of 52, Synthetic Fiber; 158, Musical

Instruments and Parts; 159, Toys and Sporting Goods; and 160, Office Supplies.

22. *Kerosene, matches.* 62, Petroleum Products.
23. *Tobacco products.* 29, Tobacco Manufactures.
24. *All manufactures.*
25. *All commodities.*

APPENDIX K

Note on Soviet Population and Employment

Population

The data on the population of the USSR which have been used in the present study are set forth in Table K-1. All data are centered on July 1. Except for that for 1940, all figures refer to the USSR within boundaries of the time. In the case of the figure for 1940, reference is to the postwar terri-

TABLE K-1

Population of the USSR, Specified Dates
(millions)

Year	All ages	Age 16 and over
1928	151.5	91.4
1937	165.2	102.7
1940	195.1[a]	122.6[a]
1944	175.0	—
1948	174.8	—
1949	177.3	—
1950	180.1	120.9
1951	183.2	—
1952	186.4	—
1953	189.5	—
1954	192.7	—
1955	196.1	135.3
1958	206.8	143.5
1965	231.9	155.6
1975	265.2	185.3

[a] Postwar boundaries.

tory of the USSR. Except as is to be explained, the cited data were compiled by the U.S. Bureau of the Census, and represent the results of an unpublished revision and elaboration of calculations described in John F. Kantner, "The Population of the Soviet Union," in Joint Economic Committee, Congress of the United States, *Comparisons of the United States and Soviet Economies,* Part I. Regarding the total population, for 1928 this is calculated from January 1 figures in Eason, 1959, p. 13. For 1944, Dr. Kantner favors a figure of about 180 millions for the total population, but Eason estimates that on January 1, 1945, the population numbered but 171.4 millions. In Table K-1, the figure cited for 1944 is perhaps as reasonable as any that might be adopted in this light.

Regarding the population of ages 16 and over for 1928, I assume these persons constitute 60.3 percent of the population of all ages, as they did in the census of December 1926.

Employment

In Table K-2 are shown the estimates of the volume of employment in the USSR to which reference was made in the text and corresponding sectoral figures from which the global estimates are derived.

TABLE K-2

Employment in the USSR, 1928–55
(millions)

	1928	1937	1940	1944	1950	1955
Civilian, nonfarm	13.8	26.5	33.0	21.5	38.1	44.8
Farm	35.0	37.4	41.5	—	38.5	37.9
Military	0.6	1.8	3.5	12.0	4.0	5.5
Penal labor	—	3.0	3.5	—	3.5	2.0
All categories	49.4	68.7	81.5	—	84.1	90.2

Civilian, nonfarm. I cite here for all years except 1944 and 1950 estimates of "civilian, nonagricultural" employment compiled from Soviet data in Eason, 1959, pp. 120 ff., 355 ff. Following recent Soviet statistical practice, Eason considers the nonfarm sector to embrace lumbering and fishing. For the branch as so understood, Eason's data supposedly are essentially comprehensive of gainfully employed civilian workers, and include not only wage earners and salaried workers, but handicraftsmen. In 1928, certain persons classified in Soviet statistical sources as "bourgeoisie" are also included. Almost certainly, however, penal workers are omitted throughout. Eason considers his estimates as representing the "labor force" in the nonagricultural sector, but for the major component, wage earners and salaried workers, he uses figures representing the average number of persons employed at different dates during the year, and, as he assumes, his estimates of the "labor force" in the whole nonagricultural sector should actually be indicative of employment in the same sense.

On the average during 1945, 24.8 million wage earners and salaried workers were employed in nonfarm occupations. See *ibid.*, p. 125. Considering the trend in employment of all hired workers, farmers and nonfarm (see Warren Eason, "Population and Labor Force," in *SEG*, p. 110), I take the corresponding figure for 1944 to be 18.9 million. In relation to employment of nonfarm wage earners and salaried workers, employment of handicraftsmen in 1944 is taken to be the same as in 1940, as given in Eason, 1959, p. 121. During 1950, employment of wage earners and salaried workers in nonfarm occupations averaged 35.8 millions. *Ibid.*, p. 125. For handicraftsmen, employment in 1950 is taken to be the same as is estimated by Eason (*ibid.*, p. 121) for 1955. I am guided here in part by data on handicraft employment in F. A. Leedy, *Monthly Labor Review*, September 1957, and in *Narkhoz-1956*, p. 202.

Farm employment, 1928. I take as a point of departure these Gosplan data on the volume and direction of "productive" work done during 1927–28 by the Soviet agricultural population:

	Man-years (millions)
Arable agriculture	11.54
Animal husbandry	11.59
Work in pastures, gardens, vineyards	2.81
Forestry, fishing, hunting	1.21
Processing of agricultural products	2.60
Carting and other activities	4.90
All	34.65

See *Piatiletnii plan*, vol. II, part 2, pp. 8 ff.

Although Gosplan is not explicit as to the nature of the fiscal year to which reference is made, presumably the situation regarding employment of the agricultural population during the calendar year 1928 was about the same as that during the period considered. Among the activities considered by Gosplan, evidently some strictly speaking lie outside the field of agriculture, but since Dr. Eason advises me that such secondary activities of the farm population for the most part are not included in his estimate of civilian, nonfarm employment for 1928, it is just as well to include them here as part of farm employment. On the other hand, some of the work devoted to forestry, fishing, and hunting and some of that devoted to other activities may well be represented in Dr. Eason's estimate. For present purposes, therefore, farm employment during 1928 is taken to be 32.0 million man-years, or somewhat less than the total volume of "productive" work reported by Gosplan for 1927–28.

Gosplan calculates agricultural employment here in terms of "full valued male" equivalent. Apparently, this entails discounting work performed by women and children in order to allow for their inferior efficiency in comparison with adult males. In Table K-2, I have sought to express farm employment in other terms more appropriate here. More particularly, the figure cited in the table, 35.0 millions, supposedly represents the volume of farm employment in terms of man-years, where work time of women is counted equally with that of adult males.

Thus, as Gosplan informs us, the agricultural population of ages 16 to 59 numbered 60.1 millions in 1927–28. In terms of "full valued male" equivalent, the corresponding figure is 54.1 millions. Since the farm population of the ages in question appears to have been divided fairly evenly at this time between males and females (see Eason, 1959, p. 55), Gosplan apparently counted a female man-year as worth 0.8 of a male man-year. Moreover, according to an unpublished calculation of Dr. Eason, farm women on the eve of the five-year plans appear to have worked about 60 percent as many man-years as farm men. Prior to the application of the Gosplan discount, therefore, farm employment should have amounted to 34.6 (that is, $M + F$, where $M + 0.8F = 32.0$ and $F = 0.6M$) million man-years.

Of the 34.65 million man-years which Gosplan reports were devoted to "productive" work during 1926–27, 2.9 million man-years were worked by persons of ages other than 16 to 59 years. As for work done by adult females, this no doubt is a discounted figure, but we should not be far from the mark if we suppose that prior to all discounts farm employment totaled (say) 35.0 million man-years.

For purposes of its calculation of agricultural employment, Gosplan considers a "man-year" of 275 to 280 days. This is of approximately the same length as the "man-year" in terms of which I measure agricultural employment in 1937 and later years.

My computation may be compared with one made by Eason. Using data from the Census of December 1926 on the number of persons by sex having a principal occupation in agriculture, and employment rates for 1924–25 reported in a Soviet study for a small sample of peasant households, Eason finds that during 1926 the Soviet farm population devoted 38.8 million man-years to gainful employment. This includes employment outside as well as within the field of agriculture. The nature of the "man-year" considered is not clear. See Eason, 1959, pp. 160–161. Eason has kindly supplied me with some unpublished details on his computation, including the breakdown referred to above of the volume of farm employment by sex.

Farm, 1937–55. In Table K-2, the data on farm employment for 1937–55 were compiled by Miss Nancy Nimitz. The underlying methods and sources will be explained in a forthcoming RAND report. Essentially, Miss Nimitz calculates farm employment by aggregating employment in different agricultural branches, as is shown in Table K-3. The cited figures for employment on the collective farm of collective farm members and MTS tractor brigade workers are in terms of a theoretic full-time man-year of 280 days, and are computed from Soviet data on the total "labor days" earned from collective farm work and the average number of labor days earned per man-day. Different Soviet sources are sometimes in conflict on the latter aspect, and Miss Nimitz feels that in selecting from among the different magnitudes available for 1940 she may possibly have overstated collective farm employ-

TABLE K-3

Farm Employment, USSR, 1937–55
(millions)

	1937	1940	1950	1955
In collective farms, excluding subsidiary plots				
Farm members and MTS tractor brigade workers earning labor days	22.5	25.6	25.5	23.1
MTS employment not included in "Farm members," etc.	0.4	0.4	0.4	0.6
Hired labor	0.3	0.3	0.4	0.5
Total	23.2	26.3	26.3	24.2
In state agricultural organizations other than MTS				
Employees of state and institutional farms	1.75	1.76	2.42	2.83
Employees in other state agricultural organizations	0.30	0.41	0.33	0.26
Total	2.0	2.2	2.8	3.1
In private agricultural production				
Employment on collective farm subsidiary plots	8.0	6.6	6.2	7.2
Independent peasants	1.9	4.4	0.8	0.2
Employment of workers and employees on private plots	2.3	2.0	2.4	3.2
Total	12.2	13.0	9.4	10.6
All branches	37.4	41.5	38.5	37.9

ment in that year by as much as 3 million man-years. Exclusive of tractor brigade workers, the average number of wage earners and salaried workers employed by the MTS during the year may be estimated with reasonable accuracy from diverse Soviet data. According to a Soviet sample inquiry, hired labor accounted for 1.2 percent of all collective farm employment in 1937. Miss Nimitz assumes that the same relation prevails in 1940. For 1950 and 1955, however, hired labor is taken to account for 1.5 and 2.0 percent of the total, respectively.

For the average number of wage earners and salaried workers employed in different state agricultural organizations other than the MTS, Miss Nimitz is able to cite official statistics. As for the collective farm, so for subsidiary plots, employment is calculated in terms of a theoretic full-time man-year of 280 days. For 1937, the volume of such employment may be estimated from farm employment statistics in Soviet sources. For 1940–55, corresponding figures had to be extrapolated by reference to data on the scale of operations of the subsidiary plots, particularly their livestock holdings and sown area. Since the estimate for 1937 may understate somewhat the level of employment on subsidiary plots, the corresponding figures derived for 1940–55 may also be too low. For independent peasants, average employment during 1937 may be estimated from calculations of Eason. For 1940–55, reference is made to Soviet data which apparently represent the volume of employment, although in what sense precisely is not clear. For workers and employees, employment again in a sense that is not entirely clear is inferred for 1940–55 from Soviet employment statistics. The corresponding figure for 1937 is obtained by reference to trends in livestock holdings and sown area of private plots of workers and employees.

Military. See Appendix E.

Penal. The number of persons engaged in penal labor in 1928 is unknown, but is believed to have been relatively small. For 1940, I cite the estimate derived from data in *1941 Plan* by N. Jasny. See his essay in *Journal of Political Economy,* October 1951. Jasny's calculations have been challenged (see A. D. Redding, *Journal of Political Economy,* August 1952), but his final result appears reasonably consistent with data on Soviet population and employment compiled in Eason, 1959, pp. 169 ff. Eason finds that in 1939 the total number of males in the Soviet labor force may have exceeded by 5.0 millions the number of such persons found among "reported" categories of workers. The corresponding figure for females is 3.3 millions. Eason makes clear that his calculations are subject to error, and one gathers that on balance they are more likely to overstate than understate the unaccounted for residuals. Moreover, as computed, the residuals would include not only employed workers who are "unreported" but the unemployed (presumably there are such persons even in the USSR). On the other hand, very likely a principal component would be inmates of "correctional labor camps" who are largely if not entirely unreported. If we consider also that according to eyewitness reports such persons are predominantly males, we see that Eason's figures provide an illuminating benchmark for the appraisal of the elusive question as to the size of the Soviet penal labor force. Referring apparently to the late thirties, Dallin and Nicolaevsky, 1947, p. 86, consider that the Soviet penal labor force numbered 7 to 12 millions, but the derivation of these figures is not explained. See also Schwartz, 1954, chapter xiii.

The government recruited many penal workers from newly annexed Western areas during and after 1939 and from Eastern Europe after the war. The extent to which the new recruits exceeded releases during these years is unknown. By all accounts the government since Stalin's death has released large numbers of workers, although the extent of the resultant change in the penal labor force is again conjectural. In Table K-2, the figures on penal labor cited for 1937, 1950, and 1955 should be read in the light of these considerations.

BIBLIOGRAPHY

Akademiia Nauk SSSR. *Politicheskaia ekonomiia,* Moscow, 1954; Moscow, 1955.

American Slavic and East European Review.

Atlas, M. S., *Kreditnaia reforma v SSSR,* Moscow, 1952.

——— "25 let kreditnoi reformy," *Dik,* 1955, No. 2.

Atlas, Z. V., *Denezhnoe obrashchenie i kredit SSSR,* Moscow, 1947.

——— "O planirovanii resursov Gosbanka i denezhnykh sredstv khozorganov i predpriiatii," *PKh,* 1937, No. 9–10.

Bachurin, A. V., et al., *Finansy i kredit SSSR,* Moscow, 1953.

Baran, Paul A., "National Income and Product of the USSR in 1940," *Review of Economic Statistics,* November 1947.

Baster, Nancy, *A Study of Economic Growth and Working Memorandum on Russian Budget Studies,* New York, 1955.

Belkin, V., "Tak li nado traktovat' natsional'nyi dokhod?" *VE,* 1956, no. 5.

Belov, P., "Ekonomicheskaia pobeda SSSR v Velikoi Otechestvennoi voine," *VE,* 1950, no. 5.

Bergson, Abram, "Comments," in *American Economic Review,* May 1947, no. 2.

——— *National Income of the Soviet Union,* CEIR A-5, November 1954.

——— "A Problem in Soviet Statistics," *Review of Economic Statistics,* November 1947.

——— "Reliability and Usability of Soviet Statistics," *American Statistician,* June-July 1953.

——— "Socialist Economics," in H. Ellis (ed.), *A Survey of Contemporary Economics.*

——— *Soviet National Income and Product in 1937,* New York, 1953.

——— *The Structure of Soviet Wages,* Cambridge, 1944.

——— (ed.). *Soviet Economic Growth,* Evanston, 1953.

——— Roman Bernaut, and Lynn Turgeon, "Basic Industrial Prices in the USSR, 1928–1950," The RAND Corporation, Research Memorandum RM-1522, August 1, 1955.

——— "Prices of Basic Industrial Products in the USSR, 1928–50," *Journal of Political Economy,* August 1956.

Bergson, Abram, and Hans Heymann, Jr., *Soviet National Income and Product, 1940–48,* New York, 1954.

——— and Oleg Hoeffding. "Soviet National Income and Product, 1928–48, Revised Calculations," The RAND Corporation, Research Memorandum RM-2544, November 15, 1960.

Berliner, J. S., *Factory and Manager in the USSR,* Cambridge, 1957.

——— *The USSR Construction Industry,* CEIR, Washington, 1955.

Bienstock, G., et al., *Management in Russian Industry and Agriculture,* New York, 1944.

Bogolepov, M., "Finansy SSSR nakanune tretei piatiletki," *PKh,* 1937, no. 3.

Bor, M., "O nekotorykh voprosakh natsional'nogo dokhoda sotsialisticheskogo obshchestva," *VE,* 1954, no. 10.

Bornstein, M., "National Income and Product," in Joint Economic Committee, Congress of the United States, *Comparisons of the United States and Soviet Economies,* Part II, Washington, 1959.

Brown, Emily C., "The Soviet Labor Market," *Industrial and Labor Relations Review,* January 1957.

Campbell, Robert, "Depreciation in the Soviet Economy," *Quarterly Journal of Economics,* November 1956.

——— *Notes on a Trip to the Soviet Union.*

Carson, Daniel. "Changes in the Industrial Composition of Manpower Since the Civil War," in Conference on Research in Income and Wealth, *Studies in Income and Wealth,* vol. xi, New York, 1949.

Chapman, Janet, "Real Wages in the Soviet Union, 1928–1952," *Review of Economics and Statistics,* May 1954.

——— *Real Wages in Soviet Russia Since 1928,* Cambridge (forthcoming).

——— "Retail Food Prices in the USSR, 1937–48," The RAND Corporation, Research Memorandum RM-707–1, January 13, 1953.

——— "Retail Prices of Manufactured Consumer Goods in the USSR, 1937–48," The RAND Corporation, Research Memorandum RM-803–1, December 12, 1952.

Chernomordik, D. I. (ed.), *Narodnyi dokhod SSSR,* Moscow, 1939.

Clark, Colin, *Conditions of Economic Progress,* 2nd ed., London, 1951; 3rd ed., London, 1957.

——— *A Critique of Russian Statistics,* London, 1939.

Conference on Research in Income and Wealth, *Studies in Income and Wealth,* vol. xi, New York, 1949.

Coogan, James, "Bread and the Soviet Fiscal System," *Review of Economics and Statistics,* May 1953.

——— "Sales Taxes in the Soviet Union." Unpublished thesis, Harvard University, 1952.

Dallin, David, and Boris Nicolaevsky, *Forced Labor in Soviet Russia,* New Haven, 1947.

Den'gi i kredit.

Dewhurst, J. F., and Associates, *America's Needs and Resources, A New Survey,* New York, 1955.

D'iachenko, V. P., *Finansy i kredit SSSR,* Moscow, 1940.

D'iachkov, M., and V. Kiparisov, *Uchet kapital'nogo stroitel'stva,* Moscow, 1948.

Dmitriev, M. V., *Voprosy formirovaniia i snizheniia sebestoimosti produktsii v legkoi promyshlennosti,* Moscow, 1957.

Dobb, Maurice, "Comment on Soviet Economic Statistics," *Soviet Studies,* June 1949.

——— "Further Appraisals of Russian Economic Statistics," *Review of Economics and Statistics,* February 1948.

Dolgov, V. G. (ed.), *Analiz godovogo otcheta i balansa khoziaistvennykh organizatsii,* Moscow, 1937.

Eason, Warren, *Soviet Manpower,* Princeton, 1959.

——— "Labor Force Materials for the Study of Unemployment in the Soviet Union," National Bureau of Economic Research, Universities-National Bureau Conference, *The Measurement and Behaviour of Unemployment.* Princeton, 1957.

Efimov, M., and A. Aleksandrov, "Kreditovanie tovaro-material'nykh tsennostei," *Dik,* 1940, no. 1, pp. 15–18.

Ekonomicheskaia zhizn'.

Evans, W. D., and M. Hoffenberg, "The Interindustry Relations Study for 1947," *Review of Economics and Statistics,* May 1952.

Finansovoe i ekonomicheskoe zakonodatel'stvo.

Finansy SSSR za XXX let. Moscow, 1947.

Gallman, Robert, "Commodity Output in the United States," in Conference on Research in Income and Wealth, *Studies in Income and Wealth,* vol. xxiv (forthcoming).

Gerschenkron, Alexander, *A Dollar Index of Soviet Machinery Output, 1927–28 to 1937,* The RAND Corporation, Report R-197, April 6, 1951.

——— "The Soviet Indices of Industrial Production," *Review of Economic Statistics,* November 1947.

Gilbert, Milton, and Irving B. Kravis, *An International Comparison of National Products and the Purchasing Power of Currencies.* Paris, n.d.

Goldsmith, R., "The Growth of Reproducible Wealth in the United States of America from 1805 to 1950," in S. Kuznets (ed.), *Income and Wealth of the United States,* Cambridge, 1952.

——— et al. *A Study of Savings in the United States,* vol. III, *Special Studies,* Princeton, 1956.

Golev, I. A., "Razvitiia dolgosrochnogo sel'skokhoziaistvennogo kredita SSSR," *Finansy SSSR,* 1956, no. 2.

Gordon, Manya, *Workers Before and After Lenin,* New York, 1941.

Gosplan. *Kontrol'nye tsifry narodnogo khoziaistva SSSR na 1928–1929 god,* Moscow, 1929.

——— *Kontrol'nye tsifry narodnogo khoziaistva SSSR na 1929–1930 god,* Moscow, 1930.

——— *Narodno-khoziaistvennyi plan na 1936 god,* 2nd ed., Moscow, 1936.

——— *Narodno-khoziaistvennyi plan Soiuza SSSR na 1937 god,* Moscow, 1937.

——— *Piatiletnii plan narodno-khoziaistvennogo stroitel'stva SSSR,* 3 vols. Moscow, 1930.

——— *Tretii piatiletnii plan razvitiia narodnogo khoziaistva Soiuza SSR, 1938–42,* Moscow, 1939.

Gosudarstvennyi plan razvitiia narodnogo khoziaistva SSSR na 1941 god.

Gotovskii, A., *Ekonomicheskaia pobeda Sovetskogo Soiuza* . . . Moscow, 1946.

Gozulov, A. I., *Ekonomicheskaia statistika,* Moscow, 1953.

——— *Statistika sel'skogo khoziaistva,* Moscow, 1959.

Graaf, J. de V. *Theoretical Welfare Economics,* Cambridge, 1957.

Granick, David, "Are Adjusted Rubles Rational? A Comment," *Soviet Studies,* July 1956.

——— *Management of the Industrial Firm in the USSR,* New York, 1954.

Grin'ko, G. F., *Finansovaia programma Soiuza SSR na 1936 god,* Moscow, 1936.

——— *Finansovaia programma Soiuza SSR na 1937 god,* Moscow, 1937.

Grossman, Gregory, Review of Bergson and Heymann, "Soviet National Income and Product, 1940–1948," *American Economic Review,* June 1955.

——— "Thirty Years of Soviet Industrialization," *Soviet Survey,* October 1958.

——— Review of Bergson, "Soviet National Income and Product in 1937," *Journal of Political Economy,* October 1953.

Gsovski, V., *Soviet Civil Law,* vol. I, Ann Arbor, 1948.

Gusakov, A. D., and I. A. Dymshits, *Denezhnoe obrashchenie i kredit SSSR, Moscow,* 1951.

Harvard Economic Research Project, "Input-Output Study No. 9020" (unpublished).

——— "Report on Research for 1953." Cambridge.

——— "Report on Research for 1954." Cambridge.

Hicks, J. R., "The Valuation of Social Income," *Economica,* May 1940.

——— "The Valuation of Social Income," *Economica,* August 1948.

Historical Statistics of the United States, 1789–1945, Washington, 1949.

Hodgman, Donald, "Measuring Soviet Industrial Production: A Reply," *Soviet Studies,* July 1956.

——— *Soviet Industrial Production, 1928–1951,* Cambridge, 1954.

Hoeffding, Oleg, *Soviet National Income and Product in 1928,* New York, 1954.

——— and Nancy Nimitz, "Soviet National Income and Product, 1949–1955," The RAND Corporation, Research Memorandum RM-2101, April 6, 1959.

Holzman, F. D., "The Adjusted Factor Cost Standard of Measuring National Income: Comment," *Soviet Studies,* July 1957.

——— *Soviet Taxation,* Cambridge, 1955.

Hubbard, L. E., *Soviet Trade and Distribution,* London, 1938.

Hunter, H., *Soviet Transportation Policy,* Cambridge, 1957.
Ikonnikov, V. V., *Denezhnoe obrashchenie i kredit SSSR,* Moscow, 1954.
Il'in, N. I., *Bukhgalterskii uchet v sovetskoi torgovle,* Moscow, 1954.
Institut Ekonomiki, Akademiia Nauk SSSR. *Ekonomika promyshlennosti SSSR.* Moscow, 1956.
Jasny, Naum, "Intricacies of Russian National Income Indices," *Journal of Political Economy,* August 1947.
——— "Labor and Output in Soviet Concentration Camps," *Journal of Political Economy,* October 1951.
——— *The Socialized Agriculture of the USSR,* Stanford, 1949.
——— *The Soviet Economy During the Plan Era,* Stanford, 1951.
——— *Soviet Prices of Producers' Goods,* Stanford, 1952.
——— *The Soviet Price System,* Stanford, 1951.
——— "On the Wrong Track," *Soviet Studies,* July 1956.
Jaszi, G., and John W. Kendrick, *Problems and Techniques of Measuring the Volume of Output,* 1953.
Johnson, D. Gale, "Allocation of Agricultural Income," *Journal of Farm Economics,* November 1948.
——— and Arcadius Kahan, "Soviet Agriculture: Structure and Growth," in Joint Economic Committee, Congress of the United States, *Comparisons of the United States and Soviet Economies,* Part I, Washington, 1959.
Joint Economic Committee, United States Congress, *Soviet Economic Growth,* Washington, 1957.
Kahan, Arcadius, "Changes in Labor Inputs in Soviet Agriculture," *Journal of Political Economy,* October 1959.
Kantner, John F., "Population and Labor Force," in Joint Economic Committee, Congress of the United States, *Comparisons of the United States and Soviet Economies,* Part I, Washington, 1959.
Kaplan, Norman, "Arithmancy, Theomancy and the Soviet Economy," *Journal of Political Economy,* April 1953.
——— "Capital Formation and Allocation," in A. Bergson (ed.), *Soviet Economic Growth,* Evanston, 1953.
——— "Capital Investments in the Soviet Union, 1924–1951," The RAND Corporation, Research Memorandum RM-735, November 28, 1951.
——— "Collective Farm Investment in the USSR," The RAND Corporation, Research Memorandum RM-1733, June 12, 1956.
——— "Some Methodological Notes on the Deflation of Construction," *Journal of American Statistical Association,* September 1959.
——— et al., "A Tentative Input-Output Table for the USSR, 1941 Plan," The RAND Corporation, Research Memorandum RM-924, September 2, 1952.
——— and E. S. Wainstein, "A Comparison of Soviet and American Retail Prices in 1950," *Journal of Political Economy,* December 1956.
——— "A Note on Ruble-Dollar Comparisons," *Journal of Political Economy,* December 1957.

——— and W. L. White, "A Comparison of 1950 Wholesale Prices in Soviet and American Industry," The RAND Corporation, Research Memorandum RM-1443, May 1, 1955.

Karcz, Jerzy F., "Soviet Agricultural Marketings and Prices, 1928–1954," The RAND Corporation, Research Memorandum RM-1930, July 2, 1957.

Kaser, Michael, "Estimating Soviet National Income," *Economic Journal,* March 1957.

Katsenellenbaum, Z. S., *Oborotnye sredstva v promyshlennosti SSSR,* Moscow, 1945.

Khromov, P., "K voprosu ob oborotnykh fondakh promyshlennosti," *PE,* 1937, no. 1.

Kobalevskii, V. L., *Organizatsiia i ekonomika zhilishchnogo khoziaistva,* Moscow, 1940.

Kolganov, M., "O metodike perescheta natsional'nogo dokhoda SSHA," *VE,* 1955, no. 11.

Kolganov, M. V., *Narodnyi dokhod SSSR,* Moscow, 1940.

Kondrashev, D., *Finplan raionnogo promyshlennogo tresta (kombinata),* Moscow, 1937.

Kondrashev, D. D., *Tsenoobrazovanie v promyshlennosti SSSR,* Moscow, 1956.

Kontorovich, V., *Tekhpromfinplan promyshlennogo predpriiatiia,* Moscow, 1953.

Korneev, A. M., *Tekstil'naia promyshlennost' SSSR i puti ee razvitiia,* Moscow, 1957.

Kurskii, A. D., *Tret'ia stalinskaia piatiletka,* Moscow, 1940.

Kuznets, Simon, "Government Product and National Income," International Association for Research in Income and Wealth, *Income and Wealth,* series I, Cambridge, 1951.

——— (ed.), *Income and Wealth of the United States — Trends and Structure,* Cambridge, 1952.

——— *National Income and Its Composition, 1919–1938,* New York, 1941.

——— *National Product Since 1869,* New York, 1946.

——— "On the Valuation of Social Income," *Economica,* February-May 1948.

——— "On the Valuation of Social Income," *Economica,* August 1948.

Lazarovich, G. C., *Uchet i kal'kulatsiia na predpriatiiakh miasnoi promyshlennosti,* Moscow, 1952.

Leedy, F. A., "Producers' Cooperatives in the Soviet Union," *Monthly Labor Review,* September 1957.

Leningradskoe ob'edinenie gosudarstvennykh stantsii "Elektrotok." *Statisticheskii spravochnik, 1913–1928,* Leningrad, 1929.

Leontief, W., "Composite Commodities and the Problem of Index Numbers," *Econometrica,* January 1936.

——— "Domestic Production and Foreign Trade: The American Capital Position Re-examined," *Proceedings of American Philosophical Society,* September 28, 1953.

——— "Factor Proportions and the Structure of American Trade: Further Theoretical and Empirical Analysis," *Review of Economics and Statistics,* November 1956.

Levine, Herbert, "On Measuring Economic Growth: A Comment," *Journal of Political Economy,* August 1958.

Levitini, M. G., and P. A. Fal'kovich, *Kommunal'noe khoziaistvo,* Moscow, 1935.

Liapin, A., *Trud pri sotsializme,* Gospolitizdat, 1951.

Lifits, M. M., *Sovetskaia torgovlia,* Moscow, 1948.

Little, I. M. D., *A Critique of Welfare Economics,* 2nd ed., Oxford, 1957.

Liubimov, N., "Voprosy primeneniia optovykh tsen dlia opredeleniia ob"ema valovoi i tovarnoi produktsii promyshlennosti," *VS,* 1955, no. 4.

Livshits, F. D., *Bankovaia statistika, s osnovami obshchei teorii,* Moscow, 1948.

Maizenberg, L., *Tsenoobrazovanie v narodnom khoziaistve SSSR,* Moscow, 1953.

Man'kov, S., and I. Pupanov, "Vsemirno-istoricheskaia pobeda sovetskogo naroda v Velikoi Otechestvennoi voine," *VE,* 1955, no. 5.

Margolin, N. S., *Balans denezhnykh dokhodov i raskhodov naseleniia,* Moscow, 1940.

——— *Voprosy balansa denezhnykh dokhodov i raskhodov naseleniia,* Moscow, 1939.

Markus, B. L., "The Stakhanov Movement and the Increased Productivity of Labour in the USSR," *International Labor Review,* July, 1936.

Maslova, N. S., *Proizvoditel'nost' truda v promyshlennosti SSSR,* Gospolitizdat, 1949.

Miller, J. P., *Pricing of Military Procurement,* New Haven, 1949.

Miterev, G. A. (ed.), *Dvadtsat' piat' let sovetskogo zdravookhraneniia,* Moscow, 1944.

Miterev, G., *Sovetskii Krasnyi Krest i narodnoe zdravookhranenie,* Moscow, 1955.

Moiseev, M., "Korennye preobrazovaniia material'noi i kul'turnoi zhizni," *VE,* 1957, no. 10.

Monthly Labor Review.

Montias, John, "Rational Prices and Marginal Costs in Soviet-Type Economies," *Soviet Studies,* April 1957.

Moorsteen, Richard, *Prices and Production of Machinery in the Soviet Union, 1928–1958,* Cambridge. (In press)

——— Review of Hodgman, Soviet Industrial Production, 1928–1951, *ASEER,* February 1956.

Moskovskii oblastnoi ispolnitel'nyi komitet sovetov R.K. i K.D. *Sbornik postanovlenii moskovskogo oblastnogo ispolnitel'nogo komiteta R.I. i K.D.* Moscow, 1933.

Narkomfin SSSR. *Alfavitnyi perechen' promtovarov po stavkam naloga s oborota i biudzhetnykh natsenok,* Moscow, 1938.

——— *Klassifikatsiia raskhodov i dokhodov edinogo gosudarstvennogo biudzheta na 1936 g.,* Moscow, 1935.

——— *Raskhody na sotsial'no-kul'turnye meropriiatiia* . . . Moscow, 1939.
——— *Spravochnik po stavkam naloga s oborota i biudzhetnoi raznitse po prodovol'stvennym tovaram.* Moscow, 1944.
——— *Stavki naloga s oborota po prodovol'stvennym tovaram,* Moscow, 1937.
Narkomzem i Narkomsovkhozov SSSR. *Sel'skoe khoziaistvo SSSR,* Moscow, 1935.
National Bureau of Economic Research, *Input-Output Analysis, Technical Supplement, Studies in Income and Wealth,* vol. xviii, Princeton, 1954.
Nifontov, V. P., *Proizvodstvo zhivotnovodstva v SSSR,* Moscow, 1937.
The New York Times.
Nicholson, J. L., "National Income at Factor Cost or Market Price?" *Economic Journal,* June 1955.
Nikolaev, M. V., *Bukhgalterskii uchet,* Moscow, 1936.
Nimitz, N., "The New Soviet Agricultural Decrees (September Plenum, 1953)," The RAND Corporation, Research Memorandum RM-1178, January 13, 1954.
——— "Prices of Refined Petroleum Products in the USSR, 1928–1950," The RAND Corporation, Research Memorandum RM-1497, May 26, 1955.
——— "Statistics of Soviet Agriculture," The RAND Corporation, Research Memorandum RM-1250, May 7, 1954.
NKTP. *Formy kontrol'nykh tsifr tiazheloi promyshlennosti na 1937 god* Moscow, 1936.
Nove, A., " '1926/7' and All That," *Soviet Studies,* October 1957.
——— Review of Bergson and Heymann, "Soviet National Income and Product, 1940–48," *Review of Economics and Statistics,* May 1955.
——— Review of Hoeffding, "Soviet National Income and Product in 1928," and of Bergson and Heymann, "Soviet National Income and Product, 1940–48," *International Affairs,* April 1955.
——— "Soviet National Income Statistics," *Soviet Studies,* January 1955.
Nutter, Warren, "On Measuring Economic Growth," *Journal of Political Economy,* February 1957 and August 1958.
——— "Measuring Production in the USSR," *American Economic Review,* May, 1958, no. 2.
Omel'chenko, A. I., *O normakh proizvodstvennykh zapasov na zavodakh chernoi metallurgii,* Moscow, 1938.
Petrov, A. I., *Kurs ekonomicheskoi statistiki,* Moscow, 1952; 2nd ed., Moscow, 1954.
Pisarev, I. Iu., N. N. Riauzov, and N. P. Titel'baum, *Kurs torgovoi statistiki,* Moscow, 1938.
Planovoe khoziaistvo.
Plotnikov, K. N., *Biudzhet sotsialisticheskogo gosudarstva,* Gosfinizdat, 1948.
——— et al., *Organizatsiia finansirovaniia i kreditovaniia kapital'nykh vlozhenii,* Moscow, 1954.

Pomanskii, N. A., *Finansirovanie prosveshcheniia i zdravookhaneniia,* Moscow, 1949.

Popov, V. F., *Rol' gosudarstvennogo banka v narodnom khoziaistve SSSR,* Moscow, 1956.

Powell, Raymond P., "An Index of Soviet Construction, 1927/28 to 1955," *Review of Economics and Statistics,* May 1959.

——— "A Materials Input Index of Soviet Construction, 1927/28 to 1955," Part I, The RAND Corporation, Research Memorandum RM-1872, February 14, 1957.

——— "A Materials Input Index of Soviet Construction, 1927/28 to 1955," Part II, The RAND Corporation, Research Memorandum RM-1873, February 14, 1957.

——— "A Materials Input Index of Soviet Construction, Revised and Extended," The RAND Corporation, Research Memorandum RM-2454, September 28, 1959.

Pravda.

Problemy ekonomiki.

Prokopovich, S. N. *Biulleten',* Nov.-Dec. 1937.

——— *Quarterly Bulletin of Soviet Russian Economics.*

Redding, David, "Reliability of Estimates of Unfree Labor in the USSR," *Journal of Political Economy,* August 1952.

Riabov, N., *Sotsialisticheskoe nakoplenie i ego istochniki . . . ,* Moscow, 1951.

Riauzov, N. N., and M. V. Tenenbaum, *Torgovo-kooperativnaia statistika,* Moscow, 1939.

Riauzov, N., and N. Titel'baum, *Kurs torgovoi statistiki,* Moscow, 1947, 1956.

——— *Statistika sovetskoi torgovli,* Moscow, 1951.

——— *Statistika sovetskoi torgovli,* Moscow, 1956.

Rice, Stuart, et al., "Reliability and Usability of Soviet Statistics: A Symposium," *American Statistician,* April-July 1953.

Robinson, Joan, "Mr. Wiles' Rationality: A Comment," *Soviet Studies,* January 1956.

Rotshtein, A. I., *Problemy promyshlennoi statistiki SSSR,* Part I, Leningrad, 1936.

Rovinskii, N. N., *Gosudarstvennyi biudzhet SSSR,* Moscow, 1951.

Rozentul, S., "Protsessy nakopleniia v SSSR," *PKh,* 1929, no. 1.

Samuelson, P. A., "Evaluation of Real National Income," *Oxford Economic Papers,* January 1950.

Savinskii, D. V., *Kurs promyshlennoi statistiki,* 4th ed., Moscow, 1954.

Schmookler, J., "The Changing Efficiency of the American Economy," *Review of Economics and Statistics,* August 1952.

Schwartz, Harry, *Russia's Soviet Economy,* New York, 1950; 2nd ed., New York, 1954.

Schwarz, Solomon, *Labor in the Soviet Union,* New York, 1951.

Scott, Ira O., Jr., "The Gerschenkron Hypothesis of Index Number Bias," *Review of Economics and Statistics,* November 1952.

Sel'skoe khoziaistvo SSSR, Moscow, 1958.

Seton, Francis, "Pre-war Soviet Prices in the Light of the 1941 Plan," *Soviet Studies,* April 1952.

——— Review of Bergson, "Soviet National Income and Product in 1937," *Review of Economics and Statistics,* November 1954.

——— "The Tempo of Soviet Industrial Expansion" (read before Manchester Statistical Society), January 1957.

Shaw, W. H., *Value of Commodity Output Since 1869,* New York, 1947.

Shchenkov, S. A., *Bukhgalterskii uchet v promyshlennosti,* Moscow, 1955.

Sherwood, Robert, *Roosevelt and Hopkins,* New York, 1948.

Shestaia sessiia Verkhovnogo Soveta SSSR . . . 1940 gg, Moscow, 1940.

Smekhov, B., "Planirovanie kapital'nykh rabot," *PKh,* 1941, no. 4.

Smilga, A., "Finansy sotsialisticheskogo gosudarstva," *PE,* 1937, no. 2.

Sobranie zakonov i rasporiazhenii SSSR.

Sonin, M., and B. Miroshnichenko, *Podbor i obuchenie rabochikh kadrov v promyshlennosti,* Moscow, 1944.

Sorokin, G., *Stalinskie piatiletnie plany,* Moscow, 1946.

Sosnovy, T., *The Housing Problem in the Soviet Union,* New York, 1954.

Sotsialisticheskoe sel'skoe khoziaistvo.

Spulber, N., *The Economics of Communist Eastern Europe,* New York, 1957.

Statistical Abstract of the United States: 1946, Washington, 1946.

Statistical Abstract of the United States: 1951, Washington, 1951.

Stepanov, A., *Rabota sovetskikh profsoiuzov v oblasti zarabotnoi platy,* Moscow, 1945.

Studenski, Paul, "Methods of Estimating National Income in Soviet Russia," in National Bureau of Economic Research, Conference on Research in Income and Wealth, *Studies in Income and Wealth,* vol. VIII, New York, 1946.

——— and Julius Wyler, "National Income Estimates of Soviet Russia," *American Economic Review,* May 1947.

Suchkov, A. K., *Dokhody gosudarstvennogo biudzheta SSSR,* Moscow, 1945.

——— *Dokhody gosudarstvennogo biudzheta SSSR,* Moscow, 1955.

——— *Gosudarstvennye dokhody SSSR,* Moscow, 1949; Moscow, 1952.

Survey of Current Business.

Trubnikov, S., "Istochniki komplektovaniia rabochei sily v SSSR," *PE,* 1936, no. 6.

TSU, *Dostizheniia sovetskoi vlasti za 40 let v tsifrakh,* Moscow, 1957.

——— *Narodnoe khoziaistvo SSSR,* Moscow, 1956.

——— *Narodnoe khoziaistvo SSSR v 1956 godu,* Moscow, 1957.

——— *Narodnoe khoziaistvo SSSR v 1958 godu,* Moscow, 1959.

——— *Sovetskaia torgovlia,* Moscow, 1956.

——— *SSSR v tsifrakh,* Moscow, 1958.

——— *Statisticheskii spravochnik SSSR za 1927–28,* Moscow, 1928.

——— *Zhivotnovodstvo SSSR, statisticheskii sbornik,* Moscow, 1959.

TSUNKHU, *Chislennost' i zarabotnaia plata rabochikh i sluzhashchikh v SSSR,* Moscow, 1936.

——— *Itogi raboty mashino-traktornykh stantsii za 1933 i 1934 gg,* Moscow, 1936.
——— *Kolkhoznaia i individual'no-krestianskaia torgovlia,* Moscow, 1936.
——— *Kolkhozy vo vtoroi stalinskoi piatiletke.* (I. V. Sautin, ed.), Moscow, 1939.
——— *Kul'turnoe stroitel'stvo SSSR 1935,* Moscow, 1936.
——— *Kul'turnoe stroitel'stvo SSSR,* Moscow, 1940.
——— *Narodnoe khoziaistvo SSSR, statisticheskii spravochnik 1932,* Moscow, 1932.
——— *Slovar' spravochnik po sotsial'no-ekonomicheskoi statistike,* 2nd ed., Moscow, 1948.
——— *Socialist Construction in the USSR,* Moscow, 1936.
——— *Sotsialisticheskoe stroitel'stvo Soiuza SSR, 1933–1938 gg,* Moscow, 1939.
——— *Trud v SSSR,* Moscow, 1935; Moscow, 1936.
——— *Zhivotnovodstvo SSSR v tsifrakh,* Moscow, 1932.
Turetskii, Sh. Ia., *Vnutripromyshlennoe nakoplenie v SSSR,* Moscow, 1948.
Turgeon, Lynn (under direction of Abram Bergson), "Prices of Coal and Peat in the Soviet Union, 1928–1950," The RAND Corporation, Research Memorandum RM-1423, February 2, 1955.
——— and Abram Bergson, "Prices of Basic Industrial Goods in the USSR, 1950 to 1956: A Preliminary Report," The RAND Corporation, Research Memorandum RM-1919, June 12, 1957.
United Nations, *Economic Survey of Europe in 1953,* Geneva, 1954.
U. S. Department of Commerce, *National Income, 1954 Edition* (Supplement to the U. S. Department of Commerce *Survey of Current Business*), Washington, 1954.
——— "United States Trade with Russia (U.S.S.R.) During the War Years," *International Reference Service,* December 1945.
——— U. S. *Income and Output* (Supplement to U. S. Department of Commerce Survey of Current Business), Washington, 1958.
Usoskin, M. M., *Organizatsiia i planirovanie kratkosrochnogo kredita,* Moscow, 1956.
Vasil'ev, N., "Nekotorye voprosy razvitiia proizvodstva kartofelia i ovoshchei v SSSR," *VE,* 1954, no. 6.
Vestnik statistiki.
Vilenskii, L., "Finansovye voprosy promyshlennosti," *PKh,* 1938, no. 10.
Volodarskii, L. M., *Statistika promyshlennosti i voprosy planirovaniia,* Moscow, 1958.
Voprosy ekonomiki.
Voznesenskii, N., *Voennaia ekonomika SSSR . . . ,* Moscow, 1947.
VSNKH, *Kontrol'nye tsifry piatiletnego plana . . . SSSR,* Moscow, 1927.
——— *Svodnyi proizvodstvenno-finansovyi plan . . . na 1926–27,* Moscow, 1927.
Whitman, J. T., "The Kolkhoz Market," *Soviet Studies,* April, 1956.
Wiles, Peter, "Are Adjusted Rubles Rational?" *Soviet Studies,* October 1955.

——— "A Rejoinder to All and Sundry," *Soviet Studies,* October 1956.
Wyler, Julius, "The National Income of Soviet Russia," *Social Research,* December 1946.
——— "Die Schätzungen des sowjetrussischen Volkseinkommens," *Schweizerische Zeitschrift für Volkswirtschaft und Statistik,* 1951, nos. 5 and 6.
Yanowich, M., "Changes in Soviet Money Wage Level," *ASEER,* April, 1955.
Zaleski, Eugene, "Les Fluctuations des Prix de Detail en Union Sovietique," *Conjuncture et Etudes Economique,* no. 3, 1955.
——— "Les Fluctuations des Prix de Detail Union Sovietique," *Etudes et Conjuncture,* no. 4, April 1955.
Zhebrak, M. Kh., *Kurs promyshlennogo ucheta,* Moscow, 1950.
Zverev, A. G., "Gosudarstvennyi biudzhet chetvertogo goda poslevoennoi stalinskoi piatiletki," *PKh,* 1949, no. 2.
——— *Gosudarstvennye biudzhety Soiuza SSR, 1938–1945 gg,* Moscow, 1946.

ABBREVIATIONS

ABM	Annual budget message
ASEER	*American Slavic and East European Review*
CEIR	Council for Economic and Industry Research, Washington, D. C.
Chapman, Real Wages	Janet Chapman, *Real Wages in the Soviet Union Since 1928* (forthcoming)
Dik	*Den'gi i kredit*
Dostizheniia	TSU, *Dostizheniia sovetskoi vlasti za 40 let v tsifrakh,* Moscow, 1957
FKhZ	*Finansovoe i khoziaistvennoe zakonodatel'stvo*
Gosbank	Gosudarstvennyi Bank SSSR (State Bank of the USSR)
Gosplan	Gosudarstvennaia Planovaia Komissiia (State Planning Commission)
GOSSTROI	Gosudarstvennyi Komitet po Delam Stroitel'stva (Government Committee on Construction)
Kaplan, Fixed Capital	Norman Kaplan, "Capital Investments in the Soviet Union 1924–1951," The RAND Corporation, Research Memorandum RM-735, November 28, 1951, as revised and extended in unpublished studies by the author
KGB	Komitet Gosudarstvennoi Bezopasnosti (Committee on State Security)
KTS 1928–29	Gosplan, *Kontrol'nye tsifry narodnogo khoziaistva SSSR na 1928–1929 god,* Moscow, 1929
KTS 1929–30	Gosplan, *Kontrol'nye tsifry narodnogo khoziaistva SSSR na 1929–1930 god,* Moscow, 1930
Kul'tstroi, 1936 ed.	TSUNKHU, *Kul'turnoe stroitel'stvo SSSR 1935,* Moscow, 1936
Kul'tstroi, 1940 ed.	TSUNKHU, *Kul'turnoe stroitel'stvo SSSR,* Moscow, 1940

MGB	Ministerstvo Gosudarstvennoi Bezopasnosti SSSR (Ministry of State Security of the USSR)
MLR	*Monthly Labor Review*
MVD	Ministerstvo Vnutrennikh Del SSSR (Ministry of Internal Affairs of the USSR)
Moorsteen, Machinery	Richard Moorsteen, *Prices and Production of Machinery in the Soviet Union, 1928–1958* (in press)
Narkhoz-1932	TSUNKHU, *Narodnoe khoziaistvo SSSR, Statisticheskii spravochnik 1932,* Moscow, 1932
Narkhoz	TSU, *Narodnoe khoziaistvo SSSR,* Moscow, 1956
Narkhoz-1956	TSU, *Narodnoe khoziaistvo SSSR v 1956 godu,* Moscow, 1957
Narkhoz-1958	TSU, *Narodnoe khoziaistvo SSSR v 1958 godu,* Moscow, 1959
Narkomfin SSSR	Narodnyi Komissariat Finansov SSSR (People's Commissariat of Finances of the USSR)
Narkomsovkhozov	Narodnyi Komissariat Sovkhozov SSSR (People's Commissariat of State Farms, USSR)
Narkomzem	Narodnyi Komissariat Zemledeliia SSSR (People's Commissariat of Agriculture USSR)
1941 Plan	*Gosudarstvennyi plan razvitiia narodnogo khoziaistva SSSR na 1941 god.* This volume was issued officially as an appendix to a decree of the Council of People's Commissars and the Central Committee of the Communist Party, January 17, 1941. It has been reissued by the American Council of Learned Societies
NKGB	Narodnyi Komissariat Gosudarstvennoi Bezopasnosti SSSR (People's Commissariat of State Security of the USSR)
NKTP	Narodnyi Komissariat Tiazheloi Promyshlennosti SSSR (People's Commissariat of Heavy Industry of the USSR)
NKVD	Narodnyi Komissariat Vnytrennykh Del SSSR (People's Commissariat of Internal Affairs of the USSR)
OGPU	Ob'edinennoe Gosudarstvennoe Politicheskoe Upravlenie (Unified State Political Administration)
PE	*Problemy ekonomiki*
PFR	Annual plan fulfillment report
Piatiletnii plan	Gosplan, *Piatiletnii plan narodno-khoziaistvennogo stroitel'stva SSSR,* 3 vols. Moscow, 1930
PKh	Planovoe khoziaistvo
SEG	Abram Bergson, ed., *Soviet Economic Growth,* Evanston, 1953
SKh, 1935	Narkomzem i Narkomsovkhozov SSSR, *Sel'skoe khoziaistvo SSSR,* Moscow, 1936

SNIP-28	Oleg Hoeffding, *Soviet National Income and Product in 1928,* New York, 1954
SNIP-28–48	A. Bergson, H. Heymann, O. Hoeffding, "Soviet National Income and Product, 1928–48," Revised Calculations, The RAND Corporation, Research Memorandum RM-2544, November 15, 1960
SNIP-37	Abram Bergson, *Soviet National Income and Product in 1937,* New York, 1953
SNIP-40–48	Abram Bergson and Hans Heymann, Jr., *Soviet National Income and Product, 1940–48,* New York, 1954
SNIP-49–55	Oleg Hoeffding and Nancy Nimitz, "Soviet National Income and Product, 1949–55," The RAND Corporation, Research Memorandum RM-2101, April 6, 1959
SNK	Sovet Narodnykh Komissarov SSSR (Council of People's Commissars of the USSR)
Sovtorg	TSU, *Sovetskaia torgovlia,* Moscow, 1956
SS, 1933–38	TSUNKHU, *Sotsialisticheskoe stroitel'stvo Soiuza SSR, 1933–1938 gg,* Moscow, 1939
SSKh	*Sotsialisticheskoe sel'skoe khoziaistvo*
SZR	*Sobranie zakonov i rasporiiazhenii SSSR*
TPP	Gosplan, *Tretii piatiletnii plan razvitiia narodnogo khoziaistva Soiuza SSR, 1938–42,* Moscow, 1939
TSU	Tsentral'noe Statisticheskoe Upravlenie SSSR (Central Statistical Administration of the USSR)
TSUNKHU	Tsentral'noe Upravlenie Narodno-khoziaistvennogo Ucheta (Central Administration of National Economic Accounting)
VE	*Voprosy ekonomiki*
VS	*Vestnik statistiki*
VSNKH	Vysshii Sovet Narodnogo Khoziaistva SSSR (Supreme Soviet of the People's Economy of the USSR)
Zhiv. SSSR, 1932	TSUNKHU, *Zhivotnovodstvo SSSR v tsifrakh,* Moscow, 1932
Zhiv-1959	TSU, *Zhivotnovodstvo SSSR, Statisticheskii sbornik,* Moscow, 1959

INDEX

The letter "n" following a page number indicates that the reference is to a footnote; the letter "t," that the reference is to a table.

PUBLISHED RAND RESEARCH

THE UNIVERSITY OF CHICAGO PRESS, CHICAGO, ILLINOIS

Water Supply: Economics, Technology, and Policy, by Jack Hirshleifer, James C. DeHaven, and Jerome W. Milliman, 1960

COLUMBIA UNIVERSITY PRESS, NEW YORK, NEW YORK

Soviet National Income and Product, 1940–48, by Abram Bergson and Hans Heymann, Jr., 1954

Soviet National Income and Product in 1928, by Oleg Hoeffding, 1954

Labor Productivity in Soviet and American Industry, by Walter Galenson, 1955

THE FREE PRESS, GLENCOE, ILLINOIS

Psychosis and Civilization, by Herbert Goldhamer and Andrew W. Marshall, 1953

Soviet Military Doctrine, by Raymond L. Garthoff, 1953

A Study of Bolshevism, by Nathan Leites, 1953

Ritual of Liquidation: The Case of the Moscow Trials, by Nathan Leites and Elsa Bernaut, 1954

Two Studies in Soviet Controls: Communism and the Russian Peasant, and Moscow in Crisis, by Herbert S. Dinerstein and Leon Gouré, 1955

A Million Random Digits with 100,000 Normal Deviates, by The RAND Corporation, 1955

HARVARD UNIVERSITY PRESS, CAMBRIDGE, MASSACHUSETTS

Smolensk under Soviet Rule, by Merle Fainsod, 1958

The Economics of Defense in the Nuclear Age, by Charles J. Hitch and Roland McKean, 1960

THE MACMILLAN COMPANY, NEW YORK, NEW YORK

China Crosses the Yalu: The Decision To Enter the Korean War, by Allen S. Whiting, 1960

The Determination of Orbits, by A. D. Dubyago; translated from the Russian by R. D. Burke, G. Gordon, L. N. Rowell, and F. T. Smith, 1961

Protective Construction in a Nuclear Age, edited by J. J. O'Sullivan, 1961

McGRAW-HILL BOOK COMPANY, INC., NEW YORK, NEW YORK

The Operational Code of the Politburo, by Nathan Leites, 1951
Air War and Emotional Stress: Psychological Studies of Bombing and Civilian Defense, by Irving L. Janis, 1951
Soviet Attitudes toward Authority: An Interdisciplinary Approach to Problems of Soviet Character, by Margaret Mead, 1951
Mobilizing Resources for War: The Economic Alternatives, by Tibor Scitovsky, Edward Shaw, and Lorie Tarshis, 1951
The Organizational Weapon: A Study of Bolshevik Strategy and Tactics, by Philip Selznick, 1952
Introduction to the Theory of Games, by J. C. C. McKinsey, 1952
Weight-Strength Analysis of Aircraft Structures, by F. R. Shanley, 1952
The Compleat Strategyst: Being a Primer on the Theory of Games of Strategy, by J. D. Williams, 1954
Linear Programming and Economic Analysis, by Robert Dorfman, Paul A. Samuelson, and Robert M. Solow, 1958
Introduction to Matrix Analysis, by Richard Bellman, 1960
The Theory of Linear Economic Models, by David Gale, 1960

THE MICROCARD FOUNDATION, MADISON, WISCONSIN

The First Six Million Prime Numbers, by C. L. Baker and F. J. Gruenberger, 1959

NORTH-HOLLAND PUBLISHING COMPANY, AMSTERDAM, HOLLAND

A Time Series Analysis of Interindustry Demands, by Kenneth J. Arrow and Marvin Hoffenberg, 1959

FREDERICK A. PRAEGER, PUBLISHERS, NEW YORK, NEW YORK

War and the Soviet Union: Nuclear Weapons and the Revolution in Soviet Military and Political Thinking, by H. S. Dinerstein, 1959
Divided Berlin: The Anatomy of Soviet Political Blackmail, by Hans Speier, 1961

PRINCETON UNIVERSITY PRESS, PRINCETON, NEW JERSEY

Approximations for Digital Computers, by Cecil Hastings, Jr., 1955
International Communication and Political Opinion: A Guide to the Literature, by Bruce Lannes Smith and Chitra M. Smith, 1956
Dynamic Programming, by Richard Bellman, 1957
The Berlin Blockade: A Study in Cold War Politics, by W. Phillips Davison, 1958
The French Economy and the State, by Warren C. Baum, 1958
Strategy in the Missile Age, by Bernard Brodie, 1959
Foreign Aid: Theory and Practice in Southern Asia, by Charles Wolf, Jr., 1960
Adaptive Control Processes: A Guided Tour, by Richard Bellman, 1961

PRENTICE-HALL, INC., ENGLEWOOD CLIFFS, NEW JERSEY

Games of Strategy: Theory and Applications, by Melvin Dresher, 1961
Information Processing Language — V Manual, edited by Allen Newell, 1961

PUBLIC AFFAIRS PRESS, WASHINGTON, D. C.

The Rise of Khrushchev, by Myron Rush, 1958
Behind the Sputniks: A Survey of Soviet Space Science, by F. J. Krieger, 1958

RANDOM HOUSE, INC., NEW YORK, NEW YORK

Space Handbook: Astronautics and Its Applications, by Robert W. Buchheim and the Staff of The RAND Corporation, 1959

ROW, PETERSON AND COMPANY, EVANSTON, ILLINOIS

German Rearmament and Atomic War: The Views of German Military and Political Leaders, by Hans Speier, 1957

West German Leadership and Foreign Policy, edited by Hans Speier and W. Phillips Davison, 1957

The House without Windows: France Selects a President, by Constantin Melnik and Nathan Leites, 1958

Propaganda Analysis: A Study of Inferences Made from Nazi Propaganda in World War II, by Alexander L. George, 1959

STANFORD UNIVERSITY PRESS, STANFORD, CALIFORNIA

Strategic Surrender: The Politics of Victory and Defeat, by Paul Kecskemeti, 1958

On the Game of Politics in France, by Nathan Leites, 1959

Atomic Energy in the Soviet Union, by Arnold Kramish, 1959

Marxism in Southeast Asia: A Study of Four Countries, edited by Frank N. Trager, 1959

The Unexpected Revolution: Social Forces in the Hungarian Uprising, by Paul Kecskemeti, 1961

JOHN WILEY & SONS, INC., NEW YORK, NEW YORK

Efficiency in Government through Systems Analysis: With Emphasis on Water Resource Development, by Roland N. McKean, 1958